THE VISION OF ROME
IN
LATE RENAISSANCE FRANCE

THE
VISION OF ROME IN
LATE RENAISSANCE
FRANCE

Margaret M. McGowan

YALE UNIVERSITY PRESS
NEW HAVEN AND LONDON

Endpapers: detail from Jean Cousin, 'Enfants jouant', Louvre, Cabinet des dessins
(see Figure 51).

Set in Bembo by Best-set Typesetter Ltd., Hong Kong
Printed in China through World Print Ltd

Library of Congress Cataloguing-in-Publication Data
McGowan, Margaret M.
The vision of Rome in late Renaissance France / Margaret M. McGowan
p. cm.
Includes bibliographical references and index.
ISBN 0–300–08535–4 (cloth)
1. France – Antiquities, Roman   2. France – Civilization – 1328–1600 – Roman
influences.   3. Renaissance – France.   I. Title.
DC33.3. M39 2000
944 – dc21   00–033556

A catalogue record for this book is available from the British Library

Published with assistance from the foundation established in memory of Oliver Baty
Cunningham of the Class of 1917, Yale College.

CONTENTS

PART II

Illustrations

PLATES (pp. 195–210)

I wish to thank the Warburg Institute (University of London) for all its help in providing many photographs for this book.

The British Museum has kindly given permission to reproduce Figures 2, 22, 46, 55 and 95 (Copyright The British Museum).

The British Library has kindly granted permission to reproduce Figures 47, 69, 70, 71, 77, 78, 80 and 84.

The Victoria and Albert Museum kindly gave permission to reproduce Delaune's drawing (Figure 24).

Illustrations (Figures 15, 16, 25, 29, 52, 54, 64, 65, 66, 67, 68, 85, 86, 87, 89, and 101; Plates IV, VIII and XII) are reproduced by kind permission of the Bibliothèque Nationale de France (clichés Bibliothèque Nationale de France, Paris).

The fresco from the château d'Oiron (Plate V) is reproduced by kind permis-sion of the Inventaire Général (c. A.D.A.G.P); and that from the château Villeneuve-Lembron (Plate VII) with kind permission of the Caisse nationale de monuments historiques et des sites (CNMHS/SPADEM). Paintings and drawings from the Musée du Louvre (Figures 51 and 60; Plates VI and IX) are reproduced by kind permission of the Agence photographique de la réunion des musées nationaux.

The Director of the Bibliothèques municipales de Rouen kindly gave per-mission to reproduce pages from the manuscript record of Henri II's *L'Entrée à Rouen*, 1550 (Figure 102; Plates X and XI).

Permission to reproduce pages from Du Choul's manuscript in the Biblioteca Reale, Turin (Plates I, II and III) was kindly granted by the Director ('su concessione del Ministero per i Beni e le Attività Culturali').

ACKNOWLEDGEMENT

I wish to thank the Leverhulme Trust whose award of an Emeritus Fellowship enabled me to research the visual material for this book.

INTRODUCTION

Bursting through the gates which guarded the Piazza del Popolo at the entrance to Rome, the Renaissance traveller would embark on the final phase of his journey to St Peter's and other sacred shrines. His course towards the Vatican would be slow and noisy for the streets bulged with activity: goods – not made in Rome – swayed lumpily on the carts as they clattered over the stones; food brought in quantities for the feasts that littered the church calendar; and, above all, people talking a hundred tongues and shuffling forward through the narrowed ways. As likely as not, the traveller's ears were assailed by the myriad church bells that sang forth the times of day; his anxious eyes confused by the din, the prospect of theft, or official interrogation; and his progress hampered by the crowd, by horses and mules whose owners thrust indiscriminately onwards. In winter mud collected around the feet; in warmer weather foul smells and dust penetrated the nostrils, especially of the walkers.[1]

This was the common experience which was rarely remembered in the records of the time and which failed to excite the imagination of artists and writers. They were looking at other scenes, at buildings and not at people. Their job – as they conceived it – was to filter out all the unpleasantness of daily experience and to dwell on timeless aspects; and it is their attitudes to Rome which form the matter of this book. The versions of the city which are considered here are multiple and complex. They recognize the changing contexts in which Rome was viewed at this time and take account of the different angles of vision so that the picture of Rome that emerges is of a place layered by time and moulded by interpretation.

The haphazard nature of the building of Rome has always been acknowledged; its forms were shaped by disaster (war, fire and flood) and through political imperatives – such as the rapid growth of the city in the time of Augustus.[2] Despite this constant process of change, the visions of the city recorded by writers (ancient and modern) usually suggest a static design often within a framed space whose size and shape could be transmitted intact across the centuries or be reconstructed at will in Renaissance galleries and palaces. The fabric of the city which artists saw belonged to different periods and the remains of the buildings exhibited diverse styles and a variety of materials, yet

1. Serlio: Ruins and Latin tag *Roma Quanta fuit ipsa Ruina docet*

both writers and artists attempted to refashion its fragments into whole structures as dictated by the rules of Vitruvius.[3]

The ruins themselves constituted a significant intellectual temptation and materially affected sixteenth-century perceptions of Rome (Figure 1). In so far as they provoked conjecture, automatically encouraging the onlooker to create forms from fragments, and from those initial forms to erect whole structures, they contributed to the complexity of the visions which were recorded. Indeed, the beckoning presence of ruined buildings often stimulated impulsive, uncontrolled and even contradictory responses such that clarity of vision was confused and meaning remained barely articulated.[4]

For these reasons, although this is a book about the transmission of visions of Rome into late Renaissance French culture, it is also about perception, about the impediments which the individual viewer placed in the way of seeing clearly, or the obstacles which the scattered ruins themselves presented. Beneath considerations on the habits of filling in absent parts of the landscape were thoughts concerning attitudes towards vision itself which, in their turn, raise issues about consistency and shifting views.

The process of seeing was made infinitely more complicated by the fact that visions of the city had already been gained by most travellers to Rome from their reading. The richness and complexity of this heritage has been studied in depth,[5] but it is important to note that some features which one might more readily attribute to modern responses were embedded in the works of classical writers. All had stressed the glory and majesty of Rome; the duration of its power; and its phenomenal destiny.[6] Ovid's *Fasti* (III) had put into relief its rituals and ceremonies and had marked the extraordinary growth of the city; while Livy (among others), overwhelmed by a sense of nostalgia for the past, had consistently overstated Rome's greatness. Their assessments were unchallenged by subsequent generations; they became part of the base of further exploration, to be repeated and embroidered upon, although some Renaissance writers (like La Popelinière) recognized the distorted nature of these views.[7]

This web of association, constituted by all those layerings which come into play at the moment of seeing – sights seen, imagined visions, and views absorbed through reading – can be disentangled best if the argument dwells on the one hand on what visitors to Rome actually saw and transported back with them to their own countries, and on the other on what could *not* be seen by them.[8] For, as they gazed on the ruins of Rome, they must have experienced the same perplexed and uncanny feelings as those Aeneas felt when – from the underworld – he looked about him and saw the site of Rome with its overgrown ruins, or the same impressions of awe as Vitruvius when he contemplated the work of providence in the placing of the city.[9] As Nathaniel Hawthorne was to write centuries later, in this whole confusion of uncontrolled association, 'the present moment is pressed down or crowded out'.[10]

Specific explorations of the legacy of Rome are legion and some have informed the writing of this present work. For instance, surviving sources and early witnesses of the city's greatness have been assembled. Scholars have studied the key transmitters of Rome's power and traced the civilizing consciousness which emerged from the interplay of political and ethical concerns. The theatricality of Roman conceptions of life and their appropriateness to the Renaissance have also been examined, as has the importance of the journey to Rome in some French writing.[11]

The ambitions of the present study are different. Its conception requires an interdisciplinary approach which recognizes the complex and multiple nature of the visions received and transported, and the many different forms in which

2. Delaune: imaginary construction of Roman remains

artists and writers chose to recreate those visions. Modes of writing varied: from poems to manuscript diary entries, from confident technical works to tentative tracings. Accident of survival and the intensity of concern with Rome have been the twin criteria which have guided the choice of text and images for study.

Sixteenth-century Frenchmen sought information on and stimulation from Rome; they wanted to possess its fragments and artefacts; and there were many ready to supply them (Figure 2). The first half of the book sets out these aspirations, their shortcomings and the opportunities and obstacles encountered in the transmission of views of Rome to France. The records (both in manuscript and in printed books) of the journeys made by French travellers to Rome in the period 1550–1614 are studied in the first chapter in order to draw out the puzzled, selective and often ambiguous approach which was adopted in these writings. The next chapter explores the variety of information and advice which was available from guidebooks in the mid-sixteenth century and assesses their inbuilt prejudices and the insights they provide into contemporary taste as well as the kinds of aesthetic judgements they implied. The argument then moves to issues of appropriation, as Chapter 3 discusses the acquisitive temper of French princes, how the goods they acquired changed attitudes and encouraged reconstruction. The contribution of two collectors (chosen from the beginning and end of the period) is studied in detail. The final chapter of Part I focuses on four writers who played major roles in introducing sixteenth-century French readers to images of Rome.

The second part of this book is concerned with the reactions of French writers (and, to some extent, artists) to the images of Rome they had received. The argument raises all the questions which are evident in their writings. Is restoration of the damaged vision possible? The ruins they gazed upon were not static entities but the remnants of a city subject to constant change, worked on by time, by the imagination and by memory: could such fluid forms be reconstituted and made whole again? These are fundamental problems; and the answers they provoked show that Rome in late sixteenth-century France remained a fertile source of intellectual inspiration and creative energy. These issues are tackled initially by a consideration of the nature and creative power of ruins. It is shown how French artists used them as a basis of reconstruction and, following the example of Palladio (and others), from close observation of the fragments and remains of buildings developed justifications for their rebuilding through a methodology founded on conjecture.

The lessons acquired from this practice of reconstitution were applied to real and imagined buildings. Artists were not alone in attempts to recover whole forms from surviving fragments: Chapter 6 examines Du Bellay's achievements in this context in *Les Antiquitez* and in other poems, considers the legacy he left for other poets to explore, and studies the *Essais* of Montaigne which privileged arguments and phrases *à pièces descousues* and set in relief the benefits of the unfinished. Not all writers in the late Renaissance period responded as positively to the broken images of Rome, and many Frenchmen (especially Protestants) attacked the notion of building from the past and attempting to re-enact its forms. Some (like Grévin and Garnier) argued powerfully, with subtlety and ambiguity, against the status Rome had acquired and turned the vision of a *Rome ruinée* into a more active agent of destruction, *Rome ruineuse*; and interestingly, it was a classical text which gave critics of Rome their strongest support – Lucan's *Pharsalia*. The final chapter looks at two distilled models of Rome which dominated the heroic imagery of the period, both of which had ambiguous characteristics: the figure of Caesar, and the Triumph. These inflated images of personal and political achievement are tempered, in a closing section, by the civilized account of Rome left to us by Guez de Balzac in his *Entretiens*.

PART I

·ALMA· ROMA ·

Part-title illustration: Roma (see Figure 14)

Chapter 1

Voyages[1]

Rome: capitale du monde, orgueilleuse, triomphante, ancienne, glorieuse, romuléane, noble, puissante, fameuse, superbe, magnifique, ornement du monde, papale, grande, admirable, pompeuse, guerrière, immortelle.

[Rome: capital of the world, proud, triumphant, ancient, glorious, Romulean, noble, powerful, famous, superb, magnificent, the world's ornament, papal, great, admirable, pompous, warring, immortal.]

Thus it was in 1571 that Maurice de la Porte in his posthumously published work *Les Epithètes* summed up the characteristics and attractions of Rome, and in one sentence brought together accumulated impressions and offered some justification for his contemporaries who undertook often arduous journeys to see the splendour of the imperial city.[2] It is noticeable that La Porte's adjectives all serve to conjure up the ancient, pagan place and to ignore – with the exception of 'papale' – its Christian mission.

The vision of Rome which this present book seeks to capture will also stress the pagan aspects since these seem to have particularly impressed the imagination, although Christian travellers like Jean Tarde who accompanied the bishop of Sarlat to Rome in 1593 (and again in 1614–15) recorded its Catholic and religious significance:

En pensant à moi, ai trouvé étrange de me voir encore une fois à Rome, jadis la première ville du Monde, maîtresse de l'Univers, reine de la Terre, et domicile de Vertu, théâtre des plus beaux esprits et l'abrégé de l'honneur, gloire et splendeur du monde, ville sainte pour être arrosée du sang précieux de tant de martyrs, et à présent chef de la religion chrétienne et catholique.

[Thinking of myself, I found it strange to be in Rome again, once the first city in the World, Mistress of the Universe, Queen of the Earth and

9

3.   Marten van Heemskerck: panoramic view of Rome

abode of Virtue, theatre of the brightest minds, epitome of the world's honour, splendour and glory, a city sacred for having been watered with the blood of so many martyrs, now the fountainhead of Christian and Catholic faith.][3]

Tarde's definition reproduces the formulae which were the conventional, lapidary phrases, blending abstract and concrete, that a long tradition of descriptions of Rome had transmitted. Apart from the word *étrange*, there is nothing personal in the depiction beyond the rising, fervent tone of the committed Christian with which the passage ends.

By contrast, an immediacy of reaction is caught in Blaise de Vigenère's lament on the destruction so evident in the city which he witnessed in 1549 and then from 1551 when he made a prolonged sojourn in Rome. He could not get out of his mind:

Le souvenir des piteuses marques qui se voient à Rome . . . de la felonnie inhumaine de ces Barbares . . . ains ruiné presque de fonds en comble ceste triomphante eternelle ville . . . Les edifices les plus superbes qu'oncques le Soleil apperceut, explanez iusques à plein de terre: tout pesle-mesle de ruines à guise d'un autre Chaos: . . . Somme, tout ce qui avoit esté là par de si longues revolutions de siecles comme surentassé par despit, gasté, diffamé, villenné d'une vraye rage et forcenerie; ou plustost par quelque secrete divine disposition.

10

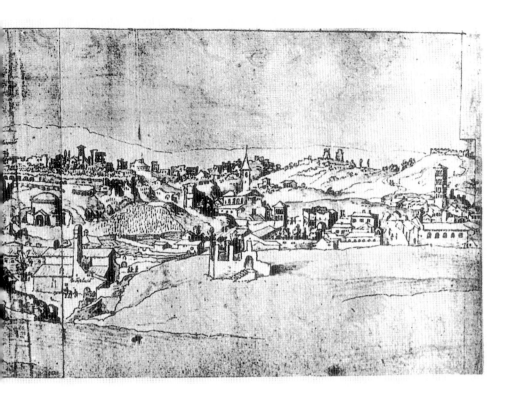

[The memory of the pitiful marks that can be seen in Rome . . . of the inhuman treachery of those Barbarians . . . who have utterly ruined this eternal and triumphant city . . . The most splendid edifices which the Sun has ever seen flattened to the ground: a jumble of ruins just such another Chaos . . . In short, all that was built up over so many centuries now piled up together through spite, spoilt and defamed, blackened through some mad rage, or rather through some mysterious divine will] (Figure 3).[4]

Embedded within his lament, which expresses the extent and the intensity of his distress, is a list of all the works of art damaged and even effaced by the fury of Rome's assailants: obelisks thrown to the ground; proud columns scorched by fire; and temples and wall paintings which had virtually disappeared. The tone is not only one of personal loss; it is also imbued with the outrage of a lover of beautiful things deprived of the opportunity to gaze upon their splendour. There is also the implication that some mysterious power has, through this destruction of Rome, avenged the brutality the Romans themselves had meted out to others. In such commentaries on Rome it is difficult to escape the moral dimension.

La Porte, Tarde and Vigenère offer three very different records of their experience. The differences are even more marked if their evocations are set beside the maps of ancient Rome drawn and engraved by Pirro Ligorio.[5] Ligorio's first map, executed in 1553 and published by Michele Tramezzino in Rome, was a small plan (*pianta piccolo* as it was termed) depicting all the ancient

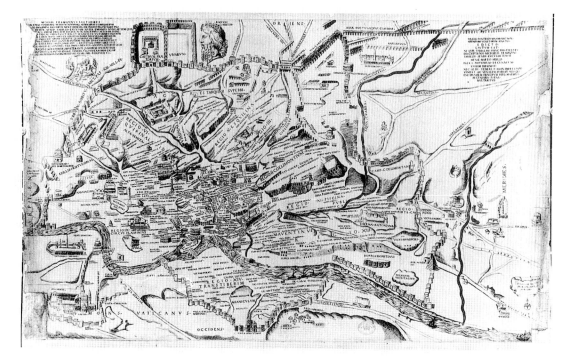

4. Pirro Ligorio: 1553 map of Rome

monuments within the circumference of Rome as if they were restored to a perfect state (Figure 4). As well as showing the principal buildings (circuses, theatres, baths, sepulchres and the Colosseum), Ligorio had indicated the main arteries of the city and slipped in the newly constructed Belvedere, St Peter's and St Paul's. His second map, which also showed the whole city, displayed the detail of each region on separate plates from the Porta Pinciana to the Porta Vaticano. Anyone looking at these delicately drawn reconstructions of Rome's most eminent buildings (Figure 5) would be satisfied that he had before him real, solid structures that could be visited and explored, although Ligorio admitted in his *L'Antiquità di Roma* that ruins had produced confusion and that the form of the city resembled a labyrinth.[6]

Ligorio's maps were eagerly sought after, printed and reprinted in Rome and Venice, engraved by Etienne du Pérac for the publisher Antoine Lafréry under the new title *Urbis Romae sciographia ex antiquis monumentis accuratiss. delineata*, and copied by Jacques Androuet du Cerceau who then produced each reconstituted building on a separately engraved sheet.[7] How far did they determine the image of Rome for those who could not travel there? La Porte and Ligorio produced idealized images for audiences who wanted to look upon the city in its pristine glory; yet Jean Tarde seems not to have been touched, scarcely seeing what was before him in his anxiety to satisfy his religious fervour. It is interesting to speculate whether the sense of shock and outrage, as exemplified by Vigenère, was intensified by the expectations aroused by Ligorio's 'false' depictions of the city. Did French travellers to Rome in the late sixteenth century

5. Pirro Ligorio: section from 1561 map of Rome

seek to measure the distance between the idealized vision and the reality of ruins, uneven ground, partial monuments and deserted stretches of land? Or is this an inappropriate question for the time? Furthermore, how far did travellers try to relate recorded images to the constantly changing face of Rome, transformed by new building projects?[8]

The purpose of this chapter is to give a sense of the varied experience recorded by French writers who visited Rome at this time, to examine the form and nature of their testimony and, in so far as it is possible, to explore their motives. The number of visits had become extraordinary. Montaigne complained, in 1580, that Rome was full only of Frenchmen,[9] and it is noteworthy that the phenomenon of travel coincided with the slowing down of French political intrusions into Italy which had been frequent since the time of Charles VIII and which had brought opportunities for plunder and gain.

THE GENRE *RÉCIT DE VOYAGE*

The genre *récit de voyage* is neither easy to determine nor straightforward in its interpretation, for travellers recorded their experience in many forms, and it is not always clear whether they were writing fictions or relating facts, or sometimes indulging in the one and then the other within the same text. Peregrination was an enriching and bewildering movement of both body and mind, and the status of the writing that emerged from that experience was often ambiguous. The writer might claim one thing for his work and demonstrate quite another.[10] In the testimony that remains of journeys to Rome, we sometimes find notes, kept secret for personal perusal only and which have survived in manuscript. There were the daily calendars of events intended as the raw material on which to build future publications such as the *Journal* of Audebert, the *Voyages* of Villamont, or the *Bref recueil* of Rigaud. There was also the record of 'choses notoires', which might be curiosities or rare works, literary texts or strange sculpted objects,[11] or which could relate to scholarly or scientific encounters such as the conversations that Jean Tarde had with Galileo or the discussions Villeroy enjoyed with Fulvio Orsini and others. Some works were styled 'commentaires/papiers journaux' such as Du Bellay's *Regrets* or Monluc's *Commentaires* where private observations were distilled and shaped for public consumption; or there were letters sent back home not only to entertain the family but also expected to be widely distributed and admired by friends, acquaintances and rivals.[12] Such were the carefully constructed letters in Latin of Pierre Paschal, or the elegant reminiscences which the ambitious young writer Guez de Balzac created. Journals of *voyages* were generally written retrospectively to preserve the memory of precious experience and to serve as guides to others, as Villamont explicitly stated; or they might be mere sketches, preliminary gestures towards literary forms, as is evident from the *Journal* of Audebert.

This mass of materials, varied and multiform, is invaluable for it not only records those features of their experience which struck the minds of observers – and it is interesting how often impressions overlap from one writer to another – but it also testifies to the effort individual visitors to Rome made to articulate fully their reactions and, abandoning the use of well-tried formulae, to pass on their view to others. Whatever their overall framework and form, these writings are uneven. The views they expressed were open-ended and seemingly arbitrary in that some objects or events are described in detail while others are merely named. They are always incomplete in so far as the record terminates abruptly or evokes objects that have not been seen and are, paradoxically, indicated by their absence.

Many wrote modestly about what they were trying to do; Villamont, for instance, asked the reader to excuse him:

> si j'ay obmis quelquechose par inadventance ou si mon langage n'a esté enrichy de quelques belles fleurs d'éloquence, comme la matière le requeroit bien.

> [If I've omitted something inadvertently or if my language is insufficiently rich in the fine flowers of eloquence that the subject would require.][13]

The plea betrays the extent to which he expected to be read critically, and reveals assumptions about the lofty style he thought appropriate to considerations upon Rome. Similarly, the young Jean Rigaud wrote a few years later:

> s'il y a du deffaut excuse m'en s'il te plaist, parce que ie l'ay fait ainsi et proprement comme sur le lieu. Ie l'avois desja escrit, seulement, depuis augmenté par moy des traductions, advis et glose en marge que j'ay estimé y estre convenables, hors d'autre embellissement.

> [if there are faults, please forgive me, because I wrote this on the spot. I had already written it, only (afterwards) I added translations and commentaries in the margin which I thought appropriate; no other embellishment.][14]

These may be insincere disclaimers; but they may also expose the will not only to describe but to do it well, with suitable adornments and erudition (although, in fact, Rigaud's marginal comments are slight and unremarkable). Notwithstanding his literary and scholarly ambitions, Rigaud insisted that he only wrote about what he had seen with his own eyes, 'pour les avoir bien veües et deüement visitees . . . Car ce seroit une trop lourde faute, d'asseurer chose que mes yeux n'eussent eu la preuve' (sig. Br) (having seen and duly visited them . . . because it would be a signal fault to assert something of which my eyes did not have proof). Such assurances about accuracy and authenticity were commonplace in travel writing even though, as will be shown, the interference of texts already written on the sights of Rome often obscured what visitors actually claimed to have seen.

15

Rigaud's apology suggests that he had reviewed his text more than once before its publication. Nicolas Audebert, too, had prepared his initial jottings very carefully with the intention of making them more widely available. The Lansdowne manuscript in the British Library is clearly a fair copy which has been much worked upon.[15] Audebert, envisaging his account as a balanced whole, shaped and organized the material, cross-referencing within the text and explaining methodically what he intended to do. He withheld, for example, detailed descriptions of the Porto S. Popolo when he first encountered it (I, 280) in order to reserve his considered comments for the time when he developed his discourse on the gates of Rome more generally. His approach is businesslike and systematic. He starts his account of Rome from the perimeter, taking his reader conscientiously round the walls of the city, counting the paces as he goes; and he describes the monuments embedded in the walls as he comes upon them, giving them detailed attention. Indeed, of all the French observers of Rome, it is Audebert who tells us most. It is evident, from the care that he has taken, that he wished to leave a record which was recognizably his own; and yet the views of 'others' are abundantly present in his work. Authors of guidebooks can be seen watching over Audebert's shoulder as he observes the monuments of Rome. He was aware of their presence, for he engages them in debate along with those 'others', authors of classical texts from which citations are frequently made. From the perimeter, his ordering mind takes the reader along the main arteries of Rome moving methodically into the heart of the city itself. Audebert's bulky *Voyage* is not without literary pretensions, and to these we shall return.[16]

Complex seem to have been the motives which led so many to undertake the journey to Rome. For some, the prospect of indulgences and of papal blessings was sufficient incentive. Greffin Affagart and his companions, for example, left Chartres on 1 March 1533 'vestuz en faczon d'hermites pour plus simplement et religieusement faire nostre voyage' (dressed as hermits in order to effect our journey with greater simplicity and devotion),[17] and they stayed in Rome just long enough to visit the seven holy places and to receive 'la benediction de nostre S.P. le Pape' before wending their way to the shrine at Loreto. By contrast, Protestants, like Gregory Martin in 1576–8, enjoyed a crude sense of satisfaction and superiority as they gloated on the Rome that was no more.[18]

From his journeys, Montaigne had sought many things: the moral and intellectual enhancement that he had advocated for others in his essay *De l'institution des enfans* (I, 26); escape from the religious strife that was overrunning France; and relief from preoccupation with his kidney stone. What he found was a source of philosophical reflection and a creative impulse. Those same ruins that had roused Martin's glee produced in Montaigne an overwhelming sense of awe. This feeling was recorded by Montaigne's secretary in a famous passage from the *Journal de voyage* where opposing notions were drawn together: 'ces petites montres de sa ruine' (these tiny signs of its ruin) which seem to

16

mpli Pacis, a Claudio Imp. inchoati, et a Vespasiano perfecti, quae supersunt ruinae, aliquibus maximis pulcherrimisq. reliquis columnis in hoc nasa et ornamenta templi Hierosolymitani seruabantur

6. G.A. Dosio: engraving of the Temple of Peace

have the same deprecatory flavour as in the reactions of Gregory Martin were, in truth, the signs that recalled the 'épouvantable machine de Rome' (fearful machine of Rome), and the city's 'gloire', 'preeminence' and 'grandeur'.[19] Montaigne's response had placed the accent simultaneously on the lingering evidence of extraordinary greatness and all-embracing achievement, as well as on the ambiguity of what he observed.

This same sense of ambiguity and paradox was felt by both Nicolas Audebert and by an anonymous traveller to Rome in 1606. The former saw the ruins of Diocletian's *Thermae* as showing 'assez la grandeur et chose merveilleuse que c'estoit quasi incroyable' (sufficiently the marvellous greatness of the thing that it is almost incredible) (II, 267), while the latter depicts the whole of Rome as 'ce fatal et admirable endroit de la terre' (this doomed and admirable place on Earth).[20] The moral uplift they had come to experience was satisfied; but there is something more, a conviction (shared by Montaigne and Italian humanists before them)[21] that they were dwelling in a unique place (Figure 6). They could not yet articulate it as Boswell was to do rather cynically – 'a man who has not been to Italy is always conscious of an inferiority, from not having seen what it is expected a man should see' – but their words transmit the sense of having been associated with something rare and precious, which would endure.

Although Frenchmen did not come to Rome in the second half of the sixteenth century as their predecessors had done, greedy for war and spoils, they did come eagerly as scholars, artists, diplomats and treasure seekers. Charles de

Neufville de Villeroy, marquis d'Alincourt ('party de Paris le 12 de Novembre, 1583'), was often perfunctory in his comments on Rome,[22] and he lazily repeated others' words and judgements. Yet it would probably be unfair to base an assessment of his reaction on the brief notes which he has left since, like Audebert, he carried letters of introduction to Fulvio Orsini. Unfortunately, he did not record his conversations with this erudite librarian of Alessandro Farnese. Both Villeroy and Audebert had gone to Italy for intellectual improvement, to copy down inscriptions, and to receive a scholarly training. The latter certainly found it; through the kind offices of Jacques Corbinelli and Piero Vettori (in Florence) he was encouraged to edit his father's poem *Roma* which was published in 1585.[23] Audebert appreciated the need to understand the technical aspects of Roman building so that he might assess the quality of what he saw; and he undertook his studies solemnly and assiduously so that, for instance, he might comprehend the water marvels at Tivoli (II, 69). Similarly, Jacques Auguste de Thou and the ambassador Paul de Foix travelled to enhance their studies and they recount how they read Aristotle with Marc-Antoine de Muret. Paul de Foix wrote in his letters to Dupuy: 'nous lisons maintenant les Politiques ayant parachevé nos Ethiques' (having read the Ethics, we are now on to the Politics). The ambassador had nothing but praise for the intellectual penetration of his companion and only regretted that his diplomatic duties prevented him from exploring the riches of Rome more thoroughly.[24] To be in Rome with evidence all around of books, art works and inscriptions also offered the opportunity of belonging to circles of scholars committed to the task of making available the great works of the past, explaining their meaning and conveying their style and sense.[25] Thus, De Thou related in his *Mémoires* how he visited the learned Sigonio and was entertained by Paulus Manutius; some years later, Jean Tarde also benefited from the knowledge of Fulvio Orsini, 'homme des grandes lettres et fort amateur de l'Antiquité' (a great man of Letters and very learned about antiquity);[26] and, later still, De Fresnes Canaye sent his three sons to Italy that they might witness 'les principales antiquitez, et choses remarquables de Rome' (the principal antiquities, and the most remarkable sights in Rome).[27]

Artists had flocked to the imperial city from the early years of the sixteenth century encouraged by the demands of princes who, like Charles VIII, admired the paintings and buildings they had seen in Italy and wished to furnish their palaces with similar splendid examples. Jean Duvet, for instance, had spent over a decade there (from 1533) studying and copying the masterpieces of Mantegna, Raphael and Leonardo.[28] Marten van Heemskerck was in Rome at the same time, and his sketchbook (preserved in Berlin) testifies to the attention he lavished on buildings and ruins. Onto his drawings he often inscribed his name as though he now owned the object; and his paintings show how imaginatively he incorporated the monuments he admired into his own compositions.[29] Their status is perhaps most apparent in the self-portrait (now in the Fitzwilliam Museum) which he painted around 1553, twenty years after his

7.   Marten van Heemskerck: self-portrait

visit to Rome. In it the artist and the Colosseum are given equal prominence, and the former is depicted in the very act of sketching the monument (Figure 7). For more than a century, a steady flow of French artists followed, sent to Rome to learn to paint and to build, or to negotiate with the papal authorities the export of precious remains to France.[30] Their activities will be explored in more detail in Chapter 5.

The value of the experience gained from travel was asserted in most *récits de voyage*. Villamont was adamant that travel refines the judgement and prepares a man for the affairs of his country much more effectively than book learning.

> Certainement l'experience nous a faict cognoistre que ceux qui avoyent beaucoup voyagé et remarqué avec jugement les façons de vivre des provinces les plus esloignees, estoient beaucoup plus propres au maniement des affaires, que ceux qui s'estoient contentez de vivre en leurs maisons et fueilleter leurs livres.

> [Certainly, the experience has made me realize that those who are much travelled and who have judiciously assessed the ways of life in the most distant places are much better suited to the management of public affairs than are those who have been content to stay at home leafing through their books.][31]

He recognized that not everyone had the chance to go. Having returned home, and wishing to reap personal advantage from the recollection, 'la souvenance des choses rares que j'y avois veües' (the remembrance of the rare things that I have seen), he determined to satisfy his mind with a reconstruction of what he had seen so that others, less fortunate, he thought, might profit.

Is it possible to trace the emotions felt by those who gazed on the city of Rome? Erasmus claimed to have left his soul there and, had it been possible, would have chosen the city for his final resting place.[32] The excited anticipation of arriving in Italy was well caught by Jean Antoine de Baïf:

> Je frétille d'aller, je désire de voir
> Les villes d'Italie et veu ramentevoir
> Les marques de Romains jadis Rois de la terre.

[I'm quivering with the desire to go and see/ Italian cities and to recall/ the traces of the Romans, once kings of the Earth.][33]

The same sentiments were expressed by Rabelais, who was filled with joy at the prospect of going to Rome, and having arrived wanted to draw everything straight away.[34] Excitement was even found in Montaigne who, having nonchalantly claimed to be indifferent to Rome, when he was within a day's journey made everyone get up three hours before dawn so anxious was he to tread the stones of the imperial city. His secretary reported: 'Nous en partismes lendemain trois heures avant le jour, tant il avoit envy de voir le pavé de Rome'.[35] Olivier de Magny, too, sang sweetly as he anticipated the pleasure of being 'En cette antique Cité', and of seeing rare treasures and his friend Joachim du Bellay:

> Là i verray les raritez,
> Et les belles antiquitez . . .
> Et nostre Bellay Angevin
> Qui plus que cela le decore.

[There, you will see rare things, beautiful antiquities, and one who adorns the place more than all that – our Du Bellay from Anjou.][36]

The emotional power of arrival could be overwhelming. One traveller, as he stood at the centre of the world in a city favoured by the planet Jupiter and predestined by God, asked 'Qui est celuy qui ne tressaillit de joye?' (who does not thrill with joy?).[37] The thought of being in Rome was so overpowering that this same visitor forgot to look around him and to describe what he actually saw; instead, he launched into the history of Rome, its growth and its successive physical states before providing a list of its current marvels. The personal emotion has given way to the style of history or to that of the guidebook.

The tendency to describe what was, rather than to say what is, was not unusual. It is perhaps partly explained by the extensive reading many had done in preparation for their journey. They came with visions of Cicero, Virgil, Ovid and Propertius, Seneca and Lucan in their heads, and they walked around where so many great men had walked and debated.[38] When they did look, they could not match what they saw with what they had expected, and their thoughts constantly turned from present prospects to pictures conjured up from the past and recorded in the lines from works they had read or in the reconstructed images which artists like Ligorio had provided.

Recognition of the gap was not always as conscious as it had been with Petrarch who, after his first effusions and astonishment, turned in his second letter to Giovanni Colonna to a reconstruction of the ancient city and its peoples: 'Here was the palace of Evander . . . the shrine of Carmentis . . . the conversations of Numa and Egeria . . .'[39] The evocation was written with fervour and with the emotion of one who had long awaited the experience. There is no sense of loss or disappointment in Petrarch's words; rather, there is a feeling of thankfulness in being given the opportunity to pen this great set-piece of evocative reconstruction. Some sixteenth-century French visitors felt more ambivalently.

Pierre de Bourdeille, seigneur de Brantôme, whose interest was rarely engaged by aesthetic considerations, nonetheless expressed his astonishment at the sight of the old buildings in Rome which continued to show their beauty and to provoke awe:

> ces orgueilleuses antiquitez, les ruines de ces beaux palais, ces superbes col-isées et grands termes, qui montrent bien encore quels ils ont esté, donnent encore admiration et terreur à tout le monde et la ruine en demeure admirable et espouvantable.

> [these proud monuments of antiquity, ruins of noble palaces, superb baths and arenas which still bear witness to what they were, inspiring the whole world with both admiration and terror, their ruin still provokes admiration and fear.][40]

Pierre Paschal, too, wrote in his letters about his complex feelings which conjured up both past heroes and heroic events and present neglect and ruin. As he described the 'vias Appias et Aurelias incultas' and the fractured columns, broken marble and tumbledown buildings,[41] Paschal's tone retains the nostalgia which a long tradition of commentators on the fate of Rome had exploited,[42] although he scarcely responded to the recreative power of the stones. In others' works, reading had transformed those stones, turning the shock of discovering a scene strewn with fragments and mounds of ruins into an active process of evocation and of building (Figure 8).

8. Marten van Heemskerck: panoramic view of the ruined Forum

This automatic and almost magical recreation is now well known. It was most memorably articulated by Sigmund Freud, for whom Rome's power was awakened by the simple act of gazing on the city and bringing to that looking the vast resources of history, art and literature. For the person who seeks to know Rome has only, in Freud's words, 'to change the direction of his glance or his position for phase upon phase of Roman history, palace upon palace, to rise before him'.[43]

Coming upon Rome from the direction of Tivoli, Florisel de Claveson, sieur de Mercurol, saw the countryside filled with old forts spread out at intervals of a mile. After enquiries, there sprang into his mind the noise of the guards who had once patrolled them:

> Retournant à Rome voyant ceste campagne, remplie d'antiennes et vieilles tours, voysines ung mille ou plus les unes des autres, me fust dist qu'en icelles jadis estoient sentinelles et corps de gardes, respondants les uns aux aultres, esquels du temps et regne des Anciens Empereurs Romains, falloit arraisonner auparavant qu'aborder leurs Majestés.

> [Returning to Rome and seeing this countryside filled with old and ancient towers at a mile's distance or more from each other, I was told that in olden times guards and sentinels patrolled there, communicating with each other, and in the reign of the Old Roman Emperors, they had to be addressed first before their Majesties could be approached.][44]

Blaise de Monluc had the same experience; when he saw the Capitol, he remembered the passage from Livy which had been read to him, and expected to meet ancient Romans: 'il me sembloit que je devois trouver là les anciens Romains' (it seemed that I must discover ancient Romans there).[45] A similar re-enactment, this time born of the author's own familiarity with historical events, can be found in Jean Tarde's visit to the Colosseum where, inside the amphitheatre (Figure 9), he and his companions proceeded to transform the ruins into the building it had been when perfect. Thus they placed along the stone seats spectators according to their rank and number, and envisioned

9.   Hieronymus Cock: view of the Colosseum

the gladiators, the wild beasts, and the Christian victims ready to meet their fate for the pleasure of the Roman people:

> Estant sur ces ruines, nous nous sommes représentés ce théâtre en sa per-fection bien couvert de peur du chaud; les trois ordres des sénateurs, cheva-liers et plébéiens assis jusques aud.nombre (octante cinq mille hommes); les gladiateurs, les bêtes farouches et les pauvres chrétiens qui y étaient exposés pour soutenir la foi chrétienne et pour donner du plaisir à ce peuple non moins superstitueux que cruel.

> [Being among these ruins, we imagined the theatre when it was whole and well covered against the heat; the three orders of senators, knights, and people were seated up to 80,000; the gladiators, wild beasts and poor Christians exposed in defence of their Christian faith and to give pleasure to this race at once cruel and superstitious.][46]

Tarde could not resist the moral sting in the tail of his story. Indeed, the next move in all these accounts of transformation was usually towards some moral or philosophical observation, as though the transforming experience was proof of the fragility of the world, 'ce monde inconstant et fragille', as Claveson had written as he entered Rome.

What is interesting here is that neither Tarde nor Claveson seems entirely conscious of the shift he was making in recreating the past, whereas the breadth of Petrarch's vision, the gathering pace of his narrative and the scope of the picture he was creating marked it out as a supremely conscious display.

Sixteenth-century travellers looked for what they had in their minds already, and they were not always aware of the nature of their engagement. Books had made them familiar with the sights of Rome as they had been in classical times and what they saw acquired extraordinary density of presence from that very familiarity.

That density might explain the unfathomable, secret and magnetic power of Rome which Du Bellay, in *Les Regrets* (lxxxvii), described as follows: 'le démon du lieu [qui] Nous y tient attachez par une double force' (. . . the spirit of the place [which] holds us fast by a double power). Yet that force only operated in a temporary way. Few French travellers to Rome elected to stay there long (Muret was an exception). Du Bellay, for complex reasons, weighed the smoke of home more heavily than the marble of Rome. The contradictory feelings which assailed travellers torn between the excitement of the unknown and the pleasure of arrival and the pull of their place of birth are well expressed by the sieur de Villamont at the end of his *Voyages*. Set to leave Italy on 13 June 1589, he wrote (choosing to express such personal sentiments in the third person, as though wishing to generalize):

> tout ainsi que celuy qui voyage en quelque region lointaine, s'efforce par tous les moyens à luy possibles, de parvenir au lieu qu'il s'est proposé: où estant heureusement abordé, après avoir enduré mille fatigues et travaux, commence à s'égayer et chanter d'allégresse, pour la joye qu'il ressent en luy-mesme d'avoir veu ce qu'il désiroit. L'amour toutefois que le lieu de sa naissance naturellement gravé au sacré cabinet de son âme l'esponçons tellement, qu'il désire incessament, s'en retourner, encores qu'il fust plus chéry et caressé en un pays estrange qu'au sien propre.

> [just as he who travels in a far off region seeks, by every possible means, to reach the place he was aiming at and where, once arrived, having endured a thousand ills and labour, he begins to enjoy himself and to sing with pleasure at the joy he feels in having seen for himself what he wanted to see, so love for one's birthplace naturally engraved in the sacred cabinet of one's soul draws him on so that – unceasingly – he wishes to return home, however more fêted and beloved he might be in a strange place than in his own land.][47]

Given such sentiments, it was imperative for Villamont to capture in words the experience that had cost him so dear and to relive it in his mind ('contenter plus longuement mon esprit', as he put it).

If we turn to the sense of place that French travellers conveyed when they were not inhibited by the tyranny of the guidebooks or by the preparation they had made through their reading, it will be seen that some were disoriented by the sight of so much rubble and by the vast empty spaces. Audebert depicted the Monte Testaccio as 'fort vaste et deshabité' (II, 16), and Rigaud similarly characterized 'la ville antique' as 'vaste et vuide' (f. 60). In contrast, others ignored the wide, open spaces, and measured monuments and counted out the distances between them step by step. One traveller marvelled at the numbers of ancient buildings believed to have been crowded on to one site and concluded that successive generations destroyed in order to build.[48] Montaigne had had the same impression, although he argued that the different stages of the buildings which time had exposed meant that earlier forms were buried many feet beneath the ground. His secretary recalled the sight and Montaigne's conviction in the *Journal*:

> [il] tenoit pour certain qu'en plusieurs endroits nous marchions sur le faiste des maisons tout entieres . . . et de vray, quasi partout, on marche sur la teste des vieux murs que la pluie et les coches descouvrent.

> [he was convinced that in several places we were walking on the roofs of whole houses – and, truly, almost everywhere one walks on the top of old walls which rain and the wheels of carriages have exposed.][49]

Many visitors, perplexed by the sheer quantity of objects worthy of note, simply cited 'un monde d'estatues', or produced long lists of buildings, art works, bridges, roads, gates and so on, often following what had become the canonical order in guidebooks and seeking, perhaps, to reassure themselves that they had indeed seen this or that famous thing. Jean Tarde is an excellent example of someone who, having thoroughly studied his subject, mastered the technical language of the architect, and forgotten no detail, still conveys no precise image of any particular piece he discusses. His detailed description of the altar in St John of Lateran illustrates the point:

> Le pape Clément VIII y fait embellir un autel d'une façon admirable. Il est entouré de grandes colonnes cannelées, pleins de terre sainte, lesquelles avec leur piédestal, chapiteaux, colevins, soubassements, feuillages et moulures, architraves, frises, frontispices, plates bandes, estatues, demi-relief et autres ornements sont de bronze couvert d'or et d'azur.

> [Pope Clement VIII had the altar embellished in wonderful fashion. It is surrounded by grooved columns filled with soil from the Holy Land, which – with their pedestals, capitals, bases, feet, leaf-work and mouldings, architraves, friezes, frontispieces, flat arches, statues, in half-relief and other ornaments – are of bronze covered in gold and azure.][50]

From this breathless list of parts and technical details it is impossible to reconstruct the actual form of the altar in question. In fact, the words block the vision entirely. Possibly Tarde did look at and admire this work of Olivieri; he may even have examined its elements closely; but he cannot convey its image to others.

The power of close observation was undoubtedly a skill possessed by Nicolas Audebert and it is worth considering several examples from his *Voyage* for, in contrast to the undifferentiated listing of elements found in some travel journals such as Tarde's work,[51] these show how valuable some accounts could be in transmitting faithful images of things seen. These examples also suggest that Audebert had literary ambitions and that, like his father, he was preparing a work that would extol Roman antiquities and give them continuing life through his words. When he described the tomb of Cestius, he first depicted its general aspect, carefully noting the interplay of cube and triangle and adding a little learned note for good measure:

> Premierement je parleray du Sepulchre de *Cestius*, qui est une forme pyramide, toute de grosse pierre quarrée depuis le pied jusques à la pointe, basty en cube et forme quadrangulaire et esgalle de chascun costé, ayant de quarré en face, et de haulteur jusques au sommet, laquelle forme de bastyment et structure a esté par les anciens appellé *Meta*. (II, 18)

> [First, I'll speak of the Tomb of *Cestius* which is a pyramid in form, made of large square stones from the base to the summit, built as a cube, with its four corners, equal on all sides and having its squared stones on the surface right to the top; this type of structure was called *Meta* by the ancients.][52]

This description reflects a careful scrutiny of the overall structure and an attempt to convey the shape of the tomb accurately. The account is then developed:

> Ceste pyramide est tellement enclavée et comprise dedans les vieux murs, que la moytié d'icelles paroist au dedans de la ville, et l'autre moytié par le dehors; estant les deux aultres costez joincts aux murailles, qui ne sont de beaucoup si espesses que la pyramide, dont elles ne couvrent que quelque partye. Il y a une inscription par dedans et dehors la ville, mais par le dedans elle ne se peult lire que demy à cause de la quantité d'herbes, arbrisseaux et ronces qui ont pris racine aux joinctures des pierres, et la mousse qui s'y est accuillye tout au tour. (II, 18)

> [This pyramid is so hemmed in and caught within the old walls that half appears inside the city and the other half outside, both parts being joined to the walls which are not as thick as the pyramid which they only partially cover. There's an inscription both inside and outside the city, but that which is inside can only be partly deciphered because quantities of weeds, small bushes and willows have taken root in the joins of the stones, and moss has invaded all around.]

The relationship between wall and structure is scrupulously, almost pedanti-

10.   G.A. Dosio: tomb of Cestius

cally, studied; no concessions are made to idealistic urges, for the mass of stone
is described warts and all, its blurred and partly effaced inscriptions, the inva-
sion of moss and weeds, the signs of age and decay seen as an integral part of
the monument. From the data which Audebert has so carefully assembled, it
would be possible to reproduce an image of the tomb (Figure 10).

The same attention to surface structure is apparent in his depiction of the
Porta Esquilina (II, 28) where the blending of polished marble and Tyburtine
stone is discussed and the different planes and surfaces are drawn out clearly
and appreciatively. The two materials are

> entremesles ensemble par rangs et ceintures, dont la pierre Tyburtine advance
> en dehors plus que le marbre et est toute martellée au lieu que le marbre
> est uny et luysant, ce qui donne grande grace l'un à l'aultre par ceste varieté
> entremeslée.

> [mixed together in bands and circles; the Tyburtine stone is more prominent
> than the marble and is hammered out while the marble is smooth and
> shining, which mixed variety gives much grace to each].

The precision might seem a little clumsy, even heavy, yet one can see how
Audebert sought to justify the aesthetic claims he had made earlier about this
gate – that it was 'la plus superbe et magnifiquement bastye' (the most superb

ANTIQVI EX PORPHYRITE SARCOPHAGI IN BACCHI AD SECVNDVM AB VRBE VIA NOMENTANA LAPIDEM *ut rudius propter marmoris duritiem vel artificis negligentiam vel saeculi sane barbariem: tum in fronte, et a tergo tum dextro ac sinistro latere totidem, et ijsdem figuris insculpti, ita sepulcri Constantiae Constantini Magni Filiae fama quamquam incerta vulgo fuerit.*

11.   Jean-Jacques Boissard: sepulchre from the Temple of Bacchus

and magnificently constructed), and to prepare his own judgement about the surface's overall grace.

A similar blend of detailed observation and praise can be found in his evocation of Bacchus' Temple whose round shape and double line of columns were described, together with the mosaic paintings of the life of the god. It was the tomb which attracted most attention and most praise:[53]

> y ayant une seule pierre de porphyre longue de six pieds, large de troys et haulte de plus de cinq, taillée par le hault en dos d'asne et tout au tour enrichie d'un ouvrage excellent eslevé en dehors, où il y a des branchages de vigne, avec force raisins et de petits enfans nuds qui en cueillent et pressurent des grappes en leurs mains, de petits oyseaux qui en mangent, et parmy tout cela y a des triomphes des fleurs suspenduz (II, 36–7)

> [one single piece of porphyry, six feet in length, three feet wide and a little more than five feet high; the top is cut in ridges, and all around it is enriched with excellent work in relief with branches of vine thick with grapes and naked little children in the act of picking and squashing the grapes in their hands; tiny birds also eat of them, and among all that are festoons of hanging flowers].

Noteworthy are the exact dimensions of the sepulchre, the description of how the stone was worked, and the liveliness of the activities depicted by the artist where both children and birds delight in the touch and taste of the grape. Audebert has sought to capture the movement and the pleasure, the quality of the material and of its design; and the judgement – 'qui est une des plus belles pieces, et plus exquises que soyent à Rome' (which is one of the most beautiful and exquisite things in Rome) – followed naturally from the implicit approval that was threaded through the description (Figure 11).

In the depiction of deities and other celebrated figures, Audebert was not satisfied with the conventional approach adopted by many of his contemporaries, who had limited their remarks to a simple naming of the god in question since they could assume that the attributes would be well known. Diana, for instance, was found in many guises at Fontainebleau and at Anet, worked in statuary, and on paintings, frescos or tapestries. Yet when Audebert came to evoke the fountain of Diana at Tivoli, he not only recalled the goddess, her dog, the beast about to be torn to pieces, her bow and arrows, but also details the exact fall of her dress, the position of her feet as though she were about to move, and the placing of her arms on the point of action and just about to inflict her wounds. Even the dog was presented as alert and ready to pounce upon the transformed Actaeon.

> Elle a son habit retroussé et tiré de l'arc ayant le pied gaulche advancé en avant et le droict à demy hors de terre s'appuyant seulement sur le bout, et près d'iceluy est un chien qui semble attentif à quand la beste sera blessée pour courir après. La main gaulche d'icelle est eslevée tenant son arc, et la droicte est demeurée en l'air comme venant encores de tirer tout à l'heure, le bras estant tout ployé, le coude en l'air et les deux doigts dont a esté tirée la corde demeurez encore recourbez et le carquois attaché derrière se montre par dessus l'espaulle, et ainsi elle semble attendante où donnera le coup . . . (II, 72)

> [Her dress is tucked up and she pulls on the bow, her left foot in front and the right half off the ground balanced only on the toe, and near it a dog, alert, waiting for the moment when the beast is wounded so that it can chase after it. The left hand is high holding the bow while the right remains in the air as though the bow has just been pulled, the arm still bent, elbow in the air, and the two fingers that released the bow still bent; behind, the quiver on her shoulder, and thus she seems to wait to see where her shot has gone . . .]

Memories of French images at Fontainebleau and elsewhere may have given greater density to this vision of the goddess of the hunt. These may have enhanced Audebert's rendering of the sense of movement frozen for an instant. This interest in figures on the move is characteristic of all the descriptions Audebert provided of forms at Tivoli, as though these marvels, so recently constructed, offered both a challenge and new territory in which to explore his narrative prowess. The concentration upon them reinforces the idea that, in his manuscript 'Journal', he was preparing an ambitious literary work which was to break new ground in the field of travel literature. Significantly, he made no attempt to describe the famous statues in the Belvedere courtyard. His father had already described them in his poem; and for the son, mere naming was now enough. The ingenuities at Tivoli were more demanding, and he was tempted to capture the movement that seemed paramount there: in the gestures of the figures (the gladiators 'tout prests à frapper et combattre', all ready to strike and fight) (II, 74) – or in the trickle of the waters whose complex travel he tried to trace.

The most difficult effect which Audebert attempted to catch was the play of sunlight beside Leda in the fountain named after her. The account is, as usual, scrupulously precise and clear. It emphasized the tiny space between the mouth of the vessel and the round piece of metal through which the water gushed before spreading and thinning out into bright radial lines and taking on diverse shapes and figures:

> Soubs le bras gaulche de Leda est un vase couché, dedans lequel sourd une Fontaine, par le moyen de laquelle le Soleil est fort naïvement representé, ayant une piece de fer blanc toute ronde en forme de soleil appliquée sur la bouche du vaisseau, sans y boucher, mais tellement proche que il ne demeure que peu d'espace d'entr'ouvert entre ledict fer blanc et la bouche du vase, de sorte que l'eau qui veult sortir en abondance . . . pousse de force contre le fer blanc, et ainsy s'espend toute platte au tour, faisant une grande rondeur puis, par ceste force et combat qui est à la sortie, l'eau venant à s'esclaircir et dilater represente une forme de rayons qui sont si brillans et de tant de diverses formes et figures, que la veue en demeure comme esblouye. (II, 70–1)

> [Under Leda's left arm rests a vase from which pours a fountain which, with great naturalness, reflects the sun, a small round piece of white metal, in the form of a sun, having been applied to the opening of the vessel, without blocking the flow but so closely fitting that there is very little space between the metal and the mouth of the vase so that the water which wants to flow rapidly . . . forces itself against the metal, spreads all around in a great circle, and through this force and effort at the point of exit, the water clears and radiates out in the form of sun rays which are so bright and in such diverse forms and shapes that one's sight stays dazzled.]

Audebert here avoids the rather didactic tone he sometimes adopted (as in the description of the theatre of Marcellus: II, 268), and to which he had recourse when words were inadequate to translate the full beauty of the antiquities.

Despite his literary ambitions, Audebert acknowledged that design and drawing could often render an object or monument more faithfully and more immediately than could words. He conceded, for example, that the Colosseum 'ne peult estre mieux descript qu'il se veoit dépeint ès livres d'antiquitez' (could not be better described than can be seen painted in books of antiquities) (II, 267). Although the whole tenor of the work suggests that Audebert was attempting something original in his account, he could not escape from the information and the images that were provided by published volumes on the sights and ancient monuments of Rome. The presence of guidebooks and *livres d'antiquitez* intruded on his consciousness. When he abandoned the new and intricate wonders of Tivoli and came to record the principal glories of Rome, he referred to drawings and engravings, for these captured the image better than words could do – 'mieux que par parolles il ne se peult descrire' (II, 270).

This sudden and frustrated refusal to describe is typical of most *récits de voyage*. Montaigne – although claiming to have studied particularly the palace and gardens at Tivoli – did not bother to describe them. As he explained:

> J'y consideray toutes choses fort particulièrement, j'essayerois de la peindre icy, mais il y a des livres et peintures publicques de ce suject.

> [I looked at everything very closely, and I would try to paint them here were there not many books and pictures on the subject generally available.][54]

Audebert had seen at Tivoli an opportunity to shine in his studied and meticulous account; Montaigne (whose *Journal* in the form that we have it was not intended for publication), merely admired.

Rome's fame was already thoroughly documented. In consequence, writers were highly selective about those objects on which they concentrated their attention; and more often than not they withdrew from the task of describing altogether. Tarde, rendered helpless by the sheer quantity of works, named the building, listed rather haphazardly and in general terms its principal features (interweaving a few new technical words), then dashed down a comment such as that there were a thousand other most remarkable things 'trop longues à réciter' (too long to enumerate).[55] So generalized and uniform in the minds of travellers was the acceptance of the external aspects of the major ancient monuments in Rome that instead of being described in travel journals, they became points of reference, standards by which other statues and buildings were judged. Their norms of excellence, often established by the guidebooks, went unchallenged, and when Villamont or André Thevet evoked the columns or obelisks seen in Egypt, or in the country around Constantinople, they referred to their knowledge and experience of Roman counterparts to give the size and form of what they described.[56]

This chapter has attempted to give some idea of the kind of testimony which French writers in the second half of the sixteenth century gave of their experience of Rome. The forms they chose for their records were varied and open-ended. In their *récits*, they often showed themselves conscious of inadequacy, of the necessity of being faithful to what they had seen, and yet of the difficulty of competing with the weight of description that was already there in classical works or in guidebooks. Reading in preparation for their journey actually seems to have inhibited the ability to see what was there and, to a certain extent, to have removed the need to describe at all. Yet the picture that emerges is more complex: modest reportage or relative silence, and a mere naming of the great things as evidence that the writer had seen what ought to be seen. An analysis of the *récits de voyage* shows the extent to which past and present coexisted in the minds of French observers in Rome. While they were anxious to find the right language and the right forms in which to express the special character of the city to which they responded, the very abundance of the objects that confronted their gaze, and their wish to absorb and re-use the new technical terms relating to sculpture and architecture, tended to screen what the onlooker was describing from the reader. In the end, the experience of Rome as recounted in these records was essentially – and perhaps unsurprisingly – a transforming process. The shifts (often unconscious) between present and past sights offered creative opportunities and these would be noted and deliberately exploited by artists and writers in France. Nicolas Audebert, however, stands by himself. He wanted to be recognized as an artist in words; this, he felt, was his destiny. He saw how the material he observed could be turned into literary performances; and, from the ruined walls of Rome, through his meticulous prose, he etched in detail complete images and evoked the vibrant forms that inhabited the gardens at Tivoli.

CHAPTER 2

The Guidebook

PREPARATION FOR ROME

Imagine hundreds of books, diversely illustrated: some are tiny and compact, made to hide in your pocket, some are so huge and unwieldy that stout reading tables are required for their use. Such was the range of guidebooks published in the Renaissance for the increasing number of travellers who wanted to go to Italy and to Rome.[1] The guidebook was a crucial aid to travellers. It not only directed their gaze, and formed their judgement in advance, but also removed the need for them to describe what they saw. Increasingly, travellers refrained from relating their own impressions in detail in their journals and, as the guidebook industry grew in volume and importance, they referred readers explicitly for information and aesthetic assessment to the published descriptions of Rome.[2]

In this context, Audebert's comments at the end of his *Voyage* may be taken as typical. When he visited the Farnese art collections, he referred nonchalantly to the attitudes of the statues and, feigning loss of memory, he reported: 'de leurs gestes il ne m'en souvient' (of their gestures, I remember nothing); similarly he would claim that an object was so famous that the reader would do well to find a picture of it in a book; in this way he failed to describe the figure of Roma, 'si bien connue vous les pourrez veoir aux livres des pourtraicts' (so well-known that you can see them in books of engravings) (II, 269). Although there was a tendency in *récits de voyage* to make sure that all the main sights had been named and recorded so that, in retrospect, the individual could claim 'I have seen', writers were ready to acknowledge the usefulness and the expertise of guidebooks. Audebert regularly referred his reader to them with specific praise for the value of the images they depicted and the precision with which they were labelled:

La plus part de ce que dessus se pourra veoir dans les livres de ceux qui ont les antiquitez, mieux que par parolles il ne se peult descrire, y ayant mesme soubz chaque piece le nom du lieu où elles sont. (II, 270)

[Most of what has gone before can be seen in books of antiquities, and better than words could describe since under each figure is the name of the place where it is to be found.][3]

Before embarking upon a study of the role of the guidebook in shaping the response of travellers to the sights of Rome, it is important to remember the extent to which visitors' reactions were also framed and articulated by memories of classical writings. Such interference was evident from the late fifteenth century at least. It has been shown, for example,[4] how a certain Giovanni from Tolentino saw and wrote about his first views of Rome by manipulating sentences from Livy, Pliny, Horace and Virgil, although he had promised (in the letter he wrote to the poet Baldassare Taccone) that he would describe 'in a more expansive manner, the ruins of Rome. I shall write about all of these things, if not elegantly, then as accurately as I can.' The power of remembrance of earlier reading was irresistible. Over and above the desire to adorn the work with memorable phrases, readers were influenced by the visions of Rome captured in a profusion of classical texts, the words of which reverberated again and again. Propertius had condensed the startling growth of Rome into a few powerful phrases drawing together a view of the city in his day and a vision of the green fields and hills that formed the original site, telescoping the movement over time:

> Hoc quodcumque vides, hospes, qua maxima Roma est,
> Ante Phrygem Aeneam collis et herba fuit. (*Elegies*, IV, 1)

[All that thou beholdest, stranger, where mighty Rome lies spread,/ was grass and hill before the coming of Phrygian Aeneas.]

His unashamed praise of Italy and its imperial city ensured its enduring and unquestioned status:

> Omnia Romanae cedent miracula terrae:
> natura hic posuit, quidquid ubique fuit. (III, 22)

[yet all these marvels shall yield to the land of Rome:/ here hath nature placed whate'er is best in all the world.]

Other writers resurrected lost monuments and gave them a new, lasting existence. The temple of Mars, long destroyed, is perpetuated in Ovid's *Fasti* (VI, ll. 191–2):

> Lux eadem Marti festa est, quem proscipit extra
> Appositum rectae porta Capoena viae.

[The same day is the festival of Mars, whose temple, set beside the Covered Way, is seen afar without the walls from the Capeae Gate.]

Similarly, the gate that led out to the Appian Way was recalled by Livy; while Persius reminded readers of the temple dedicated to Venus Erycina, his verse transforming its ruins and customs into a living entity: the temple is a place for young girls bringing their offerings to the goddess:

> Dicite Pontifices in sacris quid faciat aurum
> Nempe hoc, quod Veneri donatae a virgine pupae. (*Satire* II, ll.69–70)

> [but you, Reverend Pontiffs, tell us what good gold can do in a holy place, just as much or as little as the dolls which a young girl offers to Venus.]

Lines such as these, evocative and largely generalized, encouraged the envisioning of sights reconstituted through memory and the imagination. They shifted the gaze away from the present. This transference of attention was an important consideration too in relation to the creative processes of writers and artists in the late Renaissance, and these were themselves conditioned by the guidebook.

THE NATURE OF THE GUIDEBOOK

It may be surprising, but the greatest resistance to seeing what was actually there was provided by the nature of the guidebook itself. Enormously varied in their content, guidebooks gave the reader a definite visual image of states and their towns, supplemented by a wealth of comment, information and scholarly dispute. Their very abundance and their comprehensiveness tended to render their counsel opaque, to obscure the monuments they sought to describe, and to jumble the reception of the many facts they had assembled.

The extent of the problem was exposed by Rabelais in his introductory epistle to Cardinal Jean du Bellay which he wrote to be placed at the head of Bartholomeo Marliani's book *Liber urbis Romae topographia* (first published in Lyon by Gryphius in 1534). There, Rabelais explained how he had intended to describe Rome in detail:

> me promettais de dépeindre avec ma plume, tout comme avec un pinceau, l'aspect de la ville.

> [I promised myself to sketch with my pen, as if it were a paintbrush, the prospect of the city.][5]

He was confident that he could accomplish the task successfully since he had long prepared for it, and with method. He had amassed vast numbers of notes from texts in French and Italian, he had visited every corner and every shadow in the city itself such that he claimed 'que personne, je crois, ne connaît mieux sa propre maison que je ne connais Rome et toutes les ruelles de Rome' (that no one, I believe, knows his own house better than I know Rome and all the little streets of Rome). And yet the work never materialized; for, although it was probably not difficult to envisage the nature of the task, there was a significant problem when it came to ordering the material, as Rabelais frankly acknowledged:

> même si le sujet lui-même n'était pas difficile à concevoir, il ne me paraissait cependant pas facile d'agencer avec clarté, propriété et élégance un amas de matériaux entassés pêle-mêle. (Ibid.)

> [even if the subject itself was not difficult to conceive, it seemed to me, however, that it was not easy to arrange such a mass of material (assembled anyhow) clearly, properly and elegantly.]

Giving shape to a straggling mess and making that shape aesthetically pleasing, clear and appropriate delayed Rabelais' progress, and he seems finally to have been content to abandon his own project and to have participated in Marliani's enterprise, offering his knowledge, and checking classical quotations and inscriptions.[6]

These problems of conception and ordering were often compounded by other factors: the requirement, for example, to incorporate specialist knowledge into the text such as the requests which Rabelais himself received from André Thevet.[7] Then there was the obligation to express the sensations of 'stupor' which regularly had to accompany the first sight of Rome's ruins if the Italian translator of Marliani's text in 1548 is to be believed. In his dedicatory epistle to Giovan-Battista Grimaldi, Hercole Barbarosa da Terni boasted that nothing was more true or more vibrant, and nothing more numbing and astounding than the marvels and the ruins of Rome (Figure 12):

> de laquale, ni una cosa è al mondo, che ne possa fare, ne più vivo testimento, che la maravigliosa città di Roma, e per le cose, che vi sono hoggi, e maggiormente per quelle che ne le miraculose ruine, scampate da l'ingiuria del Tempo, con estremo stupore di tutti del mondo, vi si contemplans . . .

> [to which nothing in the world can compare nor offer a more living testimony than the marvellous city of Rome, and for these reasons: that things that can be seen there, and especially those magnificent ruins rescued from the injury of Time to the extreme astonishment of all the world who can gaze at them there . . .][8]

Further complications were introduced through the habit of incorporating into the guidebook borrowings and arguments from other texts and then by engaging in lengthy and futile debate upon them. This interweaving of borrowed facts and phrases, this copying and re-using of material, amplified verbal descriptions and also affected illustrations. The copying was sometimes left to the reader to discover but it might also be acknowledged – as in Lauro's preface to his *Antiquae urbis splendor* or in Bernardo Gamucci's use of Dosio's drawings

Foro Romano

2522.

12. G.A. Dosio: drawing of the Forum

and his expressions of gratitude to the work of Marliani.[9] Occasionally, the
requirement to incorporate enthusiastic references is announced in the title of
the guidebook. Gamucci, for instance, augmented the title of *Le antichità della
città di Roma* (1565) with the information that it had been compiled 'raccolte
sotta brevità da diversi antichi e moderni scrittori' (drawn from diverse writers,
ancient and modern). Aware that such a congestion of material might obscure
the buildings and objects he sought to describe, Gamucci tried to organize the
material so that it would not detract from an appreciation of them. He was at
pains to stress that he had arranged everything in a new order with accurate
descriptions of the most beautiful things that could be found in Rome: 'con
nuove ordine fedelmente descritte e rappresentate' (in a new order, accurately
described and represented). Ten years later, François de Belleforest (1530–85)
published his *Cosmographie universelle* in which he confidently depicted Rome,
numbering its gates and its towers without ever having visited the city, or
indeed without having set foot in many of the other towns and countries which
he described.[10] The dependence on other texts is, in this instance, total.

Intertextuality rarely secured heightened accuracy. On the contrary, borrowings encouraged the traditions and myths which people wanted to believe
rather than supporting or developing observations made by the looking eye.

37

The *Mirabilia urbis Romae*, first printed in 1475 and published many times in different versions up to 1600,[11] certainly named the principal monuments and churches which the pilgrim should see, but surrounded that naming with a sea of conjecture and romancing. It is a tribute to the hold the Catholic Church continued to have on the minds of travellers to Rome that the usefulness of the *Mirabilia* lasted so long, for the book identified the places where indulgences were granted. The sureness of that hold is demonstrated by Jean Rigaud who, while underlining his determination to write only about what he had seen with his own eyes, uses the *Mirabilia* as his most constant point of reference.[12]

Even those antiquarians who had other motives – such as the recovery of ancient Rome and the improvement of the modern city – were misled by their enthusiasm, and frequently misrepresented the state of the elements they described. The friend of Raphael, Fabius Calvus, who undertook to follow carefully and closely the various historical stages in the construction of Rome as it could be ascertained from what could be seen in the first decades of the sixteenth century, succumbed to interpretation as he tried to relate the ruins of classical antiquity to contemporary architecture conceived 'à l'antique'.[13] Moreover, he could not resist interpolating into his text effusions on the greatness of Rome, on the superabundance and quality of its buildings, reassurances on the easy availability of indulgences and on the lingering blood of its martyrs, all themes which he had also explored in a poem written two years earlier:

> Rome conserve encore l'ombre de son antique majesté, qui attire vers elle les peuples de la terre comme les membres se tournent vers la tête. Nulle part on n'a une telle abondance d'édifices, une telle pompe générale, tant de lieux saints, un pardon si efficace et tant d'indulgences . . . tant de martyrs à célébrer dont le sang répandu a tout consacré.

> [Rome still preserves the shadow of her old majesty which draws people from all the world towards her as members of the body turn towards the head. Nowhere else can such an abundance of buildings be found, such pomp, so many sacred places, pardons so efficacious and so many indulgences . . . so great a number of martyrs to celebrate whose spattered blood has consecrated everything.][14]

Inflation of this kind, coupled with the sheer quantity of facts to be imparted, seriously impeded the traveller's vision. Despite the good intentions of some authors, it proved difficult for many to avoid 'inventing' what they wished still to see in Rome, from the evidence available to them.

There were other ways of simulating the scrupulous attention to accuracy that scholars assumed in their work but only rarely achieved. Publishers started to issue compendious works, aware that they were bound to benefit greatly from continuing to feed the desire for more and more guidebooks (to Italy especially) – a desire which continued unabated for well over a hundred years. These were huge volumes designed to bring together authoritative pronouncements on Rome and clearly intended for a learned and specialist market. Masochius in Rome, Gryphius in Lyon, and Chöuet in Geneva produced a series of immense tomes: *De Roma prisca et nova. Varii auctores*, Rome, 1523; *Antiquitatum variorum autores*, Lyon, 1552; and R. Dempster, *Antiquitatum romanorum corpus absolutissimum*, Geneva, 1558. These works were frequently reprinted and they all had similar features – an enormous range of primary texts; formidable erudite references so that the scholar could chase up contentious interpretations; and pages of engravings which illustrated the many reconstructions of objects and buildings long lost to sight as well as picturing monuments that remained. Dempster's huge corpus was typical. He had searched the works of poets, historians, critics, linguists, orators and jurisconsults to fill out the 1,063 pages of the texts which he printed and which were adorned by engravings from the pen of Rosinus.[15] The very bulk of these collective works, although perhaps inviting to the persistent scholar, was hardly calculated to enlighten the mere traveller.

In circumstances of such proliferation and of hindrances to seeing, what could be done to accommodate the needs of most travellers? It was necessary to develop modes of controlling the vast material, and this realization led to the development of systematic approaches to conveying information. Thus Rome was divided into sections; its site was mapped into streets; its chief monuments were listed; and descriptions of the city proceeded hill by hill as in Lucio Fauno's popular *Compendio*.[16] Such an approach was not uncontroversial, as can be seen from the vigorous defence which Fauno made of his method against those who had attacked him. Book 1 described the growth of Rome from the time of Romulus; each of the following books was devoted to one of the seven hills, identifying its ancient monuments and temples, its churches, bridges and ruins. A companion volume provided a history of the city from the time of Augustus Caesar down to the reign of Charles V. Panvinius also, in his 'Theatrum urbis Romae' (which is still in manuscript), attempted to control the material by covering each region of the city and dividing its monuments into two columns: ancient and modern.[17] Other writers, such as Francesco Albertini, chose to concentrate on monument types: his sequence of studies on theatres and amphitheatres, on trophies and columns, on arches and on paintings and statues seemed as much designed to honour Julius II as to recall to mind surviving monuments as testimony to the achievements of the ancient world.[18] Years later, in 1569, Luigi Contarini organized his work in dialogue form,[19] chosen to facilitate the assimilation of the crowded facts he was trying to convey. Yet the structure of his volume in the end differed little from that of Fauno since Contarini also started with the origins of the city (pp. 1–74) and then, as Fauno had done, proceeded hill by hill, incorporating churches and statues, emperors and families without too much regard for accuracy in dating or in attributions. The same pattern was followed by Rosinus in his augmented edition of Dempster in 1583, although that relied on the findings of earlier scholars.[20]

13. Attributed to Etienne du Pérac, trophies of Mars, ruined and reconstructed

TROPHEA MARII.

Aeq: Giulia

Furns drizzati d'Mario qusti trofei, p hauer superato i Cimbri pop: Settentr: di Pa-
uia, e di Salauda, ma Silla gli desfece, e Cesoli ristorò, o fece di nuouo sopra un castello d'Viesqua condutta da lui p qusta regione, chiamata Giulia.

Although the pattern of narration which was based on the search for origins and then on the sectionalization of the city had become well established, guide-books continued to develop in bewildering complexity. This was due to the diversity of authors' intentions and to the fact that they often attempted much more than a mere recital of what could be seen. Flavio Biondo's aim, for instance, had been to inspire his contemporaries with a proper admiration of Rome's past greatness and an appreciation of its present potential magnificence; and this desire informed all his writing.[21] Similarly, Andreas Fulvius (a friend and colleague of Raphael) saw the greatness of the ancient city reflected in the palaces which were rising around him, and that conception permeated both his vision and his writing. He dedicated his work to Clement VII in the expectation that further improvements to the city would enhance the inflated picture he had painted;[22] and for this reason, he had penned an oration extolling the beauty of the city which he followed up with a poetic encomium on the Roman people. So easily did description give way to praise. Yet, notwithstanding the distance he had travelled from an accurate assessment of the classical buildings still standing in Rome, Fulvius' work was frequently reprinted throughout the sixteenth century, often with additional material. In 1588 Girolamo Ferrucci undertook to correct and amplify the original text.[23] He annotated Fulvius' findings and, in the spirit of Andreas himself, added accounts of new marvels built by a succession of popes to improve and beautify the city, although – for much of the sixteenth century – the piers and vaults of St Peter's, for instance, lay open to the sky, the remains of the old church jumbled around, resembling the ruins of ancient classical monuments. The emphasis continued to be placed on greatness and magnificence, yet Fulvius also recognized the devastating effects of change and decline: the triple impact of war, fire and flood; the loss of discipline and the disregard for law; and the evil work of barbarians. Such deterioration constituted a challenge for any writer who wished to leave a positive view of the city. Ferrucci, in his extensively illustrated volume, met the challenge by depicting almost side by side the ruined classical buildings as they could be seen in the sixteenth century and monuments lost to view for centuries as though they were perfect. Thus, as Etienne du Pérac had done (Figure 13), he showed the ruins on the Esquiline hill with trophies of Mars set in mounds of stones and several layers of ruins piled up one upon the other (f. 57v), and – I cite one example among many – he created a perfect rendition of the temple of Thundering Jove on the Capitoline hill (f. 38v).[24] The woodcuts stand out from the page in their simple, lined frames showing the monuments as if isolated from their immediate context and set against an imagined landscape. Thus, within the established pattern of detailing the sites of Rome, readers were accustomed to see scenes that faithfully depicted what was there alongside others that projected perfect replicas of ancient monuments. The frontispiece of Ferrucci's 1588 edition gave a good

14. *Roma*, frontispiece of Ferrucci's edition of Fulvius' book

indication of the will to maintain and broadcast a lofty view of Rome, past and present. It carried a defiant engraving of ALMA ROMA, displaying a helmeted female figure in armour holding in her right hand a statue of Fame standing on the world, with the Tiber and the seven hills of Rome shown beyond (Figure 14).[25] The tradition of praise, inherited from the ancients and from writers like Flavio Biondo, undoubtedly conjured up an inflated view of Rome and Romans in the minds of sixteenth-century readers.

Reacting against this tendency to overstate, other writers accepted the challenge of greater accuracy, although the effects in their writing could also produce another kind of disorientation. Lucio Fauno maintained that there was a role for conjecture in building images of ancient Rome. Even in the elementary and disputed area of the size of the city, he grafted his conjectural method on to the evidence provided by ancient writers such as Livy and Pliny. Conjecture, he argued, was amply justified when it was combined either with visual evidence (however meagre) or ancient sources of significance; in these circumstances 'Coniecturas seque necesse est' (conjecture is necessary).[26] This approach, which combined evidence and hypothesis, was to have far-reaching influence on writers and artists engaged in re-creating the forms which belonged to ancient Rome and in transferring those forms into sixteenth-century landscapes.

Pirro Ligorio (1510–83) tackled the challenge of accuracy in a very original way. He had planned a vast, encyclopaedic enterprise with the aim of recording and restoring every category of artefact which the city of Rome offered. In other words, his was to be a paper museum; a comprehensive resource or master archive that could be mined, added to and corrected by new generations of scholars. His was a humanist approach, using any material that came to hand – writings from classical antiquity, manuscripts, ancient remains, inscriptions, medals and coins, and the work of contemporary scholars. He compiled, classified, described, measured, invented and drew. The sheer size of the undertaking clouded the comprehensive picture he planned

43

to achieve. By his death in 1583, he had prepared over forty volumes for pub-lication; most remain in manuscript and they show how interested he was in both literary and visual approaches to his task.[27] Sixteenth-century readers – potential travellers – saw only one text: *Libro di M. Pirro Ligorio Napolitano delle antichità di Roma* (Venice, 1553)[28] in which Ligorio studied circuses, theatres and amphitheatres and challenged and refuted the common views then circu-lating about many buildings in Rome, whose inaccuracies he termed a veri-table 'labyrinth' of errors. Combativeness was typical of Ligorio's writing and this confirms the notion that he had conceived his work essentially for the specialist rather than for a wider audience. His style naturally aroused the opposition as well as the interest of other scholars who, nonetheless, used his manuscripts, copied his drawings and – occasionally – declared their indebted-ness.[29] There is, for instance, a manuscript note in vol. XIIII (f. 220), written by a French artist who was awaiting a book from Bâle on the Roman emperors. He does not complain about the delay because:

> Je suis persuadé que ce n'est que par deffaut de commodité qu'il ne l'aura pas receu que ne suis je quinze jours ou un mois avec son Pirrhus Ligorius j'y passerai mon temps bien agreablement.

> [I am persuaded that it is only by some slight want of convenience that he hasn't received it [my letter], if I'm a fortnight or a month with his Pirro Ligorio, I shall pass my time most agreeably.]

The same writer also reveals that he had copied from Ligorio manuscripts during a stay in Turin.[30]

Art historians have viewed Ligorio's work diversely. Some have criticized his own errors and 'inventions', while others have appreciated the attempts he made at restoring to sight buildings that had once existed. Although it has been shown that Ligorio frequently had recourse to images on medals in his reconstruction of ancient monuments, and that he used what Robert Gaston has happily called 'imaginative interference', the knowledge that he gained from his scrutiny of all visual remains (fragments of stone, coins or inscriptions) (Figure 15) was invaluable when he unearthed and identified new remains in Rome or at Hadrian's villa at Tivoli.[31] His influence seeped through to most artists and writers who puzzled over fragments and their reconstruction, and his work will be referred to again.[32]

Ligorio's great plan was only accessible to experts and through the con-structions he made at Tivoli for Cardinal Ippolito d'Este which many travellers visited. Nevertheless, his intense activity and the controversies he provoked prepared a larger audience for a whole series of works specializing in par-ticular aspects of Roman building, both ancient and modern; and this tendency towards specialization became more marked in the second half of the century.

Pierre Woeriot, who spent four years in Italy, dedicated his first book of

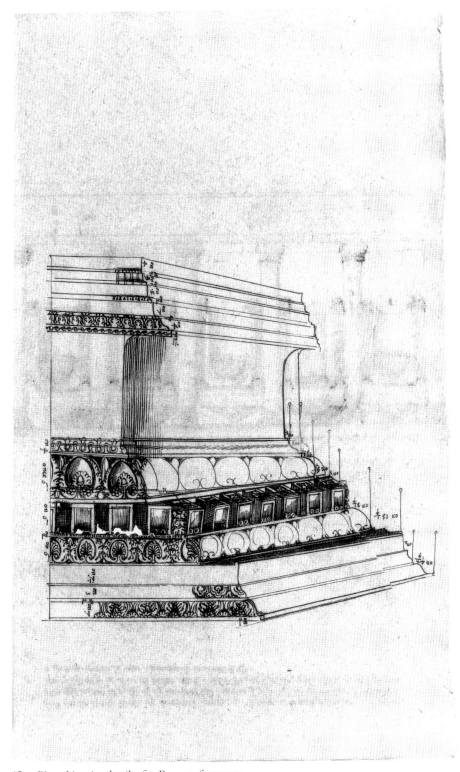

15. Pirro Ligorio: detail of a Roman fragment

engravings of Roman statues to Charles de Lorraine in 1560.[33] The statues of senators, Amazons, ancient kings, gods and goddesses were drawn directly from observations of art collections such as those housed in the Farnese palace. The figures are all dignified, their garments falling in ample folds, each one holding its appropriate device or with a carefully depicted attribute. These drawings, however, remained for the prince's eyes alone since, although the work was clearly prepared for publication, it was never issued. Woeriot's work was more obviously crafted than the figures engraved from the workshop of the Roman art dealer Lorenzo della Vaccaria whose book had the same title *Antiquarum statuarum urbis Romae* and was published some twenty years later, in 1583. These engravings were widely available and gave the reader a generous choice of figures from both public and private collections. Franzini followed this example in 1587 with his *Icones statuarum antiquarum urbis Romae* which went into several editions (1587, 1596, 1599), and he also published popular guides on palaces and churches showing them in rather crude woodcuts.[34]

The printing of engraved figures of the memorable statues in Roman collections became very fashionable and, before the end of the sixteenth century, G.B. Cavalieri and Cherubino Alberti had added their own versions.[35] Most *Icones* reproduced famous examples from the Belvedere gardens (Laocoön, Tiber and Apollo), from the Farnese palace (Hercules and Venus), or from the Campidoglio (Augustus, Constantine, Marsyas or the Marphorio); yet each engraver attempted some new variation. As the works and figures increased in number so their execution became rougher as though basic identification of the statue were all that was needed, making later works different in character from the drawings done by artists such as Woeriot who had sought both to please a powerful patron and to prepare for future projects of his own.

Alongside the production of books which catered for popular needs was the publication of numerous erudite tomes which (although not strictly guidebooks) set out for the learned reader specific areas of Roman culture. These involved a complex process of reconstruction which had several stages. It began with the study of the remains of buildings or objects that survived, which was then supplemented by ancient records whose interpretation could be difficult and controversial since they had often come down to sixteenth-century scholars only in fragmented form. Next came further enhancement by reference to comparative examples scattered across a broad geographical area; and finally there might be a collating of materials, sometimes of questionable authenticity. This staged process of re-enactment, which was then to be viewed against the fragments of the building or object which could still be seen, informed the manner in which French writers and artists saw their own tasks.

The range of these specialist volumes is enormous; it extended from the study of games to political structures, and from legal practices to obelisks. Games, their rules and procedures, their location and the size of the territory they required were studied by Onufrius Panvinius in *De ludis circensibus*, and his findings were tested, exploited and largely reproduced by Lipsius and

Boulenger.[36] A study of the organization of political structures, voting habits, the names of officials (generation by generation from the earliest times) formed the labour of Carlo Sigonio who benefited from some prior work by Panvinius.[37] Other topics were explored, too. In his *Historia fori* (1576), Francesi Polletti wrote about legal practice;[38] obelisks were discussed by Pietro Angelio in *Commentarius de obelisco* (1586);[39] and the Vatican library was treated in Mutio Panza's *Della Libraria Vaticana* (1590). It is noticeable that all these works drew on private as well as public collections and this fact is often advertised in the title of the book, as in those which emanated from Vaccaria's printing house – for example Franzini's work *Antiquarum statuarum urbis Romae quae in publicis privatisque locii visuntur icones* (1583). Thus Rome was seen not only as a repository of ancient public remains and monuments readily visible to anyone walking through the streets of the city, but also as a treasure house of precious artefacts discovered and preserved in princely private collections which had been built up over decades and which were increasingly open to visitors.

The visitor to Rome and the reader of guides to the city were invited to admire both kinds of marvels within the cultural context that had been established by the work of learned scholars, ancient and modern. Although there is abundant evidence that Nicolas Audebert himself looked hard and patiently at the detail of the monuments he visited, his training and cast of mind obliged him to refer constantly in his narrative to the support of classical writers – Caesar, Livy, Lucan, Seneca, Juvenal, Suetonius, Pliny, Polybius, Plutarch, Tacitus (to cite merely the sequence of names as they appear in the early pages of the *Voyage*), and to quote modern exponents such as Flavio Biondo, Leandro Alberti or Aldrovandi to strengthen his own words.[40] Their views intruded on his own.

At about the same time as Audebert was writing up his reflections on his journey to Rome, in 1583, Louis de Montjosieu was setting out on his own adventures in the company of the duc de Joyeuse. After two years in the city he published his ambitious *Gallia Romae hospes*[41] divided into five books in which he sought to explain the strange symbols he found on sepulchres, pyramids and obelisks. In part 2 of his book he extolled the wonderful symmetry of the Pantheon, likening it to the human body, and could not resist in his engravings decorating the outside of the building with its original ornaments.[42] In parts 3 and 4 he discoursed on the sculpture and paintings which survived from the classical world; and in his final volume he presented the Forum and St Peter's. Throughout his elucidations, two sources constantly recurred – the works of Pliny and Vitruvius. Their opinions and observations shaped Montjosieu's vision and guided his judgement.

Although images had become an integral part of later sixteenth-century guidebooks, only some parts of Montjosieu's text were illustrated, as in his depiction of the interior of the Pantheon (Book 2, p. 14) where, through a systematic use of Pliny and Vitruvius, he tried to reconstruct the temple as it was

no, di dentro hauea cinque nicchi, o' luoghi da porue statue fatti nella grossezza del muro che circuiua il corpo dela cella; et tra nicchio à nicchio era posta una colonna: la base d'uer spira erano di queste colonne per ciò che quelle che faceuano intorno portico di sette piedi largo non haueuano altro che un Toro solo per base senza Zocco per che questa posaua nel piano del portico: onde da queste parole si può dire che quel Tempio haueua questa forma qui diseguata. il Diametro di tutto il uano dela cella poteua esser da quarantacinque piedi: et il muro di cinque et un quarto fatto di opera reticulata, er incrostato di marmi sottilissimi et uaria, er per torre uia i Teuertini con che erano fermati, si le colonne come le altre cose, fu'uniuersalmente questa. Di questa medesima forma ueggamo il medesimo Tempio per riuesso di Commodo Imperadore.

Per che ad'Hercole si fu' il Tempio circulare, è forse perche egli camino' et purgo netta la Terra, di fiere, er d'huomini cattiui: onero per che egli come dice Macrobio è il sole il quale ha il suo camino circulare, et tutte le fiere intendo se no dedicate à lui, come dice Eusebio pamphilo.

16.   Pirro Ligorio: drawings of Roman remains

in antiquity with its statues and columns all in place; his reconstruction of the Septizonium (1, p. 24); or his engraving of an obelisk, borrowed from Gamucci (1, p. 11). His discussions of sculpture and of painting are devoid of engraving; and it is interesting to note that the former is entirely dependent upon the detailed use of material from Pliny while the latter is amplified by specific examples inspired by Vasari and drawn from the work of Michelangelo, Raphael, Titian and Parmigianino.[43] The absence of illustration suggests that Montjosieu believed these modern works were already in the mind of readers, although many might have regarded such an assumption as anything but satisfactory.

The combination of image and text should have given potential visitors to Rome an improved depiction of what they were to see; and certainly, Pirro Ligorio emphasized his simultaneous concern with what Robert Gaston has called 'the literary unfolding and visual representation of Roman ruins'.[44] The manuscripts show description and drawing together on each sheet (Figure 16). Unfortunately, few sixteenth-century readers — Panvinius apart — saw them.

Faced with the jumble of buildings and remains that littered the landscape of Rome, the traveller's imagination had much work to do, despite the efforts of publishers, editors, compilers, writers of guides and scholarly exploration. Some writers had indeed tried to provide stimulation. Ferrucci, for instance, had supplied images that reconstructed, from surviving medals, buildings that had long since been destroyed: the baths of Diocletian (f. 89r), of Agrippa and Nero (ff. 87 and 87v), for example, and the latter's Naumachia (f. 92). Alongside these reinvented images Ferrucci placed other sights, shown as partial, incomplete and confused. There was the Forum (f. 95v) which was little more than a hillside scene with medieval buildings set among the ruins with the occasional temple depicted as though it were still intact (Figure 17); or Trajan's forum (f. 108r) which was a medley of medieval and ruined classical buildings.[45] This double approach encouraged the reader's eye to move between the image of ruins and that of reconstruction, and the automatic movement itself began a process of conjecture whereby the reader, perhaps unconsciously at first, began to make his own pictures from the scraps available (Figure 18), guided (as the writer and engraver would have been) by buildings which had completely or partially disappeared from the landscape but which had been made whole again.

Not all authors of guides suppressed information on the true condition of buildings, although Giovannantonio Dosio was unusual in indicating on the drawings he made of ancient monuments what he had actually seen and measured, and where he had added to a fragment. He did not hesitate to draw the humblest of dwellings alongside the remains of classical structures. His conscientiousness was similarly apparent in the fact that he often provided more than one sketch of a building or scene, drawing it from different angles; such was his rendering of Trajan's column, Diocletian's baths, or the forum of Trajan.[46]

17. Marten van Heemskerck: drawing of the Forum

18. Etienne du Pérac: ruins on the Palatine

And what of the guide which Michel de Montaigne carried in his pocket when he journeyed to Rome in 1580? Lucio Mauro's *Delle antichità di Roma*, published in Venice in 1556, was a neat little book; unpretentious and without engraved images, but with the addition of Ulisse Aldrovandi's catalogue of art works preserved in Rome's private and public collections.[47] It quickly became a valuable source of information about those works which the ardent traveller must not miss. The houses and gardens of cardinals, princes, artists and those of high officials from the papal court were all presented. Outdoors, the reader is shown the city, hill by hill (in the traditional sequence): first, the Capitoline and an account of what used to be there and what is there now ('con le cose, che vi furono & che hora visono' (with the things that were there and which can be seen today), p. 5); then the Palatine, remarkable for its emptiness and for its wild and desert-like places, of which only a tiny church, St Nicholas, was still visible. In other ancient places, other shapes are clearer and better defined by time. The Colosseum which, although in Mauro's eyes was 'quasi rovinato tutto' (almost completely ruined), had sufficiently preserved its form for the rest of the original concept to be imagined: 'si puo fare congiettura del resto' (p. 31). The excursion outdoors is rapidly over; and the emphasis shifts to the art treasures housed in Rome and to Aldrovandi's account which, although centred on statuary, also refers from time to time to collections of bronze, silver and gold medals which owners courteously exposed to genuinely interested travellers, and to books and manuscripts.

The statues attracted most of Aldrovandi's attention. They were described minutely, the author attempting to catch the different postures – Venus emerging from her bath or, in another pose, again naked, holding her shift. When objects had been tampered with or modern elements added to an antique work, this is carefully noted, as in the case of the Cupid in Curtio Francipane's collection, whose head and legs were modern 'la testa e le gambe sono moderne' (p. 262), or the head of Livia owned by the sculptor Julio di Sabini which was mounted on a modern bust. Implicit claims for authenticity were anticipated, as Aldrovandi regularly identified the place where the object was found: in the Antonine Baths, for example, on the Capitoline hill, or at Frascati. Information on the aesthetic value of the statues was guided by the opinion of authorities whose judgements went unchallenged. Thus, Pliny is used on Laocoön to the effect that it was the best work ever sculpted, or Aldrovandi repeats Michelangelo's view on the statue of Hercules in the Belvedere gardens, or on the Amazon in the palace of Cardinal Cesi. Very infrequently, Aldrovandi ventured a judgement of his own, such as when he described the statues of Julius Caesar and Augustus on show in Alessandro Ruffini's house as: 'forse delle piu belle, che si veggano in Roma' (perhaps among the most beautiful that can be seen in Rome) (p. 186). Praise was not limited to the beauty of antique statues, however: the work of Michelangelo himself and of Raphael were often extolled and laudatory sentiments were also extended to gardens.

Throughout *Delle antichità* there is a pedagogical tone and every opportunity is taken to expand the reader's knowledge. At times, one might have thought that the author was writing a text on mythography, as when, for instance, having described a statue of Apollo and detailed all the attributes the sculptor had added to his work to ensure identification, Aldrovandi then listed other possible versions of the god not chosen by the sculptor. So Apollo is first seen, full figure, bending his bow as though the arrow had just left it; while other images were also anticipated – Apollo with the sun and its beneficial rays; with a lyre; seated amid the Muses and symbolizing the harmony that regulated the heavens. Similarly, the extended account of Jove's wooing of Europa can only be explained by the fact that the author assumes that his reader has little knowledge of these matters.

Yet the question must be asked: is the catalogue and the abundance of works to which it refers really an aid to understanding, as the detail of mythological stories and the attributes of deities would seem to imply? The accumulation of information was extraordinary: the succession of places; the record of their contents; the sequence of rooms carefully visited, one floor after another; the contents of the courtyards and their garden; their cabinets and libraries; the long lines of gods, goddesses and heroes, well differentiated by name and by symbols, and yet infinitely repeated and repeatable; the names of their owners and the place of their discovery. Such was the multitude of facts, the indication of numberless riches that had to be seen which Mauro and Aldrovandi offered to Montaigne and other travellers. Many many days were needed to catch a glimpse of such abundance; more days to write it all down; and even Aldrovandi himself acknowledged the impossibility of the task: 'molti giorni à vederla, non che à scriverle' (many days to see, but not to write it up) (p. 212).

Paradoxically, many guidebooks – even this one – by attempting to describe everything served to obscure what they sought to show. Multiplication did not clarify; and visitors to Rome, despite assurances to the contrary, did not always report faithfully what they had seen and were misled by the reading they had done. Theodor Zwingler, who wrote an account of his travels in 1577, was honest about the nature and degree of selectivity in his records:

> Nous allons passer en revue non pas tout ce que nous avons observé nous-mêmes mais ce que nous aurions dû observer lors de nostre passage, (autrement dit) ce qui est digne de mémoire.

> [We will go through not all the things we have seen ourselves but what we should have noticed as we went along; in other words, what is worthy of being remembered.][48]

Guidebooks were useful retrospectively, and many writers used them when writing up their own experience. Others abandoned them, as did Montaigne, who threw French guides away, finding that their information needed constant revision and persuaded that his own eyes were the surer witnesses – to the extent that, according to his secretary, 'il eust ayséement reguidé son guide' (he could easily have guided his guide).[49]

Zwingler testified to the fact that for him at least (and doubtless for other travellers) the value of what he had to see in Rome had been determined in advance as had, implicitly, the norms whereby these sights might be judged. Guidebooks helped perpetuate that predetermination in so far as they responded to and repeated patterns of information already established; they published the same sequences of views, and copied the same order of places and monuments on the assumption that the reiterated patterns responded to the motives which brought visitors to Rome. Rather than practical aids to seeing, guidebooks were often substitutes.

THE MULTI-ANGLED VIEW

It was only when artists multiplied the angles of vision, combined detailed presentation with accurate perspective, and used shading to take the viewer's eye inside the building, that the richness and complexity of what could be found in Rome was fully visible. Vincenzo Scamozzi possessed such skills. He presented the principal edifices of Rome from multiple angles;[50] he exposed the different layers of construction; he showed the buildings in different lights, representing them now in profile projecting in from the outside, and then depicting an interior scene exposing the gradient of the seats; and he set one edifice beside another so that the observer could appreciate their relative heights. From Scamozzi's work it is possible to gain some sense of the variety of what could be seen in the imperial city, to assess the different states of preservation, and even to glimpse some of the stages of the construction. The sequence of views of the Colosseum, drawn and engraved in the 1580s, offers a good example of his approach. Plate 8 shows a general view; the following plate (dated 1581) depicts the edifice both inside and out (Figure 19); plate 10 shows the entrance to the arena while the following plate presents the same view seen at midday. Plates 12 and 13 offer various scenes from the second entrance, and the succeeding plates describe the galleries inside the Colosseum. Plates 16 and 17 give more interior views but this time seen at night (Figure 20), and plate 18 is drawn in a different light in order to show the effect of light and shade. Thus Scamozzi, through these engravings and with five further views of the building, gave a sense of traversing the whole structure at different times of day, and seeing it at diverse seasons bathed in a varied play of light. The vision is observed from every conceivable aspect. His book may well have been destined for the fellow artist, who would have learned much from these measured and scrupulous engravings; but he may also have had in mind potential patrons (would-be connoisseurs) who could have appreciated the artistry and be tempted into re-creating such structures on their own land.

The image of Rome that emerges from a study of the guidebooks available

19. Vincenzo Scamozzi: engraving of the interior and the exterior of the Colosseum at midday

20. Vincenzo Scamozzi: engraving of the interior and the exterior of the Colosseum at night

to travellers in the late sixteenth century is varied and uneven. Fulvio and his commentator Ferrucci present buildings in static form, isolated and, when reconstructed as they often were, as though they were immutable. Calvus was unusual in his sensitivity to the stages of growth and decay of the edifices in Rome, although both Mauro and Lauro emphasized their then-and-now condition.[51] The predilection for resurrecting buildings that had disappeared from sight and for justifying the use of conjecture as the basis of reconstructions that were built upon the tiniest shreds of evidence prompted almost a double vision of the city. Few writers and artists sought (or were able) to transmit the reality of the experience of seeing the sights for the first time, or to give a reader the sense of having touched the object with his fingers or wetted his toes in the fountains.[52] The all-round approach of Dosio, Gamucci and especially Scamozzi came close to achieving this. But then, the words in the guidebooks were intended to attract the reader to Rome so that he could see, touch and absorb the sights for himself.

CHAPTER 3

Appropriation and Transformation

THE COLLECTING CRAZE

Perhaps the acquisitive instinct of princes ambitious to extend their cultural experience did more to transmit notions and images of Rome than guidebooks which imposed a kind of moral duty on travellers to see what earlier generations had determined should be seen. The picture we have of such transmission of remains unearthed in Rome or copied from them is very imperfect; it has to be drawn from letters, from documents preserved in archives such as inventories, and from evidence scattered in books on medals and coins written for the use of collectors. However fragmentary and random, this information serves to identify those factors which helped to contribute to the vision of Rome that was taking shape in France in the second half of the sixteenth century. The process of building up collections was initially slow and sporadic.

As far as can be ascertained, collecting of art objects began in Italy in the fourteenth century,[1] and one hundred years later it had developed into a veritable craze, with increased competition, rising prices, and shady dealing. By the late fifteenth century and throughout the sixteenth century, Rome was the centre of this frenetic activity of discovery, purchase and export,[2] and many of the recipients were French princes who associated acquisition and the display of objects with status and evidence of power. The French cardinals who lived in Rome had established a reputation for extravagant lifestyles which included the fairly indiscriminate building up of collections of antiquities;[3] although it seems that they had transmitted neither their taste nor their experience to their peers in France, for when Charles VIII invaded Italy in the autumn of 1494, he could hardly contain his astonishment at the sight of gardens filled with beautiful and rare things and at the discovery of marvellous painters. The king communicated his excitement in a letter to Pierre de Bourbon, whom he charged to be on the lookout for appropriate works to adorn his palace at Amboise;[4] and he obliged the artists who had accompanied him on his journey to copy works of art which he admired.[5] Although we cannot trace individual items, it is clear from his household accounts that the king brought back to France many treasures 'tapisseries, libraire [*sic*], peintures, pierres de marbre et de porfire et autres meubles' as well as '22 ouvriers' (tapestries, books, paintings, stone works of marble or porphyry, and other furnishings . . . 22 workmen).[6]

Charles VIII's policy of acquisition and his determination to transform his French palaces by the incorporation of architectural elements found in Rome and elsewhere in Italy was imitated with enhanced intensity by future generations of French nobles,[7] to the extent that Pope Paul III, three decades later, was obliged to appoint a special commissioner – Giovanni Manetti – whose job was to protect antique remains, to restrain (if he could not stop) clandestine digs and the indiscriminate exploitation of ruins and monuments. The pope was all too conscious of his own and his predecessors' responsibility for the devastation that had already occurred in Rome and which he publicly acknowledged at the end of his formal announcement of Manetti's appointment where he referred to 'notre propre négligence et cupidité' (our own negligence and greed) in having contributed (along with the barbarians) to the spectacle of 'les véritables monuments de l'art des Romains abattus, détruits, [et] dispersés' (the true monuments of Roman art demolished, destroyed and dispersed).[8] Although it was henceforth necessary to gain permission to export the treasures dug up in Rome, from the evidence we have of the increased volume of traffic throughout the sixteenth century, the papal appointees seem to have served as recorders of exports rather than as protectors of them.

The sack of Rome (1527) had shown how vulnerable collections of antiquities were since, during the months of occupation, many collections were ransacked, looted or destroyed. Cardinal Cesi, whose important collections of paintings, inscriptions and sculpture were to provide a focal point for French visitors to Rome for many decades, is reported to have shivered continuously at the prospect of their ruin. Throughout the weeks of looting and destruction by German troops, he remained within his barricaded palace, watching nervously over his treasures.[9] His collection is well known through Aldrovandi's detailed description of its contents which was appended to Mauro's *Delle antichità di Roma*,[10] and from various sketches of which the most notable are those by Heemskerck and Hendrick van Cleef. When Marten van Heemskerck visited Rome in 1532–36, the statues were being arranged in the gardens. Fifty years later Hendrick van Cleef depicted a scene which is still heterogeneous and with no obvious order or plan. Members of the public are shown wandering through the gardens admiring individual works; some figures are digging for further treasures while others carry heavy objects about on their shoulders; students inspect antique statues and artists are in the process of drawing them.[11]

A similar disorder seems to have prevailed inside the palace where, if we are to believe Gabriel Symeoni, one could chance upon a discovery in a dark corner or high upon the wall. Having been given permission by the *maître d'hôtel* to explore the place at will, Symeoni spied above the door of a tiny room of Cesi's palace 'un autre petit marbre faict en forme de triangle' (another small marble of triangular shape). It was doubtless the unusual shape which attracted his attention, for he immediately summoned a torch and a painter who obligingly climbed up and brought the triangular form down: a banquet scene had been sculpted on it.[12]

Amassing items for the sheer delight of observing their quantity was obviously one motive behind the collecting craze. Certainly the mass of objects inside palaces provided a bewildering spectacle of the artistic vestiges of Rome, a spectacle which was as perplexing and inviting as that of the ruins scattered around the city. Scholars had, however, begun to assemble objects (coins and medals especially) for purposes other than mere display. Aleandro, for example, at the beginning of the sixteenth century wrote to his friend Brancharius to congratulate him on his medal collection which, he claimed, would provide a rich source for scholarship; while at the end of the century, in 1584, André Thevet argued that princes were building up their medal collections because they, too, had become 'curieux des antiquités' (curious about antiquities) and took pleasure in interpreting the images engraved thereon and in deciphering 'les lettres tronquées, à demy rongées et presqu'effacées' (the broken letters, half eaten away and almost effaced).[13] Such attitudes supporting the cause of scholarship were probably more the hope of a writer seeking patronage than the conviction of the princely collector who often had a superficial approach to matters of art and antiquity. In this context, Orsini's outburst in a letter he wrote to Pinelli on 16 June 1582 has an exasperated ring of truth:

> Je déteste ces étrangers qui n'entendent rien à la peinture, rien aux livres ni aux statues, et qui me font perdre mon temps à les leur montrer ou à leur faire visiter les curiosités de Rome comme si j'étais l'homme le moins occupé du monde.

> [I detest these strangers who understand nothing about painting, books or statues, and make me waste my time showing them objects or visiting the sights of Rome as if I were the person with the most leisure in the world.][14]

Whatever the level of knowledge or of seriousness, travellers to Rome felt obliged to inspect antiquities and curiosities and, moreover, sought – in increasing numbers – to appropriate some for themselves.

It is difficult to assess the extent, scale and social range of collections and collectors at this time. Guidebooks indicated substantial holdings in many Roman palaces. Indeed some were so substantial that visitors, such as André Thevet, found themselves incapable of setting down in words the infinitude of antiquities to be seen.[15]

EXPORTS FROM ROME TO FRANCE

The export trade from Rome had always been vigorous, as papal restrictions testify. According to Bertrand Jestaz, the period of greatest activity in the trade

M. AVR. PACORVS AEDI
TVVS SANTAE VENE
RIS IN SALVST HORTIS

SPEI

ARAM CVM PAEMENTO
SOMNIO MONITVS SVM
TV SVO D D.

21. Jean-Jacques Boissard: engraving of a statue from Cardinal du Bellay's garden in Rome

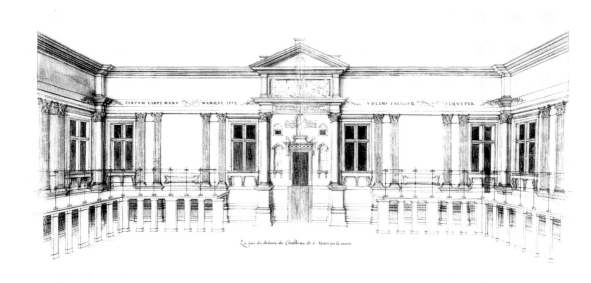

22. Jacques Androuet du Cerceau: drawing of St Maur les Fossés

from Italy to France was between the years 1541 and 1555; yet, Bertolotti has recorded crates leaving Rome for Marseille not only in 1541 but also in 1575 and 1583;[16] and almost without exception, the documents record the recipients as great princes eager to vie with each other for the possession of a choice piece. At the beginning of our period, Jean du Bellay stands out as a distinguished collector, with renowned treasures occupying the vast terrains of the baths of Diocletian which he had acquired (Figure 21). By corresponding with Pope Paul III's secretary Bernardino Maffei, he kept close watch on the excavations at Rome so that he could seize every opportunity to add to his rich store,[17] and the same papal secretary kept him informed of any finds made at Hadrian's villa.[18] Michel de l'Hospital's somewhat jaundiced report of Du Bellay's purchases gives an idea of the range of the cardinal's interests. In his poem 'Aux Muses romaines', l'Hospital noted:

> J'ai appris qu'il achetait à grands frais de magnifiques statues, qu'il payait des tableaux au poids d'or, qu'il fouillait de vastes cimetières, et arrachait du fond des entrailles de la terre les chefs d'oeuvre d'anciens artistes.

> [I learned that he bought magnificent statues at great expense, and paid for paintings with their weight in gold, that he excavated vast cemeteries and snatched masterpieces of ancient art from the depths of the earth.][19]

Of the 200 statues which Du Bellay had bought for his gardens, 134 were auctioned at his death in 1558.[20] So extensive were his purchases that he had ample treasures for his country house in France at Saint Maur les Fossés which he decorated with *antiquailles*, increasing their number every time he journeyed home (Figure 22). The zeal for collecting and the compulsion of acquisition was equally intense in the early decades of the seventeenth century when Cardinal de Richelieu was filling his new château with statues: 130 were on their way from Rome in 1633, of variable quality if one judges from the somewhat mediocre drawings by Canini. Lack of quality was not of prime concern for this cardinal, however, who modelled himself on Cicero. Like the ancient orator, Richelieu bought statues casually: anything suitable would do. He simply told his intendant Michel le Masle, prieur des Roches, to buy some statues for his new home and he recommended 'fakes' since they would be cheaper![21]

Exports, even to great princes, were not always straightforward. In 1534, one of Cardinal du Bellay's servants reported that Cardinal Pisani had given a fine sculpture to his master but that the pope did not wish to see 'le beau Pillon' (the beautiful marble) get into French hands; he wanted it himself. Negotiations were protracted and finally the pope had to concede; but he received a costlier gift from Jean du Bellay in return.[22] Authorization for export was frequently tardy in coming and papal nuncios, ambassadors and even cardinals attending conclaves sometimes had to intervene to ensure success. Even then, unforeseen difficulties might arise. A precious cargo on its way to Marseille was interrupted by Turks, who raided and scuttled the ship so that its rich and rare jewels, including 'un porphyre le plus beau qui se put voir en la chrestienté' (the finest porphyry ever seen in the Christian world), were sunk to the bottom of the sea.[23]

Despite such hindrances, Jean du Bellay not only went on collecting but was frequently helpful in acquiring treasures for others. In May 1550, for example, Le Breton de Villandry (in the cardinal's employ) wrote to the French king's financial secretary to assure him that the Leda picture had already arrived at Lyon but that the Venus would wait to accompany 'd'autres antiquailles'.[24] Du Bellay himself had written to Philibert de L'Orme to give specific details of the Venus statue which he had bought to be placed above an important door at Anet. He described the statue, assessing its quality – 'les antiquaires d'icy ont rencontré que c'est opus Phidiae' (the antiquaries here claim that it is the work of Phidias) – and also gave the dimensions and emphasized the care he had lavished upon it:

C'est une teste *di Venere* telle que je suys seur n'estre surpassée d'autre . . . Le piet et le piedouche ay fait faire icy de pierre rarissime et y a six mois que six soupelins sont dessus. Elle est à demy colossale et pour ce fault bien cinq pieds de large pour la niche et six de hault, et fauldra qu'elle soyt assise un peut haut à cause de sa grandeur.

[It's a head of Venus which, I'm sure, is unsurpassed . . . the foot pedestal, I've had made from the rarest stone; six supports have been on it for the last six months. It's huge (half-colossal) and therefore will require a niche five feet wide and six feet high; and because of its size, it will need to be placed high up.][25]

This may be the statue which was to provoke Bernini, many years later when he saw it in France, to exclaim 'que tels chefs d'oeuvre de l'art devraient demeurer à Rome sans permettre qu'ils en sortissent' (that such artistic masterpieces should stay in Rome, and not be permitted to travel).[26] There were many in Rome who watched out for material worthy of the fastidious French cardinal. Jean François Valerio, for instance, secretary of Cardinal Ippolito de' Medici, was in frequent correspondence about matters such as 'una testa dignà di lei' (a head worthy of him), or 'una testa di donna . . . che è bellissima et antica' (a woman's head which is old and beautiful).[27] Such priority had been given to statues that Cardinal François de Tournon, for example, had appended a tower to his castle (named Tour des marbres) in order to accommodate all his purchases.[28]

Of all French princes who succumbed to the fashion of collecting, François I was undoubtedly the most acquisitive and the most admired for the lavish and appropriate display of his collections.[29] He had transported to his palaces 'antiquities' from all regions. Rome, Florence, Lyon or Nîmes: any source would do as long as the works were of good quality and promptly available. He sent moneys to Rome for their purchase, as Guillaume du Bellay recorded in his letters where he assured Montmorency that the 1,000 *écus* he had received had been well spent;[30] and Vasari testified to new works of art being specifically made for the French king. Where ancient statues were not available – such as the Venus which condottiere Renzo sent to the king in 1530[31] – copies were made, for example those cast in bronze from the famous statues in the Belvedere gardens, Cleopatra, Laocoön, the Wolf suckling Romulus and Remus, Sphinxes, Apollo (Figure 23), and a Diana.[32] These casts were taken from Rome and brought to Fontainebleau where they were admired – together with the bronzes made from them – by many visitors. Nor was the admiration uncritical or ill informed, for the visitors who have left their accounts were well-travelled experts including Pierre Belon, Gabriel Symeoni and Sebastiano Serlio.[33] Serlio described, in his *Trattati d'architettura*, the placing of some statues in the loggia he built which overlooked the garden and the second courtyard at Fontainebleau,[34] and André Thevet who, in the 1550s, saw in the gardens at Fontainebleau the bronze statues 'copiées sur l'antique', wrote of them approvingly, and praised the king's appropriating spirit. According to his view, François I's anxiety to explore the darkest corners of his kingdom in order to seek out 'singularitez', to decipher inscriptions, and to ensure that rarities be put in places which would do them honour demonstrated the king's profound enlightenment. Snatching statues and inscriptions from Rome and Nîmes should be seen as a veritable service to his subjects:

SIC ROMAE EX MARMORE SCVP IN PALASIO PONI
IN LOCO QVI VVLGO DICITVR BELVEDERE
ANT LAFRERII FORMIS ROMAE M D LII

23. Antoine Lafréry: Belvedere Apollo (engraved 1552)

Le feu roy François Ier du nom, se pleut tant en ces statues, avec leurs roul-
leaux et inscriptions, en feit porter tant à Fontainebleau qu'ailleurs pour
l'ornement de ses beaux edifices. Et, qui plus est, d'autant que toute cette
Province, et Narbonnaise, et Lyonnaise, et le Daulphiné, sont [remplies] de
telles choses, ce grand Roy ne se desdaignoit d'entrer en les Crotesques,
tantost hault tantost bas, pour lire les inscriptions des Fondemens, et des
pierres que l'on avoit ostées de leurs places, àfin que s'il y avoit rien de
remarquable et notable, il le feist mettre en plus belle parade que d'estre
mesprisé de tout le monde.

[The late king, François I delighted in these statues with their scrolls and
inscriptions and had them brought to Fontainebleau and elsewhere to adorn
his noble buildings. Moreover, since the whole of this Province, Narbonne,
the Lyonnais and Dauphiné are stocked with such things, this great king
didn't hesitate to descend into caves, sometimes high and sometimes low, to
read the inscriptions on their base and on the stones that had been removed
from their original site, in order to see if there were anything new or remarkable, then he would show it off to its advantage rather than have it despised
by everyone.][35]

Pierre Belon had seen the display at Fontainebleau and had interpreted the
spectacle as showing that François I was similar to Augustus whose interest in
antiquities could be judged from the medals that survived.[36] Symeoni had seen
the king's treasures as a regeneration of Rome, transferred to France. Similar
reactions continued into the seventeenth century when Arnold van Buchel
enumerated the same images of antiquity, 'des statues de provenances les plus
diverses' (statues from diverse sources).[37] Surrounded by gods and heroes, busts
of Charles IX, Apollo, Venus, Mercury, and Emperor Commodus (as van Buchel
reports), the statues remained at Fontainebleau as embodying the spirit, and –
in some cases – the image of Rome, although the original moulds had been
given by Henri II in 1549 to the regent of the Netherlands who installed them
at Binche early in 1550, where, ironically, they would be destroyed by French
soldiers in 1554.[38]

The royal collections of François I were undoubtedly vast,[39] yet other French
princes vied with him in their eagerness to build in France their idea of Roman
palaces and collections. François, duc de Guise was both knowledgeable and
greedy. Symeoni paid tribute to his careful scrutiny of statues and medals;[40]
papal nuncios were involved in the negotiations that went on constantly to
overcome the difficulties that the duke frequently encountered as a consequence of the enormous quantities of statues he wished to export from
Rome;[41] and Italian go-betweens complained bitterly about the repeated per-
missions of Julius II issued in favour of the Lorraine family. His cardinal brother,
Charles de Lorraine was, if anything, more demanding. On his return from the
conclave of April 1550 he had twenty-five cases of statues and bronzes trans-

ported from Rome, while a Florentine agent remarked in the same month: 'Le cardinal de Guise s'applique à dérobber le plus de médailles antiques et le plus de statues qu'il peut' (the cardinal de Guise works hard at stealing as many medals and statues as he can).[42] The terms are strongly critical but they did little to halt the constant traffic from Italy into France.

Anne de Montmorency (Constable of France) benefited greatly from his position of influence and patronage, and he obliged his friends in Rome not only to search out suitable objects for the adornment of his palace at Chantilly but also to send him information in minute detail of items likely to come on to the market or which might be extorted from owners who wished to win his gratitude. The brother of the bishop of Pavia, mindful of the constable's good services, sent Montmorency two large and beautiful marble busts in the autumn of 1554, one of Severus, the other of Caracalla.[43] Two years later the Cardinal d'Armagnac was busy ensuring that a consignment of architectural and marble materials, including two marble busts of emperors together with half a dozen other good heads, was safely on its way to Chantilly via Marseille.[44] Chantilly was evidently a showplace which impressed even Jean du Bellay, used to the comfort, elegance and rare collections of his remarkable house in Rome and at Saint Maur les Fossés. No doubt wishing to flatter the powerful constable, he spoke of 'partant de l'enfer de Paris . . . je suys venu au paradis de Chantilly' (leaving the hell of Paris, I have now arrived in paradise, at Chantilly).[45] Du Bellay had himself contributed significantly to create that Elysian atmosphere, for he had supplied many of the statues which Montmorency had placed there, as the latter explained in a letter to the cardinal while Du Bellay was still in Rome; he wrote in order:

> à vous advertir que j'ay faict arranger toutes mes testes et médailles à Chantilly qu'il fait merveilleusement bon veoir mais il reste des places vuydes. Vous sçavez que c'est à dire et que vous me ferez grand plaisir si ce pendant vous que vous estes par dela vous me vueillez ayder à les remplir.

> [to let you know that I have arranged all my heads and medals at Chantilly and they look marvellous, but there are still some empty spaces. You know what it is and you will give me great pleasure if, while you are over there, you help me to fill them.][46]

The constable's appetite was insatiable. Even when he was in dire need of cash for his ransom (in 1557) he contrived to respond positively to François de Tournon who had drawn his attention to precious stones in Venice which he esteemed 'les plus belles et des plus grosses qu'il ayt encores veues' (the finest and biggest he had yet seen).[47]

The same desire to own objects, and especially statuary from Rome, had overwhelmed Catherine de' Medici who, in her letters, provides a glimpse both of the care she took over antiquities and of her purchasing power. In 1559, writing to her cousin the *maréchale* de Strozzi at Blois, she advised her to leave

24. Etienne Delaune: frieze of trophies and arms

nothing behind when she departs, 'tant d'armes, livres, medailles, marbres que autres choses semblables' (whether arms, books, medals, marble, statues and the like) (Figure 24).[48] On another occasion, when she heard that a doctor had an *Adonis* for sale, she immediately asked François de Tournon to investigate, to establish the price and to see if some kind of royal benefice might persuade the owner to sell cheaply.[49] Again, rumour reached her that at the château de Trie en Oise a group of marble statues could be found, just right for her new Tuileries palace; and she lost no time in writing to Saulx de Tavannes with an order to proceed to negotiations at once and to deliver the statues as soon as possible.[50] Even late in her life she showed persistent concern for the proper care of statues in the royal collection. In 1580, for example, she requested that a full inventory be made of the marble statues at Saint Denis, and pursued her request until the work was done.[51]

These examples of princely collectors furnish some evidence about the availability of objects and images from Rome (or thought to be from that city) in the upper echelons of French society. Their accessibility was extended through the habits of diplomacy of the time whereby gifts of statuary or paintings, costly ornaments and precious stones were seen as necessary and effective means of political persuasion. The same figures tended to be regular recipients, and donors made sure that the gifts were worthy. In 1518, Lorenzo de' Medici, for instance, ordered his gift from Raphael – a painting of St Michael overcoming the Devil, which is now in the Louvre.[52] Even a humble Venetian gentleman knew that the king would not be satisfied with less than the most perfect marble rendering of Venus.[53] Ambassadors arrived with diverse offerings: the cardinal of Ferrara – in 1540 – with gold worked by Benvenuto Cellini; antique statues; armour made by the renowned Giampetro; paintings and medals; and even a horse dressed in silver.[54] In the same year, Ippolito

d'Este turned up, sacrificing 215 coins from his own collection to please the king.[55] Both Guise and Montmorency were similarly targeted, the former in 1558 when the banker Albisse del Bene wanted to curry favour,[56] and the constable who graciously accepted a cornucopia of gifts: marble heads from the bishop of Pavia (1554); marble for beautifying his chimneys promised by Cardinal Farnese (1554); statues offered by the bishop of Viterbo (1555); and many statues and antiquities carried in the train of the papal legate (1556).[57] The pope also anticipated continuing support by sending Catherine de'Medici a hundred coins which had been unearthed in a bronze casket during the excavations at St John of Lateran in 1587.[58] Such offerings extended knowledge of Roman objects and helped to condition some French views of the ancient and modern city.

COINS AND MEDAL COLLECTIONS

Perhaps the taste for coins and medals was more remarkable and the factor that contributed most to the French vision of Rome in the late Renaissance. For coins and medals imprinted on the mind not only the visages of emperors but often, on their reverse, the buildings they had erected and consecrated, the deeds they had performed or the gods they had worshipped. Medals were especially popular because as well as their transportability, they had value; and they turned up all the time. Medal-making was an art that contemporaries had mastered to the extent that there were frequent pleas to consider modern examples equal in aesthetic value to ancient ones, as is testified by Jean Louveau who translated the work of the Mantuan antiquary Jacques de Strada and who commented: 'en ce temps on trouve tant d'excellens et subtilz tailleurs d'images, qu'à bon droit ils meritent d'estre non moins estimez que les anciens' (nowadays, there are such excellent and delicate engravers of images that they rightly deserve to be as esteemed as the ancients).[59] There were important collections under François I, the most notable being those of Dinteville and Montmorency,[60] but it was about the mid-century that large collections began to be formed by humanists and diplomats. Jean Grolier, for example, had, according to Jean Strada, 'un nombre presque infini', and Guillaume du Choul praised the treasurer for owning the most beautiful specimens that could be obtained in France.[61] Maurice Scève had a collection, as did Gabriel Symeoni who writes regularly of the constant exchange between scholars of newly found coins and of the excitement of discovery.[62] Later, Auguste de Thou started a collection, which was not surprising given his natural bent for art (as a young man, he had made copies of Dürer's work). On his travels to Italy, De Thou went to the fountainheads for information, to Sigonio and to Fulvio Orsini, the Farnese librarian who had a huge collection of his own and who had advised major collectors such as Annibale Caro, the formidable Cardinal Granvelle and French visitors including Scaliger (1565–66) and Claude Dupuy (1570–71).[63]

Evidence on the status and value of coin and medal collecting in France in the first half of the sixteenth century has recently been assembled,[64] and that evidence is corroborated for the later period by Henrich Goltzius who reported in 1563 that he had encountered over 200 worthy collections in his travels around France. That the value of coins was being recognized at the French court can be judged from the fact that Henri II, on succeeding to the throne, created the office of 'tailleur, graveur et sculpteur des cours de monnaie', of which the first incumbent was Marc Béchot.[65] Further corroboration of such interest comes in a remark made by Antoine Le Pois in his *Discours sur les medalles et graveures antiques, principalement Romaines* where he refused to give the names of princes of his time who had built up distinguished collections of coins and medals because, as he wrote, they had bought them at excessively high prices.[66]

While it might not be surprising that princes succumbed so easily to a fashionable urge, there were other reasons for the enthusiasm of humanists who also indulged similar hoarding instincts. Peiresc, for instance, at his house in Aix had huge collections which he used for scholarly enquiry; we do not know the size of his holdings of coins and medals, but they were clearly very numerous since he lost 2,000 in a single robbery.[67] Arnold van Buchel who, in his *Journal*, reported on particularly interesting French collectors mentioned all the royal palaces and collections of princes, and also expatiated on the library and coin collection of lesser mortals: La Croix du Maine 'possede des tablettes de cire et des monnaies antiques en grand nombre, entre autres des pièces à l'effigie de Camille, de Pompée, de Marius et de Cicéron' (owns wax tablets and ancient coins in great quantities, among them the effigies of Camillus, Pompey, Marius and Cicero).[68] By the 1580s, princes (for reasons of prestige), scholars (for the usefulness and the enlightenment they gave), and men of amateur/bourgeois status, collected medals and coins. Of the latter category,

Pierre de Lestoile is a good example. He saw writing as a form of collecting – his *Mémoires* were, in his own words, 'le magasin de mes curiosités' (my store of curiosities) – and he vied with his other colleagues from the *Parlement* in augmenting his collection through gifts, legacies, exchanges of duplicates or purchase when (as happened frequently) coin collections came on to the market. From the *Mémoires-Journaux* of Pierre de Lestoile, it is possible to see how what had been a princely activity a century earlier had now filtered down through humanist circles to lower social strata.[69]

Yet it was not so much the fact of collecting that is so crucial to our argument that coins and medals played a significant role in the transmission of views of Rome into France, as the reasons that were adduced by collectors for their activity. Strada argued for a two-way system, setting forth their verification value for history and the corresponding authentication of medals from the facts of history: 'Je rapporte les Medailles à la verité de l'Histoire' (I test medals against the truth of History) (sig. aa3); in other words, medals were to be read as texts. Antoine Le Pois, whose work on medals was published posthumously by his brother, was equally firm in his claim that it is impossible to understand the history of Rome, its people and its succession of magistrates without recourse to medals: 'toute l'histoire Romaine . . . ne se peut comprendre sans cela'.[70]

Categoric though this claim was, it did not reach the eloquent heights of Guillaume Roville's sentiments. Roville maintained that the honour and venerable antiquity which his contemporaries attributed to Rome had been, by fate and through the precaution of scholars, secretly preserved in medals hidden from view either within ancient monuments or underground. It was only the enquiring minds of his times which had brought to light past glories almost lost: 'pour entretenir l'eternel honneur de la venerable antiquité, et la defendre de ruine, et de perdition; celles Medalles ont esté par gens studieux diligemment cachées: en partie recueillies des antiques monumens, en partie tirées des entrailles de la terre' (to keep eternal the honour of revered antiquity, to defend it from ruin and perdition, these medals have been carefully hidden away by scholars: in part, taken from ancient monuments and in part from the depths of the earth).[71]

It might seem that only self-interest speaks here. If it is so, then royal authorization also corroborated and extended the view which Roville was expressing. In the privilege accorded by Henri II to the French translation of Strada's *Trésor des antiquitez*, we learn that the publication is intended 'pour le bien commun de nostre République' (for the common good of our land) in so far as the work offers 'illustration et intelligence des antiquitez et bonnes lettres' (examples and knowledge of antiquities and letters). Medals of Roman emperors preserve history (as Strada had argued) but they also offer enlightenment for present affairs; and they do this, as Roville argued in a publication of the same date, through the pleasure associated with figures which attract and draw in the reader, encouraging him to decipher for himself and to recreate the virtuous examples that are recorded there.[72]

Medal-hunters were fascinated by the enduring and preserving power of medals. Both Le Pois and Thevet underline this aspect. Currency of fame was well recognized by the Romans, who sought deliberately to 'perpetuer la memoire de leurs noms' (perpetuate the memory of their name) (Le Pois), and Thevet found a striking phrase to express the same thought whereby illustrious deeds and remarkable achievements were eternalized by being, as he wrote, 'engravez au cuivre de memoire' (engraved on the bronze of memory).[73] Le Pois had been interested in the capacity of medals to recall the past and, in particular, through their images to give a sense of presence to faces and objects whose contours would otherwise be lost. In his memorable words, 'les absens sont presens, et les morts sont vivans' (the absent are present, and the dead are alive) (p. 37). The status of medals was enhanced by the widely held view at this time that certain images of virtue possessed a talismanic quality which inspired in those who gazed upon them similar feelings of virtue and abhorrence of evil.[74] Thevet used such language in expatiating on the nature and merits of images at the beginning of *Les Vrais Pourtraits* where he is anxious to establish the ground on which his book should be understood and to prepare the reader for the medallion portraits soon to be encountered: 'les pourtraicts et images ont une energie et vertu interieure à nous faire cherir la vertu et detester le mal' (portraits and images have an inner power and virtue which make us cherish good and detest evil) (sig. ã vi). From such considerations, it was but a small step to use medals as propaganda – a phenomenon exploited by Henrich Goltzius in his *Fastos magistratum et triumphorum Romanum* (Bruges, 1566).

It should be recognized that, despite the quantity of coins and medals surviving in the Renaissance and despite their evident usefulness for history and for the reconstruction of ancient Rome and its customs, many collectors had a somewhat cavalier attitude to their invention. Roville, for instance, while solemnly defining them as 'profitables en vertueux exemples' (beneficial in providing examples of virtue), at the same time argued his right to invent visages on medals where no examples survived. He saw a significant role for the imagination and conjecture. The remains of faces on medals stimulated the creation of absent visages and he supplied these in abundance in the first 150 pages of his work.[75] He considered that he had an obligation to meet his readers' legitimate desire to envisage what was no longer there.

It was inevitable that the popularity of coins and medals led to counterfeiting. If De Thou's editor is to be believed, in the mid-1550s Guillaume de Marillon established in Paris 'une belle fabrique de pièces d'or et d'argent' (a good factory for gold and silver pieces). This enterprise, however, did not last because Marillon concentrated too much on the aesthetic value of the coins to the detriment of other aspects.[76] That counterfeits were in circulation is attested by Strada's view that 'les faulces et contrefaictes' should, if possible, be avoided, and by Le Pois' contention that those who sought only to perpetuate their name and reputation 'faisent forger tant de medalles' and did indeed, by this means, succeed in keeping their names alive.[77]

In order to understand how collections of medals were used, it is helpful to consider those of two outstanding French scholars; the first, Guillaume du Choul, a Lyonnais who flourished in the mid-sixteenth century; and the second Nicolas-Claude Fabri de Peiresc who, after extensive travels in Italy and having spent some time in Paris, retired to his house in Aix where he died in 1637.

Contemporaries were uniformly admiring of Guillaume du Choul. André Thevet, who gave him medals discovered on his travels, praised his work; Gabriel Symeoni, who translated *Le Discours de la religion des anciens Romains illustré*, constantly referred to his excellence; La Croix du Maine extolled his tireless search after authenticity;[78] and Jacques de Strada called him 'peritissimus', lauding his judgement, his extraordinary expertise in deciphering the meanings of images, his fine memory and his magnificent house. Louveau translated the encomium found in Strada's preface:

> Monsieur Guillaume Choul [*sic*] natif de ladite ville [Lyon], fort experimenté aux Histoires, et à déclarer le revers des Monnoyes et Medailles figurées, homme au surplus de si bon iugement et si rare, qu'on le peult bien conter entre les premiers experimentez en cest affaire, et non sans cause, tant pour sa belle memoire, que pour son bon et exquis jugement. En sa maison magnifique . . . j'ay veu grand nombre de toutes pièces de Medailles antiques.

> [Monsieur Guillaume Choul, native of this town, very learned in history and in the deciphering of the figures on the reverse of medals and coins, of such good and rare judgement that he can rightly be counted among the most experienced in these matters not only by reason of his excellent memory but also for his excellent and subtle judgement. In his magnificent house . . . I have seen quantities of all kinds of ancient medals.][79]

His collection must have been remarkable, for when van Buchel wished to convey some sense of the extent and value of the room at Fontainebleau where statues, medals and books were kept, Du Choul was his point of reference: 'j'ai vu des monnoies assez semblables chez Du Choul' (I have seen similar medals at Du Choul's house).[80]

Our purpose here is to examine how Du Choul's ownership of such riches affected the way he wrote and presented his vision of ancient Rome and its customs. In the royal library at Turin lies a manuscript of the first volume of a vast work which Du Choul planned in twelve books: 'Des Antiquitez romaines'.[81] It was apparently conceived at the request of François I, to whom it was dedicated (a portrait showing the presentation to the king, recognizably himself but dressed as a Roman emperor, is placed at the front of the manuscript) (Plate I), and it was intended to be published by Guillaume Roville who, according to Du Verdier, had charge of it. From evidence in Du Choul's other works, it seems that he had drafted at least the first seven books but these appear not to have survived. The scale of the work is ambitious, and the narrative approach adopted – whereby Du Choul organizes the material around the biographies of emperors, with their lives depicted as they had been drawn from images left of their deeds – reflects the pattern of narration and argument found in many histories of medals of the time such as those of Erizzo, Aeneas Vico or Henrich Goltzius, all of whom are used by Du Choul.[82]

Du Choul starts with Julius Caesar and, after many interruptions, the text of this first volume ends with Claudius. His method is to build his account of Roman antiquities through a careful scrutiny of images on medals and coins, and by the use of epitaphs and inscriptions; and he reproduces these details and figures in his text alongside other evidence from monuments, triumphal arches and reliefs such as Trajan's column which were still extant in Rome (ff. 27v and 78).[83] Not all the illustrations projected are actually contained in the manu-script. For instance, to enable the reader to understand the order and the cost of items purchased in ancient Rome, and – in particular – to appreciate the nature of the places in which business transactions occurred, Du Choul recon-structed Trajan's forum, which was now in a ruined state:

> Et par cecy lon peult congnoistre lordre et la despense que fairoient les romains à bien edifier les lieux publiques de Rome qui est lune des choses qui autant embellist et decore une cite qui est la cause que j'ay fait paindre le fore de Traian cy apres a present ruine a Rome. (f. 4 verso)

> [From this one can assess the order and expenditure which the Romans made when they erected buildings in the public spaces in Rome, a feature which embellishes and adorns a city the most, and the reason why I have had painted Trajan's forum which now lies ruined in Rome.]

The drawing is unfortunately missing; and likewise, he forgot to include the naumachia 'comme la figure de l'antique marbre le montre' (as the image taken from an antique marble shows) (f. 19).

Medals are frequently used as crucial sources of information: for the char-acter of the circus which is taken from a medal of Caracalla (f. 6); for the tri-umphs of Tiberius (f. 40v); or for the nature of sepulchres (f. 43v). At other times, Du Choul seeks to verify events by indicating their record on medals, such as Caesar's military successes set out in sequence (ff. 12v and 32v), or the taking of Egypt by Augustus commemorated by the presence of a chameleon on the reverse of a medal (f. 23). The interpretative range employed is consid-erable. Du Choul is able to show how Roman emperors exploited coins and medals for their own selfish intentions and not only for remembrance (f. 13v). Julius Caesar wanted to ensure that posthumously his reputation was correctly interpreted; thus his divine status is projected on the reverse of a medal which

MEDAILLE
A L'ENTIQVE.

Endroict   Reuers

25. Nicolas Favyer: medal struck to commemorate the Massacre of St Bartholomew (1572)

shows Aeneas and Anchises and establishes Caesar's own relationship with the goddess Venus (f. 18v). In similar fashion, Caesar Augustus had a medal struck showing on its reverse the planet Capricorn and the time of the emperor's birth (f. 20v); and other medals repeated the image of the planet and its connections with prosperity and abundance. Some medals showed Julius as divine, with a star on his head, or sometimes on the temple of Venus, in order to underline the august family connections (f. 21). In this context, Du Choul admired particularly the perspicacity of Tiberius who rejected the many names the Senate wished to bestow on him in his lifetime (fearful that they might be rescinded after his death), but did retain *pontifex* (as his medals testify, f. 56v) the most important title and the one which bestowed most power. Such political manipulation of coins and medals was freely engaged in by Renaissance princes. In France, for instance, Charles IX, after the massacre of St Bartholomew, instructed Nicolas Favyer to strike two medals – one showing the king enthroned trampling over rebels, its reverse inscribed 'Pietas excitavit iustitiam' (Piety excites Justice), and dated 24 August 1572; the other depicting Charles IX as emperor showing on the reverse Hercules killing the Hydra and dated 3 September 1572 (Figure 25).[84]

A first reading of Book 1 of 'Des Antiquitez romaines' suggests that Du Choul is too preoccupied with public events, with ceremonies and festivals, and with spectacle in all its diverse manifestations. He writes of circuses, naumachiae, gladiatorial combats and triumphs, bringing in, as always, images to develop and illustrate his argument. It becomes clear, however, that these shows take him to the heart of his purpose: a demonstration of the close connections between spectacle and religion for the Romans. The goddess Ceres is introduced early on for her presence at the games in the centre of the circus is,

73

according to Du Choul, 'pour montrer la religion de leurs ieux' (to show the religious content of their games) (f. 14v). The concord which Augustus established at the beginning of his reign is written on to his medals, and the trophies are displayed in ceremony and festivity (ff. 21v–22v). Achievement is inevitably linked with public confirmation of that success whether it be through triumphs or through their projection on medals; one medal shows Augustus' spoils inside the temple of Mars Ultor (f. 24); another depicts his triumph (f. 26); while on another occasion the medals are struck to consecrate a triumph with laurel and triumphal cars (f. 28v).

In Du Choul's view, religion is central to our understanding of Rome, its buildings and its citizens; and epitaphs as well as medals are used to provide information about festival banquets and offerings to Jupiter (f. 41). The functions of the aediles are clarified by the symbols found on the reverse of medals (f. 18) where sacrificial tools and the instruments of burial are also represented (ff. 49–50). Often medals were the only means available to give an impression to Renaissance readers of the appearance of many public buildings erected by Romans to please or to appease their gods. Through his close study of such images, Du Choul contrives to reconstruct whole edifices. The temple of Julia, for example, is rebuilt from the indications of Vitruvius and from the details on a medal (f. 32). The temple of Vesta comes into being again in a full-page reproduction, the round temple supported on its Corinthian columns, with the standing figure of the goddess (f. 57) (Plate II); or again shown on the reverse of a medal of Nero (f. 59). The triumphal arch built on the Appian Way to commemorate the victories of Drusus is represented here, developed from a medal, as though it were entire (f. 73) (Plate III). The full and perfect form of a Roman aqueduct is given (f. 84) and, in another place, an example of a similar structure found in Lyon (f. 86) which allows Du Choul to expatiate on the skills developed by the Romans in controlling the flow and impetuosity of water.

Although religion, the public deeds of emperors, and the preservation and consecration of those achievements in figures on monuments or medals, form the principal matter of Du Choul's book, the narration is not consistent and is often wayward. There are many strange intrusions and digressions which start spontaneously out of a simple interpretative point. So the chameleon which signified Augustus' triumph in Egypt leads to a great essay on strange animals (ff. 23 ff.). The discourse on temples and their dedication is interrupted by philosophical musings on the importance of the temple's circular form and how that shape bears resemblance to the heavens (ff. 28–28v). Then Du Choul is led to digress on the size and significance of pyramids when, realizing how far he has strayed from his text, he justifies himself, arguing that these are 'assez convenable pour noz antiquitez romaines' (sufficiently appropriate for our Roman antiquities) (f. 42v). Yet this does not prevent a similar excursion, this time on obelisks, when he cannot resist explaining their origin and the meaning of the symbols inscribed upon them (f. 69v).

Despite these interruptions, there is one guiding thread throughout the narrative. Du Choul never forgets that his principal reader is François I and he regularly refers specifically to him, addressing him directly and drawing his attention to the similarities between his own performance and that of Roman emperors like Caesar and Augustus. At first, the parallels do not seem at all novel. The initial presentation (full of wishful thinking) matches the French king's liberality with that of Alexander but then Du Choul goes on to say that a better comparison would be with Julius Caesar '[dont] vous pouvez sire estre nomme le vray successeur' (of whom you could be called the true successor), since he, like François, was immensely knowledgeable as a collector: 'amateur singulier des pierres precieuses, de la sculpture, des statues de marbre et de bronze, de tableauz et painctures et tous autres ouvrages antiques' (remarkable connoisseur of precious stones, sculpture, marble and bronze statues, pictures and all other ancient works of art) (f. 3v). Here Du Choul is touching on the major areas which the king had sought to appropriate and, throughout the 'Antiquitez', he will return to them whether it be to praise the benevolence of the emperor (this time, Augustus, f. 32) and the king, or to detail the parallels between the two in terms of their architectural plans and achievements. 'La construction des edifices' redounded to Augustus' glory; but François I has perhaps gone further for he has understood the pleasure, the utility and the dignity of grand structures and has insisted upon perfection and appropriateness of form, as is amply testified by

> vostre roialle et admirable maison de Chambort, vostre magnifique maison de Fontaine le Bleau asile de toutes antiquitez, vostre triomphant chasteau de boloigne, la restauration et embellissement de vostre chasteau capital de Louvre . . . (f. 37)

> [your royal and admirable palace of Chambord, your magnificent Fontainebleau that shelters all kinds of antiquities, your noble castle of Bologne, the restoration and decoration of your palace in the capital – the Louvre.]

The praise of the king's building programme extends over many sentences. Fontainebleau, in particular, is the place where has been concentrated 'la plus grande partie des antiquitez qui sont pour le present en nostre Europe' (the greatest quantity of antiquities at present in Europe) (f. 38). According to Du Choul, it is fitting that France should have become this repository of beauty and antiquity since François I's reign marked the recovery not only of the valuing of such things but of the very words which speak their form:

> sire cela se puisse dire de vous, il n'est personne qui le puisse ou vueille l'ignorer et iusques vostre regne les mots propres et peculiers de l'art edificatoire avoient este estaings et enseveliz avecques les anciens. (f. 37)

> [Sire, that can be said of you, no one can or wishes to gainsay it; until your reign, words appropriate and special to the art of learning had disappeared, buried with the ancients.]

There are several occasions where Du Choul exhibits proudly and somewhat profusely his own mastery of the technical language which had recently become available; the following example, where he is describing the decorations on a sepulchre near Avignon (illustrated f. 47), may be taken as typical:

> quattre colonnes rondes striez exactement a leur tierce partie et dessus les epistiliez ou architraves, le zophore ou frise est ouvert de sa couronne ou cornice condescente et raisonnable . . . Entre les quattre colonnes . . . se monstrent pilastres avecques chapiteaulx et les stilobates ou bases . . .

> [four rounded columns carefully fluted up to a third of their length, architraves or epistyles above, the frieze or carved border is open at the cornice or crown, fitting appropriately . . . Between the four columns, pilasters can be seen with their capital and base or support.]

He expected his royal reader to appreciate such sophistication and to nod with pleasure at the architectural details and alternatives he inserted liberally into his manuscript or had had drawn particularly: 'j'ay faict reduire au petit point larc triomphal dont nous parlons pour vous en donner Sire de l'architecture plus grant plaisir' (the triumphal arch about which we spoke, Sire, I have reduced it to a tiny scale to give you greater appreciation of its architecture) (f. 72v).

Although Du Choul's learning was immense (he cites more than fifty authorities), and although he regularly refers to the author he is using, his text remains eminently readable, and this is due in large part to the enthusiasm which infuses all he writes. There is no doubt that he had a deep and abiding admiration – veneration, even – for Rome and its antiquity such that he could hardly find words enough to express his feeling: 'l'antiquité que j'ay toute ma vie comme saincte et sacrée, honorée et estimée' (Antiquity which, all my life, I have honoured and esteemed as something saintly and sacred) (f. 48v), and towards the end of his manuscript he repeats with evident approval the definition of Nerva: 'Rome, royne de tout le monde et dame de toute la terre' (Rome, queen of everything, and mistress of the whole world) (f. 83).

This work ends on a twin theme: first with an acknowledgement of the king's interest in and commitment to the study of Roman history and antiquity; and secondly with robust assertions of his own achievement in this text. It is vital, he claims, that his readers appreciate the extraordinary task he has accomplished, the difficulty not only of making 'les choses antiques nouvelles' (old things new) but of giving that which is newly created authority and, moreover, 'donner splendeur, aux obscures lumiere, aux facheuses grace, et aux doubteuses foy' (of giving splendour and light to the obscure, grace to the ugly, and faith to the doubtful) (f. 88). In the end, Du Choul is confident that he has given enlightenment and opened up a new way for others to walk: 'i'ay ouvert le chemin d'une forestz obscure' (I have opened the way through a dark forest).

We do not know whether the 'Antiquitez' was ever completed. It was never published although, in the *Discours de la religion des Romains*, Du Choul cites his work as though it were finished and about to appear: when discussing further medal examples, he writes: 'la description desquelles se verra plus amplement en plusieurs passaiges des douze livres que i'ay faict des Antiquitez de Rome' (their more detailed description will be found in the twelve books on the Antiquities of Rome which I have written) (p. 17). In many ways, the *Discours* follows the pattern of the 'Antiquitez'. It is similarly based, as its title page announces, on 'un grand nombre de medailles, et de plusieurs belles figures retirées des marbres antiques qui se trouvent à Rome, et par nostre Gaule' (a large number of medals and on several fine images taken from ancient marbles which can be found in Rome and in Gaul), such as the tablet which recorded a banquet scene, depicted by Du Choul and described later by Tarde (*A la Rencontre*, p. 39). This resource, and the wide geographical range it implies, is supplemented continually by new discoveries – gold medals found at Toulouse in 1553; silver medals unearthed at Rheims; or a medallion presented to him only six months before; by engraved stones from his collection, kept by 'pour l'intelligence de l'Antiquité' (for the understanding of Antiquity); and by drawings and engravings which he has ordered from artists who worked in Rome and from some who had sojourned in France, such as Antonio Fantuzzi.

The *Discours* is more narrowly focused, yet the subject matter is still vast. The same veneration of the Romans is present but Du Choul is not uncritical of their habits. The number of names they gave to Jupiter, for example, he describes as 'folles et superstitieuses' (foolish and superstitious); he uses exactly the same derisive terms to characterize the canonization of their emperors, and he cannot understand why they took so long to accept the coming of Christ. He thinks of their beliefs with exaggerated sadness: 'Pouvres Romains, pouvres Gentils aveuglez d'ignorance, dignes certainement de grand pitié et de compassion' (poor Romans, poor Gentiles blinded with ignorance, certainly worthy of great pity and compassion) (p. 263). Such moments are rare in a work dedicated to the religious customs of non-Christians where attention is lavished on the details of pagan sacrifices and on the gods, their demeanour, their attributes and responsibilities. The work is, in fact, not a discourse in the sense that Du Choul sees his role as defending ancient beliefs and customs. His concern is more historical: to reconstruct from the evidence available modes of worship and the reasons for them.

In this context, he is concerned to represent accurately the temples erected in honour of the pagan gods: that which was created by Hadrian; the temple of Peace which housed all the booty brought back from Jerusalem by Titus and still displayed on his arch in Rome; or the temple of Jupiter which would not otherwise be known (Figure 26). Du Choul is conscious that all these

LE TEMPLE DE IVPITER
retiré de l'antique.

26. Guillaume du Choul: temple of Jupiter

images of temples are, in a sense, reconstructions made from medals and there-fore subject to error and poor definition. He expressed his reservations espe-cially when some renderings on medals are tiny or indistinct: 'il est bien difficile d'en retirer la certaine congnoissance, pour les lineaments, qui sont si subtils et deliez, qu'à grand'peine, et labeur on peu[t] juger l'ordre des colonnes' (it is very difficult to derive certain knowledge from them as the lines are so subtle and fine that one can just make out the order of the columns, and then only with great trouble and labour) (p. 40).

Notwithstanding these difficulties, Du Choul does frequently re-create from somewhat flimsy material, since such images are essential to his demonstration. Thus, the temple of Peace is given in two versions from bronze medals of Ves-pasian and Titus respectively; the temple of Janus Quadriform appears in full-page presentation thanks to the gift from Jacques de Strada of a medal from the time of Augustus, but which only depicts the three heads. Finally, there are the four reconstructed temples which can only be dimly perceived from the poor state of the medals which inspired them; yet they appear crisp and whole enough in the text (Figure 27). Du Choul gazed at medals and saw vanished buildings of Rome rise up. He could not resist communicating their presence any more than he could resist sharing the beauty of a small Bacchus which he had in his possession and which he reproduces – even though it does not bear on his argument – simply because it is beautiful, 'faict d'un tel artifice, qu'il mérite bien d'estre veu' (made with such skill that it is worthy of being seen) (p. 133) (Figure 28).

27.   Guillaume du Choul: 'Jeux séculaires des romains'

28. Guillaume du Choul: his Bacchus

Du Choul was a prolific writer. He dedicated to Henri II a treatise *Des Bains et antiques exercitations grecques et romaines* (1557) (the translation into Italian was dedicated by Symeoni to Montmorency), with a frontispiece borrowed from Fabius Calvus' *Balneum* (f. Fr).[85] He also offered Henri II his *Discours sur la castramentation et discipline militaire des romains* (1559) which, inspired by Trajan's column, depicted the costumes of the various military.[86] Other works mentioned in the *Discours* but probably never published are 'De la Nature des dieux' (p. 93); 'De imaginibus deorum' (p. 13) (which is possibly the same work); and 'Des Epigrammes de toute la Gaule' (p. 142).

In the two works which we have examined, Du Choul, whether consciously or not, was transferring his collection of medals, stones and engravings on to the pages of books where they became rearranged, thematically ordered, and given a logic and explanation. In this transference he was going beyond those books of drawings which reproduced the lineaments of a statue or a relief. I have in mind Aspertini who, around 1530, formed his drawing collection.[87] Aspertini had a natural affinity with battle scenes and violent actions, and drew the famous statues of Rome, but his drawings, like those of Girolamo da Carpi,[88] were often copied from sketches of others rather than from the original sculptures. They were carefully made, providing an accurate record even of broken pieces, and their purpose was to form a private cache of materials suitable for interpolation in future work. These were records, as were Du Choul's books, but Du Choul sought to go behind the images, to explain their sense with an abundance of erudite commentary, and to offer to a French public views of Rome and its customs. Through his ordering process and the thematic approach he adopted, his enterprise anticipated in some respects the paper museum of Pozzo where the whole means of recording gave rise to a new way of seeing the ancient world, matching fragments, comparing sculptures, and laying the ground for arriving at aesthetic judgements.[89]

Similar enthusiasm but couched in an infinitely more informed style characterized Nicolas-Claude Fabri de Peiresc who, on his death in 1637, left over 17,000 medals and many antiquities of other kinds including books, manuscripts and a large collection of vases. He published nothing, but he has left a huge correspondence (edited in 1894 by Tamizey de Larroque) which shows his contact with leading figures in Rome, Paris and Antwerp – Cardinal Barberini, Gassendi and Pozzo (from whose collection he had drawings made),[90] Auguste de Thou, Gabriel Naudé and the Dupuy brothers, and Rubens. He trained in the law, travelled to Italy,[91] and spent some years in Paris, but for the most part he lived comfortably in Aix or at his country house in Beaugency. In both places he surrounded himself with rare things which he bought continuously, and he inherited some notable collections, such as that of Guillaume du Vair.[92] For him, medals were historical documents, texts to be read and deciphered, and of significant status because they represented official records: 'pour qui cherche à porter de la lumière dans l'histoire de l'antiquité, les médailles ont plus d'importance' (for whoever seeks to throw light on the history of antiquity, medals are very important).[93] His letters reveal a good judge of aesthetic quality, and an eager yet systematic mind which stressed the value of close observation and of seeing for oneself.[94] On the subject of Holstenius' visit to Italy, for example, he wrote to the brothers Dupuy in 1628:

> j'ay fort loué son dessein d'aller voir les païs d'à l'entour de Rome sçachant bien qu'une vëue occulaire a un merveilleux advantage sur toute sorte de relations ou portraictures faictes à boulle vëue, comme on dict. (*Correspondance*, I, 547)

> [I much praised his project of going to see the country around Rome, knowing that seeing for oneself has an immense advantage over all kinds of accounts or engravings done with 'a sure throw', as one says.]

Notwithstanding this observation, since his fragile health prevented him from returning to Rome himself, he used all ways to keep in touch with new discoveries. He kept up with publications on medals, requiring Dupuy to send him Savot's new book as soon as it was available so that he could send a copy 'à quelque amy d'Italie' (to some friend in Italy) (ibid., 129–30);[95] and he wrote constantly to Rubens reminding him to send details of antique images (medals and reliefs) while he would furnish drawings of rare objects from his collection in return. Conversely, Rubens brought the best examples from his own collection for Peiresc to study, as the latter tells Rambervilliers in November 1622: 'pour l'amour de moy [Rubens] apporta tout plein de belles et des plus precieuses pieces de son cabinet' (for love of me, he brought a quantity of fine and precious examples from his collection).[96] Peiresc valued accuracy above all and therefore prized the faithfully drawn engravings which he found in the cargo destined for De Thou (*Correspondance*, II, 181). In this regard, when Holstenius was on his way to Rome he charged him to take exact measurements of buildings and make true records of faces, although Peiresc recognized that copyists often misunderstood the material and were inaccurate.[97] If Holstenius wanted models on which to base his work he should consult Andrea Palladio (*Correspondance*, V, 357 and VII, 229); or – writing to Aubéry – study the books of Sebastiano Serlio whose drawings Peiresc had himself copied.[98] He admired the sieur de Templery for the quality of his work in restoring medals, sculptures and broken ancient vases (*Correspondance*, I, 598). For his own collection, he had had copies made by famous artists of the most celebrated examples of ancient vases that had come to light, 'qui fussent à Rome de mon temps, comme estoit le congius du Cardinal Farnese' (which were found in Rome when I was there, such as the congius belonging to Cardinal Farnese); and in their fabrication, he had – as usual – made sure that the measurements were accurate (*Correspondance*, II, 301–2).[99] Perhaps his most valued possessions were the antique bracelet 'trouvé dans un tombeau antique quand j'estois à Rome' (found in an ancient tomb while I was in Rome) (*Correspondance*, VI, 2) and the cameo representing the apotheosis of Emperor Augustus and his family of which he has left a minute description in manuscript.[100]

He was not selfish in his demands. On the contrary, his generosity shines through his letters, where he is seen constantly on the lookout for books for his friends: Erizzo's *Discorsi*, for instance, despite their shortcomings (*Correspondance*, II, 435).[101] He kept a careful check on the sale of collections: after the death of Monsieur de Fontenay in 1628, he urged Pierre Dupuy to acquire the best pieces for him, though he conceded that Monsieur (the duc d'Orléans) would, of necessity, have the choice pick (*Correspondance*, V, 697); he monitored exports from Rome; and he even reported on weather conditions, the routes and schedules of cargoes, and on the movements of ambassadors, so anxious was he to have sight of the latest treasure. He was exceedingly gratified, for instance, when Cardinal Barberini sent him advance copies of the plates destined to illustrate Bosius' *Roma subterranea* (*Correspondance*, III, 136). Then there is the story of De Thou's *coffre* that got waterlogged and which so discoloured antique medals that they acquired a modern appearance (*Correspondance*, II, 147); he gives an account of the fifty-three cases destined for the collection of the duc d'Orléans (*Correspondance*, II, 244); and he provides valuable information about the large quantity of marble statues sent from Rome to 'monseigneur l'Eminentissime Cardinal de Richelieu' by his agent Monsieur Frangipani (*Correspondance*, II, 547), and to the Queen Mother (*Correspondance*, VI, 184).

Some exchanges – particularly with Alphonse de Rambervilliers and with his agent in Rome, Claude Menestrier (*Correspondance*, V, 491) – are exclusively concerned with medals. With the former, he discussed extensively the nature of medals and each person's taste when it came to building up a collection: 'car chacun y a le sien particulier' (because each person has his own particular taste);[102] and he informed the latter in 1627 that he had sent the artist Mellan to Rome (*Correspondance*, I, 211) so that he might make good drawings from extant works and from manuscripts at his own expense. At home, he employed Jean Rabel, whose careful work he admired.[103] Claude Menestrier worked in the employ of Cardinal Barberini and had hoped to make a successful career within that cultured prelate's orbit but he was forced to eke out his existence by establishing a *cabinet des curiosités* and serving the demands of scholars like Peiresc.[104] The latter was – in Menestrier's view – stringent in his instructions (*Correspondance*, VII, 198) and concerned about the state of conservation of what he was purchasing (*Correspondance*, V, 494–5), questioning the cost of each item with meticulous care, and reinforcing his requests with statements about his own particular taste. Peiresc did, nonetheless, trust Menestrier's judgement and he usually paid what was asked as he accepted Menestrier's contention that it was difficult to find good copiers in Rome when all the world, it seemed, wanted them.

Few collectors would have had the knowledge and experience of a Peiresc who knew precisely what he wanted done. A significant example is when he directed Menestrier to have Pirro Ligorio's manuscripts in the Vatican copied:

> Si vous me faisiez portraire des volumes de Ligorio qui sont au Vatican tout ce que vous y trouverez en cette matière [statues et marbres de bronze], vous m'obligeriez bien. (*Correspondance*, V, 786)

> [If you were to draw all you can find on this matter in Ligorio's volumes in the Vatican [statues, marble and bronze], you would greatly oblige me.]

Peiresc had recognized on his visit to the papal library, over thirty years earlier, the quality and value of Ligorio's drawings of Roman remains and some examples of the copies he had made survive in his own manuscript collections (Figure 29).[105] His ability to recall the details of drawings and engravings which he had seen only once was extraordinary. He explained to Pierre Dupuy, for example, that drawings 'tirez des peinctures antiques de Rome où sont representez divers animaulx estranges' (taken from ancient Roman paintings where several strange animals are represented) were in fact printed in Rome in 1547, and could be found on several large plates in Auguste de Thou's collection (*Correspondance*, I, 138). For all his distinctiveness, Peiresc is an interesting

Apollo cum tripode in Arcu Constantini M.

29. Drawing made from Ligorio, in Peiresc's collection

witness in that his urbane yet erudite approach to collecting, and his wide
network of contacts across Europe with other collectors, artists and intellec-
tuals, offer insights into attitudes towards Rome at a time when appropriation
of its artefacts – either literally or in copies – had significantly expanded in
France. By the end of the sixteenth century, the habits of collecting already
extended far beyond court and scholarly circles.

THE TWELVE CAESARS

The kinds of appropriation and literal incorporation into imaginative writing
and into the creation of buildings in France in the late Renaissance will be
the matter of the second half of this book. It suffices for present purposes to
see how the rapid and sometimes indiscriminate building up of collections
encouraged the assimilation of objects from Rome, which were transferred on
to the decoration of buildings and there, in turn, affected notions of acquisition. Images of the twelve Caesars may be taken as illustrative. An abundant
stock of such images was available in print, made accessible in Andreas Fulvius'

Illustrium imagines as early as 1517, and reproduced with elaborate commentary and other images associated with the reign of each emperor by artists and print-makers such as Aeneas Vico (the friend of Aretino) in his *Omnium Caesarum verissimae imagines ex antiquis numismata descriptae* (Venice, 1553), or Sebastiano Erizzo in his *Discorso sopra le medaglie antiche* (1559) to which was appended a learned explanation of the moneys and medals struck for each emperor. The texts of Vico and Erizzo were republished frequently,[106] and were undoubtedly used as models by architects – as Antoine Le Pois made clear when he wrote: 'Et nos Architectes et maçons les imitent et usurpent fort pour le present, en cheminées et autres ouvrages domestiques' (and our architects and masons imitate them [medals] and currently place them on chimneypieces or on other domestic works).[107] What had become routine by the 1570s for interior decoration and for collecting (Throckmorton had a set of bronze medallions of the twelve Caesars on approval to place before Elizabeth I in 1561, and Catherine de' Medici ordered a set from Rome in 1577)[108] was still novel in the first decade of the sixteenth century. Then it had been customary to display one's taste on outside walls. In this way, the twelve Caesars were incorporated into the walls of the hôtel Allement at Bourges, they were added for Flori-mond de Robertet into the façade of the hôtel d'Alluye along a band of white stone,[109] and they similarly adorned the courtyard of Robertet's friend's castle at Gaillon where, among many other signs of Roman influence and imitations *à l'antique*, Georges d'Amboise had the twelve Caesars placed around the inner courtyard in roundels.[110]

In this chapter, an attempt has been made to trace the extent and nature of collecting of antiquities in France in the Renaissance. This indicates the basis of knowledge of Roman antiquities current at the time from which might be created French equivalents, through acquisition and absorption, through adjust-ment and modification. The most easily transportable objects – coins and medals – have been seen as providing evidence of an extensive interest which stretched from princes to more humble folk and which recognized the value of such objects as historical witness on the one hand and as indicating artistic potential on the other. The scholars and artists who developed a more general understanding of their merit and applicability and of the imaginative resources bound up in these artefacts must now be considered.

CHAPTER 4

The Transporters

NEW IMAGES AND A NEW VOCABULARY

Mental attitudes towards images of Rome were shaped by experts, by architects, numismatists and humanist historians who wrote abundantly about
Roman antiquities and whose works were illustrated and available in France.
It might be argued, however, that France was not yet ready to receive (or at
least understand) such works. According to contemporary writers themselves,
the French language could hardly accommodate the technical terms needed to
transmit the images of ancient Rome accurately. Although the enriching power
of architectural terms became a commonplace, that the French struggled to
absorb the necessary words[1] is evident from the description in 1531 of Queen
Eleonore's present, offered on the occasion of her entry into the capital and
whose details have been preserved in the *Registres et délibérations de la ville de
Paris*. The anonymous author attempts to describe the shapes and symbolism
of a pair of candelabra and, after detailing the various tiers of gods, triumphs
and scenes 'faites à l'antique', he comes to the final level which formed a circular platform on which danced fauns and satyrs. Above their dance was fixed
'une assiette ronde et carré [*sic*] garnie d'une cornice et art qui traive' (a round
platform and a square decorated with a cornice and architrave).

Despite the apparent precision, the overall shape of the top of the candelabra remains unclear; and this is a direct consequence of the technical terms
used. Are *cornice* and *architrave* being applied correctly, especially since the writer
patently does not know the second term? Such hesitancy was not uncommon.
Du Choul, in his Turin manuscript, had claimed that the vocabulary of architecture was not known in France until the reign of François I although, in
making this claim, he may simply have been preparing the ground to show off
his own mastery of this novel language.[2]

Following the tradition established by Vitruvius and Alberti who had been
at pains to emphasize the new and rare nature of the art they were building
and the terms used to describe it,[3] the historiographer royal – Denis Sauvage
– presented the king in 1553 with Martin's posthumous translation of Alberti's
work *L'Art de bien bastir*, warning Henri II, in his preface,

vous y trouverez vostre langue enrichie de mille mots, paravant cachés dedans les boutiques des seuls ouvriers

[you will find here your language enriched by a thousand words which were hidden away in workmen's stores and known only to them].[4]

The accent here is on the enriching process that Joachim du Bellay had so enthusiastically advocated for poetry in *La Deffence et illustration de la langue françoise* (1549) and yet, in 1567, Philibert de L'Orme was still obliged to acknowledge the poverty of the French language for his purposes and the necessity, as he saw it, either to invent, to import foreign words, or to have recourse to circumlocution:

Pour dire verité nostre langue Françoise en l'explication de plusieurs choses, est si pauvre et sterile, que nous n'avons mots qui les puissent representer proprement si nous n'usurpons le langage ou mot estranger: ou bien que nous usions de quelque longue circonlocution.

[To tell the truth, for the explanation of many things, our French language is so poor and sterile that we can only describe them properly if we borrow foreign words and if we indulge in long circumlocutions.][5]

Fortunately, no inhibitions resulted from the recognition of these difficulties. Until his death, Martin had persisted with his valuable translations; and Philibert de L'Orme bequeathed long and admiring accounts of his own architectural enterprises.

In persisting with their efforts to introduce up-to-date architectural terms into French, Martin and De L'Orme were following in the footsteps of four scholars – Serlio, Symeoni, Vigenère and Lipsius – whose work is of particular significance. They are considered here in turn as, in their several ways, they were responsible for conditioning French attitudes to Rome for many decades.

SEBASTIANO SERLIO (1475–1554)

Sebastiano Serlio's seven books of architecture made him one of the most important transporters into France of images of Rome, ancient and modern. At the behest of François I, he came to Fontainebleau in 1540 and stayed in France for the remainder of his life. Serlio's significance lies not only in the fact that his work was profusely illustrated and that the drawings carried the burden of the argument, for the first time in such a work, but also in the fact that these were accurate renderings of the buildings observed and were presented by Serlio with sure judgement and in a fully comparative way. His contemporaries called him 'consumatissimo ne le antichità' (consummate in the art of antiquity),[6] and in his work, Serlio stressed how vital it was to measure buildings accurately and to study and draw them *sur place*; to read voluminously in ancient and contemporary writing on painting and architecture; to scrutinize modern works as well as those left by the early Romans; and to communicate what he saw unambiguously in word and image.

It is the interaction of images and Serlio's commentaries which makes his work so remarkable and so influential. Rabelais, who was in Rome when Serlio came to do his measurements and complete his drawings, testifies to his seriousness. He evokes Serlio burrowing away with Peruzzi among the ruins of the theatre of Marcellus (slavishly, according to Rabelais) advocating the authority of Vitruvius, discoursing with Ligorio from whose manuscripts he borrowed, and enjoying the hospitality of the great French households in Rome – the Du Bellays and Pellicier.[7]

The terrain had been well prepared for his arrival in France. François I had been the willing recipient of Italian translations of Vitruvius,[8] and he had ordered casts of the famous statues from the Belvedere court. French artists came back from Rome with new notions; and French patrons generally were ready to respond to fresh ideas. Serlio, who had advised Guillaume Philander and Jean Martin on their version of Vitruvius,[9] was assured of a good reception which Pellicier confirmed in a letter to the queen of Navarre:

> messer Sebastiano Serlio m'a escript le bon recueil qu'il vous a pleu luy faire et le bon traictement qu'il a eu du roy par vostre faveur.

> [Master Sebastiano Serlio has written to me about the warm welcome it pleased you to give him and, through your influence, about his good treatment by the king.][10]

Almost as important as the favour of the monarch were the reactions of his peers; and it is interesting to note the warmth with which Goujon pays tribute both to the value of Serlio's contribution to the knowledge of ancient architecture in France and to the role he played in introducing the principles of Vitruvius to the French and extending the vocabulary of architecture.[11] In his remarks which preface the 1547 translation by Martin of Vitruvius, Goujon (having listed the fine artists whose legacy was essential to good artistic work) wrote of Serlio:

> Et encores pour ce iourd'huy avons nous en ce Royaume de France un messire Sebastian Serlio; lequel a assez diligemment escrit et figuré beaucoup de choses selon les regles de Vitruve, et a esté le commencement de mettre teles doctrines en lumiere au Royaume. (sig. Diiij)

> [And also we have now in this kingdom of France, a certain M. Sebastiano Serlio who has written and engraved diligently many things, according to the rules of Vitruvius, and has been responsible for beginning to circulate such ideas throughout the land.][12]

The compliment should be seen in the context of a close working relationship between the two artists since elsewhere Goujon notes Serlio's approval for a figure he had made.[13] Jean Cousin also praised Serlio's work, setting it beside that of Vitruvius and Alberti, for having measured the true proportions of ancient forms of architecture.[14] Even Philibert de L'Orme – not noted for his generosity – was explicit in his praise of Serlio who had already provided such good descriptions that his own explanations could, he wrote, be more succinct.[15] In Book 7 of his work he applauded the figures Serlio had drawn of Roman antiquities, and praised his careful measurements and the quality of the architect's own inventions:

> C'est luy [Serlio] qui a donné le premier aux François, par ses livres et desseings la cognoissance des edifices antiques et de plusieurs fort belles inventions estant homme de bien, ainsi que ie l'ay cogneu, et de fort bonne ame, pour avoir publié et donné de bon coeur, ce qu'il avoit mesuré, veu et retiré des antiquitez. (f. 202v)

> [It is Serlio who, by his books and drawings, first gave knowledge to the French of ancient edifices and of several excellent inventions, being a man of honour as I have known him and of strong mind, for having – with good will – published and given to the world all that he had measured, seen and drawn from antiquity.][16]

Serlio's work went on being influential both in Italy and in France after he had ceased to be active, and long after his death; Vasari used him a great deal but did not acknowledge the fact, and Peiresc had Serlio's texts copied.[17]

The history of Serlio's publications is tangled and complex, but has been ably elucidated by William Bell Dinsmoor.[18] Initially Serlio's aim may have been to carry through a project which had been contemplated by his master Peruzzi: that is, to publish a work on the antiquities of Rome. Serlio's own plan took on larger dimensions. The first publication (Book 4) came out in Venice in 1537, and there Serlio outlined the scope of his whole enterprise, which projected seven volumes in all. Book 3, dedicated to François I, appeared next, in 1540, and dealt with the antiquities of Rome. Books 1 and 2 came out in 1545, in French and Italian; the fifth book, also in both languages, appeared in 1547 and was followed by the *Libro extraordinario* (designs for doors and gateways), published in Lyon in 1551, which was to become the sixth book in the collected edition (1584). The final book – the seventh – eventually appeared in Frankfurt in 1575, some twenty years after the author's death.

Although, in these volumes, Vitruvius is cited as the ultimate authority on rules for perspective, on proportion, and on technical aspects of the five orders of architecture, Serlio does not find him infallible as a guide and, with objective attention and an ability to detach himself from the weight of authority which were unusual at this time,[19] he repeatedly draws attention to ancient ruins that do not adhere to Vitruvius' conceptions, and to successful modern works that break his rules:

io trovo gran differenza dalla cose di Roma et d'altri luoghi d'Italia gli scritti de Vitruvio. (IV, f. 141v)

[I find great differences in buildings at Rome and in other places in Italy from the writings of Vitruvius.][20]

Even more interesting is Serlio's regard for modern masters of painting and of architecture, who are presented as points of reference and of emulation throughout his work. Thus Bramante is remembered for his knowledge of perspective and his rare architectural skill, for initiating the design of St Peter's which encouraged Raphael to make 'one of his fayrest draughts to be found',[21] and for having built the Tempietto which was to appear in later French designs (Figure 30). The praise which Serlio awards to modern masters is accompanied by specific comments on quality and style: Raphael's loggias, for example, are extolled for their good order and the harmonizing of so many varied elements (*Tutte l'opere d'architettura*, Venice, 1584, III, f. 120v), and, in Serlio's view, his capacity to make images seem real and to transfer life so faithfully to canvas made him exceptional (1584, IV, f. 192v). Unusually, Michelangelo is only mentioned once, although Caravaggio (and others) are praised for the quality of light that filters on to the canvas (ibid., f. 191v); Giulio Romano for the fantastic and original works he wrought in Rome and in Mantua (ibid., f. 133v); Girolamo Genga for his expertise in perspective (ibid., III, f. 18v); Titian for the light and colour which radiate from his paintings and for his figures which stand out in high relief (ibid., f. 50); and Dürer for the range of his experimentation (ibid., II, f. 47).

Two names emerge as commanding special respect: Balthazar Peruzzi who taught Serlio all he knew and whom he mentions with reverence and affection;[22] and Mantegna, whose triumphs he admired for

la profundità del disegno, la prospettiva artificiosa, la inventione mirabile, la innata discretione nel componimento delle figure, e la diligentia estrema nel finire. (ibid., IV, f. 192v)

[the profundity of the design, the skilful perspective, the marvellous powers of invention, the innate delicacy in the attitudes of the figures, and the extreme carefulness in the finishing of the work.]

Although Serlio's judgements tend to evoke general aesthetic categories, they do – in the case of Mantegna – address all the major concerns that come into play when assessing a work of art. In this way, Serlio's readers are given clear and diversified images of the work of modern masters.

The images of earlier times are transmitted with equal care and clarity. In Book 3, *De gli antichità di Roma e molti d'Italia*, words and figures combine to give portraits of ancient monuments. Serlio presents first the Pantheon (ibid.,

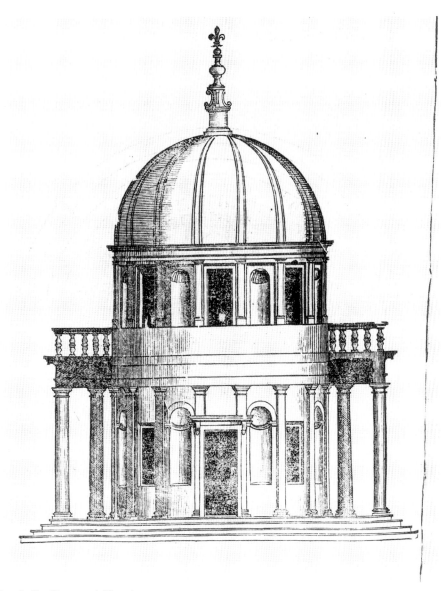

30.   Serlio: Bramante's Tempietto

ff. 50–6) and the perfection of its round form with an initial view of the exterior; then the interior is opened up, shorn of its ornaments; and gradually the parts which compose this perfect whole are systematically revealed (Figure 31). Serlio analyses each, gives individual measurements, calls attention to striking features, and builds his comments so that they justify his overall assessment of a 'maraviglioso edificio' (marvellous edifice).

This was his method: first a view of the whole building, or of its plan if no

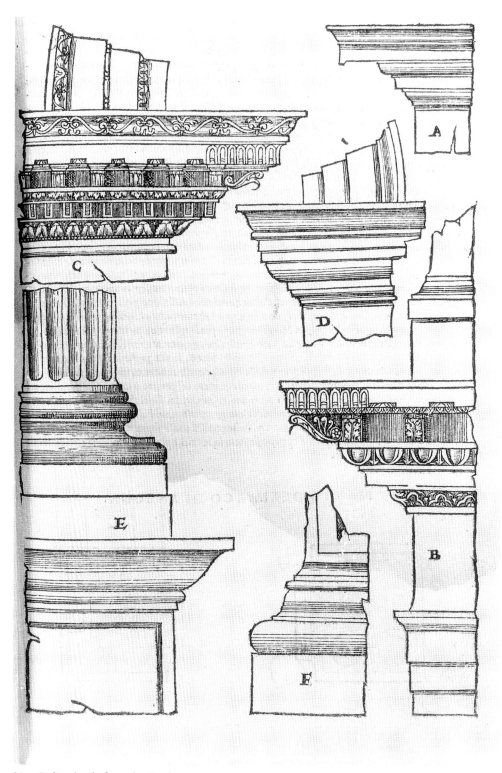

31. Serlio: details from the Pantheon

structures survive above ground (as for the temple of Bacchus); then a sight of the interior, and finally drawings of columns, capitals, cornices, floors and ceilings, each receiving due consideration, with buildings in Rome often being compared unfavourably with others in Verona, Ancona or Tivoli.

The baths of Diocletian (ibid., III, ff. 94–6) fascinated him partly by reason of their size, the evident richness of decoration in what remained, and the huge proportions and number of the columns, and partly because the variety of invention and style went far beyond the dictates of classical rules. The arch of Constantine, so admired by contemporaries for its harmonious form, for the richness and consistency of the symbolism of its reliefs and decorations, and for its 'bella maniera' (fine manner), was beautiful to the eye, yet like so many triumphal arches which were erected in a hurry and under pressure (the arch of Titus, for example: ibid., III, f. 99v), it was constructed from the ruins of many other buildings: che detti archi sono fatti di spoglie d'altri edifici (ibid., III, f. 99v) (the said arches are made from the spoils of other buildings).

Despite this knowledge, the image Serlio leaves of the arch of Constantine is that of a perfect and unified edifice (ibid., III, f. 106).

Alongside the Pantheon, the building that Serlio most admired from ancient Rome was the theatre of Marcellus, to which he returned on several occasions. Only fragments of this building remained,[23] and Serlio reproduced these pieces to scale in his text (ibid., III, f. 197v). He was persuaded that the positioning of the arches and their proportion were the best he had ever seen (ibid., f. 196v) and, as examples of Doric cornices or Ionic columns which should be imitated, he cites and draws those he had found in the rubble around the theatre (1584, II, f. 171).

Serlio was aware that Leonardo da Vinci had left a relatively small corpus of finished work because he was unable to make his hands shape the ideas that came to him. Serlio perceived a similar gap when it came to interpreting the ruins of buildings that remained in Rome and when he tried to conceive the complete edifice that had once existed. In order to help his readers to understand the full import of the images he was transmitting and, if that reader were an architect, to enable him to make use of the images in his own compositions, Serlio deconstructed the ancient buildings that still stood entire. Like the Pantheon they were first illustrated whole, and only then were they decomposed into their constituent parts.

The process also worked the other way. Where no building remained, Serlio studied the fragments that survived, mapped out the overall plan, and then offered a reconstructed building. Peruzzi, he claimed, had been able to conceive the whole of the theatre of Marcellus from the fragments he had unearthed (1584, III, f. 69v), 'per quella parta scoperta comprese il tutto' (from the parts discovered, the whole could be understood). Another example was the temple found at Tivoli, near the river, which was in a completely ruined state:

Ma io l'ho cosa disegnato per ornamento, che ancor cosi potria stare, e ave nelle mura, nè delle bande di dietro si vegonno alcune fenestre; io nonimento le, ho volute porre nella pianta in quei luoghi, dove elle per miso parere, stariano bene. (ibid., f. 64)

[Yet I wished to draw it thus with ornaments because it might have been so, even though there are no windows on the walls, nor on the sides or at the back; I have introduced them on the plan there where it seemed good to me.]

There is something almost cavalier about this reconstruction, and it is noticeable that Serlio has not justified his approach (as Palladio did) with arguments about the ability to build wholes from fragments. The English text of 1611 had amplified the reasons for Serlio's addition of doors in the walls of the temple, arguing:

I have drawne it out thus to make the more show for I judge it had been so (f. 15; the French text of 1550 also added the gloss: 'là où il m'a semblez bon').

Clearly, the translators felt the need to explain. Serlio, however, in the original version simply argued the difficulty of interpreting the ruins of Rome, 'Tra le rovine di Rome si trovano molte cosa per lequali non si può comprendere che cosa fossero' (many things are found digging in the ruins of Rome which one cannot understand) (1584, III, f. 88v).

Nevertheless, the single, massive yet elegant Corinthian column (Figure 32) which had prompted this remark stimulates the imagination if not to re-create the building it helped to support, at least to conjure up the mighty ambitions of the Roman mind that conceived it (as Serlio acknowledged, 'dalle quali si comprendere la grandezza di gli animi Romani'). With equal honesty, Serlio had presented completed figures of the temple of Peace (ibid., f. 60). While admitting that 'e molto rovinato, nè visi vegono vestigii di finastre' (is much ruined and the vestiges of the windows cannot be seen), he added, 'I have put them in places where I thought it fittest for them to stand' ('nondimeno io le ho poste nella pianta in quei luoghi dove sariano piu convenienti') (ibid., f. 59v).

Serlio added elements to a ruined building because he thought they should be there, and in order that his reader might – in the Dutch translator's words to his English audience – 'satisfie our eyes . . . [and] the desire we have to see such incredible works . . . [and] to have the contemplation thereof'.[24] Such expectation moved Serlio to advocate the transferability of his designs, to argue for the incorporation of the old into the new, and to urge the cultivation of the unfinished effect in architectural design.

Transferability of design ideas from altars to arches, from doors to windows, was not only a valuable practical tactic for any architect, it was fundamental to the incorporation of the vision of Rome into French practice and habits. In

32. Serlio: engraving of a single Corinthian column

33. Serlio: design for a gateway

his own designs in Book 4, Serlio argued: 'Di questa segnente figura, il giudicioso Architetto si potrà accommodare diverse cose' (from the following image a judicious architect can adapt many things) (f. 149v), and he then elaborated on the transfer of the same idea to several different surfaces. Similarly in Book 7 he has several chapters where he discusses the blending of old and new; how to incorporate ancient columns on to the façade of a temple (ch. 47, p. 114),[25] and how to use columns and other fragments so that the finished building has a harmonious look (ch. 50, p. 118). Elsewhere, in Book 6, he is concerned to create designs which while questioning the status of classical lines and forms serve to reinforce their power. There is the design for a gateway for example, where he attempts to make the brickwork seem to absorb the marble Doric columns, but only partially (f. 4v, 'la presente porta è tutte dorica mista col Rustico' (the order of this gateway is entirely Doric, blended with rustic); or, on the next page, a door designed to give the impression of columns not yet finished: 'come sono le colonne non finite'; or again, in another effort to disturb, playing with the marble so that it resembles wood (Figure 33), as Serlio writes, in order to give variety to the work.

At times, there is a visible urge in Serlio's designs to break out of the classical mould to satisfy those 'huomini bizarri' who search for the new, and to indulge his own wish for an untrammelled style. Thus he devises gateways where, as in example XXVIII (f. 16v), he deliberately breaks down the form and Doric purity of the columns. It is not perhaps surprising that this book of designs was originally called 'Libro extraordinario'.

Such conscious deviations from the norm reinforced the classical criteria by which buildings and paintings were judged excellent or beautiful. One of the notable services Serlio rendered was not only to import into France details of those norms but also to provide an extensive vocabulary to support and elucidate that detail. French writers and artists were predisposed to give such criteria a favourable reception since they had been evolving their own aesthetic ideas and values from classical sources and these closely paralleled the notions that had been debated in Italy and which Serlio had absorbed.[26] Thus there was a strengthening of prepared attitudes which facilitated the absorption of images of Rome which reflected aesthetic standards that had already been set.

Harmony, proportion and grace are terms authoritatively applauded by Vitruvius and Alberti and which constantly recur in Serlio's work. They are exemplified in the two arches in Verona discussed and figured in Book 3 (1584, ff. 112 and 115), the first praised for its 'buona forma & proportione' (excellent form and proportion); the second extolled as full 'di gracilità e molto gracioso' (full of grace and most elegant). Grace comes from the ability to combine beauty and embellishment, and from decorum, which means ensuring that variety is controlled, made harmonious and appropriate to the object or building being created. Variety, too, is an essential ingredient if a work is to be deemed perfect: indeed, Serlio was to maintain in his final work that

> La varieta delle cose è di grand contentezza all'occhio humano, et di sodisfattione all'animo. (1584, VII, ch. 38, p. 92)

> [The variety of things provides much contentment to the human eye and satisfaction to the soul.]

And yet few architects achieved the necessary balance. The baths of Diocletian astonish by virtue of their inventiveness, but their ingenuity breaks all the rules and has to be labelled 'licentiousness'. On the other hand, the arch at Ancona (1584, III, f. 107v) achieves its great beauty by being varied because the parts correspond and harmonize with each other just as Raphael's loggias (ibid., f. 120) were 'varieto concordamente' (harmoniously varied).

The most important factor of all – *giudicio*, or judgement, especially preoccupies Serlio. Judgement is the most difficult skill to acquire, to define and to exercise effectively. He knows men of undoubted judgement who have performed acts which suggest the contrary, and vice versa. Good judgement, he thinks, comes from experience and from listening to the opinions of many. If judgement is applied to architecture, how – Serlio asks – does one distinguish *architettura giudiciosa* which is defined as 'soda [solid], semplice [simple and unadorned], schietta [plain], dolce [sweet], e morbida [soft]' from an architecture that is weak and fragile, affected and crude or obscure and confused ('una debole, gracile, delicata, affetata, cruda, anzi oscura et confusa')? Typically, Serlio tries to answer his own question by offering four illustrations of works which

34. Serlio: examples of columns designed with good and bad judgement

were of both types. He asks us to consider example C (1584, VII, ch. 53, f. 124) which is graceful and dainty, but also crude and harsh. He analyses the drawing explaining *grace* by looking at the subtlety and sveltness of the columns; and the *daintiness* by the polish the author has given to the work. The *crudeness*, on the other hand, is apparent in the darkness of the columns and in the decision to mix different stones. Thus, the left side with mixed and marked stone on the columns and pedestals is harsh and contrasts strongly and unfavourably with the unadorned right side, described by Serlio as 'morbida, dolce e semplice' (soft, sweet and simple) (Figure 34).

Such a demonstration is very practical in its effect, for Serlio is not only attempting to overcome his own puzzlement, but is simultaneously teaching the reader how to achieve good results by explaining and illustrating the difference between simplicity and superfluity. In addition to the technical terms which identified the parts of a building, Serlio has introduced a set of aesthetic terms which matched sentiments that had developed in his new country and that were acquiring their verbal equivalents in French. This suggests that, whatever the reservations articulated by De L'Orme concerning the expressive power of the French language regarding architecture, these doubts may have been unfounded. Serlio's work served to give ideas, confidence and added impetus to those who sought to transform their French compositions by the incorporation of newly minted images from across the Alps.

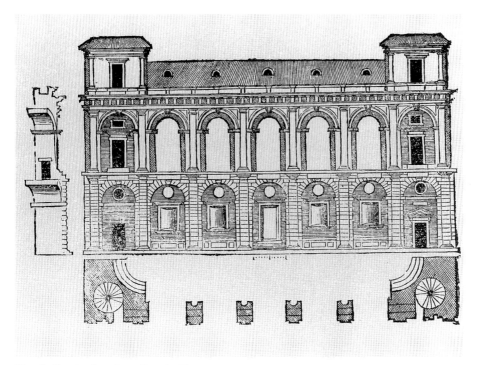

35.   Serlio: the Loggia at Fontainebleau

Serlio had also an unusual capacity to persuade. Indeed, it has been argued that he knew Delminio's *Idea dell'eloquenza* and owed something to rhetorical traditions,[27] and he communicated many of his ideas through memorable (if somewhat commonplace) metaphors. The surface stone of a building, for instance, is likened to flesh while 'le pietre vive' that support the edifice are described as its bone structure (1584, III, f. 188v). When Serlio is attempting to persuade the reader not to be impressed by a surface overladen with ornament, he thinks of a beautiful woman, richly clad, dressed sparsely with jewels, 'in fronte un bel gioiello, et ell'orecchie due belli et ricchi pendenti' (on her forehead, a fine jewel; and in her ears, two beautiful, rich pendants): a touch of sparkle that corresponds to her form is all that is needed (1584, VII, ch. 54, f. 126). Beside her, he sets the vision of a woman dressed from top to toe in jewels and ornaments, an indiscriminate show that blurs rather than surprises, and concludes that such superfluity is monstrous. The metaphor has made the argument, just as it does a little later (ibid., ch. 66, f. 168) where, having difficulty in defending a façade that is not symmetrical and finding the topos 'una discordia concordans' inadequate, he resorts to a musical analogy where four performers ('il Soprano, il Contrabaso, et il Tenore, et il Contralto') intervene in the composition, apparently singing against each other – the depth of tone of one contrasting sharply with the piercing pitch of the other – and yet the overall effect on the listeners is one of pleasurable and intense harmony.

Serlio's presence and work in France doubtless had a lasting influence on the taste for grottoes, and on the style of gateways, doors and arches.[28] The modifications he made to the *loggia* at Fontainebleau (Figure 35), where the casts from the Belvedere gardens and other precious statues and bronzes were housed, brought him fame.[29]

His written monument, too, secured for him the posthumous reputation referred to by Philibert de L'Orme, and continued to serve in the practical way that its author would have wished.[30] Constantly pillaged by later writers on architecture for ideas, designs and information, the *Seven Books of Architecture* also provided an invaluable source for careful humanists such as Peiresc who, in his 'Recueil d'antiquitez',[31] found no better way of paying tribute than by copying verbatim Serlio's opinions and descriptions of the ancient baths of Titus and Diocletian.

GABRIEL SYMEONI (1509–*c*.70)

An Italian author who pursued an active career in France was Gabriel Symeoni. Now largely forgotten (except by specialists), he carried images of Rome and its antiquities on his many journeys back and forth between Italy and France, and made them readily accessible in the books he published in the 1550s. Symeoni was an intellectual adventurer who used his writing as a vehicle to obtain influential friends and patrons; but he never achieved the high position at the French court which he craved and felt he had been promised.[32] In his search for recognition, he tried everything. He was poet, historian and antiquary; collector of medals, visionary and translator; writer of political pamphlets and – at the end of his life – decorator; and in all these fields he wrote books, publishing his multiple talents to the world. Given his aspirations, the majority of his works were in the form of miscellanies designed to attract the attention of some great patron. The *Interpretation* (1555) was dedicated to Henri II; his translation of Caesar's *Commentaries* (*Le César renouvellé*) to the Dauphin; a book of letters was offered to the duchesse de Valentinois; and several works carried dedications to the duc de Montmorency and to Charles, cardinal de Lorraine. His prefaces routinely praised their love of antiquity and their knowledge of classical remains; and they are presented as worthy recipients of Symeoni's work because they shared his enthusiasm and his erudition. The cardinal de Lorraine, for instance, is called 'grandissime amateur de toutes choses anciennes et rares' (a marvellous connoisseur of all ancient and rare things); his mansion at Meudon is likened to the palace Hadrian had built at Tivoli and it is especially commended as the place where the prelate had attempted to imitate and present 'la plus grande partie des anciennes singularitez de la ville de Rome' (the greater part of the ancient marvels of Rome).[33] We know that the taste for medals and other antiquities was enjoyed by most wealthy men at this time, but Symeoni makes a particular point when, in developing arguments about the benefits the young dauphin will derive from Caesar's example, he draws attention to virtues evident in François' regard for 'medalles, pourtraicts, statues et autres nobles choses antiques' (medals, images, statues and other fine antique things).[34] The prince's own natural inclinations prepared him for the lessons in tactics and strategy which, in *César renouvellé*, Symeoni offered as part of his own commitment to the French crown ('suyvant l'envie que tousjours des longtemps, j'ay eüe et auray toute ma vie de faire service à la couronne de France' (following the desire I have long had, have now and will always have, to serve the crown of France), sig. ã iij).

That commitment had already been spelt out in Symeoni's strange work *Interpretation grecque, latine, tuscane, et française du monstre ou enigme d'Italie* in which he saw Henri II as destined by the laws and interactions of the planets to assume an imperial role and to bring harmony and freedom to Europe, uniting the principalities of Italy under one head. This vision of concord and imperial dominion is shown, in an engraving which depicts Henri II victorious at the centre of the planets, and is explained as:

> nouveau portrait ou globe de son ciel ainsi bien disposé par le divin vouloir à l'homme que Sa Maiesté nacquit pour rendre au monde sa pristine liberté, la paix, le salut et le repos. (*Interpretation*, p. 40)

> [a new image or globe of his planetary system, by divine will, well disposed towards man, showing that His Majesty was born to bring back to the world its original liberty, peace, salvation and repose.][35]

This language of imperial pretension gives a flavour of Symeoni's enthusiasms, and prepares for an analysis of the images he brought into France from Rome.

He had spent four years (1542–46) in Rome where he claimed to have 'étudié tous les marbres antiques de Rome' (studied all the ancient marble reliefs of Rome),[36] and he went there again in 1557 in the entourage of the duc de Guise. Symeoni drew from the earlier experience and from this later journey (when he spent only just over a week in Rome) to write *Les Illustres Observations antiques* (Lyon, 1558). In this work, dedicated to Charles de Lorraine, he described precise examples of classical works: the *Feste des Cybelles* whose image sculpted in marble could be seen in Cesi's palace courtyard (p. 18); the *Baccanale* preserved in the same cardinal's house (pp. 42–3); or the contents of the palace of the Della Valle (pp. 43 ff.). The Italian version (which is more complete and written after the French text) emphasized the evidence that could be gleaned from epitaphs and medals, as the title makes clear: *Illustratione de gli epitaffi e medaglie antiche* (Lyon, 1558). Although the pieces themselves were often worn and disfigured by time, Symeoni underlined their value as records of the true visage of Rome and its customs: such were the medals of Nero and Augustus showing the imperial chariot seen full face at the entrance of the Golden House.[37] Symeoni owned a large collection of medals and his affection for them was so great that he carried 500 around with him wherever he went. As he declared dramatically: 'si j'allais sans icelles, il me sembleroit estre sans mains' (if I went without these, it would seem as if I had no hands).[38]

Where Symeoni writes of medals or inscriptions on marble, these objects are presented as if they had been personally observed and the images recorded on the spot. Perhaps they had. But he also relied on his profound knowledge of guidebooks on Rome. When describing Nero's palace, for example, he uses exactly the same terms and evokes the same details as Andrea Fulvius had done, using words also repeated by Lucio Mauro in his *Delle antichità*.[39] Similarly, when Symeoni discusses the form of ancient circuses (*Illustratione*, pp. 145, 148), he relies heavily on the research of Onufrius Panvinius.[40] It is not unsurprising that Symeoni omits to cite his sources, since acknowledgement of ownership or of debt was not a necessary condition of being an author in the sixteenth century. Furthermore Symeoni was fully aware of the advantages of presenting material as if freshly seen by his own eyes. The impact of authenticity and of an eyewitness account was then, as now, considerable.

Whatever their origin, Symeoni's images of Roman antiquities were greatly appreciated by his French contemporaries. When he settled in Lyon in 1554, after so many extensive and weary wanderings, he seems to have found his spiritual home. Lyon was a place where his enthusiasm for Rome would be given a warm reception. He was immediately welcomed into the intellectual circles established by Claude Bellièvre who, on his return from Italy in the late 1520s, had turned his garden into a vast museum of antiquities. He joined the group of antiquaries represented by Jean Grolier and Guillaume du Choul, and entered into contact with printers and booksellers like Guillaume Roville and Jean de Tournes. Symeoni paid tribute to their friendliness and erudition, recorded memories of fruitful daily intercourse when medals were given and exchanged, and retold conversations in which questions of attribution and the authenticity of medals and their interpretation were discussed. Symeoni praised Grolier for his encouragement and commended his deep knowledge of medals[41] and singled out Jean de Tournes for his diligence and publicly thanked him for having given him medals found in his garden.[42] Above all, Du Choul is extolled – evoked on numerous occasions as a friend whose qualities of mind, knowledge and resource were infinite.[43] For Symeoni, Du Choul was 'un grandissime amateur et restaurateur des antiquités romaines' (a great connoisseur and restorer of Roman antiquities).[44]

Symeoni had a particular obligation to Du Choul since the latter's collections of medals, antiquities and books provided him with a generous and readily accessible resource; and he was proud to translate into Italian two of Du Choul's works – the *Discours de la religion des anciens romains* and the *Discours sur la castramentation* – thus passing images and scholarship back across the Alps. The second work, with its abundant engravings of the Roman military, captains and soldiers in their appropriate dress, carrying their badges and symbols, and accompanied by their musicians, gave one of the most detailed insights at this

IMAGINIFERI, PORTEN-
seignes de l'image du Prince.

36.   Guillaume du Choul:
Roman dress: *imaginiferi*

time into Roman customs and dress (Figure 36). Symeoni's translation of the
Discours de la religion is interesting for the modifications which he made to Du
Choul's original text. In order to concentrate in Rome all the examples of
beautiful monuments and significant ancient remains, he systematically added
'a Roma' to the text wherever he could, and eliminated all the comparative
examples which Du Choul had originally supplied.[45]

Rome, its greatness and its survival, are the main themes in Symeoni's mul-
tifarious works, almost to the point of obsession. The admiration is unalloyed,
as can be seen in his letters where Rome is depicted as a magnet drawing all
nations to her and encouraging them to work for her glory. Writing to Messire
Dominique Guidi in 1549, he stressed 'combien que vous ayez à Rome un
grand avantage' (what a great advantage you have, being in Rome); and in the
final phrase to a psalm which he had composed in 1553 for *Monsieur Carnavalet, premier écuyer du Roi*, he underlined the inspirational quality of Rome:

Cependant que Romme entretint tous les hommes de bon esprit, non
obstant qu'ilz fussent estrangiers, elle augmenta tousiours son empire.

103

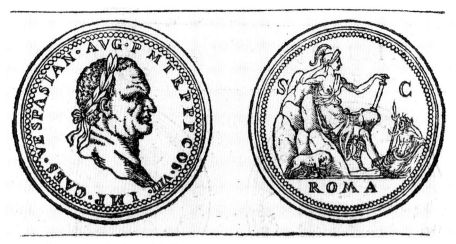

37.   Guillaume du Choul: medal of *Roma*

[while Rome maintained all men of good mind, even if they were foreigners, and continued to increase her empire.][46]

The same inflated tones occur in his *César renouvellé* (1558) which provides a veritable panegyric on Rome: on the vitality, discipline and virtues of its citizens; and on Caesar whose faults are quickly excused or justified.[47]

In the context of his praise of Rome, Symeoni gave Pope Paul III a special accolade in the *Dialogo pio et speculativo*[48] – published in the *Sententiose imprese* (1560) – since the pope had prevented Rome from being completely denuded of her ancient treasures by the activities of agents, many of whom were working for French patrons. According to Symeoni, thanks to papal energy Rome had kept her monuments: 'ses vieux ornements qui sont demeurés témoins de sa grandeur' (her old ornaments which stand witness to her greatness). The city itself, symbolized on medals and coins (Figure 37), was lovingly described by Symeoni who analysed these representations in bronze, silver and gold and, on occasion, had them engraved for his books. There is, for example, the silver medal given to him by his cousin François Massey on which Rome is shown helmeted like Minerva and seated, with the wolf and Romulus and Remus beside her. Symeoni compares the image to that on a similar medal owned by Du Choul which symbolized the origins of the city, and where the wolf and twins are represented, but this time with a shepherd and a tree.[49] Both versions were familiar and their ready availability ensured that the image of Rome as an armed goddess with the wolf and its twin charges was embedded in the mind.

Pictures of the buildings in Rome are also found depicted in his works and are mostly derived from coins and medals. Yet it is the abiding presence of Rome in Symeoni's work which constantly reminds the reader of the city's various forms and images. The city is the major (and often the only) point of reference. If Symeoni wished to praise Anet or Meudon, he did so by comparing them – to their advantage – to Nero's golden palace: after a visit to Meudon, he was so amazed at the construction of the Grotto and at the large number of statues which the cardinal de Lorraine had assembled there that he exclaimed 'Vive Roma resurgens' and, he added, 'que la maison dorée de Neron n'eust sçeu être ni plus riche ni plus belle' (Nero's Golden House couldn't have been richer or finer).[50] If Symeoni seeks to comment favourably upon the duc de Guise's military exploits, he remembers Metz and the rout of the Spaniards, and then immediately interjects the martial triumphs of the Romans, and dwells in particular on the successes of Caesar.[51] The best tribute Symeoni could pay the modern city to which he was most attached – Lyon – was to conceive of it as Rome. He saw the ancient riches found daily among the ruins on La Forvière as just like those which were unearthed every day in Rome. He remembered the contribution to Lyon of Emperor Caligula who had recognized the quality of its inhabitants, the beauty of its site and its Roman potential.[52] He responded to the scattered fragments on the deserted hills surrounding Lyon as if they were ancient relics of Rome itself:

> il n'est resté en ce lieu autres enseignes que certaines piecetes de tuiles consumez, de vases et statues brisees, de conches de terre cuite, de Porfires, serpentins, alabastre, marbre, mosaic, voutes par dessous terre, fondemens hauts et de merveilleuse grandeur, les reliques de ces pouvres miserables acqueducs, avec autres edifices. Comme le palais Senatorien, ou de Severe; les vestiges de l'Amphitheatre sur la coste Saint Sebastien . . .

> [in this place, there remains no other signs except some burnt fragments of tiles, broken statues and vases, shards of clay, porphyry, serpentine, alabaster, marble, mosaic, vaulting lying on the ground, foundations of wonderful size, remains of those poor, miserable aqueducts, with other buildings: like the palace of the Senators or of Severus, the relics of the Amphitheatre on S. Sebastian's hill.][53]

In the decades which followed, French writers would try to emulate the sense of loss and to capture that double spectacle of ruins and the shades of the buildings which they recalled.

It is possible to measure the extent of Symeoni's obsession with Rome by studying the first half of his *Description de la Limague d'Auvergne en forme de dialogue* (1561). From its title,[54] the work would seem to be about the Auvergne, and the dialogue is intended to take place in or near the château de Beauregard owned by Symeoni's patron, Bishop Guillaume du Prat. However, the opening shifts quickly from the quiet solitude in which all such dialogues conventionally took place to an evocation of Lyon, its site, its walls, its hills and valleys and its magnificent rivers. As we have seen, the picture of Lyon is soon overlaid by and fused with that of Rome. The same theme occupies Symeoni again as, for nearly a hundred pages, he explains Rome's images on medals, recalls the piety of the Romans, and their respect for the gods. Momentarily he remembers Auvergne and the château de Beauregard, but only briefly before being sucked again into evoking those monuments built by the Romans to extend 'la brieveté de nos noms' (the short-lived nature of our names). Instantly, he is launched on the Appian Way, obliged to contemplate the classical beauty of the Pantheon, and to gaze on the Colosseum which is depicted intact and entire from a medal of Vespasian illustrating the different orders circling around each level. On the opposite page is shown the restored forum of Trajan, also reconstituted from a medal (p. 83).

Although Symeoni may not have been fully aware of the extent to which the city of Rome and its monuments dominated his writing, he was clear as to his overall purpose. Beyond the permanent practical concern to please someone who could give him a job, Symeoni had higher intentions, which he set out in his opening remarks to *Les Illustres Observations* (1558):

> j'espère que ces autres miennes antiques donneront courage, ouvriront l'esprit et monstreront le chemin à maints autres sçavans antiquaires. (sig. A3)

> [I trust that these, my antiquities, will give hope, open the mind, and show the way to many other antiquaries.]

The sentiments are similar to those expressed a decade or so earlier by Du Choul in his address to François I.

The last known contribution which Symeoni made to French knowledge of Roman antiquities was the repair of Antoine du Prat's small country house at Vanves and the installation there of a 'salle d'études' (a study) and a 'cour ornée d'antiques' (a courtyard decorated with antiquities). The idea was to create a retreat where the owner could study in surroundings that recalled the villas built by Romans in classical times.[55] Within this courtyard Symeoni had niches constructed in which to place the statues:

> una testa di bronso di Petrarcho . . . un Laocoonte . . . un Apollo bronzato, simile à quella di Belvedere di Roma . . . un Daphne . . . una testa di Cesare era quella d'Augusto . . . due Termini rustici.

> [a bronze head of Petrarch . . . a Laocoön . . . a bronze Apollo similar to the one in the Belvedere gardens in Rome . . . a Daphne . . . heads of Caesar and Augustus . . . two rustic statues.][56]

The text makes clear that the intention has been to reproduce at Vanves an effect such as that seen in the Belvedere courtyard, and even to duplicate some of the statues. Despite the significant parallel, it appears that Du Prat did not appreciate Symeoni's work in the way the scholar had anticipated. Certainly, Symeoni did not receive adequate financial reward, nor did he secure a position in the Du Prat household.[57] Disappointed, he withdrew to Lyon where he composed at the end of the *Dialogue* an extraordinary piece of self-assessment and self-justification. Beneath his engraved portrait, he wrote out in full his life's prediction and his own epitaph, setting out the range of his activities; and the great peroration ended with claims which were never much evident in his writing. If no others were prepared to praise him and to recognize his worth, Symeoni was constrained to supply what was missing: he was sharp in his judgement and counsel, possessing rare acumen, and endowed with the gift of verbal sobriety: 'in consilio perspicax, in iudicio acer, inventionis acumine clarus, risus et sermonis parcus . . .' (perspicacious in counsel, acute in judgement, [with] clear-sighted acumen in ideas, homely and sober in speech).[58]

BLAISE DE VIGENÈRE (1523–96)

Blaise de Vigenère, who spent his life in the employ of the Nevers family,[59] was a faithful secretary and an industrious scholar whose knowledge of Rome and its remains was that of an enthusiast and an expert. His busy life can largely be reconstructed from the series of erudite tomes which he wrote from 1570 after he had given up travelling and had settled down in Paris. In particular, his *Traicté des chiffres ou secretes manières d'escrire*[60] tells us that he first visited Rome in 1549 and stayed there three or four years (f. 36); he returned again to Italy for three more years in 1566 when, as *secrétaire du roi*, he accompanied Juste de Tournon, the king's ambassador. In the first of these sojourns, he inspected closely all the ancient buildings in the city and, as he wrote, did all he possibly could to deepen his knowledge of antiquity:

> par six ou sept ans que j'ay demeuré à Rome, j'ay faict autrefois tout ce qui m'a esté possible, et par la communication des gens doctes les plus versés en l'antiquité Romaine, et en revisitant tous les marbres, bronzes, medalles, et camaieux antiques, dont l'on en peult tirer quelque cognoissance et instruction, mais j'en ay peu rien redresser.

> [during the five or six years I lived in Rome, I did all that was possible – talking to learned men versed in Roman antiquity, visiting and revisiting the marble reliefs, bronzes, medals and ancient cameos from which one might draw knowledge and instruction – but I couldn't restore anything.][61]

Although direct experience was to be the most powerful influence on his response to Rome, he also delved into printed books. These he read carefully and critically, citing Vitruvius whom he used to identify columns belonging to the temple of Jupiter[62] and Flavio Biondo whose opinions he challenged: 'car ce n'est pas un autheur bien certain' (because he is not a reliable author). He quoted from Du Choul and freely acknowledged his borrowings from Tomasso Porcacchi, and from Lilio Gregorio Giraldi.[63] The 131 illustrations which formed such an important part of the argument in his lengthy annotations to the first ten books of Livy's *History* are not original, owing much to the work of Gamucci and to the engravings of the workshop of Lafréry which Vigenère does not acknowledge.

He made scholarly friends in Rome, and sought them out for their counsel, argued with them about attributions and shared their enthusiasm for the regeneration of ancient Rome. The most pervasive in his influence was Pirro Ligorio, whom Vigenère described as 'peintre et antiquaire tres excellent, avec lequel nous avons eu très-familière conversation et accointance à Rome' (painter and excellent antiquary with whom I was on familiar terms in Rome) (L. 589). Elsewhere he praised Ligorio's diligence, dexterity and an ability to recognize details and decipher inscriptions such as no one before had achieved (L. 1145–6).[64] Although the illustrations in his annotations on Livy also borrowed from Ligorio's reconstructions – Augustus' mausoleum, for example, which he depicted partly from his own observations of what was left and partly 'de la coniecture de Pyrrho Ligorio sur ce qui s'en peult veoir dans les autheurs' (from the drawing by Pirro Ligorio of what can be seen in other authors) (L. 877–8)[65] – he did not always agree with the latter's opinions. In trying to determine where three columns which had survived intact should be placed, he rejected Ligorio's view that they belonged to the temple of Jupiter and placed them instead on the portico of the temple of Augustus (L. 715).

His experience of ancient Rome was enhanced by his visits to the *cabinet* of Cardinal Farnese whose palace housed the most recent finds from excavations as well as numerous objects which were given to him or which he bought for the collection. Vigenère listed some of the contents, referring to a heap of gods and goddesses fashioned in semiprecious stones which he saw in 1566 and which had been unearthed the previous year (L. 868).[66]

When, therefore, Vigenère retired to write in 1570 he was undoubtedly well equipped to inform his contemporaries about Rome. His works tended to be large, erudite and unusual in the topics he chose to tackle. Some were celebration pieces like his account of the entry of Henri III into Mantua (1576) and others were translations of Greek or Latin texts supplemented by long and learned commentaries: the *Histoire de la décadence de l'empire Grec* of Chalcondylas (1577); the commentaries of Caesar (1576), the histories of Livy (1583) and the works of Philostratus (1578), or Onosander (1605).

In all this writing, Vigenère sought to explore areas which were difficult of access, either because the information was recorded in languages understood by few (such as Greek), or because the terrain was shrouded in uncertainty. He was ever conscious that perceptions of Roman antiquity would be blurred. In his mind, 'ceste trouble antiquité' (this obscure antiquity), as he called it in his annotations on Livy, was:

> plongée et ensevelie dans de si profondes ruines de tant de revolutions de siècles, d'une si longue suitte de temps; parmy l'incertaine varieté d'un ouy

dire, d'une traditive inconstante de main en main, tout en l'air sans aucun fondement asseuré . . . (L. 464)

[plunged and buried in such a depth of ruins for so many centuries and for such a long time; at the mercy of the ever-changing nature of hearsay, of wayward transmission from hand to hand, all in the air without any sure footing . . .]

Within this frame of obscurity and haphazardness his task of demonstration and explanation was formidable, yet he determined to elucidate the past for his 'concitoyens' (fellow-men) (L. 503) as well as satisfying his learned peers.[67] To fulfil this aim, he tried to ensure that the context of what was being recounted was thoroughly understood, and, in his comments on the texts he was translating, to relate them to contemporary experience.

He recognized that, if he were to achieve his ambitions, he would have to attend to making images of the past clear and visible. This led him to think deeply about writing and about the necessity of giving a living presence to what he was attempting to evoke. He regarded writing as very important and, having rehearsed Socrates' arguments for not committing thoughts to paper, he discoursed eloquently on the virtues of writing facts and ideas down to preserve them for posterity:

Ils diront tout ce qu'ils voudront, mais de moy ie tiens l'escriture pour la plus singuliere, excellente et necessaire invention qui tomba oncques en l'esprit de l'homme, et le vray et seul remede de perpetuer la memoire des choses, et les garentir du gouphre de l'oubliance, voire digne d'être preferer [*sic*] à la parole qui ne peut servir que de presence à presence, au seul instant, et au lieu ou l'on la profere et desploye; là où l'escriture peut parcourir d'un bout du monde jusqu'à l'autre, et se maintenir en une éternité des siècles.

[they can say what they like, but I hold that writing is the finest, the most unique and necessary invention that has come from man's mind, and the only true way of keeping the memory of things and saving them from the abyss of ignorance; indeed it is to be preferred to speech which can only serve those present at a single moment in time and in the place where it is offered and deployed; whereas writing can go from one end of the world to the other, and last for an eternity of time.][68]

Vigenère was sensitive to nuance in the use of language, and could discover differences in style in both Latin and French.[69] He justified the use of the latter in his works because he aimed to interest those who knew no other language (L. 768), and recommended that best practice could be obtained by frequenting 'la cour des Princes'. But his was not a succinct or pared-down style. On the contrary, he advocated verbal exuberance in order to awaken the interest and choice of young readers:

Cette longue queue et trainasserie de mots enfilez inutilement, a esté mise de moy tout exprès; à ce que parmy une telle copie, la jeunesse puisse choisir et tirer ce qui luy viendra le plus à propos. (*Les Images*, 1578, f. 16)

[This long string and trail of words, put uselessly together, has been done on purpose by me so that, from such a text, the young can choose and take out what seems most appropriate.]

Although the tone is deliberately self-critical, it is obvious from the later development of his argument that in exuberance he saw the opportunity to reach 'une heureuse perfection d'un riche, orné, propre et élaboré langage' (a happy perfection of language, rich, ornate, suitable and elaborated) (ff. 158–158v). Du Verdier was later to argue that the style of Vigenère 'est plus profitable à un français qui veut orner son langage' (was more useful to a Frenchman who wanted to embellish his language).[70] Certainly Vigenère never gives the impression that he is holding anything back in his honest appraisal of the facts, although he may not always have interpreted them correctly.[71]

As far as Latin was concerned, he admired the simplicity of the language used by Caesar and tried to imitate it in his own rendering of the text in French.[72] He was a severe critic of the ambiguity that coloured Livy's use of terms, describing him as 'un tres grand affectateur de mots equivoques, ambigus et doubteux' (a great coiner of ambiguous, doubtful and equivocal words) (L. 1648). In interpreting and transmitting the meaning of this master of equivocation, Vigenère used clearcut images which stay in the mind. He seems to have had a natural gift for descriptions that move: on the arch of Septimus Severus at the north end of the Forum, for instance, he paints the captured kings:

le bonnet ou chapeau Royal en la teste, et les mains liees derriere le dos, en captifs qui montrent assez à leur triste chere, l'angoisse de leur desconvenue et misère; comme si le marbre en avoit quelque doleance et ressentiment. (L. 527)

[the royal hat on their head, hands tied behind their back, as captives who, from their sad mien, show their grief at their miserable plight; as if the marble itself felt some sorrow and distress.][73]

The transfer of feeling to the stone is, of course, a conventional rhetorical device, yet it does convey the vividness and immediacy of Vigenère's own response to the lively depiction of fallen princes.[74] The response also shows how keen were Vigenère's powers of observation. He had an eye for the telling detail whether he was differentiating the crude from the refined on the arch of Constantine (Figure 38) which he deemed 'd'ouvrage grossier, et sentant desja bien son rabaissement des arts et des sciences, hormis en quelques endroits où il y a des pieces excellemment taillees' (to be of crude workmanship, signifying a decline in the arts and sciences, except for a few places where the

38. Attributed to Etienne du Pérac: arch of Constantine

stone is excellently cut) (L. 647); or establishing that the columns said to belong
to the temple of Concord (in truth, the temple of Saturn) could not be of the
same period because they had dissimilarities; or again, explaining why the figure
of Roma on medals was always covered with a helmet (L. 1160). Such acute-
ness suggests that Vigenère was extremely well acquainted with architectural
sources and vocabulary and also had developed close contact with the
practitioners.[75]

   Beneath this succession of images runs a current of unmistakable moral

111

intent. In the domain of art, he was eager to leave clear messages which could impact on the progress of French art already infected by images of ancient Rome and by fables from Philostratus. In a wider sphere, he regarded images themselves as mirrors of human activity. Reflecting on the collapse and semi-destruction of Rome, and pondering how successive generations 'n'ont cessé de la despouiller à leur tour' (have not ceased to despoil it, in their turn), Vigenère concluded that there was no distinction to be made between that city and its empire and the lifespan of a human being: 'Car cette presente cité et l'Empire qui en dépendait, ont eu presqu'un même cours que la vie d'un homme' (because this city and its empire have almost the same course as a human life) (L. 824).[76] For both, man and the city, there was an inevitability in decline and loss from which there were lessons to be learned.

Our discussion of Vigenère's contribution to the French view of Rome in the late Renaissance will concentrate upon his annotations to Livy, as they provide abundant evidence of ruin and reconstruction and are characteristic of his approach. In focusing on Livy, Vigenère's stock of images was in no way exhausted, for in other works too he created memorable representations of Roman figures. A typical sample would show the Nile, drawn with careful precision in *Les Images* from medals and from the statue in the Belvedere gardens; the figure of Venus depicted from Vigenère's scrutiny of the statue owned by the pope and the copy made for François I at Fontainebleau; or the conjuring up of Hercules – as seen in the Farnese palace where the god is shown leaning on his club, with his:

> despouille de Lyon, à demy mangée des vers; la main droicte reiettée en arrière dessus ses reins, tient trois pommes de coing dedans, dont il semble se iouer tout ainsi que s'il avoit vie;

> [lion skin half eaten by worms; the right hand thrown back above his thigh holding] three quinces which he is playing with as if he were alive;][77]

or on display in the Conservatori palace, a younger version of Hercules 'tenant en la main droicte sa massue, et qu'il semble remuer des doigts' (holding his club in his right hand, and seeming to move his fingers) (L. 726). The texture of the marble seems to vibrate with life through Vigenère's words which evoke the physical eating up by Time and the urge of the limbs to break out of the stone.

Vigenère dedicated *Les Décades de Tite Live* to Henri III in 1578, announcing in the preface that, because of the difficulties presented by the author whose terms were often obscure and who had held 'en suspens ce qu'il veult dire' (in suspense, what he wanted to say), he had appended to his translation of volume I a series of annotations and illustrations 'pour l'intelligence de l'antiquité Romaine' (for the understanding of Roman antiquity).[78] Vigenère was familiar with earlier French versions of Livy's work and he was determined to avoid the Frenchified Rome which could be found there – in the edition of Philippe le Noir in 1514, for example, the woodcuts show figures in medieval armour and these are distributed indiscriminately through the text and often repeated regardless of the context to which they purport to refer.[79] The most recent translation by Amelin (1557) was principally concerned with Livy's *harangues* and the fact that his books were filled with good sayings (*sentences*).[80] In Vigenère's version, the vast network of commentary is systematically organized. The structure was a conscious one, designed to contrast with those works made up of bits and pieces filched from ancient texts and fitted together anyhow. Vigenère had vehement views on such unprincipled compilers, which he expressed in his *Trois dialogues sur l'amitié* (1579) and which are relevant to the rather rigid shape he imposed on his Livy. He fulminated against:

> Ceux qui tout ainsi que du Colisée, ou des thermes Antonianes et autres exquis bastiments antiques de Rome, ausquels l'on a barbaresquement advance [*sic*] leurs jours pour en faire je ne say quels petits Figurions, appendiz et meschantes cabanes; affin de bien tost depescher un livre, prennent, empruntent et desrobent à toutes mains ça et là dans les vieils autheurs.

> [those who, in order to make up a book quickly, snatch, borrow and steal wholesale and haphazardly from ancient authors, just as in the exploitation of the Colosseum, the Antonine baths and of other exquisite buildings in Rome others have barbarously hastened their decline by making out of them small figures, wretched huts and other appendages.][81]

In contrast, he had engaged in original research, explaining 'j'ai pu sans y épargner mon huile et ma peine, de faire ça et là une quête, et y contribuer encore du mien' (I've managed, without stinting on candle and labour, to do some research and to contribute what is mine) (L. 503). He traced, emperor by emperor, the buildings erected by each in turn, discussing their original construction and providing illustrations of their state in ancient times and then as he had seen them. To take one example: after a detailed analysis of the history and making of the Colosseum, the building itself appears in his text complete and perfect, copied from one of Titus' medals, immediately followed by a figure which 'monstre l'estat en quoy il est reduict à ceste heure' (which shows the sorry state it had been reduced to at this time) (L. 509–12).

As for the city of Rome itself, he adopted a structure well known from guidebooks, presenting first its site, growth and hills, then its gates, bridges, aqueducts, baths and fora, before moving to the detail of each of the fourteen regions established by Augustus. There follows a sequence of sections on sepulchres, customs (civic and religious), festivals, triumphs, and on the organization of empire. Throughout his presentation, although the pattern is now very familiar and in that sense adds little to our knowledge, concern with authenticity is paramount. Vigenère will not accept unsupported evidence and he carefully matches data found on medals and inscriptions with the records found in histories.

He recognized, however, that many areas of the past remained obscure and that the surest ground on which to proceed was, therefore, the resurrecting of physical objects which could be evoked, sited, observed, measured and rebuilt. The decision to illustrate his text was, as Vigenère argued, itself a discipline. Portraits had to be drawn from life (even if that life was only recorded on a medal) and not left to the painter's whim such as those 'pourtraictes fortuittement et à la volée, selon qu'il a pleu à la fantaisie du peintre' (painted anyhow and in haste according to the whim of the painter). And if the result seems rough or unconvincing, this must be attributed to the limitations of the woodcut, whose effect was never as satisfactory as images engraved in metal.[82]

The process of resuscitation, Vigenère knew, was fraught with problems: lack of evidence, disagreement among the sources, accident of survival, changes through time, and so on. To overcome these, he had recourse to the method based on conjecture advocated by Ligorio and Palladio (among others).[83] Vigenère makes frequent reference to this approach about which he was, at times, quite categoric.[84] In the absence of written records (on parchment or on stone) 'nous ne pouvons avoir autre lumiere de toutes ces antiquités sinon par des coniectures' (we cannot throw any light on all these antiquities, except through conjecture) (L. 588). In such an uncertain field he proceeds with caution: 'és embrouillemens de ces antiquitez où l'on est contrainct d'aller à tastons' (with the muddle presented by these antiquities, one is obliged to go carefully) (L. 595). Nonetheless, he is fairly confident that by relying on medals which can be dated with reasonable accuracy, and on the findings of archaeologists like Ligorio who not only excavated the soil but also read widely in ancient sources, his representations would be faithful.

His respect for the accuracy of the evidence displayed on medals is considerable. Vigenère acknowledged his great obligation to the glimpses they gave into dark areas of Roman antiquity and the elucidation they offered on linguistic matters:

> Et certes nous leur sommes fort obligez, car sans cela nous demourerions en tenebres d'infinis choses de l'antiquité Romaine qui nous sont revelees par là, et lesquelles toutes les escriptures du monde ne nous scauroient si bien representer que font ces revers. (L. 1493)

> [Certainly, we must be grateful to them, for without them we would be in the dark on a large number of things from Roman antiquity which are revealed (through medals); all the writing in the world could not be plainer than what is found on their reverse.]

The tone is somewhat inflated; yet it is understandable for, without the revealing power of medals, Vigenère's attempts to reconstruct lost buildings or damaged texts would have been – in his view – of no avail.

Vigenère transferred the same methodology to problems of philology and to language. In the annotations to his translation of Caesar's *Commentaires* he is at a loss as to how he might reconstitute the language that was spoken in Gaul at the time of the Roman conquest; and he concludes: 'n'est possible d'en dire rien d'asseurance, n'y d'en parler autrement que par coniectures' (it is not possible to state anything with assurance, nor to speak other than through conjecture) since books, archives, records are all lost, and medals and inscriptions are also wanting (*Les Commentaires*, f. 99v).[85]

In this context, his references in the commentary on Livy to the reconstruction work of Scaliger on Festus' *De significatione* is of particular interest for they assumed a process of reasoning that is common to art and language, and illustrate how the philologist and art historian treated their defective material – whether texts or buildings – in similar ways. In recording facts about one of the tribes of ancient Gaul, Festus' text is corrupt and fragmented and it seemed that only a miracle could restore its completeness. Scaliger, through the exercise of conjecture, was that miracle:

> les fragmens de Festus au reste quant à ceste Tribu, avoyent besoin de quelque oracle pour les remettre en leur entier. Toutesfois le sieur de la Scala par coniecture l'a remply en la sorte. (L. 1405)

> [to be given their completed state, the fragments in Festus about this tribe needed some oracle. Scaliger – through conjecture – filled in the gaps required.]

He then cites the reconstituted text, achieved despite the fact that nothing was known about this particular tribe. Such success encouraged Vigenère to hazard his own conjectures.

His attitude to Rome is straightforward, and the opening of the preface sets the tone:

> Et de faict ceste brave et superbe cité, dame et maistresse de toutes les nations, ayant par de si longues revolutions de siecles maintenir une telle gloire d'Empire, et une si puissante dominion sur toutes les nations de la terre . . . (L. sig. ã v)

> [And indeed, this brave, proud city, queen and mistress of all nations, having maintained such a glorious Empire over so many centuries, and such powerful dominion over all the races of the world . . .]

The long, sustained phrase (of which only part is given here) states the bare facts of Rome's greatness in general terms, and in its direct and undisguised admiration, warns the reader of further praise to come. For, although Vigenère was critical of the quality and accuracy of some of the individual images he inherited, when it came to an overall view of the city his attitude is one of deep approbation, and words of esteem pour from his pen. Disputing Rome's splendour is a challenge which Vigenère easily turns aside: 'il ne faut pas s'esmerveiller si la plus belle, opulente et magnifique cité qui fut oncques, a esté Rome' (one should not be astonished if the finest, the most opulent and magnificent city that ever was, was Rome) (L. 466), he roundly asserts at the beginning of his annotations. He then exemplifies this conviction with ample proofs, reminding us that the few remains of Nero's palace testify to the exquisite quality of the workmanship (L. 514), or evoking the prodigious size, magnificent conception and brilliant style of Roman baths which are lasting memorials to the extraordinary grandeur of the ancient city. Vigenère's eloquence rarely reached such heights:

> Mais de ce peu qui reste de ceux-cy [the baths of Caracalla and Diocletian] nous pouvons comprendre à peu pres qu'elle [*sic*] devoit estre leur somptuosité et magnificence; presque incroyable, pour le nombre et desmesure grandeur des colonnes, la superbe hauteur des voultes; la longue estendue des Portiques et galleries . . . (L. 593–4)

> [But from the little that remains, we can more or less appreciate their former splendour and magnificence, almost unbelievable by reason of the number and extraordinary size of their columns, the superb height of the vaulting, and the extended stretches of porticos and galleries . . .]

Unbounded praise and wonderment there is in plenty, feelings tempered by a sensitivity and sympathy for the pathetic signs of what had been lost. The piteous lament on the ruins of Rome which Vigenère penned at the end of the *Traicté des chiffres* was cited at some length at the outset of this book. There are other passages, too, in the annotations on Livy which show the same intensity of feeling. For example, Vigenère was lost in amazement as he contemplated the work of Apollodorus on the gallery which once surrounded Trajan's column of which 'il s'en voit encore des pieces estranges' (one can still see some strange pieces). The pieces which astonished him roused his imagination so that he saw capitals, great bronze and gilded horses along the cornice, and intermingled trophies and spoils of war (L. 515).

Vision fed by artistic emotion did not always provoke such positive images. One day, on the Palatine, walking on ground which was once filled with princely palaces but was now an uninhabited place (Figure 39), Vigenère suddenly fused in his mind two images: the first, palatial splendour as sign of civic achievement; the second, empty, desert space, the home of sheep. In a vast historical sweep, he read into that fusion lessons of human incertitude:

> Le Mont Palatin: toutes les cours et demeures des Princes ont été appellées de là Pallais . . . En quoy fait bien à considérer l'inconstante variété des choses humaines: Car estant monté ce petit lieu là, qui ne sçauroit contenir plus de mille pas de circuit, d'un désert vague et inhabité, ou pour le mieux une simple retraitte de brebailles; à un si hault comble d'honneur par l'espace d'environ mille ans, il seroit retourné en ses derniers iours à son premier estre. (L. 768)

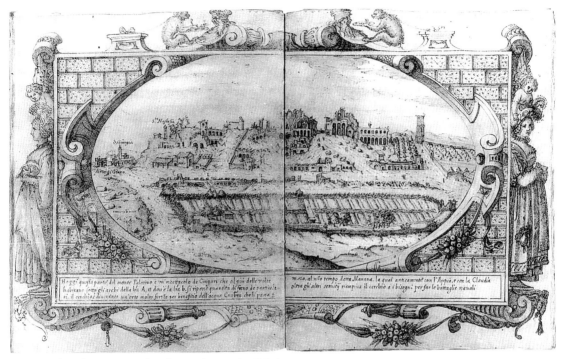

39.　Attributed to Etienne du Pérac: ruins on the Palatine

[The Palatine Hill: all the courts and dwellings of princes which have been named palaces were there . . . From which, it is good to consider the inconstant variety of human affairs; having climbed up to that place, no more than a thousand paces in circumference, one now finds an empty, uninhabited desert, or rather a simple refuge for sheep; thus, from the utmost height of honour for over a thousand years, it has returned in its last days to its first condition.]

The proud Palatine hill, returned to the shepherds who had first lived there, has been cut down to size.

The pristine state of monuments then and their present collapsed aspect is a constant theme in Vigenère's work, captured regularly by the illustrations which show both forms, and commented on by a turn of mind which moved naturally and persistently between the two. About the Septizonium for instance (Figure 40), Vigenère wrote: 'cette première figure monstre quel il devoit estre à peu près' (the first image shows, more or less, how it should look). Such remarks occur almost on every page and, as here, they are cautiously phrased.

It was a small step from emphasis on the 'then and now', to modern emulations of ancient works, and to judgements which tried to evaluate the respective quality of each. Nero might spend a million gold pieces on wall decorations for one chamber but these could not match in quality and value the Scipio tapestries which belonged to the French crown (L. 494). Hadrian's villa at Tivoli

40.   Attributed to Etienne du Pérac: Septizonium – reconstructed and ruined

LE RVINE DEL SETTIZONIO DI SEVERO.

hoggi è rimato la meta, e chiamasi la Scuola di Virgilio vedisi che è stato
occupato da particolari per altro tempo, i quali se ne son serviti, p habita
none serando i vani tra le colonne con muri

was unquestionably, Vigenère agreed, one of the most excellent *chefs d'oeuvre* of all Roman structures (L. 519); yet its strange and sumptuous ruins represented a challenge to Ippolito d'Este, cardinal of Ferrara who built his own palace at Tivoli, surmounting the emperor's achievements, and filled it with antiques of the rarest kind (L. 1781).

Readers of Vigenère's books acquired clear, trustworthy images of ancient Rome and, in addition, learned to know modern works inspired by the antique. In the *advertissement* to his translation of Philostratus, Vigenère stated unequivocally that the quality of modern works, in their conception and in their making, was equal to anything achieved by the ancients.[86] From other comments it is clear that he had in mind especially Michelangelo, who is cited several times,[87] but also Raphael for his *Banquet of the Gods* and Mantegna for the *Triumphs of Caesar*, both works referred to in a way that suggests they were well known and required no further description. Vigenère knew and admired the frescos of Giulio Romano, and described the paintings of Sebastiano del Piombo.[88] Nor were French artists forgotten. He praised Lescot, Du Cerceau, Pilon and Goujon,[89] and kept his warmest statements for a certain Jacques d'Angoulême who was working in Rome in the mid-century and whose statues (here Vigenère claimed to be repeating the judgement of Michelangelo himself) were equal in quality to those of the Italian master.[90] Moreover, Cardinal de Lorraine had acquired one of Jacques d'Angoulême's statues for his retreat at Meudon, a figuration in marble of Autumn 'en forme d'un beau jeune adolescent couronné de raisins et de pourpre, qu'il fit à Rome l'an 1550 extremement loué de tous, et presque à pair des antiques' (in the form of a handsome youth, crowned with grapes and purple, which he made in Rome about the year 1550 and which was much praised by everyone, and almost equal to the ancients) (L. 727). It is that same statue which Ronsard described in his *Chant pastoral à Monseigneur de Lorraine*:

> Et au petit Bacchus qui dans ses doigts marbrins
> Presse un rameau chargé de grappes de raisins.

[And that tiny Bacchus who in his marble fingers squeezes a vine laden with bunches of grapes.]

Few contemporary writers refer directly to Vigenère's achievements, although André Thevet recognized that – with Antoine de la Faye who translated the remaining books of Livy – he had brought ancient Rome to life again.[91] His deeply researched commentaries on Livy, on Caesar and on Philostratus created reliable images of Rome, both old and new; but his own assessments of his contribution were modest and measured, so aware was he of the uncertainties surrounding information that survived and of the frailty of human transmission.[92] In contrast to many of his fellow travellers to Rome he really saw what was there and recorded it as faithfully as he could. He had digested what he had read and considered the views of other authors with healthy scepticism.

And he was not diverted by the new vocabulary which attached to art and architecture. On the contrary, he thoroughly understood the technical foundations of both arts in their theory and practice, as is evident from the technical discussions which often invaded his discourse in *Les Images*. His gaze did not inhibit his mind or feed his imagination with many fantasies. In all these ways he was very different from the fourth transporter of images of Rome into France – Justus Lipsius.

JUSTUS LIPSIUS (1547–1606)

It is appropriate to consider Justus Lipsius in this context; although not a French writer, his works were extraordinarily popular in France where they quickly became standard texts and were much cited, discussed and pillaged. Professor Momigliano's observation, that although it is still a matter of dispute whether Lipsius significantly added to our knowledge of Tacitus, he certainly made the Latin author famous, is still highly pertinent.[93] The same could be said of Rome. That this erudite scholar believed profoundly in the greatness of Rome and its empire, and that he sought to bring to life the forms and the virtues which caused that greatness so that his contemporary world might profit from his resurrection, cannot be denied. Lipsius' vast work is marked with Rome in all its aspects: concerns about its politics, its morals, its heroes and its military strength ooze out from every sentence. And yet, paradoxically, the visualizing of the city and its grandeur are not placed centre stage. They are relegated to a backdrop despite the engravings of the Colosseum and other amphitheatres which adorned the *De amphitheatro* (1584).

Lipsius' attitude to Rome and antiquity was complex. His knowledge of writings on Rome and the empire was phenomenal; his reading of early and modern texts was critical; his remarks were judiciously articulated and based on well-founded data; and he tells his reader straight what his judgements are and why. Two writers stand out in his admiration and for the time he lavished on them – Tacitus and Seneca. He responded with vigour to the political manoeuvrings exposed by Tacitus and to the acuity of his observations; and he read with evident pleasure the works of Seneca and was deeply moved and excited by the tenor and style of the *Letters*.

His enthusiasm was contagious, and was all the more effective in being based on enormous erudition. No one can read the work of Lipsius without being persuaded that ancient Rome was central to his thinking. Propaganda for Rome and its greatness is there in abundance and every sixteenth-century reader would have recognized its presence and its importance. And yet, where is the city itself in Lipsius' extensive writings?

Lipsius made his only visit to Rome when he was just over thirty, and he stayed there for some eighteen months.[94] He had gone as secretary to Cardinal Granvelle to whom he had dedicated his first work, the *Variorum lectiones* in 1566. Our information about his sojourn in the city comes largely from Lipsius himself, from the *Antiquae lectiones* (published in 1575), and from his first biographer Ambertus Miraeus. From these two sources we learn that he knew and conversed with leading scholars such as Muret, Paulo Manutio, Fulvio Orsini, Benci, Mercurialis, Sigonio and Pietro Victori,[95] and that he spent much time among the manuscripts and books in the Vatican Library.[96] In his spare time he inspected stones and monuments and visited the remains of the ancient city and those in the country surrounding Rome,[97] and the extent to which he internalized the experience of these walks can be suggested by what Lipsius has to say about travel.

In the dedication to Ortellius of that part of the *De amphitheatro* (1584) concerned with the arenas outside Rome, while conscious of the many tribulations which regularly beset the traveller in the Renaissance, he praised travel as a means of broadening and maturing the mind.[98] In the letter he had written four years earlier to Philippe de Launoy (who was himself embarking on a journey to Rome) he had developed his views more fully.[99] Lipsius seems to be writing from his own experience when he assures De Launoy that, in Rome, the shades of great writers (Pliny, Virgil and Propertius), the places where they lived, and the stones that survive to tell of the magnificence that surrounded them (temples, theatres, triumphal arches and sepulchres) have acquired a presence that is real and compelling. Not only do they rouse the spirit but the mind expands with their encounter. The chief stimulus is to have been so close to them and to their experience, in Lipsius' words 'to touch those places which they themselves have touched', that their writing, their ideas and their customs are embedded in our own. Once absorbed and retained, they become an active and integrated part of that which guides judgement and feeds the creative process.[100] From this letter it is clear that Lipsius saw a close relationship between the lived experience *en voyage* and the future writings which he will undertake. A continuum of conversations, of sights observed, of people(s) assessed and of customs examined, nourished both his approach to establishing authentic texts and his communication with scholars of repute across Europe.

Implicit in his advice to De Launoy was a deeply felt conviction of Rome's importance. In the *Inscriptions antiques* (1588), he wrote of the flourishing empire whose greatness has never been nor will ever be equalled.[101] In *De admiranda, sive de magnitudo romana* (1598), the title eloquently states his intention of setting out the richness and variety of Rome's grandeur. It is interesting that his personal contribution to that picture related essentially to the collecting of quantifiable data which established the size of the city, the extent of its empire and its organization, the number of citizens, and the stupendous gifts of the Caesars (*effusa* and *stupenda* are the words he uses). His conviction of greatness found support in the many records of praise of the city of ancient authors. These he cites at length to bolster his argument: Martial, Frontinus and Claudian are quoted at the outset to fix ideas of greatness in readers' minds;[102]

and Ammianus Marcellinus is used on the imperial virtues of Rome (*De admiranda*, *Opera*, Book 3, p. 376). He remembers the Athenian (Polemon the Sophist) who made his name for having coined the phrase 'Rome is the epitome of the world',[103] and cites Cassiodorus who – having listed all the marvels of the world – came finally to his climax represented by Rome: 'Universa Roma dicatur esse miraculum' (the whole world pronounces Rome a miracle) (ibid., p. 428). Above all, Lipsius repeats the words of Aristides who, in the time of Hadrian, had penned a glowing account of the city. This panegyric had been frequently referred to over the centuries; and Lipsius used it as the conclusion to *De admiranda*.[104] The scholar in Lipsius took for granted such expressions of amazement, while recognizing the reverberative advantages of recalling well-known passages of praise; and it was his job to provide the detailed material which substantiated such views. The extent of Lipsius' use of other people's words is extraordinary; the work began by underlining God's benevolence towards the city, its predestined status and its continuing prestige and power. Rome, claimed Lipsius, in his 'Advice to the Reader', was first renowned for its might in conquest, then for the soundness of its laws; and, when the force of these diminished, the city became the centre of the major religious cult of the western world.[105]

Lipsius was not interested merely in recording greatness, he sought to understand it, and to criticize when this was appropriate, as when he challenged the style of those great writers Caesar and Livy – a fact which La Popelinière was to remember.[106] The wish to understand came not only from his scholarly instinct but also from his belief that Rome and the empire in the two hundred years which started with Augustus' reign represented the theatre of contemporary life. This expression he reiterated in his books, notably at the beginning of his edition of Tacitus' works where he announced that imperial Rome, as it were, was a simile of his own age (*quasi theatrum hodiernae vitae*);[107] and in the commentary to his third edition of the *Annals* and *Histories* (1585) where he spelt out their relevance.

> The History of Tacitus does not present the spectacle of wars and triumphs ... but you see there kings and monarchs, in brief the theatre of life today. I see a prince who sets his face against laws and customs, subjects lined up against their king; I discover the manoeuvres and machinations designed to oppress liberty and the pathetic struggles involved in trying to recover freedom; I read of the fall and ruin of tyrants, of the uncertainty of power when it has become excessive. I find the ills of freedom once recovered, the confusion, jealous emulation among equals, cupidity, theft, and public goods diverted from public benefit.[108]

The parallels with the wars in the Netherlands or with civil strife in France are obvious; and Lipsius sought to provide practical applications of what he uncovered from the past to lighten present distress.[109] Rome offered an arsenal of experiences which could be applied to contemporary Europe in decline.[110]

In his view, appreciation of the full eminence of Rome and an understanding of the nature of its decline and fall were essential first steps in a process of resurrecting authentically the monuments of the ancients (whether written or sculpted in marble), and of making that process available to his contemporaries. Understanding meant preparing for action in the modern world.[111] The prospect was attractive as he contemplated at the end of the *De admiranda* the unity of the known ancient world bound by language, culture, trade and law – that contemplation being imbued with a longing to import such commonality into his own times.

The nostalgia is all the more poignant when one remembers that the discourse on Rome's greatness began with an evocation of the frailty and brevity of human life and of all things built by man (p. 370). Rome's greatness too was fleeting; its collapse – visible in the ruins of the city – mirrored the disappearance of men, of those who had realized its splendid creations. As Lipsius and his companion contemplate the fragments that remain, he is aware that in a few months, years, days, they will be no more than 'poussière, ombre, rien' (dust, shadow, nothing).[112] Rome could, however, be caught, resuscitated and used.

How did Lipsius display Rome's greatness which he sought so fervently? What methods did he use beyond affirmation and quotation? It must be stressed that Lipsius did not wish to differentiate between fragments of old statues, coins or medals and fragments of old writing. The latter were, he argued, to be esteemed as much as the former (*Antiquae lectiones*, I, 15, writing on Plautus), and were to be revivified by similar careful shaping and placing in context. As far as his texts are concerned (Plautus, Propertius, Tacitus, Seneca), Lipsius used conjecture aided by his knowledge of the immediate context of composition, historical information, cross-fertilization from his immense knowledge of Latin literature (its vocabulary and style), and recent archaeological findings.[113] His method can be seen at work in his earliest publications – the *Variorum lectiones* of 1566 where many of his suggestions with respect to Propertius, for instance, have been retained by modern editors[114] – and it is strikingly apparent in his two masterpieces, the works of Tacitus and Seneca.

In all these works, he displayed the inner state of Rome, but of the city itself his evocations are less precise. Words somehow seemed powerless to convey ruins and his response to them.[115] At the beginning of the *De admiranda,* as he depicted himself walking among the ruins with Florentius, he noted the broken and scattered structures still breathing the spirit of ancient Rome and throwing forth – as it were – sparks of the city's former splendour ('Scilicet haec ipsa ruta et caesa spirant etiam Romam veterem, et velut scintillas emittunt priscis splendoris', p. 557). Here is an opening for him to respond to those sparks and fashion them into visions from the past. Yet the emotional tone temporarily drops and there follows instead a simple list of well-known monuments. Later, he returned to the ruins, looked at them with consternation, and saw there not the potential for creative resurrection, but the image of destruction and confusion (as had been recorded by Heemskerck). Confronted with this spectacle, Lipsius was at a loss and withdrew from further comment. Similar evasion occurs when, in the Colosseum, his companion Florentius has drawn attention to forms that are now without defined shape, to masses of stone broken and in pieces leaving only a shadow of the work, more like a corpse (*cadaver*), he ventures. Florentius laments that he cannot visualize the original forms and asks for Lipsius' aid. But the latter evades the issue and launches into a discourse on the different names given at diverse times to the buildings, indulging in long citations from Dio Cassius explaining the functions of amphitheatres.[116] In the *De admiranda* the same reluctance to dwell on aesthetic details occurs even when they have been promised; in Book 2, ch. 9, 'On statues' (p. 440), he announced that he would write not only about their number but also on their value and beauty. In fact, he does nothing of the sort. He gets side-tracked into thinking about the signs of destruction that surround him, and he reflects instead on their bleak moral implications.

There is thus more than a simple retreat from exposing aesthetic judgements in his own words. Lipsius was a scholar and not a creative artist. When it came to describing the Pantheon, he dutifully wrote of its artifice and symmetry, and about its singular order, and then he passed the pen to an expert: that is to Serlio 'vir peritissimus' (a most learned man) in whose writings all details measured and illustrated may be found. If Lipsius wanted an image of ancient baths, he referred his reader to Flavio Biondo and Sigonio; for aqueducts he counselled the use of Leandro Alberti; on roads, Onufrius Panvinius is the man to consult; on theatres, Vitruvius or Andreas Fulvius will provide all the expertise needed; while if the theatres are outside Rome, Sebastiano Serlio is the best source, 'eximio architecto' (the best of architects).[117] Although many of Lipsius' books on Rome are illustrated, the engravings too are borrowed, chiefly from Serlio and Mercurialis. Thus a composite picture of Rome emerges, with conventional images of ruined buildings denoting splendour underpinned with a sense of their significance for the late Renaissance; and that significance is enhanced by Lipsius' vast erudition and by the connections he drew with contemporary life.

Lipsius' impact was immediate. The wide network of scholarly contacts he had built up through his correspondence ensured speedy and progressive recognition of his work. Many of those contacts were leading French scholars and statesmen: Auguste and Jean-Jacques de Thou, Michel de l'Hospital, Frédéric Morel, Pierre Pithou, Florimond de Raemond, Turnèbe and Nicholas Bruslart. The most famous correspondent was Montaigne who used the *De amphitheatro* extensively in the *Essais*, marvelling at the technical detail which Lipsius had assembled on the machines invented by the Romans to change scenes with extraordinary speed and at the light, floating coverings designed to protect the audience from the weather.[118] Montaigne appreciated Lipsius' profound and secure knowledge, his ability to amass vast quantities of facts or measurements about Rome and the empire and to organize them in a coherent fashion.[119]

Abel l'Angelier, printer of the 1582 French translation of Tacitus' *Oeuvres* (by Estienne de la Planche), provides evidence of the speed of sale of the first printing. At the end of seven or eight months he was obliged to issue another set, proof as he put it 'comme la France estoit affamee de la lecture d'un tel historien' (that France was thirsty for the book of such a historian).[120] In the annotations which followed the translation, Lipsius is a constant point of reference. The author had accepted all his textual corrections, considering him the most informed and clear of all those who had ever touched 'nostre Tacite'.[121] When Paschalius had published his Latin observations on Tacitus in Paris the previous year, he had used Lipsius' original text of 1574.[122] Lipsius remained authoritative, finding a place in George Graevius' great thesaurus of Roman antiquity (issued between 1694 and 1698).

'Sous le signe de Rome' (under the sign of Rome) is how Jean Jehasse has described the pervasive influence of the city on Lipsius.[123] However, the most immediate and lively representation of Lipsius' work on Rome and antiquity (and the most fitting to end this chapter) came from his panegyrist who published *Justus Lipsii principatus litterarius a Gaugerio Rivio, I.C.* in 1607. There he evoked Lipsius in Rome groaning and lamenting before the disfigured ruins of the ancient city. He ran through the whole gamut of devastation – temples, statues, images of illustrious men, the Senate and so on. And then he remembered the names that had gone; literary monuments destroyed or mutilated – and the list from Cicero to Pliny, Seneca to Plautus seemed endless. At first, rooted to the spot, Lipsius merely suffers; then gradually visiting their piteous vestiges, depicted as belonging to souls in prison, he frees them from the chains, the dust and filth, marked by the iron 'à demi-rasés, à demi-morts' (half-demolished and half-dead). He restores them, and makes them visible and available.[124] This was his achievement.

PART II

Part-title illustration: Roma (see Figure 71)

CHAPTER 5

Visions Transported:
the Creative Power of Ruins

I FRENCH ARTISTS' RESPONSE

THE ENIGMATIC POWER OF RUINS

Ruins are tantalizing; they command attention, but in challenging the viewer to explain their fragmented form, they remain essentially ambiguous, resistant to such explanation, forever signs of larger and completer structures beyond themselves. The incomplete and open character of ruins invites participation from the observer who seeks to recognize, and perhaps define, the whole structures of which the ruins now represent only a part. These general considerations apply equally to the ruins of Rome which were not neutral entities, but relics possessing strong magnetic power. In the sixteenth century, individual ruined pieces or collections of fragments were seen not so much as valuable in themselves, but as evidence of something else: that is of larger forms waiting to be made anew. Ruins, in the Renaissance, set the imagination of poets and artists alight and, in Thomas Greene's words, 'they inspired a will to form'.[1]

The significance of the fragment or the ruin lay in its referential power. Although Renaissance artists and writers did not always articulate that sense, architects like Peruzzi working on important sites respected the style of the ancient structures and in building afresh seemed almost to be restoring them.[2] By the next century, ruins attracted less respect but more reverence, and antiquarians were supremely aware that the delight they derived from the contemplation of antique relics was linked to the opportunity to let the imagination run riot and to visualize scenes that were superior to the present. The process of imaginative recreation was well observed in 1790 by Archibald Alison, who tried to understand the role emotions played in the perception of beauty, and his remarks are so pertinent to our present enquiry that they are worth setting out in full.

In a passage on Rome which, in its analysis of unconscious remembrance and the associative play of the mind, anticipates more modern views on perception, he explored the seemingly elastic shape of things seen close at hand and from a historical distance.

> And what is it that constitutes that emotion of sublime delight which every man of common sensibility feels upon the first propect of ROME? It is not the scene of destruction which is before him. It is not the Tyber diminished in his imagination to a paltry stream flowing amid the ruins of that magnificence which it once adorned. It is not the triumph of superstition over the wreck of human greatness, and its monuments erected upon the very spot where the first honours of humanity have been gained. It is ancient Rome which fills his imagination. It is the country of Caesar and Cicero, and Virgil which is before him. It is the mistress of the world which he sees, and who seems to him to rise again from her tomb, to give laws to the universe. All that the labours of his youth, or the studies of his maturer age have acquired with regard to the history of this great people, open at once before his imagination, and present him with a field of high and solemn imagery which can never be exhausted. Take from him these associations, conceal from him that it is Rome that he sees, and how different would be his emotion.[3]

Alison here speaks not only for the man of science, the artist or the writer; he extends his comment to include 'every man of common sensibility'. Pronounce the name of Rome and the idealization is automatic. Detailed objects from the past seem nearer, offering untold sources of imagery on which memory and fancy together can work, and the emotional satisfaction attaching to this experience is unfathomably powerful.

The fascination exerted by apparently incomplete forms was not new.[4] At the end of the first century AD, Silius Italicus in his manuscript epic poem (found by Poggio Bracciolini in 1416–17)[5] evoked men who gazed on the ruins of the city at that time, but whose heads resounded with the claims for Rome's eternal dominion even though – in the continuing building process they were observing – signs of decay were everywhere apparent. The ruins of the city were in the Romans' minds as they moved around the streets which were still untouched by Hannibal's arms; for, after the battle of Cannae, rumour quickly found its way to Rome and the citizens, in their fear, thought they saw the houses burning and the temples pillaged. Conversely, for Hannibal's men, the destruction of Rome, the image of whose greatness stood before their eyes and whose name rang in their ears, signalled their victory over the whole world.[6]

The compelling effect of the relics' survival arrested the attention of even the most reluctant admirers of Rome. In the mid-seventeenth century, when over a hundred years of descriptions of the imperial city had been accumulated, Nicolas Bralion was still overwhelmed and emotionally disturbed by the sight of the ruins (Figure 41):

41. Marten van Heemskerck: view of ruined Roman landscape

C'est une chose estrange que toute ancienne et abbatuë qu'elle est, on ne peut la voir et considerer en cheminant, et s'arrestant entre ses ruines sans des sentimens d'admiration, de veneration et d'amour, et i'adiouste, sans être saisi et surpris tout ensemble de plaisir et de ioye.

[It's a stange thing that, however old and battered she is, as one rides around one cannot help looking, contemplating and stopping among the ruins filled with feelings of admiration, veneration and love; and, I may add, without being seized and completely overwhelmed with pleasure and joy.][7]

The sentiments are strongly felt (*admiration, veneration, amour*) and, as Bralion assesses them, he sees their contradictions: his curiosity is delightfully aroused, yet his mind is filled with melancholy as he senses the gap between what he sees and what he knows was once there before him. Similar tones of veneration – even of awe – had been used by Giorgio Vasari when he wrote of the relics of buildings which remained in Rome. He honoured them 'as something holy', worthy of all the labour involved in imitating them, for such work would produce structures that were 'really beautiful'.[8]

The same contradictory impulses are found in Marliani's *L'Antiquità di Roma*, where he testified to the wonder that was Rome while emphasizing that the sense of the marvellous came directly through 'le miraculose ruine' (miraculous ruins) which, shaped by the rigours of Time, aroused in the observer profound amazement (*estremo stupor*).[9] In a different spirit, Vigenère saw in the ruins pathetic signs of loss (*piteuses marques*), but they were also *chiffres* (signs) belonging to some secret language which the viewer had to decipher.[10] The drawings of Marten van Heemskerck had taken even further this idea of the difficult

131

42.   Marten van Heemskerck: ruins seen through the arch of Titus

recovery of meaning in the ruins. His depiction of the Roman Forum seen through the arch of Titus, for instance, resembles the scene of a lost city (Figure 42). Often he stretched a panoramic view across the canvas, amalgamating old and new, and setting them side by side with seeming indiscrimination. In this prospect, the ruins become like fossils of an extinct nation and civilization.[11] Ruins gave a palpable presence to the heritage of Rome, a presence whose meaning was not immediately graspable but which provided an evident continuity.

COLONNA'S ENTHUSIASM FOR RUINS

In some respects then, ruins were enigmas beckoning to the viewer to read, to decipher and – even – to reconstitute. There were writers, however, who revelled in the puzzling, incomplete and mysterious character of ruins. Such a one was Francesco Colonna whose famous book *Hypnerotomachia Poliphili* (*Discours de Songe de Poliphile*), with its novel woodcuts, exerted enormous influence on art in Italy and France for many decades after its publication in 1499.[12] As far as mystery is concerned, Colonna deepened that feeling by presenting Poliphile's journey as a dream, thus blurring the lines which separated reality from a fictional world where the dreamer believes his experiences to be real while the reader recognizes that, though real, they may be happening only in a made-up world. The mystery is further complicated by an issue concerning language. In his translation of Colonna's text in 1546 Jean Martin (as in other works) laments the paucity of the French language in matters of technical specification. The description of an arch, for example, is interrupted:

> ie ne sens point en moy tant de savoir que ie le puisse suffisamment descrire, considéré qu'en nostre temps les vocables vulgaires propres et communs à l'architecture, sont enseveliz et esteints avec les oeuvres.

> [I do not detect within myself sufficient knowledge to be able to describe it properly, since – in our time – terms in the vulgar language appropriate and common to architecture have been buried and made extinct along with the works of art.][13]

Such expressions of limitation occur frequently in Martin's translation and were a common feature in the work of sixteenth-century French artists who sought to enhance their scholarly reputation and distinctiveness by attributing to themselves alone the capacity to speak and write fully about difficult architectural matters. Aids to understanding were provided by the many woodcuts which adorned the book; Colonna evidently considered image and text to be mutually supportive; and words frequently refer to the form depicted which, in its turn, reflects the details developed in the prose.[14]

Colonna positively delighted in describing ruins; and in his enthusiasm he

43.   Colonna: ruins adjacent to a dark forest

explores all their forms, for ruins are the agents which entice Poliphile to explore; and they are everywhere, drawing him on by their unexplained presence. There are ruined temples and theatres, broken tombs and fractured funerary monuments; there are obelisks lying their full length and columns in pieces on the ground; cracked portals which are no longer able to bear the weight of the buildings they once gave access to; and inscriptions are disordered and incomplete. Notwithstanding their broken state, every detail is lovingly rendered. No aspect of the fallen object is omitted, whether it be the columns which Poliphile discovered as he found his way out of the dark forest at the beginning of his adventure (Figure 43), or the temple dedicated to Pluto and which was now in ruins (Figure 44).

At times, the narrator even apologizes that his story is delayed by the obsessive attention he has given to the ruins, yet the intense engagement he has with them seems ample justification: 'ie ne me povoye (par verité) saouler de veoir choses tant merveilleuses' (truly, I could not exhaust my desire to see such marvellous things) (f. 18v). Marvelling at the impact of these fragments upon him, right down to the dust they would become ('voire quasi la pouldre d'icelle'), he wonders what effect ancient buildings found intact might have.

When, in the *Discours de Songe de Poliphile*, structures are entire, they are uniformly magnificent. Some are imagined extravaganzas; others have been found by art historians to owe their form to designs imprinted on coins or to ele-

44. Colonna: ruined temple

ments of surviving monuments. Rome is the source of reference when Colonna seeks to stress the magnificence of a structure: the Pantheon (f. 15v) which secures the harmonious proportions of the gate Poliphile encounters at the start of his travels; the Colosseum which conveys the size and the splendour of the amphitheatre he explores at the end of the book (f. 124); the round temple inspired by Bramante's Tempietto (f. 72); and the obelisk in Rome (f. 86v) which serves as a measure for the one found behind the ruined temple. The pleasure of discovery and a keen aesthetic awareness are uppermost, and as he walks around the ruins sniffing out new signs and better designs, Poliphile turns into a veritable architect with his measuring-rod, verifying his judgements:

> Mon plaisir estoit merveilleux en regardant ces ruines tant glorieuses, et desiroie tousiours trouver quelque nouveauté: parquoy m'en alloie fouillant par ces monceaux de pierre, comme fait un Beuf qui en paissant chemine, cuydant trouver plus avant de meilleure pasture. Ainsi ie vey plusieurs grandes pièces de colonnes, et d'autres entieres: l'une desquelles ie mesuray. (f. 95)

> [My pleasure was enormous as I looked at these glorious ruins, and I searched always to find some new discovery, digging around among these piles of stones like a grazing bullock shifting forward in the hope of finding better pasture. So it was that I saw several large fragments of columns and some whole ones, one of which I measured.]

The ruins have become a school for the builder, and the eagerness and thoroughness with which Colonna sought out and examined these broken pieces is comparable to the behaviour of French artists who flocked to Rome in the first decades of the sixteenth century.

FRENCH ARTISTS IN ROME

Artists had some knowledge of what they might find not only from the guidebooks but also – and more accurately – from the moulds of the great statues in Rome which had been sent into France by order of François I. The moulds needed attention when they arrived at Fontainebleau, and Bontemps got to know them well as he repaired the damage done to them by their rough journey from Italy.[15] The bronze statues cast from these moulds were on public display, available to artists for study, and frequently described: in manuscripts dedicated to the king (Piero Pietrasanta, Du Choul),[16] or by visitors to the château (Symeoni, Van Buchel).[17]

Direct copies of statues, monuments and fragments observed were much more valuable to the artist than vague complaints about the inadequacy of the French language to define the characteristics of ancient building techniques or generalized claims of works being made *à l'antique* – an expression that probably did no more than signal a perception of difference.[18]

Most artists relied on their notebooks and on sketches recording their impressions, which they later exploited on their return to France in works executed for their patrons. Among the many sketchbooks compiled in the sixteenth century, some French examples survive. Those, for example, of Jacques Prévost, who studied the architectural details of Corinthian columns and capitals, provided measurements of them, and indicated their precise location.[19] There are also the sketches found in the album of Pierre Jacques (*c.* 1570) which recorded his visits to the great art collections in Rome: of Andrea della Valle, Cardinals Cesi and Carpi, the Farnese palace and the famous statues in the Campidoglio and the Belvedere courtyard.[20] In both these examples, the artists were concerned to learn about the lines and measurements and to study the movement of the forms; and their albums are, accordingly, filled with details and fragments of independent elements of ancient sculpture and architecture which caught their eye.

As far as we know, Prévost's knowledge, acquired in Rome, was not transferred into surviving works in France, although there is some evidence from his son that the expertise filtered into his work as sculptor. To judge from inventories taken at artists' death, designers and sculptors kept such sketchbooks beside them all their working lives and regularly dipped into equivalent sources of ideas such as engravings. For example, when he died in 1570, Ponce Jacqueau (Jacquiot) left a large collection of drawings and engravings of Rome in his library including '60 pièces de pourtraictures faictes à la main et au pinceau après les Antiquitez de Rome' (60 images of the antiquities of Rome, drawn by hand and by the pen).[21] Of other French artists who visited Rome in the sixteenth century we know rather more, and I shall dwell upon the work of three of them: the first two, Philibert de L'Orme and Jean Bullant, because they designed and built major structures in France on their return from Italy, and Jean-Jacques Boissard because his contribution to the recording of ancient monuments in Rome was so comprehensive.

The evidence for Philibert de L'Orme's journeys to Rome comes from his books – *Nouvelles inventions pour bien bastir et à petis frais* (Paris, 1561) and *Le Premier tome d'architecture* (Paris, 1567) – which provided the kind of detail which cannot be matched by any other French artist at the time. His first visit, lasting three years, from 1533 to 1536, was undertaken to pursue his studies and to deepen his knowledge of architecture (f. 90v, *Premier tome*); and further visits may have been made in 1553, and in 1560 during a temporary period of disgrace. While he was in Rome, he made good contacts with the French community there (notably with Rabelais),[22] and he gained entry into the houses of the great collectors. The importance of his Roman experience cannot be exaggerated. Rome is a constant presence in his written work and quotations from his observations there appear in many of his buildings in France. In some respects, the buildings he admired in Rome and which formed a regular source of reference provided the credentials for his own future creations. He praised the Belvedere court and the 'infinity of beautiful works' located there which he enumerated in full (f. 124, *Premier tome*), and he incorporated the exedra design into the garden staircase at Anet; he admired the size and proportion of the Roman baths (ibid., f. 147v); and, above all, he celebrated the Pantheon, whose portico he found wonderfully harmonious: 'oeuvre digne d'alleguer et meriter grande louange, pour estre belle à merveille' (a work worthy of meriting great praise by virtue of its marvellous beauty) (ibid., f. 184v). Overall, he was impressed by the antiquities he studied, evaluating them as 'divinement bien faites' (divinely well made) (ibid., f. 145v), and created by architects who were eminently wise and gifted: 'fort bien advisez et pleins de grande industrie et artifice' (well endowed and full of great inventiveness and industry) (ibid., f. 191v).

Philibert's knowledge of the works he judged so enthusiastically was pro-found. It came from his close and judicious reading of Vitruvius, Pliny and Alberti whose works he cited frequently; and it also came from his perusal of historians and classical writers such as Varro, Virgil and Columnella, whose names are added to the roll call of experts at the beginning of the *Premier tome* (f. 15). His knowledge was supplemented by his acquaintance with the think-ing of contemporary mathematicians and their commentaries on Euclid, by the scholarly thoughts of François de Candale and of Forcadel (ibid., f. 116), and even by Dürer (f. 164). These secure theoretical foundations were infinitely developed by Philibert's direct contact with ancient buildings.

In Rome, in the same way as many other architects, he observed closely the details of structures still standing and inspected minutely the broken pieces that lay scattered about. He measured everything and, almost incessantly, referred to the authenticity such measurements ensured:[23] triumphal arches, the columns of the Pantheon, the remains of the Roman baths, or fallen capitals and archi-traves. And he accomplished those operations surrounded by a crowd of onlookers, some of whom were there to earn a few pence; others were keen to profit from what Philibert found:

> les autres pour apprendre comme estoient ouvriers, menuisiers, scarpelins ou sculpteurs et semblables qui desiroient cognoistre comme je faisois, et par-ticiper du fruict de ce que ie mesurois. (f. 131)

> [Others came to learn – like workmen, carpenters, stone carvers or sculp-tors and the like – who wanted to know what I was doing and to benefit from the outcome of my measurements.]

Such a group did not go unnoticed, and Philibert described how a cardinal and his entourage stopped one day to engage in debate about the best measuring schemes, and that same cardinal – who later became Pope Marcel II – invited him into the great houses of Rome. It was an invitation which Philibert eagerly accepted. The French architect claimed much for his thor-ough manner of recording the essential elements of antiquities; and he was con-vinced that these forms 'mesurees, deseignees et retraites par leurs proportions' (measured, designed and drawn in their proportion) constituted a unique source which no other Frenchman had found or made available.[24] His scrupulous observation gave him rare insights into the fabric of Roman buildings.

Philibert was singular among Frenchmen for having had a predominantly technical interest in Roman remains. On the Colosseum, for instance, he provided no details on the overall shape and structure of the building, remind-ing the reader that these could be found (if needed) in Serlio's excellent works

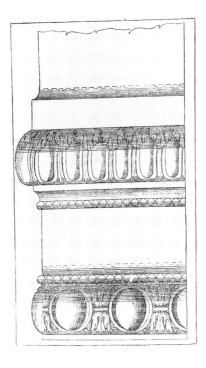

45. Philibert de L'Orme: fragment from Hadrian's villa

(f. 202v, *Premier tome*), but he did observe the holes on the uppermost layer which allowed him to specify the nature of roof coverings in Roman amphitheatres (f. 34, *Nouvelles inventions*) – an observation on which Lipsius later elaborated. Philibert's approach to the ruins was essentially unemotional and businesslike. He was moved, of course, by the way that lime-burners were destroying interesting fragments so that, on one occasion, when he went back to check his measurements of a fallen piece of masonry, he found that it had disappeared (f. 152v, *Premier tome*). Yet he was able to walk past the Colosseum without noticing it, so intent was he on locating a cornice nearby which had previously aroused his interest (ibid., f. 197).

Despite his careful assessing of the size and proportions of ancient remains, Philibert by no means advocated slavish adherence to his findings. These were necessary preliminaries, required for a thorough understanding of classical forms. Once they had been absorbed, it was then up to the architect to design his own creations and to incorporate in them the appropriate size and proportions (ibid., f. 197).

It was necessary to advance beyond accumulated knowledge to an intuitive and critical understanding. Thus Philibert was able to perceive that columns in the Pantheon belonged to different periods (ibid., f. 184v); that the columns in Notre Dame de Trastevere had similarly been amassed at various times; and that the Ionic capitals were diverse and brought together from several edifices and from ancient ruins (ibid., f. 162).[25] Mouldings for use on windows and

139

doors he had picked up in many places, particularly in the soil among the foundations of Hadrian's villa near Tivoli, of which he offered the first published fragment (Figure 45); and, concerned to introduce diversity into French design, he gave the budding architect a range of cornices from which to choose, from eleven different sources. From this variety of ideas, it is obvious that Philibert saw himself first and foremost as an enlightener. He was conscious of offering a new language and new forms. He never underestimated the difficulty of attempting to convey through words and writing his architectural observations and inventions,[26] so he often resorted to images to convey his meaning: 'la prochaine figure vous pourra proposer ce que ma plume en peu de paroles ne sçauroit expliquer' (the following image will explain to you what my pen could not do in a few words) (ibid., f. 112v).

His notion of a good architect was clear and unequivocal. His status is high; he should have due concern for his reputation (ibid., f. 11v); prudence and caution should be his watchwords and the figure of Mercury, as god of prudence, is therefore appropriate to his skill (ibid., f. 50).[27] Architects converse with monarchs and dedicate their works to them (as indeed Philibert did to Charles IX and Catherine de' Medici). True architects are few in number and they should guard their status jealously for architecture is a science, founded upon mathematical skills. It is the architect who provides the model of the building to be created, and who controls the work and the workmen (ibid., ff. 30, 81).

This lofty view of the standing of his profession required Philibert to accept the responsibility of speaking both to great princes (he had himself been in the king's employ since 1544), and to his own kind: to those 'gentilz esprits' (cultured spirits), the nobles who understood what he was trying to do (ibid., f. 61), and to the next generation of minds, with skills similar to his own (ibid., f. 282v). His many references to Vitruvius and Alberti showed Philibert's appreciation of their good counsel; but, more importantly, they created the context in which his own works were to be viewed and judged. These architects were not his masters but his equals, and when he praises them, the words reflect upon his own performance.[28] Although contemporaries (including Ronsard),[29] considered Philibert's behaviour and claims on behalf of the architect to derive from his innate arrogance – as when he bitterly decried what he termed the *abastardement* (bastardizing) of architecture (ibid., f. 129v; that is to say the demands of bourgeois and tradesmen to have houses built like those of nobles) – he was expressing his deep sense of a proper hierarchical order of things as well as defending his territory.

Philibert's works are highly self-conscious constructions containing frequent references to the need to be clear, and to have polished style that will be appreciated by connoisseurs. This preoccupation with clarity and with the avoidance of prolixity has to be set in the context of Philibert's awareness of the dense obscurity of Vitruvius' text, which he described as 'enveloppé, confus, obscur et difficile' (entangled, confused, obscure and difficult) (f. 134v, *Premier tome*).

One day he aimed to unravel its difficulties but, in the meantime, Philibert had amply demonstrated his own abilities. In the *Nouvelles inventions* (1561), he had considered the problem of the weight of wooden roofs which spanned the space in single wide beams and which were inflexible and subject to damage and decay. His solutions came from finding a way of linking short pieces of wood satisfactorily to form one firm arch that could be thrown across a broad space to provide lasting security. The discovery was much admired and commented upon – by Vigenère, for example.[30] Philibert was proud too of the suspended bays and rooms he built immediately on his return from Italy: at Lyon in 1536 for the 'general de la Bretaigne, monsieur Billan' (f. 90v, *Premier tome*), and at Anet for the king's private room (ibid., f. 51v). Both were ingenious and elegant solutions to lack of space.

Forced by such constraints to exercise his imagination and powers of invention, Philibert was in his element. Underlying his texts were concerns about the variety of forms that might be devised and the virtuosity with which they might be accomplished. His models of the projected buildings were only the first stage in the excited anticipation of what might be achieved. Once basic forms were understood then he moved swiftly towards variation – in the columns of the Tuileries palace which were under construction at the behest of Catherine de' Medici or, as he had done for Henri II, in the portico of the chapel at 'Villiers Coste-Rets' which he illustrates in detail (Figure 46). He revelled in the virtuoso challenges of adapting old buildings to new requirements, and was especially excited when brand new projects – Saint Maur, Anet and the Tuileries – gave him the opportunity to try out new ideas, maximize the expressive possibilities of the design, offer variations and render the fabric richer. The prospect of overcoming difficulties stimulated his genius and his will to pass on to the next generation the solutions he had devised. The suspended 'cabinet' of Henri II could serve as the prototype for many others, yet Philibert could not resist expatiating on the even more complicated 'trompe sur un coing' (closet suspended on a corner) (ibid., f. 99v).

A thorough understanding of classical forms was the essential first step in his campaign to promote French architecture and other forms of art in France. Throughout his work, Philibert stressed the quality of French materials such as marble, stone and gravel (ibid., f. 27) and the need to upgrade and rehabilitate fine French structures. As he put it to Henri II, who had encouraged him to write the *Nouvelles inventions*, he had undertaken this task 'pour le profit de son peuple et décoration de son royaume' (for the benefit of his people and the decoration of his kingdom) (sig. Aij). The phrases were to be repeated almost verbatim at the beginning of the *Premier tome* (f. 1) 'pour la decoration de son Royaume, et illustration de nostre architecture' (for the decoration of his kingdom and representation of our architecture). Philibert was persuaded that there were an infinite number of beautiful and ingenious touches in French architecture which were not known, or properly appreciated.[31] His written works were intended to remedy this oblivion, and his examples were

Dessin de la chappelle qui est au parc de villers costé res

46. Portico of the chapel at Villers-Cotterêts, designed by Philibert de L'Orme, drawn by Jacques Androuet du Cerceau

French: La Muette (*Nouvelles inventions*, f. 14), Saint Germain-en-Laye (ibid., f. 14), Saint Maur des Fossés (ibid., f. 52v and *Premier tome*, f. 250), Fontainebleau (ibid., f. 124v), Villers-Cotterêts (ibid., f. 156v), and the Tuileries (ibid., f. 62, 156v).

Philibert de L'Orme is acknowledged by art historians as the first great French architect. From 1544, he was involved with the construction or repair of nearly all royal buildings and to this work he applied the knowledge he had acquired in Rome.[32] The forms he had seen there infiltrated new conceptions: the chapel at Villers-Cotterêts, or the ceiling of the Salle de Bal at Fontainebleau. Ideas from Rome were absorbed into structures that remained essentially French in conception. The extent of the Roman influence can be seen in Philibert's plans for the dormitory at Montmartre (Figure 47). This was designed to replace a structure which had burned down, but it was never built. Inspired by the Pantheon, it was conceived as a circular building which would allow the light to penetrate only from the oval aperture in the roof. Philibert admitted that it was 'quasi ainsi qu'est le Pantheon de Rome' (almost like the Pantheon in Rome), although he claimed that his construction would encourage more light than did its Roman source. Just like the Pantheon, its roof was circular; two tiers of porticoes divided the interior into cells which were supported by Ionic columns with their architraves, friezes and capitals (*Nouvelles inventions*, ff. 32–33v). Although the work was not put in hand, the plans were well known through Philibert's publications, for his standing as architect and writer was such that his books were avidly read by fellow experts. It is known, for example, that he was read in Palladio's circle and that Scamozzi owned a copy of the *Premier tome*.[33]

We know much less about Jean Bullant (*c*. 1515–78) who was the architect of *connétable* Anne de Montmorency and who was responsible for the elevation of the château of Ecouen (see Figure 97, p. 329). He went to Rome in the early 1540s[34] and, from his own testimony, he undertook there activities similar to those of Philibert, measuring *à l'antique* and generally providing himself with a stock of ideas which he could incorporate into his building programme on his return.[35] His *Reigle générale d'architecture des cinq manières de colonnes*, published in 1568, was fully alive to the intricacies of geometry, perspective and 'horologiographie', and was intended for the workmen who laboured with compass and set-square.[36] He constantly refers with reverence to Vitruvius and praises Jean Martin for the quality of his translations (notably that of Alberti), yet the needs of workmen were uppermost: 'ma principale intention, en ce mien nouvel oeuvre, a esté de travailler pour les ouvriers . . . afin de leur donner à entendre quel a esté le iugement de noz bons maistres antiques' (my principal aim, in this my work, has been to labour for workmen in order to permit them to understand the judgement of our fine ancient masters) (sig. A. ii v). As a consequence, the book provides little insight into Bullant's impressions of Rome. Indeed, he ventures few aesthetic judgements, confining himself to a businesslike style and to matters of professional and technical orientation.

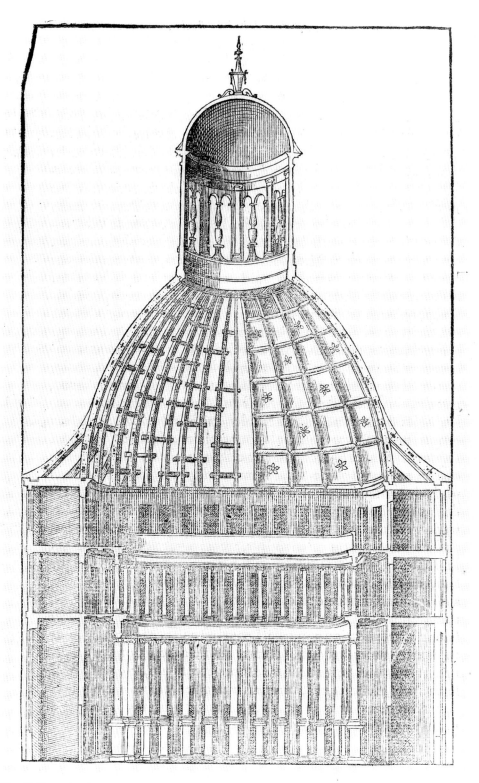

47. Philibert de L'Orme: design for a dormitory at Montmartre

However, the examples of the different orders of columns he provides, and upon which he comments, are mostly taken from buildings in Rome: 'cest ordre Dorique est au theatre de Marcellus' (this Doric order is from the theatre of Marcellus) (Bii v and Div). Other evidence comes from the Ionic capitals of the temple of Fortune; Corinthian columns from the Pantheon; from the three columns left standing in the Forum; from the temple of the Sibyl at Tivoli; and a composite order is drawn and measurements given from Titus' arch. At the end of his book, Bullant makes his view of the role of ancient monuments clear. In a sonnet addressed to all French architects, he appeals to them, urging them to bring to life and to reconstitute 'Les vrais pourtraictz des bastimentz antiques' (the true images of ancient buildings), as he has done himself.[37]

Bullant's most notable achievement was the work he carried out at Ecouen where the inner courtyard, with its monumental Corinthian columns on the south side that rise from ground level to reach the roof, provides clear evidence of inspiration from Rome.[38] After the death of the *connétable* in 1567, Bullant seems to have entered the employ of Catherine de' Medici; and he was described in a legal document in 1571 as 'Maistre architecteur de la Reyne'.[39] His new patron ensured that Bullant's son was adequately versed in the fundamental elements of classical remains in Rome before she employed him, too, as her architect. Bullant's widow did not have the means to send him into Italy, so Catherine – at her own expense – ordered that his journey there be paid 'affin qu'il puisse veoir les belles choses qui y sont pour son art' (so that he might see there those fine things appropriate to his art).[40]

Jean-Jacques Boissard (1528–1602), who spent a decade in Rome from 1551, was in the employ of Cardinal Caraffa.[41] His impressions of Rome and his intentions in his publications were very different from those of the working architects Philibert and Bullant. Boissard returned temporarily to Metz in 1576 and finally settled there for the rest of his life in 1583, participating in public events.[42] He was not concerned with technical self-improvement, and he did not particularly desire to build new things. Rather his purpose was to record the antiquities he had seen in Rome: written inscriptions, and sculpted or painted objects. Boissard admired the grandeur of Rome profoundly and claimed that he used all his leisure hours there 'à peindre ou à sculpter; je recherchais sans cesse les vestiges de l'antiquité' (to paint and to sculpt; I searched unceasingly for the vestiges of antiquity).[43] His record was built up over a long period, accumulated day by day (especially for his project on inscriptions). Since he considered that it was important to list everything, he visited all the extant remains scattered around the city and made a systematic review of the great collections in Rome. From all this labour, Boissard produced two works relating to Rome: the *Inscriptionum antiquarum*, originally dedicated to Charles de Lorraine in 1559 but which was not published until 1599;[44] and the *Antiquitatum Romanorum*, a vast encyclopaedic record, conceived in six parts, drawn by Boissard and engraved by Theodore and Robert de Bry,[45] and published in Frankfurt between 1597 and 1602 (Figure 48).

145

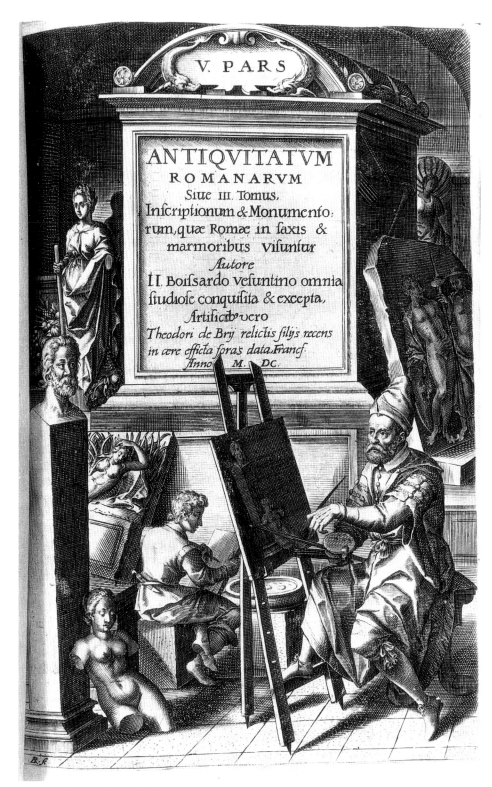

V. PARS

ANTIQVITATVM
ROMANARVM
Siue III. Tomus,
Inſcriptionum & Monumento:
rum, quæ Romæ in ſaxis &
marmoribus viſuntur
Autore
I I. Boiſſardo veſuntino omnia
ſtudioſe conquiſita & excepta,
Artificib° vero
Theodori de Brij relictis filijs recens
in ære efficta foras data.Francf.
Anno M. DC.

48. Jean-Jacques Boissard: showing Theodore and Robert de Bry engraving

The book of inscriptions, which Raymond Chevalier praised for their accuracy,[46] was compiled via a network of relationships with other scholars who took the trouble to give Boissard their own copies of writings on tombs and sarcophagi, found in both Germany and Italy. The record of Rome was no longer an individual's interpretation of what he had seen, but a common enterprise. Boissard took examples from accounts published by established experts, as he acknowledged in his reference to 'Gabrielis Simeonis Florentini';[47] from manuscripts of the antiquarian Roussati or of his friend Giulio Rosci.[48] Such collaboration took a different form in the *Antiquitatum*. These books, containing more than 500 engravings, were based on Boissard's life's work, drawn from sketchbooks made in Rome. The task of leaving a comprehensive monument was complicated by the fact that the artist lost major parts of his collection in 1587,[49] and the loss might explain the character of Boissard's volumes with their disorder and the haphazard selection of elements to be illustrated. The six parts of the work are, however, clearly delineated: part 1 records the day-by-day visits to the collections; and the reader is invited to accompany Boissard around the city, discovering each street in turn, gradually absorbing the treasures and disposing his time so that nothing is left out. Part 2 concerns the site of Rome and the growth of the city; part 3 publishes the work on inscriptions and epitaphs while part 4 is given over to funerals and their ceremonies; and parts 5 and 6 offer more inscriptions and a miscellany of statues.

Interspersed among Boissard's own testimony are huge blocks of text extracted from others' work. In part 1, for instance, thirty pages of Panvinius' account of the buildings of Rome are inserted, followed by Piero Victori's discourse on the districts of the city. In part 2, Marliani's text is given in its entirety with some additions. Giraldi is the expert used for funerals, and part 5 opens with a formidable list of authorities to whom Boissard appeals – thirty-one in all.[50] Such an approach suggests that Boissard sought to provide a monument to his predecessors by incorporating their work into his own, and that he saw recycling as a form of collaboration.

His method was a simple one. Each engraving is provided with a precise location: in this cardinal's garden (the Juno or Ceres of Jean du Bellay); in that prince's collection (Della Valle, for example); found in the Borgo or the Forum, and so on. Such an encyclopaedic endeavour ought to arouse our applause; yet the very multitude of objects, all with an air of familiarity, all stylized and isolated from their context, lacking any sense of perspective or of the past, disappoints. Although the drawing is always confident, Boissard could not discriminate true from false; he gave equal importance to each aspect of what he was depicting and provided no light or shade. Nor was he interested in the technical dimension of what he observed. From time to time there are some realistic touches which suddenly enliven the page, such as the women hanging sheets out to dry in the Forum, or the couple who wander among the ruins near Naples (in 1554), lizards sunning themselves upon the stones, and the birds ignoring the lady about to enter the grotto.[51] The overall effect is, however, that of flatness and sameness. It has to be noted that the drawings in the manuscripts show a finer line and greater delicacy than do the engravings, although, in one respect, they have similar characteristics: when heads are depicted, they resemble late sixteenth-century models attached to Roman sarcophagi.

As a source book illustrating the sheer quantity of items available, Boissard's text was invaluable. As inspiration, it was severely limited. Nevertheless, contemporary opinion was favourable, as mutually dependent scholars tended to praise each other's work. Lipsius, for instance, paid Boissard a fine tribute and the author responded with his own compliment: 'Magnus Lipsius ille . . .' (that great Lipsius).[52] Modern critical opinion is divided on the value of Boissard's work. Callmer compared him to Ligorio who, without discretion, collected authentic and false material;[53] Choné recognized his limitations, with the unique focus on the object separated from its historical and artistic context;[54] Chevalier admired his epigraphic accuracy; whereas Bruce Mansfield accused Boissard of fabrication and interpolation.[55] In any event, whatever their merits or flaws, his volumes were reprinted and provided the foundation for seventeenth-century compilations which attempted to leave nothing unrecorded.

INSPIRATION FROM ENGRAVINGS

The visits of artists to the city itself were only one means of absorbing and transmitting images of Rome, and they may have been less effective than the numerous prints and engravings which were made by French engravers in Rome and which were sent in quantities across Europe.[56] There is ample evidence of the collecting of such prints at this time and of a growing interest in engravings and etchings. The latter had, by the end of the fifteenth century, become a recognized art form and was an important source of revenue for artists.[57]

The principal source of such engravings was the workshop of Antoine Lafréry (1512–77) who established his enterprise in Rome in 1544 and whose products found their way to most major cities. He used French and Italian engravers including, among the former, Nicholas Béatrizet, Etienne du Pérac and Claude Duchet (Lafréry's nephew) (Figure 49).[58] For specialist prints, he used experts: the circus of Caracalla (engraved 1566) was measured and reconstructed by Onufrius Panvinius, and that of Flaminius came from Pirro Ligorio.[59] Such names helped to enhance the reputation of the workshop, and by 1571 Lafréry was ready to publish his first large catalogue. This had five sections: A – maps; B – seventy-nine engravings of antiquities; C – seventy-two engraved mythological subjects; D – seventy-two prints from the Bible; and E – twenty-six portraits. Usually each print was dated and signed. The range of subject matter can be gauged from the work of Béatrizet who engraved all the

49. Claude Duchet: engraving of three columns from the Forum

major monuments in Rome: the equestrian statue of Marcus Aurelius, the Pantheon, and the Castel di Sant'Angelo. He also reproduced friezes from the reliefs of Trajan's column, depictions of the famous statues in Rome, and engravings of modern buildings such as the Farnese palace. Independent prints were sold singly like postcards,[60] but could be made up into entire volumes like Du Pérac's *I Vestigi dell' antiquità di Roma* (1575) which was devoted exclusively to the ruins, as the title makes clear; or they could be worked into large albums for princely collectors. These had the advantage of being open-ended, forming a kind of personal dictionary or scrapbook of famous scenes and objects which could be added to, almost infinitely. Several copies of these albums, entitled *Speculum Romanae magnificentiae*, survive, of which the largest (now the property of the University of Chicago) contains 996 engraved pieces.[61] Sometimes the albums were a miscellany of drawings and engravings such as that assembled by Salamanca in 1588, or they could be augmented by single sheets with illustrations from published works.[62] A letter from Marc-Antoine de Muret to Pierre Dupuy (dated '2 novembre 1572') shows how collections of engravings

149

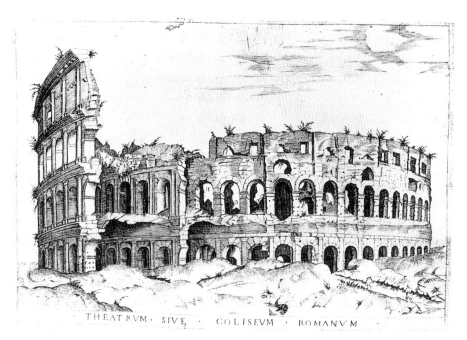

THEATRVM · SIVE · COLISEVM · ROMANVM ·

50. Antoine Lafréry: engraving of the Colosseum

were gradually assembled. Lafréry had promised to show Muret all that had been engraved in the last year and a half, so that he could report in detail to his friend in Paris; Muret was obliged to delay his letter as the engraver was not at home, despite earlier assurances.

> Il [Lafréry] me remist à auiourd'hui pour voir tout ce qui a esté fait despuis un an et demi. J'i ai esté par deux fois et ne l'ai sceu trouver. Et c'est la cause que ie suis mis à heure si tarde à vous rescrire. J'i envoie encores un mien serviteur tout à cest heure.

> [Lafréry put me off till today to see all that has been done in the last year and a half. I have been twice without being able to see him. That's the reason why I'm writing to you at such a late hour. I'm sending one of my men there, even at this hour.][63]

The images themselves are interesting. Lafréry's shop had over a hundred engravings of Rome and they were advertised as 'accuratiss. delineata repraesentans' (images accurately rendered) (Figure 50). Yet the title of the volume also stressed that the images were 'partim iuxta antiquam partim iuxta hodiernam formam' (in part, forms from ancient times and in part what could be seen today). Elsewhere, in Lafréry's volume, the engravings of Rome by Ligorio (1573) and Duchet (1582) were cited as perfect – 'Antiquae urbis perfecta imago' (a perfect image of the ancient city) – and from the engravings it is clear that we must understand *perfecta* to mean *reconstructed* rather than accu-

150

rately rendered.[64] Thus we have views of ancient Rome that are interpreted and reconstituted alongside images that show the buldings in their ruined state. Lafréry was perhaps the first to spread abroad such double visions of Rome (which were to become the hallmark of Du Pérac's work later), and these related not only to monuments but also to the activities of the Romans, as can be seen from the reconstructed naumachia where ships are shown engaged in a brisk sea battle. Within the picture frame, the image appealed directly to the reader/observer, for in every scene are spectators viewing the monument or ruins; they provide a sense of scale and draw the reader (who tends to identify with the spectators) into the process of remaking.[65]

It was inevitable that such a mass of visual material so readily available and portable should find its way to France and influence French artistic ideas. These sources may well have encouraged the extensive use of ruined landscapes in the second half of the sixteenth century. Ruins are present in surviving drawings and in many anonymous designs;[66] they can be seen in the *martyre d'un saint* of Jean Cousin where classical architectural forms, broken pillars, ruins and obelisks are sketched in across two-thirds of the design, dominating the principal subject, which is confined to the left foreground.[67] Similarly, in *Enfants jouant près d'une fontaine*, vast ruins (like those of the baths in Rome) rise up filling almost all the available space, a spiralling column cuts through the centre of the image, other ruins – broken columns and obelisks – are shadowed in behind (Figure 51). The tiny children in the foreground seem almost an afterthought.[68] Although it is rare for ruins to invade the whole picture in this way,[69] ruined landscapes were dominant in the engravings Léonard Thiry made to illustrate the story of Persephone, and they appeared in contemporary Books of Hours where the illuminators specialized in using them to frame the action. They are present in the *Heures Henri II*, those of Gouffier, and in the extraordinary resurrection scene in the *Heures Dinteville* (Plate IV) where an obelisk topped by a globe (like that in Rome) is flanked by tall, ruined arches.[70] It may well be, as Vigenère argued, that such features were intended to enrich the image and to fill in space which would otherwise be empty,[71] yet the symbolism of the obelisk and the ruined arches has clear affinities with the open tomb and skeleton stretched out below. Ruins so dominate Jean de Gourmont's painting of the *Nativity* that the human forms seem reduced to insignificance (Plate V). Landscapes with classical ruins, in fact, appeared everywhere, and they were undoubtedly inspired by the ruins of Rome (Figure 52). They became a regular feature in mid-sixteenth-century designs for interior decoration, and appeared on many models for furniture – chimneys, buffets, bedheads and the like. They were, for instance, worked into the stained-glass windows made for the library at Anet;[72] they filled the background of frescos VIII and IX in the long painted gallery at Oiron where Noël Jallier (who may have been in Rome in 1544–45) chose to depict ruins and a view of Rome[73] which was obviously intended to be recognized (Plate V); and they appeared on the walls of the château Villeneuve-Lembron (Plate VII).

51. Jean Cousin: drawing of 'Enfants jouant'

52.   Jacques Androuet du Cerceau, landscape design – *paysage en ruines*

The habit of 'quoting' well-known features was widespread and often took the form of singling out a motif – Bramante's Tempietto, an obelisk, a triumphal arch or a broken column – chosen to indicate the whole. Although a modern building, the Tempietto (and various versions of it) was, because of its harmonious classical proportions, especially ubiquitous; also perhaps because in addition to its elegance it had been illustrated by Serlio[74] and because the round temple was revered at this time as the most perfect form. It figured on three of the illuminations in the *Heures Montmorency*; it was reproduced by Du Cerceau in his *Vues des Monuments antiques* and appeared as a motif on his designs for chimneys;[75] it was conspicuous in Antoine Caron's designs for Amphion (published in Vigenère's *Les Images*); and it was the central feature in one of the 'Destruction of the Huguenots' paintings – the *Wounding of Coligny* – which Pope Gregory XIII had personally selected for the Sala Regia in the Vatican.[76]

Although such conscious use of an individual element deliberately pointed to Rome, inspiration could be even more direct. When the chapel in the château de Saint Jouy was being built in 1544, the *marché* (contract) specified that the columns were to be made exactly like those of the Pantheon, or better if possible ('faictes en tout à l'imitation de celles qui sont dedans l'eglise de la Rotonde à Rome ou mieulx s'il est possible').[77] Perhaps the most remarkable and explicit reference to Rome came in the paintings of Marten van Heemskerck, as seen in his self-portrait and in the colossal statue of Hercules which he set within the Colosseum in his design for the eighth wonder of the world.[78]

No French painter attempted anything quite so audacious; into his painting the *Massacre du triumvirat* (1566), Antoine Caron contrived to pack all the major monuments of Rome (Plate IX). He depicted the Colosseum in the centre of the picture, the Castel di Sant'Angelo in the background on the left, the Pantheon, the Septizonium, the Forum, the arches of Septimus Severus and Constantine, and the Campidoglio with the equestrian statue of Marcus Aurelius. Trajan's column and an obelisk covered in hieroglyphics act as focal points for the neatly arranged and serried heads of the massacred; and on each side of the picture, in the foreground, on their pedestals opposite each other, stand Apollo Belvedere and the Hercules Commodus. Each monument seems a faithful copy of its original, and the onlooker immediately assumes that s/he is gazing at Rome. On the other hand, the ruins seem to have been tidied up, and the interior of the Colosseum is exposed to display a show in progress watched by the triumvirs Antony, Octavius and Lepidus. Moreover, the buildings, while carefully replicated, are all in the wrong places. Caron has had little regard for topography and has arranged his material artistically so that the larger elements fill the central space or frame the action. The dreadful scenes of massacre in this picture (similar to one that had been owned by Anne de Montmorency)[79] shrink into insignificance and it is the imperial and architectural context which predominates. Now Caron had never visited Rome, and – as far as we know – did not even travel to Italy. How then could he paint the buildings with such accuracy, and at the same time show such ignorance of the topography of Rome? The answer lies in the engravings. It has been shown that Caron copied the prints that came out of Lafréry's workshop and these gave him the detail of each building which he subsequently painted, but they failed to explain the relationship of one structure to another.[80]

The presence of Rome is powerful in all his work. In his paintings inspired by festivals, Caron juxtaposed real French sites with buildings inspired by Rome. In his *Triomphe de l'hiver* he shows Fontainebleau framing the back of the picture while, just off centre, there sits his adaptation of the Tempietto (Figure 53). The same temple appears again, in modified form and flanked by two obelisks, in a French garden setting in the *Triomphe de l'été* (1568–70). Obelisks, triumphal arches and columns provide the somewhat scattered structures of two other paintings: *Astronomes observant une éclipse* (1571–72) and *L'Empereur Auguste et la Sibylle de Tibur* (c. 1580).[81] It is possible that Caron's addiction to Rome was encouraged by Vigenère, for whom he worked; in any event, the insistence on Rome is so overwhelming that no attempt is made to

53.   Antoine Caron: 'Le Triomphe de l'Hiver'

blend the different architectures. Caron presents a double vision of Rome and France. The dominance of the imperial city and the fact that Caron copied single monuments from prints may explain why his pictures seem to have no central focus. Each individual figure or group is carefully drawn, and seems surrounded by air as it retains its independence and does not relate to other elements in the picture – except in the *Massacre du triumvirat* where the individual buildings cumulatively spell Rome.

Another French artist significantly dependent on prints for his work was Jacques Androuet du Cerceau (1510/12–1585/86), although he may have spent some years in Rome at the beginning of his career (1530–33).[82] His output was voluminous and of interest because Du Cerceau absorbed the images and transformed them. Du Cerceau is best known for his engravings of French palaces – *Les Plus Excellents Bastiments de France* (1576, 1579) – which he claimed to have drawn *sur place* and at the behest of Catherine de' Medici.[83] The labour took many years and suggests a preoccupation with French architecture and, as he put it, a diversion from the painful spectacle of war which surrounded him. It should also be remembered that he published his *Livre d'architecture* in 1559 on the assumption that architects would no longer have to have recourse to foreigners for their building needs.[84] The engravings, however, often reveal the influence of Rome. His depiction of the Louvre, for instance, emphasizes the motif of the triumph incorporated into the façade of the inner courtyard and at the entrance of the Great Hall.[85]

For his other publications, Du Cerceau copied ideas from Lafréry or from Ligorio, as in his map of Rome (1578) and his *Edifices antiques* (1584) where he simply engraved on separate sheets the reconstructed buildings which Ligorio had drawn some twenty years earlier. His *Vues d'optique* (1551) were borrowed from Michel Crecchi's *Prospectiva et antichita di Roma*[86] and, although one of the engravings depicts the artist standing beneath an arch in Rome in the act of drawing its decorations,[87] his book on ruins (*Praecipua aliquot Romanae antiquitatis ruinarum*, 1561) came from a work by Hieronymus Cock published in 1550 at his workshop in Antwerp which he had set up to rival the printing presses of Lafréry in Rome. Du Cerceau did, occasionally, attempt to break the mould to escape from his attachment to other artists' ideas. In 1560 he designed the château de Verneuil as radically different from all previous French castles with its circular *porte d'entrée*, its theatrical conception of niches designed to accommodate statues of Assyrian kings sculpted by Ponce Jacqueau; yet some of the niches in the inner courtyard were copied from the antique. Hercules (for instance) was ordered to be made 'comme l'on treuve aux anticques' (as one finds in ancient examples).[88]

Du Cerceau's work generally depended on the ideas of others. Yet his prolific production of designs for every conceivable object served as a channel of imitation and stylization for others to use professionally.[89] One of his first publications, *Exempla arcuum* (1549),[90] which contained twenty-five designs for arches invented by himself and drawn from monuments still surviving in Rome, was specifically addressed to all students of building ('omnes aedificandi studiosi'); and similarly, one of his last works,[91] his *Edifices antiques* (1584), copied from Ligorio, was explicitly engraved for the curious and especially for architects ('pour servir à ceux qui sont curieux de l'antiquité, et encore plus (à mon jugement) à ceux qui sont maistres en l'Architecture' (to serve those who are eager to know about antiquity, and those – more so, in my judgement – who are experts in Architecture)). His works served as reference books for furniture makers, painters, embroiderers, gold and silversmiths, and tapestry makers not only because of their number but also through the variety and range of images and patterns made available. He did not restrict his use of the ubiquitous Tempietto motif to chimneys. He also adapted ruins to fill the central space of his designs. According to the size required he drew palaces, baths, obelisks, columns or church towers. On furniture (a bedhead) he designed scenes of triumph with trumpeters, soldiers with trophies, the Triumphator on horseback; or, for a double buffet, a triumphal arch design crowned with the picture of Laocoön and his sons (Figure 54).[92] His work had added value as it was engraved on metal, which gave greater refinement to the finished image and allowed for fuller detail to be represented. In this respect, Du Cerceau's work stands up well against the images printed in the books of Serlio and Philibert which were made from a cruder process based on wood.

In Du Cerceau's more fanciful designs – the *Grandes et petites arabesques* and the *Grotesques* – it is interesting to see how building elements, columns for

54. Jacques Androuet du Cerceau: design for a buffet

instance, no longer have solid supporting functions and, in the imaginative play of the artist's pen, have become mere decorative features. The twisted columns (erstwhile a device of Charles IX) seem in the *Petites arabesques* to have shed any structural significance for the columns are intertwined and woven into the overall design of a pavilion and support nothing (Figure 55). Similarly, in the design for a ceiling, twisted columns are placed on either side of an obelisk and they demonstrably have no supporting role.[93] In another design from the *Grandes grotesques* a temple is placed at the centre but its walls have lost their solidity. As in some earlier designs by Ligorio (Figure 56), they seem as if made of glass and the four rivers which decorate each angle of the drawing also have this transparent quality.[94]

55.   Jacques Androuet du Cerceau: design from *Petities arabesques*

With Du Cerceau's decorative designs, we have come a long way from the faithful copying of classical fragments and the careful measuring of antiquities by Philibert or Bullant. Their records had provided rich sources of ideas for buildings and for their decoration. Prints had widened the availability of images from Rome, and had provided painters like Caron with a series of images which had an air of authenticity and which could be lifted off the page entire and set within a picture frame or incorporated in a fresco, giving them renewed life in a new context. Du Cerceau marks a temporary end to the process of absorption. In his arabesques and grotesques one has to look hard to discover what had been such prominent motifs in ruined landscapes or in Caron's painting, since they have all but disappeared within the playful, decorative web of design. *À l'antique* has returned to its vaguely indicative associations – as Du Cerceau himself used the term in *Temples antiques* where he offered designs 'Pour ung devant de pallais selon l'antique' (for a palace, according to the antique, plates 5 and 6) '. . . pour une galerye selon l'antique' (for a gallery, according to the antique, plate 10) '. . . pour ung vestibule selon l'antique' (for a vestibule according to the antique, plate 23) '. . . pour une cheminée selon l'antique' (for a chimneypiece according to the antique, plate 24).[95]

56. Pirro Ligorio: grotesque design

Another kind of transference of images of Rome allowed the imagination to play on the fragments that remained and to reconstitute the pieces into whole structures. In this reconstruction, the city was no longer a static entity framed within its walls and bounded by them; instead, its individual elements became manipulable, conceived as in a process of becoming.[96] A long tradition lay behind this and one of its most celebrated exponents was Petrarch, in his epic poem *Africa* and in his account of his own impressions of the city which he first visited in 1337.

In many respects, Rome is the central theme of *Africa*. Its enduring might and unique renown are celebrated in Book 2 (ll. 165–7, 378–80); though fallen, Rome is not vanquished, and the physical signs of strife serve to perpetuate its greatness (ll. 420–4). Rome in triumph is evoked on many occasions, conjured up in particular by Sophonisba in Book 5 (ll. 993–1003), and by Scipio in Book 6 (ll. 234–40). The most complete depictions of the city occur in Books 8 and 9 with Hasdrubal's famous visit to Rome when excitement had prepared him in advance to see something glorious in what he had christened 'the whole world's capital'. Guided through the Appian gate, he ascends to the Capitol where he views Jupiter's temple whose threshold had witnessed a thousand triumphs and where enormous piles of treasure captured from their foes gave witness to the power of Rome and Romans. Statues, arches and other emblems of triumph surround Hasdrubal and his companions as they make their way through the city to the summit of the Quirinal, past the temple of Minerva and down again to the Tiber. The idealization of the city mirrored Hasdrubal's expectation, and the exalted impression was underlined at the end of the epic with the triumph of Scipio. He journeys along the same path which Hasdrubal had followed; and the spectacle of triumph in the streets and hills gives the city added lustre.[97]

In *Africa*, Petrarch projected a splendid and inflated view of the city which provided a suitable frame for the contemplation of great deeds and for admiring the visual expression of them. Although he was excited and interested, Hasdrubal's reaction to the glories of Rome was essentially passive in that he merely observed and marvelled at the spectacle. Scipio, too, remained aloof; he is shown as the severe commander of divine aspect, above the mêlée, the noise and paraphernalia of his triumph.

Although leaning heavily on the information gleaned from his reading of Roman histories, Petrarch injected into his poem something of his own experience, for in his letters to Cardinal Giovanni Colonna di San Vito he wrote of the same expectation and anticipated excitement. Like the *Africa*, his letters are literary works where traces of personal experience have been moulded to impress.[98] They transmit the whole process of travel, recollection and re-enactment. The first letter (*Rerum familiarum*, Book 2, no. 14) withholds from his correspondent any description of the place. Books had provided him with a preview of Rome, and he had been fearful that the gap between his mental image and the real experience of the city would be too great to bear. It is also as though he can only stutter his overwhelming wonder and the greatness of his astonishment for, as he wrote: 'In truth Rome was greater, and greater are its ruins than I imagined'.

The second epistle records his experience of Rome and that of the cardinal to whom he writes and who had accompanied him on his daily walks. The historical sweep is even greater here than in his epic, as Petrarch combines his deep knowledge of history and myth.[99] These vast tracks of history which Petrarch traces assume that the reader will supply the detail since the evocation remains at a very general level.[100] He evokes places (the palace of Evander, shrines, caves, the spot where Romulus' fig tree grew, and the place where Numa and Egeria conversed), refers to events (the rape of the Sabines), recollects people and their deeds, and names the seven hills of Rome. As the narrative gains momentum, individuals seem to live again: Lucretia and Brutus, Virginia and Coriolanus, Caesar and Pompey, Augustus and Trajan, St Peter, St Paul and St Stephen; the names tumble out at ever increasing speed. Then, abruptly, the rhythm changes; with the tag 'nowhere is Rome less known than in Rome', Petrarch suddenly ends on an image that contrasts sharply with the crowded canvas he had been painting and where centuries and layers of history had been made to exist simultaneously. Rome has become deserted; it is now an infinite space of silence and of solitude; the two walkers climb up on to the roof of Diocletian's baths (Figure 57); from that height, they gaze down upon the remains of a broken city and the remnants of all the ruins, and it is time for philosophical reflection.[101]

In this context, it is suggestive to recall Freud's analysis of the mental processes whereby events which were spread out over time and places built at different periods are brought into one dense and charged simultaneous experience, and where disparate fragments are shaped into larger, coherent forms.[102] In his analysis, Freud – probably without knowing them – articulated the endeavours writers and artists had made in the sixteenth century as they constructed wholes out of parts and reconstituted the monuments of Rome. As he tried to trace a particular thought sequence from its origins, Rome came to his mind. Freud reminded his readers of its beginnings, evolved from the oldest part of the city (the *Roma quadrata* – the fenced settlement on the Palatine), then traced its growth and phases of development. He then reversed the process and showed that, however carefully he stripped away the growth and excrescences, it was literally impossible to find the ancient area, the *Roma quadrata*, or even some scanty remains. Freud then transferred this building and stripping, and saw Rome not as a physical place but as a psychical entity. In this rendering, nothing is lost: all phases of growth survive and are simultaneously

57.   G.A. Dosio: the baths of Diocletian

present; in other words, one space contains more than one content. It was just this simultaneity, underscored by his repeated *hic*, that had been important for Petrarch.

THE URGE TO RECONSTRUCT AND THE ROLE OF CONJECTURE

Imaginative recreation was essential if you were to be a successful artist at this time, and the ability to visualize an entire structure from a few fragmentary remains seems to have been highly prized. There is the famous story about Brunelleschi, repeated by Vasari from Manetti's life of the architect: such was the architect's profound knowledge of ancient buildings and their technical construction 'that he became completely capable of seeeing Rome in his mind's eye, just as it was before it was ruined'.[103] Although Brunelleschi left no evidence of this static view of the city, the urge to reconstruct its ancient forms was shared by many.

Flavio Biondo (1388–1463) may, in some ways, be seen as the fountainhead for those artists and humanists who succumbed to this urge to reconstruct. As archaeologist and as apostolic secretary to four popes, he was well placed to influence changes to the landscape in Rome, and this he accomplished through

163

his counsel and by his books. His *Roma triumphans* (*c.* 1459) was infused with a sense of kinship with the classical past, and it assumed the possibility of close interactions between the achievements of ancient times and the potential of the present. As its title suggests, it was concerned with the reconstruction of the glory of ancient Rome. Biondo advocated a building programme there that would reconstruct classical buildings, and he also set out a vision of ancient Rome as a civilizing power, through its strict adherence to religion, its family organization, its military and constitutional machines. All these achievements were relevant to his own time and others recognized that fact. *Roma triumphans* proved very popular and was influential both as an inspiration and as a source book.[104]

What impressed Biondo was the coherence of the structures of ancient Rome: a single language extending across a multitude of peoples; and one legal and administrative system throughout the empire. Although such coherence could be no more than a powerfully attractive ideal, there was something that could be done about the ruins of the city, which Biondo regarded as tangible proof of Rome's glory.[105] He was convinced that the ruins provided an invaluable resource for remaking Roman culture and values and, in *Roma instaurata* (1446), Biondo had set about building the topography of the ancient city with information based on his observations of its remains and supplemented by an impressive array of other aids: literary and historical sources, numismatic evidence, inscriptions, archives and regional catalogues.[106] He counselled the use of conjecture, particularly in considering the siting of buildings which he knew to have been on the Palatine hill but whose location was then undetermined: 'For that reason [related to the Palatine], I came to ponder every so often what conjecture I am at liberty to make about the rest of Rome when I see those three hills, the first and only ones in the early city, now stripped almost bare of their buildings as though Rome had not yet been founded.'[107] It is interesting that he sees the rebuilding process as the same as that of retrieving a corrupt text, stressing in his work of reconstruction the philological and historical dimensions. Biondo had set himself a formidable task; but what we have in *Roma instaurata* is an incredibly learned and enthusiastic venture, packed with information on chronology: the dates when gates and bridges were built; when additions were made to buildings by previous popes and about the functions of those structures; about the origin and nature of obelisks; who inhabited which hill at which time; on baths, arches, temples, churches, theatres and circuses. Nothing was omitted.

Perhaps most significant is his comparison of the old and new Rome,[108] where senators are transformed into cardinals. There was no more succinct way of expressing the change from one kind of imperialism to another. Biondo wanted to leave a vision of ancient Rome, written down, so that the memory could live for ever, and to use that vision as a source of inspiration for magnifying the modern city. In essence, his aims were political for he saw immediate connections between reconstruction, inflation and idealism linked to the service of princes. The connections suggested between power and building at this early date are important. They also have a personal dimension. The power of the great city which Biondo had restored (in his mind) inspired in him a belief in his own building capacity; and that feeling had more general significance, especially for artists who would benefit from the juxtaposition. Biondo spelt out the aims and the power potential in his address to Pope Eugenius IV and, in full detail, outlined the enormous amount of restoration work to be done.[109]

If we now leap to the mid-sixteenth century, it will be seen that reverberations of the spirit and practice of Biondo were widespread. Motifs and fragments acted as stimulants to the imagination, and conjecture in the cause of reconstruction was generally applied. While Jean Martin recognized that anyone could construct an entire building in his mind: 'Certes un homme peult bien imaginer en sa pensee des maisons toutes accomplies, sans y rien employer de materiel' (of course, a man – without using any concrete materials – can imagine in his mind houses that are completely finished),[110] when it came to the business of planning or building from ruins, the matter was more problematic. At least, the builder felt constrained to justify the result even if he acknowledged simultaneously that some fragments were so ruinous that it was impossible to envisage any shape to which they might belong,[111] while also declaring that he could reconstitute the size and greatness of an original structure from the remains.[112] Thus Serlio confidently inserted windows into his version of the temple of Peace 'where I thought them fittest to stand'.[113]

As far as I know, no one has criticized Serlio for the additions he 'conjectured' because he thought them right, yet Pirro Ligorio has been denounced by some historians for having 'improved' the original sculptures by giving them completed form in his drawings when only fragments survived. This urge to complete came from Ligorio's desire to bring the ancient world fully alive;[114] and, in his creations, he made that world grander than it had really been.[115] Again, the artist's approach to reconstruction was via conjecture,[116] as he admitted in his bringing to light of the Circus Flaminius: 'Desiring with all my heart to revive and preserve the memory of ancient things . . . I have often made use of conjecture, where the ruins, which are few, were lacking.'[117] Ligorio was usually open about the extent of his own contribution to the reconstructing of a building or the perfecting of an object; and in some instances the licence he took was considerable. In the case of a relief of Diana, although he supplemented conjecture with the study of comparative material, out of a few fragments which remained around the feet, he reconstituted the entire figure: 'Above the inscription was a statue of Diana with nothing left visible but a few vestiges of sculpture at the bottom near her feet. Nevertheless I have drawn her figure complete, taking as my starting point the position that remains and supplying the rest from other statues of Diana in the same action.'[118] Attitude and gesture were the salient features, and they indicate how removed the finished drawing was from anything like a copy. The ability to convince the viewer that the piece had an authentic air was prized at this time, as is evident from the praise Vasari heaped on Giovan-Maria from Spoleto (called Falconetto) who was able to restore antiquities 'by furnishing the parts wanting, with the utmost truth and in all their integrity'.[119]

THE PROCESS OF RECONSTITUTION IN ANDREA PALLADIO AND ETIENNE DU PÉRAC

As far as French artists were concerned, it was the reconstitution of ancient buildings which most interested them because from the rebuilding process not only did they learn valuable techniques, but their own creative ideas were also stimulated. In this sphere, no one was more influential than Andrea Palladio (1508–80) who knew the work of Ligorio well and whose own works, *L'antichità di Roma* (1554) and *I quattro libri dell'architettura* (1570), were to have lasting authority in both France and England. Of these two texts, there were three or four issues each decade,[120] and they became standard source books for generations of architects.[121] His use of conjecture was guided by an impressive scholarship which even embraced the latest findings in archaeology.[122]

At the outset, Palladio affirmed that he would use no source other than the most authoritative (Vitruvius especially), and no surviving fragment of classical architecture which he had not himself seen and measured. As he stated in the dedication to Count Giacomo Angaranno in 1570, he had seen with his own eyes ('con egli occhi proprij ho veduto') and handled with his own hands ('con le proprie mani'), and had measured fragments 'di molti edificii antichi' in Rome and in other parts of Italy.

His remodelling of ancient forms benefited from the widespread acceptance of man's ability to contemplate a whole building from its surviving fragments;[123] but there was still a sizeable gap between conceiving a building in the mind and calculating – for building purposes – the relationship of its parts and its decoration. Nonetheless, having declared in his preface to the reader of his *I quattro libri*, that he was able 'from such fragments to comprehend what the whole must needs have been, and so make Draughts accordingly' (that is to say move from conjectured form to draft plan),[124] he went further. Sure in his method of reconstruction, he announced in Book 2:

> I shall therefore in this book show the form and ornament of several antient Temples, whereof the ruins are yet to be seen, and of which I have made the Designs; that everyone may know in what form, and with what orna-ments Churches ought to be built. And tho' of some of these Temples but very little is to be seen above ground, yet from this little, consider'd together with the foundations that could otherwise be seen, I have made by Con-jecture what they must have been, when they were entire. (IV, ii, 42)

The prescriptive *ought to be built* and the confident statement *must have been* are striking. There are several examples in Palladio where it is clear that the work is carefully and systematically done. Like Serlio, he was sure that he could display the whole of the temple of Peace from the fragments that remained (IV, vi, 54–5); and, as for the temple of Neptune, although nothing of the structure had been left standing, the remains were so numerous that 'it was possible to come to the knowledge of the whole' (IV, xiv, 88–9), and the reconstructed plan and building are engraved in the text (Figure 58). Such reconstructions, Palladio believed, could serve as models and as norms for future experimentation. The models offered new sources of knowledge of technique and of proportion, enabling further understanding of classical forms and of the criteria which governed them, and a fuller appreciation of Roman virtue and greatness, and they stimulated artists to draw from them 'manifold and noble Inventions' of their own (Figure 59).

The artist's own imagination was already engaged in the shift from fragments to the composition of whole buildings; its freedom was increased when it was a question of ornamentation. Palladio, judging from the beautiful vestiges that remained of the temple of Mars the Avenger that it 'must have been much more wonderful *in toto*', used that hypothesis as justification for inventing ornaments and tabernacles to adorn his drawing of the temple, since its beauty implied that there must have been such decoration. Deploying similar arguments, he added statues to the temple of Antoninus and Faustina, porticoes to the temple of Jupiter, and for the temple of the Sun and Moon, 'I have made the Fore-galleries, and the Ornaments of the inside, according as I fancy ("come me sono imaginato") they ought to have been'.[125] The word *fancy* 'imaginato' here does not imply a whim but is synonymous with *imagine*, another word for *conjecture*.[126] It will be seen that *conjecture* has lost its tentative associations – the conjuring up of possible whole forms from surviving vestiges – but has acquired the affirmative tones of Palladio's own judgement of what *ought*, or even *must* properly be drawn in a particular context.

In Palladio's work, the reader is mostly shown the finished conception, complete and perfected. The ruins which generated them are absent from the text. In other reconstructions, however, ruins continued to be shown alongside their reconstituted form, offering a double vision of Rome. A systematic coupling of ruins and reconstructions occurs in a manuscript dating from about 1574 and thought to be the work of Etienne du Pérac (1525–1604).[127] This Parisian lived in Rome from about 1559 to 1578 when he returned to France. He engraved for the Lafréry workshop, and was clearly preparing himself for renown greater than he was ever to enjoy. He was helped by Orsini,[128] worked on the engravings for Panvinius' projected volumes on the antiquities of Rome,[129] and was a friend of Ligorio, who lent him his manuscripts.[130] In addition to his work for Lafréry, he published a plan of ancient Rome (copied from Ligorio and dedicated to Charles IX in 1574), the *Vestigi dell'antiquità di Roma* (Rome, 1575),[131] and a plan of modern Rome in 1577.[132]

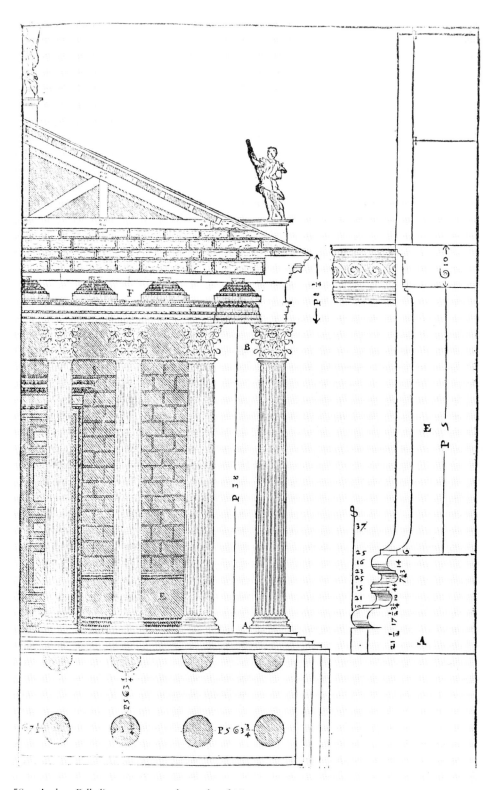

58.   Andrea Palladio: reconstructed temple of Neptune

59. Andrea Palladio: reconstruction of decorative elements from the temple of Neptune

A manuscript of drawings from antique marble reliefs and fragments relating to Roman religious customs is preserved in Paris, and it shows Du Pérac's admiration for the Romans. In the opening lines of his text, he draws attention to 'la Majesté, la grandeur, la vieillesse et l'authorité des exemples qui se voyent sculptez et gravez aux marbres Antiques' (the majesty, grandeur, age and authority of the examples which can be seen sculpted and engraved on ancient marble reliefs); so impressive is their quality that, beside them, Du Pérac declares, 'nous ne soyons que leur ombre' (we are their mere shadows).[133] Other manuscript drawings which testify to the thoroughness of Du Pérac's preparatory work are now in the Louvre. There are three stout volumes, of which the second is devoted to Egyptian images and hieroglyphs copied from marble remains, and the third 'contenant plusieurs Temples, faux Dieux, Autels, Sacrifices, Inscriptions, Epitaphes et ceremonies observees en la religion des anciens Romains, retirez des marbres antiques qui sont à Rome et autres lieux d'Italie, par Estienne Du Pérac, 1575' (containing several temples, false gods, altars, scenes of sacrifice, inscriptions, epitaphs and religious ceremonies of the ancient Romans, taken from ancient marble reliefs that can be found in Rome and in other places in Italy, by Estienne Du Pérac).[134] In many ways, the Louvre drawings can be seen as an advance on the other Paris manuscript: in that, while the subject matter is similar, the scope is more comprehensive. The topics announced in the title are all covered, but the ordering is somewhat heterogeneous, suggesting that Du Pérac was not yet ready to publish. On the one hand, the work resembles a sketchbook since the drawings are copies rather than inventions, and precise locations are given;[135] on the other, the thematic arrangement implies a volume being prepared for an audience. The quality of drawing is sometimes exceptionally fine as when Du Pérac depicts Mercury with a cornucopia balancing on the world (Figure 60), or in his four different versions of the goddess Diana.[136]

The manuscript which is of particular interest here, and which presents a double vision of Rome, was clearly destined for a rich patron: the frontispiece is carefully constructed and shows putti holding up the symbols of Rome at the centre, flanked by the pope and Moses on either side within an elaborate frame. The sequence of drawings is designed to follow the itinerary that had become standard for visitors to Rome.[137] The double image invites the eye to move backwards and forwards from the fragments to the perfected view, from a wilderness inhabited by cattle and caravans to a perspective drawn in neat, confident lines. The conjectural skill of the artist is openly displayed. Trajan's column, for example, is first shown set upon uneven ground, with more recent, modest buildings behind; although the column itself is fairly intact, its base is flawed and buried in excavations. The second image presents the column with surroundings reconstructed, the base reworked and the ground levelled. Similarly, the Forum on a double-page spread is given in true perspective (Figure 61), while a second view depicts a scatter of ruins lying about among the heaps and mounds of earth (Figure 62). The scenes are contained within

60. Etienne du Pérac:
'Mercury'

the same elegant oval frames; both are drawn with the same care: the ruins –
'ombres d'aujourd'hui' (as Du Pérac called them) – finely sketched, the reconstructions boldly drawn, as though they had emerged *toutes faites* from Du
Pérac's pen.

Yet Du Pérac had, even in this manuscript, expressed considerable hesitations
about his ability to interpret ruins accurately. In his *Disegni* he refrained from
a description of the Palatine hill and of the dwellings of emperors which were
once there and of which a few ruins remain that 'still make those who see
them marvel . . . because to attempt to speak of it [the hill] completely would
in any case be impossible'.[138] The second book of the Bibliothèque Nationale
manuscript, devoted to illustrations of temples, gods and scenes related to sacrifice, begins with worries about the difficulties of copying material remains,
and Du Pérac begs the reader to excuse him 'considérant la difficulté qui y
peut estre à cause des Ruynes qui ont levé la congnoissance du temps' (considering the difficulty that can be here in that the ruins have taken away all
knowledge of the time).[139] Despite his fears and excuses, it is amusing to note

171

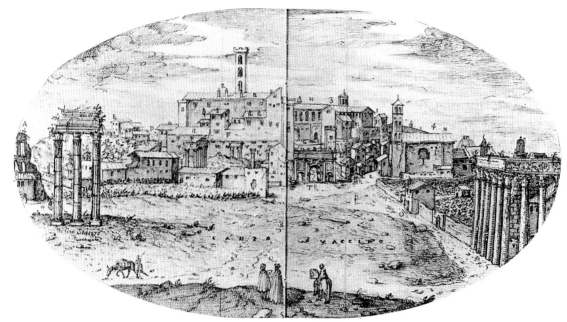

61. Attributed to Etienne du Pérac: drawing of the ruined Forum

62. Attributed to Etienne du Pérac: drawing of the Forum reconstructed

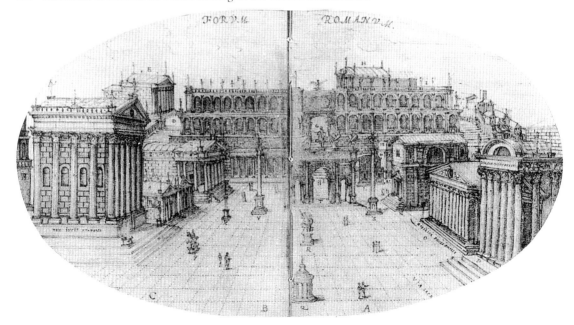

that, in following up his written account of Roman temples, he proposes to 'representer par figures ceux de qui nous avons recognus quelques vestiges' (represent in images those of which we have recognized some traces) (f. 35v), and these images all show the temples complete and perfect in form! While the artist has reservations, he assumes that the viewer wishes to see whole buildings.

An exemplification of this attitude in action may be seen today in central London. In the model room of the house of the eminent English architect Sir John Soane, which he bequeathed to the nation in 1833, the entire organizational strategy of the museum, dedicated to antiquities, is displayed. Like Etienne du Pérac, their founder recognized the value of preserving fragments and appreciated the power of reconstruction. In this room fragments are set out, separated from each other so that they might independently evoke the actual whole buildings whence they came; while, alongside, there are scaled-down, scientifically measured models of real buildings representing in miniature an idealized view of antiquity.[140] The visitor is thus encouraged to allow his gaze to drift from one to the other and to reflect on the processes which led from the fragment to the whole. Similar ways of proceeding had been used by Philibert de L'Orme as he constructed the models of the new palaces he was commissioned to build such as Saint Maur des Fossés, or of the modifications he undertook to existing establishments.

ANCIENT MODELS RECREATED: THE COUNTRY RETREAT

Fontainebleau, 'rebasty à neuf par le grand Roy François Ier' (rebuilt anew by the great king François I),[141] was the earliest royal palace to be shaped in part by influences from Rome. From the time when Primaticcio sent back from Italy moulds of the most important statues there and when Serlio settled in France (1540), Fontainebleau began to be seen as a new Rome. It was so called by Petrasanta, and Du Choul described it as 'l'asile de toutes les antiquités' (the refuge of all antiquities), a view confirmed by Du Cerceau in 1567 and by Thevet in 1575.[142] The most detailed accounts of the absorption of the Roman statues into the Fontainebleau landscape came from Serlio himself, who described the modifications to the gallery intended to house them, and from Arnold van Buchel, who visited the palace in 1585. In the gardens, the latter traveller saw Diana the Huntress, Laocoön, the Tiber and the Wolf suckling Romulus and Remus, Cleopatra, and many other statues he was unable to identify. There were busts of gods and princes – Charles IX, Apollo, Venus, Mercury, Hercules and Commodus – and he noted the treasures acquired by Henri II and the transformations this king had made to the palace. He admired the great Gallery, the sumptuous apartments, and the Chapel decorated by Italian artists (Sebastiano del Piombo and Giovanni di Bologna); and he evoked the villas built around the palace by members of the court.[143]

It seems clear that, for many observers at this period, the sight of abundant antiquities, and especially statues, sufficed for a place to be christened Rome or Roman. And yet, at the same time, Philibert de L'Orme saw in Fontainebleau an example of French genius, claiming the palace as one of the 'beaux traicts en France' (fine features in France) (*Premier tome*, f. 124 v). It was, however, in the new country retreats which French princes began to build, on the model of villas and palaces found in Rome and its surroundings, that the influence was most marked and where those visions were shaped to accommodate French taste, and to reconcile the apparent paradox of Fontainebleau as at once a new Rome and an example of French inventiveness.

In order to understand the forms and functions attributed to the country retreat, where the intellectual and aesthetic advantages of *otium* (leisure) could combine with evidence of connoisseurship, it is necessary to go back to Hadrian's villa begun in AD 118. From Cicero's letters and from those of Pliny, Renaissance readers knew about the construction and content of classical villas; but of the buildings themselves nothing remained. In contrast, Hadrian's villa had been known since the mid-fifteenth century, and although Pius II and Biondo,[144] Raphael and Bramante had visited the site, our knowledge of the palace derives principally from Pirro Ligorio's manuscript account.[145] Ligorio began digging there in 1551 and many of his findings, especially sculptures, were transported either to Cardinal Farnese in Rome or to the cardinal of Ferrara in Tivoli.[146] The architect was overwhelmed by what he found, and his description starts with an assertion that the villa was so sumptuous and so incomparable that it deserved to be classed among the seven wonders of the world (*Descrittione*, f. 11). The site was enormous (about 300 acres), and within its confines Ligorio found some sixty buildings: academies, baths, theatres, libraries arranged according to their subject, halls, porticoes, hippodromes and temples. Their conglomeration was so great that it is astonishing that Ligorio was able to write so confidently about the detail of the structures and their decoration. According to his account, all the buildings were peopled with statues and adorned with images of the gods wrought in marble of different colours, with columns of diverse form and mosaic pavements. Occasionally, he did admit failure. Some buildings were so ruinous that he could only guess at their ornamentation, although – even here – Ligorio improvised virtuoso possibilities: as, for instance, with the vestibule of the Teatro inferno which 'dovevano esse finte' (must have been finished) with pictures, stucco and sculpture retelling the story of Orpheus and Eurydice and of the rape of Proserpina, both of which evoked lively scenes of Hell.

What has been conjured up is a vast space filled with a multiplicity of buildings, diverse in their form and function, remarkable for the scale of their structure, and impressive in their decoration. Hadrian had incorporated many styles into the building; for, alongside references to traditional and Roman contemporary style, he inserted copies of famous works and buildings inspired by Greece and Egypt.[147] The villa was an imperial residence and court as well as a retreat dedicated to repose, to philosophical enquiry and debate, and to artistic endeavour; and its excavation in the mid-sixteenth century provided a special impetus and source of inspiration for the design of Renaissance villas.[148] It reinforced the notion of a multi-purpose dwelling and, above all, it provided rich resources for decoration and design. The very first example to be published was a detail taken from an architrave included in *Le Premier tome de l'architecture* (1567, f. 213) by Philibert de L'Orme who had visited the site and had copied many decorative motifs (see Figure 45, p. 139).[149]

It is not surprising that, when Ligorio came to design Ippolito d'Este's residence at Tivoli, he imported many ideas from the discoveries he had made from Hadrian's villa. Tivoli was famous in the second half of the six-teenth century and served as an important source of inspiration. It attracted visitors from all over Europe, and travel journals testify to the great interest of Frenchmen in the palace and gardens of the cardinal of Ferrara. The palace, which was constructed a few kilometres distant from Hadrian's villa, came into being in that particular place because the pope had refused permission for Ippolito d'Este to build a mansion in Rome. The cardinal had planned it to be close to the Vatican, and intended it to compete with the papal residence in the vastness of its conception and in its aggressive design. According to Nicolas Audebert, Pius V considered the project 'trop superbe, voire dangereux' (too proud, even dangerous). To this rebuff, the cardinal immediately retaliated with his ambitious developments at Tivoli, retorting (as reported by Audebert) 'puis qu'il ne luy estoit permis avoir un chasteau en Rome, qu'il vouloit avoir Rome en son chasteau!' (since he was not permitted to build a palace in Rome, he would have Rome in his palace).[150] Thus he had Ligorio design a palace and gardens which, in size, magnificence and ingenuity, outdid the splendid edifices of rival princes. The rooms were decorated lavishly and filled with sculptures and other precious works of art;[151] while the gardens were even more elaborate than those at Pratolini and astonished all who walked within them by their fantastic water works. Moreover, in a prominent position on the terrace was the fountain of Rome, theatrical in design, and reproducing in miniature all the major buildings of Rome (Figure 63). A large statue, the personification of Rome herself (made by Pierre de la Motte to Ligorio's design), was erected at the centre of the structure, all the elements of which can be recognized from Ligorio's map.

The model of Rome aroused much comment; Du Pérac engraved several versions of it and Audebert left a scrupulous account of every detail he observed. He wrote of:

une *Platteforme* sur laquelle est bastye une petite ville toute de massonerie, qui est *la ville de Rome* non plus hault eslevee de quattre ou cinq pieds, et en icelle se recongnoissent tous les principaux lieux fort bien representez et reduicts en petits comme les sept montz, et le Vatican, les eglises St. Pierre, St Jean de Latran et aultres, l'obelisque de Jule Cesar, le Colisee, la Rotonde,

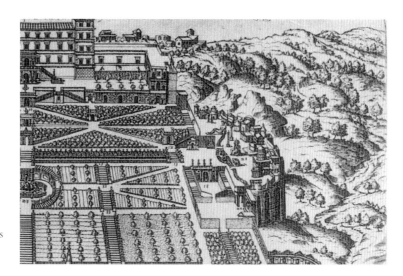

63. Etienne du Pérac: detail from engraving of the gardens and the fountain of Rome at Tivoli

les colomnes d'Antonin, et de Trajan, le Chasteau St. Ange, les principales places, et ce qui y est de plus remarquable.

[a *platform* on which was built a small town, all in stone; it was *the city of Rome*, not more than four or five feet high and in which one could recognize all the principal buildings, excellently represented in miniature such as the seven hills, the Vatican, the churches of St Peter and St John of Lateran and others, Julius Caesar's obelisk, the Colosseum, the Pantheon, the columns of Antoninus and of Trajan, St Michael's castle, all the main places, and anything that is considered remarkable.][152]

The fountain of Rome seems to have been intact in 1660 when Monconys went to Tivoli and described it as 'une representation de relief de l'ancienne Rome' (a representation in relief of the ancient city of Rome); but it was eventually destroyed in the nineteenth century when part of its retaining wall collapsed.[153]

From this model, visitors were reminded of what they had seen in Rome and, thinking further about the functions of the place, they could reflect on life there and the beauty of the situation. They could recall their appreciation of antiquities and modern works of art, their amazement at the skill in hydraulics, and their enjoyment of books and debate. Learned men stayed with the cardinal at Tivoli. Lipsius visited him there, and every summer Marc-Antoine Muret came and engaged the cardinal in scholarly discussion, talking well into the night about Ippolito d'Este's favourite books – the *Odes* of Horace, and the *Lives* of Plutarch.[154] News of the marvels created at Tivoli were sent back to France by Muret in his letters; brought home by travellers like Audebert and Montaigne; and even came first hand from the cardinal himself who, as papal legate, was at the French court from 1560 to 1563.

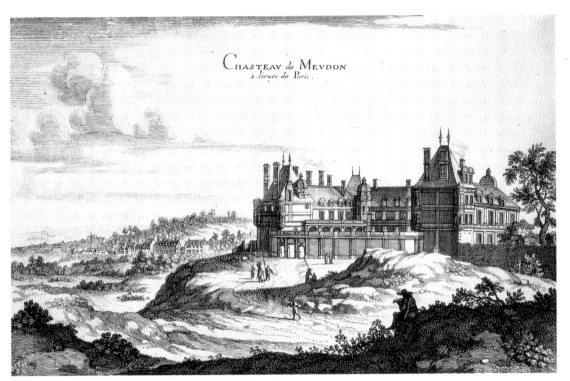

64. Israel Sylvestre: engraving of the château of Meudon

In parallel with these developments, French princes began to conceive their own country retreats in order to display their collections of antiquities and to indulge in literary and intellectual pursuits appropriate to their status. How far the evidence of poets, artists and scholars was just so much wishful thinking and how far wealthy French patrons did in fact desire to imitate classical models, shaping their lifestyle and their dwellings by them, must remain an open question; but their expenditure on libraries and art treasures provides suggestive evidence of their priorities.

Apart from the royal palaces which François I, Henri II and Catherine de' Medici had modified or built from scratch, the country retreat which aroused most attention among contemporaries (if we are to judge from the abundance of comment that survives) was Meudon (Figure 64).[155] The mansion and its Grotto were designed for Cardinal Charles de Lorraine, who had had ample opportunity to admire such dwellings in his journeys to Italy and who was (according to Symeoni) 'grandissime amateur de toutes choses antiques' (great connoisseur of all ancient things).[156] Symeoni's praise of Meudon was unconstrained. He wrote in his *Illustres observations* of how the impact of the buildings and antiquities at Meudon was such that the only words that would issue forth were VIVE ROMA RESURGENS.[157] 'Rome reborn' and the abundance of statues were the impressions vaunted in the writings of others: André Thevet extolled the antiquities in marble and in bronze;[158] Colletet stressed how the

177

Grotto was designed 'à l'imitation des anciens Romains, qui souloient bastir ainsi leurs edifices' (in imitation of the ancient Romans who used to erect their buildings like this) – sentiments that were repeated by Jean Rabel in 1588, and echoed by Estienne Cholet in 1614.[159]

Charles de Lorraine bought Meudon from the duchesse d'Estampes on 19 December 1552, and immediately set about transforming the place; indeed, only a few days later the sculptor Ledoux was at work inscribing the cardinal's arms and devices on the walls. In the following years, Charles showed an obsessive interest in his new purchase, buying antiquities in such large quantities that the papal nuncio – Lenzi – complained that he would not attend to urgent business and he could not see the cardinal who had gone to see 'il suo bel luogo di Medun' (his beautiful place, Meudon).[160]

The most remarkable creation at Meudon was the Grotto begun in 1552 in the grounds of the château. Although it was not the first such grotto to be created in France (Cardinal du Bellay had had one constructed in the early 1540s at Saint Maur, and D'Urfé had built one in 1548 to house the collection of marble statues he had brought back from Italy), it was clearly seen to be something out of the ordinary.[161] We have a good idea of it both from contemporary descriptions of its brilliant interior and precious contents, and from the seventeenth-century engravings by Israel Sylvestre and Jean Marot. These show an ambitious structure on three floors, and a central pavilion rising up with two further storeys. Below ground was a crypt with statues placed in each niche; a gallery ran the length of the building; and a central salon was placed on the level of two halls situated in each wing.

A bevy of famous artists were employed in its creation: Primaticcio and Niccolò dell'Abate together with Ponce Jacquiot worked on the murals, the stucco reliefs and marble panelling; and Domenico del Barbieri (Dominique Florentin) decorated the vault with *stucco groteschi*, perhaps inspired by the recent discovery of Nero's Golden House. It is not easy to visualize the startling effects of lacquer, mosaic and porphyry combined in diverse colours, and of walls painted with swirling arabesques, their panels filled with shells, crustations and bright coral.[162] The entrance to the Grotto was guarded by Pallas, Bacchus and the figure of Autumn made by a certain Jacques d'Angoulême when he was in Rome and thought by Michelangelo to be the finest statue he had seen.[163] The central pavilion was supported by statues of immense size depicting the Virtues. Inside was part of the cardinal's collection: a series of busts of Roman emperors and – as a tribute to his learning and eloquence – the heads of Aristotle, Demosthenes and Cicero. Van Buchel's account gives many further details. The Grotto, he tells us, also housed sculpture brought from Rome representing pagan legends and gods – Europa lying full length; Diana with her hounds; a marble statue of Venus and Cupid; and two others of the same goddess carrying shells to denote her birth – while in the palace itself were many portraits of emperors and monarchs. There was also a series of historical pictures showing the coronation of Henri II, the *colloque de Poissy*, the marriage of François II and Mary Queen of Scots, and the Council of Trent, all recalling those occasions at which Charles de Lorraine had played a dominant role. Other rooms held further treasures from Roman antiquity, with more busts of emperors and monarchs, and marble statues representing Bacchus, Mercury, Minerva, Perseus and Cleopatra.[164]

Considering why the cardinal de Lorraine had lavished such care on his Grotto, Symeoni drew attention to the obvious parallel with Hadrian's villa at Tivoli, and to Charles' determination to transport into France and to shape anew the notable antiquities which had belonged to Rome:

> Le magnanime Empereur Hadrien, apres sa longue peregrination feit en sa maison de plaisance au païs de Tivoli peindre et representer au naturel toutes les provinces, et plus nobles citez qu'il avoit veües, aussi comme vous (Monseigneur) avez entreprins de renouveller en vostre royal chasteau de Medon toutes ou la plus grande partie des anciennes singularitez de la Cité de Romme.

> [The magnanimous Emperor Hadrian, returning from his long journey to his country retreat near Tivoli, had represented and painted there all the provinces, the most noble cities he had seen, just as you (my lord), in your royal palace at Meudon, have undertaken to renew all – or rather the greatest part – of the remarkable antiquities from the city of Rome.][165]

When one asks what precisely did mid-sixteenth-century French observers mean when they referred to this 'renewal', the answer seems principally to have been: simply the purchase and display of sculptures brought from Rome or made from the moulds of ancient statues.

François de Belleforest, however, in his description suggests something more:

> Vous avez encor de ce mesme costé Meudon, plus cogneu et recommandé des singularitez, que d'antiquité qu'on vous en sçache dire . . . Cardinal de Lorraine . . . est aussi amoureux de tout ce qui est de rare, exquis, singulier, et gentil en la nature et imitation d'icelles: ce qu'il fait voir en cette Grottesque artificielle, et à demy naturelle de Meudon, où il n'y a sorte d'antiquailles soit en colonnes, Architraves, soubassemens, Cornices, statues, Medailles et autres singularitez, ou en superbe et industrie de l'architecture (bien que ce soit une rustique) qui ne soit pratiquée en ce lieu, où ce grand Cardinal a comme renouvellé la gentillesse Romaine, et la curiosité ancienne des hommes de plus grand, et gentil entendement, comme aussi il est non imitable que par soy-mesme.

> [In this region, you also have Meudon, well-known and appreciated for its marvels, as much as for its acknowledged antiquity . . . Charles de Lorraine . . . is also a lover of everything that is rare, exquisite, unusual, and noble as fashioned in the nature of these antiquities which he has displayed in that

Grotto at Meudon, made by art and yet half natural and where there is every kind of ancient thing: columns, architraves, bases of pillars, cornices, statues, medals and other marvels; that Grotto, although rustic in style, is superbly and carefully constructed, the like of which does not exist elsewhere; through this edifice, the cardinal has (it seems) renewed that Roman nobility and that ancient curiosity of men of greater and more polished understanding, and he is inimitable (except by himself).][166]

In this long, convoluted sentence, the initial message is familiar enough – Meudon houses antique treasures acquired or imitated by a refined and learned connoisseur. The reference to 'cette Grottesque artificielle, et à demy naturelle' raises new considerations as does his phrase 'a comme renouvellé la gentillesse Romaine et la curiosité ancienne'. Belleforest implies that the use of artifice to simulate the natural produces a double effect where the blending of skill and nature remains obvious and where a new style (French) recalls Rome, assumes knowledge of ancient models, yet has become more polished – 'plus gentille'.

Ronsard immediately recognized the substitution when, in the *Chant pastoral* on the marriage of the duc de Lorraine to Claude de France, he depicted the Grotto as

> . . . un si beau bastiment:
> Le plan, le frontispice, et les piliers rustiques,
> Qui effacent l'honneur des colonnes antiques.

[such a beautiful building: the plan, the frontispiece, the rustic pillars which efface the honour of ancient columns.][167]

The blend and the counterfeit were what Michel Bouterone found most remarkable when he paid a visit to Meudon in 1609:

> Grotte de marbre et de porphire
> Où l'artifice a contrefaict
> Un rocher que nature admire
> Et croist qu'elle mesme l'a faict.

[Marble and prophyry Grotto whose artifice has simulated a rock, admired by nature who thinks it is her own creation].[168]

The reshaping process did not ignore the needs of letters. When, for instance, Cardinal du Bellay had dedicated his château Saint Maur des Fossés to François I, he caused to be inscribed directly below a bust portrait of the king – on a plaque above the main entrance – a verse conferring this place on the monarch, on Diana and on the three Graces. These guardians of the hunt and of virtue were also figured in relief, with the nine Muses above the architrave making the point that king and nymphs were mutually supportive and dependent (see

Figure 22, p. 60).[169] In like manner, at Meudon, Charles de Lorraine named Henri II,

Quieti et musis Henrici II Galline[170]

marking the spot as both a prince's retreat and the home of the Muses. Ronsard saw the Grotto as divine and sacred, belonging to the monarch, 'dieu-donné' and as the 'demeure éternelle' of the Muses, guarded by the twin gods of poetic and prophetic inspiration – Pallas and Bacchus. Whoever approaches this sacred haven will be moved to create and to foretell:

> . . . se voirront l'ame pleine
> De saincte Poësie . . .
> Phébus leur apprendra les choses à venir.

[will have their soul filled with sacred Poetry . . . Apollo will teach them about the things to come].[171]

This unusual grotto was demolished by the Grand Dauphin in 1706; but in the sixteenth century its fame had encouraged others to compete.

Sometimes the modifications to existing buildings were not very extensive. François de Tournon had (as we have seen) transformed a tower room to accommodate his collection of statues and sculptures imported from Rome, and François d'Andelot used his hall at Tanlay for a similar purpose, and had the ceiling painted with members of the French court depicted as gods and goddesses. Antoine du Prat, *prévôt de Paris*, required a little more from Symeoni who had accompanied him to Rome in 1547. In 1560, Du Prat asked his erstwhile scholar/companion to install at his seat at Vanves a library sufficient for his needs when he wished to stay in the country, and to fill the courtyard with antique statues and images. Symeoni, in a manuscript autobiography, left a list of the *termini* (herms) and columns he had devised, and of those antiquities which he had ordered for Vanves. These were busts of Caesar and Petrarch; a version of Laocoön; a bronze of Apollo; Daphne painted in relief; busts of Augustus and Marcus Aurelius; a distant imitation of Pasquino and other ancient heads. There seems to be no particular pattern except that, in his comments, Symeoni (somewhat incredibly) refers to the Belvedere court.[172] With such heterogeneity, it is hardly surprising that both men were dissatisfied: Symeoni because he was neither paid nor thanked, Du Prat because the transformations seem to have fallen far short of his expectations. This episode at Vanves does, nevertheless, offer insights into the rush to have customized versions of elements of Rome in France in the 1550s and 1560s.

'L'HISTOIRE DE LA REINE ARTHEMISE'

A project which, over the years, has been much studied and which belongs to the same sphere of influence which was responsible for Meudon, is the

'Histoire de la reine Arthemise' of Nicolas Houël. The four books dedicated to Catherine de' Medici (and which are preserved in a sumptuous manuscript)[173] were never published, and the drawings which Houël commissioned to accompany his text from Antoine Caron and others were never made up into wall decorations in the queen's lifetime.[174] Houël was an antiquary and remained close to his sources. His manuscript demonstrates what a re-enactment of earlier Roman customs (funerals, sacrifices, triumphs) would have been without artistic interference, and the drawings show how faithful in overall conception and in detail Caron was to the engraved sources which had, in turn, inspired him.[175]

Apparently, Houël composed his history at the request of Catherine de' Medici, although no document confirms the command. His purpose was to please the queen and to provide material for artists, as he stated:

Pour ces occasions (Madame) estant adverty par plusieurs hommes doctes, que la lecture des histoires vous apportoit un singulier plaisir, et speciale-ment quant elles estoyent mises en bonne peinture, sculpture, broderie, ou tapisseries je me suis esvertue en toute diligence. (f. 8)

[For these occasions (Madam), having been alerted by several learned men that reading history gave you extraordinary pleasure, and especially when it is represented in fine paintings, sculpture, embroidery or tapestry, I have laboured diligently.]

Houël had in mind the Tuileries which were then under construction.[176] He was also concerned to draw attention to the parallels between the history he was writing and his own times, 'à propos pour le temps' (appropriate for the times) as he says, and between the life of Queen Arthemise and that of Catherine herself.[177] Both queens were respected for their prudence in the conduct of public affairs; both had to deal with insurrection and war; both had lost martial husbands; both sought to consecrate their memory with appropriate and lasting memorials; and both, of course, supported writers and artists.

Houël's writing and powers of organizing his narrative are very uneven.[178] The story of Arthemise is frequently interrupted by long and learned digressions: on the origin of statues, for instance (f. 22), on games in the ancient world (f. 26), or again on Roman funeral monuments, pyramids and epitaphs (Book 2, chs 5, 6 and 8). At other times, his account diverges into considera-tion of contemporary affairs: strong denunciation of civil war 'qui se faict de citoyen contre citoyen, le subjet contre son prince, de frere contre frere, cousin contre cousin' (which is waged between citizen and citizen, a subject against his prince, brother against brother, cousin against cousin) (f. 86v); the Assemb-lée des Etats held in 1560 (f. 37); or on the education of princes, where he leans heavily on Ronsard's *Institution pour l'adolescence du roy* (ff. 87v–94).

The digressions, especially those related to the ancient world, reinforce the

65.   Antoine Caron: drawing of procession of soldiers carrying trophies

Roman spirit that pervades both the text and the drawings.[179] Hoüel lost no opportunity to expatiate on Roman funeral customs and on the arrangements for the disposal of King Mausolus. He describes the effigy, the tabernacle, its paintings and the hall in which the elaborate ceremonies took place; the processions of soldiers and others carrying trophies of the king's victories (Figure 65); and the chariots, pyramid, obelisks, sacred songs and sacrifices. All the paraphernalia, which hardly differentiated funeral from triumph, were there – even to a competition for the best funeral oration and the frequent, obligatory references to the experts, Vitruvius and Alberti. A glance at the drawings reveals how close was their conception to designs for sixteenth-century triumphs and princely entries: classical arches, figures in Roman military attire, vases filled with perfumes, chariots piled with spoils, and images of towns and countries conquered.[180]

From this plethora of allusions to Rome, it is worth selecting a few dominant motifs. The first depicts a scene from the beginning of Book 2 and shows the queen seated in front of an extravagant arch that fills almost all the space. She is receiving homage from her people, and through the centre of the arch, which is supported on Corinthian columns and decorated with an elaborate

66.   Antoine Caron: drawing of *L'Equitation* for 'Histoire de la Reine Arthemise'

frieze, can be seen a round temple recalling once again the Tempietto. A similar circular building is used for the design of Mausolus' monument within which a recumbent figure of the king, wrought in marble, is displayed.[181] Perhaps the most striking double reference to Rome occurs in the drawing made to illustrate *L'Equitation*, where the young King Lygdamis (Charles IX) has lessons in riding (Figure 66). In the foreground, the queen observes the instructor and the king in action; beside them stands the imperious figure of Hercules; while – in the centre of the picture – the Colosseum is represented, broken open to reveal spectators watching a sword fight. Hercules and the Colosseum are shown virtually as they were in Caron's painting *Massacre du triumvirat* (1566), and are clearly borrowed from Lafréry's *Speculum*. The different levels within the drawing – in the foreground, the young king; in the background, a Roman combat; and in the text at the base, contemporary reference to Catherine and her son Charles IX – demonstrate how easily the author's mind moved across all three. It is also noteworthy that, in this multiple comparison, the bloody spectacle familiar to the Colosseum in Roman times has given way to the noble exercise of the sword.

At the end of Arthemise's story, Hoüel evoked the country retreat she built in order to live 'en grand repos et tranquillité d'esprit' (in great repose and

184

calmness of mind). Rather than the reshaping which had characterized the residences actually built in France at this time, Arthemise's abode is closely modelled on classical sources, chiefly Pliny the Younger from whom Hoüel took all the elements he describes.[182] Planned on a vast scale, the house was 1,000 feet long and 200 feet wide and was surrounded by a semicircular colonnade designed for walks. There was a temple dedicated to Jupiter, gardens with marble fountains, and galleries supported by columns of diverse orders. The interior was embellished with further galleries, halls, cabinets and a library, with rooms set aside for painters, sculptors, embroiderers and tapestry makers. In order to press further the opportunities offered to Catherine, Hoüel envisaged for Queen Arthemise decorations of the same type which he had commissioned for his own project from Caron, dell'Abate and Lerambert. Thus the walls of this country mansion were crowded with scenes depicting battles and the triumphs of her ancestors, while her own apartments were lined with the portraits of gods and princes of renown from antiquity. She also had a pavilion constructed where many precious vases were displayed alongside memories of Mausolus, his life-size portrait, and images of the gods to whom she offered sacrifice. In this retreat, Queen Arthemise passed her days in conversation with learned personages – to whom she allocated pensions – and in pursuit of agriculture. Arguments supporting such activities as appropriate for princes are taken from a wide range of authors: from Horace, for example, and from Budé, Boistuau, Cardan and Estienne, although the most frequently cited are verses from Ronsard and Du Bellay who had exhorted Henri II to practise the art of agriculture as 'nos bons pères Rommains' (our good Roman fathers) had done.

No doubt the intensification of civil strife after 1560 prevented Catherine from responding to Hoüel's project. La Croix du Maine saw the manuscript and the drawings when he visited Hoüel, as they were still in his *cabinet*.[183] According to La Croix du Maine, the history had been composed at the express command of the queen mother, although Hoüel had received no recompense for the large amounts of money he had expended on the project. La Croix du Maine implied that Hoüel had exhausted his resources, an opinion which seems to be corroborated by a letter which Hoüel wrote to Lord Burghley in 1571,[184] inviting him to place (for purchase) before Queen Elizabeth I his large collection, built up over twenty-five years, which included Italian and French drawings and engravings, pictures, medals and precious vases. We do not know what response Lord Burghley made, but clearly Hoüel had given up on Catherine de' Medici.

Biondo, Ligorio, Palladio, Philibert de L'Orme and others had wanted to see building programmes in their own times that matched the quality and the values they attributed to those erected in ancient Rome; and, in order to fulfil their wishes, they blended their deep knowledge of the structures remaining in Rome and other parts of Italy with inspired guesses as to what the originals were actually like. In parallel, the tradition which reshaped and reinvented in drawings and in books was continued by artists like Du Pérac and anti-quaries such as Hoüel. The new building and the sketchbooks, the drawn reconstructions and the historical re-enactments, all testify to the strength of sixteenth-century preoccupations with Rome and its inheritance.

CHAPTER 6

Fragments and Wholes

I   DU BELLAY

DU BELLAY'S APPROPRIATION OF ANCIENT ROME

No one disputes that the sight of Rome which he experienced for the first time in 1553 provided Joachim du Bellay with rich poetic inspiration. His *Antiquitez de Rome, Les Regrets* and *Poematum libri quattuor*[1] provoked an immediate response, and their reverberations continued to be heard by writers in France and in England long after the poet's death in 1560.[2] What continues to be cause for argument and disagreement is the precise nature of Du Bellay's inspiration, especially with respect to *Les Antiquitez*. Did he really believe that his poems could resurrect and keep alive the splendid shapes of ancient Rome, by delving for its fragments and reassembling the ruins that remained? Did his appeal to the shades of Virgil, Horace, Ovid, Propertius and Tibullus, and to so many other Latin poets whom he had read, admired and absorbed, really effect the magical transfer from past to present, from broken pieces to visions of whole monuments?

   Critical opinion is divided. While all modern interpreters have stressed the allusive character of *Les Antiquitez*,[3] it is this very denseness and the concentrated power of the poems that has led to fundamental disagreements as to their meaning. Thomas Greene, in his chapter entitled 'Du Bellay and the disinterment of Rome', saw in *Les Antiquitez* the expression of 'a will to imitate the poets who are buried beneath the shattered landscape of Rome and to learn from the excavations of the archaeologists'.[4] He also argued that, for Du Bellay, the creative act was always a double gesture: 'first penetrating depths to bring up some one or something from them, and secondly restoring it to being and form'. MacPhail supports Greene's hypothesis in seeing reconstruction (*rebastir*) as the refrain that haunts Du Bellay's Roman poems, although he concedes that the vision of rebuilding is underscored with irony and paradox.[5] Emphasis on irony and on the exploration of an elaborate network of textual associations and influences (from classical and neo-Latin poems and contemporary guidebooks) pushed Tucker to reach an opposite position: despite Du Bellay's evident wish to reconstruct Rome, its rebirth has to be viewed negatively, a conclusion which (in Tucker's opinion) is amply borne out by the final sonnet in the series.[6]

It is not my purpose here to attempt to reconcile such contraries, but rather to place Du Bellay's creative theory and practice within the larger frame of artistic reconstruction and shared knowledge of Rome. It will be remembered that Du Bellay ended his *Deffence et illustration de la langue françoise* (1549) with a rousing appeal: 'marchez couraigeusement vers cete superbe cité romaine: et des serves despouilles d'elle . . . ornez vos temples et autelz' (march with courage towards this superb city of Rome, and from its remaining spoils . . . decorate your temples and altars). With such soaring tones ringing in his ears, he arrived in Rome and, like Michel de l'Hospital some years later, 'Depuis ce moment-là, je me suis mis à rouler dans mon esprit de nouvelles pensées' (from that moment, new thoughts began to turn in my mind).[7] Du Bellay's exploitation – for that is the right word – of Roman remains was to be energetic (brutal even), as he likened the process to plunder, stripping bare, and to rapine (*pillage, despouilles*). This violent act of appropriation applied both to texts and to fragments of stone which Du Bellay named in the same terms, 'les sacrées reliques de l'antiquité' (the sacred relics of antiquity) (*Deffence*, p. 97); these texts from the past, like the ruins, still throbbed with life and stimulated his poetic ideas.[8]

The nature of these initial stimuli are well demonstrated in the two Latin elegies which Du Bellay composed in 1553 and early 1555.[9] The first, *Romae descriptio*, was dedicated to Louis de Bailleul who had accompanied Du Bellay on his walks around Rome and whose knowledge of the ancient monuments was unequalled.[10] As the title suggests, the poem is a celebration of the city; the poet is overwhelmed by its physical presence and, above all, by the special atmosphere of the place. The city imposes; it exudes power and imperial domination; and everywhere the past intrudes through its broken walls, still full of menace:

> Moenia quae vastis passim convulsa ruinis
> Antiquas spirant imperiosa minas. (ll. 19–20)

[These walls, vast ruins collapsed in every place, and yet imperial, still breathe their former threats.]

There seems to be no differentiation between the grandeur of the pope's abode, Saint Peter's, the painted halls of palaces, the Belvedere, and the marvels of ancient Rome that are alive, brought forth from the soil as the poet watches:

> Multaque praeterea veteris miracula Romae,
> Undique de fosso nunc rediviva solo. (ll. 38–9)

[and yet other marvels from ancient Rome now emerge all fresh from the soil as it is dug.]

Here, there is richness beyond expression as the poet tries to suggest the living quality of the famous statues of which some are named, others evoked (ll. 75–95). While Du Bellay reflects upon the opportunities for writing which such a scene offers, he remains hesitant about his capacity to do justice to such opulence. His task is further complicated by the ambiguity of the messages sent forth from this city of signs. Giant structures are mutilated; theatres are sad and silent; walls represent an undifferentiated mass as herbs and wild grasses cover their surface and screen their meaning. Not only is it difficult to read significance into this formless heap, but the ruins add a further layer of complexity. They seem to move. Summits of monuments tremble and anticipate their own fall. Yet, it pleases the poet to look upon 'les colonnes rongées' (columns eaten away) and 'les temples ensevelis' (buried temples), and then to name (just as Petrarch had done, using the same technique of evocation introduced by repetitive *hic* and *nunc*) the places which bring to life again past events and people long dead:

> Nunc Martis campum, Thermas, Circumque Forumque,
> Nunc septem Colleis et monumenta virum.
> Hac se victores Capitolia ad alta ferebant,
> Hic gemini fasces, Consulis imperium. (ll. 117–20)

[Now the field of Mars, baths, Circus and Forum, now the seven hills, and all that recalls the memory of heroes. Along here the victorious went on their way to the Capitol. Here were the rods of the two Consuls, symbols of their power.]

This enthusiastic excursus into past glories is brought to an abrupt end. With the realization that *that* Rome is dead, and that the city he contemplates is the tomb of its former grandeur, moral concerns interrupt the poet's vision:

> Ipsaque nunc tumulus mortua Roma sui est. (l. 130)

[The city of Rome, dead herself, is today her own tomb.]

But, asks the poet, is the city only a tomb? And if it is, cannot its splendour be revived for, although the Great Rome is dead, writing lives on?

> Roma ingens periit, vivit Maro doctus ubique,
> Et vivunt Latiae fila canora lyrae.
> Nasonis vivunt, vivunt flammaeque Tibulli,
> Et vivunt numeri, docte Catulle, tui. (ll. 133–6)

[Great Rome is dead: but Virgil, he lives on everywhere; the harmonious chords of the Latin lyre still live on; the passion of Ovid is living and that of Tibullus; learned Catullus, your rhymes – too – live on.]

The presence of these poets whose souls inhabit the subterranean regions on which Du Bellay stands, and the living quality of their verse is underlined by the insistent *vivunt* of the lines. The interrelationship of past poetic rhythms and present creative processes is so close that they are nearly coextensive, so that the genius of the place can easily effect their fusion. From these benevolent forces – the city of Rome and the noble writers whose presence permeates the atmosphere and to whom the poet now appeals as *cendres*, *poètes sacrés* and *prophètes* of *La Rome glorieuse* – Du Bellay will invent a new form of poetry which, he claims in a final flourish, may survive.

> Hactenus et nostris incognita carmina Musis
> Dicere, et insolito plectra movere sono . . .
> Forte etiam vivent nostri monumenta laboris. (ll. 141–2, 145)

[Let me sing verses hitherto unknown to our Muses, let me play new sounds on the bow . . . perhaps, even, the monuments that emerge from our labour will survive.]

The kind of new poetic enterprise which Du Bellay had in mind can be seen in the second Elegy which he wrote to welcome Jean d'Avanson to Rome in March 1555 when he came as Henri II's ambassador to the papal court.[11] Recalling the huge sculptures of the Nile and the Tiber that reclined at their ease in the Campidoglio, Du Bellay gave his words of salutation to the great Roman river, depicted here as an authoritative god, surrounded by the busy, dancing nymphs that customarily decorated fountains (ll. 1–50). The scene which the river god invites D'Avanson to contemplate (with a succession of *aspice*) is one of immediate contradictions. The visitor is furnished with a double vision. Before him was *Rome, the Great* (Maxima Roma fuit, l. 62), which now lies abandoned, a wilderness bristling with bushes whose luxuriant growth renders the old shapes unrecognizable. Yet, in contrast, there is the Capitol, enduring for ever, and proud temples on lofty columns which prove

> Aspice templa Deum sublimibus alta columnis,
> Et quam nunc similis Roma sit ipsa sui.
> Aspice quae passim Romana palatia surgant,
> Quaeque sit antiqui frons rediviva loci. (ll. 67–70)

[How much the Rome of today is like unto herself. Look at the Roman palaces that stretch up everywhere, and recognize the brow of this ancient place; it lives again.]

The interrelationship of past and present which Du Bellay had drawn in the earlier poem is here much developed. The new buildings which have risen up echo, in size and ambition, those of former times; and, although they have not obliterated the sight of crumbling structures, they have given back to their decayed presence both status and significance. Past and present have, in this way,

67. Jacques Androuet du Cerceau: engraving of artist drawing the ruins of Rome

been almost conflated, and the river turns attention to future events and encounters that are predicted for this venerable place: a triumph here in the imperial city – for Henri II, no less. Tamer of the lion, victor over the eagle, and architect of peace, the king is shown in triumph 'dressé sur un quadrige' (erect in a chariot) (l. 123), distributing largesse, his *croissant* device now grown full to englobe the world. On this high note of prophecy which sees Rome not only reconstituted in the splendour of its buildings but also renewed through victory and triumph, the poem ends:

> Sic iterum antiquos spectabit Roma triumphos,
> Henrici festos instituetque dies. (ll. 135–6)

[Thus again, Rome will enjoy the spectacle of ancient triumphs, and institute feast days to celebrate Henri.]

However implausible this vision,[12] it is possible to discern Du Bellay's new enterprise. He is using the experience of Rome to extend the creative powers of poetry; he has learned from architects and seeks to follow their methods which had transformed the spectator's view of crumbling stones (Figure 67).

That Du Bellay thought in such comparative terms is evident from his writings on creative theory and from his poems. In a letter to Jean de Morel, written

191

only a few months before he died, Du Bellay suggested the appropriateness of his poetic offering to the dead Henri II in 'Le Tombeau latin et françois', and he couched his thoughts in architectural terms. A Doric tribute, substantial and solid, was fitting to the occasion rather than a more elaborate and decorated Corinthian style:

> Mais il m'a semblé que pour la dignité du subject et pour rendre l'oeuvre de plus grande Maiesté et durée, un ouvraige Dorique, c'est à dire plein et solide, estoit beaucoup mieux séant qu'ung Corynthien de moindre estoffe, mais plus élabouré d'artifice et d'invention d'Architecture.

> [It seemed to me that for the dignity of the theme and to render the work enduring and of greater Majesty, a Doric work – that is to say full and solid – was much more appropriate than a Corinthian one of lesser weight, more inventive and elaborate in architectural design.][13]

Many critics have also pointed out how the vocabulary of the poems invites the reader to gaze upon a spectacle:[14] verbs of perception abound like the injunctions *vois, regarde*, or his own observations (*Je les ay veuz* or *Il fait bon voir*); and he suggests outlines, shapes and gestures to be completed – the colourful, swaggering hangers-on at the papal court, or the rush of the bull at carnival time.

Du Bellay attempted to do more than simply record or paint scenes from the vast theatre of Rome. Draughtsman and builder, in sonnet CXLIX of *Les Regrets* (addressed to Pierre Lescot), he constructs a palace for the Muses, using as its context the transformations Lescot had effected at the Louvre while assuring the architect that he – the poet –

> Avec d'autres compaz, et d'autres instruments (l. 5) . . .
> Aux Muses je bastis d'un nouvel artifice
> Un palais magnifique à quatre appartemens. (ll. 7–8)

> [with a different kind of compass and other instruments I build a magnificent palace dedicated to the Muses, with four rooms and in a new style.]

The language is that of the architect: the four orders are the principal columns of classical architecture; the tools and the techniques are claimed to be novel. The palace is an ideal structure, built in the mind; or rather not yet built, as sonnet CL indicates:

> De ce royal palais, que bastiront mes doigts,
> Si la bonté du Roy me fournit de matière. (ll. 1–2)

> [this royal palace which my fingers will build if a generous king provides the means.]

Creative processes (whether architectural design or poetry) depend for their effectiveness on the encouragement and performance of princes, on the beneficence of the Muses, and on recognition of the vital importance of creative activity itself.[15] Even with all this support, the process was difficult, especially if (continuing the building analogy) the poet/architect sought to incorporate fragments from the superb edifices of the past. Of these, as Du Bellay explained in the *Deffence*, a significant part has been reduced to dust – 'une partie devint poudre' – and the rest is nothing more than a heterogeneous mass: 'et l'autre doit estre en beaucoup de pieces, lesqueles vouloir réduire en un [en une unité] seroit chose impossible' (and the rest is a mass of broken pieces which are impossible to assemble into a coherent whole). Working with 'les sacrées reliques de l'Antiquité' required caution and skill. Old bricks will not make new buildings unless they are renewed, integrated, absorbed and thereby changed. However intrinsically attractive, they may not blend, the pieces may not fit and make a whole. Other strategies, therefore, had to be devised if satisfactory structures were to be made.

In the sixteenth century, it seems to have been generally agreed that fragments had value in themselves, for philologists and archaeologists and also for princes. Jacques de Vintemille in the dedication of his translation of Herodian's *Histories* to the constable of France reminded Anne de Montmorency:

> si nous sommes tant amateurs des ouvrages antiques que nous voulons en tout imiter leurs bastimens, si nous sommes tant curieux de leurs statues et medailles que bien souvent une teste, une main, un fragment ou piece rompue, nous est si precieuse que nous l'honorons à merveilles et mettons en tresor, combien devons nous estimer l'Histoire?

> [If we are such connoisseurs of ancient works that we want to imitate their buildings, if we are so keen on their statues and medals that often a head, a hand, a fragment or a broken piece is so precious to us that we treat it with supreme honour and keep it as a treasure, how much more should we esteem History?][16]

This obvious way of arousing interest in his book implied a common understanding about ancient remains (of whatever kind). Appreciation of fragments and the desire to own them was widespread and the sentiments expressed in a letter to Ippolito de' Medici, about some scraps of Valeriano's manuscripts which had come into Pietro Mellini's hands, may be taken as typical:

> I thought it much better to put this mutilated and disjointed work into your hands than to suppress it, in this matter following our example, and especially your own, since because you are gripped by a remarkable desire for ancient works you are accustomed to admire even a single foot or a hand or a head of some statue, nor do you seek these out with less diligence than you would the whole since even from these you assess the talent, workmanship, and skill of the artist.[17]

The value lies in the way broken or unfinished fragments expose the technical processes which went into their making. In other words they may reveal details of fabrication which often disappear in the finished whole.

Yet the urge to repair flawed objects/texts remained; for although they were regarded as precious they were also mutilated, and in making good those parts that were maimed, authors, like artists, had recourse to conjecture. There are many examples of scholars who responded to this pressure. It is evident, for example, in Henri Estienne's *editio princeps* of the pseudo-Anacreon, and in Lambin's edition of the *Nicomachean Ethics* (1558) where he had announced in the preface, 'I emended many passages partly by relying on the trustworthiness and witness of ancient manuscripts, partly induced by some conjecture'.[18]

RECONSTRUCTIONS: SCALIGER'S SUCCESSFUL CONJECTURES

In considering how far this process of repair and the envisaging of whole structures is relevant to an analysis of Du Bellay's response to the ruins of Rome, it is instructive to digress slightly to examine the work of Joseph Justus Scaliger (1530–1609). In his time, Scaliger was certainly one of the most renowned critics and editors of ancient remains.[19] He was in Rome in 1565 and 1566 (in the suite of the French ambassador, Louis Chasteigner), and there had the opportunity to study the ruins of the city, to deepen his knowledge of antiquities through his talks with Panvinius, Muret and others,[20] and to strengthen his resolve to mend what he called 'textes désespérés' (hopeless texts).[21]

Scaliger's methods of repair and reconstruction began with the drawing of a clear picture of the hypothetical lost archetype of the text he was establishing. He then used parallels in sculpture to justify the additions he made, additions gleaned from his wide knowledge of comparative material, particularly texts of the grammarians which were available to him in compilations and compendia. He liked to piece together the scattered words and phrases from Roman drama, for example: 'I take the greatest possible delight', he exclaimed, 'in these remains'. Once he had drawn together three or four quotations from a given play he would 'glue them up' (as he said) into a coherent speech. He did not try to disguise what he found or what he invented and added from an authentically transmitted text as a poet might have done, or as Du Pérac and Ligorio did in the interests of conserving harmony and proportion. On the contrary, drawing a parallel with sculpture, Scaliger explained:

> We have set off what is Festus' from what is ours, so that we may convince the reader that we neither believe nor wish to persuade others that what does not belong to Festus belongs to him. I have imitated the men who love and study old images and statues. They sometimes have an elegantly carved marble which, perhaps because of its age, is mutilated and lacks a section, as often happens. They seek out skilled craftsmen to fill the missing space with

DES ANTIQVITES ROMAINES
PREMIER LIVRE FAICT PAR LE
COMMANDEMENT DV ROY PAR
M·GVILLAVME CHOVL LIONNOYS
CONSEILLIER DVDICT SEIGNEVR ET
BAILLY DES MŌTAIGNES DV DAVLPHINE

I.   Frontispiece from Guillaume du Choul, 'Antiquitez romaines', Turin, Biblioteca Reale, Ms Var. 212.

II. 'Temple of Vesta', Guillaume du Choul, 'Antiquitez romaines', Turin, Biblioteca Reale, Ms Var. 212, f. 57.

III. 'Arch of Drusus', Guillaume du Choul, 'Antiquitez romaines', Turin, Biblioteca Reale, Ms Var. 212, f. 73.

IV.   'Resurrection of Lazarus', *Heures de Dinteville*, Bibliothèque Nationale, Ms lat. 10558, f. 73v.

V. Noël Jallier, 'Combat entre Paris et Menelaus'; fresco, château d'Oiron.

VI. Jean de
Gourmont,
'Adoration
des bergers'
(*c.* 1550),
Musée du
Louvre.

VII.   Emblematic window panel from the chambre de la Bergère, château Villeneuve-Lembron.

point du iour, & que par mes ex‑
plorateurs la choʒe me fut confer‑
mee . Ie enuoyay toute ma cheua‑
lerie pour leur donner ſur la queue
& en baillay la conduyte a Quint⁹
Pedius,
& a Lu‑
cius a‑
runcu‑
leius Cot‑
ta, et cõ‑
manday
a Labie‑
nus de les ſuyure auec troys legiõs.
℄ Si diligẽment cheminerent mes
deux legatz Quintus Pedius, & .
Arunculeius/quilʒ les trouuerent
& en les pourſuyuent leſpace de

Lucius Arũ‑
culeius
Cotta .

VIII.   Godefroy le Batave, 'the Connétable de Montmorency as Lucius Cotta', Bibliothèque Nationale, Ms fr. 13429, f. LII.

IX. Antoine Caron, 'Massacre du Triumvirat' (*c.* 1566), Musée du Louvre.

Templa focos Vrbes f
Caſsatas naues

X. [Henri II], 'L'entrée du très Magnanime . . . Henry deuxisme . . . à Rouen', 1550, Rouen, Bibliothèque municipale, Ms Y 28 (1268).

. Sex Elephanti

castra gerunt,

Augustum : fortun...

Henricum titu...

XI. [Henri II], 'L'entrée du très Magnanime . . . Henry deuxisme . . . à Rouen', 1550, Rouen, Bibliothèque municipale, Ms Y 28 (1268).

et: largita Secundum.
rs eademq decet,

XII. '*Le grand camée de France*', Bibliothèque Nationale, Cabinet des médailles [Bab, 264].

their own work. All who see the statue know both what portion of the old craftsmanship has been lost and what has been added by the new.[22]

To those who might be astonished by such evident interference, Scaliger replied that without it nothing useful could appear at all since the overall shape would be absent, the sense obscure or lost, and the work maimed and incomprehensible. He argued:

> Yet the addition is often so important that, without it, the remaining proportion and symmetry of the whole statue would be impossible to detect. This is what we have done in this passage of Festus [Epitome of Flaccus' *De Verborum significatione*]. For without the limbs as we have added, it would be very difficult to tell what the truth was. Now as far as we can tell, we have done something most useful for scholars. For by our diligence we have restored this building that was almost levelled to the ground, from its foundations, and set it in good repair.[23]

Scaliger is not claiming authenticity but the inspired creation of a text that can be *useful*, and by that word *useful*, he means a text that can be understood, interpreted, argued about and capable of further change as future scholars perceive its meaning. He has created a whole, a composite whole which keeps an open form in so far as the joins and stitches remain apparent, open to questioning and to further adjustment as other fragments come to light. His enterprise remains tentative and incomplete, while all the time he lays stress on the necessity of being able to envisage the whole. Scaliger's recovery of classical texts, working by collation and by conjecture in equal amounts, was, in Grafton's words, 'as much an act of imagination as of criticism, as much an invention as a rediscovery'.[24]

DU BELLAY'S IMAGINATIVE RECONSTRUCTIONS OF ROME

Evident in *Les Antiquitez de Rome* is a similar concern with parts and wholes; and in attempting to move from the one to the other, the poems bring into play both discovery and invention amid the ruins.[25] *Le Premier Livre des Antiquitez de Rome contenant une generale description de sa grandeur, et comme la deploration de sa ruine . . . Plus un Songe ou Vision sur le mesme subiect* was published in Paris in 1558 by Frédéric Morel. From the title, it appears that Du Bellay projected more than one volume (as many writers of guides to Rome had done) and that, by *Antiquitez*, he understood the ancient buildings and remains of Rome.[26] The title also juxtaposed two different modes of viewing the city: an evocation of its greatness, and lamentation on its ruin. To put it another way, Du Bellay planned a celebration of the magnificence of its structures, and a moral and generalized response to their damage. This antithesis prepares the reader for tensions and contradictions as the poet seeks to bring both views into the same frame, and for the continual movement between past and present which assumes a knowledge of the site and of its buildings. Thus the poet implied from the beginning of his Roman collection shifts from ruins to reconstruction and back again.

The dedicatory poem 'Au Roy' reminds the king that the poems he is about to read constitute that new enterprise which had been announced in the second Elegy.[27] Du Bellay, in *Les Antiquitez*, made clear that he was offering a poetic equivalent of 'ces ouvrages antiques' (these ancient works) which filled the royal palaces at Fontainebleau and, increasingly, at Saint Germain-en-Laye where Philibert de L'Orme was incorporating extensive new structures. Poet and monarch, according to Du Bellay, share the responsibility of building future greatness; but, most of all, the king must recognize the poet's extraordinary feat,

> . . . d'avoir hors du tombeau
> Tiré des vieux Romains les poudreuses reliques. (ll. 7–8)

[. . . of having torn from their tomb the dusty relics of the ancient Romans.]

Du Bellay's plan has many similarities to that which Philibert undertook; he intends to rebuild in France that renewed greatness through the agency of verse, 'De rebastir en France une telle grandeur' (l. 10). Whether it be with real buildings or structures made by the pen, the aim is to let the world know that France vies with Rome in all respects – architecture, letters, political power and domination – and that the first step is to celebrate the imperial city.[28]

To achieve his purpose, Du Bellay built on the work of Roman poets of old: on Virgil, Ovid and Horace, on Propertius and Tibullus. Their celebration of the city sounds continuously beneath his own, and Du Bellay assumes that we hear their voice too. His contemporary readers certainly did.[29] His appeal to revered poets in the first sonnet of the series turns into a kind of ritual whereby he draws out their divine afflatus to infuse his own songs which are designed to promote the glories of *their* poetic achievements. Their physical presence has no more substance than 'la poudreuse cendre' (powdery ashes) beneath the city walls, yet their glory (their marvellous verse) lives on, in part through this new poet of Rome, Du Bellay himself:

> J'invoque icy vostre antique fureur. (l. 12)

> [And for your antique furie I here doo call.][30]

The inspiration was, on occasion, almost blatant as in sonnet 6 where Du Bellay reaffirmed Virgil's prophecy concerning the great destiny of Rome (*Aeneid*, VI, ll. 777–87), asserted Rome's greatness and uniqueness:

> Rome seule pouvoit à Rome ressembler,
> Rome seule pouvoit Rome faire trembler (ll. 9–10)

> [Rome only might to Rome compared bee,
> And onely Rome could make great Rome to tremble]

and conflated his vision with that of Virgil without the specificity given in the epic. So the presence of Rome, haunting the landscape in *Les Antiquitez*, is often mysterious, even veiled, as Du Bellay relied on other accounts of the city, shaded in just enough to stimulate the reader's memory.

Readers are also required to appreciate (and puzzle over) the ambiguous signs painted by Du Bellay's complex picture of Rome which had been announced in his title. These are revealed in sonnet 3 (adapted from Jean Vitalis)[31] where the emphasis is on paradox:

> Nouveau venu, qui cherches Rome en Rome
> Et rien de Rome en Rome n'apperçois (ll. 1–2)

> [Thou stranger, which for Rome in Rome here seekest,
> And nought of Rome in Rome perceiv'st at all]

and on the double, contradictory aspect which the city presents: 'Voy quel orgueil, quelle ruine' (l. 5). The words *orgueil* and *ruine* can be read in two ways. Both refer to a physical state: *orgueil* conjures up the proud, tall structures that still soared skywards, and *ruine* points to their collapsed condition which strikes the eye immediately; and both have moral connotations, of pride coupled with decadence and fall. Although the two states (physical and moral) are both suggested, it seems that the stress is placed on the visible presence of the city transmuted into symbolic form and meaning. Form and symbolism coexist.[32] At line 9, as the poem gains a new impetus, paradoxes and ambiguities are strengthened, with

> Rome de Rome est le seul monument. (l. 9)

> [Rome now of Rome is th'onely funerall.]

The word *monument*, too, is double-edged, supporting two contrasting meanings: on the one hand presenting evident signs of decay; on the other referring to a greatness still visible and acknowledged in the choice of the word (monument = a lofty eminence or memorial). The paradox it represents is succinctly summed up in a later sonnet in the phrase 'la grandeur du rien' (the greatness of nothing) (sonnet 13).[33] This use of terms which work on different planes of meaning is carried through right to the end of sonnet 3 where, in the tercet, the opposites *fuite/resistance* and *ferme/inconstance* are intertwined, and gain their force from the interplay of physical and moral levels of meaning.[34] Such vacillation – between past and present, concrete and abstract, picture and imagination – enhances the already dense texture of the verse.

For the poet, just as much as for the artist/architect, ruins were an invitation to construct, and together with the 'daemon du lieu' (the Genius of the place) (*Les Regrets*, LXXXVII; *Les Antiquitez*, sonnet 27), inspired vision of reconstituted structures (Figure 68). In sonnet 5, fragments stimulate such reconstruction: 'Qui voudra voir [Rome]?' (who lists to see Rome?) The first answer to this proposition is categoric: 'Rome n'est plus . . . Le corps de Rome en cendre est dévallé' (Rome is no more: . . . The corpse of Rome in ashes is entombed).

68. Attributed to Etienne du Pérac: drawing of reconstructed Rome

Yet the poet poses a series of other hypotheses: what if through some magical process of transposition and penetration the 'corps de Rome' could be revived, made perceptible through writings that have survived and seen among the shadows cast by the stones:

> . . . et si l'architecture
> Quelque umbre encor de Rome fait revoir,
> C'est comme un corps par magique sçavoir
> Tiré de nuict hors de sa sepulture. (ll. 5–8)

> [. . . but if the shade of Rome
> May of the bodie yeeld a seeming sight,
> It's like a corse drawne forth out of the tombe
> By Magicke skill out of eternall night.]

The vision is cerebral and fragile despite the fact that it depends for its form on processes fed by knowledge and by magic. The surface ruins which led to the pronouncement 'Rome n'est plus' (Rome is no more) are also the essential medium through which the whole shape of the city is to be rediscovered.[35] Although almost reduced to powder – 'en cendre' – they entice and attract, inviting the poet/archaeologist to probe and dig down to the divine presence which lies below the soil. These phenomena which constitute the body of Rome are able to reappear, and although the effort required to snatch them from their tomb is huge, writings on Rome can effect the reawakening:

> Mais ses escripts, qui son loz le plus beau
> Malgré le temps arrachent du tombeau,
> Font son idole errer parmy le monde. (ll. 12–14)

[But her brave writings, which her famous merite
In spight of time, out of the dust doth reare,
Doo make her Idole through the world appeare.]

Together, the stones of Rome and the power of poetry have pulled off a miracle. 'Le corps de Rome' can be seen, its spirit[36] walks abroad and, although insubstantial, its presence is sufficient encouragement.

In some sonnets (numbers 6 and 8, for example) the greatness and extent of ancient Rome are sung without reservation. These counterbalance those poems (like sonnet 15) where the building achievements of architects seem entirely obliterated by Time. 'N'estre plus rien qu'une poudreuse plaine' (l. 14) (ironed out of existence and reduced to dust) is the image which dominates this sonnet, where every permutation of words associated with dust is used: 'Umbres poudreuses' (l. 1), 'reliques cendreuses' (l. 4), 'images umbreuses' (l. 8), 'poudreuse plaine' (l. 14), strengthened by assonance and by their rhythmic position at the end of each line, all in the cause of evoking extremes of pulverization. The scraped-clean flatness of 'plaine' (rhyming with 'peine') serves to complete the image of destruction. Even in this ghastly landscape, however, the shadows of mighty structures still haunt the place, conjured up by the words 'cest orgueilleux séjour' (l. 3) (this proud place).

If Du Bellay needed encouragement to delve beneath the ruins in order to create anew, he had only to respond to the astonishing spectacle that greeted him every day: that of Rome recreating itself (almost spontaneously) from its own entrails. In the first two quatrains of sonnet 27, Du Bellay had named all the elements which had constituted 'l'antique orgueil' of the city, sharpening their presence with demonstrative adjectives – 'ces vieux palais . . . ces murs . . . ces arcs . . . ces temples' – taking it for granted that the reader would reconstitute their shapes. Then, in the tercets, comes the shift to the incredible activity of renewal; independent of the poet, a magical force stirs the soil:

> Regarde apres, comme de jour en jour
> Rome fouillant son antique sejour
> Se rebastist de tant d'oeuvres divines:
> Tu jugeras que le daemon Romain
> S'efforce encor d'une fatale main
> Ressusciter ces poudreuses ruines. (ll. 9–14)

> [Then also marke, how Rome from day to day,
> Repayring her decayed fashion,
> Renewes herselfe with buildings rich and gay:
> That one would judge, that the Roman Daemon
> Doth yet himselfe with fatall hand enforce,
> Againe on foote to reare her pouldred corse.][37]

In this process of probing, revival and restoration, Du Bellay recognized the creative process itself, which began with the necessity to envisage whole structures that could probably not be built, but could be imagined. And that was enough. The will simply to stretch out towards a possible structure began the process of revival and restoration.[38] The point is illustrated in sonnet 25 where, in order to build, the poet wishes to be those shades who had created ancient Rome; or to be another Amphion whose music had breathed life into the brittle walls; or to assume Virgil's pen and design in words palaces that would endure. So enthused is he at the prospect he is painting that he sees the chance of fashioning temples that would outdo the products of the builder's hand:

> J'entreprendrois, veu l'ardeur qui m'allume,
> De rebastir au compas de la plume
> Ce que les mains ne peuvent maçonner.

> [I would assay with that which in me is,
> To builde with levell of my loftie style,
> That which no hands can evermore compyle.]

This seems more than a challenge. It is, rather, the assertion of poetry's superior power, and of the poet's supreme draughtsmanship.

It must not be forgotten, however, that these are desires, conditioned by *ifs* (*if* I were an ancient architect, Amphion, or a kind of Virgil) and future determinations (*J'entreprendrois*). The same hesitancy (heightened here by modesty) is present in the final sonnet of the sequence (no. 32). As he closes his first book on Rome, Du Bellay thinks of his readers, of his muse's powers of survival, and reminds himself of the precarious condition of living 'sous-ciel'. He invites his verses to imagine a world without mortality and all the inadequacies that go with that condition; and, in this context, then:

> Les monuments que je vous ai fait dire,
> Non en papier, mais en marbre et porphyre,
> Eussent gardé leur vive antiquité. (ll. 6–8)

> [These moniments, which not in paper writ,
> But in Porphyre and Marble do appeare,
> Might well have hop'd to have obtained it.]

The very posing of the issue of immortality brings its reality closer. Du Bellay believed that the poet is capable of reassembling the fragments towards the making of a possible work which, although it can still only be conjectured and implied, can be projected in a way that will last. Despite all the conditions and reservations, the attempt is worth making:

> Ne laisse pas toutefois de sonner,
> Luth . . . (ll. 9–10)

Indeed, Du Bellay implies, the attempt has already been made. *Les Antiquitez* has shown that the poet could build and live on to be read, repeated, interpreted and rearranged by future generations. Moreover, the poet's building was original. However much he had relied upon the absent spirits of classical Rome, on the beckoning ambivalence of the ruins, and upon the visible renewal of Rome itself, Du Bellay had created something new: he was (he claimed in tones mingled with modesty and pride) the first to sing in French the ancient honour of the Romans:

> Vanter te peux, quelque bas que tu sois,
> D'avoir chanté le premier des François,
> L'antique honneur du peuple à longue robe. (ll. 12–14)

> [Well maist thou boast, how ever base thou bee,
> That thou art first, which of thy Nation song
> Th'olde honour of the people gowned long.]

Rome, although unique in her greatness, is an integral part of Nature in *Les Antiquitez*: she shares the same phenomena and the same destiny (sonnets 28 and 30). In drawing moral lessons from Rome's greatness, decline and fall, and thus depicting the city as a symbol of humankind and of a world where imperfection is inevitable, Du Bellay had also kept glowing the image of that original splendour. The very sound of the name of Rome reverberating through the poems helped to sustain the fiction of that greatness, especially in lapidary formulations such as,

> Rome fut tout le monde, et tout le monde est Rome. (sonnet 26, l. 9)

> [Rome was th'whole world, and al the world was Rome.]

It is the property of ruins to provoke moral meditation and, at the same time, to encourage reconstruction. Du Bellay recognized that double call in which he also perceived for himself a role in raising poetry to the overwhelmingly significant position he believed it should occupy.[39]

Le Songe, the sequence of sonnets which followed the *Antiquitez*, continues to puzzle its commentators.[40] Du Bellay clearly saw it as constituting part of his Roman collections as he announced in his title, *plus un Songe ou Vision sur le mesme subiect*. Did he conceive it as a commentary on *Les Antiquitez* or as a complement to that series of poems? Both collections sought to actualize a vision related to destruction, although there are significant differences in the way such visions were handled. In *Les Antiquitez*, the disintegration is progressive over time; Rome is depicted as subject to repeated and intermittent assaults, but demonstrates an impressive power of resistance to destruction. By contrast, in *Le Songe* the destruction is immediate and total, and there is no suggestion of possible recuperation. In each of the fifteen sonnets, Du Bellay describes an event which shows the same kind of movement: collapse, explosion and general dissipation. There are further disparities in the ways the fabric of the city is presented in each volume. No detailed, graphic reality is attempted in *Les Antiquitez*, where Du Bellay has relied on his reader's understanding, knowledge and powers of recognition. *Le Songe* specifies objects,[41] and brings into our view frail, transparent and idealized structures that recall some of the tall and slender buildings that inhabit the landscapes of Jean Cousin's or Antoine Caron's pictures; shining brilliantly for a moment and disappearing as though their delicate outlines had merely been imagined. The temple of Doric design (sonnet 2) has walls 'd'un luysant cristal' (of shining crystal), which shimmer with a jewelled finish made of diamonds, gold, jasper and emerald; the obelisk (sonnet 3) is like a gigantic diamond laced with gold; and the arch (sonnet 4) is conceived in ivory with transparent columns of alabaster and crystal. Although their form recognizably derives from ancient Roman paradigms, their fabric is improbable – the stuff of dreams (*vision*).[42] Moreover, Du Bellay claimed no responsibility for their making. In *Le Songe* the poet is the agent of a higher order that directs his gaze and the series of spectacles he is to witness:

> . . . Voy (dit-il) et contemple
> Tout ce qui est compris sous ce grand temple,
> Voy comme tout n'est rien que vanité. (sonnet 1, ll. 9–10)

[Observe and contemplate (saith he) all that is beneath this great temple, see how all is nothing but vanity.]

Inspired directly by Ecclesiastes (1,2), these lines situate the poet as a distant, passive observer of sights and forces outside his control. By contrast, *Les Antiquitez* was written from a privileged site of the poet's own choosing: from Rome, Du Bellay projects out to his readers the record of building activities inspired by the ruins, and he is in control of their evocation, of their shape, and of the future programme destined for France. Thus, the perspectives from which the two series were conceived are very different.

The realization of the instability and inconstancy of the world he has been required to contemplate makes the poet of *Le Songe* turn that sequence of poems into a kind of emblem book, as subsequent translators and publishers of these sonnets recognized.[43] After the representation of an event or object, each tercet offers to the reader a moral lesson to absorb: 'n'espere rien qu'en la divinité' (believe in nothing but divinity) (sonnet 1), 'O Vanité du monde' (O Vanity of the world) (sonnet 2), or 'Las, rien ne dure au monde que tourment' (Alas, nothing lasts in the world but torment) (sonnet 3). The moral is explicit in these three examples; while in later sonnets the lesson is implied by the drama of destruction which the poet has witnessed and described.

In the transference from evocation of ruins to the imagining of future completed forms, Du Bellay relied heavily on the complicity of his readers. In fact, the presence of readers (either contemporary or future) loomed large in all Du Bellay's poems; and he had acknowledged their importance in his elegy 'Patriae desiderium' which ended, 'Les vers aiment l'approbation des grands et les applaudissements de la foule, et celui qui plaît à peu de lecteurs se déplaît à lui-même' (Verses love the approbation of the great and the applause of the crowd, and he who only pleases a few readers is displeasing to himself).[44] In *Les Antiquitez*, the poet's self-conscious, direct appeal seated the reader beside him as he addressed Rome, or evoked monuments and ruins which were not named but pointed out with the poet's finger, for he could assume a special kind of reader – one completely familiar with the buildings of Rome, sensitive to the allusiveness present in the poems and able to appreciate the references to the Latin texts Du Bellay had pillaged,[45] and equipped to play his role in understanding and completing the structures which Du Bellay had begun. Between poet and this specialized audience there was a kinship, a sharing of mutual interests and endeavour.

Immediate responses to the publications of Du Bellay's poems in 1558 testify to the accuracy of the poet's predictions regarding his readers' taste. The chancellor of France, François Olivier, in a letter to Jean Morel which was published as a preface to the *Poematum libri quatuor* in 1558 declared: 'Since you left I have re-read Du Bellay's poems three or four times, and they appeal to me more and more all the time'. He also acknowledged their density and the difficulty he sometimes had in penetrating their meaning, and he envisaged that a perfect reader of Du Bellay's work would need to be 'a thoroughly refined man of far-ranging and diversified learning and most discerning taste'.[46] The appreciation which Olivier publicly voiced seems to have been generally shared in France if we are to believe Scévole de Sainte Marthe who, on the subject of *Les Antiquitez* and *Les Regrets*, reported in his *Eloges*: 'Jamais ouvrage françois ne fut lu plus volontiers ni avec plus de plaisir que ces deux premiers livres qu'il composa sur le sujet de la ville de Rome.' (Never was a French work so willingly read and with such pleasure than the first two books which he composed on the subject of the city of Rome.)[47]

DU BELLAY'S HERITAGE

Reading with pleasure inevitably encouraged attempts to imitate and to expand on Du Bellay's creative ideas and, in the case of Edmund Spenser, to translate *Les Antiquitez* and *Le Songe* into English. Although only at the beginning of his own poetic career, Spenser recognized the originality of what Du Bellay had done in his poems on Rome and in an envoi (appended to his transla-

69. Jan van der Noot: the
Obelisk

tions in 1568, revised 1591)[48] offered this tribute: Du Bellay had achieved immortality for having managed

> Olde Rome out of her ashes to revive,
> And give a second life to dead decayes. (ll. 5–6)

So great was the immediate impact of *Les Antiquitez* and *Les Regrets* that they became a significant reservoir of inspiration for other poets and, more generally, a means of extending the vision of Rome. Some idea of the extent of Du Bellay's influence might be gathered from the fact that Malcolm Smith identified twenty-eight poems in eight languages which 'echo just one of Du Bellay's sonnets' (sonnet 3 of *Les Antiquitez*).[49]

It was the moral content of *Le Songe*, in particular, that attracted Protestant writers. When Jan van der Noot, a Dutch refugee in London, published in 1568–69 a series of adaptations of Du Bellay's sequence of fifteen sonnets in several languages (Spanish, French and English), he was developing their emblematic nature more fully, manipulating Du Bellay's text to sharpen his own condemnation of Rome, and supplying the pictures which regularly appeared in emblem books. *A Theatre for Worldlings* bears on Rome as spectacle, on elements – temple, arch, obelisk and so on – instantly recognizable as belonging to that show, and draws out messages that could support the Protestant cause.

70. Jan van der Noot: the Triumphal Arch

These are made blatant in the sonnets of Van der Noot's own invention such as the cry 'Now for truth great Babylon [Rome] is fallen' at the end of sonnet 13, or 'The Holy Citie of the Lorde' displayed in the woodcut attaching to sonnet 15.[50] It is interesting that the images which belong to Du Bellay's poems in this book show two scenes simultaneously. In the foreground looms the perfect, completed edifice: the powerful temple (sonnet 2), the obelisk covered with hieroglyphs (sonnet 3) (Figure 69), and the arch inscribed with Augustus Caesar's name and surmounted by a triumphal chariot (Figure 70). A little behind and to the side lie their shattered fragments.[51] Thus the poet's double vision (fragments becoming wholes) is here reversed with no apparent hope that the broken pieces can be made good. On the contrary, Van der Noot sees them replaced by entirely new structures – visions like the City of the Lord which ends the sequence. It might be argued that arch, obelisk and temple do not necessarily belong to Rome, but the words of the poem clearly identify them as buildings in the imperial city, and actual edifices in Rome (Castel di Sant'Angelo and the Tempietto) are visible behind *Roma* as she strides forth, accompanied by her trophies and hundreds of vanquished kings in sonnet 11 (Figure 71).[52]

Remakings of Du Bellay's poems were sometimes clumsy when the adaptor tried to reproduce too closely the structures and rhythms of the original with

71. Jan van der Noot: *Roma*

its detail little altered. Such were the sonnets of Claude Pontoux who in sonnet 266 in his *Oeuvres*, merely listed the famous places in Rome as though they were still glorious sights to see:

> O qu'il fait beau marcher à la fraiche diane . . .
> Allons au Capitole, allons au Palatin . . .

[O how delightful to walk in the fresh early morning . . . Let us to the Capitol, let us to the Palatine . . .]

but then deliberately deflates the image in the tercet,

> Mais quoy que voyons nous icy nous arrestons,
> Toute vieille ruine; et qu'est ce que de Rome,
> Voilà que c'est, froissard, toute chose a son temps.

[But wait, what do we see here, stop; everything is old ruins; and what about Rome? this is what it is – broken; everything has its day.]

Here, the final trite comment and the awkward phrasing take away all the spring that had been suggested by successive verbs in the quatrains 'allons . . . admirons . . . voyons'.[53] Although Pontoux was undoubtedly attracted by the opportunity to appropriate the language of triumph in order to celebrate Charles IX's entry into Paris (1571) with new structures, his lines rarely soar:

> Iô doncques Paris eslieve tes Trophées,
> Et les arcs triomphaux aux tympanes coiffees,
> Aux bases de relief . . .

[Io then Paris, erect your trophies, your triumphal arches, crowned with spandrels, low reliefs . . .]

Nor do long lists of *antiques artifices* – 'D'Ionics, de Dorics, et de Corynthiens' – capture the tone of triumph and celebration.[54]

Pontoux, as he wrote, had in front of him *Les Antiquitez*. For Jean de la Jessée, however, it was *Les Regrets* which was a constant point of reference, as he readily acknowledged when he addressed Du Bellay directly in the fourth book of *Les Jeunesses*:

> Ainsi loing de ma terre ores je me lamente,
> Regrettant mes parantz, comme tu regrettois
> Ton sejour Angevin . . .

[Thus far away from my homeland, I now lament, sorrowing for my parents, as you yearned for your home in Anjou . . .]

This poet, in his choice of theme (exile) and in the elegiac tones that dominated his work could not rid himself of Du Bellay's influence. Yet, despite the closeness of his feelings, the similarity of experience, the linguistic parallels, and the evident initial impetus deriving from Du Bellay's account of his sojourn in Rome, the influence was more complex than a one-to-one relationship, as has been shown.[55] There is closeness yet independence, for the voice of La Jessée states its individuality by defining itself as not that of an imitator.

Similar absorption occurred in the sonnets composed by Jérôme Hennequin entitled *Regrets sur les misères advenues à la France par les guerres civiles* (1579).[56] The tones, vocabulary and rhythm of *Les Antiquitez* are instantly recognizable:

> Esprits, dont les saints os dans le cercle oublieux
> Reposent au giron de la masse poudreuse . . . (sig. A iij)
> . . . Palles esprits, et vous ombres poudreuses . . . (f. 10)
> . . . Toy estranger qui viens ici chercher la France. (f. 4v)

[Spirits, whose saintly bones rest in a forgotten circle in the bosom of a powdery mass . . . Pale spirits, and you dusty shades . . . and you, foreigner, who comes here to find France.]

Hennequin has simply borrowed Du Bellay's terms and themes and transferred them virtually unaltered. The ruins of Rome become the metaphor to describe the appalling spectacle of collapse and desolation in France ('le païs ruyné, les

Eglises bruslées' (the country destroyed and the churches burnt)), and the spirits are not the ancient poets of Rome but those of pious Frenchmen, long dead and forgotten by all but this sorrowful voice. In these bleak poems there is no room for hope or reconstruction; the transfer, so specifically made, seems to close down possibilities of fresh creative expansion.[57]

However, in the sonnets written by Simon Goulart 'sur les pourtraits des antiquitez Romaines' (on the images of Roman antiquities), the interpretation is more dynamic.[58] The references both to Du Bellay's Roman poems and to engravings of ruins are clear; and, although Goulart emphasizes the size and extent of the destruction, he perceives behind the vestiges that remain the quality of the artist and the power of survival of his work. In his poems, Goulart is contemplating the pictures of ruins and these show that despite the fact that 'L'art permit que son art en ruine fust mis' (art condones that his art was reduced to ruins), art also has left marks of its original conceptions that can be admired by future generations, and perhaps emulated:

> . . . Quelques traits excellens de son premier ouvrage,
> Ouvrage desmonstrant à toute creature,
> Les merveilles du ciel, de l'art et de nature. (sonnet 13)
> . . . Venerables pourtraits, en vos ruines paintes,
> Nous voyons aujourd'huy tres vivement empraintes,
> Du monde, la grandeur, la pompe, et la beauté. (sonnet 14)

[A few excellent traces of earlier work, work which shows to every creature the marvels of the heavens, of art and of nature . . . Venerable images, painted in your ruined state, today we see strongly imprinted there the grandeur, the pomp and the beauty of the world.][59]

It would be a tiresome task to trace all the detailed dependences on Du Bellay's text whether it be (for example) the play on the metaphor 'ces poudres cendreuses' in the *Sonnets* of Nicolas Ellain which he composed from 1561 and dedicated to Eustache du Bellay in 1571;[60] or the focus on the destructive power of Time, which reduced shining marble to fragments 'mutilés et massacrés' (mutilated and destroyed), which was later explored by Jean Jacquemot.[61] There is one poet, however, whose work is hardly known and whose poems offered fresh insights into the vision of Rome which was developing in French writing at this time.[62] Adrian de Gadon, seigneur de Saussay was in Rome at the age of twenty,[63] and he has left a series of sonnets, composed while he was there, which introduce new strands into texts inspired by ruins. In the first of the *Sonnets de l'auteur faits à Rome*, expecting to find solace and inspiration among the ruins, the poet found only 'un peu d'ombre' (a little shade) and flimsy traces of what the city once was. His mind is filled with incredulity, distress, reminiscence and conjecture. Moved beyond endurance, he attributes to the city all the civil disorder that has invaded France. Some secret force, unknown to the poet and to Rome, is at work:

> . . . civile discorde
> Fille pour mon païs une secrete corde
> Dont elle attache, un iour, nostre aise à vos malheurs. (ll. 12–14)

[civil disorder weaves a secret thread for my country with which, one day, she attaches our ease to your misfortune.][64]

The mysterious threads binding the two countries together are made manifest in powerful, bloody images of war. They are evoked by Gadon through repeated expressions of incredulity – 'Feu-ce en cest endroit?' (Was it really in this place?), so ruined and devastated, that such cruel deeds were performed? (f. 20v). Unlike other French poets (and notably Du Bellay himself), Gadon has selected for his themes civil strife, murder between brothers, and internecine battles that cause death in the same family and among members of the same race.

Like Du Bellay, however, Gadon also calls on spirits long dead: on the 'Quirites genereux' (f. 21r) to interrogate their feelings as, powerless now, they look upon ruined Rome and brood over the fact that verse and paint do not represent (as in *Les Antiquitez*) positive guarantors of survival, but are instead the mere hints of *all* that survives. Such vestiges which poet and artist conceive, although incomplete and seemingly unsatisfactory as a consequence, are nonetheless (the poet suggests) reminders of greatness even if its recollection is painful:

> Sentez-vous quelque deuil, dont en prose et en vers,
> Elle est, sans plus, vivante, ou en carte ou en toille (ll. 7–8),
> . . . Celle qui tant de monde a mis à sa mercy,
> Plus vie ne tenir que de peintre ou d'histoire (ll. 10–11),
> . . . Sentez-vous augmenter vos peines, et vos maulx,
> Par le seul souvenir de vostre grande gloire? (ll. 13–14)

[Do you feel any sorrow for her who lives only in prose and verse, or in drawing or tapestry . . . she who had so much of the world at her mercy, no longer has life outside painting or history . . . Do you feel your pains and misfortunes increase from the sole memory of your great glory?]

Although the visible evidence of history is slight in the marble fragments that remain, the poet draws out from them precise historical events which Du Bellay had avoided, and Gadon's imagination actualizes the deeds and gestures. He shows, for instance, the victory of Horatio and the slaughter of his sister (f. 20v); he recalls the rape of the Sabines, the wolf suckling the twins, and the murder of Remus by Romulus.[65]

From time to time, the poet appropriates to France the power and glory usually attributed to Rome, declaring for example,

> Or vostre empire est poudre, et France
> Triomphe . . .[66]

[Now your empire is as dust, and France triumphs.]

Such an assertion is a sign of the unsteady focus of this sonnet sequence. Du Bellay lurks in the background as Gadon strains to renew and extend the poetic possibilities found among the ruins, and the effort is visible in the contorted phrasing and jerky rhythms of the poems. Ultimately, Gadon's concern is less with a sense of loss (except for the poem addressed to the *Quirites*) and more on the city as a place of violence and murder, as a melting pot for mixing the evils of civil disorder capable of seeping out everywhere. Yet, above all that, there is the desire to transfer the glory that was Rome to France.

THE REVERBERATIONS OF VITALIS' *ROMA PRISCA* AND *ROMA INSTAURATA*

The whole business of borrowing, appropriation and extension is complicated by the reverberations surrounding the poetic diptych *Roma prisca* and *Roma instaurata* which Janus Vitalis published in his *Elogia* in 1553. This double portrait of Rome, and in particular the 'Roma prisca' which invited the reader to meditate upon the ruins and (in a series of compelling paradoxes) to assess the destructive power of Rome, had been prepared by a long-standing literary interest in the themes of ruins and time. Vitalis' forceful articulation of the motif relaunched the idea and sustained its influence, and Du Bellay's own interpretation in sonnet 3 of *Les Antiquitez* ensured its popularity for decades.[67] Sonnet 3 is therefore of special significance. The creative atmosphere in Rome in the 1550s was such that the interaction of poets writing in different languages (Latin, Italian, English) was intense. Louis des Masures who was exiled in Rome (1547–50) likened the circle of poets in the entourage of Cardinal Jean du Bellay to that which had surrounded Caesar Augustus, 'Les nouveaux Quirites rappellent ici les siecles anciens, lorsque César Auguste entendit *L'Enéide* chantée de la bouche divine du grand [Virgile]' (new nobles recall here the centuries of old when Augustus Caesar heard the *Aeneid* sung by the divine lips of Virgil).[68]

In this tangled web of influences, we know that, when he is expressing appreciation of 'une épigramme bien faite' (a well-turned epigram), Estienne Pasquier is referring directly to Vitalis because he says so.[69] Similarly, Jean Doublet announced his debt to Vitalis in the subtitle to his poem 'Sur les ruines de Rome', 'tiré de l'épigramme latin' (taken from the Latin epigram).[70] However, when Philibert de L'Orme wrote, 'on ne cognoistra plus Rome à Rome' (one no longer recognizes Rome in Rome), he may have been thinking of either Du Bellay or Vitalis;[71] and by the time Pierre le Moyne writes in 1672, 'Rome n'est plus dans Rome' (Rome is no longer in Rome), the source may no longer be recognized even though the idea was evidently still very much alive.[72]

The memorable phrase rang in the ears of French travellers to Rome in the late sixteenth and early seventeenth centuries, conditioning their response to the city, as can be seen from Pierre Bergeron's manuscript account of his journey: 'cherchant Rome dans Rome on ne trouve rien moins que Rome qui ayant vaincu tout le monde s'est trouvée enfin vaincue et accablée soubz sa propre grandeur' (looking for Rome in Rome, one finds nothing other than that Rome which, having conquered the world, found herself vanquished and buried under the weight of her own greatness).[73] Although the accents of Du Bellay are recognizable in Bergeron's text, Jean-Jacques Bouchard (who travelled to Rome in 1632) made the reference to the poet explicit. He had sojourned in Rome for eight months, and had returned to the city after a stay in Naples. Suddenly, he was struck by the city's emptiness and (like Montaigne) missed the sight of bell towers and the sound of bells. He tried to analyse the feelings he experienced through this abrupt sense of loss: first there was 'une certaine horreur religieuse' (a certain religious horror) which came upon him, then (almost immediately) 'une certaine aise et tendresse' (a certain ease and tenderness) for, as he entered the city, he felt as if he were coming back home. As his gaze lingered on the 'ruines de tant de temples, sepulcres, arcs, palais, acqueducs, chemins publics, la desolation et peu de culture de la campagne si fertile autrefois, et la solitude et peu d'habitans et d'habitations' (ruins of so many temples, sepulchres, arches, palaces, aqueducts, public ways, desolation, and a land which was once so fertile now little cultivated, emptiness, few inhabitants and few dwellings), he could not find the words to bring out the feelings that had invaded his soul until he thought of Du Bellay's Roman poems. And that recollection was sufficient. There was no need to delve further into the experience, for the poet had already done that for him:

> Je me suis mis à faire en l'esprit tous les regraits que jamais
> Bellay fit en ses sonets sur ceste mesme matière.

[I began to fill my mind with more regrets than those which Du Bellay made in his sonnets on this same subject.][74]

The vibrancy of Du Bellay's 'Romae descriptio' was never matched in *Les Antiquitez* and yet, in these sonnets, the poet found ways of making the reader scan back and forth across the glorious past of Rome and its ruined present. Visible and verbal associations encourage the reader to make the connections and to project images of this place, to see the shapes paradoxically built out of the poet's intense belief in and fear of the ephemeral.[75] Though its fabric might be ruined, the sound of Rome beat on[76] – in poems that denied the city's power, and in the work of new generations – and opened up (as Du Bellay dared to hope) areas of meaning as yet unrealized where the present seemed coextensive with the past, a living part of a vast literary and visual culture.[77]

Like other travellers to Rome, Montaigne carried in his head fully developed images of the city which he had derived from his reading.[79] His first view of Rome itself was glimpsed from afar, as he tells us in his *Journal*: 'a quinze milles nous descouvrismes la ville de Rome, et puis la reperdismes pour longtemps' (at fifteen miles we discovered the prospect of Rome, and then we lost it again for a long time).[80] The apparition served to whet his appetite; yet the initial eagerness to set foot on the *pavé* of Rome was tempered by the spectacle of remnants of mediocre buildings and by the barren landscape that confronted him as he rode the last kilometres into Rome. Even the brickwork did not compare favourably (he thought) with the size and density of similar old classical ruins found in France. Another distant view was experienced some months later as Montaigne left Rome for Tivoli, on the *via Tiburtina* whence he could contemplate 'une plaine infinie de toutes parts et cette grande Rome' (an infinite plain on all sides and that great Rome) (p. 128). Direct experience of the city, as well as the changed angle of viewing, had transformed his original disappointment in the grandeur of Rome; but they did not remove all his doubts since his reactions to the city were still characterized in both the *Journal* and the *Essais* by ambiguity — by contradiction, even.

Although Montaigne's meditations upon Rome and its site are well known, critics have tended to reduce their complexity to his one negative statement 'Rome is a tomb', or to stress the positive picture he painted of a modern city bustling with life and corruption.[81] It is worth recalling, however, the rich and ambiguous texture of Montaigne's observations of the ruins in particular, since the processes whereby he attempted to revisualize the Roman buildings of the past and to see the plan of the ancient city are akin to those he used in the composition of his *Essais*.[82]

In Montaigne's opinion the ruins had totally transformed the city; and its hills and slopes were forever changed by the piling up of different generations of buildings, difficult to distinguish one from another. In the *Journal*, this opinion developed through study of specific places. The valley of the Velabrun, which formed a triangle between the Palatine hill, the Capitol and the Tiber, had originally been a lake but was now filled in with fragments of buildings decayed over time; and the Monte Savello was built from the ruins which had been broken from the theatre of Marcellus.[83] Such observations are based in part on information provided in guidebooks, and in part on close scrutiny of the places themselves. Every day Montaigne paid extended visits to the old parts of the city, and his remarks on the fabric of buildings testify to the detailed attention he had given to their bulk and massive character, to their layered construction and to the shards of inscriptions that remained:

Les ruines de Rome ne se voient pour la pluspart que par le massif et espois du bastiment. Ils faisoient de grosses murailles de brique, puis ils les encroutoient ou de lames de marbre ou d'autre pierre blanche, ou de certain ciment ou de gros quarreau enduit par dessus. Ceste crouste, quasi partout, a esté ruinée par les ans, sur laquelle estoient les inscriptions; par où nous avons perdu la pluspart de la congnoissance de telles choses. (pp. 116–17)

[The ruins of Rome are only to be seen, for the most part, by the massiveness and thickness of the buildings. They made thick walls of brick, then encased them either with sheets of marble or another sort of white stone, or a kind of cement or large bricks plastered on top. Almost everywhere, this crust on which there were inscriptions has been worn away over the years, so that we have lost the greater part of our knowledge of such things.]

The practical craftsman is fascinated by the methods of construction while the humanist laments the irretrievable disappearance of words that might enlighten and bring forth exact forms from the past. Although, according to his secretary, Montaigne spent many of his days in Rome studying the city and its site – 'il ne s'amuse qu'à estudier Rome' (he only delights in studying Rome)[84] – he was not persuaded that ancient Rome could in any way be reconstructed from the remains he observed. Only the sky remained the same and, he maintained, an ancient Roman coming back to life in 1580 would not even recognize the overall plan of his city: 'un ancien Romain ne sauroit recognoistre l'assiette de la ville quand il la verroit' (p. 101).

It is just at this point in the recollection of his sojourn in Rome that Montaigne launches into his famous description of the ruins of the city which he sees as the remains of an admirable structure and as signs of pre-eminence and of a grandeur that was at once powerful and extraordinary.[85] Although the ruins represent the sepulchre of Rome, they are also reminders of 'une si espouvantable machine' (such a frightening machine) which is recalled with reverence (Figure 72). The description is tinged with nostalgia and with the powerless acquiescence of a mere mortal faced with decisions made by destiny. In Montaigne's presentation, the whole corpus of the city is present and visible in all its beauty and its dignity, while the process of the determined destruction is re-enacted. This is given in detail:

Le monde, ennemy de sa longue domination, avoit premierement brisé et fracassé toutes les pièces qu'encore tout mort, renversé et desfiguré et luy faisoit horreur, il en avoit enseveli la ruine mesme. Que ces petites montres de sa ruine qui paroissoient encore au dessus de la bière, c'estoit la fortune qui les avoit conservées pour le tesmoignage de cette grandeur infinie que tant de siècles, tant de feux, la conjuration du monde réitérée à tant de fois à la ruine, n'avoient peu universellement esteindre. (p. 100)

[The world, antagonistic to her long dominion, had first broken and shattered it all to pieces; and, even completely turned upside down, dead and

72.   G.A. Dosio: the baths of Caracalla

disfigured, the city still inspired horror, so its ruins were themselves buried. And these little signs of her collapse which still stick out above the sepulchre, it was Fortune which preserved them as witnesses to that infinite greatness which so many centuries, so many fires, the conspiracy of the whole world determining so many times on her ruin, failed to extinguish entirely.]

Montaigne's interest, evenly distributed between resistance to destruction and the determination to destroy, is unusual. While maintaining this double projection, Montaigne continued to argue that recreating a vision of ancient Rome was neither possible nor plausible. Those who claimed it could be done were appealing to 'une science abstraite et contemplative de laquelle il n'y avoit rien qui tombast sous les sens' (an abstract and contemplative science which has nothing to do with practical issues) (p. 100). Those who sought to reproduce plans of ancient Rome, marking therein the place of each monument and detailing its lineaments, had no credibility – 'plusieurs conjectures qu'on prend de la peinture de cette ville ancienne n'ont guiere de verisimilitude, son plan mesme estant infiniment changé de forme' (several conjectures that are made about this ancient city are scarcely credible, even its site has changed its form infinitely) (p. 101). Montaigne has in mind the celebrated maps of Rome which Pirro Ligorio had drawn in 1553 and 1561 and which were reprinted and

73. Etienne du Pérac: section of engraving for Antoine Lafréry of Ligorio's map of Rome

modified by Etienne du Pérac in 1574 (Figure 73). He was also thinking of
the many French nobles who wasted their time measuring and comparing, and
ascertaining 'combien de pas a Santa Rotonda . . . combien le visage de Neron,
de quelque vieille ruine de là, est plus long ou plus large que celuy de quelque
pareille medaille' (how many paces has the Pantheon . . . how long is Nero's
nose on some old ruin and is it larger or longer than its equivalent on some
medal) (I, 26, l53).

Notwithstanding such ironic statements, Montaigne himself indulged in
conjecture. In the *Journal*, for instance, he used the arch of Severus as the mode

231

74. Etienne du Pérac: arch of Severus

of establishing how far above the original ground level of classical times he was now walking in 1580 (Figure 74). From this spot he saw himself strolling two pikes' length above that ground on old rooftops exposed by the rain and by wheels of carriages.[86] Moreover, even as he argued the impossibility of resurrecting ancient Rome, he speculated on the meaning of what remained and why it survived: 'ces membres des visages qui en restoient' (these limbs of vestiges that remain) (p. 100) were assuredly the least significant remains since they had been allowed to outlast the general destruction and, he continued to surmise, destiny itself required that some traces of Rome remained 'pour faire sentir au monde leur conspiration à la gloire et pré-eminence de cette ville, par un si nouveau et extraordinaire tesmoingnage de sa grandeur' (to make the world aware that they conspire to produce the glory and pre-eminence of this city through such a novel and extraordinary witness to its greatness) (p. 101). Montaigne saw the incongruity of the juxtaposition – greatness and ruin – so that what might be interpreted as a negative appraisal of Roman ruins emerged, in fact, as an expression of admiration fittingly matching the emotive eloquence of his description.

There are other examples in the *Journal* where Montaigne leaps from the observation of a fragment to visualizing a larger entity. The ruins he encountered on the way to Ostia drew forth the remark that the road was strewn with great signs of former beauty, and he saw the whole road from Rome to the coast as 'garni d'habitations' (adorned with dwellings) (p. 116). The ruins are admired for their own quality and because they suggest larger concepts – those entire structures, now missing, from which they came. The possibility of giving a shape to absent forms is facilitated by the knowledge store which Montaigne had acquired through reading and through observation.

Calling forth forms from the past was further complicated by the multiplicity of signs that remained of them, and – in particular – by the multi-

Etienne du Pérac: engraving of the temple of Peace showing piled up earth and stones

layered nature of those remains and the diverse angles from which they could be viewed.[87] The digging that went on in Rome often revealed the crown of a lofty column with its base hidden in the ground many feet beneath (Figure 75); indeed, Montaigne claimed, it was not unusual to find traces of roads thirty feet below those on which one regularly walked (p. 101). And then there was the question of how to accommodate the twenty-five or thirty temples said to have been erected on the same site along with several private houses. Such questions and observations supported Montaigne's view that reconstituting the plan and buildings of ancient Rome was a vain activity, but its difficulty did not diminish the temptation to try, nor did it remove any of the layers of the city whose presence survived under the stones. Montaigne obviously understood all that was involved in any attempt at reconstruction and, although he resisted any thoroughgoing effort to reconceive the complex structures and their relationships, he recognized the value of such processes in writing his later *Essais*.[88]

Montaigne's acknowledgement of the reverberative power of ruins is evident from the way he wrote about them in his *Journal*; and he also recognized their usefulness in providing material for new building works. In commenting on the cathedral at Pisa, for example, he noted the different columns, their diverse form and order, and added:

cette eglise est ornée de diverses dépouilles de la Grèce et de l'Egypte, et bâtie d'anciennes ruines, ou l'on voit diverses inscriptions dont les unes se trouvent à rebours, les autres à demi tronquées. (p. 260)

[this church is decorated with diverse spoils from Greece and Egypt, and is built from ancient ruins; one can see several inscriptions, some are upside down and others half broken away.]

The observer here is acute but offers no judgement as to the aesthetic consequences of such composite forms beyond noting the incoherent jumble of
inscriptions which, because of their haphazard assemblage, resisted explanation.
In constructing the cathedral, no attempt was made to place the classical elements in knowing fashion,[89] and in considering this heterogeneous blend of
elements, Montaigne was in fact witnessing a similar process of borrowing 'les
dépouilles des anciens' (the spoils of the ancients) to that which Du Bellay had
recommended for writing some thirty years before.[90]

READING AND WRITING — À PIÈCES DESCOUSUES

It is precisely in the context of discussing his preferred style that Montaigne
recalls the ruins of Rome:

> J'ay veu des maisons ruynées et des statues, et du ciel . . . et si pourtant ne
> sçauroy revoir si souvent le tombeau de cette ville, si grande et si puissante,
> que je ne l'admire et revere. (III, 9, 996)

> [I have already seen elsewhere ruined palaces and sculptures of things in
> heaven . . . Yet, however often I were to visit the tomb of that great and
> mighty City, I would feel wonder and awe.]

He had virtually made the connection between his own writing and a building process, achieved by accumulating fragments, in the *Defence de Seneque et
de Plutarque* (II, 32, 721) where, using terms relevant to construction and repeating the word *dépouille*, he describes his book as 'massonné purement de leurs
despouilles' (entirely built out of their spoils). In *Des livres* (II, 10, 413), too, he
had acknowledged that both Seneca's and Plutarch's manner of writing in short
opuscules or *essais* had furnished him with knowledge immediately accessible,
quotable and manipulable, 'à pieces descousues' (pieces not sewn together),
ready to be absorbed into his own jaunty discourse.[91] While Montaigne was
justly critical of commonplaces accumulated without real thought or purpose
('ces pastissages de lieux communs' (those meat-pies stuffed with commonplaces), III, 12, 1056), he knowingly appropriated thoughts and phrases from
others – as he insisted – the better to express himself: 'Je ne dis les autres, sinon
pour d'autant plus me dire' (I only quote others the better to quote myself)
(I, 26, 148), and these proverbial phrases often served, in the *Essais*, to maintain a balance between the parts or fragments of experience and the whole
human condition.[92]

Montaigne's habits of borrowing rarely neglected the context of meaning
from which the fragments came,[93] but (as in his counsel in *De l'Institution des
enfans*, I, 26, 152) he stressed the extent to which they became his own words
and were changed and fused into new forms and matter.

Reworking Aristotle's original notion of literary composition as comparable
to bees sucking nectar from flowers, as many had done before,[94] Montaigne

moves the metaphor from gathering food (inspiration) to its absorption and metamorphosis into one's own mental energy:

> Les abeilles pillotent deçà de là les fleurs, mais elles en font après le miel, qui est tout leur; ce n'est plus thin ny marjolane; ainsi les pièces empruntees d'autruy, il les transformera et confondera, pour en faire un ouvrage tout sien: à sçavoir son jugement. (I, 26, 152)

> [Bees ransack flowers here and flowers there: but then they make their own honey, which is entirely theirs and no longer thyme or marjoram. Similarly the boy will transform his borrowings; he will confound their forms so that the end-product is entirely his: namely his judgement.]

Here the emphasis is on the transforming process which gave fragments of old texts new substance, although the new work – 'un ouvrage tout sien' (a product entirely his own) – may have retained an apparently heterogeneous and haphazard character, induced by the borrowing and of which Montaigne was proud.[95] His expansive statements in *De la vanité* (III, 9, 994–6) on what he called 'l'alleure poétique à saut et à gambades' (the gait of poetry, all jumps and tumblings), and which he associated with the discourse of Socrates as much as with the writing of Plutarch and Seneca, underlined his preference for jerky, disjointed utterance which threw into relief the parts or phrases of an argument, and tended to fragment its overall shape.

It is interesting that by the early seventeenth century the power of this kind of writing was no longer appreciated. Guez de Balzac, for instance, who was not without admiration for Montaigne's political acumen and moral stance in a period of civil disarray, completely misunderstood the purpose behind the essayist's disordered and dismembered text. In his *Entretiens* where he had reviewed the style of many authors, Guez de Balzac made this assessment of Montaigne's style.

> Son Discours n'est pas un corps entier: c'est un corps en pieces; et sont des membres couppez; et quoy que les parties soient proches les unes des autres, elles ne laissent pas d'estre separées. Non seulement il n'y a point de nerfs qui les ioignent; il n'y a pas mesme de cordes, ou d'aiguillettes, qui les attachent ensemble; tant cet Autheur est ennemy de toutes sortes de liaison, soit de la Nature, soit de l'Art; tant il s'esloigne de ces bons exemples, que vous imitez si parfaitement.

> [His Discourse is not a whole body: it's all in pieces; and its parts are all cut up; and although they are related to each other they are, for all that, separate. Not only are there no nerves to join them up, there are no veins or knots to bind them together; this Author is so antagonistic to all forms of liaison, either natural or through artifice, so distant is he from those good examples which you imitate so perfectly.][96]

The final flattering flourish closes a text that assumes the best writing to be a seamless structure, that cannot conceive an author who willed that his borrowing be visible, and that the broken course of his thought be evident, or that the surface of his text should resemble a 'marqueterie mal jointe' (a piece of badly joined marquetry). In writing such as Montaigne's, a reader has the opportunity of making reference back to the texts from which the borrowings came, and of probing the dense hinterland of reading experience which informed the *Essais*.[97] He may also study the interplay of the parts – 'pieces descousues' – on which Montaigne laid such stress and the whole implied by the 'marqueterie mal jointe'. Another contemporary shared Montaigne's view. The historian La Popelinière appreciated the powerful and distorting effect incomplete texts could have. In *L'Histoire des histoires*, he recalled that Cato's works and speeches have only come down to us in fragmented form, and those 'lambeaux qui nous restent' (fragments that remain to us) make us 'd'autant plus desirer les corps entiers de ses ouvrages, et nous les [font] penser plus beaux, et peut-estre plus recommandables qu'ils n'estoient' (all the more long for whole works and make us think of those that remain as fine and more remarkable than they really were).[98]

The principal emphasis in the *Essais* is on the fragments, on the 'membres descoupez', whether Montaigne is describing his reading habits – 'sans ordre et sans dessein, à pieces descousues' (disjointed, without order or design) (III, 3, 828); noting his capacity to penetrate through to the motives and impulses of behaviour in his friends which he does 'par articles descousus et à tastons' (in bits and cautiously); or defining the activities of his mind. In claiming so much for an approach to reflection that privileged process, Montaigne was at one and the same time stating his own limitations and criticizing those philosophers who moved so effortlessly and so rapidly to make general statements about the human condition. His own contribution was much more modest. He depicted wisdom as 'un bastiment solide et entier' (an edifice solid and entire) (III, 13, 1076), and saw himself as providing a few bricks towards the construction of that edifice. In speculating about the difficulty of capturing on the page the myriad traits and diverse details which make up the human form, his mind turned to the artist; perhaps painters might give some order and coherence.[99] But no: while a landscape with mountains or clouds can be created through artists' illusion, because we are relatively ignorant of these forms, when it comes to the lineaments and colours of more familiar subjects such as the human face, the process is more exacting (II, 12, 536).

Montaigne recognized the difficulty of translating into words what the mind perceived in sudden flashes of concentration, or of giving an adequate record of those moments when an idea hovers darkly on the edge of his mind and refuses to sharpen into focus:

> J'ay tousjours une idée en l'ame et certaine image trouble, qui me presente comme en songe une meilleure forme que celle que j'ay mis en besongne, mais je ne la puis saisir et exploiter. (II, 17, 637)

[I always have in my soul an ideal form, some vague pattern, which presents me, as in a dream, with a better form than the one I have employed; but I can never grasp it nor make use of it.]

In an early essay, he had already noted the wayward yet accretive nature of his mind, which moved hesitantly 'chancellant, bronchant et chopant' (swaying, stumbling, tripping over), often not towards a given object but into unknown dim territory: 'je voy encore du pais au delà, mais d'une veüe trouble et en nuage, que je ne puis desmeler' (I have a troubled cloudy vision of lands beyond, which I cannot make out) (I, 26, 146). And, in a later essay – *Des boyteux* (III, 11, 1029) – he reinforced the point when, translating freely from Seneca, he declared: 'Nostre veüe represente ainsi souvent de loing des images estranges, qui s'esvanouissent en s'approchant' (thus does our sight often produce strange visions in the distance, which vanish as we draw near) (III, 11, 1029).[100] Montaigne's stress on man's inability to grasp the whole of an experience flows directly from the conviction that the activities of the mind are transient and incomplete; and that the best that can be hoped for is to monitor its diverse and changing course, its unfinished ideas and its contradictions: 'C'est une conterole de divers et muables accidens, et d'imaginations irrésolues et, quand il y eschet, contraires' (This is a register of varied and changing occurrences, of ideas which are unresolved and, when need be, contradictory) (III, 2, 805).

It is in the context of this multiple, moving experience that Montaigne's criticism of the ambitious edifices erected by the philosophers must be placed: their complete and overblown 'architecture' (Montaigne used the building metaphor to accommodate the riotous forms of their imagination). Yet an architecture so ordered, assembled and enriched cannot contain every shift, every harmony that can occur (II, 12, 537). In Montaigne's opinion, such a fixed, all-embracing, monumental container – painted or written – is inappropriate to man's experience.

There is another need about which Montaigne wrote positively (though rarely) and which was closely associated with the wish to pin down in words an idea or a sensation as it happened. It concerns the ability to give adequate expression to thought at the moment of its conception and, simultaneously, to express reflection on the nature and manner of that thought. Matching the movement of mental change, the process of becoming, as Pouilloux has aptly termed it,[101] required renewing the capacities of language. It was a question of delving deep into the chest of words or the box of tropes not to find a perfect match as Horace had done, but rather for the idea to give new growth to language: stretching and bending its elements, deepening and strengthening meaning, inserting unexpected energy into the phrase. The most eloquent expression of this renewal is given in *Sur quelques vers de Virgile* where Montaigne reflected on the extraordinary efficacy of the Roman poet's words. The power of the thought drove the language, 'l'estirant et ployant . . . [ils]

appesantissent et enfoncent leur signification et leur usage, luy apprenant des mouvements inaccoustumés' (by extending and deploying it . . . (they) deepen their meanings and tie down their usage; they teach it unaccustomed rhythms) (III, 5, 873).

Fragmentation and discontinuity were thus deliberate writing strategies for Montaigne; their effect on the reader (whose response Montaigne constantly anticipated) was redoubled by the fact that phrases were not only discontinuous and jerky in their form but more often than not were couched in terms that left the idea unfinished and, moreover, offered the opportunity of recognizing old texts embedded within the new.[102] Montaigne had noticed in his reading of Plutarch the many places where a thought had been merely touched on, suggested by a sign which left the reader to follow at will the hint that had scarcely been formulated. While there were undoubtedly many sustained passages in the ancient writer's *Oeuvres morales*, conversely:

> Il y a dans Plutarque . . . mille [discours] qu'il n'a que touché simplement; il guigne [fait signe] seulement du doigt par où nous irons, s'il nous plaist, et se contente quelquefois de ne donner qu'une attainte dans le plus vif d'un propos. (I, 26, 156)

> [There are in Plutarch . . . hundreds of points which he simply touches on: he merely flicks his fingers towards the way we should go if we want to, or at times he contents himself with a quick shot at the liveliest part of the subject.]

Without apparently intending to imitate this manner observed in an acknowledged master, of his own way Montaigne had noted 'je n'entasse que les testes' (I merely pile up the heads of argument) (I, 40, 251), an approach which, he claimed, often provoked better, richer and more rewarding ideas. The partially formed notion, or the hint suspended, was, Montaigne admitted, engineered by him partly 'pour moy qui n'en veux exprimer davantage' (because I do not wish to press more out of them) (a selfish reason perhaps engendered by the need to protect himself at a time when words were weighed and measured so precisely in order to find fault),[103] and partly for the enjoyment of readers 'qui rencontreront mon air' (who get my gist).[104]

Critics of Montaigne have rightly grown suspicious of interpreting his ironies literally or of taking his dismissive remarks about the *Essais* at face value. When Montaigne referred to his work in an apparently derogatory way as 'ces petits brevets descousus' (flipping through my notes) and then went on to liken them to 'des feuilles Sybillines' (the leaves of the Sybils) (III, 13, 1092), he was making a joke at his own expense (using the *Essais* as a source of consolation and of retrospective prediction), and he was claiming some authority for his writing. When he referred arrestingly to 'ce fagotage de tant de diverses pièces' (all the various pieces of this faggot), he was drawing attention to the exact nature of his *Essais* whose composite fabric, like the arch of Constantine (see Figure 38,

p. 111), was 'basty à diverses poses et intervalles' (assembled at intervals and at different periods), and where each idea, each fragment could be separately identified, 'et qu'on voye chaque piece en sa naissance' (revealing each element as it is born) (II, 37, 758). It was, he argued late in life, easier to gloss the work of others than to create one's own (III, 13, 1065–6), and having largely opted for the latter he determined that the stages of his structure be visible in all their incompleteness.[105]

There were, however, reasons more telling than self-protection or the reader's satisfaction to explain the attention Montaigne gave to the unfinished in his work. In addition to the manner in which the haphazard, ever-changing beat of his thoughts was captured in a style that mirrored such unevenness, Montaigne determined not to complete an argument on the grounds that since he could never have a complete view of anything, it was not appropriate to do more than offer shards of thoughts cut out of their original context, and assembled without design and without promise of greater consistency. The consequences of this resolve were intended, in Montaigne's words, to reinforce his sense of uncertainty and doubt, and to render public, and in its proper form, his fundamental, defining character – a state of ignorance. The fullest account of his defence of the unfinished can be found in the opening paragraph of *De Democritus et Heraclitus* (I, 50, 302) where Montaigne reflected on the form he had given to his *Essais* and why. Having stressed the testing and watchful approach he adopted to both difficult and well-worn topics, accepting any subject (easy or hard) indiscriminately, in a late addition to the essay he developed this approach:

> Et ne desseigne jamais de les produire entiers [C] car je ne voy le but de rien . . . De cent membres et visages qu'a chaque chose, j'en prends un tantost à lecher seulement, tantost à effleurer; et parfois à puiser jusqu'à l'os . . . Semant icy un mot, icy un autre, eschantillons despris de leur piece, escartez, sans dessein et sans promesse . . . et me rendre au doubte et incertitude, et à ma maistresse forme, qui est l'ignorance. (I, 50, 302)

> [I never plan to expound them in full for I do not see the whole of anything . . . Everything has a hundred parts and a hundred faces: I take one of them and sometimes just touch it with the tip of my tongue or with my fingertips and sometimes I pinch it to the bone . . . Scattering broadcast a word here, a word there, examples ripped from their context, unusual ones, with no plan and no promises . . . I can surrender to doubt and uncertainty and to my master-form, which is ignorance.]

THE SHADOW OF THE WHOLE

Although Montaigne admitted frequently that he did not have the power to see or to record anything in the round, like the reconstructors of classical buildings who worked from the scattered fragments that remained, he could not resist the temptation at least to envisage the whole. 'Mon livre est tousjours un' (My book is ever one), he claimed; and such overall consistency was made up of 'membres descoupez'.

In the context of the relationship between the whole and its parts, it is instructive to consider the metaphor of the state which Montaigne used several times in the *Essais*. He presented it as an architectural structure, its diverse parts slotted together so expertly that, in contrast to his own compositions, the joins are not visible. Any disturbance to any part of this state/structure affects the whole and threatens to cause its ruin:

> une police, c'est comme un bastiment de diverses pieces jointes ensemble, d'une telle liaison, qu'il est impossible d'en esbranler une, que tout le corps ne s'en sente. (I, 23, 119)

> [a polity is like a building made of diverse pieces interlocked together, joined in such a way that it is impossible to move one without the whole structure feeling it.]

So much for the general hypothesis which a political philosopher might have conceived. A few sentences later, Montaigne considers a particular political structure (the French monarchy), and he shows it to be of a different kind; its parlous state, broken over the years, is vulnerable to further damage, and it resembles some great ruin as its parts decay and fall off:

> la liaison et contexture de cette monarchie et ce grand bastiment ayant esté desmis et dissout, notamment sur ses vieux ans, par elle [la nouveauté], donne tant qu'on veut d'ouverture et d'entrée à pareille injures. (I, 23, 119)

> [Once the great structure of the monarchy is shaken by novelty and its interwoven bonds torn asunder – especially in its old age – the gates are opened as wide as you wish to similar attacks.]

Once the joints loosen and the building becomes unsteady, the danger of collapse is predictable. Yet conceiving of the state as a well-knit building whose parts are weakened by time and stress has no practical consequence. The perception is philosophically interesting and of little political import; and the example from *De la coustume* (I, 23) was offered more as a cautionary tale to deter those who sought political change.

What emerges from any study of the interplay of parts and wholes in the *Essais* is evidence of the enormous distance between those completed, abstract entities which the mind creates and everyday experience where the tiniest element can impinge and hurt. The most telling example occurs in *De la diversion* where, after generalizing about the impact small and even superficial events can make, Montaigne homed in on a favourite subject, death.

Je voyois nonchalamment la mort, quand je la voyois universellement [en gros], comme fin de la vie; je la gourmand [domine] en bloc; par le menu, elle me pille. (III, 4, 837)

[When I looked upon death as the end of my life, universally, then I looked upon it with indifference. Wholesale, I could master it: retail, it savaged me.]

The distanced, abstract and generalized conception was easy to believe and therefore simple to control. In succumbing to the temptation to create such images, Montaigne was aware that he was giving in to a common human weakness, to the ability of the mind to create anything out of a fragment, a given assumption; out of nothing, even. The game is easy and, once a basis has been posited, it follows logically, inexorably, that the whole edifice should be constructed. There is no lack of building materials and no absence of patterns to be followed. Were the following passage not to come from *De l'apologie*, its rising tone and confidence might have been interpreted as indicating Montaigne's enthusiasm:

Il est bien aisé, sur des fondemens assurez, de bastir ce qu'on veut: car, selon la loy et ordonnance de ce commencement, le reste des pieces du bastiment se conduit ayséement, sans se démentir. Par cette voye nous trouvons nostre raison bien fondée, et discourons à boule veue. (II, 12, 540)

[Base yourself on admitted postulates and you can build up any case you like; from the rules which order the original principles the remainder of your construction will follow on easily without self-contradiction. This method allows us to bowl our arguments with the jack in view (and to be satisfied that our foundations are rational ones).]

In a late essay Montaigne asked ironically: why should one restrict human capacity to the building of one argument or one philosophy? Why not let the mind conceive of multiple worlds?

Nostre discours est capable d'estoffer cent autres mondes et d'en trouver des principes et la contexture. Il ne luy faut ny matiere, ny baze; laissez le courre; il bastit aussi bien sur le vuide que sur le plain. (III, 11, 1027)

[Our reason has capacity enough to provide the stuff for a hundred other worlds, and then to discover their principles and construction. It needs neither matter nor foundation; let it run free; it can build as well upon the void as upon the plenum.][106]

Here Montaigne has taken several leaps forward, disdaining the arts of rhetoric and dialectic which he was exposing in *De l'apologie* and letting his irony run riot. Building worlds out of air, supported by no discernible fragments of matter in their make–up, has the vaporous, empty quality which he attributed to most human mental constructions. The building prowess presented in *De l'apologie*

241

was, in the end, nothing but dreams and smoke ('tout le demeurant . . . n'est que songe et fumée' (all the rest . . . is dream and vapour), II, 12, 540). The hundred worlds tossed up out of pure air were also no more than modes of escape from the realities of living, from the limitations of being human; and, paradoxically, such building fantasies were themselves – when performed – the most convincing proofs of human imbecility.[107]

Even the greatest minds were not exempt from such strictures; indeed, their evidence confirmed Montaigne's realistic view that their ability to capture a complete and coherent explanation of the world in which they lived (whether by atoms, ideas or numbers) was so much subtlety and conjecture, of surface value only (III, 12, 511). Ultimately, the ease with which man stretched his mind to encompass everything, while he simultaneously ignored the detail of experience, led Montaigne to conclude that he, and others, could best be described as so much wind. In his final chapter *De l'experience*, this conclusion summed up his opinion of the unstable yet variable activities of the mind and provided terrain for further speculation. The wind marvellously characterizes inflated and wayward power, yet with its free moving qualities sufficient unto themselves, showing no concern for the stable and solid anchorage which man yearned for despite the uncontrolled flights of his imagination, even the wind is superior:

> Moy . . . n'y trouve quand j'y regarde assez finement à peu pres que du vent. Mais quoy, nous sommes partout vent. Et le vent encore, plus sagement que nous, s'ayme à bruire, à s'agiter, et se contente en ses propres offices, sans desirer la stabilité, la solidité qualitez non siennes. (III, 13, 1106–7)

> [I . . . find virtually nothing but wind in them when I examine them in detail. But then we too are nothing but wind. And the wind (more wise than we are) delights in its rustling and blowing, and is content with its own role without yearning for qualities which are nothing to do with it such as immovability or density.]

It is important to recognize that the sharpness and depth of Montaigne's criticism derived from his view that what man was constantly tempted to create and then to hold in his grasp belonged to God's domain. Seen from this perspective, man's ideas are properly termed 'masse informe, sans façon et sans jour' (formless mass, unenlightened and without shape) (II, 12, 447), his knowledge 'une pièce, et bien petite, de nostre ignorance' (part of our ignorance, and a small part at that) (II, 12, 501), and as to the world, 'cette pièce n'est rien au pris du tout' (the tiny bit that we know, is nothing compared with all).

If we transfer the metaphor of parts and wholes from fragments of buildings reassembled and made into new structures to those mental constructs projected and criticized in the *Essais*, it is clear that, although the metaphor helps to clarify the distance which Montaigne perceived between the fragments of living and the large entities created by the mind, by placing man's best achievements in the context of the divine, he has changed the terms. Neither parts nor whole have validity within the immensity of *le Grand Tout*, Montaigne affirmed (quoting Lucretius). In fact, although words can name that immense whole, the mind cannot grasp its nature, so great is the disjunction between specifying and properly conceiving it: 'Quand nous disons que l'infinité des siecles tant passez qu'avenir, n'est à Dieu qu'un instant . . . nostre parole le dict, mais nostre intelligence ne l'apprehende point' (when we say countless ages – ages past and ages yet to come – are but a moment to God . . . we utter words, but our intelligence cannot grasp the sense) (II, 12, 528).

The principal consequence of Montaigne's devastating analysis of man's general incapacity was to turn his attention inwards, to scale down his aspirations, and to study his own self. But there, in this new orientation, despite a feeling that some kind of inner consistency did exist within and that there was an internal pattern ('un patron au dedans') which regulated his behaviour, despite also the indisputable presence of common traits in all men, Montaigne concentrated on the fragments. The philosophy of writers, like Seneca, who had encouraged him to build, from his observation of those fragments, a self whose strength and regularity would withstand the vagaries of external events, was abandoned in the face of discoveries that showed a multiple person.[108] In *De l'exercitation* he had resolved to show himself entire to the reader. The whole would be exposed like a skeleton with its well-delineated shape that could be taken in at a glance, its muscular structure, and nervous and circulatory systems intact:

> Je m'estalle entier: c'est un *skeletos* où, d'une veüe, les veines, les muscles, les tendrons paroissent, chaque piece en son siège (II, 6, 379).

> [I am *all* on display, like a mummy [skeleton] on which at a glance you can see the veins, the muscles and the tendons, each piece in its place.]

This vision of a completed form, exhibited in full, was never achieved in the *Essais*. As Montaigne explored himself, that self disintegrated as he looked, and the whole dissolved into myriad parts. Self-scrutiny meant observing behaviour over time, from one minute to the next, and such observation revealed a succession of selves: 'Moy à ceste heure et moy tantost sont bien deux' ('I' now and 'I' then are certainly twain) (III, 9, 964). As he tried to project the diverse changes and movements over time, Montaigne saw his *moi* as if it were a double propelled outside him, objectified and taking on a life of its own. It became another human form, dimly perceived and stumbling into the distance: 'C'est un mouvement d'yvroigne titubant, vertigineux, informe, ou des joncs que l'air manie casuellement' (but it is a drunkard's progress, formless, staggering, like reeds which the wind shakes as it fancies, haphazardly) (III, 9, 964). On other occasions, too, he tried to reassure the reader of the accuracy of his scrutiny through similar objectifying modes; at the end of *De l'art de conferer*, for instance, where the self is seen at a distance, as if it were other, 'comme un voisin, comme un arbre' (like a neighbour or a tree) (III, 8, 942). The different perspectives of looking matched the mobile changeability of the being Montaigne was observing, and what he discovered about his own self he readily transferred to human experience in general. Thus, in *De l'inconstance de nos actions*, he argued the impossibility of evolving a sure line of future behaviour. Pieces cannot be arranged without some notion of the form of the whole, and that was not possible as we function only through small fragments of things:

> Il est impossible de renger les pieces, à qui n'a une forme du total en sa teste. A quoy faire la provision des couleurs à qui ne sçait ce qu'il a à peindre? Aucun ne fait certain dessain de sa vie, et n'en deliberons qu'à parcelles. (II, 1, 337)

> [It is impossible to put the pieces together if you do not have in your head the idea of the whole. What is the use of providing yourself with paints if you do not know what to paint? No man sketches out a definite plan for his life; we only determine bits of it.]

These assertions gathered strength from Montaigne's own experience, which permitted him to develop a series of general affirmations about the varied and shapeless nature of man who was made up of parts that played independent roles, reacting separately to successive moments of time. Degrees of difference are measured not only from one man to another, between the self and the other, but also between those different selves belonging to the same person and made manifest through the play of the individual parts:

> Nous sommes tous de lopins, et d'une contexture si informe et diverse, que chaque piece, chaque moment, faict son jeu. Et se trouve autant de difference de nous à nous mesmes, que de nous à autruy. (II, 1, 337)

> [We are entirely made up of bits and pieces, woven together so diversely and so shapelessly that each one of them pulls its own way at every moment. And there is as much difference between us and ourselves as there is between us and other people.]

This stress on the pieces of man's make-up neither hides the presence of a whole form nor dispels the urge to give it visibility. In this discussion of the fragment in the *Essais*, and our exploration of how consistently Montaigne avoided closure and the reasons for that determination (whether it be in his statements about the broken and unpredictable nature of thought, behaviour or external events, or whether expressed in his own practice of writing), it has not been easy to resist the temptation to complete the many deferred conclusions, and to find an overall unity in the *Essais*.[109]

Unity and completion are comforting and reassuring notions; and perhaps it was for this reason that Montaigne went to such lengths (insistence, repetition, irony) to engage the reader in the argument, and to make him experience those flashes of confusion and even of shame when the urge to conclude, to overdefine or offer definitive statements was irresistible. The reader's share in the making of the *Essais* was important for Montaigne, both as reader himself (a matter upon which he had expatiated at length),[110] and as a writer anxious to be heard. He had examined the receptive power of different forms and approved them when they reached that point of expression where author and reader/listener are over-whelmed: in poetry, the 'saillies qui emportent . . . et ravissent hors de soy' (those creative ecstasies which transport a poet and carry him outside himself in rapture); in rhetoric, where gestures take the orator beyond his original inten-tion ('ces mouvemens et agitations extraordinaires, qui les poussent au delà de leur dessein' (stirrings and perturbations, outside their natural order; which impel them well beyond what they had planned)); in painting, where touches exceed the artist's plan and astonish him ('des traits qui eschappent surpassans sa con-ception et sa science qui le tirent luymesme en admiration, et qui l'estonnent' (painting . . . which sometimes escapes free from the brush-strokes of the painter's hand, surpassing his own conceptions and artistry and bringing him to an ecstasy of astonishment which leaves him thunderstruck)); and in his own writing, for which he craved a well-furnished mind which could extend the meaning of the text through his own perceptions:

> un suffisant lecteur descouvre souvent és escrits d'autruy des perfections autres que celles que l'autheur y a mises et apperçeües, et y preste des sens et des visages plus riches. (*Divers evenemens de mesme conseil*, I, 24, 127)

> [a competent reader can often find in another man's writing perfections other than those which the author knows that he put there, and can endow them with richer senses and meanings.]

Montaigne's reader cooperates in the creation of the text. Fragments leave him space to develop the idea, to disagree or to protest. This participation was so essential that Montaigne went to considerable lengths to stir his reader: by shocking him with themes such as suicide or torture; by using subtle ways of drawing him in – understatement and, for example, withholding detail of the civil war; or by outrageous overstatement: 'ce sont icy, un peu plus civilement, des excremens d'un vieil esprit, dur tantost, tantost lache et tousjours indigeste' (here, a little more decorously, you have the droppings of an old mind, some-times hard, sometimes squittery, but always ill-digested) (III, 9, 946). The triple adjectives reinforce the unpleasantness of the image *excremens* which perfectly captures the experience of struggling with the *Essais*. In another place, Montaigne offered an overall view of his work which took as its measure an ordered structure, well regulated and harmonious in its proportions. Against such a form, the *Essais* are depicted as a monstrous body: their pieces thrown together haphazardly, they are irregular, impermanent and unbalanced:

> Que sont-ce icy . . . que crotesques et corps monstrueux, rappiecez, de divers membres, sans certaine figure, n'ayants ordre, suite, ny proportion que fortuite? (I, 28, 183)

> [what are these . . . if not monstrosities and grotesques botched together from a variety of limbs having no defined shape, with an order, sequence and proportion which are purely fortuitous?]

What we now understand is that such a strange structure is the willed product of a writer whose strategy was to match the words and phrases to his thought processes, who laid emphasis on the parts with little regard for the shape of the whole, and who deliberately eschewed contemporary standards of aesthetic judgement.[111] He knew these well and, in this passage, reminded the reader of such norms in order to make a typically Gascon statement signalling a certain pride in his 'monstrous' achievement.[112]

RETURN TO ROME

The discovery of the New World had led Montaigne to reflect on the Old and to observe how forms of all kinds multiply and change, and how our knowledge of these is regulated by the accident of survival. Among the survivals which drew his admiration were the spectacular games performed under the emperors for the people in the Colosseum at Rome (Figure 76).[113] In his evocation of them there is a mixture of admiration for and irony at the magnificence and ingenuity of the building, the machines involved, and the size and excess of the conceptions. In particular, apart from fertility in inspiration, he praised the beauty of the buildings:

> ces grands amphitheatres encroustez de marbre au dehors, labouré d'ouvrages et statues, le dedans reluisant de plusieurs rares enrichissemens. (III, 6, 905)

> [those great amphitheatres encrusted on the outside with marble and decorated with works of art and statuary, the inside gleaming with rare and precious stones.]

The only modern spectacle to arouse the pleasure which Montaigne derived from this recollection of ancient festivals was the chariot race he witnessed at Florence in 1581 on his way back from Rome, about which he declared,

> ce spectacle me fit plus de plaisir qu'aucun de ceux que j'eusse vus en Italie par la ressemblance que j'y trouvois avec les courses antiques. (*Journal*, p. 254)

76. Attributed to Etienne du Pérac: the Colosseum

[this sight gave me more pleasure than all those others I saw in Italy because of its similarities with ancient races.]

In reconstructing a vision of these spectacles, Montaigne leaned heavily on Justus Lipsius;[114] but also threaded through descriptions in *Des coches* were reminders of his own experience. There was the sight of the amphitheatre in Verona which was 'le plus beau bastiment qu'il eust veu en sa vie' (the most beautiful building he had seen in his life), and which he had described in detail in the *Journal*, noting 'qu'il y en a assez de reste pour descouvrir au vif la forme et service de ces bastimens' (that sufficient remained for discovering the form and function of these buildings) (p. 65). There was also the evidence of Mantegna's *Triumphs of Caesar*, located at this time in Cardinal Clesius' Castello del Buon Consiglio and which Montaigne admired greatly (p. 59).[115]

Similar memories returned as he pondered in *De la vanité* the mutability and durability of states. The supreme example of the way gods play with mortal things is, of course, Rome. And here, Montaigne picked up again the idea he had elaborated in *De la coustume* of states conceived of as great buildings. In this instance, however, the image is slightly changed: the age of the building rather than its joints holds it together. Then gradually the image slides into an evocation of the ruins of Rome:

Tout ce qui branle ne tombe pas. La contexture d'un si grand corps [Rome] tient à plus d'un clou. Il tient mesme par son antiquité: comme les vieux bastimens, ausquels l'age a desrobé le pied, sans crouste et sans cyment, qui pourtant vivent et se soustiennent en leur propre poix. (III, 9, 960)

[All that totters does not collapse. More than one nail holds up the frame-work of so mighty a structure. Its very antiquity can hold it up, like old buildings which, without cement or cladding, are propped up their own mass.]

Nostalgia for those ruins, and for what they represented, is accepted by Montaigne, who came back to them later in the essay when he expressed his profound affection for Rome as much in its flourishing state – 'cette vieille Romme, libre, juste et florissante' (of ancient Rome, free and just and flouri-shing) – as when it was ruined.

The magnetic pull of that city which had housed so many of his heroes was mysterious but real. Montaigne remembered both Cicero and Quintilian as he explored the power that inhabited such places, capable of so stirring the imagi-nation that it brought alive those heroic beings and made them walk again on the stones of Rome in company with him. He recalled the dignified old city entire, the ruins that stretch down to the Antipodes, the faces, steps and talk of his companions from classical Rome, and the noise of the modern inter-national city; all these recollections, memories and reconstitutions are given equal status and seemingly simultaneous presence in this eloquent passage filled with yearning:

Me trouvant inutile à ce siecle, je me rejecte à cet autre, et en suis si embabouyné que l'estat de cette vieille Rome libre, juste et florissante . . . m'interesse et me passionne. Parquoy je ne sçauroy revoir si souvent l'asiette de leurs rues et de leurs maisons, et ces ruynes profondes jusques aux Antipodes, que je ne m'y amuse. [C] Est-ce pas nature ou par erreur de fan-tasie que la veuë des places que nous sçavons avoir esté hantées et habitées par personnes desquelles la memoire est en recommendation, nous esmeut aucunement plus qu'ouïr le recit de leurs faicts ou lire leurs escrits? (III, 9, 996–7)

[Finding myself useless for this present age I fall back on that one. I am such a silly baboon about it that the state of ancient Rome, free and just and flourishing . . . is of passionate concern to me. That is why I could never so often revisit the site of their streets and their palaces, and their ruins stretch-ing down to the Antipodes without lingering over them. Is it by nature or an aberrant imagination that the sight of places which we know to have been frequented or inhabited by those whose memory we hold dear moves us somewhat more than hearing a recital of their deeds or reading their writings?]

The movement across time is unimpeded, and the interplay of past and present fluent and uncomplicated. It is as though Montaigne sees all the layers of the city at once, from its state when it was in its prime to its magnificent ruins.

In this evocation of Rome (then and now) it is noticeable that Montaigne stressed the closeness of his association with those who had lived there; in doing so, he was drawing on his direct experience of Rome and on phrases recollected from his reading of classical texts – his favourite authors and the ancient rhetoricians. Quintilian, in his exposition of the artificial art of memory, had explained this experience as a common one:

> For when we return to a place after considerable absence, we do not merely recognize the place itself, but remember things that we did there, and recall the persons whom we met and even the unuttered thoughts which passed through our minds when we were there before.[116]

When Montaigne re-read *De la vanité*, although he recalled Quintilian's remarks, he also remembered the opening lines of Book 5 of Cicero's *De finibus*. Montaigne's question of whether the mysterious power of place is greater than heroes' deeds or writers' words is a direct quotation from the ancient orator:

> Whether it is a natural instinct or a mere illusion, I can't say; but one's emotions are more strongly aroused by seeing the places that tradition records to have been the favourite resort of men of note in former days, than by hearing about their deeds or reading their writings.[117]

After translating Cicero's text word for word, Montaigne then uses another quotation from the same source (without acknowledging it), this time citing the text in Latin, 'tanta vis admonitionis inest in locus' (such powers of suggestion do places possess) (V, I, ii). To emphasize his point about the reverberative power of Rome further, Montaigne juxtaposes yet another phrase from Cicero, taken from a later passage in *De finibus*: 'there is no end to it in this city; wherever we go we tread historic ground' (id quidem inifinitum est in hac urbe; quacumque enim ingredimur, in aliqua historia vestigium ponimus). Had Montaigne gone on to remember Cicero's *De legibus*, he would have found an even more explicit statement of the strange ways in which we are affected by the *vestigia* of loved ones and of the places they had inhabited. This time, the city was Athens; it had attracted Cicero less for its beauty and ornaments, or for the exquisite works of antiquity which could be seen there, than for the great men who had loved and disputed in the city.[118]

The collapsing together of all the stages of growth and decay which was evident in the evocation of Rome in *De la vanité* (III, 9, 996–7) was sometimes expressed by Montaigne more abruptly. At the end of the evocation and of the re-enacting of that companionship Montaigne felt with figures from ancient Rome, he inserted into the essay four brief sentences:

- Sa ruyne mesme est glorieuse et enflée.
- [C] Laudandis preciosior ruinis [Sidonius Apollinarus, *carmina*, 23, line 62].
- [B] Encore retient elle au tombeau des marques et images d'empire.
- [C] Ut palam sit uno in loco gaudentis opus est esse naturae [Pliny, *Natural History*, book 3, ch. 5] (III, 9, 997).

[Even in ruins it is glorious and stately/ More precious for her ruins which deserve our praise/ Even in her tomb she still retains the signs and ghost of empire/ so that it should be obvious that in this one place nature delights in her work.]

Three of the phrases juxtapose the ruins of the city and images of its former greatness, while the last emphasizes how fragments of ancient Rome acted as additional signifiers of the city as a unique place, favoured by nature.

This is the context Montaigne prepared for citing, in its entirety, the papal bull which conferred upon him the citizenship of Rome: '[la ville] la plus noble qui fut et qui sera oncques' (the noblest City there ever was or ever shall be).[119] Montaigne's pride in such ownership, however bashfully expressed, is underlined by the picture of Rome which he had drawn.

Inevitably, Montaigne's responses to Rome were conditioned by the Wars of Religion. His journey to the imperial city had, in part, been triggered by the wish to escape the appalling sights which civil strife had brought to France; once in Rome, he was confronted by sights no less moving, by the ruins of those places where his heroes had lived, walked and talked. He acknowledged the emotional pull of such places; and the evidence of their destruction, compounded by the devastating sights he had left behind in France, deeply affected his thinking. The suggestive power of ruins, those enigmatic signs which encouraged interpretation, seems to have strengthened his resolve to continue writing *à pieces descousues* in the *Essais*, a manner designed to arouse the imaginative capacity of his well-prepared reader.

CHAPTER 7

Negative Responses
and Reverse Appropriation

The experience of civil war in France transformed attitudes to Rome. Writers became more selective in their use of images of the ancient city; ruins were given moral readings and became signs of deserved destruction; and memories of ancient texts and of privileged places in the imperial city concentrated on the extent to which they could throw light on contemporary conditions in France. Rome, the city, its history and its principal actions were appropriated for reasons almost opposite to those which have been explored so far. They furnished material for argument in tragedies designed to move audiences away from admiration to pity, and incited reflections on the spectacle of Rome torn apart by ambition and greed. Emulation had given way to critical assessment of Rome and, in some poems, to downright condemnation.

Many powerful thinkers had actually opposed attempts to identify contemporary forms and issues with counterparts from ancient Rome. Their reasons were complex. Guicciardini had counselled against adopting political, judicial or organizational forms from Rome since they were imperfect and inappropriate to modern times, and he considered that even to think about them did disservice to contemporary customs. In his view, antiquity was often praised more than it should be.[1] Likewise Erasmus, concerned about the neglect of current problems, had condemned excessive praise of antiquity and satirized those who spent their time dreaming of ancient Rome. The city itself, he declared, 'is not Rome. It has nothing but ruins and rubble, the scars and signs of the disasters that befell long ago', and he castigated those unfortunates who did not realize that the world had changed, and that a citizen of Rome was no more significant than a bourgeois from Bâle.[2]

Montaigne was equally suspicious of past/present comparisons, recognizing their inexact match. 'Tout exemple cloche' (every example limps), he maintained in *De l'experience* (III, 13, 1070), though he reluctantly conceded – and with evident disapproval – that it was possible to manipulate parallel images and make them fit together in some way: 'on joint toutesfois les comparaisons par quelque coin' (we can nevertheless find some corner or other by which to link our comparisons). For his part, René de Lucinge acknowledged that Rome provided the most generous source of images and examples ('la Romaine est la plus copieuse en exemples'), but he thought, nonetheless, that the whole business of building images or arguments on fragments gleaned from the past was a doubtful exercise and one to be deplored. Rome is too far from us, Lucinge argued, to provide points of reference that are proportionate to our need; past and present issues are inevitably different in scale and context. In setting forth his opposition to facile comparisons with the past, Lucinge's principal target was Lipsius, whose laborious attempts to mould sixteenth-century civil wars 'sur le modelle de celles de Cesar et de Pompee dans Rome' (on the model of those of Caesar and Pompey in Rome) were misguided and only served to distort the truth. Lipsius' method, he contended, was no more than 'une chymerisee science qui n'a point de consistence pour en conclure l'assortissement' (an imaginary science with no consistency to effect any bringing together). Comparisons (Lucinge agreed) may be ingeniously stretched to fit into predetermined moulds, but they do not produce a sound result; they are inaccurate and misleading, distorted and obscure. In between the points of comparison, too much has slipped and changed:

> Si on en collige quelque traict qui se ressemble, cela est plustost sophistiqué que pris d'une juste appariation pour en rendre l'image et le pourtraict relatif de ces vieilles pieces aux nostres. C'est chanceller par tout, et aller à tastons vers l'humeur, le maintien, le port et les causes de tant d'accidens advenus du passé aux nostres d'aujourd'huy pour les apparier. Il n'y a ciment qui puisse conjoindre, attacher et coller des pieces tant inesgalles, raboteuses, et des parties si disproportionnées.

> [If one sticks together some forms which resemble each other, it is through cunning in order to make the image or likeness of these old pieces akin to our own rather than through some just appearance. It's a chancy method, groping towards the humour, attitude, stance and the causes of so many happenings from the past to fit them to those of today. There is no cement that can join, attach or glue together such unequal and craggy fragments and such disproportionate bits.][3]

Whether Lipsius struggles to keep alive some sense of the discordant tones related to each part, or strives to subsume one image into the other, according to Lucinge it does not matter: the outcome is always unsatisfactory.

However powerful the voices which considered such stitchings together of questionable value, they did not undermine the will to create structures inspired by ancient vestiges, nor did they inhibit what seems to have been a natural, almost automatic tendency for French writers to have recourse to Rome in developing their ideas and feelings on civil war. After all, writers perceived close connections between the literal pillage of antiquities to which they were often witness and the literary plunder which Du Bellay had advocated at the end of the *Deffence*. There were also links with the pillage and devastation experienced by everyone who had participated in the civil wars: and this relationship engendered hostile interpretations of Rome and its ancient remains.

Negative readings of the ruins had always formed part of travellers' response to Rome: from Poggio's lament onwards, ruins had been interpreted as evidence of the destructive power of Time and Fortune, and as symbols of man's fallen state. In France, in the second half of the sixteenth century, such interpretations were less abstract notions. The ruined city was evoked with greater intensity and precision in order to provide the material on which to base attacks on Rome and all the city stood for.

Hostility towards Rome has to be seen in the more general context of increasing antagonism towards Italy, especially after the outbreak of civil war in 1560. The hatred (which is not too strong a term) had been nourished from complex sources and its expression shaped by diverse strands of prejudice, political manoeuvring and personal ambition.[4] Protestant diatribes against Rome became more blatant as the war and their sporadic successes flourished and as the crown's control over the fighting weakened. Attacks upon Italianism at court and against the dominance of Italian advisers on royal policies were also more explicit as writers like Henri Estienne sought to protect the purity of the French language, or to stem the tide of influence of Machiavelli.[5] After Henri III's assassination, the departure of many Italians from the court was greeted with extravagant relief, expressed luxuriously in pamphlets such as the anonymous *Discours de la fuite des imposteurs italiens* (Paris, 1589). The tones of excess which characterized these works also invaded writing which sought to paint Paris as the successful rival to Rome.

In the first of his Latin epistles addressed to the Roman Muses, Michel de l'Hospital strove to attract Jean du Bellay back to France. As bait, he promoted the glories of France and, especially, the splendour of Paris. Let us set aside, he argued, that old, deep-rooted renown, that prejudice 'attaché au seul mot de Rome!' (attached to the name of Rome). Consider, instead, the treasures of Paris: its people, its palaces and its temples, and 'sachez que Paris s'approche du ciel et lève la tête plus que Rome' (know that Paris raises its head higher towards heaven, than does Rome). The motif – 'Paris, rival de Rome' – occurred more than once in his poems.[6] Some writers went even further, arguing that the French capital was a more ancient foundation than Rome.[7]

A hectoring tone criticizing Rome and praising all things French was also present in the first attempts to define the elements which made up French identity, and to affirm the strength of the nation's originality and traditions. In this context, Pasquier gibed that he could not see that Italy had served as anything but a graveyard for Frenchmen. He was exasperated by the prevailing view that nothing good could be done in France unless it had been inspired by Rome, and wrote to Sebillet in uncompromising terms: 'nous devons rien à ce superbe Rome' (we owe nothing to this proud Rome). Although he recognized that all young men were eager to see Rome, he counselled sobriety:

reactions to ancient remains should be subdued, to the extent that he advised Paul de Foix not to let his (Pasquier's) son waste time on *antiquailles* 'qui ne me semblent de grande edification' (which do not seem to me to provide much enlightenment). In fact, he viewed them with such scorn that when he dedicated his first book of *Recherches* to cardinal de Lorraine, he expressed the hope that his patron would pay due attention to them, and certainly more than the fleeting glance of ownership accorded to the fragments of ancient statues which came into his possession:

Mais tout ainsi qu'en vos maisons de parade, chacun s'estudie de vous apporter quelques anticailles de marques, desquelles paraventure vous repaissez seulement une fois à la traverse, vos yeux, demeurant au surplus, contents de les avoir une fois en vostre possession: aussi vous envoyant ces fragments que j'ay tirez des anciennetez de nostre France, j'espère, qu'encores que ne les couriez que de l'oeil, si en ferez-vous estat comme des vostres.

[But just as in your magnificent houses each one seeks to bring you some notable ancient fragment which — as likely as not — you take in fleetingly, your eyes being merely content to own it, similarly in sending you these fragments which I have drawn from ancient relics of our France, I hope that not only will you cast your eye upon them, but that you will take them as your own.][8]

The severity of the Protestant attacks on Rome was boundless. St Bernard had long ago christened the imperial city 'la putain purpurée' [the crimson whore]; and the name stuck. It was used again and again (with variations) in polemical writing during the French civil wars, and culminated in the anthology of Protestant writing *La Chasse de la beste romaine*, where *Rome/la Paillarde* forms the unchanging structure to a vast work of monotonous verbal diarrhoea.[9] This text contains no arguments but merely states opinions purporting to be true, building one on top of the other into a huge edifice of vacuity. It is as though the insistent affirmations are themselves acts of destruction, exactly like the series of statements found in a sonnet attributed to Jodelle and addressed to Du Bellay. The opening quatrain sets the tone and the no-nonsense affirmative structure:

> Je sçay bien, Du Bellay, que Rome est le bordeau,
> Où l'on voit paillarder sans fin le corps et l'ame!
> Le corps y est espris d'une bougresse flamme,
> L'esprit paillarde avec l'antechrist son bourreau.

[I know well, Du Bellay, that Rome is the sink,/ Where one witnesses endless debauching of mind and body!/ The body is seized with passionate sodomy,/ The spirit couples lecherously with Antichrist, her executioner.]

The affirmations continue to accumulate in the tercets: Rome is 'la fine lar-roneuse' (the cunning thief), 'la fausse revenderesse' (the false haggler), 'La source de tout mal, le gouffre de tout bien' (the source of all evil, the well of all good), and 'cette pute immonde' (this shameful whore). This string of abuse hardly prepares the reader for the city being termed 'à bon droit', 'le chef de tout le monde' (rightly . . . the head of all), until the lame ending explains that *all* is worth nothing.[10]

The same virulent temper was present in George Buchanan's satirical poem on Rome. In his epigram 'In Romam', Buchanan reminds the reader how the city, now in ruins and resembling a corpse, was once the haunt of wolves and, he asserts with emphatic and wearisome alliteration, those wild animals still dominate the place:

> Hic colles, ubi nunc vides ruinas
> Et tantum veteris cadaver urbis,
> Quondam caeca LUPIS fuere histris
> . . . Nihil comperies nisi LUPERCOS,
> LUPERCALE, LUPOS, LUPAS, LUPANAR.[11]

Despite crude play on words and monotonous repetition, whose aim seemed to be to obliterate a reverential image of Rome and to replace it with the picture of an uninhabitable, dangerous place, Protestants were hungry to see Rome. They sought special passports and disguised themselves to escape detec-tion.[12] Once inside the city, they stood before the remains of classical build-ings and gloated at their ruined state, recording their glee with relish, and painting the rubble and the piles of stones with malevolent satisfaction. Gregory Martin described his 'delight to see the ruines thereof, and how they are neglected', and he enjoyed watching the crumbling of 'the triumphal vaultes [which] come daily to nothing'. Nicolas Filleul reduced the former greatness and authority of Rome to a mere 'ornement misérable . . . quelque monceau de ruinez palais' (miserable ornament . . . a heap of ruined palaces), and the only evidence he finds that a city once existed is in the one durable object that survives – the bronze which depicts a wolf suckling the twin founders of Rome.[13]

RUINS IN FRANCE

But why go to Rome at all when France itself was a thesaurus of Roman ruins? Scattered around French towns, especially in the south of the country where the Romans had penetrated and settled, were visible signs of their occu-pation. Temples, arenas, sarcophagi and columns could still be seen and admired in places such as Autun and Lyon, Xaintes, Nîmes, Arles and Orange, and Bordeaux. In the sixteenth century, observers began to record their impressions of the remains:[14] Bernard Palissy used the 'ruines antiques' (ancient ruins) at

Xaintes as inspiration for his work; Michel de l'Hospital and Jacques Auguste de Thou noted the many monuments – marble doors, sculptures, triumphal arches and palaces – which reminded them of Roman supremacy in France; while André Thevet emphasized how every day the soil unearthed new treasures – coins, fragments of columns and statues, and broken architraves.[15] There were three towns which attracted particular attention: Lyon whose origins were debated by several scholars;[16] Nîmes and Bordeaux, plans of which were issued by Braun and Hogenberg in 1572.[17]

Nîmes' rich remains had, in part, been pillaged by François I, yet they were still sufficiently numerous to attract visitors from many countries on their way to Rome and to command the admiration of those who studied these vestiges of Roman power whose magnificence (as De Thou argued) outdid all modern building in the city.[18] In 1560, Poldo d'Albenas published an account of the origins of the city and of its ancient buildings. The folio volume is richly illustrated with engravings and with preliminary poems indicating contemporary attitudes to the ruins. The columns and arches of the Arènes (as they were called) were admired for their order and proportions; and Jacques Pineton, in an ode addressed to Poldo, marks out for special appreciation the engraved epitaphs and paving stones, the columns and vases, the capitals and medals which had emerged – almost haphazardly – from the ground:

> Tant d'épitaphes gravés,
> Et taillés en pierre dure
> Et tant de riches pavez,
> Trouvez aux champs d'aventure,
> Tant de Beaux marbres brisés,
> Colomnes, chapiteaux, bases
> Tant de medailles et vases
> Pour l'oeuvre et la main prisés.

[So many engraved epitaphs/ Cut into the hard stone/ And so many rich pavements/ Found fortuitously in the fields/ So many magnificent marble pieces/ Columns, capitals, bases/ So many medals and vases/ prized for their workmanship.][19]

Inhabitants of Nîmes were proud of their ancient architecture and boasted about its qualities; and, although their claims for its grandeur and perfection might seem extravagant, they undoubtedly valued the city's remains and saw them as a source of inspiration for new building. Poldo's erudition shines forth alongside his evident affection for the antique remains of his native city. His treatment of the *Maison quarrée* is a good example of his approach. First, there is a representation of the entire building, which is followed by detailed examples of individual elements of construction (of the columns, their base and capitals, and their dimensions); and similar care is given to the depiction of cornices, friezes and architraves (Figure 77). In short, the structure is studied as

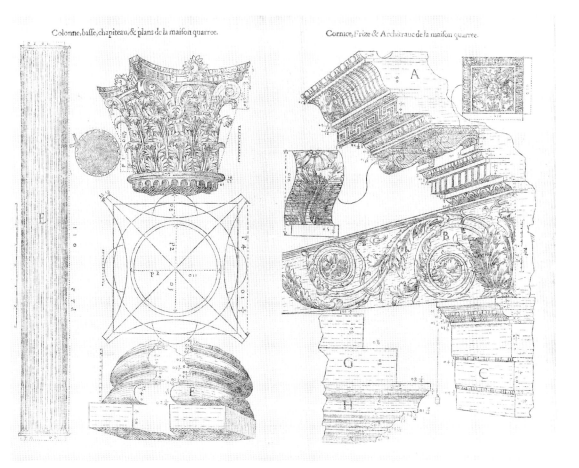

77. Poldo d'Albenas: engraving of detailed elements of the construction of the *Maison quarrée* at Nîmes

meticulously as if it were a ruined building in Rome.[20] Poldo examines these surviving remnants of classical architecture with pride, to assess the quality of their structure and to give an idea of the lost splendour of his city (Figure 78).

A similar attitude prevailed in Bordeaux, where Elie Vinet had carefully researched the Roman origins of the city. He presented his findings to Charles IX who visited Bordeaux on his grand tour in 1565. The volume specified the exact dimensions of the Palais Tutelle and the Palais Galliene, and gave illustrations of their surviving forms (Figure 79).[21] Another author, Pierre de Brach, meditating upon Rome, its rise and fall and its ruined greatness, and upon the architectural remains in Bordeaux, saw no difficulty in comparing Bordeaux and the imperial city:

> Et de Bordeaux à Rome avec iuste raison
> D'un égal contre-pois je fay comparaison.

[And from Bordeaux to Rome, I – with good reason –/ Make comparison of equal weight.]

257

78. Poldo d'Albenas: engraving of the *Fontaine* at Nîmes

79. Elie Vinet: engraving of the *Palais Tutelle* at Bordeaux

LE PALAIS TVTELE DE BOVRDEAVS.

80.   Elie Vinet: engraving of the amphitheatre at Bordeaux

Their equality is demonstrated by another detailed description of the Palais Tutelle, where Corinthian and Doric orders are properly attributed, decorative motifs and the channelling on the columns evoked, and by an account of the remains of the amphitheatre (Figure 80). Interestingly, in this bold comparison, Pierre de Brach does not claim more than he should. He compares his picture of the antiquities of Bordeaux to the work of a painter who also struggles to depict forms whose shape has been obscured by Time and who allows us to glimpse them as through a veil of cloud:

> Et comme estant caché au repli d'un nuage,
> La fait voir seulement ainsi que par ombrage.[22]

[And as if hidden in the fold of a cloud/ Allows glimpses only as through a shadow.]

Alongside these distinguished vestiges from the past were other ruins freshly made, and far less agreeable. In the late sixteenth century the French country-side presented scenes of devastation, the product of civil war: cottages burned to the ground, small towns broken up and pillaged, country houses smashed to pieces, churches shattered and destroyed. Histories, memoirs, political writing,

259

pamphlets and letters all paint the same gruesome pictures, which Le Roy summarizes:

> Nous avons veu batailles et rencontres données, villes asieges, prinzes et sacagees, maisons pillées, plat pays fouragé, temples desmolis, sepultures ruinees . . .

> [We have seen battles and military encounters, towns taken and sacked, houses pillaged, the countryside ravaged, temples demolished, sepulchres destroyed . . .][23]

In this, his *Consideration sur l'histoire françoise*, Le Roy makes clear (as others had done) that the experience of war was immediate; a visible, relentless, seemingly unending presence that each one witnessed daily. Princes and peasants, churchmen and women were assailed by cruel and odious soldiers who might once have been loving brothers or fathers, or by those hated foreigners, the *lansquenets* who, motivated only by greed, fought for any side that paid.

It is hard to differentiate the ruined scenes that characterized France at this time, since the devastation seems to have been indiscriminate and its spectacle produced a numbing air of sameness in those who saw and tried to write down their feelings.[24] But in one case, at least, the sight of a ruin drew forth the same kind of lamentation as that provoked by the ruins of Rome. The fortress at Lusignan was of ancient design, revered for its strength and because it was thought to be the home of magical powers, and the palace of Melusine. Civil war had flattened its superb towers and its ruined site rapidly became a spectacle for visitors to admire and to bewail. Catherine de' Medici, for instance, went out of her way to see what she termed 'cette perle unique',[25] and Odet de Turnèbe composed sonnets for the Dames des Roches which imported the style, structures and models of writers who had meditated upon the ruins of Rome. In a series of questions 'Qui eust pensé? . . .' (who would have thought?), Turnèbe moves from 'la grandeur de Rome', its temples and palaces, its baths and triumphal arches, to the more amazing sight: the collapse of Lusignan 'un si brave Rocher/ Un tel chasteau' (such a proud rock/ Such a palace). The size and speed of the loss is measured by setting Lusignan in the context of Rome and her ruins: just as that city had encouraged reflection on the vanities of the world, so, too, does Lusignan whose strong edifice returns to the fragments of rock which first gave it being.[26] However disproportionate the comparison, the transposition to the French context was deliberately forged.

FRANCE AND ROME: PARALLEL CONDITIONS

On the larger scale, the fate of France and of Rome were deplored in similar terms and using the same structures. Jean de la Jessée wrote a sequence of sonnets where the term used by Du Bellay – *deploration* – figures in his title to the fifth book of *Les Jeunesses*: *la France desplorée*.[27] In De la Jessée's words, Rome and France 'l'un et l'autre s'esgalle' (both are equal): and just as 'Rome n'est plus dans Rome' (Rome is no longer in Rome) in *Les Antiquitez* so 'La France n'est plus la France' (France is no longer France) in *La France desplorée*. Both poets exhibit in their work (and for the same reasons) 'ces champs depeuplez/ Ces chasteaux demolis, ces murs demantelez' (these deserted fields/ These castles destroyed, these walls dismantled). Perhaps the most ingenious transfer of an evocation of Rome to France occurs in a sonnet by Jérome Hennequin where he has made his poem according to the model provided by Du Bellay (*Les Antiquitez*, sonnet 3) in order to attack Frenchmen themselves for their contribution to the civil war. The first quatrain follows the pattern which sonnets on Rome had elaborated; the rhythms are the same and, as far as possible, words are repeated:

> Toy estranger qui viens ici chercher la France,
> Si rien de France, en France, esbahy n'aperçois
> Fors que ces vieux Palais, et ces murs que tu vois
> De nouveau efforcez tomber en decadence.

[You stranger who come here to look for France,/ Yet – astonished – nothing of France in France can you see/ Except for these ancient palaces and these walls that you see/ Once again overcome and fallen into ruins.]

In the tercets, while Hennequin maintains the theme of the inconstancy of human affairs found in earlier poems, he avoids their general moralizing tone and heaps the responsibility for his countrymen's distress on the French alone.

> La France, de la France est le seul monument,
> Et seulle France, France a vaincu seullement,
> Le païs ruyné, les Eglises bruslées,
> Sont le reste de France, ô par trop grand malheur,
> O future inconstante, ô trop grand creve-coeur,
> De voir par ses subjects les villes desolées.

[France is the only living monument of France,/ And France alone has vanquished France herself,/ The country destroyed, the churches burned down,/ Are all that remain of France, Oh! what great misfortune,/ Oh! uncertain future, calamity too great to bear,/ To see towns desolated by their own subjects.][28]

Some plays on words are retained, but Hennequin has forgone the ingenious balance of *fuite* and *résistance*, *ferme* and *inconstance*, which Du Bellay introduced in his final tercet, in order to underline yet further the self-destructive power of the French.

Sentiments such as these were widespread as writers sought to attribute

261

blame for the horrors that were witnessed every day in France. Rome and its loss of empire became the sources which were scrutinized in depth to find reasons for the civil strife and answers to the endlessness of war.[29] They searched for the first signs of conflict and, as Hennequin had done, located them in the citizens themselves. Le Roy cites Sallust's anticipation of civil war, destined to destroy Rome:

> I'estime, puisque toutes choses commencees finissent, alorsque par destinee la ruine de Rome approchera, citoyens combattront contre citoyens, et ainsi lassez et affoiblis seront exposez en proye à quelque Roy ou nation estrange . . .

> [I believe that since all things in being come to an end, when – through destiny – the ruin of Rome approaches, there citizens will slay citizens, and thus weakened and tired, they will fall prey to some king or foreign nation . . .]

And, Le Roy adds, 'Autant en peut on dire de ce Royaume' (one can say as much of this kingdom).[30]

The parallel with his own time was apt, and yet the warnings went unheeded so great was the will towards self-destruction. This suicidal fixation became a major theme in the literature of the time, as exemplified in Ronsard's 'Discours' where he likened his country to Rome, which 'jadis . . . Tournant le fer contre elle' (in former times, turned the sword against herself).

For Renaissance observers the most disturbing feature of the Roman civil war was not so much the wilful destruction of buildings, intended to leave a permanent scar on the city (the demolition of the property sent citizens, like Cicero, into exile), but rather the contamination of holy places. Caesar gave licence to such acts when on his return to the city he raided Jupiter's temple and the treasury of Rome to finance his wars.[31] His crime was no different in kind from the indiscriminate pillaging of churches and temples by the Germans in the most recent sack of the city (1527), exploits which were all too frequent during the French religious wars when foul intentions desecrated churches and brought them crumbling down. Ronsard did not mince his words:

> Le desir, l'avarice et l'erreur insensé
> Ont sens dessus dessous le monde renversé
> Ont fait des lieux sacrez une horrible voirie (*Discours*, 1562, p. 548)

> [Greed, avarice and wayward madness/ Have turned the world upside down/ And made sacred places into pestilent dunghills.]

Such reversal of functions engendered further evils even more alarming since they attacked the means whereby men communicated with each other: in seditious times when all was turned upside down, the meaning of words was no longer secure. As standards collapsed and morals faltered, the naming of activities became highly dubious – a process of falsification well caught by Le Roy. In his translation and commentary on the *Politics* of Aristotle, he was aware that Book 5, *Des Changemens, ruines et conservation des estats publics, avec les causes des emotions civiles, leurs maux et remèdes*, was particularly relevant to his times. Convinced that examples were more powerful persuasive tools than precepts, he analysed the cruelties of the factions in the civil war in Rome, and from them drew conclusions for his contemporaries:

> Tous les maulx qu'ils [the Romans] faisoyent, ilz les appeloyent par noms nouveaux et inusitez: Car ils nommoyent la temerité magnanimité tellement que les temeraires estoyent nommez deffenseurs vertueux de leurs amys: et la tardité et froideur ilz nommoyent une honneste crainte; et la modestie, pusillanimité couverte; l'indignation precipitée, virilité et hardiesse; la consultation et deliberation prudente, tergiversation palliée.

> [All the evils which they did, they called them by new and unusual names; because they named temerity, magnanimity such that the fearless are called virtuous defenders of their friends; coldness and belatedness they termed honourable fear; and modesty, concealed pusillanimity; hurried indignation was strength and virility; prudence and cautious deliberation was weak flinching.][32]

In a world which had thus become muddled and difficult to read, the greatest danger was to become accustomed to its chaotic moral atmosphere. In 1570, Michel de l'Hospital urged Charles IX to give peace back to his subjects for he believed that the prolongation of war would produce that condition diagnosed in Rome during its civil wars: 'les plus meschants et détestables forfaicts se rendirent familiers par accoustumance' (the most detestable and wicked crime becomes habitual through custom).[33]

As writers identified the many ills which beset their society, it became almost natural to turn to Rome as providing the example *par excellence* of their problems. Rome's fall was due to the sale of offices (Pierre de La Place); to the excessive ambition of individuals – notably Caesar and Pompey (Michel de l'Hospital, *Harangues*); or to greed and the lure of gold and luxury items brought in from the East (Michel de l'Hospital, *Poemata*).[34] Although these claims kept the city foremost in the mind, some thinkers questioned the act of writing at all at a time of war. For Pasquier, pens were double-edged swords, difficult to manage and uncertain in their effect so that he concluded, 'Brief c'est chose fort chatouilleuse de vouloir desployer sa plume à bon escient' (in short, it's a ticklish thing to want to wield one's pen in good faith).[35] This observation did not deter him from writing and, as Montaigne remarked, there is a singular correlation between civil war and the business of pouring forth words and yet more words:

L'escrivaillerie semble estre quelque simptome d'un siècle desbordé. Quand escrivismes nous tant que depuis que nous sommes en trouble? Quand les Romains tant que lors de leur ruyne? (*De la vanité*, III, ix, 946)

[Scribbling seems to be one of the symptoms of an age of excess. When did we ever write so much as since the beginning of our civil wars? And when did the Romans do so as just before their collapse?]

As well as serving as a court of appeal for every ill that civil war could muster, the ruins of Rome and the history of its civil wars provided the best incentives for peace. On the one hand, in the harmonious relations and established loyalties between Rome, its emperor and its many tributary states, Michel de l'Hospital saw the possibility of creating similar links and networks between the French monarch, the nobles and the people: 'comme le peuple Romain disoit sa ville heureuse, invincible et éternelle par la concorde des estats, ainsy dirons-nous d'un accord que par ceste paix le roy et la France seront heureux' (as the Roman people declared their city happy, invincible and eternal by virtue of the concord among its states, so may we all say that through this peace the king and France are happy). The networks, established on the basis of faith and merit and without regard for status, maintained their equilibrium until the ambitious and greedy sought power. Then like a noble edifice, the city and the empire must crumble, irrevocably broken, unless some noble architect (such as Augustus or the king of France) repairs, rebuilds from the ruins, and creates afresh:

ny plus ny moins qu'ung superbe bastiment dont les colomnes ne le soustenoient sont sapées, ne faillit pas à deschoir si lourdement, que jamais plus on ne l'a sceu relever, encores que, sur les ruynes d'iceluy, le grand et victorieux Auguste ayt rebasty ung aussy superbe edifice en apparence que le premier.

[Neither more nor less than a stately building, whose supporting columns are undermined, inevitably falls heavily to the ground so that never can it be set up again, and yet the great and victorious Emperor Augustus was able to rebuild on those ruins as magnificent an edifice in appearance as the first.][36]

On the other hand, Pasquier, meditating in 1560 upon the role of Cato in the war between Pompey and Caesar, saw ample evidence to suggest that war should be avoided at all costs, since whoever was victor would ensure the desolation and ruin of the Republic and the beginnings of a new sort of tyranny. Pasquier dwelt on Cato's reflections on the forthcoming struggle at Pharsalia, the elder Roman statesman 'prevoyant que de quelque costé que fust la victoire, c'estoit non seulement la desolation et ruine de la Republique de Rome, mais aussi le préparatif de nouvelle tyrannie, à celuy qui seroit le victorieux' (foreseeing that whichever side was victorious, it was not only the desolation and ruin of the Roman Republic but also the beginnings of a new tyranny, that of the victor). On such evidence, Pasquier argued, it was unwise to take up arms,[37] but his counsel and De l'Hospital's vision of harmony between Rome (France) and its peoples were unattainable goals. In the French context from 1560 onwards, they were more like unrealizable ideals which few wished even to recognize.

Given that war was inevitable, what kind of war was it to be? Brantôme (with many others) was clear that it was *our* war, Frenchmen against each other. Unperturbed by the slaughter, unquestioning as to the motives for war, and with no interest in the outcome of the conflict, incredibly he concerned himself only with the business of making war nobly, keeping the order, the well-tried, traditional French customs, and the martial music, keeping it all in the family – 'entre-nous'. To support his case, Brantôme cites Lucan and the *Pharsalia* where the same national considerations came into play and where the Roman military machine prevailed. The absence of any concern about the calamities that civil war brought to France for two generations, the emphasis on the right mix of combatants for the fighting to be suitably noble, and the point by point analogies with Lucan make the text worth quoting in full:

> Et quant tout est dict, puisque c'estoit une guerre intestine de nation à la mesme nation, nous la devions desmeler entre nous autres ensemble, sans y appeler la nation estrangere, comme l'on faict d'estranger contre estranger.
>
> Certes, la guerre en fust esté plus noble, voir en mesme campagne mesmes enseignes, pareilles et mesmes armes, mesmes sonneries de tabourins et trompettes et mesmes façons et ordre de guerre; ainsi qu'on vist aux plaines de Pharsalle mesmes Romains (dit Lucain) mesmes aigles, mesmes armes et pareilles ordonnances des gens et formes de guerre; si bien que Pompée mist force estrangers ramassez et vraie racaille. Cesar en avoit aussy mais plus disciplinez et aguerris pourtant à la milice romaine.

[And when all is said and done, since it was an internecine war, one nation against the same nation, we ought to fight it out amongst ourselves, without involving foreigners as one does, one foreigner against another. Truly, it would have been a more noble war, to see on the same field of battle the same standards, the same arms, the same sound of tambourine and trumpet, and the same methods and order of battle; just as one saw on the plains of Pharsalia (as Lucan reported) the same Romans, the same eagle standards, the same arms and the same order of troops and forms of combat; so that Pompey involved many foreigners whom he had picked up – the scum of the earth. Caesar had some too, but they were more disciplined and trained in Roman military ways.][38]

Lucan's graphic rendering of the fighting was naturally attractive to the combative Brantôme who, in his leisure moments, translated several harangues from the epic which he dedicated to Marguerite de Valois. However, he was not the only Frenchman at this time to pay such close attention to Lucan's text.[39]

Other French writers had learned not the latent nostalgia and stupidity manifest in Brantôme's writings but rather to provide eyewitness accounts of atrocities like those which Lucan had presented. His epic reinforced their sense of the endlessness of war (particularly civil war); his depiction of countless dead bodies unidentified and of the ghoulish physical damage wreaked on human form matched their own experience. Such details were sometimes a source of aesthetic satisfaction, and Lucan provided models for articulating the physical pain inflicted by brother upon brother, father on son, comrade upon comrade. Some, sickened by these sights, refused to bear witness, fearful of increasing the horror. Jean de Serres, in his *Mémoires*, was of the view that the calamities which had erupted all over France were so appalling that publicizing them would undoubtedly 'redoubler l'horreur et la misère' (redouble the horror and the misery), though he did concede that such discourse would recall 'la splendeur, excellence et dignité en laquelle elle [la France] s'est veue auparavant ces troubles' (the splendour, excellence and dignity in which France was viewed before these religious troubles).[40] This conjunction of an ideal state and its ruin had been present in the address which Lucan made to Rome in Book 7 of the *Pharsalia*, in that battle where the Romans by destroying themselves also destroy Rome itself, and in so doing, are reminded of an idealized conception of the city.[41]

The vision of Italy abandoned, homes half demolished and walls tottering with only a few inhabitants picking their way among the stones of ancient sites is powerfully evoked at the beginning of the *Pharsalia* (I, ll. 24–32). Lucan keeps the possibility of Rome's destruction alive throughout his poem, from the speech delivered by Laelius to Caesar after the crossing of the Rubicon where he envisaged that fate – 'even if the city you doom to utter destruction be Rome' (I, ll. 384–5) – to the leitmotif 'terrified Rome' which describes the state of the city whenever Caesar comes close, and on to Troy (presaging the fate of Rome) which Caesar visits, 'the very ruins [of which] have been destroyed': the ancient city is covered with bracken and choked with ivy, and 'a legend clings to every stone' (IX, ll. 961–99). These are the elements which contributed to the vision of ruined France. French writers appropriated them and, in some cases, extended the spectacle to a personalization of the country's grief. Ronsard depicted the spirit of his native land, torn apart by war

> L'idole de la France foible et sans confort
> Comme une pauvre femme attainte de la mort.

[the spirit of France, weak and comfortless/ Like a poor woman close to death.]

D'Aubigné imported Rome into 'Les Misères', witnessing her arrival as she quakingly attempted to defend her domain against Caesar:

> Il vit Rome tremblante, affreuse, échevelée,
> Qui en pleurs, en sanglots, mi-morte désolée,
> Tordant ses doigts, fermoit, défendoit de ses mains
> A Cesar le chemin au sang de ses germains.

[He saw the figure of Rome trembling, wild and dreadful,/ Who, in sorrow and with tears, stricken half-dead,/ Twisting her fingers, defended and closed with her hands/ The way to Caesar who sought for the blood of her kin.][42]

Lucan was an obvious source of inspiration. His work was readily available, reissued regularly from the middle of the century, and the terrible scenes that he evoked were corroborated by the histories of Appian, long accessible and translated into French by Claude de Seyssel, and published in 1544. As Le Roy reminded his readers, no place in history nurtured civil war with greater frequency, more intensity and deeper cruelty than Rome, and he referred to Appian for the detail:

> Cela est certain, qu'il n'y eut iamais lieu ou les particularitez pleines de toutes sortes de maulx fussent tant frequentes et longues, ny les factions des guerres civiles plus cruelles qu'à Rome, Dont Appian a dressé un traitté à part.

[It is a fact that no other place has endured so fully every kind of evil, so frequently and for so long, nor suffered the factions of civil war more cruel than Rome, on which Appian has written a special treatise.][43]

ATTACK UPON ROME – THE WORK OF JACQUES GRÉVIN

In the context of attempts to redress the ills that had swept through France with the wars of religion, two poets – Jacques Grévin (1538–70) and Robert Garnier (1544–90) – gave Rome a central place in their work. Some time after 1567, Grévin fled the war in France and sought consolation in Rome; as he put it:

> J'aimay mieux aller voir les ruines d'autruy
> Et m'en esmerveiller.

[I preferred to go and see others' ruins and be astonished.]

As he gazed on the broken columns and arches, and contemplated the crumbling theatres which still stood in 'le grand tombeau' (the great tomb) of the city, he saw not Rome but the continuing spectacle of 'la France ruineuse'.[44]

From beneath the ruins of the ancient city rose up a vision of the shattered stones of his native land. The fusion in his mind of the ruins of both countries conveys the strength of the presence of his homeland as he walked the streets of Rome. France was in his consciousness although, in the twenty-four sonnets on Rome which he dedicated to Madame, duchesse de Savoie, the principal focus is the imperial city. The poems were composed towards the very end of his short life (between 1568 and 1570), and until recently remained in manuscript among Pierre de Lestoile's papers. The hostility to Rome which he shared with many other Protestant poets was prepared for in earlier works: in his play *César* (adapted from Muret's play of the same title) where in a rousing speech that opens the action, the emperor predicts that his fall will bring the collapse of the fabric of the city, and Rome will be reduced to a wandering shade –

> Et ne restra sinon que ton idole errante
> Pour servir d'une fable à l'aage suivante,
> Dont tu seras la proye et le riche butin
> D'un grand peuple ennemi plus farouche et mutin (I, ll. 83–6)

[Nothing will remain except your wandering spirit/ To serve as a fable for the ages to come/ And of which you will be both the prey and the rich booty/ For a great enemy, more wild and seditious][45] –

and in sonnets from his 'Gélodacrye' where he anticipates disillusion, remembering in one sonnet the self-constructed sepulchres made by Troy and Rome, and in another (addressed to his friend Jean Patouillet who lived in Rome) voicing his disappointment:

> . . . Je pensoy que Romme
> Fust le commencement du paradis de l'homme;
> Mais comme je puis voir, j'ay bien esté trompé.

[I thought that Rome/ Was the beginning of paradise for man/ but I can now see that I was sorely mistaken.]

The intensity of Grévin's feelings against Rome in his Roman sonnets is seen in his uncomplicated approval of the fact that the city was ruined at least twice (in ancient times, and then again through the ministrations of the 'emperor of spirituality' [the pope], sonnet 10); in his direct condemnation of Rome's violent victories (sonnets 12 and 18); and in the irony that such a place – synonymous with ferocity – should build a temple of Peace (sonnet 16). The antagonism is further evident in the serenity with which he describes the destruction of Rome. Sonnet 5 calmly specifies how all the forces of nature conspired to bring about the city's ruin. Touches of satisfaction intrude in sonnet 8 with the word play on *sepulture/sepulcre*, and with the quiet appeal to the Senate of Rome, its people and its emperors to accept that their striving has been for naught. Against the backcloth of vanity which inspires the poem's message words like *grands/belle*, *orgueil* and *majesté* acquire derisive tones and meaning:

> Des *grands* arcs triomphaux la *belle* architecture . . .
> Des coulomnes encor *l'orgueil* et *majesté*. (ll. 5 and 7)

> [the *beautiful* architecture of these *grand* triumphal arches/ And again, the *pride* and *majesty* of the columns . . .][46]

Even more pointed was Grévin's play upon *ruine* on which the whole of sonnet 13 is constructed. Ruin belongs to the place and to the Roman race. The city emerged from the ruins of Troy, its founders established Rome through an act of murder, and its progress had depended upon the ruins of others. Sober, repetitive, insistent phrases communicate the bare facts of ruin and murder, and the theme is carried on into the next poem, which depicts the city in ruins – 'Rome n'a rien d'entier' (Rome has nothing whole). And, in a final flourish, the poet asserts that this broken, incomplete state is everlasting: 'Sa ruine jamais ne puisse prendre fin' (l.14) (Her ruin will be never ending).

Throughout the poems, the attack is unrelieved. It is sustained by ironic juxtapositions of all kinds, as in sonnet 6 where Rome is depicted as a collection of grand-sounding names with no substance, their surface glitter immediately undermined. A sequence of rhythmically balanced phrases – 'O palais enterrez . . . Tombeaus ensevelis . . . Colonnes . . . en poudre . . . Theatres affaissez . . . Arcs vaincus et rompus . . . Colosses empoudrez . . . Portiques ruinez' (Oh! entombed palaces . . . buried sepulchres . . . columns rendered into dust . . . theatres flattened to the ground . . . arches broken and vanquished . . . huge statues dissolved into dust . . . porticoes destroyed) – evoke monuments which simultaneously convey beauty, achievement, style and nobility alongside their ruin and their disappearance.

Perhaps Grévin's most original contribution to the critical vision of Rome adopted by Protestants is his reversal of inherited attitudes towards the famous sculptures in the city. He brings alive (in sonnet 17 for instance) the icons of beauty and models of sculpture universally admired and imitated; but Cleopatra, Venus, Flora and Faustina are shown in the Belvedere gardens, which Grévin has turned into a kind of brothel which the pope visits furtively.[47] One of these beauties/concubines gave birth to Aeneas, another to Romulus (founder of Rome), and another caused the Trojan war. In history and legend they are creatures of disaster, and together they demonstrate the rottenness at the core of Rome (Figure 81). Grévin provides a similar, unusual reading of Laocoön and his sons in sonnet 19. The sculpture (found entire in 1506) was considered in the Renaissance as a wondrous example of ancient art. Grévin detaches the figures from their aesthetic environment and puts them back into history and legend where Laocoön bore some responsibility for the burning of Troy and was punished by Pallas as a consequence. Far from being objects of admiration, Laocoön and his sons are 'ce signe ruineux' (this sign of ruin),

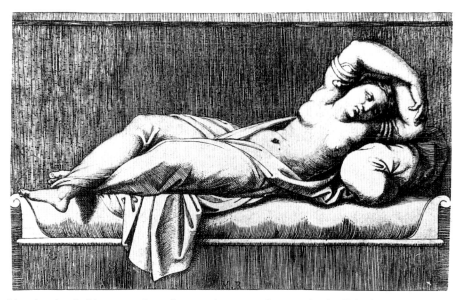

81. Antoine Lafréry: engraving of a recumbent nymph, statue in the Belvedere court

those by whom 'Troie fut mise en cendre et Priam ruiné' (Troy was reduced to cinders and Priam ruined) (l. 8). This ruinous sign also signals Rome's own rotting condition:

> Les Romains ruinez se ruinent encore,
> Car ils ont retenu toujours au milieu d'eux
> Un vieil Laocoon que le serpent dévore. (ll. 12–14)

[Ruined Romans go on ruining themselves,/ Because they have always retained in their midst/ An ancient Laocoön whom the serpent devours.]

By this turning upside down of the reader's expectation (Laocoön and his sons as an object to be praised), Grévin succeeds both in sustaining the original positive view of the group as well as using it for his own critical purposes and, because that view was well entrenched, Grévin's rejection of it is all the more powerful.

Thus gods and the figures Rome worshipped are made into symbols of the city's parlous state.[48] Even the ancient representations of the Nile and the Tiber, with their urns flowing with water and their hair garlanded with reeds, are no longer appreciated as objects of art or sources of embellishment: they are merely witnesses of Rome's ruin. Grévin takes a further step, attributing the rivers' perpetual movement to the city itself,

> Romme sans fin poursuit sa course périssante (l. 12)

[Without end, Rome pursues her ruinous course],

and he plays on the different meanings of *flow* in order to emphasize the inevitable and relentless course to ruin.

Grévin acknowledged that his first vision of Rome arose from books and engravings (sonnet 3): 'Je portois le portrait de cette grand'cité' (I carried the image of this great city) (l. 1); the image which he formed was splendid 'semblable à son antiquité' (similar to its antiquity) (l. 5), and its glowing face tempted him into journeying to the city to see for himself. His disappointment (though anticipated) was immense, for he saw nothing but 'une ruine aperte' (an obvious ruin) (l. 10), and he concluded that only traces of that glorious vision of Rome survive – its name, a picture lingering in the mind, and a great sense of loss:

> . . . et de ceste grand'Romme
> Ne reste que le nom en la bouche de l'homme,
> L'image dans l'esprit, et le regret en l'oeuil. (ll. 12–14)

[. . . and of this great Rome/ All that remains is its name in the mouths of men,/ The image in their minds and regret in their eye.]

The gap between desire and experience was too great to be bridged, and it might be said that the shock of discovery of the real condition of Rome provided the springboard for all the other sonnets. Chastising himself for such a vain pursuit, which had taken him daily, from morn to night, from the Colosseum to the Rotunda (Pantheon) and beyond (sonnet 4) only to find 'Romme ensevelie' (Rome buried), 'un sepulcre apparent', he turned from self-preoccupation to wider explorations of the phenomenon of loss. His search and explanations were to have a distinctive voice, not only by providing new ways of seeing old favourites but also from the very sound of his verse, as he had announced in sonnet 1. Just as a mighty pine, huge with age, finally falls, its deep roots torn out of the ground, so Rome will be heard: 'Par son bruit ruineux porté *dedans mes vers*' (by its crashing fall sounding within my verse) (l. 13). Although Rome is the place where all ruin and ills have been concentrated – 'la marque de ruine et de malheur' (the mark of ruin and of evil) – Grévin will not follow Petrarch in bewailing the city's fate; his verse will celebrate the wonder and the fear that reverberate from Rome's fall. The second sonnet establishes Rome as a 'ville destruite' (a destroyed city), a 'cité . . . en poudre réduite' (a city reduced to dust), and as exemplary ('un merveilleux exemple') of the fact that the utmost greatness conceivable is as nothing. His moral point, however, depends on being able to envisage Rome at the peak of its splendour, and the poet's close scrutiny of the remains brings a flash of recognition of that earlier state:

> . . . les vers que je compose
> Ne peut représenter à vos yeux autrechose
> Que ce rien descendu d'un grand tout ancien. (ll. 9–11)

[the verses that I write/ Cannot present anything other/ Than this nothing descended from a great ancient everything.]

The ability to keep simultaneously in play positive and negative views of the city gives Grévin's poems their tightness and tension, and keeps the reader waiting since the balance is usually sustained equally between the grandeur and the ruin. A variation of such equilibrium is found in sonnet 23 where every nameable element in the city is listed, each accompanied by some approving adjective: 'Aqueducts eslevez . . . Colosses monstrueux . . . Obelisques pointus . . . Trophées somptueux . . . Asile autorisé . . . Braves ponts . . . Campidole honoré . . .' (aqueducts upright . . . huge statues . . . pointed obelisks . . . sumptuous trophies . . . authorized refuge . . . proud bridges . . . honourable Campidoglio . . .), and so the roll call goes, extending uninterruptedly over twelve lines. Then, without pause (the rhythm of the long sentence which stretches from line 1 is unbroken), comes the reversal of all our expectation:

> Vous n'est rien que cendre, et quiconque vous voit,
> A la cendre et à rien compare toute Romme. (ll. 13–14)

[You are naught but dust, and whoever sees you,/ To dust and to nothing compares the whole of Rome.]

There is a certain gratification in the extent of the deception practised here, and a pleasure at ending on the negative entities of dust and nothingness.

Terms such as these characterize the last work of Jacques Grévin. Pessimism predominates and the presence of ruin and decay, the hopelessness of war and its endlessness exemplified by the extent of the ruins of Rome which still offer glimpses of her greatness. Here is a melancholy spirit nurtured by this site of destruction.

GARNIER'S DRAMATIZATION OF ROME

Robert Garnier's representation of Rome in three of his tragedies – *Porcie* (*c.* 1563–67), *Cornélie* (1574) and *Marc Antoine* (1578)[49] – is grander, more complete and more powerfully alive than many other depictions penned by his contemporaries. In his plays, the city's rich and paradoxical nature emerges clearly: great yet violent, exemplary but calamitous, eternal though visibly fallen.

Although Henri Estienne, while arguing for the usefulness of history (which encouraged meditation upon events long past and discovered their relevance to the present), had questioned the truth of the same events when represented in plays, he used the analogy with the theatre to stress how important it was for the reader to be engaged in the actions he recounted, and to respond emotionally to the lessons that were implicit in his narrative: 'Considère ces deux commentaires historiques comme deux Théâtres où se jouent les comédies, les tragicomédies, les tragédies d'alors' (Think of these two historical commentaries as two theatres where comedies, tragicomedies and tragedies of the past are played).[50] Reading the past to reflect on the present was, of course, a well-entrenched practice. Montaigne had also acknowledged the irresistible magnetism attaching to any account of 'ces confusions des autres estats' (the disorders in other states) (*De la physionomie*, III, 12, 1046). He eagerly pondered their dreadful appropriateness, and recognized that historians, seeking to accommodate man's natural tendency to be aroused to pity and fear, concentrated on significant and tragic events, and that these dramatized stories had a compelling effect:

> Comme je ne ly gueres és histoires ces confusions des autres estats que je n'aye regret de ne les avoir peu mieux considerer present, ainsi faict ma curiosité que je m'aggrée aucunement de veoir de mes yeux ce notable spectacle de nostre mort publique, ses symptomes et sa forme . . . Si cherchons nous avidement de recongnoistre en ombre mesme et en la fable des theatres la montre des jeux tragiques de l'humaine fortune. Ce n'est pas sans compassion de ce que nous oyons, mais nous nous plaisons d'esveiller nostre desplaisir par le rareté de ces pitoyables evenemens. (ibid.)

> [I rarely read in my history books about the disorders in other states without regretting that I could not have been there to study them more closely: so, too, my desire for knowledge leads me to find at least some satisfaction in being able to see with my own eyes this remarkable spectacle of the death of our institutions, the manner of it and its symptoms . . . After all, we make great efforts so that we can eagerly witness performances of fictional portrayings of the tragedies of human fortunes; it is not that we lack sympathy for what we hear there but that we delight in awakening our grief by the exceptional nature of those pitiable events.]

Garnier shared such attitudes and, in the prefaces to his plays, he made the parallels explicit between the wars he depicted in his drama and those which surrounded him in real life. *Porcie*'s enlarged title reads: 'Tragedie françoise representant la cruelle et sanglante saison des guerres civiles de Rome: propre et convenable pour y voir depeincte la calamité de ce temps' (French tragedy depicting the cruel and bloody time of the civil wars in Rome: suitable and appropriate for seeing painted there the calamity of our time). In *Cornélie*, he laments how the subject of his tragedy is all too fitting for the 'malheurs de nostre siecle' (the evils of our century). The playwright's address to Guy du Faur de Pibrac in *Marc Antoine* carries the analogy further: to whom could he better dedicate

> les représentations Tragiques des guerres civiles de Rome? qui avez en telle horreur nos dissentions domestiques, et les malheureux troubles de ce Royaume, aujourd'huy despouillé de son ancienne splendeur et de la révérable maiesté de nos Rois, prophanée par tumultueuses rebellions.

[the tragic spectacle of the civil wars in Rome; you who hold in such horror our domestic quarrels, and the unfortunate strife in this kingdom, today denuded of her ancient splendour and of the venerable majesty of our kings, violated by such tumultuous rebellion.]

There is no doubt that his contemporaries read into the experience of reading or watching Garnier's plays their own perilous state and, as the printer Robert Estienne remarked, they served as a warning to Frenchmen: 'France, fuy donc la guerre' (France, take flight then from war).[51]

Rome is given an overwhelming role in the three dramas. It is the place where all the action happens as well as being the tragic heroine whose destiny is intimately linked to the lives of her heroes and whose physical presence is rendered poetically by Garnier, now in huge blocks of architectural structure,[52] now by allusive references to parts of the city quintessentially Roman. Rome is the supreme example of the play of Fortune as sung by the Chorus at the end of Act I (*Porcie*):

> Nostre Rome qui s'eslevoit
> Sur toutes les citez du monde . . .
> Maintenant d'autant plus abonde
> En cruelles adversitez . . . (*Porcie*, ll. 191–2, 195–6)

[Our Rome who rose higher/ Than all other cities in the world . . . / Now abounds even more/ In cruel adversity . . .]

and such sentiments echo through the dramas, where the exemplary functions of the city are a recurring theme. Rome is the centre of misplaced ambition (exemplified by Caesar and Pompey), 'Méchante Ambition . . .' (wicked ambition), 'Mortelle Convoitise' (deadly greed) track their course, and although the city seems 'immortelle, immuable' (immortal and unchanging), individual greed brings civil strife:

> La civile fureur, plus que vous [Rome] redoutable,
> A presque renversé cette ville indomtable,
> Terreur de l'univers . . . (*Cornélie*, ll. 23–5)

[Civil strife, more redoubtable than yourself,/ Has almost overturned this indomitable city,/ The terror of the universe.]

Behind the war, behind the self-destruction,[53] looms that vision of a remarkable place, visibly rent and shaken yet still projecting ideals of power and performance. It is also the abode of calamities and a dreadful warning to all humankind.

These exemplary notions were well understood; it was Garnier's job to give them new life and make his spectators appreciate them fully and afresh, and be moved by them. He achieved this by giving the city a material presence so palpable and animated that it seems not only a real place where buildings, sights and decorations are named and given substance, but also a sentient being that feels, exults and suffers. The links between characters and Rome are close, so intimate indeed that their actions have immediate effects upon the city, and their mental states find echoes in the place itself.

Marc Antoine enters on stage and, in an expansive, exultant address to Rome expresses his excited mental state:

> O beau séjour natal esmerveillable aux dieux,
> O terre florissante en peuple glorieux,
> Coustaux sept fois pointus, qui vostre teste aigue
> Portez noble en palais iusque aux pieds de la nue:
> Soit où flanquez de tours vous honorez Jupin
> Dans un temple basti du roc Capitolin,
> Soit où vous élevez en bosse Célienne,
> En pointe Vaticane ou en Esquilienne,
> Soit où vous recourbez sous le faix Quirinal,
> Sous l'orgueil Palatin ou sous la Viminal,
> Joyeux je vous salue. (*Porcie*, ll. 1013–23)

[Oh! noble birthplace, held in awe by the gods,/ Oh! land flourishing in a glorious people,/ Hills, seven times pointed, who hold your sharp head high/ Supporting noble palaces right up to the foot of the clouds,/ Either flanked with towers you honour Jove,/ In a temple built of Capitoline rock,/ Or you rear up on Caelian heights,/ On Vatican or Esquiline mounds,/ Or you bend under Quiriline weight,/ Under proud Palatine or Viminal,/ Radiant, I salute you.]

The glories of Rome, almost envied by the gods, are the same as his achievements; they reflect his performance.

In his greeting to the city, Caesar's tone is also exultant but with added notes of triumph. Rome's power and beauty, its high status and victorious appearance match Caesar's own. His flamboyance heightens the city's splendour as the inflated apostrophes tumble one after the other to reach the point where, in his enthusiasm, Caesar sees the whole world (including Rome) prostrate at his feet to pay him homage:

> O superbe Cité, qui vas levant le front
> Sur toutes les citez de ce grand monde rond,
> Et dont l'honneur, gaigné par victoires fameuses,
> Espouvante du ciel les voûtes lumineuses!
> O sourceilleuses tours! ô coustaux décorez!
> O palais orgueilleux! ô temples honorez!
> O vous, murs que les dieux ont maçonnez eux-mesmes,
> Eux-mesmes étoffez de mille diadèmes,

Ne ressentez-vous point de plaisir en vos cueurs,
De voir vostre César, le vaincueur des vaincueurs . . .
. . . mesme ceste Cité . . .
Ploye dessous ma force. (*Cornélie*, ll. 1333–42, 1381, 1383)

[Oh! proud City, who raises her brow/ Above all the cities of this rounded globe,/ And whose honour, bought with famous victories,/ Brings terror to the luminous vaults of heaven,/ Oh! frowning towers, oh! ornamented hills!/ Oh! proud palaces oh! honoured temples!/ And you, walls which the gods themselves fashioned,/ Themselves ornate with a thousand diadems,/ Do you not feel pleasure in your hearts,/ To behold Caesar, the victor of the victorious . . . even the City/ Bows beneath my power.]

Rome is Caesar's stage, and its people are his applauding audience. The city is part of the dramatic argument for, like a chameleon, it changes as the action moves from triumph to disaster.

At moments of such transformation (real or imagined) Rome is depicted as a person experiencing the pain of defeat or the excitement of triumph. 'Tu souffres, pauvre Rome, hélas!' (you suffer, poor Rome, alas!), exclaims Porcie's nurse as the civil war seems unending; and Porcie herself extends the personification, showing the figure of Rome bent and crippled beneath Caesar's yoke:

Courbe son dos suject sous le pouvoir d'un homme,
J'affecte plustost voir nostre dolente Romme . . . (*Porcie*, ll. 563–4)

[As a subject bows her back beneath the power of a man,/ I would rather see our Rome sorrowing.]

Cornélie paints Rome's degradation using a transposed version of a Roman triumph and here a visual subjugation is effected as she dwells on each detail appropriate to a victim. Rome becomes a being, head bowed and hands tied behind her as she walks in front of the glorious chariot of her victors (ironically, her own children) who, in the civil war, had left their fellow Romans dead, unburied with their bones sucked clean by fishes or picked bare by birds;

Tu sers, superbe Rome . . .
Tu iras désormais la main au dos liée,
La teste contre bas de vergongne pliée,
Devant le char vainqueur, et ton rebelle enfant,
Le diadème au front te suivra trionfant.
Tes chefs si courageux, et de qui la vaillance,
Jointe avec si bon droit levoit nostre esperance,
Sont morts atterrassez, pasture des oiseaux,
Pasture des poissons qui rament sous les eaux. (*Cornélie*, ll. 781, 785–92)

276

82. Guillaume du
Choul: Roman
soldier

[You serve, proud Rome . . . / Henceforth you will have your hands tied
behind your back,/ Your head held low, bent with shame,/ Walking before
the triumphal chariot, and your rebellious child,/ Crowned will follow you,
triumphing,/ Your courageous captains whose courage,/ And the right cause
raised our hopes,/ Are dead, sprawling on the ground, Food for birds,/ Food
for the fish that row the waves.]

Rome's enslavement is Caesar's triumph; her condition is the same as that projected in *Porcie*, for all to see

> Tu nages dans le sang de tes pauvres enfans
> Que n'aguère on voyoit marcher si triomphans! (ll. 437–8)

[You swim in the blood of your poor children/ Who were once seen marching so triumphantly!]

The physicality of a place, swimming in the blood of its own offspring, is portrayed literally.

At other times, from the vast common fund of knowledge about Rome, the
reader's participation is assumed in filling out the sketch where the pen has
simply named a few features: the opening scene of *Porcie*, for example, where
Mégère — accentuating the desire to *see* with her own eyes ('Je veux voir'
repeated) — invites the spectator to visualize the Roman soldier and to dress
him in 'morion cresté' (crested helm) and 'double cuirasse escaillée' (double
scaled breastplate) (Figure 82). Lost grandeur is recalled as the reader ponders

the list of past heroes: 'Les Marcels, les Torquats et encore/ Les Scipions vainqueurs' (*Porcie*, ll. 1703–4), the trophies of victory, or the statues dedicated in a triumph (*Cornélie*, ll. 957–60). The Capitol comes alive with a mere reference to the sacrifice of oxen or the naming of Jupiter's temple (*Porcie*, ll. 1329–30); *Cornélie*, ll. 825–30). Garnier takes for granted his spectator's knowledge of history so that when the Nourrice (in *Porcie*) nostalgically remembers the foundation of Rome and traces the city's progress, the details so lovingly retold by Livy come to mind to fill out the great historical sweep that is intended to involve the spectator in Rome's fall. The extent of the disaster is doubly felt as, at the end of Act IV, after the death of Brutus, Porcie recalls exactly the same historical sequence of accumulated greatness suddenly cut off.

Rome's fall is made all the more appalling by the irony injected into events through Garnier's references to the fall of Troy and the destruction of Carthage. The reader/spectator knows that Rome was born from the former, that Trojan blood at one and the same time built the city and infected it with the seeds of disaster, and that Rome itself annihilated Carthage and now meets the same fate:

> [Rome] Semblable à l'antique Troye,
> Le séjour de tes ayeux,
> Tu seras l'ardente proye
> D'un peuple victorieux. (*Marc Antoine*, ll. 848–51)

[Rome, resembling ancient Troy,/ The home of your ancestors,/ You will be the burning prey,/ Of a victorious people.]

> Tu souffres, pauvre Rome, hélas! tu souffres ores
> Ce que tu fis souffrir à la cité des Mores,
> A la belle Carthage, où tes fiers empereurs
> Despouillez de pitié commirent tant d'horreurs. (*Porcie*, ll. 339–42)[54]

[You suffer, poor Rome, alas! You suffer as/ You made the city of the Moors suffer,/ Noble Carthage, where Rome's proud emperors/ Devoid of pity, committed such outrage.]

For the hatred of Mégère to be appeased, the sound of Rome's fall must reverberate around the world, but the show of the city's collapse must also be visible to all, and so sings the Chorus in *Marc Antoine* (Act II):

> . . . de flammes impétueuses
> De toutes parts ravageant,
> O Romme, ira saccageant
> Tes richesses orgueilleuses
> Et tes bastimens dorez,
> Dont les pointes envieuses
> Percent les cieux éthérez. (*Marc Antoine*, ll. 835–42)

[. . . impetuous flames/ Make havoc on all sides,/ Oh! Rome, they will sack/ Your proud possessions/ Your buildings of gold,/ Whose envious roofs/ Pierce the heavens.]

The spectator has the opportunity to visualize in detail the collapse or progressive ruin of each building. Further pleasurable participation is assumed as Garnier expects the reader to recognize Lucan's descriptions of the dire effects of civil war on the battlefield and in the city; and to appreciate the great blocks of rhetoric inspired by Seneca.[55] The spectator who is really attentive may also admire bold juxtapositions – 'Tu sers, superbe Rome' (You serve, proud Rome); appreciate the paradoxes and unexpected turns of phrase – 'Cette cité riche de violence' (*Cornélie*, l. 138), and relish the descriptive set-pieces such as the messenger's account of Brutus' death (*Porcie*, Act IV). In these ways, Garnier engages readers/spectators in his discourse and encourages them to complete the dreadful scenes he paints.

The views of Rome are rich and multiform and the meanings attached to this variety are manifold. Crucially, Rome still stands – however crippled. Towering over the disasters it has experienced, it signals defiance to destiny. Rome lives in its heroes' souls; their minds return to the city as to a sacred point of reference guiding their view of themselves; their joy radiates out over the hills; their fears and sorrows are painted on the walls and the buildings; their achievements and Rome's greatness are inseparable. The imperial city is a place of grandeur and of strength, and when Caesar or Mark Antony mentions the Capitol – 'Allons au Capitole' (Let us to the Capitol) – its sound rings out as a mark of supreme distinction. The Capitol means the place of worship, the abode of Jupiter who guards the city, the summit towards which all triumphs are directed and where the Triumphator pays homage to the gods.

Rome is also a place of violence. *Porcie* ends with lamentations on Rome's calamities, and Garnier's characters bid the city goodbye signalling her reputation as a place of ill fortune: 'Adieu Romme,/ Qui renommé malheur pour tout jamais renomme' (Goodbye, Rome,/ Who, renamed Evil, will carry the name for ever). Evil is part of its make-up, present in its stones and ever ready to break forth into civil disobedience and strife. The Chorus in *Marc Antoine* (end of Act IV) advocates foreign wars (as did many of Garnier's contemporaries) rather than domestic ones 'qui rongent l'estat' (which eat away the state). Civil war fills the city with mercenaries 'horribles en leurs armes' (dreadful in arms). It brings suffering and ghastly deaths, all graphically described by Garnier. Sometimes it is an individual like Porcie dying from swallowing hot coals, or Caesar murdered and his corpse sprawling on the streets of Rome, mocked by the populace. Sometimes it is a spectacle of more general slaughter: on the battlefield (*Cornélie*, Act IV), or at Rome with the hundreds of decapitated heads adorning the Forum (*Porcie*, ll. 541–4). The scenes are horrible, designed to shock, and to serve as warnings to sixteenth-century Frenchmen.

Perhaps the most effective means of emotional provocation used by Garnier was his manipulation of the Triumph. Viewers of this era were very familiar with the sight of the monarch entering a city in triumph. They had also seen images of ancient Triumphs in Rome (on which many royal entries were based) when the Triumphator entered the city on a chariot preceded by the kings and princes of the countries he had vanquished, and by spoils and pictures of the towns he had captured.[56] In *Cornélie*, the ceremony of the Triumph grows in the heroine's mind. She first sees it in her dreams associated with the figure of Pompey who appears not as she remembers, in triumph with vanquished kings dragging along in his cortège, but pale and haggard, hollow-eyed and drawn with a long shroud trailing behind. Remembrance underlines the magnitude of Pompey's fall. Similarly, the extent of Rome's fall is measured by Caesar seen in triumph, lauding it over his fellow citizens. Cassius' prejudiced mind has exploited the elements of the Triumph to paint a terrifying picture of the Dictator, trampling over his people and over Rome itself:

> Nous le voyons terrible en un char élevé,
> Traîner l'honneur vaincu de son peuple esclavé;
> Ainsi Rome à César donne un pouvoir suprême,
> Et de Rome César trionfe en Rome mesme. (*Cornélie*, ll. 1087–90)

[We see him, terrible, standing in his chariot,/ Leading the vanquished honour of his enslaved people;/ Thus, Rome gives to Caesar supreme power,/ And Caesar triumphs over Rome in Rome itself.]

So deeply merged were the ideas of the Triumph and of Rome that for Cleopatra the two were synonymous: the Triumph was Rome victorious, and the most appalling prospect she could imagine was to be preserved by Caesar so that she might be exhibited in his Triumph. Her fears were well grounded, for Caesar did have such a plan and already enjoyed the picture of her wealth and beauty (suitably humbled) being displayed to foster his glorious image: 'à fin d'en décorer/ Le triomphe qu'à Romme on nous doit préparer' (in order to adorn/ The Triumph they are preparing for us in Rome) (*Marc Antoine*, ll. 1703–5). These legitimate fears of Cleopatra are used at the end of the play in an attempt to dissuade the queen from suicide when her servant exposes the scenes of Caesar's Triumph in Rome adorned with the presence of Cleopatra's children; she also should be present. She recoils from the sight and shows how, from the viewpoint of the victim, Triumphs were barbarous.

A factor which lifted Garnier's conception of Rome on to a higher plane was the ease with which his characters communed with spirits from the underworld, and the confidence with which they assumed the interest of the gods in their affairs. Rome, they believed, was ruled both by good and malign forces; the very walls of the city had been built with divine assistance and those gods admired their work and rejoiced in the splendour of the structures erected by Romans to do them honour. The closeness of their presence is notable, especially in *Porcie*; and, although one might expect the fury Mégère to have a direct line to the other infernal demons whose aid she seeks, the intimacy of Porcie's own relation to the spirits of the underworld, her knowledge of 'les romaines ombres' (the Roman shades), and her mental familiarity with 'les rives umbreuses' (the gloomy shores) are remarkable.

Often, in the French Renaissance, Rome was called a tomb. This was a complex image, almost always implying criticism, but it rarely acquired the startling significance which Garnier gave it at the end of the first scene of *Porcie*:

> Desjà par les cantons mille tableaux meurtriers
> Des malheureux proscrits saisissent les gosiers.
> Rome n'est qu'un sépulchre à tant de funérailles,
> Qu'elle voit entasser en ses froides entrailles. (*Porcie*, ll. 143–6)

[Already through the streets a thousand murderous images/ Of unfortunate outlaws catch at the throat./ Rome is all tomb with so many funerals,/ As she watches them pile up in her cold entrails.]

Here, the brutality and quantity of deaths jostle in the cavernous regions of Rome depicted as a physical entity, a body with entrails. If the quiet stillness of ruined monuments to the dead is evoked, the teeming mass of bodies freshly slaughtered is also present.

This double image of Rome is maintained throughout the dramas in the chants of the Chorus and in their commentaries where they insist both on the lofty grandeur of the city and on the realities of cruel adversity. Their remarks broaden out the implications for the spectator to include all humankind, but especially – as Garnier announced in his dedications – the inhabitants of France in the late sixteenth century. The tone is set in the first Chorus of *Porcie*:

> O combien roulent d'accidens
> Des Cieux sur les choses humaines! (*Porcie*, ll. 151–2)

[Oh! how many events/ Sent by heaven flow over human affairs!]

Although these meditators on human affairs sometimes focus specifically upon a dramatic moment in Rome's story, their comment is usually generalized while still maintaining a double, balanced approach. Peaceful rural activity is disrupted by the violence of war; hopes are sung while the fear of ruin lurks in the background; soldiers deplore 'que les Romains/ S'entre-massacrent de leurs mains' (that the Romans/ Kill each other with their own hands). Of exemplary Rome: '. . . il ne reste de sa grandeur/ Que la ruine' (there only remains the ruin of her greatness) – and yet, if something of the former grandeur could still be seen, the ruin could serve as a lesson.

Although there was some hesitancy on the part of writers who were critical of Rome's dominance, at a time of civil war, the same writers exploited for multiple purposes the rich spectacle of the city and of the ancient ruins from Roman times that were still scattered across the French landscape. They used Rome to dilute their share of the responsibility of war and to give expression to their horror at the atrocities they witnessed. They harnessed the image to provide the substance of their attacks upon Catholicism, to uncover the causes of war, or to illustrate the universal mutability of all earthly things, of which Rome had become the emblem. Their meditations brought new approaches to the vision of the city as they turned upside down the significance of its inherited images – both sculpted and ceremonial forms. Yet, in most works, positive and negative readings coexisted, in recognition of the fact that full appreciation of Rome's ruin relied on the onlooker's ability to perceive its former greatness.

CHAPTER 8

Two Distilled Models of Rome

I CAESAR

SELF-FASHIONING IN ROMAN WRITERS

In the Renaissance, certain features of ancient Rome came to stand for the city and its power. It was as though all the city's force was concentrated into a single, representative form: either the imperial figure frozen into the concept 'Caesar'; or the triumphal arch rich in its association with both Rome and its empire. In large part, Roman writers had themselves created these imperial symbols,[1] and their images were passed down from generation to generation, fixed in their form and impact but, with time, their inner content was elaborated and filled out with later views and prejudices.[2]

Early Roman writers themselves made Rome the essential point of reference for every action and for all judgements on behaviour. In Livy's *Histories* for instance, from the city's foundation to the author's own times, Rome was the hero. Caesar, in his *Commentaries*, when he punished his enemies, did so not from personal animosity but because he had discovered that they were plotting against Rome. Augustus' writings (the *Res gestae*, drafted and redrafted 23–22 BC, and discovered in the sixteenth century)[3] projected the view of Rome, and of the emperor who guided its destiny, which he wished his readers to adopt. Emperors, like Caesar and Augustus, thus became their own historians and were able to shape their own images for general consumption. Although the substance of the *Commentaries* had obvious connections with his private self, Caesar – writing in the third person – was concerned to provide a public version of himself which could be shaped and refined according to events which he ordered and linked for his own purposes. Likewise, the *Res gestae* served to organize and direct public opinion, and to mould perceptions of Rome and of the person of Augustus, whose acts were geared to promoting the greatness of the city and to securing its power and dominance.[4]

Although in the minds of many subsequent writers – Petrarch,[5] Dante and Erasmus for example – Caesar Augustus had become the accepted model to be emulated by later emperors, for historians, numismatists and medieval French writers, Julius Caesar (regarded as the first emperor of Rome) remained the dominant figure. His image and his myth were widely known in

C·IVLIVS
CAESAR
DICTATOR
PERP·

83.   Aeneas Vico: engraving of Julius Caesar, flanked by Venus and Mars

sixteenth-century France, and the following discussion will focus upon them (Figure 83).

Self-fashioning of the kind found in Caesar's and Augustus' writings was also a pre-eminent characteristic in the design of coins. These provided a primary way of fixing the image and registering any changes of emphasis; for, while the topside of the coin figured the emperor's stylized and named countenance, its reverse showed significant events of his reign such as triumphs, games, construction of buildings, important legislation or victories. A fair idea of the variety of possible combinations can be gained from Hubert Goltzius' work *C. Julius Caesar sive historiae imperatorum caesarumque romanorum*[6] where he arranged the order of the coins to match his narration of Caesar's life, and then elucidated each engraved portrait with a scholarly commentary pulling out the meaning and linking the interpretation to the previous event or a following one. In this way, coins (and their commentary) reflected the fusion of the emperor's visage, usually crowned with the laurels of victory, with the symbols of his deeds and of Rome itself. In public perception, therefore, the power of the two were synonymous; to evoke the greatness of one automatically brought to mind that of the other. Caesar was Rome.

The simultaneity of concept recorded on coins had been established in writing by Cicero in the speech which he delivered before Caesar in 46 BC, in the Senate after the victory at Pharsalia. The orator argued that henceforth Caesar was no private man whose personal wishes could command his life. On the contrary, his prowess includes the salvation of the citizens of Rome and of the whole Republic. When Rapin translated this oration in 1610, he dedicated it to Henri IV, arguing the perfect appropriateness of the comparison between the king and Caesar, and rendered Cicero's conclusion:

Ce n'est donc point à vous de definir le temps de votre vie, à la mesure de la douceur de votre esprit, mais au poids et à la balance du bien universel de tout le monde et de l'estat public.

[It is not for you to define the length of your life by measuring it upon your gentleness of spirit, but according to the weight and balance of universal good towards all and to the state.][7]

In addition, Cicero had claimed, Caesar's own renown was tied up with, and dependent upon, the soundness and good order of Rome itself. Remove Caesar, his good influences, his wise laws and edicts and the city will fail, and Caesar's own good name will wander fruitlessly abroad, unanchored and empty of meaning:

Pourtant si cette cité n'est restablie et refondue par vos bons conseils et bonnes ordonnances, votre nom courra comme un vagabond au long et au large. (Rapin, *Oeuvres*, p. 215)

[However, if the city is not re-established and built again through your good counsel and sound laws, your name will travel here and there like a vagabond.]

The closeness of Rome's destiny and of Caesar's own became a regular theme in medieval French renderings of Caesar's *Commentaries*. In Du Chesne's account, the vision which assailed Caesar as he was about to cross the Rubicon – 'cel ymage pour vray representoit la cité et le pays de Romme' (this image truly represented the city and landscape of Rome) – Caesar appropriated to himself.[8] Similarly, in the tapestry tradition, Rome was frequently personified in the figure of Caesar.[9]

THE *LIVES* OF THE CAESARS

The admiration accorded to Caesar has to be seen in the context of two strong traditions, both of which gave sixteenth-century readers detailed knowledge of his life and deeds. The first was constituted by series of illustrious men whose visages were painted on walls or sculpted in marble and presented, in long lines, in princely galleries; the second – *Lives* of the Caesars – spawned multiple books graced with portraits of the emperors, their medallions and potted biographies. The first tradition came from ancient examples deriving from knowledge of Augustus' statue collection of those who had been worthy of Rome and extended the boundaries of empire.[10] This collection had inspired designs for wall paintings and portraits such as the engravings of the Roman heroes by Etienne Delaune at Chantilly;[11] Fulvio Orsini's *Imagines romanorum*;[12] French translations of the statue collection of ancient and modern heroes brought together by Paolo Giovio at his house in Como (*Les Eloges et vies briefvement descrites sous les images des plus illustres et principaux hommes de guerre . . . qui se voyent à Como*, 1589);[13] and finally André Thevet's *Les Vrais Pourtraicts des hommes illustres* produced in two handsome volumes in 1584. In this last example the accent was on the authenticity of the images and the facts associated with them, for, in immobilizing the features of his great men, Thevet sought to provide what he called 'un trésor et cabinet de mémoire' (a treasury and memory place) which would (he confidently claimed) energize and uplift the minds of all those who perused his work.[14]

The other inheritance which interacted with the first tradition was that of the *Lives* of the Caesars which had evolved in various forms: some stemmed from the *Historia augusta*, that miscellaneous collection of biographies of the emperors from Hadrian to Carinus; others were read and translated from the twelve Caesars' *Lives* written by Suetonius; some were shaped as a sequence of medal portraits with learned commentaries by numismatists and historians; and others came from translations and adaptations of Caesar's *Commentaries*. Each genre was modified by others and, in the sixteenth century, strongly influenced by Plutarch's *Vies des hommes illustres*, and his separate accounts of Pompey and Caesar.[15]

Copies of the twelve Caesars in medals, portraits or statues were owned by most princes of the Renaissance. Queen Elizabeth, for example, turning down the offer of another set from Nicholas Hoüel, boasted that she had three splendid versions already, collected by her father.[16] Scholars, less fortunate in worldly possessions, had their own series of the first twelve emperors' *Lives* either in summary form such as the potted biographies provided by Charles Fontaine in 1554,[17] or in La Boutière's translation of Suetonius: *Suetone Tranquille de la vie des douze Cesars* (Lyon, Jean de Tournes, 1556). Not content with the mere rendering into translation of Suetonius' original work, authors continually added to the father text, either (as did Egnatius in 1551) by supplementing it with biographies of later emperors,[18] or by adorning the volume with medallic representations of the Caesars. Aeneas Vico had inaugurated this practice in 1552, and his example was followed by many up to the end of the century.[19] Vico stressed the truthful nature of the images he depicted (as Thevet was to do), and it is interesting to note that, by 1560, Vico's entire text, with its scholarly commentary and engraved portraits and medals in multiple aspects, had expanded into a study exclusively devoted to Julius Caesar – an approach imitated by Goltzius three years later.[20] In all these texts with images, their composer worked on the assumption that the coins on which they based their drawings were designed to perpetuate the memory of those whose deeds merited immortality.[21] In extending renown beyond the lifetime of an emperor and linking it to the city which he had served, writers brought together, under the banner of fame, Rome and Caesar.

Renaissance writers played variations on classical texts, stuffing their commentaries with learned references and with details gleaned from an impressive array of Latin sources. In this, they were perpetuating habits developed by their predecessors in the vast number of surviving manuscripts, usually entitled *Les Faicts des Romains* and, more often than not, dedicated to the life and deeds of Julius Caesar.[22] Those which focused on Caesar suggested wider horizons, such as Nicolas Boyvin's 'Miroir hystorial' (Ms fr. 15456), tending to attribute to the conqueror of Gaul responsibility for the larger picture of Rome. Many of these manuscripts were simple compendia of Roman history built up from a range of Latin authors (chiefly Caesar, Livy and Lucan),[23] and some were published, like the *Recueil des histoires romaines extraicts de plusieurs historiographes c'est assavoir Tite Live/ Valere/ Orose/ Justin/ Saluste/ Cesar/ Lucan/ Suetone/ Eutrope et autres* (Paris, 1528). Whatever their orientation, these texts appropriated Caesar and his deeds, and absorbed them into their own culture and ideals. So it is that, in the miniatures that adorn the manuscripts, Caesar is often attired in medieval dress and his achievements are presented as belonging to the art of chivalry. For these writers, Caesar was the *chevalier par excellence*.[24]

In any consideration of Caesar's impact on the French vision of Rome in the sixteenth century, attention must be given to the phenomenal number of editions, translations and adaptations of his *Commentaries* which were often produced at the request of princes.[25] Gaguin's rendering, published in 1539, was executed for Charles VIII. In the same year, Estienne de Laigue, seigneur de Beauvais, issued his translation, in which he acknowledged Gaguin's translation and set out the reasons why Caesar's work was important. In addition to his undoubted magnanimity and military prowess, De Laigue outlined the following advantages: from a study of the *Commentaries*, one acquired prudence in the orderly conduct of public affairs; the strength to lead military campaigns valiantly; and the ability to ponder wisely the prospect of war.[26] Although some authors, like Pierre de la Ramée, exploited the *Commentaries* as a tool for their own purposes,[27] most recognized the political and military benefits to be derived from a close reading of Caesar's work. Above all, their relevance in particular to war which first threatened and then overwhelmed France in the second half of the century was appreciated. Symeoni, in his *César renouvellé* (1558), signalled their timeliness in his title as he rearranged Caesar's text to illustrate his own propositions about making war. This text was reissued in 1570 by François de Saint Thomas who, at first, hesitated to publish a book on war at a time of civil strife; but, nevertheless, acknowledged the pertinence of Caesar's work to the third wave of violence in France. The adaptation was intended to have practical use. Of similar intent were Palladio's engravings which interleaved Francesco Baldelli's translation, reissued in 1575. These showed the dispositions of Caesar's troops in all the major encounters in Gaul, implying that tactics, troop formation and weapons had changed little since Roman times and, as was argued in the preface to Palladio's book, the example of Julius Caesar provided an antidote to the miserable conditions of the current *époque*.[28] Even more authoritative was the monster edition produced by Blaise de Vigenère in 1589. He, too, underlined the practical usefulness of Caesar's strategies and yet, in his copious annotations, he seized the opportunity to expand, not on these, but on related topics such as the nature of the legions, the art of fortification, bridge building, and Roman armour as evidenced on surviving marble monuments in Rome.

It became customary to gloss the *Commentaries* with additional information until, eventually, the original text was overwhelmed with supplementary details from a vast network of ancient sources which scholars explored to enhance their knowledge of Caesar and of Rome. These were all available to sixteenth-century readers. Livy's *Histories* were read and discussed by those who wished to lead in political and military affairs. Sallust, a protégé of Caesar in whom he considered the greatness of Rome to reside, had written on the conspiracy of Catiline; Dio Cassius had furnished details of the political manoeuvrings of Caesar and Pompey; and Appian left an account of the civil wars which was translated into French at the request of Louis XII, and subsequently published in 1544.

These historians not only provided detailed narratives of Caesar's campaigns and of the ever-changing political situation in Rome at that time; they also penned portraits of the man. Their often laudatory versions may have owed something to the various encomia by Cicero, who expatiated on Caesar's virtues on at least three occasions. In his *Brutus or Remarks on Eminent Orators*, in the voice of Atticus, he described Caesar's studious application to literature, and praised him for having the purest and most elegant command of the Roman language in speech and in writing, describing his style as 'plain, correct and graceful, and divested of all ornaments of language, so as to appear in a kind of undress'. So the style admired in the Renaissance, that direct and colloquial expression, came from intense and prolonged study.[29] In the *De provinciis consularibus* (delivered about 56 BC), Cicero had extolled the genius of Caesar in conquering the whole of Gaul. But his most extended account of Caesar's qualities occurred in *Philippic II*, which was never delivered. There, he listed many virtues:

> wit, genius, learning, penetration, deep reflection, unwearied assiduity, and a fine memory, were the characteristics of Caesar,

and then he examined his principal aims and objectives. He shows Caesar to have been a man given to deep premeditation, who had planned his success from a long way back:

> though he waged a pernicious and fatal war against the republic, yet in every stage of that war, he shone a HERO. His plan of reigning was deep and permanent. By incredible labour, and through almost insuperable difficulties, he executed that plan. By acts of munificence, and public works, by royal largesses and with splendid entertainments, he soothed and gained the unthinking multitudes. By presents, and a pretended moderation, he lured his adversaries to his purposes. And what is still more, he brought us, partly by our fears, partly by his moderation, to bear the yoke of servitude without repining. The love of domination was indeed congenial in both [Caesar and Mark Antony], but in no other instance did the least resemblance appear.

Although implicit in Cicero's comment lies some criticism of Caesar's ambitions, the orator contrived to turn this to the benefit of Rome.[30]

Cicero's views were enormously influential in his own time and in the Renaissance, although their glow was somewhat tempered by Suetonius and by the slightly later assessment of Sallust who picked up some of the aspects highlighted by Cicero. In his account, Caesar was a being of extreme activity, vigilance and application who, from an early age, aspired to play a significant role on the world stage. But Sallust added other features, to end on a distinctly critical note: Caesar was generous, careless, clement and gifted beyond the norm as strategist and writer. Only one thing marred his portrait – ambition was his ruling passion, and that very ambition not only helped make Rome great but also contributed to the city's distress and downfall.[31]

Such was the image of Caesar transmitted to the Renaissance, either directly from the perusal of these texts, or through the versions passed on by medieval commentators and translators. Yet many sixteenth-century readers preferred to shape their own image from first-hand acquaintance with Caesar's *Commentaries*. We know from recent work that reading at this time was not a passive activity.[32] As often as not, noble men and women were read to and engaged in lively discussion, debating the merits (or otherwise) of what had been heard. Brantôme reported, for example, that Marguerite de Valois provoked such 'discours et disputes' (debates and discussions), and one day talking of Julius Caesar and commenting on his qualities and extraordinary achievements, she 'en pristes la parole et l'allastes exalter par de si gentils et briefs mots . . . la plus belle gloire qu'eurent jamais les Romains, Cesar la leur avoit acquise, et Cesar estoit digne plus que de Rome' (took on the discussion and praised him with a few kind words . . . that the greatest glory which the Romans ever had, was achieved by Caesar, and that Caesar was worthier than Rome).[33] Action was often the outcome of reading, as has been shown with respect to Sir Philip Sidney whose knowledge of Livy and Machiavelli (whose work he had pondered with Gabriel Harvey) informed his approach to the diplomatic exchanges he was to have on the continent.[34]

When Erasmus recommended the *Commentaries* for study he may have had Caesar's style principally in mind;[35] he could hardly have imagined that an active soldier like Philip Strozzi would have laboured to translate them into Greek 'et luy-mesmes escrits de sa main, avec des commentaires latins, additions, et instructions pour gens de guerre' (and, with his own hand, wrote Latin commentaries, additions, and instructions for men of war), or that François de Carnavalet would have learned them by heart – in the Latin – notwithstanding Symeoni's later injunction that, without knowing them by heart, it was virtually impossible to take proper direction of wars.[36] In his soaring praise addressed to Caesar, with which he ended Book 1 of the *César renouvellé*, Symeoni asked:

> Qui sera celuy tant envieux, aveugle, sourd, maling, ou du tout despourveu d'entendement, qui ne loüe, invite et ammire tes faicts merveilleux et memorables?

> [who would be so envious, blind, deaf, malicious, or so lacking in understanding that does not praise, extol and admire your marvellous and memorable deeds?]

Blaise de Monluc liked to have books read to him and he relished the deeds of 'ces braves Scipions, Catons et Césars' who seemed to come alive as he listened.[37] Above all, he cherished Caesar, the greatest commander who ever lived and whose book (Monluc frankly admitted) he had imitated. Like his master, he called his work *Commentaires* and he regarded them not as fodder for the learned (which, in many ways, Caesar's had become – especially with Vigenère's giant edition), but for the soldier still active and anxious to extend his knowledge of tactics and experience of war. To win battles, he counselled, 'Regardez les Commentaires de César et de tous ceux qui ont escrit de luy' (consider the Commentaries of Caesar and all those who have written about him); follow his practice, be diligent, alert and speedy in your resolution: 'toutes ses victoires luy sont advenues pour estre diligent, vigilant et prompt exécuteur' (all his victories came about through his diligence, alertness and speed of action).[38] Monluc's immersion in Caesar not only prompted him to action but served as authoritative justification for his own precipitous acts.

PARALLELS BETWEEN FRENCH PRINCES AND CAESAR

It was hardly surprising that Renaissance princes were eager to compare themselves to such a paragon as Caesar and that their encouragement of scholars' translation efforts had much to do with their wish to appear in his image. A very large number sought so to depict themselves and the verb *cesariser* entered the language, automatically conjuring up those qualities which brought lasting renown, as Louys Papon summed up at the end of the century:

> Dire *Cezarizant* ie vins, vis et vainquis.

> [Say, as Caesar, I came, I saw, I conquered.][39]

Virtually every prince was compared to Caesar, and the parallel was as much a compliment to powerful performances as an incitement to perform even better.[40]

It could be argued that the Holy Roman Emperors legitimately claimed affinities with Caesar, with more justice at least than some princes like Caesar Borgia or Pope Julius II, who revelled in the comparison. The former flaunted the motto *aut Caesar aut nihil* (either Caesar or nothing); while the latter was delighted to see the apothegm *veni, vidi, vici* (I came, I saw, I conquered) attributed to himself and inscribed on a triumphal arch on Palm Sunday 1507.[41] Maximilian I (whose personal copy of the *Commentaries* can still be seen in Madrid) had actually planned a triumphal entry into Rome as Caesar; Charles V was universally known as *sa Cesarée Magesté* and regarded as a reincarnation of Caesar to the extent that, in an account of the Roman commander's life, he himself became the point of reference: 'come fece Carlo Quinto' (as did Charles V); and Rudolph II's sense of himself was unmistakably as *ex utroque Caesar* (another Caesar).[42]

What is interesting in the parallels drawn between French princes and Caesar is the specificity of the comparisons. These are not timeless, empty gestures of praise. Du Chesne, for example, in accepting Charles le Téméraire's commission to translate Caesar's *Commentaries*, saw his duty as measuring Caesar's achievements against those of his master. He had no hesitation in concluding that the Burgundian's mode of governance was superior in every way to the one adopted by Caesar in Rome, and the translation turned into an apology for the personal power of Charles.[43] Charles VIII, having also adopted the apothegm *veni, vidi, vici*, enjoyed seeing himself as another Caesar on the monuments erected to greet him as, for example, at Lucca. On his triumphant journey through Italy, the images charted his succession of victories and provided the substance of the imperial pretensions that dominated themes in French literature and art of this period.[44]

These themes were to be taken up with even more verve under François I, and were applied much more systematically. The mirror image – King/Caesar – was, from the earliest period of his reign, embedded in the culture of his court. It can be seen in the portrait preserved at Chantilly,[45] in the monarch's entry into Rouen in 1517 where an immense equestrian statue of the king was erected to emulate the Triumph of the Romans, with the inscription: 'Rome, avec un tel César, devient une autre/ Rome' (with such a Caesar, Rome becomes another Rome). Among the many histories, drawings and tributes written to please François I and incorporating the Caesar parallel were Du Choul's 'Antiquitez romaines', and a sketch by Luca Penni (*c.* 1541–45) showing the king in the guise of Caesar: seated and contemplative, dressed for battle *à la romaine*, he ponders the conflict to come.

The most thoroughgoing attempt to show the king in the image of Caesar was made by François Demoulins in three manuscripts, dated 1518–20, beautifully illuminated by Godefroy le Batave. Commissioned by the king to commemorate his victory at the battle of Marignan, the manuscripts invite the royal reader to see himself in conversation with Julius Caesar, discoursing on the political and military implications of the *Commentaries*.[46] The youthful and victorious warrior-king 'interrogea subtilement' (subtly questioned) the venerable sire dressed in military garb and wearing his imperial cloak. The physical dissimilarities are emphasized to underscore the astounding similarities in achievement – conquest over the Swiss and German mercenaries. Very precisely, the day, the hour and the content of each encounter between François I and Caesar are recorded. At the first meeting (30 April 1519, at Saint Germain-en-Laye) François I is the 'secund Caesar victeur et domateur des Souyces' (second victor and conqueror of the Swiss); Caesar comes as the 'premyer subjugateur des helvèces' (first master of the Swiss); they both fought at night and both had been eager to avenge wrongs inflicted on their parents. The manuscript is illustrated with a series of battle scenes showing Caesar's exploits, and Demoulins, in the margin, repeatedly draws the king's attention to the exact nature of the parallel: 'Sire ne voyez vous clerement que la similitude de vous et de Caesar?' (Sire, do you not see the clear likeness between yourself and Caesar?) (Ms Harleian, f. 37). The second manuscript (narrating the meeting at Fontainebleau

Le trefcreftian Roy
Francoys
Demande a Cæfar
EN quantez partiez eft diui.
fee toute la gaule qui vous
a aultreffoiz tant donne de peine.
Cæfar dictez le moy ie vous prie

Cæfar refpond
Oy liberal & pacifieque vray
heritier de ma gloire et fortu

84.   Godefroy le Batave:
François I and Julius Caesar

at the beginning of August) is chiefly adorned with a succession of medallion portraits; on the same page François I is placed above Caesar (Figure 84), and on other pages members of Caesar's entourage are painted (possibly by Jean Clouet) in the features of François I's chief officers. Thus Artus Gouffier stands for Quintus Pedius (Caesar's legate), Lautrec for Quintus Titurius Sabinus, Anne de Montmorency for Lucius Cotta (Plate VIII) and so on. This degree of inter-changeability anticipates Caesar's response to the king's question: 'Invincible Caesar, dictez moy verite, que vous semble de nostre temps?' (Invincible Caesar, tell me the truth, what do you think of our time?) With admirably brevity, Caesar replies: 'Il est imperial' (It is imperial) (Ms fr. 13429, f. 6).

Towards the end of his second manuscript Demoulins informed the king: 'Je

85. Niccolo della Casa: engraving of Henri II as Emperor

86. G.A. Rossi: Henri II as *Imperator*, medal to commemorate the King's victory at Calais and Guisnes

mettray peine, Sire, de trouver aultres figures antiques, et en feray declaration els livres qui s'ensuiyvrent' (Sire, I will try to find other antique figures and will show them in the other books which follow) (ibid., f. 94). The intent to model his work on the antique is clear; but unfortunately only one other manuscript in the series has survived, recording the third encounter at Cognac on 27 February 1520, a short time before François I met Henry VIII at the Field of the Cloth of Gold. Although it is impossible to say whether further work was executed, the parallel habit exploited so obviously by François Demoulins and his contemporaries had become ingrained, and successive Valois kings were also drawn in the image of Caesar. Henri II, at the beginning of his reign, was depicted as *imperator* by Niccolo della Casa (Figure 85), and again – retrospectively – by Antoine Caron for *L'Histoire françoyse de nostre temps*;[47] he was labelled 'plusque Caesar' (more than Caesar) by Ferrand de Bez in the *épistre héroique* he wrote on the king's entry into Paris in 1549;[48] and a medal was struck depicting Henri II as *imperator* in commemoration of his victories at Calais and Guisnes (Figure 86). So familiar was the comparison that Vigenère set medallion portraits of Henri III and of Caesar side by side because both men loved arms and letters.[49]

And the taste for such parallel depictions prevailed. Particularly apt were the comparisons drawn, and in fine detail, between Henri IV and Caesar and their deeds:

> Que Cesar et Henry, deux vainqueurs indontables;
> Tellement qu'on pourroit comme d'un mesme cours,
> De Cesar, et Henry former mesme discours.

[Caesar and Henry, two victors so indomitable that one can trace the same career and write the same discourse for Henry and for Caesar.]

Thus began the most systematic set of parallels ever attempted between Roman emperor and French monarch. In couplet after couplet, the careers of the two were inextricably intertwined, matched and assessed, and in the midst of the praise appears Sully, the *bon serviteur* who composed the piece (published by Toussainct du Bray in 1615).[50] It must be acknowledged, however, that Anthoine de Bandole had already familiarized readers with the comparison in 1609 when his elaborate *Les Parallèles de Cesar et de Henri IV* was published in Paris by Jean Richer, accompanied by political maxims of the author's own invention, and by Vigenère's learned annotations and, perhaps most striking of all, introduced by a frontispiece which displayed both heroes crowned with laurel leaves, seated on horseback, in full armour and carrying the symbols of imperial majesty (Figure 87).

This trend in French art and literature, which encouraged parallels that took account of the minutiae of political and military events, was supported by current approaches to history. The comparative method of Jean Bodin or Louis le Roy necessitated constant reference to the great men of the past, to Caesar and to Rome; and the genius of Caesar, in particular, was the peak to aim for and the proper expression of a truly remarkable performance. In Lipsius' view, Caesar was altogether out of the ordinary and his military gifts (as strategist and warrior) made him and kept him the foremost man of war of all times.[51]

HOSTILITY TO CAESAR AND THE CONTEST BETWEEN HIM AND POMPEY

And yet, despite the fame and the glamour attaching to his name, Caesar's achievements were not always viewed with such favour in the Renaissance. Major thinkers made him responsible for the fall of the Republic, and ultimately for the destruction of Rome. Lucan's hatred was well known; and his *Pharsalia*, written as a deliberate counterpoise to Caesar's *Commentaries*,[52] had penetrated much writing on the French civil wars. Readers of Machiavelli's *Discorsi* (1531), too, of whom there were many in sixteenth-century France, would have known the violence of his attacks upon Caesar. He had drawn attention to what he regarded as mistaken opinions of Caesar's reputation; it was absurd (Machiavelli claimed) to go on extolling a man whose achievements had been distorted 'by the long continuance of the empire . . . ruled under that name'. For the purposes of his condemnation, however, Machiavelli exploited that very longevity, and he rolled under the name of Caesar all the appalling deeds of the bad emperors, attributing to him all the ills that befell Rome by the dynasty he had founded:

He [the reader] will see Rome burnt, its Capitol demolished by its own citizens, ancient temples lying desolate, religious rites grown corrupt, adultery rampant throughout the city . . . In Rome he will see countless atroc-

Hercule. Thesée. Achile. Alexandre.

CVCTA DOMAT VIRTVS. IN FEROCES FEROX. VINCERE AVT MORI. SOL SOLVS IN ORBE.

AVT CÆSAR AVT NIHIL. CEDIT VICTORIA FORTI.

LES
PARALLELES
DE CESAR, ET
DE HENRY·IIII.
PAR ANTHOINE DE
BANDOLE,
Avec
Les Commentaires
de CESAR, & les Annotations de BLAISE
DE VIGINERE,
De nouueau Illustrez
de Maximes Politiques
par ledit DE BANDOLE
DEDIE
A Monseigneur
le DAVLPHIN

A PARIS,
Chez IEAN RICHER rüe S. Iean
de latran a l'arbre verdoyant
et en sa boutique au Palais sur le
perron Royal.

Cæsar. Henry IIII.

SIC VIRESCIT IVSTVS. HONOS DVCIBVS VBI LABOR. AGITATA VIRESCO.

Auec priuilege du Roy. L. Gaultier sculp. 1609.

87.   A. de Bandole: Henri IV and Caesar

ities perpetuated; rank, riches, the honours men have won, and, above all, virtue, looked upon as a capital crime. He will find calumniators rewarded, servants suborned to turn against their masters, freedmen to turn against their patrons, and those who lack enemies attacked by their friends. He will thus happily learn how much Rome, Italy, and the world owed to Caesar.[53]

The picture Machiavelli paints is thick with irony and its portentous peroration streaked with prejudice. No less violent was Symphorien Champier's attack on what he called the tyranny of Caesar, to whom he assigned all the crimes which stained Roman history, disregarding – in his effort to promote the value of French traditions – the atrocities instigated by Sulla and Marius or the later emperors.[54]

The most nuanced hostility towards Rome and Caesar can be found in the writings of Estienne de la Boëtie, published by Montaigne after his friend's death. It was, paradoxically, Caesar's apparently good qualities which La Boëtie divined were at the root of Rome's destruction; their effect was more insidious than the most savage cruelty ever encountered. La Boëtie did not mince his words:

à la verité ce fust ceste sienne venimeuse douceur qui, envers le peuple romain, sucra la servitude.

[in truth, it was this venomous clemency towards the Roman people that sweetened their servitude.][55]

His disgust is evident in the deliberate juxtaposition of 'venimeuse douceur' and 'sucra la servitude', and from his sad reflections on the behaviour of the Roman people who, after his death, baptized Caesar 'Father of the Roman people', and erected a mighty column in his honour. It will have been remarked that those who sought to emulate Caesar concentrated chiefly on his military exploits while his critics tended to harp on his political career and on the role he played in bringing the Roman state to ruin. Estienne de la Boëtie was unusual in discerning the rotten consequences of Caesar's virtues.

Views of Caesar were complicated especially by the debates concerning the relative merits of Pompey and Caesar. Discussions of this issue had raged since the time of the civil war, and Cicero was the major source of the ambiguities and shifting attitudes towards the behaviour of Pompey and Caesar. The evolution of his views was most clearly demonstrated in his letters to Atticus, from which it is possible to chart Cicero's changing opinion and hesitations almost day by day. Obviously, his judgement was clouded by the fact that his own political career was bound up with theirs. So, in all the preliminary skirmishes, Cicero veers from one side to the other: 'I see it would be better to be beaten with Pompey than win with Caesar. Shall I choose the other course?'[56] Yet, finally, it was his devotion to the needs of the Republic and to the liberty essential to the future power of Rome which gradually made him disenchanted with Caesar's cause and caused him to side with Pompey. He rehearsed the complex nature of the issues involved, traced the paradoxical reception of the behaviour of both men, was incredulous at Pompey's decision to leave Rome with members of the Senate, and gave some inkling of the inextricable problems with rhetorical questions such as: 'Is there a more wretched spectacle than that of Caesar earning praise in a disgusting cause, and of Pompey earning blame in the most excellent?' (II, viii, p. 127). Throughout, despite his shifts and turns of fear and genuine perplexity, Cicero recognized that 'Absolute power is what he [Pompey] and Caesar have sought . . . Both want to be kings' (II, xi, pp. 131–3).

The historian Dio Cassius, at some distance from the events, exposed the motives of both men. He described Pompey as guileful, a master in the art of deception, 'always in the habit of pretending as far as possible not to desire the things he really wished'. Caesar was similarly painted, plotting for the longer term, voting for measures he might one day want passed on his own behalf, and heaping plaudits upon Pompey whom he wished to render 'more envied and odious as a result of the honours conferred upon him, so that the people might get their fill of him more quickly'. Neither emerges as a hero in this account, and both were obliged to share the responsibility of Rome's ruin. Dio Cassius is quite explicit: 'Because of them, Rome was being compelled to fight both in her own defence and against herself, so that even if victorious she would be vanquished.'[57] The cruel fate of Rome, both city and empire diminished by the prolongation of the civil war, is aptly caught in this paradoxical sentence which also reveals how finely balanced the judgements on the two protagonists had to be. Both Pompey and Caesar had undoubted qualities, and for this reason, attribution of praise or blame required nice assessment. It was not easy to choose which side to support; as Velleius Paterculus put it: 'A man of probity and sound judgement would approve Pompey's party; a man of prudence would rather follow Caesar's; deeming the former more honourable, the latter more formidable.'[58] That very difficulty kept the debate alive.

It was reignited by Lucan, whose poem promoted the cause of Pompey, and although the facts of history required him to show Caesar triumphant at Pharsalia, this was grudgingly done and, at the end of his epic, the poet left the victor wandering and uncertain, with his readers waiting for the final catastrophe – the murder of Caesar in the Senate. In the Renaissance, concerns about freedom provoked further discussion, and controversy broke out in Florence in 1435 between Poggio Bracciolini and Guarino Guarini, the former attacking Caesar because he had destroyed Roman liberty, the latter stoutly defending his accomplishments. The quarrel raged on for years. It reiterated many of the arguments which had been deployed by earlier writers – whether Rome, in Caesar's day, had become ripe for the rule of one man; or whether Caesar and Augustus had instituted the tyrant rule and, thereby, had reduced the cultural energy of Rome.[59]

Sixteenth-century Frenchmen were also fascinated by the struggle between Caesar and Pompey, though not always because they were interested in the conflict *per se*. Often they sought to apply the ingredients to contemporary situations. A miscellany of examples provides an overview of the range of responses found in France at this time. Henri II, for example, wore parade armour on which was engraved the struggle between Pompey and Caesar. The armour, now in the Louvre, fashioned from designs by Etienne Delaune, tells the whole story: the death of Julia on the vizier, the battle of Durazzo on the back, Pompey vanquished on the gauntlets and Pompey's head being presented to Caesar on the breastplate.[60] In recalling the pact between Pompey and Caesar before the outbreak of war, and then the conflict itself, Du Bellay exploited – in *Les Antiquitez* (xxiii) and in his *Elegy to Avanson* – passages from Lucan's epic to evoke the dying strength of Rome and its present new resurrection.[61] Before him, Guillaume Budé, preoccupied with the dignity of the French monarchy, had been impressed with Pompey's majesty and triumph, about which he reminded François I in detail. Many pages of the *Institution du prince* (1547) are devoted to Pompey's virtues, and to his determination not to deprive the Roman people of freedom; in Budé's vision, Pompey is 'le vray exemplaire de protocolle de vertuz nécessaires à tous grans princes' (the true exemplar of all protocol and virtues required of great princes).[62] By contrast, a mere paragraph suffices for Caesar, whose emulation of Alexander is Budé's principal preoccupation. Symeoni did remember the civil war, took sides with Caesar and castigated Pompey as ambitious.[63] Michel de l'Hospital took the opposite stance, condemning Caesar for having put his personal ambition above the fate of his countrymen, and seeing the struggle between Pompey and Caesar as evidence of wider human failings, which drew him to express approval for the former (representing the cause of freedom) and denunciation of the dictator.[64]

Estienne Jodelle had a quite different preoccupation. In his *Discours de Jules César avant de passer le Rubicon*' (addressed equally to Charles IX and to himself)[65] he represents as the solution to his country's dilemma (and his own) a re-enactment of the thoughts that assailed Caesar on his way to conquer Rome. The poet appropriates the Rubicon and turns it into a metaphor with which to express the difficulties in opening his mind to the king on the vexed topic of war:

> . . . un estroit Rubicon à passer se propose
> A moy comme à César . . .
>
> [A narrow Rubicon confronts me, as it did Caesar . . .]

Just as Caesar's thoughts shifted hither and thither, contemplating war and justice, so Jodelle's mind is filled with contradictory notions that agitate him and make him fearful of inflicting pain and doom. He postpones advice, puts off the moment when he must come to a decision, and – instead – takes up the metaphor again, this time applying it to the king who himself has 'à passer/Maint nouveau Rubicon' (to cross many new Rubicons). Back and forth go his thoughts, swinging from prompt action to patient waiting, hesitations, and sudden determination as quickly set aside; so the poet and Charles IX's mind (as conceived by the poet) meander through this long, indeterminate and unfinished poem. The work is of interest to us, despite Colletet's strictures that it was the most boring poem he had ever read,[66] because it is the first time that a writer had tried to get inside (so to speak) and to interiorize Caesar's thoughts and use them for his own. He makes no judgement. Not so Innocent Gentillet, whose vehement attack on the *Discorsi* set aside Machiavelli's dire opinion of Caesar; although, in a parenthesis during his long diatribe against the sale of offices, he makes Julius Caesar and Pompey jointly responsible for the ruins of the Republic, he reassures his readers about the 'grandeur de Pompée' and the 'magnanimité de César'.[67]

MONTAIGNE'S VIEW OF CAESAR

The fullest account of Caesar in French in the sixteenth century was written by Montaigne; and, although consideration of Caesar offered the author of the *Essais* a perspective on the Roman world at large, Montaigne's interest is sharply focused on Caesar himself.[68] His knowledge of Caesar and his writings was profound; he read the *Commentaries* in detail between February and July 1578,[69] and his reactions to that perusal and the impressions he gained from reading Suetonius, Dio Cassius, Lucan and others are chiefly recorded in the first [A] version of the *Essais*.[70] The depth of his knowledge is evident from the ways in which Caesar's thoughts and actions are threaded into Montaigne's argument: his courage in the midst of seditious troops who owe him loyalty is set beside De Moneins' behaviour in an uncontrolled crowd of angry citizens in Bordeaux (I, 24, 130) (Montaigne leaving the reader to ponder the different consequences); or Caesar's view that the unknown is always overvalued and mistaken, which happily coincided with his own opinion (I, 53, 309–10). Montaigne's knowledge can be seen, too, in the sheer delight he experienced in reading Caesar's pure and simple prose, and in the care with which he assessed Caesar's qualities: his 'douceur' (clemency) for example – was it feigned or part of a strategy? (II, 33, 732). His questioning and probing allowed him to divine that Caesar courted his own destruction rather than suffer the shame of being vanquished (II, 34, 740).

Montaigne's assessment of Caesar was mixed. At times, he is so close to the Roman statesman that he has internalized Caesar's views and then used them to corroborate his own, as on those occasions when objects, images and feelings seem to loom larger from afar than nearby (I, 20, 90). At other moments, in critical mood, he strips Caesar's image of its glowing associations: Caesar's courage marching at the head of his troops, bareheaded, is diluted by being set in a list of dress customs (I, 36, 226); and his famous clemency is eroded when Montaigne reminds us that it merely consisted in strangling his pirate enemies before having them crucified (II, 11, 430). If one were to draw up a balance sheet, in terms of quantity of items, almost the same number would weigh on the favourable side as on the side of disapproval. Common to both is the affirmative language used by Montaigne and, more often than not, extreme statements – in the superlative.

On the positive side, Montaigne was attracted by the dash displayed by Caesar in all his military enterprises (I, 24, 131); admired his history; thought that the *Commentaries* should be 'le brévaire de tout homme de guerre' (the breviary of every man of war); and went on to justify this view with fifteen developed instances of Caesar's prowess and wisdom (II, 34, 736–43). Caesar's deeds were miracles (II, 10, 412–17). The noun is repeated on his copy of Caesar's text where Montaigne had written:

> Caesar un des plus grands miracles de Nature . . . le plus disert, le plus net et le plus sincère historien qui fut jamais . . . et le chef de guerre en toutes considerations des plus grands qu'elle fit jamais. Quand je considère la grandeur incomparable de céte ame, j'excuse la victoire de ne s'être pu défaire de lui, voire en cette très injuste et très inique cause.

> [Caesar, one of the greatest miracles of nature . . . the most eloquent, the most pure and sincere historian that ever was . . . and in all respects, one of the greatest commanders that ever was. When I think of the incomparable greatness of his soul, I forgive victory for not having been able to abandon him, even in the most unjust and iniquitous cause.][71]

These notes, probably written immediately after Montaigne had completed his reading of the *Commentaries*, assert the extent of his admiration, which even condones the victory at Pharsalia. In *L'Histoire de Spurina* (II, 33), Montaigne developed his notes. First, he examined Caesar's powers of oratory and praised them; and he then considered the spirit of the commander who could withstand such stress and activity. As his thoughts multiplied so his tone grew enthusiastic, and the admiration poured out in triple adjectives and words denoting exception: 'fut-il jamais ame si vigilante, si active et si patiente en sa labeur que la sienne? . . . Il estoit singulierement sobre' (was there ever a man's soul so vigilant, so active and so long-suffering in toil as his? . . . He was uniquely lacking in self-indulgence) (II, 33, 731). Montaigne waxed eloquent, almost lyrical, in his assessment of Caesar's abundant natural gifts: so much so that his mind leapt away from the real Caesar, and indulged in conjecture: 'et sans doubte encore estoit elle [Caesar's soul] embellie de plusieurs rares semences de vertu, je dy vives, naturelles et non contrefaictes' (for without doubt it was rendered beautiful by many a rare seed of virtues – living, natural ones I mean, not counterfeit). Back to the facts, Montaigne recalled examples of Caesar's clemency (this time unfeigned), and marvelled at his self-confidence and the extent of his courage.

Montaigne gave enormous weight to Caesar's qualities but demonstrates that their emotive power was irreparably damaged by his faults. To become Caesar ('pour devenir Caesar'), he amassed huge debts (I, 14, 63); he bypassed the laws of his country, and needlessly prolonged the civil war (I, 23, 122); his motives for waging war against Pompey were unworthy and false (II, 10, 416); he was no more than a brigand, treading underfoot the ancient liberties of his father-land (II, 11, 424). Thus Montaigne accumulated the evidence for his indict-ment of Caesar. The most crushing condemnation came with Montaigne's outrage at 'l'ordure de sa pestilente ambition' (the filth of his pernicious amb-ition) (II, 10, 416). He is as passionate about Caesar's great flaw as about the fanatical drive that characterized the conqueror of Gaul. In *L'Histoire de Spurina* Montaigne had calculated the structure of his essay so that the glowing image of Caesar which he had lyrically built is demolished at one stroke:

> Mais toutes ces belles inclinations furent altérées et estouffées par cette furieuse passion ambitieuse, à laquelle il se laissa si fort emporter qu'on peut aisément maintenir qu'elle tenoit le timon et le gouvernail de toutes ses actions. (II, 33, 733)

> [Yet all these beautiful dispositions were stifled and corrupted by that fren-zied passion of ambition by which he permitted himself to be so totally carried away that it is easy to show that it was the rudder which steered all his actions.]

There is no redress. Montaigne beats the drum of disapproval, doubling up his words, and underlining the inveterate and overwhelming nature of the passion. Then follow the consequences: the liberal mind became a public thief, exploit-ing and recompensing anyone (criminal or not) willing to serve his ends. Montaigne's own passion soars to a climax as he details Caesar's vanity, his dis-regard for the forms of the Senate and the Republic, his ready acceptance of divinity. The final thrust is no mere flourish but reflects the devastated feelings of an admirer who had grown intimate:

> Somme, ce seul vice, à mon advis, perdit en luy le plus beau et le plus riche naturel qui fut onques, et a rendu sa memoire abominable à tous les gens de bien, pour avoir voulu chercher sa gloire de la ruyne de son pays et sub-version de la plus puissante et fleurissante chose publique que le monde verra jamais. (ibid.)

> [To sum up, that one vice alone, in my judgement, undid the most beau-tiful and the most richly endowed nature there ever was, making his name abominable to all good men for having willed to seek his own glory from the destruction and overthrow of his country, the most powerful and flour-ishing commonwealth that the world will ever see.]

Montaigne has spelt it all out and, in doing so, has coloured his judgement with traces of make-believe; the rosy view of the Republic hardly matches the historical facts about the condition of Rome in the first century BC. The ideal-ization does, however, serve to heighten Montaigne's sorrow. Caesar's amb-ition continues to sear at Montaigne's heart; and he returns to it again in *Des plus excellens hommes* (II, 36, 755) where he sees that passion as not only respon-sible for the ruin of Caesar's homeland but also for 'l'empirement universel du monde' (the debasement of the entire world).[72]

There is nothing straightforward, however, in Montaigne's account. The opin-ions are clear enough – emotional approval and passionate condemnation – but they do not cancel each other out. The picture is complex, affected by Montaigne's personal involvement and by the complicated nature of the issues which he discusses subtly. Take Caesar's murder, for instance. His death is deserved and his 'massacreurs' are deemed 'genereux' (great-souled) (II, 10, 413); yet Cassius and Brutus ('tueurs de Cesar' (killers of Caesar)) did not appreci-ate that one evil – the murder – would bring ills that were more pernicious and uncontrollable (III, 9, 958). Moreover, Montaigne was personally moved by Caesar: his ambition wounded him as if he had sustained some personal injury (II, 33, 731). On the other hand, he was filled with amazement and pleasure at Caesar's extraordinary feats and his phenomenal confidence in himself (II, 34, 740), while experiencing that exasperation which comes from close attachment at Caesar's habit of expanding on the detail of his engineering feats (the bridge across the Rhine) while being succinct and mean when it came to speaking about himself.[73]

The complexity can perhaps best be illustrated from Montaigne's thoughts on the rivalry between Pompey and Caesar. He has no doubt that his sym-pathies lie with Pompey (II, 32, 722), and he castigates Dio Cassius for the support he gave to Caesar (III, 9, 994). Behind the horrors that the very idea of civil war provoked in Montaigne, he perceived the quality of mind of both Pompey and Caesar:

> Toutesfois il me semble reconnoistre en ces belles ames une grande moder-ation de l'un envers l'autre. (III, 10, 1014)

> [Yet I believe I can detect in these fair, noble souls a great moderation towards each other.]

While lesser and more superficial worldly virtues (honour and the will to dominate) took over and tipped them into war, in their conduct of that strife Montaigne detected a mutual respect, a high-mindedness and a sobriety that suggested the possibility that they might have come to some accommodation. Montaigne entertained this remarkable notion, conjuring up the spectacle of Caesar and Pompey being prepared to sacrifice each one his own cause: 'chacun d'eux eust desiré de faire son affaire sans la ruyne de son compaignon plustost qu'avec sa ruyne' (each of them would have wished to achieve his ends without the downfall of his fellow rather than with it) (ibid.). He expressed this hypo-thesis at the very moment that he himself is pondering what stance he should take in the French civil wars. He hoped fervently that, by some miracle, peace might be achieved between the warring Protestant and Catholic factions; and that hope is here touchingly transferred back to an unrealistic projection of the relations between Caesar and Pompey in the Rome of 48 BC.[74]

Inevitably, Montaigne's view is influenced by his experience of civil war. His criticism of Sulla and Caesar for having relentlessly pushed the war to the very end without recourse to law (I, 23, 122) is as much a comment on his own times as a judgement on the past. Similarly his view of Caesar is infected by his reading of Lucan, whose poem he often quotes. The strength of his disgust at Caesar's advice to his soldiers (to shoot at the face of their opponents) – 'j'abomine les enhortemens enragez de cette autre ame des-reiglée' (I hold in abomination the frenetic exhortations of that other man with his disordered mind) (III, l, 802) – was fomented by lines from Lucan which he cites immediately:

> [Sed] dum tela micant, non vos pietatis imago
> Ulla, nec adversa conspecti fronte parentes
> Commoveant; vultus gladio turbate verendos. (Book 7, ll. 320–2)

> [while your weapons flash, let no thought of duty to your parents move you, nor the sight of your fathers on the other side; slash with your swords at the faces which you should venerate.]

Lucan distorted Caesar's instruction, which was to shoot at the youthful recruits in Pompey's army since their regard for their appearance would then make them retreat. Lucan has introduced sentiment and venerable fathers into the frame and it is against these that Montaigne was aroused. It is interesting, too, that in this passage Montaigne does not mention Caesar (referring to 'cette autre ame des-reiglée' (that other man with his disordered mind)), and only a knowledgeable reader would know that it is he who speaks in Lucan's verse. However, in *Couardise, mère de la cruauté* (II, 27, 698), he is explicit and cites Caesar's instruction as a necessary (and acceptable) military ploy.[75] Montaigne relies on poets again when he criticizes Caesar's bombastic utterances, his inflated sense of his own importance, and the absurd assumption that the heavens are concerned about the death of a man and react accordingly. The burden of such claims ('piperies' (deceits)) are shouldered by Lucan, Virgil and Pliny (II, 13, 606).

If we read the *Essais* seriatim, Montaigne had prepared us to see Caesar as man and as hero. In an early essay, he cited Caesar as evidence of every gesture revealing the inner being: 'tout mouvement nous descouvre. [A] Cette mesme ame de Caesar, qui se faict voir à ordonner et à dresser la bataille de Pharsale, elle se faict aussi voir à dresser des parties oisives et amoureuses' (Anything we do reveals us. The same soul of Caesar's which displayed herself in ordering and arranging the battle of Pharsalia is also displayed when arranging his idle and amorous affrays) I, 50, 302). There is a certain levelling down in the balanced juxtaposition which doubtless Montaigne intended since, in *De l'experience*, while arguing that Caesar is no different from anyone else when it comes to reviewing the experience of a human life, he still sees Caesar as the peak of human endeavour (III, 13, 1073–4), and an example of 'singularité' (uniqueness) (II, 26, 156). Thus, although he is incontestably *Caesar* in the *Essais*, he remains essentially human. Montaigne argues that Caesar's extraordinary deeds ('sa grande besongne') are demonstrations of natural pleasure bringing to these violent and mind-stretching activities the rigours of ordinary life:

> Quand je vois et Caesar et Alexandre, au plus espais de sa grande besongne, jouyr si plainement des plaisirs [C] naturels, et par consequent necessaires et justes, [B] je ne dicts pas que ce soit relascher son ame, je dicts que c'est la roidir, sousmetant par vigueur de courage à l'usage de la vie ordinaire ces violentes occupations et labourieuses pensées. (III, 13, 1108)

> [When, in the thick of their great endeavours, I see Caesar and Alexander so fully enjoying pleasures which are natural and consequently necessary and right, I do not say that their souls are relaxing but that they are giving themselves new strength, by force of mind compelling their violent pursuits and burdensome thoughts to take second place to the usages of everyday life.]

It might seem that Montaigne has cut Caesar down to size, but he has, in fact, used his career to demonstrate how extraordinary human life is. A final addition sums up Montaigne's intent: '[C] Sages, s'ils eussent creu que c'estoit là leur ordinaire vacation, cette-cy l'extraordinaire' (wise if they were to believe that to be their normal occupation and the other one abnormal).

CAESAR CONQUERS ROME — HIS TRIUMPH

When Montaigne thought of Alexander or Caesar engaged in war, he tended to see them as in a drama; and it may be that residual memories of seeing Caesar stride across the stage in a college performance lingered deep in his mind. Three French dramatists had attempted re-creations of the political and human consequences of Caesar's exploits: Marc-Antoine de Muret in his tragedy *Caesar* which was composed about 1544; Jacques Grévin in *César* (*c.* 1561); and Robert Garnier in *Cornélie* (1574).[76] The focus in Muret's play was the tragic loss of liberty and the demise of the Republic. Grévin's drama, by contrast, although borrowed substantially from Muret's pedantic text, is much more interesting and exploratory. It examines the states of mind prior to Caesar's murder, the reverberations following that act, and the restoration of the image of Caesar's greatness in a final spectacle.

The opening of Grévin's play shows Caesar at war with himself, a being no longer worthy of his name and a prey to apprehensions: 'Quel mal va furetant aux mouelles de mes os?' (What illness peers into the very marrow of my bones?) This first line announces the exploratory tone of the speech, studded with 'soucis' (cares), 'présages', and 'soupçons' (suspicions) such that the emperor is a 'César, non plus César, mais esclave de crainte' (Caesar, no longer Caesar but a slave to fear) (l. 7). Exploration of inner feelings, and of how Caesar's fate was intimately linked to that of Rome, was Grévin's major concern. Those personal doubts and fears which shame the spirit of a general prepare Caesar so that he will favour honour over suspicion, listen to Brutus' arguments and reject the warnings of his wife Calpurnia. Since Caesar's power and the might of Rome are conterminous, as Caesar claims:

> Ce m'est assez de voir la Romaine hauteur
> Ores estre borné avecque ma grandeur, (ll. 29–30)

[It's enough to see the Roman heights coextensive with my greatness],

his fall will precipitate the collapse of the city and the decline of empire. Only such an outcome, in Caesar's eyes, would justify the murder that is threatened:

> Que la mort de Cesar soit de Rome la mort (l. 142)

[that the death of Caesar means the death of Rome].

This line, neatly balanced, summarizes the action of Grévin's play.

Marcus Brutus and Cassius, together, make out the case for killing what they saw as a proud, arrogant, authoritarian ruler, but who, in conversation with Mark Antony (Act I, scene i), had shown himself curiously world-weary and ready to die. His acquiescence undermines the violence of his adversaries' speeches: for Brutus (Act II), Rome itself fears the desires and ambitious greed of Caesar, whose dissimulation he condemns: 'ce traistre, ce cruel, cest ingrat eshonté' (this traitor, this ingrate – cruel and shameless) (l. 315); these are sufficient reasons for murder, 'Pour . . . estouffer ceste royale audace' (for snuffing out this royal audacity) (l. 352). Brutus' picture of Caesar hardly fits the emperor we have just seen, nor is Cassius' portrait a more exact likeness. He castigates 'Ce traistre, ravisseur de la franchise antique/ Ce larron effronté' (this traitor, robber of ancient freedom, this shameless thief) (ll. 445–6). Although the abuse from both speakers is personalized, it is the freedom of Rome and a return to the Republic which exercise both Brutus and Cassius.

Caesar's dead body haunts the rest of the drama. It is displayed as a spectacle in Calpurnia's dreams (Act III), exposed and massacred, with blood running freely from the many wounds; it is proclaimed with exultation by his murderers (Act V, scene i) who justify their deed with words which blend condemnation and resuscitation: Caesar is 'le tyran', 'oppresseur du pays', 'ce bourreau d'innocens, ruine de nos loix', 'la terreur des Romains', 'le poison des droicts' (the tyrant, his country's oppressor, this executioner of the innocent, destroyer of our laws, the terror of Romans, the poisoner of rights). Rome is unbound, 'la liberté remise' (liberty returned), Rome can breathe freedom again. Then, there is a final apparition. The emperor returns, his figure evoked by Mark Antony who brandishes Caesar's cloak, a sight both taunting and inspiring:

> . . . ceste robbe sanglante
> C'est celle de César qu'ores je vous présente:
> C'est celle de César magnanime empereur,
> Vray guerrier entre tous, César qui d'un grand cueur
> S'acquit avecque vous l'entiere jouissance
> Du monde . . . (ll. 1076–80)

[. . . this bloody robe,/ It is Caesar's which I present to you/ It is Caesar's – that magnanimous emperor/ The truest warrior of all, Caesar whose great heart/ With you acquired the entire possession/ of the world.]

This vision re-establishes Caesar's greatness and Rome's dependence. The spectator is left to ponder his achievements: his magnanimity, his military genius and his courage. Ironically, Cassius' list of iniquities seems, by contrast, faded and hollow. The murder has preserved the name and the glory, and Mark Antony's final gesture has consecrated both. The myth of Caesar and of Rome has begun.

Garnier's portrait of Caesar in *Cornélie* exposes the tenacity and the extent of his ambition – nurtured through deception and the crafty courting of Pompey's friendship; through the meticulous training of his army in Gaul; and through the conscious coupling of his power with the might of Rome. From the beginning of his play, Garnier anticipated the triumphant arrival of an exulting emperor. First, Cicéron analyses the parlous state of the city, rich in violence, deprived of freedom, and where men's ideas of paradise are measured by the extent of their possessions. Cicéron's view makes 'méchante ambition' (wicked ambition) and 'convoitise' (greed) (ll. 23, 25) rule in Rome; they are passions concentrated in Caesar and they are amplified later by Cornélie and by Cassius who address Caesar as parricide, tyrant and dictator. The title *Dictator* (Cassius argues) is a mere shift, adopted by the emperor to mitigate any fears that might dwell in Roman hearts prejudiced at the very sound of the name *king*. Yet, as Cassius pointed out: 'Il peut tout, il fait tout, bref il est roy' (He can do everything, he does everything, in short – he is king) (l. 1151). In his mind, Rome and Caesar are as one, each recognizing the dominion of the other and their interdependence. Although Cassius paints Caesar as supreme and triumphing over the city:

> Ainsi Rome à César donne un pouvoir suprême,
> Et de Rome César trionfe en Rome mesme (ll. 1089–90)

[This Rome has given supreme power to Caesar, and Caesar triumphs over Rome in the city itself], actually, the emperor needs Rome in order to give expression to and receive recognition of his victorious deeds.

In the play, Caesar's arrival seems endlessly postponed; and it is only in the middle of Act IV that he finally bursts on to the stage, jubilant, rejoicing in his glory. Rome (he unquestioningly believes) shares in the joy and congratulation, its lofty towers signalling from their height and their decoration pleasure at the sight of this 'vaincueur des vaincueurs' (victor of the victorious) (l. 1302). Even the Tiber quickens its flow to carry forth the happy news. As Caesar's excitement mounts, he strides the stage, the very embodiment of Cicéron's predictions and of Cassius' portrait. He is that appalling dictator who brooks no opposition, and who tolerates no one above him. He gloats over Pompey's fall, and even revels in his hold over Rome. And if (from the warnings imparted by Mark Antony) he knows that fate promises death at the hands of those he nourished and saved from slaughter, he regards that end as a fitting climax to his career:

> Je vole dans le ciel sur l'aile de mes faicts.
> Puis n'ay-je assez vescu pour mes jours, pour ma gloire? (ll. 1426–7)

[I fly through heaven on the wings of my deeds/ Have I not lived long enough for my days and for my glory?]

Caesar is on the way to becoming a monster.

And yet Garnier sees justification in the emperor's claims. The picture he leaves is of Caesar, the commander, engaged in the thick of battle against the superior forces of Scipio. There, in contrast to the mere generalized evocation of the activities of Scipio and his troops, Caesar is individualized. All the action of battle is concentrated in him: in his glistening eyes, in his ability to be everywhere at once and to take in every gesture, dire or glorious; and in his fearless presence that provoked, and frightened his men into victory:

> Les poussoit, enflamboit, les emplissoit d'horreur. (l. 1728)

[He pushed them on, inflamed them, and filled them with horror.]

However unacceptable in times of peace, in war Caesar is magnificent.

The logical outcome of such military achievement was for Caesar to enjoy Rome's recognition of his prowess through the granting of a series of Triumphs. We have seen, however, that Garnier's view of such celebrations was highly equivocal. Nonetheless, in the eyes of his contemporaries, the climax of Caesar's career was in the five triumphal entries he made into Rome, just as they also represented the highpoint of Renaissance perceptions of Caesar's military genius. Triumphs were granted by the Senate in gratitude to a general who had brought countries to peace under Roman rule and customs. Four of Caesar's Triumphs (the Gallic, the Alexandrian, the Pontic and the African) were celebrated in the same month, and the final one (the Spanish) after his defeat of Pompey's sons.

Ancient sources (Suetonius, Appian, Dio Cassius and Plutarch)[77] provided ample details of these splendid occasions which were copied and adapted by medieval and Renaissance commentators, such as 'De la faction de tryumphe rommain' (In the fashion of a Roman Triumph) in Charles of Burgundy's copy of the *Commentaries*.[78] And we have shown how the Triumph had become incorporated into the psychology of characters in Garnier's dramas.[79] The most influential Renaissance *Triumphs of Caesar* was that painted by Andrea Mantegna for the Gonzagas and now housed at Hampton Court. Mantegna had found his inspiration in these ancient sources, and from reading the tenth book of Biondo's *Roma triumphans* and Valturius' *De re militari* where there was a chapter on Triumphs,[80] and also from studying reliefs on sarcophagi, on Trajan's column, and on Triumphal arches – from copies and from originals.

Mantegna's extraordinary celebration of Caesar was famous even before he had finished the nine immense canvases. Artists copied and engraved scenes direct from Mantegna's drawings and designs. In 1504, Benedetto Bordone obtained a ten-year privilege from the authorities in Venice for a twelve-block woodcut frieze of the *Triumphs of Caesar* which Jacopo de Strasbourg had completed.[81] Although Jacopo may not have seen the paintings, he had knowledge of other engravings (of the 'Elephants' and 'Trophy Bearers'), and of the 'Senators' composition.[82] Simon Vostre pirated Jacopo's engravings and printed them at the end of his Book of Hours in 1502 where – in fifteen woodcuts accompanied by a commentary – *Le Triumphe de Jules Cesar* is detailed, showing wagons of triumph, soldiers carrying treasures, banners of victory, elephants, the mourning faces of kings and princes taken prisoner, and Caesar himself in triumph accompanied by writers and soldiers, princes and many others of noble estate.[83]

It is not easy to assess just how many people saw the actual paintings of Mantegna. They were used in festivals until they were finally installed in a room specially made for them in the palace of San Sebastiano (1506–7). There henceforth, princes, art enthusiasts and travellers could view and admire them. Vigenère had studied them there, Henri III perhaps saw them in 1574 on the occasion of his royal entry into Mantua, and Montaigne admired them some six years later.[84]

There were many ways in which images of Caesar's Triumphs could filter through into French experience. There were secondhand ways, from the frieze that had been mounted at Gaillon between 1502 and 1510; from the reconstructed triumphal entry of Caesar which students at Caen organized in 1513; or from the plates of engravings which were transported to France.[85] Mario Equicola's account of Mantegna's *Triumphs* was published in his *Commentari Mantuani* in 1521.[86] Serlio praised Mantegna's genius in composing *The Triumphs of Caesar* in his fourth book (*Tutte l'opere*, 1619, ff. 191v–192), and it is perhaps because of this architect's influence that a frieze of Caesar's triumphs appeared on a sixteenth-century house at Gisors.[87] They also figured on French enamel, on a casket at Ecouen, and on tapestries, and were incorpor-

88.　A. Andreani: engraving from Mantegna's *Triumphs of Caesar*

ated by Symeoni in designs for devices which might be used by grand personages.[88]

The idealized figure of Caesar, dressed in gold and purple, raised high above the mass of spoils, the procession of prisoners, the images of all the towns he had conquered, and the faithful chanting cohorts of soldiers who followed on behind, was a fitting and satisfying spectacle to French Renaissance viewers, many of whom were fascinated by Caesar the man, in awe at his feats as general, still marvelling at his fate, and eager to adapt forms of triumph to their own use (Figure 88).

II   THE TRIUMPH

By the Renaissance, the Triumph had become a topos which conveyed notions of Roman authority and greatness. It constituted both a *model* and an *idea* which embodied a vast repertory of conceits and motifs that could be explored, developed and made relevant to any occasion. So thoroughly absorbed was it into sixteenth-century experience that the Triumph was immediately recognizable as having a universalizing effect, and its meanings were readily understood.[89] It had played a fundamental role in welding together concepts of city and empire in the Roman mind; and its cultivation had explained and reinforced Rome's divine foundation and the city's imperial destiny.[90] For instance, Flavio Biondo's determination to resurrect triumphal forms was designed to restore Rome's imperial status and to make the city a source of inspiration for princely conduct.

There were, apparently, some 320 Triumphs celebrated in Rome up to the reign of Vespasian; but these processions through the city were only the most prominent aspect of triumphalism, for the Triumph took on multiple forms. There were triumphal arches in Rome and scattered across the landscape of empire; trophies of war, powerful reminders of victory and defeat; amphitheatres like the Colosseum, decorated with the statues of conquered races; temples built on columns constructed in accordance with classical architectural norms; imperial statues such as that of Augustus embossed with symbols of *imperator*, or the equestrian statue of Marcus Aurelius; chariots of Triumph, originally conveyances of the Triumphator and later the decorative feature which crowned the triumphal arch; obelisks; and columns of achievement like those of Trajan or Antoninus. Each element of triumph developed its own independent life, became an object of individual study,[91] and in becoming a kind of icon, the fragment acquired the power to stand for the whole. Thus the Colosseum lost its specific relation to the emperors who built the amphitheatre (Vespasian, and dedicated by Titus), and assumed a wider sphere of reference, conjuring up Rome itself. Even Trajan's column, named from the deeds of the emperor it carried and celebrated, came to have a more universal import: it stood for Roman military achievement and power.

The very heterogeneity of triumphal forms was attractive to Renaissance scholars and artists, who used all the available motifs either severally or together in the larger panorama of a triumphal entry. Léonard Limosin, for example, depicted Henri II with the imperial stance and gestures of Marcus Aurelius; the image was enhanced by the association with pictures of past glory. Such familiarity provided artists with extra zones of meaning, simultaneously upgrading their own design and inviting the observer to make the connections.

Familiar images, fixed in their form, invited exploration and development,

and their potential was recognized.[92] One might point to the Dutch humanists who, inspired by Heemskerck, produced a series of engraved moral triumphs under the composite title *The Triumph of Patience* (1559); these were
printed with a verse inscribed below each picture emphasizing the moral implications and explaining the elements of the engravings. The designs were elaborate and included triumphs of Abraham, Joseph, David, Job, Tobias, St Stephen
and Christ; and they show how the triumphal car had become an independent
motif capable of carrying the weight of moral meaning. These allegorical victories were so popular that a further eight engravings were produced, representing the *Cycle of the Vicissitudes of Human Affairs* (1564);[93] while, at this same
period, Léonard Limosin was enamelling his own series of moral triumphal
cars, *Le Triomphe de la Foi* and *Le Triomphe de l'Eucharistie*.[94]

All the elements belonging to the Triumph were used in the Renaissance as
the most appropriate means of expression in the ambitious courtly contexts
that had grown up all over Europe. Information on triumphal forms, images
of them and their meaning was to hand; and it was opportune. Ancient
texts describing the details of triumphal entries into Rome were now easily
available in print; coins which had triumphal forms engraved on their reverse
were found in abundance. The technical know-how for recreating triumphal
structures from the past and for adapting them to suit contemporary taste had
come to light through editions and commentaries on the works of Vitruvius,
and through Alberti. These facts and access to expertise coincided with
political need since, above all, Renaissance princes required triumphant projections of their aspirations and achievements to reinforce the theatricality
which attached to their function and characterized their courts. A propagan-
dist impetus was abroad, blending the authority and status of the ancient world
with sixteenth-century visions of what fitted the person and the court of a
prince.[95]

Not only did the Triumph assume diverse forms, it also supplied multiple
meanings. Out of the rich repertory of forms inherited from Rome, the focus
here will principally rest on the triumphal arch and on the royal entry in
France; and in order to appreciate the directness of their impact it is necessary
to gain some notion of the forms, functions and meanings of the ancient
Triumph. These have been studied by Robert Payne, who has stressed that the
Triumph's context was the power of Rome, with its mission of conquest and
domination, and the courage of the Roman soldier. He has shown how significant were the Roman beliefs that attended the Triumph, how the triumphal
procession followed a route consecrated by tradition and directed towards the
Capitol where, as the climax of the proceedings, the Triumphator did homage
and sacrificed to the gods, offering thanks for his victories and for his good
fortune.

To be granted a Triumph was the greatest honour a Roman citizen could receive. It allowed him – surrounded by all the paraphernalia of war – to pass through the city as a general with his army. Payne has described his chariot, his garments and accoutrements; the detail of the procession, and the games which often followed the Triumph on succeeding days; and he outlines the conditions which had to be met before a Triumph was voted by the Senate and approved by the people of Rome.[96] The Triumphator was required to demonstrate that the war was necessary for Roman survival and that the scale of the victory, the number of dead and vanquished, the towns and countries conquered were sufficient.

The Triumph represented the apotheosis of Roman pride, made manifest in the display of captured riches and in the vigour of the soldiers who walked and sang jubilantly in the procession. It was an affirmation of power and of the durability of victory. Rome and the Triumphator shared the spectacle as the endless line of booty, treasures and prisoners provoked extraordinary emotion: rejoicing at the signs of conquest, fear at the immensity of what had been done, and sorrow for the plight of some of the vanquished. The spoils (piled up on decorated cars) and those who walked beside them gave those who watched an *idea* of victory, and the spectacle provided an inkling of what war was like.

The occasion celebrated a named individual whose attributes and achievements were inscribed on every object that passed before the spectator's eyes. It was a performance with a multiple cast, as everyone waited for the sight of the originator of it all – the Triumphator, standing in his two-wheeled chariot, crowned with laurel and holding a branch of laurel. Rome was filled with a sense of theatre and a quality which the city never lost, as Du Bellay reminded us in *Les Regrets*:

> Rome est de tout le monde un public eschaffaut
> Une scène, un theatre . . . (lxxxii)

[Rome is the public scaffold of the whole world, a stage, a theatre.]

The Triumphator was honoured because he had gained significant victories, and in doing so he had demonstrated his *felicitas*, showering Rome with treasures, and blessings which protected the citizens from ill luck.[97] For that good fortune he thanked Jupiter, and ended his day of triumph with a religious act.

Triumphalism is a complex phenomenon, and Renaissance artists and humanists took on all that complexity.[98] Paradoxically, the Triumph brings together faces of defeat and victory: chants of rejoicing contrast with the doleful visages of the vanquished. Military valour spelt out good fortune and the support of the gods, and had implications for the future, as success breeds confidence and faith.

89. Jacques Androuet du Cerceau: engraving of triumphal arch according to Vitruvius

THE TRIUMPHAL ARCH

Were it not for the descriptions by ancient historians and the Renaissance reconstructions such as Mantegna's *Triumphs of Caesar*, there would survive no record of the nature, function and meanings of Triumphs. In contrast, some seventy to eighty triumphal arches (Figure 89), which were not originally an integral part of the Triumph but which were also dedicated by the Senate and people of Rome, are still standing. They were erected either to bear witness to extraordinary feats of arms such as the conquest of Jerusalem sculpted on the arch of Titus, or to legitimize a dynasty as did Septimus Severus when, in AD 203, he used traditional and classicizing forms and symbols to produce an impressive and coherent design which celebrated the emperor's victories against the Parthians.[99] Scattered across the empire as reminders of Roman supremacy, arches were sometimes set up at the entrance of a city or incorporated into its walls (Verona) and sometimes built in open spaces, isolated in their grandeur (Glanum, St Rémy, Provence).[100] Wherever they stood, they were permanent manifestations of achievement, an essential part of imperial magnificence,[101] and – as such – they attracted the attention of travellers.[102]

If one were not disposed to travel to see these splendid structures for oneself, then Serlio's *Architecture* (Book 3) would give an excellent idea both of the

315

arch's general appearance and of its constituent parts. He explained, for example, how the arch of Constantine (the last of the great Roman arches) had been made from reliefs, heads and statues taken from Trajan's frieze.[103] Despite its fabricated nature, this arch acquired considerable status and influenced the design of many similar structures in later times. A replica, for instance, was hung in front of the Vatican to greet Julius II (a second Caesar) when he made his triumphant entry into Rome on Palm Sunday (1507);[104] when Emperor Charles V made his entry into the imperial city in 1536, the arches erected to celebrate his dominion in Europe were inspired by that of Constantine; and Palladio modelled his arch for the reception of Henri III into Venice (1574) on this same ancient prototype, for that was how the arch of Constantine had come to be perceived.

Triumphal arches were a rich source of information about Roman customs. As Manuel Chrysoloras put it, the images on their surface spoke. According to him, the figures were 'as if really alive' showing forth 'the stamp of the Roman mind', and he characterized them as 'rather not a history so much as an exhibition, so to speak, a manifestation of everything that existed everywhere at that time'.[105] The ability to penetrate the meaning of such figures was a prime condition underlying the construction of the monument. Artists and emperors assumed that future observers would read their significance and, in that reading, relive and remake the episodes recorded there. That reading ability was even extended to the inscriptions and symbols engraved on their façades, a fact which was to be exploited in later periods with confidence (if not with passion) as symbolic images and their mysterious messages proliferated over the surface of triumphal arches.[106] Yet, to aid his understanding in 1536, Charles V had required the *conservatores*, dressed in Roman togas, to walk beside his horse and to explain the meaning of the antiquities and the mysteries of the signs inscribed on monuments dedicated to himself.[107]

In the Renaissance, triumphal entries into cities and the erection of imperial arches became a European phenomenon involving great artists (Leonardo, Dürer and Palladio, for instance) and, in France, the most gifted poets (Maurice Scève, Ronsard and Jean Dorat). Influential examples of triumphal forms came from the papal city itself and perhaps more especially from Florence whose authorities vied in status with Rome and where Lorenzo the Magnificent had mounted a re-enactment of Paulus Aemilius' Triumphs (1491).[108] Moreover, Colonna's famous book had shown images of several triumphal arches and discussed their meaning, and had depicted four chariots of triumph on which his hero Poliphile had gazed with amazement (Figure 90).[109]

In short, pictures of Triumph invaded every surface, and the collections of drawings and sketches preserved in major archives testify to artists' awareness that these forms would be in demand everywhere.[110] Botticelli had represented the arch of Constantine in the centre of his picture *The Punishment of Korah, Dathan and Abiram*, destined for the Sistine Chapel, and other painters followed suit.[111] Triumphal cars appeared on *cassone*; they were woven into tapestries;[112]

90.   Colonna: engraving of the Triumph of Venus

and, following the inspiration of Alberti, they were incorporated into the design of churches and princely dwellings, with Palladio using the idea in his conception of Loggia del Capitano at Vicenza, and contemporary French architects (De L'Orme, Bullant and Goujon) using then at Anet, Ecouen (Figure 91), and in the Great Hall of the Louvre.[113] At Ecouen, even keyholes were designed to look like triumphal portals (Figure 92);[114] and they formed the frame of frontispieces and edged the borders of illuminated manuscripts.[115] Nor was it unusual to find triumphal forms worked into onyx jewel cases, and they appeared on the present which the city offered to Charles IX to celebrate his entry into Paris.[116] Their influence on poetic forms was equally widespread and has been studied elsewhere.[117]

   The sources for this mass of material are well known. They should be reviewed here, however, since they informed French examples of Triumph which will be then examined in some detail. Apart from Dionysius of Halicarnassus who limited his remarks to praise of the simplicity of Romulus' Triumphs,[118] other historians of ancient Rome were fortunately lavish in details when describing Triumphs. Appian (died *c.* AD 165) left an account of the form of the Roman Triumph and then itemized all the elements which accompanied Scipio when he entered Rome as Triumphator. Plutarch (born between AD 46 and 49) described the Triumph of Paulus Aemilius (which had lasted

317

92. Anonymous design for a keyhole at Ecouen

91. Part of Jean Bullant's design for the inner courtyard at Ecouen

Lvne des faces du dedans de la court d'Escouan opposite a celle ou sont les grandes Colomnes.

three days), enumerating the 150 chariots laden with the spoils of the Macedonians, the 3,000 participants in the procession, the 750 vessels filled with money, the 120 oxen prepared for sacrifice and the 77 skilfully engraved sacred vases made of precious materials, before focusing on the general himself, in purple raiment streaked with gold and riding high on his chariot.[119] For the triumphs of Caesar and Pompey, Dio Cassius deftly sketched the essential parts of their entries into Rome, while Suetonius dwelt on both the triumphs and the games (theatrical and military) which followed Caesar's triumphs.[120]

These texts provided the basis on which Flavio Biondo (*Roma triumphans*, (*c.* 1459), Robertus Valturius (*De re militari*, 1474), and Alexandri ab Alexandro (*Genialium dierum*, 1522) constructed their analyses of the Roman Triumph, and these works, too, were to be major sources of information.[121] Later compilations of ancient texts, reconstructions and overviews of all the available material on the Triumph were published, mostly towards the end of the sixteenth century – the works of Panvinius, Modius and Boulenger, the commentaries of Vigenère on Livy, and the engraved reconstruction of the Triumph by Giacomo Lauro – although this mass of scholarly exegesis coincided with the decline in the communicative power of the princely entry.[122]

PETRARCH AND THE CONCEPT OF TRIUMPH

There is one more triumphal tradition which must be mentioned because of its vigour and the extent of its influence. The *Triumphs* of Petrarch were widely read and frequently illustrated, if we are to judge from the number of manuscripts that are still extant (over 300, and many of them in France),[123] and from the printed editions in Italian and French which poured out of the presses in the first half of the sixteenth century. Although Petrarch described only one triumphal car in his poem, the visual tradition 'triumphalized' all six parts of the work, and the same pictures were transmitted from manuscript to manuscript and from edition to edition.[124] In France, like the military Triumph inspired by Rome, Petrarch's Triumphs invaded all modes of art. It suffices to recall a few examples to illustrate the force of impact and the persistence with which artists and patrons favoured this theme. Petrarchan Triumphs were copied, repeated, modified and endlessly adapted. They were engraved on glass, incorporated into tapestries as, for example, when François Robertet's translations of the *Triumphs* were woven into the borders of tapestries which depicted scenes from Petrarch's poem;[125] they decorated libraries; were owned in fine illuminated manuscripts by Louis XII, Claude d'Urfé and Anne de Montmorency; in printed editions they were dedicated to noble personages such as Anne de Montmorency, Bauffremont, Maurice Scève and Marguerite de Valois;[126] and they were displayed in a relief frieze on the walls of the Galerie François I at the hôtel de Bourgthéroulde in Rouen (a feature not unrelated to Henri II's triumphal entry there in 1550).[127]

Petrarch's triumphal vision reinforced the effects of the Roman Triumph in France in so far as it had developed the particular element of the triumphal car, either seen from the side sweeping across the page or frontally presented as though leaping out of the frame. The two traditions also interacted, since the poet's *Triumphs*, through their naming of the historical personages who had enjoyed earlier Triumphs, activated the reader's knowledge of the past and, if this happened to be deficient, the extensive commentaries which often surrounded Petrarch's text triggered the memory.[128] In fact, Triumphs in Petrarch were less real events than cultural concepts evoking the power of Rome, so that the reader is placed inside the text, on a par with the poet, as he observes and refers back to experience long since read and absorbed.[129]

The Triumph had never been static in its form, but there were certain properties which continued to characterize its reconstructions in the Renaissance. Excess and enhancement had marked it since the time of the emperors and, in its decline at the end of the sixteenth century, the Jesuit fathers (who, at this period, were regularly called upon to invent the overall schema and the detailed political, moral and philosophical images for a princely entry, a city's commemoration or a religious triumph) pushed their symbolic decorations to effervescent limits.[130] The layers of meaning built up from acquaintance with earlier Triumphs meant that, in re-enacting a Triumph in the sixteenth century, whether in words on the page or on monuments erected in urban space, humanists could simultaneously show a dazzling display of knowledge of the past and parade the celebration of a contemporary subject.

The process of thus creating a density of impact was not new. When the arch of Constantine was built using the spoils taken from the victories of Trajan, Hadrian and Aurelius, and when their heads were, with the approval of the Senate of Rome, replaced by those of Constantine, the emperor was not only appropriating the deeds of these earlier emperors, he was also absorbing their reputation and the associations that had since accrued to them.[131] The spoils served as visual quotations embedded in the overall structure waiting to be recognized, weighed and savoured, and – in their effect – were halfway between the citations which Montaigne acknowledged in the *Essais* and those he did not. They were visual fragments which, at one and the same time, belonged elsewhere but were made to speak again in their new context and to harmonize with it.

In a similar way, Triumphs continued to be fundamental to the meaning and purpose of the city which – although it was 'disguised' and to some degree transformed by the temporary classical monuments imposed by the organizer – had the opportunity to display its own power and resources within a very familiar pattern of movement. The processional route through the city was traditional; each of the stopping places had its own ritual and themes – religious, judicial or political. At the climax of the Triumph (at the temple of Jupiter or before a Christian cathedral) the same prayers of thanksgiving for victories achieved and hopes for continued prosperity were reiterated.

Yet within these broad conventions, there was evolution. While the shape of the Triumph had become predictable, there were few fixed rules regulating its performance. From the records, it seems that Pompey's Triumphs exceeded in splendour and extravagance all those which had gone before, and that Caesar's carefully orchestrated triumphal entries into Rome were personalized to a degree never before encountered. By the time of Augustus, the Triumph was restricted; taken away from the conquering generals, it became the emperor's right alone;[132] and, in late antiquity, it tended to accentuate imperial majesty.[133] Thus, what had originated as a demonstration of achievement had turned into the celebration of an idea of majesty. This fluidity allowed Renaissance imitators plenty of scope to develop individual pathways within an accepted and easily recognizable frame; and it is perhaps not surprising that its reconstructed evolution shows the same shifts as those which had occurred in ancient times, ceremonies of achievement being replaced by visionary projections of ideal performers.[134]

TRIUMPHS IN FRANCE

Although, in the sixteenth century, French forms of triumph could vary from place to place, they shared general characteristics with other European countries. Our own analysis of images from Rome present on triumphal occasions in France, will concentrate on the middle years of the century (1548–50) when the urge to reconstruct ancient forms reached a peak and when records of Henri II's royal entries into cities of his realm are most abundant, and then on Henri IV's entry into Lyon at the end of the period, when changes are clearly visible.[135]

Philibert de L'Orme provides some guidance to the significance attached to triumphal forms by his contemporaries because, during his sojourn in Rome, he made a particular study of the triumphal arch. He was partly attracted to it for the technical information which he could derive from his observation of the detail of its construction and from the measurements he made of its proportions, and he provided illustrations in *Le Premier tome de l'architecture*.[136] But it was also the status that triumphal arches enjoyed at this time which attracted his attention. The following passage gives some idea of the depth of his concern. He explains the origins of the arch, expounds the range of things recorded on its surface, and ponders on its role as a lasting witness of achievement:

Qui me faict penser que tel ordre de colomne composée fut trouvé du temps que l'on faisoit les arcs triomphants aux Empereurs et vaillants Capitaines, apres avoir obtenu quelques grandes victoires: car oultre les grands honneurs et magnifiques entrées, on leur faisoit aussi des arcs triomphants, les plus riches dont on se pouvoit adviser, avec sculpture sur les marbres, representant (comme histoire) les païs et royaumes qu'ils avoient conquestez: voire iusques y mettre les Roys, Princes et Capitaines, qu'ils avoient subiuguez et amenez prisonniers, sous mesmes habits desquels ils avoient en leurs païs, àfin qu'il fust mesmoire longue des triomphes de leurs victoires . . . (f. 201v)

[which reminds me that such a composite order of column was found at the time when triumphal arches were being built for emperors and valorous captains who had achieved great victories: because in addition to the great honours and magnificent entries, triumphal arches were also made, as rich as they could possibly be, with sculpture in marble showing (as in history) the countries and kingdoms they had conquered: even to putting kings, princes and captains there whom they had subjugated and brought back as prisoners in their native dress so that the memory of their triumphant victories might be long lasting.]

In this context of hands-on learning, it is not surprising to find the authors of accounts of triumphal entries in France at this period underlining the accuracy of the classical reconstruction, the authenticity of the monuments that were erected, and referring to Vitruvius as the model that has been followed.[137] In this way, these accounts played an important role in introducing precise classical terms from architecture into French. However, the structures they describe were rarely the permanent monuments built by the Romans. Renaissance triumphal arches were, for the most part, temporary; they were made to order and under great time pressure, as often as not in the form of canvas stretched across wooden frames and painted to simulate sculpted reliefs. Sometimes their detail has been visually preserved in the engravings which adorned some accounts,[138] or in pictures (Henri III's entry into Venice), or in the illuminations of manuscripts for Henri II's entry into Rouen, 1550. Yet, it is as well to keep in mind that records of festival occasions are not easy to interpret. Different accounts of the same event can contradict each other; the 'official' record was sometimes written beforehand, or was adjusted in order to accommodate its inventor's desire to leave an ideal version of what he wanted his readers to see.[139] Nevertheless, in attempting to assess the impact of Rome on French triumphal entries, it is at least possible to state that they combined the strength of local traditions with the excitement of newly understood ideas and images from ancient Rome, and that they witnessed an exhibition of the balance of power between the king and the city authorities.

Imperial claims had long been sought by French monarchs, and signs of these aspirations could be found in many places. For example, the tombs of Louis XII and of François I at St Denis show each king enjoying military triumphs, with Louis XII in a triumphal car[140] and with François I resting with his queen on a triumphal arch. Henri II announced his imperial claims right from the beginning of his reign when he was engraved as emperor by Niccolo della Casa (see Figure 85, p. 294); appointed artists of note to the Royal Mint; and had imperialist coins designed by Etienne Delaune. The gift he received after

93. *Magestas*, Triumph at the Châtelet, Charles IX's entry into Paris, 1571

his entry into Lyon in 1548 was a gold statue depicting a seated king arrayed in Roman armour.[141] Imperial pretensions became more and more insistent as one weak Valois king followed another so that, by 1571, when Charles IX entered Paris, at the Châtelet – where the king traditionally saw a spectacle designed to show him dispensing justice – he faced a large perspective in which the figure of *Magestas* dominated and where justice is depicted as one of the instruments of the king's majesty (Figure 93).[142] The relationship between Majesty and Justice, between king and *Parlement* has radically changed. There is no longer any doubt about the supremacy of the king, and this message was underlined in the symbolism of the present which the city gave Charles IX. It showed a triumphal car with Cybele (the Queen Mother)[143] gesturing towards her son whose equestrian statue, reminiscent of Marcus Aurelius, was erected above two Corinthian pillars bearing the king's motto *Pietas et Justitia*. His imperial form was further emphasized by the presence of an eagle hovering above the king's head and threatening to place thereon an imperial crown

323

94. Charles IX's present, entry into Paris, 1571

(Figure 94). The same imperial spirit coloured the language used to describe the king and his subjects in accounts of royal entries; in 1549 (for instance), Henri II is designated as 'Roy triumphateur' (king triumphant) and his people as 'aussi bien triumphateurs que les Romains' (as triumphant as the Romans) (*L'Entrée à Paris*, 1549, f. 13v).

The inventors of entries were as ambitious as the princes for whom they worked in that they prepared themselves for such occasions by storing up engraved records of their compositions, and by blazoning abroad the quality, range and erudition of their designs. Their confidence was supported by contemporary observers: of the Paris entry (1549), Gilles Corrozet remarked that it was the most magnificent he had ever seen; and Guillaume Paradin declared that if one were to list its beauties one would, in fact, be compiling a veritable inventory of antiquity itself! – 'des quelles en vouloir inventorier le promptuaire de toute l'antiquité'.[144]

It has to be remembered that, though temporary, the structures designed to greet the monarch as he entered the cities of his realm were massive, and often fifty or sixty feet high. The arch at the Bourgneuf (Lyon, 1548) was of this height, and forty feet in depth. Yet, despite its ephemeral nature, the images and the inscriptions painted on its surface were detailed, the latter taken from authentic classical texts,[145] the former often borrowed from medals in contemporary collections.

THE ENTRY INTO LYON (1548)

There was an undoubtedly antiquarian tone to this entry. Its general theme was invented by Maurice Scève who was himself heavily dependent on the advice of both Guillaume du Choul, whose scholarship is evident on the monuments (particularly with respect to the inscriptions and medals), and of Serlio who had come to live in Lyon and who was subsequently to organize the entry of cardinal de Tournon in 1552. Apparently the king, who liked ritual and the imperial allusions, approved. However, with the possible exception of the arch at Bourgneuf, the engravings in the official account of the entry are too sketchy to allow an adequate assessment of how far the antiquarianism actually went in practice. When the text claims that a particular image or structure reproduces the authentic style and appearance of an original found on monuments in Rome, was the author indulging in make-believe or reporting something that was really there? Sometimes it is possible to check against a surviving piece of marble; and, certainly at Lyon in 1548, a deliberate attempt was made to recreate a Roman townscape. All observers agree on that. The preface to the reader of *Le Grand Triumphe* (published in Paris, 1548) wrote:

> Et ne puis croyre que le triumphe tant renommé de César fust de si grande valeur et estime que cestuy-cy

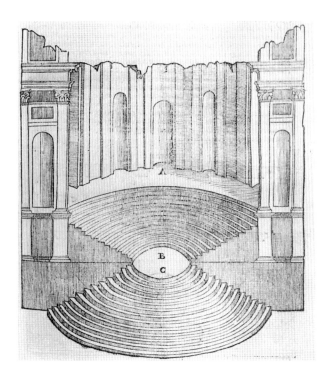

95. Serlio: the exedra from the Belvedere court

[and I cannot believe that the famous Triumph of Caesar was as great in prestige and esteem as this one].

Conegrani, in his dispatches back to Mantua, wrote in similar vein: on the platform above the arch of Honour 'era tra loro tre vi erano ritratti gli triomphi di Cesare' (there were there representations of the triumphs of Caesar); while Denis Sauvage opened his judgement on the occasion with,

Et fust ceste entrée assez magnifique et superbe, pour estre parangonnée aux triomphes des Scipions, Pompées et Cesars tant vantez aux hystoires Rommaines.

[and this entry was so magnificent and superb as to be compared to the Triumphs of the Scipios, the Pompeys and the Caesars so extolled in Roman histories.][146]

He then elaborated on their Romanness, listing the portals, arcades, obelisks, temples, perspectives, columns and amphitheatres covered in figures and reliefs.

An overview of the structures built to celebrate this entry, as given in Scève's official account, bears out the impression that a determined effort had been made to reconstruct a triumph evoking a composite vision of Rome. On the river bank there was an obelisk modelled on the one erected in front of the

96.   Exedra at the port de l'Archevesché, Lyon, 1548

Vatican; there were five arches of huge dimensions, built following classical rules of architecture, their niches and architraves filled with scenes and statues inspired by Rome; there were three columns, two Corinthian in design and the third according to the Doric order; a painted perspective meant to represent the city of Troy; and, behind the cathedral, an exedra imitated from the one in the Belvedere court, engraved by Serlio (Figure 95) and of which Scève gives a careful description. From the port with its porticoes built on twelve columns,

l'on descendoit en la riviere par seze degrez bas: les huict premiers suyvantz la ceincture du demy centre, devalantz sur une petite plateforme ronde reprenant sur centre en autres huict ordres de degrez forgettez en rond jusques sur l'eau. (H4 v) (Figure 96)[147]

[one went down to the river by sixteen steps: the first eight following a half circle leading to a small round platform which lay at the centre, and the eight other steps were rounded and went right down to the water.]

Another feature at Lyon in 1548, this time recalling contemporary rather than ancient Rome, consisted of the simulated ruins which had been constructed alongside the splendour of the triumphal arches:

A costé dudict Arc [that at the Bourgneuf] ioignoit une muraille à la rustique ruinee en plusieurs lieux, et audessus de laquelle estoient encor resté

327

quelque fragmentz de cornices avec bases, et demy Colonnes pour mieux representer son antiquité. (*L'Entrée à Lyon*, E3 v)

[at the side of the said arch was a rustic wall, ruinous in several places, above which there still remained some fragments of cornices with their bases and half columns – the better to show their antiquity.]

Although this introduction of ruins might recall Gallo-Roman circuit walls, they also conjure up the juxtaposition of ruins and noble structures in Rome.

Throughout his text, Scève was at pains to characterize the structures he is describing as *à la romaine*. Immediate comparisons were suggested by their very shape: arches, obelisks and columns. The trophy at the Griffon, a column soaring fifty-three feet into the sky, decorated with victorious arms (French, but in the guise of Roman weapons) was one of the first sights to greet Henri II after he had passed through the main gate of the city and had advanced from the arch at Bourgneuf.[148] He saw a statue of France atop this Corinthian column, held in place by a mighty figure H [HENRI]. The column was flanked by statues of Time and Fame, and by Immortality and Virtue, themes that recur throughout the entry.

One of the most ambitious structures was *l'Arc triomphal du temple d'Honneur et Vertu* which not only multiplied the levels of surfaces on which images and inscriptions might be engraved or sculpted, but also sought to resurrect an arch that had long since been lost to Rome. About 100 BC, Gaius Marius Marcellus built a temple to Honour and Virtue from the spoils of the Cimbri and the Teutones.[149] He gave it only one door in order to demonstrate the indissoluble relationship between Virtue and Honour. Du Choul discussed the temple in his *Religion des romains* (pp. 33–4) where he made the point about the necessary interaction of the two qualities, and doubtless it was he who gave the idea to Scève for this arch on the place St-Eloy. The engraving (ibid. f. G3) which, like most illustrations in festival books, detaches the building from its context and leaves it in splendid isolation, shows all the levels of the structure: the broad sides of the arch depicted pairs of herms supporting a pediment whose entablature was inscribed with words which dedicated the temple of Honour and Virtue to the victorious Henri II. Immediately above was the figure of Honour, flanked by Faith and Love. Standing out against the sky were three statues – Victory, Fame and Eternity – with attributes well known from classical times. Higher still on this sixty-foot arch was a square tower with a parapet beneath which ran a frieze showing two Triumphs: the first of Honour whose triumphal car was drawn along by elephants; the second that of Virtue showing her seated in a car which was pulled along by unicorns. Sitting on top of the structure was a dome with six columns around its circular form, crowned by Henri II's device, the crescent moon (Figure 97).

The temple of Honour and Virtue gives a good idea of the multiple messages and forms that could be incorporated by an arch. It also illustrates that

Within the illustration:

HONORIS VIRTVTISQ PERPETVAE HENRICO PRINC INVICTISS
SACRVM·   D D

PERPETVO HONORI   VIRTVTI PERPETVI

97. Arc triomphal du Temple d'Honneur et de Vertu, Lyon, 1548

the influence of Rome had penetrated the antiquarian interest so far that mere imitations of existing images from the imperial city were no longer enough. The organizers resurrected forms lost for centuries to express their aspirations for the king, and – in doing so – they were following the same urge to reconstruct that dominated the work of artists, engravers and architects.

The same classicizing spirit dominated the arches, columns and obelisk erected for the king when he made his entry into the capital in June 1549. Specifically Roman references are absent from the text and from the *registres* of the hôtel de ville de Paris where Jean Martin (who had translated the major works on classical architecture from Latin into French; that is, Vitruvius and Alberti) emerges as the chief planner of the event. It is clear, however, from the remarks of an impartial observer that the buildings and general decoration of the city were interpreted as belonging to Rome.

> Antiquam speciem et imaginem triumphi Romani videre mihi viderer, qualem in historiis descriptam et expressam legimus . . .

> [I could see there an antique spectacle and the image of Roman Triumphs which are described in the history books where their representation can be traced . . .]

wrote the Scotsman John Stewart who happened to be in Paris and who thought that he was witnessing a Roman Triumph.[150]

A ROMAN TRIUMPH AT ROUEN (1550)

Had he been at Rouen the following year, he would also have thought that Rome had been transplanted there. The king's entry into that city in 1550 is interesting from many points of view. The sources are abundant, comprising a prose account with woodcuts showing not only the structures erected but also the tableaux vivants that had been devised for the occasion, and the details of the extended procession that passed before the king prior to his entry; a poem preserved in manuscript with ten miniature illustrations; and detailed archival records.[151] They reveal that, although the authors of the entry claim to have created a Triumph – 'à l'imitation expresse des Romains triumphateurs, chose bien deue à ung si magnanime et victorieux prince . . . Pareil triumphe à tous ceulx des Caesars' (*L'Entrée . . . à Rouen*, Diii) (in deliberate imitation of the triumphing Romans, a suitable thing for such a magnanimous and victorious prince . . . a Triumph similar to all those of the Caesars) – and that by the number of arches built they had outdone the ancients ('bien d'autres arcz/Que ceulx qui ont esté faictz pour Césars', *L'Entrée*, Ms Y28, p. II (many other arches/than those which were made for Caesar)), they also retained medieval traditions of tableaux vivants and the invention of ingenious mechanisms.

From structural and aesthetic points of view, this entry falls into two parts: first, the procession of the citizens of Rouen in triumph before the king seated in a magnificent gallery constructed on the edge of the town; and secondly, the king's journey through Rouen itself where, although he passed under two arches, the principal *spectacles* – in their design – looked back to a previous era. The first part is unequivocally modelled on a Roman Triumph, and the main discussion here will focus on that since, in significance, it displaced the usual show of strength by the town and, instead, produced an extraordinary display of the king's recent victories, giving him (as they thought) the satisfaction of experiencing a Roman Triumph dedicated to him and his deeds.

The preface to the reader of the official account had stressed Henri II's achievements; and, after the town's representatives had marched through the arch of the gallery in which Henri sat with his court around him, straightway before the king came 300 arquebusiers, marching five by five, the 1,500 soldiers chosen from the town's elite, again five by five, all bearing on their clothes and weapons the king's device. These troops were followed by eighteen cavaliers remarkably turned out, their dress and equipment 'Pareil à celluy dont l'antique chevalerie Romaine souloit user' (similar to that which the Roman chivalry of old used to wield) (*L'Entrée . . . à Rouen*, D1 v), who entertained the company with a military show demonstrating an agility and expertise which matched that of gladiators of old (or so the recorder predictably claimed).[152]

This martial display, designed to recall military exercises of ancient times,[153] heralded the Roman Triumph proper. Fifty captains in Roman garb led the procession which was to exhibit all the necessary apparatus: triumphal cars, and soldiers carrying weapons and standards; footmen sounding trumpets, shawms and tubas; soldiers lifting aloft models of the forts that had been captured (Figure 98); others bending under the weight of heavily carved vases; and another band, crowned with laurel, and brandishing wreaths of laurel. Other soldiers, with Henri's crown emblazoned on their breast, held up images of the places that had been conquered; and yet more, similarly attired, came with trophies of arms, followed by a band of men carrying lambs for sacrifice. Henri II's device on a huge flag came next, on its own, supported by a troop of soldiers. This demonstration of personal power prepared the way for six elephants carrying urns and bronze vases exuding scents from the Orient (Plate X). They led the prisoners, dishevelled and dejected, 'de triste representation' (of sad appearance), whose despair was intensified by the triumphant music that came close after.

The parallels with Mantegna's *Triumphs of Caesar* are striking, and the engravings testify to a knowledge of the picture bearers, the vase bearers, the elephants and the musicians.[154] Not only are the same gestures depicted but details, such as those of the military spoils, match closely. A verse epitome summed up the Roman nature of the Triumph:

La premiere bande.

98. Soldiers carrying images of captured forts, Rouen 1550

> Pareil triumphe à tous ceulx des Caesars
> Chars, Elephantz, Trophées, Escussons,
> Theatres, Parcz, et les triumphantz arcz . . . (*L'Entrée . . . à Rouen*, R2 v)

[a triumph like all those of Caesar/Chariots, elephants, trophies, shields/ Theatres, landscapes and triumphal arches . . .]

The Triumph, it is claimed, was no less delectable than the third Triumph of Pompey which he had enjoyed on his birthday and which was, reputedly, the most extravagant seen in Rome up to that time.[155] The official account stressed the Romanness of the costumes ('le morion en teste bien gravé et doré' (the helm finely engraved in gold)); of the weapons ('la targe ou Imbraciature, ennoblye d'hystoires de platte peinture, ou à demy rellief' (the shield or *imbra-ciatura* embellished with stories in painted marble or in half relief)); and of the pattern of the Triumph as it unfolded from offering a living expression of the celebrants ('l'effect des choses vives et mouvantes' (the effect of living and moving things)) to the celebration of Henri II's military achievements.

In the course of the procession came three triumphal cars: that of Fame triumphing over death; that of Religion drawn by four unicorns carrying Vesta, Royal Majesty and Victorious Virtue; and of Good Fortune displaying the living image of the king himself. It has been argued that these elements of the Triumph derived from the tradition of Petrarch's *Triumphs*;[156] and there are undoubtedly reminiscences in the chariot of Fame where Death is enchained and the spoils of battle are prominently displayed.[157] Yet the authentic Roman flavour is dominant, especially in the six companies of soldiers who flanked the cars, as the text underlines. The second group's vases were 'moullez de diverses antiquailles' (moulded with diverse ancient figures) and they carried 'un Paludament militaire' (military shield); the banners held aloft by the fourth company were painted 'par bonne perspective' (in good perspective); the spoils brandished by the fifth group were 'de toutes sortes d'armes antiqués' (of all kinds of antique arms); and the live lambs carried by the final group were 'à l'imitation des anciens triumphateurs, qui rendantz graces aux Dieux, dont offroient oblations et victimes' (in imitation of the triumphators of old who gave thanks to the gods offering oblations and victims) (*L'Entrée . . . à Rouen*, G1 v).

It is significant, however, that all the references to Rome are redirected towards Henri II. The forts 'reduicts au petit pied' (reduced to a small scale) are those which the king took 'au pays de Boullonoys' (in the country around Boulogne); the banners painted in good perspective represent the countryside around Boulogne, 'Geografiquement pourtraict, en sa dimension le paysage des environs de Boullogne'. The absorption of Roman custom into French practice could not be plainer; and the transposition is made manifest by the sight of Henri II's own image on the *Char de l'Heureuse Fortune* (Plate XI). *Felicitas* was an essential feature in the ancient Roman Triumph, reassuring the citizens of Rome and giving them confidence in their future well-being. Here that power and security is conceived in the figure of Henri II dressed, not in Roman imperial garb, but in the majestic robes of state belonging to the French crown. He carries both sceptre and laurel branch. His hair is cut 'à la cezarienne' (in the mode of Caesar), and above his head the goddess Fortuna holds the imperial crown. The fusion of French and Roman was complete.

It would be possible to cite many examples from the French royal entry tradition in the sixteenth century to show similar appropriation. But it is noteworthy that the imperial parallel seems to have been particularly emphatic at periods when the king was weak and when the comparison was used to bolster unrealistic aspirations of empire and to impress important foreign visitors with outward displays of a strength which had no substance. The disproportion between pretension and reality was perfectly exemplified in the entry of Charles IX into Paris in 1571.[158]

HENRI IV — A NEW DYNASTY AND THE TRIUMPH FOSSILIZED

By 1595 there were better reasons for mounting Roman Triumphs in France. For Henri IV, they seemed especially appropriate as he had scored victory after victory against his foes, had been received into the Catholic Church, and had enjoyed the pope's blessing. Triumphal entries were a time-honoured way of authenticating a new dynasty, and at Moulins in 1595, when the king entered the town, this intention was made explicit as the devices of the House of Bourbon appeared on all the monuments constructed according to classical rules, and Antoine Laval, the author of the account of the entry, wrote long and intricate explanations of the origins, strengths and successes of this royal House.[159]

Contemporaries saw strong affinities between Henri IV and Caesar, and these were spelt out on the vast canvas which stretched across the gateway at Montluel, put up to greet the king on his arrival there, after his visit to Lyon. In the picture, on either side of a temple stood Caesar and the king, depicted in the act of forgiving their enemies. Both men were renowned for their clemency, and both resisted unnecessary shedding of native blood during the civil wars. It was easy to pass from a very detailed comparison which evoked precise acts at Pharsalia or at Ivry to hyperbolic claims such as the assertion that ancient heroes were turned into shadows by the mere presence of Henri IV (Lyon, 1595).[160] His actual presence was sometimes very difficult to secure as his realm continued in a turbulent condition which required him to rush hither and thither to quash the latest uprising, often provoked by foreign interference. It was not surprising, therefore, that royal entries were commanded at very short notice, or put off for several weeks. Occasionally (as for the queen's entry into Lyon in 1600), the king never arrived at all. Fortunately, a ready supply of materials from past entries was kept in stock although – even with such aid – the time pressure was sometimes so acute that not all the projected monuments could be constructed.[161]

Henri IV's entry into Lyon in 1595 is especially interesting in that regard. Pierre Matthieu, who wrote the official account, declared that half the work was left undone:

> le peu de temps . . . De maniere qu'on fut contraint laisser la moitié de la besongne imparfaite comme la statue du Roy à cheval, l'Apollon tirant le serpent Python, le chariot de Triomphe, la bataille des deux gallères sur la riviere, deux arcs triomphants à l'antique. (*L'Entrée . . . à Lyon*, p. 5)

> [the shortness of time . . . such that we were constrained to leave half the work imperfect, such as the equestrian statue of the king, Apollo killing the Python, the triumphal chariot, the naval combat between two galleys, and two triumphal arches in the antique mode.]

Moreover, he was aware of the vast resources available from earlier Triumphs, and he listed them: sixteen accounts from Roman times, and thirty-nine modern examples taken from all over Europe (p. 4); and he acknowledged that it was unlikely that anything new could be found that might prove richer than the ancients or more elegant than the moderns. For the 1595 entry, it had been resolved to follow neither the one nor the other and if, perchance, an observer – well versed in such matters – were to detect some borrowing, it should be judged to have been by accident rather than by design.

Such sensitivity and self-consciousness indicate the extent to which royal entries had become fossilized, their form predictable, and their erudition an elaborate game that scholars loved to play. Matthieu shows some impatience at their attitude and at the architectural expectations surrounding these events. His record, he warns, will be straightforward 'tout simple et cru' (simple and unadorned); he proposes to offer a strictly faithful account of what happened, unadorned with pictures or portraits. 'C'est une histoire non un recueil d'Architecture ou de Perspective' (it's a history not a manual on architecture or perspective), he expostulated. Despite these resolves, Matthieu's approach remains complex. He anticipates readers' reactions, knowing that they await structures modelled on ancient Roman Triumphs (albeit 'feints de marbre' (simulated marble)); he is keen to stress the truthfulness of his record; and he immediately supplies an engraved pull-out of all the structures whose representation he had previously denied – six arches, an arcade with fountain, four statues on columns, two altars, an obelisk, and column (Figure 99). The regular elements of the Triumph are all here: columns made according to the classical orders, arches inscribed with the detail of Henri IV's recent victories on which Matthieu elaborates in his text,[162] allegorical statues and so on.

Despite the determination not to be overwhelmed by ancient or modern forms of Triumph, the climax of Henri IV's entry in 1595 came when he confronted the column built before the Petit Palais. Like that which had been designed by Bandinelli for Leo X's *Entrata* into Florence (1515),[163] it replicated the column of Trajan, as Matthieu admits, and thus managed to imitate both modern and ancient models (Figure 100). It had ten scrolled bands, and as each one curled around the column, it was engraved with some remarkable event 'de ces derniers troubles' (of our recent troubles). The first five concentrated on military activities: the help the king had received from Henri III; his succession to the crown of France; sieges of towns; the taking of the Paris suburbs; the King's contests against Farnese. Then came the moral and religious concerns (scrolls 6–8), followed by a representation of Henri's sea power (scroll 9), and finally, pictures of the collapse of all opposition (scroll 10).

So palpable a reference to the column still standing in Rome, and from which historians drew knowledge of the emperor's victory over the Dacians, helped to establish visually the authority of the king and of the new dynasty, and to reinforce all the reasons behind the statement of obedience which Monsieur le Doyen de Chalmazel had uttered on behalf of the citizens of Lyon at

99.   Attributed to Jacques Perrissin: engraved view of all the monuments, Lyon, 1595

100.   Antoine Lafréry: engraving
of Trajan's column

the beginning of the ceremonies: 'nous vous avoüons pour nostre Roy et vous recognoissons pour la vive image de Dieu, representant parmy nous sa Maiesté éternelle' (we accept you as our king and as the living image of God, representing among us His Eternal Majesty) (*L'Entrée . . . à Lyon*, p. 9). However blatant the parallel might seem, the traditions of Triumph, as renewed and interpreted in Renaissance Europe, had made it acceptable – and even apposite. Structures from ancient Rome thus had a role to play in getting the French people to appreciate and to accept the Bourbon line of kings.

So familiar was the Roman tradition in Renaissance France that it was even possible to exploit it by a process of inversion. Thus, long before, in order to set forth the achievements of Anne de Montmorency, Jean de Luxembourg had argued *against* using the relics of Rome. In a convincing demonstration of his deep knowledge of the history and evolution of the Roman Triumph, he decried the excesses and presumption of those generals (from Publica to Caesar, and beyond) who successively tried to outdo their predecessors in display, exoticism, and even eccentricity. After Pompey's elephants, 'cerfs, tigres et lyepartz'

338

(deer, tiger and leopards) followed 'Autres plusieurs bestes de toutes parts' (many other beasts from all regions). How, he asked, could one associate glory with such beasts? Brutality was more appropriate. Let us leave all that aside, let the real presence of the man and his deeds speak for themselves (Jean argued); and he tried to persuade his fellow writers to cease offering praise based on such inadequacies:

> Cessez de plus tant louer et prescher
> Un tas d'aerins, de marbres et médailles
> De vieils pourtraicts, rouillées antiquailles
> De bronze, d'or, d'arcz boutans et statues,
> Qui par le temps ont esté abbatues.

[Cease advocating and praising so much/ A heap of brass, of marble and medals/ Old images, rusty antiques/ Of bronze and gold, flying buttresses and statues/ Which have all been knocked to the ground by Time.][164]

Jean de Luxembourg's attack on the Triumph and his dismissal of other signs of Roman grandeur could, of course, be read as an ingenious exploitation of such things. The very turning upside down of their value served to enhance Montmorency's claim to honour and praise. In a strange way, denying their existence gave them a sharper presence.

There was, however, alongside the obvious, calculated imitation of (or playing with) the Roman Triumph used to foster the imperial aims of French princes, a persistent current of criticism. To some extent, reproof had been inherent in some of the earliest triumphs when part of the experience had been to weep as well as to applaud at the sight of the great brought low, and even to sympathize with the plight of the little children of conquered princes.[165] Disapprobation had been explicit in the response to the Triumphs of Caesar when, despite his care not to inscribe any Roman names in his Triumph, he had, for example, exhibited images of his victories over Pompey, Scipio and Cato. At this spectacle, which brought to mind the misery and sufferings of civil war and which the people could easily interpret as Romans triumphing over their fellow citizens and as Caesar rejoicing at the ruin of some of the greatest men of Rome, there was much groaning and many expressions of regret, although other deaths were applauded.[166]

It was less the impact of the images which bothered Renaissance critics, and more the display of superfluities and the indulging in conspicuous expense at a time when poverty was so visible all over Europe.[167] La Popelinière's condemnation of triumphal shows was forthright and very thoughtful.[168] He considered that they fed the naturally vain propensities of their recipients. Such 'vaines magnificences' were only acceptable if the princes to whom they were addressed strove to emulate the character and deeds of those to whom they were compared, 'pour tirer profit et se conformer aux vertueux exemples de ces grands personnages y représentés' (to benefit and conform to the virtuous examples of the great persons represented there). Unfortunately, in La Popelinière's observation, the effect of such triumphs on princes was the opposite of beneficial. They rested their eyes only momentarily on the images, attracted instead by superficial paraphernalia:

> ils ne se plaisent qu'en la diversité des formes et couleurs; et en la riche estoffe qu'on leur fait admirer; simples et nouvelles creatures. (f. 380v)

> [They delight only in the diversity of forms and colours, and in the rich stuff which they are made to admire; simple and naive creatures.]

The most deleterious effect was on their minds, for – lacking good judgement and a proper upbringing – they were flattered into believing that these grandiose fictions actually represented their true state; they 'se persuadent joüer de ces mêmes surnaturelles magnificences qu'on leur fait regarder' (persuade themselves that they are playing these same supernatural magnificences which they are shown). As a consequence, they placed themselves so high upon a pedestal that they lost contact with their own people, thinking only of surrounding themselves with 'ces vaines imaginations d'extraordinaires excellences'.

This distancing from the people is also at the heart of Michel de Montaigne's observations, although his attack on modern triumphs *à la romaine* was more direct and more radical. He challenged the approach adopted by his contemporaries to the training of princes. Notions of liberality and magnificence were not, in Montaigne's view, in the interest of the monarch; and those who advocated largesse were, in fact, concerned to fill their own pockets. As for Triumphs, Montaigne saw these as the mark of limitation of mind and even of cowardice:

> C'est une espèce de pusillanimité aux monarques, et un tesmoignage de ne sentir point assez ce qu'ils sont, de travailler à se faire valloir et paroistre par despences excessives. (III, vi, 902)

> [It is a sort of lack of confidence in monarchs, a sign of not being sure of their position, to strive to make themselves respected and glorious through excessive expenditure.][169]

For Frenchmen who had witnessed the civil wars, their ideal monarch had been drawn by Hotman in the *Franco-Gallia*:

> the king is not shown in military guise on horseback, or riding on a four-horse chariot in the manner of a Triumph, but robed and crowned, seated on his throne, with the royal sceptre in his right hand and the sceptre of justice in his left.[170]

Here sits not a military commander or triumphing victor but a wielder of justice.

Despite these counter-voices, the tradition of modelling the representation of the achievements of French princes on ancient examples which brought to mind images of Rome was astonishingly vigorous. And yet, although the determination to imitate is clearly articulated in many of the surviving texts, we know comparatively little about how the monuments really looked. At Rouen (1550), the engravings in the official account are relatively crude; and, although the parallels with Mantegna's *Triumphs* are patent, the engraved figures for the entry are only approximations, and the manuscript illuminations follow manuscript traditions. Many designs for monuments were never actually realized and, as Pierre Matthieu put it, the design remained 'au crayon' (only drawn in pencil). In addition, before publishing their accounts, authors like Maurice Scève were careful to reshape the experience. One might say that the printed account gave a performance of the event, an account which was sufficiently flexible for the reader to remake and retell the experience of the entry as he progressed through the script. The text provided an opportunity for further exploration and interpretation, rather than offering a truthful record of what had happened. The reader's mind (well stuffed from his reading and his visual experience) could play between remembered images of monuments in Rome and those drawn by the recorder. There was a sense in which the text became more than a substitute for the real experience. It permitted an overall view of the occasion as though the reader was privileged to be in the company of the prince. Furthermore, it often offered an improved version of the event.

These advantages had been recognized at the beginning of the century by Emperor Maximilian I whose 'paper Triumphs' have largely been preserved: the *Arch of Honour*, engraved by Dürer and completed for distribution by 1518; the *Great Triumphal Chariot*, designed and engraved by Dürer and Pirckheimer; and the *Triumphal Procession* of which 137 engravings (out of some 200) were completed. These paper pageants have survived, bearing the political and moral intentions of the emperor and his artists, free from the manipulation of intermediaries or interpreters, as testimony to the virtues of Maximilian I and his imperial office.[171]

In many respects, the Triumph, and the texts which recorded the occasion, sum up Renaissance attitudes to the vision of Rome in France. They borrowed fragments, set them in a French context and thereby changed their meaning, although their shape continued to mirror their original form. They slavishly copied images, simulated reliefs, and inscribed on the surface of arches (for instance) medals drawn from princely or scholarly collections, and applied them to new circumstances.[172] One might have expected that this most quintessential form denoting Roman greatness – the Triumph – would have retained its purpose intact. Certainly, it kept its essential structures – arches, obelisks, theatres of honour, processions and triumphal cars loaded with spoils. And yet, the same transforming processes observed in other forms which had been transported into France can be seen here. As the Triumph was accommodated to local conditions, its symbolism changed, and its meanings multiplied and became more complicated (its authors would say, more sophisticated). Assimilation into French culture brought inevitable modifications. The flexibility of the Triumph and its capacity to be adapted in multiple ways offered rich opportunities for the artist and writer to develop their own inventiveness while believing that they remained faithful to the models they copied.

CODA

In the autumn of 1619, the young and ambitious Jean-Louis Guez de Balzac set out for Rome. He spent eighteen months there and, like many visitors before him, wrote down his impressions and composed a collection of letters analysing his feelings and giving an idea of the moral reflections which had been stimulated by the city. First published in 1624, his letters were immensely popular. They ran into many editions; and they made his reputation. The experience of the imperial city was fundamental to all Balzac's future writing and his works were to influence French attitudes to Rome for at least a generation.

Balzac's works provide evidence of significant shifts in reactions to Rome and to what it stood for and in the techniques for recording and developing these responses. Interest was no longer centred on the effort to recover ancient Rome or to parallel its many features in French building and writing. Nor were observers any longer primarily concerned to discover what ancient Rome was like. The emphasis now was to marshal all the collected evidence from Rome, apply it to the majesty of France, and thereby demonstrate the greatness of Paris which, transformed into the new Rome, came to displace the old imperial city. Thus, while historians of the French capital, Corrozet and Rabel for instance, used primitive archaeological techniques to establish the ancient origins of Paris and to unearth its own antiquities, Henri IV and his advisers set about aggrandizing the city.[1] Something of this changing spirit may be seen when, in 1609, the military engineer, Benedit de Vassilliev dit Nicolay, offered a map of Paris to Henri IV in his book *Portrait de la Ville, cité et université de Paris avec les faubours di celle, dédié au Roy*. In the upper right corner of the map an equestrian portrait shows the king trampling over his enemies and below is inscribed the following quatrain:

> Soubs le regne de ce Grand Roy
> Tresclement, tresvaillant, tresiuste
> Paris est comme soubs Auguste
> Fut Rome du Monde l'effroy.

[Under the dominion of this great king/ Very clement, courageous and just/ Paris is as Rome under Augustus/ When it was the terror of the world.][2]

101. Vassilliev dit Nicolay: section from map of Paris, 1609

The king, with an imperial gesture, underlines the parallel with Augustus (Figure 101). Just as this emperor had refashioned Rome, so Henri IV has transformed Paris.

As we have seen, Rome and its ruins had proved a remarkably fertile source both of ideas and forms which could be played upon by artists and writers, and of artefacts which could be acquired and cherished by princes and scholars. In French art and literature the reverberations of the city and of its fragments were complex and far reaching. They provoked both positive and negative responses, extended aesthetic experience and artistic practice, and took them into new imaginative zones. But responses to Rome were complicated by the vast weight of remembrance. The very preparation made by visitors, and the sheer quantity of detail available in the sixteenth century, often impaired critical vision. Frenchmen were excited and overwhelmed by the range of images and materials transferred from Rome through guidebooks, journals, engravings, mouldings of statues, copies of reliefs and inscriptions, and by the increasingly accessible medals and coins which had secured the survival of images of long-vanished buildings of ancient Rome.

The transfer of ideas and images of Rome to France in the late Renaissance was opportune: French writers and artists had prepared for their reception, and had seen their relevance to contemporary life – on the one hand in heightening the status of artist and poet, and on the other in the duplication of the experience of civil war. Ruins, in particular, were powerful stimuli to the imagination and, given the close connection between the experience of travelling and writing, in the records left by travellers to the city the act of description itself became a transforming process. Despite all their claims of faithful recording, the ancient city was depicted as grander than, in fact, it was. At the opposite end of the spectrum, however, those hostile to Rome used the impact of the ruins to condemn civil war, to dramatize the spectacle of devastation, and to bring to light Rome's rotting condition.

Nevertheless, in general, ruins inspired positive reconstructions, for the urge to turn fragments into whole forms proved irresistible and both artists and writers displayed the same tendencies. Ruins impelled them to try to give shape to what was only partially there. As Françoise Joukovsky pertinently observed:

> le Forum n'offre pas au pèlerin le spectacle de la gloire antique, mais seulement la possibilité de la recréer.

> [The Forum offers the pilgrim not the spectacle of ancient glory but rather the possibility of recreating it.][3]

That recognition was even more keenly felt by the artist and writer who appreciated the value of the broken and the incomplete, and especially its indicative power. In some profound, almost subconscious way, they believed that the whole temple was implicit in the fragment, and that the ruins of Rome offered endless possible regroupings (like tones in music). Whether they were reconstituting a text or a building, or making new forms out of old ones, they were fascinated by the interplay of fragments and wholes.

The method used by artists and writers to move from the parts to a conception of the whole form was a process of conjecture: on the one hand explicitly advocated by historians such as Flavio Biondo or Andreas Fulvius, by architects like Palladio, and by critics and linguists such as Scaliger and Vigenère; and on the other hand implicitly used by creative writers like Du Bellay and Montaigne. This process of conjecture may have been connected with an experience which many writers and artists recount. As they walked among the ruins of Rome, or wandered across the desert-like stretches of the Palatine hill, they felt the simultaneous presence of key moments in the history of Rome. At one and the same time, they were aware of the present ruined landscape and saw mirrored there the city of Evander, remote in time and yet present now; and then they perceived the splendour of classical Rome when the hill was studded with magnificent dwellings. The experience was translated into the illustrations in guidebooks where idealized reconstructions and the reality of ruins are found together, often side by side, so that readers can ponder the then and the now, make the shifts between the two, and draw their own conclusions. Involuntary memory was at work in the feeling which conflates vast tracts of time into a single moment; and the density of meaning which came from such conflations was imported by artists and writers into their work. Sculptors, architects and painters introduced motifs – 'quotations' – from ancient style which they expected to be recognized. They incorporated images whose meaning would be understood. Writers, in like manner, hinted at the huge reservoir of words and images from classical authors which lay beneath their texts, sometimes suggesting a name allusively, sometimes frankly citing lines for the reader to enjoy.

Layered meanings of this kind implied a significant role for readers and spectators, and their share in the creation of new forms from the fragments of the old was considerable. From those elements which had been taken, absorbed, reprocessed and thereby changed, a new style had emerged. It was a style which aimed at the *gentillesse romaine* (Roman elegance) as Philibert, Belleforest and Ronsard made clear, although in their view it was now more refined, blending natural and artificial effects. While not hiding his admiration for Rome, Philibert de L'Orme promoted French forms. Joachim du Bellay, despite misgivings and hesitations, was confident that new forms could be created out of old ones even if their shape could be only dimly divined. His poems were evidence of that resuscitation both in themselves and in the resonances they had for later generations of poets and travellers. The château of Fontainebleau, although shaped in part by influences from Rome and praised by contemporaries for its collections of Roman art, was – in the early decades of the seventeenth century – criticized by Italian *cognoscenti* as defective, resembling a 'monster in stone':

Il n'y a point d'architecte d'Italie, qui ne trouve des défauts en la structure de Fontainebleau; et qui ne l'appelle un Monstre de pierre: Ce monstre néantmoins est la belle demeure des Rois, et la cour y loge commodément.

[There is no Italian architect who does not find fault with the structure of Fontainebleau and who does not term it a Monster in stone; nonetheless, this monster is the noble abode of kings, and the court resides there commodiously.][4]

In this view, the Roman connection had entirely disappeared.

It was perhaps in forms where the power of Rome had been most concentrated – frozen into the figure of Caesar or into manifestations of Triumph – that the fusion of French and Roman elements was most obvious, although the result was not always creatively effective. Caesar, retaining all his attributes, was reconceived in the person of François I or Henri II. The Triumph provided rich and multiple meanings which could be read on the surfaces of the arches beneath which French princes rode – arches whose symbols displayed reputations, achievements and associations that had accrued over time together with those attributed to the monarch currently being honoured. Such forms appeared immutable, and from that static state they derived their strengths and their weaknesses.

The constantly changing nature of the French vision of Rome at this period can be set into relief by a brief study of Guez de Balzac's responses.[5] His view of Rome (both in the letters he wrote during his sojourn in the imperial city, and in his later work)[6] sought to demolish the significance of those features which had inspired earlier visitors. Of the antiquities, he is dismissive. Marble and paint are good enough for the *hoi polloi*, but not for those who dedicate themselves to higher things:

Ce n'est point toutesfois que j'aye beaucoup de curiosité pour ces choses-là [antiquities], ny que j'admire du marbre qui ne parle point, et des peintures qui ne sont pas si belles que la verité. Il faut laisser cela au peuple, dont les mesmes objects bornent l'imagination et la veüe.

[It isn't, moreover, that I've much curiosity for that sort of thing, nor that I admire marble which has nothing to say, or paintings which are not as beautiful as the originals. All that should be left to the plebs for whom these same objects limit both sight and imagination.]

The very ruins and their representation which had stimulated the imagination so successfully are here ironically shown as generating an opposite, limiting condition.[7] In another letter, Balzac railed against the relentless pursuit of medals which scholars, their enthusiasm unabated, still continued.[8] And, most devastating of all, he criticized those who abandoned 'la force, la vigueur et la lumière de Rome' (the force, vigour and light of Rome), represented by the Roman literary heritage, for the study of the ruins of Rome – 'sa carcasse . . . son sepul-chre et . . . ses cendres' (its carcass . . . its tomb . . . and its ashes).[9]

Yet Balzac's response was more nuanced and more ambiguous than these citations imply. The ruins which he rejects are nonetheless 'precieuses' since they provided the environment in which he sought refuge every day that he was in Rome, in order to dream of his own big projects.[10] The remarkable thing about Balzac is that, for him, the value of ruins resided in the atmos-phere they create. He was not interested in them *per se*. He was not concerned with authenticating their origin or identifying their style. What they provided was a context for reflection on moral truths; in themselves, they counted for nothing even though they might recall tales from long ago, as Balzac warned cardinal de la Valette who, in June 1623, was setting out for Rome:

> A Rome, vous marcherez sur des pierres qui ont esté les dieux de César et de Pompée: vous considérerez les ruines de ces grands ouvrages, dont la vieil-lesse est encore belle, et vous vous pourmenerez tous les jours parmi les his-toires et les fables. Mais ce sont des amusements d'un esprit qui se contente de peu.

> [In Rome you will walk upon stones which were the gods of Caesar and Pompey: you will contemplate the ruins of these great works which remain beautiful in old age, and you will wander every day among story and fable. But these are entertainments for a mind which is satisfied with little.][11]

The unexpected deflation of the rising tones in the earlier part of this passage conveys Balzac's full meaning. Walks which have as their only goal the contemplation of ruins of the past are idle pursuits, divorced from the bustle of the real world. Yet Balzac had himself conceded that the Palatine hill and the Capitol transported his spirit and turned his thoughts towards loftier concerns:

> Je ne monte jamais au mont Palatin, ni au Capitole, que je n'y change d'esprit et qu'il ne m'y vienne d'autres pensées que les miennes ordinaires: cet air m'inspire quelque chose de grand et de généreux que je n'avois point auparavant.

> [I never go up the Palatine hill or to the Capitol without my spirit being refreshed and without thinking thoughts very different from my usual ones, because that air inspires in me something great and generous that I did not feel before.][12]

From experiences such as this, Rome remained an abiding influence even on the reluctant Balzac, despite the claim by the chevalier Méré that he had con-fessed before he died that he did not believe half the good things he had written about Rome.[13] While Balzac refused to offer any detailed account of the physical presence of the city and deliberately withdrew from developing his thoughts on topics such as 'tous les triomphes des anciens' (all the triumphs of the ancients),[14] Rome remained a constant point of reference in all his writing, notably in *Le Prince* where the city was at the centre of his argument. The works of Cicero were a regular source of consolation; they had provided a core of social serenity which masked, and even displaced his individual uncertainties and tensions;[15] and when he wished to signal his approval of a contemporary, he attributed to them Roman qualities.[16] Balzac even wrote to his cousin some fifteen years after his sojourn in Rome that he had given his heart to Italy, and that, if it had been in his power, he would already have become a citizen of Rome in 1620.[17]

If the stones and the paintings had lost their magnetic power, what was it – beyond the personal consolation he found in the writings of classical authors – that drew Balzac to Rome? When he had stayed about half his time in Rome, Balzac wrote to his old tutor Nicolas Bourbon giving an assessment of the city and of its importance for him and for his contemporaries. His tone and his words (whether he realized it or not) were reminiscent of those of Flavio Biondo nearly two centuries before.[18] Above all, it was the civilizing power of Rome that had impressed him: her gifts in the fields of religion and law; her manifold examples of civilized behaviour; and her inspiration in the arts – literature, music and poetry.

> Rome est cause que vous n'estes plus ni Barbares ni Payens, car elle vous a appris la civilité et la Religion: elle vous a donné les loix qui vous empeschent de faillir, et les exemples, à qui vous devez les bonnes actions que vous faites. C'est d'icy que vous sont venuës les inventions et les arts, et que vous avez receû la science de la paix et de la guerre. La Peinture, la Musique et la Comedie . . .

> [Rome is the reason why you are neither barbarous nor pagan because she has taught you civility and religion; she has given you laws which prevent you from failing, and examples to which you owe the good actions that you perform. From her come invention and the arts, and the sciences of peace and of war. Painting, Music, Theatre . . .]

All this added up to a formidable legacy and, although expressed in very general terms, Balzac's emphatic statements are pregnant with meaning for him. They prepare the ground for that ideal of urbanity which, he was subsequently to argue, characterized all that is best in French society, and in particular the entourage of Madame la marquise de Rambouillet for whom he wrote the *Discours de la conversation des Romains* (1644) where *urbanitas* is defined as: 'un certain air du grand monde, et une couleur et teinture de la Cour, qui ne manque pas seulement les paroles et les opinions, mais aussi le ton de la voix et les mouvements du corps' (a certain atmosphere of high society, the colour and tones of the court which are evident not only in words and opinions but also in the timbre of the voice and in the movements of the body).[19] Rome's physical presence has been covered over with the smooth façade of social politeness.

It was essentially these virtues which Balzac found to praise in Corneille's *Cinna* (1643) when, modifying the words which Augustus himself used of his own performance, he commended the playwright: 'Aux endroits où Rome est de brique, vous la rebastissez de marbre' (where Rome was once brick, you have refashioned it in marble). Rome's lofty pride, Corneille has transmuted into the style of Paris: '[vous] l'advertissez de la bienséance, quand elle [Rome] ne s'en souvient pas' (you alert her to good manners when she had forgotten them). And he spells it out,

> Vous nous faites voir Rome tout ce qu'elle peut être à Paris, et ne l'avez point brisée en la remuant.

> [You have made us understand all that Rome might be in Paris without breaking anything in the move.][20]

Corneille had discovered a new Roman style which was in tune with Balzac's own writing. As Jean Jehasse has concluded, *Cinna* was the 'chef d'oeuvre d'Antiquité repensée' (masterpiece of Rome rethought),[21] as serene as *Le grand camée de France*, inherited so long ago (Plate XII). Scattering one's text with fragments from ancient and honoured authors was no longer a tenable procedure. For Balzac, such 'larcins des anciens' (thefts from the ancients) were simply old-fashioned. Modern French style required a complete remoulding. Ancient remains were to be so absorbed that they disappeared in the mix. The emergent form was to be a seamless structure which also remodelled the Roman mind and character. This was Corneille's achievement in *Cinna*. And it was an achievement which Balzac applauded.

Balzac's views were very influential; and they suggest that, in the early decades of the seventeenth century in France, Rome's status depended on French reinterpretation. While consideration of antiquity, and of ancient Rome in particular, had helped Balzac see more clearly the nature of his modern world and to define it better,[22] those reflections had led to a more radical metamorphosis of the imperial city, its people and empire than any earlier appropriation by French artists and writers. In stark terms, Rome had moved to Paris, and many contemporaries recognized that fact. The historian André du Chesne stated categorically: 'Paris qui est nostre Françoise Rome . . . ne cède en rien à ceste vieille Rome' (Paris is our French Rome . . . and yields nothing to the ancient city of Rome).[23] And Louis d'Orléans, when he came to explain the structure of the *Parlement* in 1607, divided the capital 'nostre Françoise Rome' (our French Rome) into three regions. The first is the city – *Roma vetus* – not a mass of ruins, but 'féconde en citoyens, superbe en édifices' (fecund in citizens, splendid in buildings). Secondly, the Louvre and its surroundings become the new city. Finally, there is the *Civitas litterarium*, home of the Muses:

les Muses fugitives de la Grece et absentes de Rome se sont réfugiées pour
être françoises.

[the Muses having fled Greece, and absent from Rome, have found refuge
in becoming French.][24]

The complex vision of Rome which had stimulated French writers and artists
in the mid-sixteenth century and which had encouraged partial reshapings and
then wholesale reconstructions had, by the end of Henri IV's reign, become
detached from the viewer's gaze. The idea of Rome had been fundamentally
changed, refashioned into a French conception of classical styles and character,
and the imperial city was now embodied in the fabric of Paris.

NOTES

Introduction

1 A superb evocation of the dangers and grubbiness of Renaissance Rome, especially for the individual traveller, is given by Ingrid D. Rowland, *The Culture of the High Renaissance: Ancients and Moderns in Sixteenth-Century Rome*, Cambridge, 1998, first section of ch. 1, 'Initiation', pp. 7–10.

2 The haphazard nature of building in Rome is described by Paul Zanker, *The Power of Images in the Age of Augustus*, Ann Arbor, 1993.

3 The freedom of interpretation exercised by Renaissance architects has been studied by Gérard Labrot, *L'Image de Rome: une arme pour la contre réforme, 1534–1677*, Champvallon, 1987, pp. 41–8, 92–102.

4 For a discussion of such uncontrolled responses, see my article 'Contradictory impulses in Montaigne's vision of Rome', *Renaissance Studies*, vol. 4, no. 4, 1990, pp. 392–409, and the work of Charles Burroughs, *From Signs to Design. Environmental Process and Reform in Early Renaissance Rome*, Cambridge, MA, 1990, where he shows the city as a constant process of change whose ruined monuments are worked on by the imagination, by memory and by expectation. Thomas L. Greene argued in *The Light in Troy*, New

Haven, 1982, p. 234 that 'the encounter with the fragmentary and the formless automatically produced an answering movement towards form'. The interplay of ruins and completed forms continued to be a major theme in art and architecture; see, for example, Hubert Robert's imaginary view of the Grande Galerie du Louvre in ruins (Salon, 1796 – Louvre), or the watercolours of Joseph Gandy depicting Soane's Bank of England under construction and resembling the venerated ruins of antiquity (*Sir John Soane. Master of Space and Light*, ed. Margaret Richardson and Mary Anne Stevens, Royal Academy of Arts, London, 1999, pp. 220–1; and an imaginary view of the Rotunda in ruins, ibid., cat. no. 133.

5 See Philip Jacks, *The Antiquarian and the Myth of Antiquity: the Origins of Rome in Renaissance Thought*, Cambridge, 1993; J. Hubaux, *Les Grands Mythes de Rome*, Paris, 1945; K.J. Pratt, 'Rome as eternal', *Journal of the History of Ideas*, vol. 25, 1965, pp. 25–36; David Thompson, *The Idea of Rome from Antiquity to the Renaissance*, Mexico City, 1971.

6 I refer in particular to Virgil (*Aeneid*, VI); Horace (*Epodes*); Tibullus; Dionysius of Halicarnassus (Books I, V and VIII); Livy; Statius; and Silius Italicus (*Punica* III, VII and IX). Many readers may also

have admired the Oration in praise of Rome by Aelius Aristides which had been available from the Aldine Press since 1513: see J.H. Oliver 'On the Roman Oration of Aelius Aristides', *Transactions of the American Philosophical Society*, vol. 43, part 4, 1953, pp. 871–1003; see also C.M. Bowra, 'Melinno's Hymn to Rome', *Journal of Roman Studies*, vol. 47, 1957, pp. 21–8.

7 See, for example, La Popelinière, *L'Histoire des histoires avec l'idée de l'histoire accomplie*, Paris, M. Orry, 1599, p. 266.

8 For an initial appraisal of this double and contradictory reception of the image of Rome, see my article 'Impaired vision: the experience of Rome in Renaissance France', *Renaissance Studies*, vol. 8, no. 3, 1994, pp. 244–55.

9 Virgil, *Aeneid* VII; and Vitruvius, *Architecture*, translated by Jean Martin, Paris, H. de Marnef, 1572, f. 89.

10 Nathaniel Hawthorne, *The Marble Faun*, London, 1906, p. 6.

11 Additional recent works on Rome which have informed my writing are: Erich S. Gruen, *The Image of Rome*, Englewood Cliffs, NJ, 1969; Lidia Mazzolani, *The Idea of the City in Roman Thought*, London, 1970; Edward K. Rand, *The Building of Eternal Rome*, New York, 1972; Sabine G. MacCormick, *Art and Ceremony in Late Antiquity*, Berkeley, 1981; P.A. Ramsey (ed.), *Rome in the Renaissance*, Binghamton, 1982; Charles L. Stinger, *The Renaissance in Rome*, Bloomington, 1985; Leo Braudy, *The Frenzy of Renown*, Oxford, 1986; Richard Jenkins (ed.), *The Legacy of Rome*, New York, 1992; Alain Schnapp, *La Conquête du passé. Aux origines de l'archéologie*, Paris, 1993; and Jas Elsner, *Art and the Roman Viewer*, Cambridge, 1995. Recent work on France: Gladys Dickinson, *Du Bellay in Rome*, Leiden, 1960;

George H. Tucker, *Les Antiquitez. The Poet's Odyssey*, Oxford, 1990; and Eric MacPhail, *The Voyage to Rome in French Renaissance Literature*, Stanford, 1990.

Chapter 1   Voyages

1 Some ideas elaborated here were first formulated in my article, 'Impaired vision', pp. 244–55.

2 *Les Epithètes*, f. 232v. La Porte adds to his definition in all editions (1571, 1593 and 1612) the following: 'Romme, ville capitale d'Italie et iadis le chef de tout le monde, a esté ainsi appellee de Romule son fondateur. On dit qu'anciennement elle a eu en ses murailles 634 tours et 37 portes: mesmes que l'entour de la ville estoit de 20,000 pas' (10,000 in the 1593 edition). (Rome, capital of Italy and at one time the head of the world, called thus from the name of her founder, Romulus. It is said that the city once had 634 towers along its walls, and 37 gates, even though the circuit was 20,000 paces.)

3 Jean Tarde, *A la rencontre de Galilée: deux voyages en Italie*, ed. F. Moureau and M. Tetel, extracts of the manuscript preserved in Périgord, no. 106, which recounts two journeys to Rome (1593 and 1614–15), Geneva, 1984, pp. 67–8.

4 Blaise de Vigenère, *Traicté des chiffres ou secretes manieres d'escrire*, Paris, 1586, ff. 336–7.

5 Pirro Ligorio left a vast collection of manuscripts which are chiefly preserved in Rome, Naples, Turin, Oxford and Paris. There are over 50 volumes and these were intended to cover all aspects of ancient Roman life. Some manuscripts are illustrated with medals, scenes from sarcophagi and statues. As will be seen, his manuscripts were used by many artists (like Serlio) who were to exert significant influence in

France. Such was their reputation that Christina of Sweden (for instance) owned a copy of all the manuscripts of Ligorio: C. Volpi, *Il libro di Pirro Ligorio all'Archivio di Stato di Torino*, Rome, 1994, p. 53. The maps are reproduced in Amato Pietro Frutaz, *Le Piante di Roma*, 3 vols, Rome, 1962. For 1553, see vol. II, plate 25; for 1561, vol. II, plates 26–32. Both maps were copied and engraved in 1573 (*piccola*) and in 1574 (*grande*) by Etienne du Pérac, who dedicated his work first to Charles IX and then to Henri III; these were published by Antoine Lafréry in 1577. G. Braun and F. Hogenberg's map of Rome was published with a paean to the city in 1575: *Civitates orbis terrarum*, no. 46.

6 P. Ligorio, *Libro delle antiquità di Roma*, Venice, 1553, f. 25v: 'à me pare, che in vece di rappresentare l'imagine, et la forma di Roma, ci habbiano più tosto fatto védere lo schizzo, el disegno d'uno strano laberinto'. (It seems to me that rather than having presented the image and form of Rome we have shown instead the sketch and design of a strange labyrinth.)

7 The accuracy of Ligorio's reconstructions has frequently been questioned and his reliance on ancient texts criticized. For a review of the evidence for and against, see Ginette Vagenheim, 'La Falsification chez Pirro Ligorio', *Eutopia*, vol. 3, 1994, pp. 67–114. Jacques Androuet du Cerceau, *Livre des edifices antiques romains*, Paris, 1584, sig. ã iv, acknowledged that his map was copied from an Italian, and – in his dedication to the duc de Nemours – he explained that he had drawn each building separately so that both the 'curieux de l'antiquité' and 'maistres en l'Architecture' could find matter for their work and inventions. Such an approach was probably necessary as many plans of

Rome published in the sixteenth century were very unclear. Take, for example, those in Guillaume Guéroult, *Epitome de la corographie d'Europe*, Lyon, 1583, or in Antoine du Pinet, *Plantz*, Lyon, 1564, p. 126.

8 Jean Delumeau argues that no other century transformed Rome so radically as the sixteenth century when, for example, 63 new palaces were built, *Rome au XVIe siècle*, Paris, 1975, pp. 58–71.

9 Michel de Montaigne, *Journal de voyage*, ed. François Rigolot, Paris, 1992, p. 91.

10 For consideration of the quality of writing in travel accounts see the article of Wes Williams, 'Salad days: revisiting pilgrimage in the sixteenth century', in *(Ré)interprétations: études sur le seizième siècle*, ed. John O'Brien, *Michigan Romance Studies*, vol. 15, 1995, pp. 151–76, and his recent book, *Pilgrimage and Narrative in the French Renaissance*, Oxford, 1998. Friedrich Wolfzettel, *Le Discours du voyageur*, Paris, 1996, has studied travel discourse especially in early accounts of journeys to America.

11 A typical traveller who conscientiously notes down all the famous objects he saw in Rome is the anonymous author of Bibliothèque Nationale Ms fr. 5550, 'Voyage de Provence et d'Italie' (1588–9).

12 Pierre Dupuy, for instance, showed Lestoile the letters which he had received from his brother who was visiting Rome, P. de Lestoile, *Journal*, VIII [1607], pp. 310 and 326.

13 Sieur de Villamont, *Voyages*, Arras, 1598, sig. ã iiij; Villamont's account of his journey was enormously popular and went through a further twenty-five editions before 1620.

14 Jean Antoine Rigaud, *Bref recueil de choses rares, notables, antiques, citez, forteresses principales d'Italie*, Aix, 1601, sig. A4v.

15 Edited and published in full

(though without the drawings) by Adalberto Olivero, *Nicolas Audebert, Voyage d'Italie*, 2 vols, Rome, 1983.

16 Wes Williams has provided an excellent account of the extent to which expression of experience in these accounts belonged in part to others (*Pilgrimage*, pp. 8, 136–75); he also has underlined the ways in which travel stories are linked to other literary genres (see his two chapters on 'Narratives of experience').

17 Greffin Affagart, *Relation de la Terre Sainte, 1533–1534*, ed. J. Chavanon, 1902, p. 4; on the experience of travelling at this time see J. Céard and J.C. Margolin, *Voyager à la Renaissance*, Paris, 1987.

18 See Gregory Martin, *Roma sancta*, ed. G.B. Parks, Rome, 1968. His uncompromising enjoyment at the ruin of Rome was expressed through lines borrowed from a work of the neo-Latin poet J. Vitalis whose succinct '*Rome* in Rome is no more' echoed through the poetry devoted to Rome in the sixteenth century; see Tucker, *The Poet's Odyssey*, for a synthesis of this continuing tradition.

19 Montaigne, *Journal de voyage*, pp. 100–1; for an analysis of these apparently contradictory impulses which the sight of Rome provoked in Montaigne, see my article: 'Contradictory impulses'.

20 Michel Bideaux has edited this anonymous text, *Voyage d'Italie*, [1606], Geneva, 1981, p. 72.

21 Fifteenth-century Italian writers had stressed the role of Fate in reducing Rome to the ruins which nonetheless evoked its ancient splendour; see, in particular, Poggio Bracciolini, *De fortunae varietate urbis Romae et de ruina eiusdem descriptio*, 1448 [begun in 1431], and Bernardo Rucellai, *De urbe Roma*, 1494.

22 Bibliothèque Nationale, Ms fr. 14660, Villeroy, 'Memoire de tout mon voege fait en italie, l'an 1583, avec les choses remercables que l'i ay veues'. Villeroy is less laconic about his dancing and fencing lessons.

23 His father, Germain Audebert, was very anxious that his son should meet the most learned and profit from his journey as he himself had done in the 1540s when he studied in Bologna. The poem *Roma* which describes the principal statues of Rome (Laocoön, Apollo, Cleopatra, two Venuses, the column of Trajan and the equestrian statue of Marcus Aurelius) was dedicated to Cardinal Alessandro Farnese. His poem in praise of Rome was published in Paris by J. du Puy in 1585.

24 *Mémoires de la vie de Jacques Auguste de Thou*, 16 vols, London, 1734, I, 33; and Paul de Foix, 'Lettres', Bibliothèque Nationale, Ms Dupuy 712, f. 18.

25 The activities of Muret and his friends recalled the erudite academy founded on the Quirinale some hundred years earlier by Pomponius Laetus and his antiquarian colleagues.

26 Tarde, *A la rencontre*, p. 39; and Audebert acknowledged the benefits he derived from Carlo Sigonio on his visit to Bologna, *Voyage*, I, p. 187.

27 A letter to Cardinal du Perron in Rome, 26 May 1607, published in the cardinal's correspondence, *Les Oeuvres diverses*, Paris, Antoine Estiene, 1629, pp. 620–1.

28 See E. Jullien de la Boullaye, *Etude sur la vie et les oeuvres de Jean Duvet* [1485–c. 1555], Paris, 1976, p. 17.

29 C. Malcolm Brown has explored the significance for Heemskerck of the painter's stay in Rome, 'Martin van Heemskerck. The Villa Madonna Jupiter and the Gonzaga correspondence files', *Gazette des Beaux Arts*, vol. 94, 1979, pp. 49–60. The sketchbook was edited by Hülsen and Egger, *Die Römischen*

Skizzenbücher von Marten van Heemskerck, Berlin, 1916.

30 A typical hunter after art and intellectual improvement in the next century was Monsieur de Monconys, who recorded his experiences in detail in his *Journal des voyages*, Paris, 1665, especially pp. 438–71.

31 Villamont, *Voyages*, sig. ã iij.

32 Writing to an unidentified Roman prelate, Erasmus exclaimed: 'Certe animus est Romae, nec usque libentius huius corpusculi Sarcinam deposuero', cited in P. de Nolhac, *Erasme en Italie*, Paris, 1898, p. 118.

33 Jean Antoine de Baïf, *Oeuvres*, ed. Marty Laveaux, 5 vols, Paris, 1881–90, IV, p. 278.

34 See A. Heulhard, *Rabelais, ses voyages en Italie, son exil à Metz*, Paris, 1891.

35 Montaigne, *Journal de voyage*, p. 90.

36 Olivier de Magny, *Oeuvres*, Paris, 1885, pp. 112–15, 'Ode sur son partement de France pour aller en Italye, à Pierre de Pascal, Historiographe du Roy'.

37 *Voyage d'Italie*, ed. Bideaux, p. 72.

38 The extent to which travellers had come prepared by their reading is examined in several communications given at the international conference devoted to *Montaigne et l'Italie. Atti del congresso internazionale di studi di Milano–Lecco, 26–30 ottobre, 1988*, ed. E. Balmas, *Biblioteca del Viaggio in Italia*, no. 38, Geneva, 1991.

39 Petrarch, *Rerum Familiarum*, Book VI, no. 2, letter dated 1337, translated by Aldos Bernardo, New York, 1975, II, 14.

40 Brantôme was in Rome in 1559 and in 1565; see Robert D. Cottrell, *Brantôme. The Writer as Portraitist of his Age*, Geneva, 1970; and G. de Piaggi, 'Les Voyages de Brantôme en Italie', *Annales de la Faculté des Lettres et Sciences Humaines d'Aix*, vol. 40, 1966, pp. 79–116; the passage from Brantôme is cited in Piaggi, pp. 84–5.

41 *Petrus Paschali oratio de legibus, Romae apud sanctae Eustachium habita*, Lyon, 1548, cited at length by Pierre de Nolhac, *Ronsard et l'humanisme*, Paris, 1966, pp. 277 ff.

42 See Roland Mortier's survey, *La Poétique des ruines en France*, Geneva, 1974. The automatic link between ruins and greatness became a commonplace: see L. Meilliet's translation of Scipione Ammirato's *Discorsi* [1574], *Discours politiques et militaires*, Paris, 1619, p. 123.

43 Sigmund Freud, *Civilization and its Discontents*, ed. James Strachey, London, 1982, pp. 6–8.

44 Florisel de Claveson, 'Voyage', Bibliothèque Nationale Ms Clairambault 1006, f. 29v.

45 Blaise de Monluc, *Commentaires*, ed. Paul Courteault, Paris, 1964, p. 341.

46 Tarde, *A la rencontre*, p. 74.

47 Villamont, *Voyages*, f. 218.

48 *Voyage d'Italie*, ed. Bideaux, p. 74: 'd'autant que l'opinion de plusieurs est que, dans la Rome ancienne, toutes ces choses que l'on represente à présent ne furent jamais toutes ensemble et à un coup, ains successivement, comme il advient qu'un roy ou seigneur ruine une chose pour en ediffier une autre, l'enclos de Rome me semblant par la veue du lieu trop petit pour avoir peu contenir tant de choses à la fois' (especially as in the opinion of several scholars, all those things that are currently shown were never together at a single time in ancient Rome, but successively, as it happens when a lord or king destroys one edifice to build another; from looking at its site, the compass of Rome seems to me to be too small to contain so many things, all at once!).

49 Montaigne, *Journal de voyage*, p. 92.

50 Tarde, *A la rencontre*, pp. 69–70.

51 The same list of generalizations and technical terms recurs in his description of St Peter's, ibid., p. 68: 'sera la plus grande et la plus belle

église du monde, les surpassant toutes en grandeur, forme, artifice, embellissements, voutes, incrustations, pavés, niches, colonnes, moulures, rétables, revêtements, et bref, en toutes choses' (will be the greatest and most beautiful church in the world, surpassing all others in size, form, invention, embellishment, vaults, decorations, pavings, niches, columns, mouldings, reredos, surfaces; in short, in all things).

52 Rigaud, *Bref recueil*, f. 59, provides a good example of less careful accounting in his description of that minor official Cestius' tomb: 'certes c'est une belle grande oeuvre, grand antique, formée à quatre carres, et en pointes de Piramide, toute de grosses pierres de marbre, plus haute de beaucoup que les tours et murailles, la montre de chasque costé d'icelle, le carré esgal, et presque douze pas à chascun' (certainly, it is a beautiful work of great antiquity, built in four squares with Pyramid points, all of large marble stone, much higher than the towers and walls, and visible from each side; the four squares are of equal length, almost twelve paces each one).

53 It is interesting to contrast Villamont's more abrupt mention of the Temple and tomb of Bacchus, where he remains at a much greater distance from what he describes: *Voyages*, f. 31, 'D'avantage ie ne passeray soubs silence qu'à un bon mille de Rome, est le temple de Bacchus soustenu pareillement sur colonnes de marbre, où l'on void son sepulchre, faict d'une grande piece de porphire couronnée d'autres petits Bacchus qui tiennent chacun une coupe en la main et le raisin en l'autre.' (In addition, it shall not pass unremarked that at a good mile's distance from Rome is the temple of Bacchus, similarly supported on marble columns

where one can see his tomb, made out of a great piece of porphyry, crowned with tiny bacchic figures, each one holding a cup in one hand and a bunch of grapes in the other.)

54 Montaigne, *Journal de voyage*, p. 128.

55 Tarde, *A la rencontre*, p. 76.

56 Villamont, *Voyages*, ff. 292–2v; André Thevet, *La Cosmographie du Levant*, Lyon, Jean de Tournes and G. Gazeau, 1554, p. 93.

Chapter 2   The Guidebook

1 The general design and development of guidebooks has been charted by Ludwig Schudt, *Le guide di Roma*, Vienna, 1930.

2 Among the many texts which refused to describe and referred the reader to existing guidebooks are Capgrave (1450); André Thevet, *Cosmographie* (1554); Sir Thomas Hoby (1549); le sieur de Villamont, *Voyages* (1598; in Italy, 1588–92); Jean Rigaud, *Bref recueil* (1601); Pierre Bergeron, 'Le Voyage d'Italie' (1601–3); J.J. Bouchard, *Journal de voyage* (1606); and anonymous travellers (1611–12), Bibliothèque Nationale, Ms fr. 19013.

3 Throughout his *Voyage d'Italie*, Audebert refers to the most obvious authorities on the subject, both ancient and modern: these include Pliny, Silius Italicus, Livy, Lucan, Dionysius of Halicarnassus, and, among modern writers, Flavio Biondo, Fauno, Lambin, Leandro Alberti, Sigonio and Guicciardini.

4 Giovanni's complete dependence on the words of others to describe what he saw has been set out in full by Richard Schofield, 'Giovanni da Tolentino goes to Rome: a description of the antiquities in Rome in 1490', *Journal of the Warburg and Courtauld Institutes*, vol. 43, 1980, pp. 246–56.

5 Rabelais' text is given in Richard

Cooper's *Rabelais et l'Italie*, Geneva, 1991, pp. 99–103 (translated pp. 103–4); Marliani's work is discussed briefly by Schudt, *Le guide*, pp. 370–4.

6 For the detail of Rabelais' contribution, see Richard Cooper, 'Rabelais and the *Topographia Antiquae Romae* of Marliani', *Etudes Rabelaisiennes*, vol. 14, 1977, pp. 71–87.

7 Thevet visited Rabelais in Rome in 1548, see ibid., p. 59.

8 Bartholomeo Marliani, *L'antiquità di Roma*, translated into Italian by Hercole Barbarosa da Terni, Rome, A. Bladum, 1548.

9 Giacomo Lauro's engravings were published in 1612 in Rome; his preface to Sigismond III lists all the writers to whom he is indebted; Gamucci's text, *Libro quattro dell'antichita della città di Roma*, was published in Venice in 1565, by Gio. Varisco & Compagni, the reference to Marliani is on p. 107; sixteen drawings were taken from Dosio and these reappeared in the latter's own work, engraved by Cavalieri, *Urbis Romae aedificorum*, Rome, 1569. Pirro Ligorio borrowed from others (notably Andreas Fulvius) and, in turn, his work became a significant resource for engravers and architects in particular; Serlio and Du Pérac made use of his manuscripts as well as Lauro.

10 *La Cosmographie universelle* was published in Paris in 1575 by Michel Sonnius. Belleforest's most recent biographer, Michel Simonin, has found no evidence to suggest that Belleforest travelled to Italy, *Vivre de sa plume au XVIe siècle ou la carrière de François de Belleforest*, Geneva, 1992.

11 See Schudt, *Le guide*, for an analysis of these editions, pp. 185–232.

12 Rigaud, *Bref recueil*; all the marginalia, in fact, refer to the *Mirabilia*.

13 On Calvus' powers of invention, see Phillip J. Jacks, 'The simulacrum of

Fabio Calvo: a view of Roman architecture *all'antica* in 1527', *Art Bulletin*, vol. 72, September 1990, pp. 453–81, and his book, *The Antiquarian, passim*.

14 Cited and translated by André Chastel, *Le Sac de Rome, 1527*, Paris, 1984, p. 204. Calvus' book, *Antiquae urbis Romae cum regionibus simulacrum*, was published in Rome in 1527, the year of his death.

15 These works were published many times. Dempster's approach, for example, is at once comprehensive and concerned with detailed linguistic niceties. He lists buildings no longer there, and describes minutely gods whose form had been forgotten. His citations are precise and factual and his own comments are interspersed among the quotations. Dempster's work was published with substantial notes by J. Rosinus, *Antiquitatum Romanorum Corpus Absolutissimum*, Amsterdam, Blaviana, 1685.

16 Fauno, *Compendio di Roma antica*, Venice, 1552; and *De antiquitatibus urbis Romae*, Venice, 1549.

17 Panvinius' 'Theatrum' is discussed in full by Labrot, *L'Image de Rome*, pp. 73 ff.

18 Francesco Albertini, *Opusculum di mirabilia novae et veteris urbis Romae*, Lyon, 1520 (first edition, Rome, 1510).

19 Luigi Contarini, *L'Antiquita, sito, chiese, reliquie et statue di Roma*, Naples, 1569.

20 J. Rosinus, *Romanorum antiquitatum corpus*, Bâle, 1583 and *Romanorum antiquitatum libri decem*, Lyon, 1585.

21 Flavio Biondo, *Roma instaurata* (written about 1446, published 1481) and *Roma triumphans* (written about 1459, published 1482), were translated by Fauno in 1542, and reprinted in both Latin and Italian many times.

22 Andreas Fulvius, *Antiquitatis urbis*, Rome, 1527, ff. ciii–cvir.

23 Girolamo Ferrucci, *L'antichita di*

Roma di Andrea Fulvius antiquario Romano, Rome, 1588.

24 Details are given on f. 219v in the Italian, 1543 Venice edition, of Fulvius' Latin text.

25 The helmeted figure would be well known from its depiction at the base of the column of Antoninus Pius; from the collection of Cardinal Cesi, and from the engraving in Cavalieri, *Antiquarum statuarum*, Rome, 1561, plates 1–6.

26 The 1549 edition of Fauno, *De antiquitatibus urbis Romae*, sig. Tv r.

27 Details on the early ownership of Ligorio's manuscripts and their compilation are given by David R. Coffin, 'Pirro Ligorio on the nobility of the arts', *Journal of the Warburg and Courtauld Institutes*, vol. 27, 1964, pp. 191–210. Eighteen manuscripts are in Turin; others at Oxford, Naples and Paris. I have looked at the Bibliothèque Nationale, Ms it. 1129, dedicated to Ippolito d'Este, which gives drawings and a careful description of each edifice, often with measurements, and at the manuscripts preserved in Turin; I have also consulted the photocopies of the manuscripts available in the Print Room at the Warburg Institute. Thomas Ashby has analysed in detail the Oxford manuscript, 'The Bodleian Ms of Pirro Ligorio', *Journal of Roman Studies*, vol. 9, 1919, pp. 170–201. Essays in the collection *Pirro Ligorio, Artist and Antiquary*, ed. Robert W. Gaston, Silvana, 1988, in particular that of Howard Burns, 'Pirro Ligorio's reconstruction of ancient Rome', pp. 19–92, discuss the important interplay of text and image in Ligorio's manuscripts.

28 The extension of Ligorio's title announces the contentious tone: 'con le paradosse del mesismo auttore, quasi confutano la commune opinione sopra varii luoghi della città di Roma' (with paradoxes by the same author, mostly disproving the common view of various places in the city of Rome).

29 Ligorio lent his manuscripts to artist friends like Du Pérac, and it is known that Panvinius copied and even traced many of Ligorio's designs from his manuscripts; see the discussion in E. Mandowsky and C. Mitchell, *Pirro Ligorio's Roman Antiquities. The Drawings in Ms XIII B 7 in the National Library in Naples, Studies of the Warburg Institute*, London, 1963. They were also used by Dal Pozzo, who had drawings copied from Naples, Turin, and from the Vatican libraries; see C. Vermeule, 'The Dal Pozzo album. Drawings of classical antiquities', *Art Bulletin*, 38, 1956, pp. 31–46, and by the Lafréry workshop in Rome; see Claude Duchet's acknowledgements, plates 35 and 36 in the British Museum copy of the *Speculum Romae magnificentiae* (174 c 31).

30 The text reads: 'Je suis parfaitement obligé à Dom Grossedo; je voudrois l'avoir desja veu evesque et Cardinal et tout ce qu'il voudroit en recompense de son honnesteté et de son erudition. J'ay cherché dans les brouillons que je desseigné à Turin dans sa chambre et ay trouvé que les deux medailles dont je voudrois avoir les desseigns exacts sont de l'empereur M. Aurele . . .' (I am deeply obliged to Dom Grossedo. I would have wished to see him already bishop and cardinal or anything he likes as recompense for his civility and erudition. I have examined the sketches I made in his room at Turin and have found that the two medals of which I wanted to have exact copies are of the emperor Marcus Aurelius) (f. 220). The comments have been glued to the page of the manuscript and do not appear to relate to its immediate context.

31 Pirro Ligorio, *Descrittione della superba et magnificentissima Villa Tiburtina Hadriana*, in *Thesaurus antiquitatem et historiarum Italiae*, ed. J.G. Graevius, Leiden, 1723; and Ligorio's manuscript in the British Library. For a discussion of the value of Ligorio's reconstruction of Hadrian's villa, see William L. Macdonald and John A. Pinto, *Hadrian's Villa and its Legacy*, New Haven, 1995. For Ligorio's work at Tivoli, consult D.R. Coffin, *The Villa d'Este at Tivoli*, Princeton, 1990.

32 An indication of the extent of that influence can be seen in the letters of Peiresc in which he asks his agent in Rome (Claude Menestrier) to make copies of Ligorio's manuscripts in the Vatican Library which recorded series of 'statues et marbres de bronze', *La Correspondance de Claude-Fabri de Peiresc*, ed. Tamizey de Larroque, 9 vols, Paris, 1894, V, p. 786.

33 Bibliothèque Nationale, Estampes Fb7a Rés; Woeriot had also developed an interest in Roman funerals, basing his information on Lilio Gregorio Giraldi; he engraved the funeral rituals in *Pinax Iconicus. Antiquorum de variorum in sepulturus ritum*, Lyon, 1556, published and therefore more widely available, and dedicated this time to the duc de Lorraine himself.

34 G. Franzini later added these further books depicting palaces and churches, *Palatia procerum Romae urbis*, and *Templa dea et sanctis eius Romae dicata*, both Rome, 1596.

35 G.B. Cavalieri, *Antiquarum statuarum urbis Romae*, I and II in 1574; III and IV in 1594; C. Alberti, *Antiquorum statuarum urbis Romae . . . icones*, Rome, 1585.

36 Panvinius' work, *Respublicae Romanae commentarium libri res*, appeared in 1558; and Jules César Boulenger's *De circo romano* in 1598. Graevius in his *Thesaurus antiqui-*

tatem Romanorum, IX, Lyon, 1698, made available all the sixteenth-century works on this subject: Panvinius, *Respublicae romanae*, pp. 1–574, and pp. 1061–144; Boulenger, *De circo romano*, pp. 575–1060; Lipsius, *De amphitheatro*, pp. 1161–270.

37 Panvinius, *Respublicae Romanae*. For a detailed discussion of Sigonio's labours, his problems and his borrowings in composing *De regno Italiae* see William McCuaig, *Carlo Sigonio. The Changing World of the Late Renaissance*, Princeton, 1989.

38 Polletti's text was also republished in Latin in Douai in 1591 as *Forum romanorum*.

39 Three years later Angelio wrote a long epistle on the public and private buildings of Rome, *De privatum, publicorumque, aedificorum urbis Romae*, Florence, 1589.

40 It is interesting to note that Leandro Alberti's *Descrittione di tutta Italia* (which Audebert used extensively during his journey through Italy) was dedicated (in 1550) to Henri II and Catherine de' Medici.

41 The full title of Montjosieu's work is *Gallus Romae hospes ubi multa antiquorum monumenta explicantur*, Rome, 1585.

42 Labrot, *L'Image de Rome*, note 11, p. 392 translates Montjosieu's text: 'nous n'avons pas voulu laisser l'extérieur du Temple [Pantheon] sans ornement, ainsi en avons-nous reconstitué la forme primitive, autant qu'il était possible, dans son intégralité' (we did not wish to leave the exterior of the Temple without decoration, so we have, as far as possible, given it back its primitive form in its completeness).

43 Montjosieu's debt to Vasari is made plain by G. Rèpaci-Courtois, 'Vasari, source de Blaise de Vigenère', *Revue de l'Art*, vol. 80, 1988, pp. 48–51.

44 See Gaston, *Pirro Ligorio*, p. 14.

45 Antonio Labacco had detailed the

varied fragments of buildings which could still be seen in Trajan's forum, *Libro appartenente a l'architettura*, Rome, 1576, ff. 7–16 (first edition, Rome, 1557).

46 Dosio, *Urbis Romae*, plates 35 and 36 (Trajan's column), plates 39 and 40 (Thermae), plates 43–6 (Diocletian's baths). For the care which Dosio took in drawing objects and buildings observed, see Carolyn Valone, 'G.A. Dosio and his patrons', Northwestern University Dissertation, North Western, 1972, pp. 115 ff., and her article, 'Giovanni Antonio Dosio: the Roman years', *Art Bulletin*, vol. 58, 1976, pp. 528–41.

47 Aldrovandi described ninety-three collections although he did not list all their contents; for a discussion of his approach, see Phyllis Pray Bober, 'Francesco Lisc's collection of antiquities. Footnote to a new edition of Aldrovandi', *Essays in the History of Art Presented to Rudolf Wittkower*, London, 1969, pp. 119–22.

48 Theodor Zwingler, *Methodus apodemica*, Basle, 1577, cited and translated in Michel de Montaigne *Journal de voyage*, ed. François Rigolot, Paris, 1992, p. xx.

49 Montaigne, *Journal*, p. 103.

50 Vincerzo Scamozzi, *Discorsi sopra l'antichità di Roma*, Venice, 1583; Ligorio also presented multiple drawings of different aspects of the same building: see his plans of the Pantheon, Ms [Turin] lib. xiiii, ff. 48–54.

51 On each engraving, Lauro inscribed a short explanation of the building represented and added its current [*hodie*] state and name, *Antiquae urbis splendor*, Rome, 1612, plate 4, 'Roma vetus et nova' (Rome, old and new).

52 André Thevet assured his reader that such was 'la realité . . . icy exhibée avec une telle naifveté, que sans vous mouiller le pied, dans vostre cabinet vous pouvez apprendre les plus beaux et signalez secrets de la marine' (the realism evident here, in all its simplicity, so that without wetting your toes you can, in your study, learn the most important and delightful secrets of navigation . . .). And, later in the same manuscript, 'àfin de vous faire toucher au doigt plus assurément la cognoissance que devez esperer' (in order to make you more confidently touch with your finger the knowledge that you hope to gain) *Le grand Insulaire et pelotage* [1583], Bibliothèque Nationale, Ms fr. 15452 ff. 6 and 7.

Chapter 3   Appropriation and Transformation

1 Art objects were admired and collected in ancient times, but – as far as can be ascertained – such collecting was not resumed until the fourteenth century. On collecting, see J. Alsop's article in the *Times Literary Supplement*, 1948, p. 891, and his book *The Rare Art Collections*, London, 1982. There is now a considerable body of work on this phenomenon: *The Origins of Museums. The Cabinet of Curiosities in the Sixteenth and Seventeenth Centuries*, ed. O. Impey and A. McGregor, Oxford, 1985; K. Pomian, *Collectors and Curiosities: Paris and Venice, 1500–1800*, Venice, 1990; and *The Cultures of Collecting*, ed. J. Elsner and R. Cardinal, London, 1994.

2 For an account of the great Italian collections of the second half of the sixteenth century, see R. Weiss, *The Renaissance Discovery of Classical Antiquity*, Oxford, 1969, pp. 171–80, where he argues that coin collecting had become such a mania by the mid-fifteenth century that good coins became scarce; and David R. Coffin, *Gardens and*

Gardening in Papal Rome, Princeton, 1991, who traces to Pomponio Leto in the 1470s the earliest collection of antiquities to decorate a residence. Most recently, Clare Robertson has provided a portrait of a great collector (advised by humanists such as Fulvio Orsini) in *'Il gran Cardinale': Alessandro Farnese, Patron of the Arts*, New Haven, 1992.

3 Burroughs, *From Signs to Design.*

4 Charles VIII, *Lettres*, Paris, 1903, IV, pp. 187–8.

5 The use of painters and sculptors to copy works which Charles VIII admired on his journey is recorded by J. Jacquiot, 'Des Médaillons italiens, diplomates et voyageurs', *Voyager à la Renaissance*, ed. J. Céard and J.C. Margolin, Paris, 1987, pp. 115–22.

6 Bibliothèque Nationale, N. a. fr. 7644, ff. 195–5v, *reçu* dated le 24 décembre, 1495. A further manuscript note (Ms fr. 11350, dated 1497–8) published by A. Montaiglon in the *Archives de l'art français*, 1851–52, I, pp. 100–25, gives the wages paid to the 'ouvriers et gens de mestier qu'il a fait venir de son royaume de Secille pour ediffier et faire ouvrages à son devis et plaisir, à la mode d'Ytallye' (workmen and skilled labour whom he invited into his kingdom from Sicily to carry out works in Italian style for his schemes and pleasure). Charles VIII shipped Neapolitan bindings from the collections of the Aragonese kings in 1495 to the château de Blois; see A. Hobson, *Humanists and Bookbinders*, Cambridge, 1989, p. 178; for the effect of the king's descent into Italy, see Silvia Fabrizio Costa and Frank La Braxa, 'La Descente de Charles VIII vue par l'humaniste Filippo Beroaldo l'Ancien', pp. 215–24, *Actes du Colloque International*, Université de la Sorbonne nouvelle, 1990, published Paris, 1992.

7 La Popelinière was, perhaps, the first historian to recognize the influential role of Charles VIII on the dissemination of Italian taste into France. Towards the end of his *L'Histoire des histoires*, p. 266, he claimed that 'Les François ne firent oncques estat de l'Architecture que depuis le Roy Charles Neufiesme [*sic* for VIII], qui retournant avec les despouilles d'Italie en France, amena nombre des plus rares ouvriers en bois, pierre, et autres matieres propres à edifices. Lesquels apres qu'on eust veu l'artifice du chasteau qu'il fit par eux eslever sur le bord de Loire en Amboise, furent enfin suyvis et comme semez par toute la France.' (The French paid little attention to Architecture until King Charles brought back spoils from Italy into France along with a number of workmen gifted in shaping wood and stone and other materials suitable for building. After people saw the craft of the château which he built at Amboise, on the Loire, others followed suit and were scattered all about through France.)

The taste was shared by the king's servants: Robertet, for instance, had a copy of a bronze David by Michelangelo made for his château de Bury, near Blois; see Edith Balas, 'Michelangelo's *Concetti* (1505) in the château de Blois', *Gazette des Beaux Arts*, vol. 101, 1983, p. 33.

8 Cited and discussed in full by Chastel, *Le Sac de Rome*, p. 293.

9 For the number and range of antiquities known in the Renaissance, see P.P. Bober, 'The census of antique works of art known to the Renaissance artists', *Acts of the XX International Congress of the History of Art*, 3 vols, Princeton, 1963, II, pp. 88–9.

10 Mauro, *Delle antichità di Roma*, pp. 122–40.

11 See M. van der Meulen, 'Cardinal Cesi's antique sculpture garden',

Burlington Magazine, vol. 116, 1974, pp. 14–24.

12 Gabriel Symeoni, *Les Illustres Observations antiques*, Lyon, 1558, p. 48.

13 Cited in J. Paquier, *Jerome Aléandre: lettres familières*, Paris, 1909, no. xxxv, p. 59; and André Thevet, *Les Vrais Pourtraits et vies des hommes illustres*, Paris, 1584, sig. b i; Thevet refers particularly to the collections of Henri II, Michel de l'Hospital, Catherine de' Medici, and Maurice Scève. For Thevet's own collection of coins, see the comments of Arnold van Buchel, *Journal* [1585], Paris, 1899, p. 177: 'C'est là (dans l'église des Franciscains) qu'était le moine André Thevet, géographe du roi, qui a rapporté des divers pays qu'il a visités une collection de monnaies anciennes, de statues, de pierres variées et de toutes sortes d'objets des pays exotiques.' (It is there – in the church of the Franciscans – that the monk André Thevet, geographer royal, lived; he brought back from many countries a collection of ancient coins, statues, different stones, and all sorts of objects from exotic lands.)

14 Cited in Pierre de Nolhac, *La Bibliothèque de Fulvio Orsini*, Paris, 1887, p. 56.

15 '. . . et autres infinies antiquitez que je pourrois vous déduire n'estoit que j'évite prolixité, tant qu'il m'est possible' (and an infinity of other antiquities which I could list were it not that I seek to avoid prolixity as much as possible), *Cosmographie*, II, f. 731 bis.

In addition to guidebooks there were, of course, pattern books of artefacts which were copied in France; see Agostino Veneziano's *Recueil de vases*, drawn in the 1550s and reissued in 1680 in Paris.

16 Bertrand Jestaz, 'L'Exportation des marbres de Rome, 1535–1571', *Mélanges d'archéologie et d'histoire*, vol. 75, Ecole française de Rome,

Paris, 1963, pp. 415–66; and A. Bertolotti, *Artisti francesi in Roma*, Mantua, 1886, pp. 49–50.

17 Richard Cooper, *Litterae in tempore belli. Etudes sur les relations littéraires italo-françaises pendant les guerres d'Italie*, Geneva, 1997, p. 238 draws attention to this correspondence.

18 Pirro Ligorio was excavating the villa from 1550, and Cardinal Maffei wrote regularly to Jean du Bellay commenting on his progress: see Macdonald and Pinto, *Hadrian's Villa and Its Legacy*, p. 289.

19 Michel de l'Hospital, *Poésies complètes*, translated from Latin into French by Louis Baudy de Nalèche, Paris, 1857, p. 5.

20 A full description of the growth of Cardinal du Bellay's collection can be found in Coffin, *Gardens*, pp. 67–8. Details of the sale are in Bibliothèque Nationale, Ms Dupuy 264, ff. 39–40, 'Atto di vendità delle collezioni del card. du Bellay, Roma 29–30 mai, 1556'; see also L. Clédat, 'Le Musée de sculpture du cardinal du Bellay à Rome', *Courrier de l'Art*, vol. 3, 1883, pp. 99–100, 206–7.

21 Marie Montembault and John Schloder, *L'Album Canini du Louvre et la collection d'antiques de Richelieu*, Paris, 1988, p. 31.

22 The detail of this incident is in the *Correspondance du Cardinal Jean du Bellay*, ed. R. Scheurer, Société de l'histoire de France, 2 vols, Paris, 1969 and 1975, I, no. 184. Other purchases and exports are reported in letters pp. 404 and 415.

23 Reported by Heulhard, *Rabelais, ses voyages . . .* , p. 319.

24 Ibid., p. 315. It should be pointed out that the traffic was not always one way; see the books and bindings purchased in Lyon and sent to Rome by the papal nuncio in 1558, *Correspondance des nonces en France, Lenzi et Gualterio, légation du Cardinal Trivultio*, ed. J. Lestocquoy, Rome, 1977, p. 115.

25 Heulhard, *Rabelais, ses voyages . . .* , p. 344.

26 Montembault and Schloder, *L'Album Canini*, p. 41.

27 Letters of 2 July and 27 August, 1534, in Bibliothèque Nationale, Ms Dupuy 264, ff. 37–8, 39–40. On François I's almost indiscriminate buying of antiquities and objects, see Caroline Elam, 'Art in the service of liberty. Battista della Palla, art agent for François Ier', *I Tatti Studies. Essays in the Renaissance*, vol. 5, 1993, pp. 33–109; letters to Filippo Strozzi stressed the need to have 'large quantities of excellent antiquities of whatever sort' (21 January, 1529).

28 See *Correspondance du cardinal François de Tournon*, ed. Michel François, Paris, 1951, pp. 515–16.

29 His collections were eagerly scrutinized by foreign ambassadors, who reported the marvels to their masters; see, for example, the letter of Wallop to Henry VIII concerning the diverse moulds which François I had ordered, W. McAllister Johnson, 'On some neglected images of the Renaissance diplomatic correspondence', *Gazette des Beaux Arts*, vol. 79, 1972, pp. 51–4; for the contents of his collection, see Janet Cox-Rearick, *The Collection of Francis I: Royal Treasures*, New York, 1996.

30 'Des mil escuz que le Roy me fist bailler pour luy acheter ici livres et antiquailles, par le compte que j'envoye par l'homme de Mr d'Arranches [Jean de Langeac], vous verrez que j'en ay employé plus de 700 et pense qu'il ne les trouvera pas mal employez' (of the 1,000 écus which the king sent to me in order to buy books and antique objects, you will see from the account which I've sent via M. d'Arranches that I have used up 700 of them, and I do not think I've used them badly): 21 November 1526, Ferrare to Mont-

morency, cited in V.L. Bourrilly, *Guillaume du Bellay, seigneur de Langey, 1491–1543*, Paris, 1905, p. 37.

31 The statue had been found in the soil near Naples, and when François I had it installed at Amboise, it excited universal approbation; see Emile Picot, *Les Italiens en France au XVIe siècle*, Bordeaux, 1918, p. 243.

32 According to the most recent work on these moulds, Primaticcio bought 125 pieces and sent 133 crates to Fontainebleau 'esquelles estoient toutes les medalles et figures de marbre antique, et aussy plusieurs mousles en plastre, mouslés à Rome sur autres figures antiques' (which were all models and antique marble figures as well as plaster moulds made in Rome from other ancient figures), quoted by S. Favier from *Les Comptes des bâtiments du roi* in 'Les Collections de marbres antiques sous François Ier': *Revue du Louvre et des musées de France*, vol. 24, 1974, pp. 153–6. The quantity of objects commissioned from agents in Rome is testified by Vasari: see his comments on the merchant Giovanni Battista Puccini, *Lives of the Most Eminent Painters, Sculptors and Architects*, translated by J. Foster, 8 vols, London, 1881, III, pp. 198, 204–6. See also Sylvie Pressouyre, 'Les Fontes de Primatice à Fontainebleau', *Bulletin Monumental*, vol. 127, 1969, pp. 223–39; and C. Scaillerez, *François Ier et ses artistes*, Paris, 1992.

33 Pierre Belon, *Les Observations de plusieurs singularitez et choses memorables*, Paris, 1553, f. 116; Symeoni, *Les Illustres Observations*, sig. A 2r; Sebastiano Serlio, *Tutte l'opere d'architettura*, Venice, 1584, Book 7, ch. 40, p. 96.

34 Serlio, *Tutte l'opere*, pp. 96–7 where he details: 'Et per che il Rè Francesco haveva condotto da Roma di molte statue, si vede in

questa loggia molti luoghi per allogar le. Ma nè quattro nichij maggiori v'andava il Laoconte, il Tevere, il Nilo et il Cleopatra. Et nel mezzo v'è una fenestra, che mirò sopra il giardino.' (And because the King François I had had brought from Rome many statues, there are many places to put them in this loggia. But in four large niches are placed the Laocoön, the Tiber, the Nile and Cleopatra. In the middle is a window which looks on to the garden.)

35 Thevet, *Cosmographie*, II, f. 536; he refers to the multiple sources of the king's acquisitions again later: II, f. 573v.

36 Belon, *Les Observations*, f. 116, and the *De admirabili operum antiquorum et rerum suspiciendarum praestantia*, Paris, 1553, preface.

37 Van Buchel, *Journal*, pp. 160–5.

38 See Bruce Boucher, 'Leone Leoni and Primaticcio's moulds of antique sculpture', *Burlington Magazine*, vol. 123, 1981, pp. 23–6; Henri II had a habit of giving precious things away: the two slaves of Michelangelo which had been acquired by Roberto Strozzi who had given them to the king were passed on to Anne de Montmorency in 1550; see Picot, *Les Italiens en France*, p. 247.

39 See Jean Adhémar, 'The collection of François Ier', *Gazette des Beaux Arts*, vol. 30, 1946, pp. 4–16; and C. Malcolm Brown, 'Major and minor collections of antiquities in documents of the later sixteenth century', *Art Bulletin*, vol. 46, 1984, pp. 296–507.

40 Symeoni, *Les Illustres Observations*, sig. A2v. On the patronage of the Guise and their collections, see I. Wardropper, 'Le Voyage italien de Primatice en 1550', *Bulletin de la Société de l'Histoire de l'Art Français*, 1981, pp. 27–31.

41 Lestocquoy (ed.), *Correspondance*, letter no. 105 (Paris, le 12 janvier 1559).

42 Cited in Lucien Romier, *Les Origines politiques des guerres de religion*, 2 vols, Paris, 1913–14, I, pp. 47–8. The same complaint was voiced by Vasari later: see Marie Geneviève de la Coste-Messelière, 'Pour la République florentine et pour le roi de France: Giovanbattista della Palla, des "orti oricellari" aux cachots de Pise', *Il se rendait à Rome: études offertes à André Chastel*, Paris, 1987, pp. 195–208.

43 Letter from Cardinal d'Armagnac to Montmorency (le 20 novembre 1554), cited in Charles de Grandmaison, 'Bustes antiques envoyées de Rome au connétable de Montmorency, 1554–1556', *Archives de l'Art Français*, Documents, IV, Paris, 1855–6, pp. 69–71.

44 Ibid.

45 Jean du Bellay, *Correspondance*, no. 87 (1530).

46 Bibliothèque Nationale, Ms Dupuy 265, f. 236 (letter of 26 July 1535); also cited in full, *Correspondance du cardinal Jean du Bellay*, I, p. 31.

47 *Correspondance du cardinal François de Tournon*, no. 676. Some idea of the size of Montmorency's collection can be gained from the inventories taken at various points and published by L. Mirot, 'L'Hôtel et les collections du connétable de Montmorency', *Bibliothèque de l'Ecole des Chartes*, vol. 79, 1918, pp. 347–69. One notes, for example, paintings of the overall plan of Rome, numerous statues (Mars, Pallas, Jupiter and Semele, Jupiter and child, Cupid), and a table inset with the heads of the twelve Caesars.

48 *Lettres de Catherine de Médicis*, ed. La Ferrière, 10 vols, Paris, 1880, X, pp. 23–4 (lettre du 21 janvier 1559). On Catherine's art collections see E. Bonnaffé, *Inventaire des meubles de Catherine de Médicis en 1589*, Paris, 1874.

49 *Lettres de Catherine de Médicis*, II, p. 394 (lettre du 20 octobre 1566).

50 Ibid., III, p. 1 (lettre du 9 janvier 1567).

51 Ibid., VII, pp. 296 and 517 (lettre du 24 novembre 1580).

52 Information provided by Anne Marie Lecoq, *François Ier imaginaire*, Paris, 1987, pp. 444 and 446.

53 See E. Müntz, *Les Antiquités de la ville de Rome aux XIV, XV et XVIe siècles*, Paris, 1886, p. 55.

54 Romier, *Les Origines politiques*, I, p. 90.

55 See Cooper, 'Collectors of coins . . .', p. 10.

56 Romier, *Les Origines politiques*, II, p. 325. The order was countermanded when Montmorency returned to power the following year.

57 *Lettres du cardinal Georges d'Armagnac*, ed. Tamizey de Larroque, Paris, 1874, p. 63 (letter from Rome to Montmorency, le 20 novembre 1554); Bibliothèque Nationale, Ms fr. 20442, f. 7 (letter from Lanssac to Montmorency, le 10 avril 1554); ibid., f. 267 (Lanssac to Montmorency, le 26 novembre 1555); and Romier, *Les Origines politiques*, II, p. 62.

58 *Lettres de Catherine de Médicis*, IX, p. 481.

59 Jean Louveau, *Trésor des antiquitez de Jaques de Strada*, Lyon, 1553, sig. ãã 4v. Strada's own collection, preserved in Vienna (Codex Minatus 21, 2), is titled *Antiquam statuarum tam deorum quam dearum . . . ad vivam depictae atque quam fidelissime repraesentatae*.

60 See Cooper, 'Collectors of coins . . .', p. 10.

61 Louveau, *Trésor*, sig. bbv; Guillaume du Choul, *Discours de la religion des anciens Romains illustré*, Lyon, 1556, p. 32. La Croix du Maine characterizes Grolier as 'l'un des plus curieux d'antiquitez (et surtout des Medailles) qu'autre qui fust de son temps' (one of the most knowledgeable about antiquities (and

especially medals) of his time), *Bibliothèque françoise*, Paris, 1584, p. 231.

62 Thevet, *Les Vrais Pourtraits*, f. 490v; Gabriel Symeoni, *Illustratione de gli epitaffi e medaglie antiche*, Lyon, 1558, p. 154. La Croix du Maine, *Bibliothèque*, p. 20, also lists Antoine de La Porte: 'Il a un cabinet fort excellent, remply de beaux livres et de medailles antiques' (He has a notable study filled with fine books and ancient medals), and (p. 110) Georges du Tronchay, sieur de Balladé. For other collectors at Lyon, see F. Planet, 'Jacob Spon et la science des médailles', *Jacob Spon. Un humaniste lyonnais du XVIIe siècle*, ed. R. Etienne and J.C. Mossière, Paris, 1993, pp. 129–36.

63 Thou, *Mémoires de la vie de . . .*, I, pp. 14 and 22; see also Pierre de Nolhac's account of French voyagers to Italy in search of enlightenment, in *La Bibliothèque*, pp. 5, 9, 13, 31, 65 and 68; another important *homme d'état* who built up a vast collection of medals was Guillaume du Vair who went to Italy at the same time as De Thou.

64 Cooper, 'Collectors of coins . . .', pp. 4–24.

65 *Actes de Henri II*, Paris, 1979 [1547], p. 270.

66 Antoine Le Pois, *Discours sur les medalles et graveures antiques, principalement Romaines*, Paris, Mamert Patisson, 1579, sig. ẽ iv.

67 Writing to the brothers Dupuy (le 6 décembre 1623, *La Correspondance*, I, p. 9), Peiresc specified: 'Parmy tout cela j'ay eu un si sensible desplaisir, m'estant apperceu que pendant mon absance on avoit vollé mon cabinet et emporté plus de 2,000 escus de medailles d'or, pierreries et autres singularitez.' (And amid all that, I suffered a great misfortune, noticing that in my absence my study had been broken into and over 2,000 écus of gold coins, gems, and other rarities had been stolen.)

68 Van Buchel, *Journal*, pp. 142–3.

69 For an overview of Lestoile's collecting habits and those of his time, see Margaret M. McGowan, 'Pierre de L'Estoile: amateur collector of medals and coins', *Seventeenth Century French Studies*, 1993, pp. 115–27. In order to show that he had really risen in the world, the merchant Ludovic Dadiaceto, having bought an *hôtel* in the rue Vieille-du-Temple, filled it with marble busts and statues brought from Rome, and with sixty portraits of historical subjects bought from the Gouffier sale; see Jacqueline Boucher, *La Cour de Henri III*, Paris, 1986, p. 103. By the early seventeenth century, collections by people of relatively humble status seem to have been more common; see, for example, the apothecary Samuel Veyrel from Xaintes who published the contents of his cabinet with a commentary in 1635, *Indice du cabinet de Samuel Veyrel*, Bordeaux, 1635.

70 Le Pois, *Discours*, f. 46v; Antonio Agustin was similarly convinced of the value of coins, which he regarded as more trustworthy witnesses than literary texts: see Charles Mitchell, 'Archaeology and romance in Renaissance Italy', *Italian Renaissance Studies*, ed. E.F. Jacob, London, 1960, pp. 455–83.

71 Guillaume Roville, *La Première Promptuaire des medalles*, Lyon, 1553, sig. ã3v.

72 Ibid., sig. ã2v.

73 Le Pois, *Discours*, f. 37; Thevet, *Les Vrais Pourtraits*, sig. ã iv v. On modes of perpetuating achievement consult Stephen K. Scher, *The Currency of Fame*, New York, 1994.

74 See my discussion in *Ideal Forms in the Age of Ronsard*, Berkeley, 1985, pp. 56–8.

75 Roville, *La Première Promptuaire*, sig. ã2v.

76 De Thou, *Mémoires*, II, p. 382.

77 Louveau, *Trésor*, sig. ãã4, and Le Pois, *Discours*, p. 13.

78 Thevet, *Cosmographie*, p. 135; Symeoni, *César renouvellé*, Lyon, 1558, pp. 11, 60, 73; and La Croix du Maine, *Bibliothèque*, p. 144.

79 Strada, 'Antiquam statuarum . . .', Vienna, Codex Minatus, 21, 2, sig. A2; Louveau's translation, *Trésor*, sig. bbv. For a collector of similar strength, see Suzanne Grunner von Hoerschnelmann's article, 'Basilius Amerbach and his coin collection', M.H. Crawford, C.R. Ligota and J.B. Trapp (eds), *Medals and Coins from Budé to Mommsen*, London, 1990, pp. 25–52.

80 Van Buchel, *Journal*, p. 162. See also Antoine du Verdier's comments on Du Choul's knowledge of Italy and his extensive collections, *La Bibliothèque*, Paris, 1585, p. 476.

81 Guillaume Du Choul, 'Antiquitez romaines', Biblioteca Reale [Turin], Ms Var. 212. I am indebted to Professor Richard Cooper for drawing my attention to this manuscript and for providing me with a photocopy. He plans to publish the manuscript together with other unpublished material from the Bibliothèque Nationale (Paris). He has worked extensively on Du Choul, see 'Collectors of coins . . .', pp. 7, 8, 21, 15–18 where he refers specifically to the antiquary's collection. There are two illustrations from the manuscript in Bruyère's article, 'Lyon romain retrouvé', *Jacob Spon*, ed. Etienne and Mossière, pp. 88 and 90.

82 Du Choul used the books of three numismatists and collectors; he was especially indebted to Aeneas Vico, the curator of the Este collection of coins, marbles and gems.

83 The habit of illustrating texts with drawings sent direct from Rome or copied from medals was fairly widespread; another example is Hieronymus Mercurialis whose *De arte gymnastica* (composed between

1569 and 1573) contained engravings furnished by Panvinius and Ligorio, who had copied them from medals; see Du Verdier, *La Bibliothèque*, p. 476.

84 Nicolas Favyer, *Figure et exposition des pourtraicts et dictons contenus es medailles de la conspiration des rebelles en France, opprimee et estaincte par le Roy Tres Chrestien Charles IX, le 24 jour d'Aoust, 1572*, Paris, 1572; the preliminary notes make clear that the king himself ordered the medals: sig. Aij, 'Exposition de deux sortes de medailles forgées par le commandement du Roy' (representation of two kinds of medals struck by order of the king).

85 Initially, Du Choul's works were often published separately and then, later, bound together as *Des Bains* and *Discours de la Castramentation* in 1557. His borrowings from Calvus are discussed by Jacks, *The Antiquarian*, note 150, p. 343.

86 A copy of this text was owned by a Parisian surgeon in 1567 (an indication of the range of interest in such matters); it is now preserved in the Scott Collection (City of Glasgow Art Gallery) where it is bound into a copy of *Le Discours de la religion*. The title page is signed 'François Rasse Des Neux, Chirurgeon à Paris, 1567'.

87 P.P. Bober, *Drawings after the Antique by Amico Aspertini. Sketches in the British Museum*, London, 1957.

88 See Norman W. Canedy, *The Roman Sketchbook of Girolamo da Carpi*, London, 1976.

89 Between 1625 and 1650 Cassiano dal Pozzo assembled in twenty-three volumes drawings 'after the antique' and classified thematically. He had sought both accuracy and completeness and had commissioned several skilled craftsmen to do the work; see C. Vermeule, 'The Dal Pozzo album'.

90 A report and instruction on the drawings he wishes to have made from Pozzo's collection was drawn up for 'Monsieur d'Arene, allant en Italie [1621]: il faut faire la cour au cavalr del Pozzo' (M. d'Arene, in going to Italy you must go and pay homage to Cavalier del Pozzo) (Peiresc, *Correspondance*, VII, p. 198). Later, Peiresc was to correspond with Pozzo: see *Lettres à Cassiano dal Pozzo, 1626–1637*, ed. Jean-François Lhote and Danielle Joyal, Adosa, 1989. In the Bibliothèque Nationale (Paris), Ms fr. 9532 preserves some of the drawings which Peiresc had made.

91 Cecilia Rizza has provided a detailed itinerary for Peiresc's Italian journey, *Peiresc in Italia*, Turin, 1965.

92 Peiresc referred to this particular inheritance in his letter to Alphonse de Rambervilliers, ed. Anne Reinbold, Paris, 1983, p. 63, no. 32. (lettre du 29 janvier 1622). It is mentioned by Marc Fumaroli, *Nicolas-Claude Fabri de Peiresc, prince de la République des Lettres*, Brussels, 1993, p. 4.

93 Cited in Georges Cahen-Salvador, *Un Grand Humaniste, Peiresc*, Paris, 1951, p. 251.

94 Agnès Bresson, 'Peiresc et le commerce des antiquités à Rome', *Gazette des Beaux Arts*, vol. 85, 1975, pp. 60–72, has drawn attention to the importance of this correspondence for the art of collecting, especially of the letters to Claude Menestrier (secretary to Cardinal Barberini) in volume V of the *Correspondance*.

95 Peiresc bought seven or eight copies of the book based on Jacques de Strada's collection of medals in 1615, then discovered he had given them all to friends and found himself without a copy (ibid., I, 150).

96 Peiresc, *Lettres*, ed. Reinbold, no. 39, p. 72.

97 See Peiresc's remarks in his letter to Holstenius (1628), *Correspondance*, V, 291.

98 The letter to Aubéry is ibid., p. 231. See Bibliothèque Nationale, Ms fr. 9532, ff. 15 ff. for Peiresc's copies from Serlio's *Terzo libro*, 1544.

99 For these drawings, see the 'Antiquitez du cabinet de Peiresc dessinées par le Poussin, Rubens et autres', Bibliothèque Nationale, Estampes Aa 53 and 54 Rés.

100 See Bibliothèque Nationale, N. a. fr. 1209, ff. 12–21.

101 On his search for books and manuscripts, and on the binding of his books, consult C. Coppens, 'Ein Bibliofiel van formaat: Nicolas-Claude Fabri de Peiresc (1580–1637)', *Ex Officina*, no. 2, Louvain, 1990, pp. 89–110.

102 See Peiresc, *Lettres*, ed. Reinbold, p. 11; Rambervilliers responded with enthusiasm, repeating Peiresc's lesson and attributing to medals, 'le tesmoignage de la vérité de l'histoire qu'on en peut tirer, aussy il y a de quoy contenter l'esprit en contemplant l'excellence de la sculpture ou graveure qui estoit alors florissante' (p. 12) (witness to the truth of history which one can derive from them as well as the pleasure which fills the mind as one contemplates the excellence of the sculpture or engraving of what flourished then).

103 References to the work of Rabel may be found in Peiresc, *Correspondance*, V, pp. 97, 119, 122, 125, 135, 136 and 140–1.

104 Claude Menestrier's *Medales* was published posthumously by his cousin in 1642, *Medales illustres des anciens empereurs et imperatrices de Rome*, Paris.

105 Bibliothèque Nationale, Ms fr. 9532, ff. 82–91.

106 The number of editions is clearly a sign of their popularity and of publishers' belief that they would make money from frequent reissues. It is interesting to note that Erizzo pays particular tribute to his publisher Girolamo Ruscelli, whom he describes as 'un huomo di molta dottina, et di perfetto giudizio' (a man of great learning and of perfect judgement), *Discorso* p. 57. Peiresc (le 6 février 1633) refers specifically to the need to have another copy of Erizzo's works (*Correspondance*, II, pp. 435 and 464) but he finds the price extortionate.

107 Le Pois, *Discours*, p. 46.

108 Letter from Nicholas Throckmorton, dated 19 September 1561, published by le comte de la Ferrière, *Le XVIe Siècle et les Valois: les documents inédits du British Museum et du Record Office*, Paris, 1879, p. 65. Bertolotti, *Artisti francesci*, p. 50 gives the details of Catherine's order.

109 See the discussion of D. Bentley Cranch, 'A sixteenth-century patron of the arts, Florimond Robertet, Baron d'Alluye and his "vierge ouvrante"', *Bibliothèque d'Humanisme et Renaissance*, vol. 50, no. 2, 1988, pp. 317–33; and Louis Courajod, *L'Imitation et la contrefaçon des objets d'art antiques au XVIe et au XVIIe siècles*, Paris, 1887.

110 See J.A. Deville's work, *Comices de Gaillon*, Paris, 1850, and the account of Cardinal d'Aragon's visit to Gaillon in 1517–18: A. de Beatis, *Voyage du Cardinal d'Aragon . . . 1517–1518*, Paris, 1913.

Chapter 4   The Transporters

1 On the state of the French language at this time and on the significance of the role translators played in its enrichment, the following works are helpful: Glyn Norton, *The Ideology and Language of Translation in Renaissance France and their Humanist Antecedents*, Geneva, 1984; Valerie Worth, *Practising Translation in Renaissance France: the Example of Etienne Dolet*, Oxford, 1988.

2 Du Choul, 'Antiquitez romaines', f. 69v.

3 See Jean Martin's version of Alberti (*L'Architecture de Jean Baptiste Albert*, Paris, 1553, f. 120): 'vous sçavez bien que j'ay promis de parler si clairement en ce discours, que s'il est en ma puissance, ie pourray estre entendu: mais si ie veuil parvenir à ce poinct, il convient necessairement que ie signe ou invente des Termes tous nouveaux, au moins si ceulx qui sont en usage, ne suffisent; et si ie le fay, ie prendray mes similitudes sur des choses non fortes à entendre ou eslongnées de cognoissance, mais approchans de ce que ie diray' (You know well that I promised to speak clearly in this discourse so that, if it is in my power, I may be understood; but if I am to achieve this, I shall necessarily be obliged to indicate or invent entirely new terms, because those currently available are insufficient; and if I don't do that, I'll take my comparisons from things easy to understand, not remote but close to what I have to say).

4 The opening of Book 5 in Martin's translation of Vitruvius (1547) stresses the same difficulties (f. 67): 'considéré donc que ses mots ne sont usitez ny cogneuz, mesmes qu'ilz se trouvent estranges entre les communs . . . Pource que donc qu'il me convient user de nominations occultes si je veuil exprimer les choses requises en cest endroit . . . ie me delibere n'y employer grande parole, afin qu'on les puisse mieux retenir en memoire, cognoissant que la brieveté les rendra moins difficiles, et plus aisees à comprendre' (considering therefore that his terms are neither known nor currently in use, and they appear strange to ordinary people . . . Thus, since it is appropriate to use obscure words if I'm to express properly what is needed in this place . . . I have resolved not to use great eloquence, so that they can be retained in the memory more efficiently, knowing that brevity will render them less difficult and easier to understand).

5 P. de L'Orme *Le Premier tome de l'architecture*, Paris, 1567–68, f. 136v.

6 Compliment coined by Marcantonio Michiel; see Jennifer Fletcher, 'Marcantonio Michiel: his friends and collection', *Burlington Magazine*, vol. 123, 1981, pp. 453–67. There has been renewed interest in Serlio's work in France: see the most recent international gathering at Lyon (7–10 December 1998), 'Sebastiano Serlio à Lyon. Architecture et imprimerie', whose deliberations are to be published.

7 See A. Heulhard, *Rabelais, ses voyages . . .* , p. 78.

8 Translations of Vitruvius into French are indicated several times by La Croix du Maine in his *Bibliothèque*, pp. 1, 70, 227. In his preface to his own translation of Vitruvius in 1547, Martin recalls that in 1521 Augustini Gallo had offered François I his Italian translation of the work.

9 This is made clear in Goujon's tribute which appeared in the foreword he wrote for Jean Martin's translations of Vitruvius, Paris, 1547.

10 See *Correspondance politique de Guillaume Pellicier*, ed. A. Tausserat-Radel, Paris, 1899, letter dated 10 novembre 1541, no. 297.

11 For an assessment of Serlio's influence on architectural vocabulary, see Deborah Howard, *Jacopo Sansovino. Architecture and Patronage in Renaissance Venice*, New Haven and London, 1975, p. 3.

12 Having previously listed Raphael, Mantegna, Michelangelo, Sangallo and Bramante as worthy of particular commendation, Goujon then turns to Lescot and Philibert de L'Orme whose capacities he also admired.

13 Goujon's words (Vitruvius, *Architecture*, trans. Martin, preface sig. Diiij) are as follows: 'mais pourceque un jour fust communiquée à messire Sebastian Serlio une figure que i'en avois faicte, et qu'il trouva qu'elle estoit bien selon la reigle de l'autheur (Vitruve)' (but, because one day M. Sebastiano Serlio was given an image which I had made and which he found according to the rules of Vitruvius).

14 Jean Cousin, *Livre de perspective*, Paris, 1560, f. M. iij v: 'les proportions et mesures d'Architecture combien que ie ne vueil m'amuser à la declaration d'icelles mesures, parceque plusieurs personnes de bon esprit en ont assez amplement descrit, ayants si soigneusement cherché la perfection d'icelles, extraites des Antiques: comme pouvez voir en Marc Vitruve, Sebastian Serlio, et Leon Baptiste' (the proportion and measure of Architecture, I shall not indulge in giving their details because several excellent minds have fully described and carefully researched their perfection, modelling them on the antique, as can be seen in Marcus Vitruvius, Sebastiano Serlio and Leon Baptista).

15 De L'Orme, *Le Premier tome*, f. 202.

16 When he was preparing Serlio's seventh book for publication, Jacopo Strada was struck by the 'clarity and facility' and 'an order so beautiful' of the architect's explanations; preface to Serlio, *Settimo libro*, Frankfort, 1575, cited and translated by William Bell Dinsmoor, 'Sebastiano Serlio's literary remains', *Art Bulletin*, vol. 24, 1942, p. 77.

17 Patricia Lee Rubin, *Giorgio Vasari. Art and History*, New Haven, 1995, p. 169 discusses Vasari's unacknowledged debt to Serlio; for Peiresc's use of Serlio, see Bibliothèque Nationale, Ms fr. 9530 (*Recueil d'antiquités*), ff. 15ff, and his *Correspondance*, VI, p. 231. In his *Livre*

d'architecture (Paris, 1559), Jacques Androuet du Cerceau plagiarized a good deal from Serlio's work: see David Thomson, *Renaissance Paris: Architecture and Growth 1475–1600*, London, 1984, p. 18. For recent assessments of his influence on architectural practice, see J.J. Gloton, 'L'Influence de Serlio en France', *Les Traités d'architecture*, ed. J. Guillaume, Paris, 1985, pp. 407–23; and H. de la Fontaine Verwey, 'Pieter Coecke van Aelst and the publication of Serlio's book on architecture', *Quaerendo*, vol. 6, 1976, pp. 166–94; and Myra Nan Rosenfeld, *Sebastian Serlio. On Domestic Architecture*, New York and Cambridge, Mass., 1978.

18 Dinsmoor, 'Sebastiano Serlio's literary remains', pp. 55–154.

19 Most French contemporaries were in fact impressed by Serlio's frequent reference to Vitruvius, attributing the former's authority to his deep knowledge of the ancient writer.

20 Unless otherwise stated, all quotations are taken from *Tutte l'opere*, the composite edition of Serlio's works published in Venice in 1619.

21 Cited from the truncated English translation by Robert Peake, London, 1611, f. 15v.

22 The references to Peruzzi are frequent: *Tutte l'opere*, II, f. 18v; III, ff. 65v, 69v, 118v, 126; IV, f. 190v; VII, f. 52.

23 Serlio shared with Peruzzi this admiration for the forms of the theatre of Marcellus; according to Serlio, Peruzzi was able to conceive the whole building from the measurements he took of the fragments that remained: *Tutte l'opere*, III, f. 69v.

24 Robert Peake, 1611, 'Address to the Reader'.

25 There are clear parallels with Du Bellay's advocacy of incorporation in *La Deffence et illustration de la langue françoise*, 1549.

26 For an account of such criteria, see my *Ideal Forms*, ch. 2, pp. 51–88.

27 See the arguments of Françoise Choay in 'Serlio Redivivus', *Bibliothèque d'Humanisme et Renaissance*, vol. 57, no. 1, 1995, pp. 119–25.

28 See L. Golson's article, 'Serlio, Primaticcio and the architectural grotto', *Gazette des Beaux Arts*, vol. 77, 1974, pp. 95–108, and Gloton, 'L'Influence de Serlio' for these influences. Serlio also influenced the design of the château de Madrid, see Monique Chatenet, *Le Château de Madrid au bois de Boulogne*, Paris, 1987; and when the hôtel de Joannis came to be built in 1583, the *maîtres maçons de Draguignan* were instructed 'à édifier une porte semblable à celle figurée au f. 39 du Livre IV de Serlio' (to erect a gateway similar to that shown on f. 39 of Book IV of Serlio), Jean Boyer, 'L'Influence de Serlio en France: la porte de l'hôtel de Joannis à Aix en Provence', *Gazette des Beaux Arts*, vol. 127, janvier 1996, pp. 11–14.

29 Serlio, *Tutte l'opere*, 1584, f. 96.

30 According to the inventory of his belongings made after his death, Ponce 'Jacqueau' owned three of Serlio's texts, as well as other works on Rome: Labacco, sixty drawings 'faictes à la main et au pinceau apres les Antiquitez de Rome' (made by hand and with the pen after the antiquities in Rome), twenty other drawings on the same theme, and a sketch of the Colosseum; recorded in C. Grodecki, *Archives nationales. Documents du minutier central des notaires de Paris. Histoire de l'art au XVIe siècle*, 2 vols, Paris, 1986, II, p. 101, no. 618 (1570).

31 Bibliothèque Nationale, Ms fr. 9530, ff. 15–59.

32 T. Renucci, *Un Aventurier des lettres au XVIe siècle. Gabriel Symeoni*, Paris, 1943, has provided a detailed account of Symeoni's life based on a manuscript autobiography pre- served in Florence; he has made clear the questionable motifs behind some of Symeoni's work. The disappointments are evident in the letters Symeoni published, Symeoni, *Epitome de l'origine et succession de la duché de Ferrare . . . avec certaines épistres à divers personnages*, Paris, 1553.

33 Symeoni, *Les Illustres Observations*, sig. A2v; a more detailed discussion of cardinal de Lorraine's retreat at Meudon is given in Chapter 5 p. 177 ff.

34 Symeoni, *César renouvellé*, sig. ã ii v.

35 This work was published in Lyon in 1555 one year after Symeoni settled there. It has been analysed by Victor E. Graham in the context of Henri II's imperial ambitions, 'Gabriel Symeoni et le rêve impérial des rois de France', in *Culture et pouvoir au temps de l'humanisme et de la Renaissance*, Chambéry, 1978, pp. 299–309; and by Richard Cooper with regard to the intellectual currents which linked to Symeoni's apparently curious views: 'Gabriel Symeoni visionario', *Studi di Letteratura Francese*, XIX, Florence, 1992, pp. 279–97.

36 Renucci, *Un Aventurier des lettres*, p. 39, citing from the Florence manuscript, 'Apologia generale'.

37 Symeoni, *Illustratione de gli epitaffi e medaglie antiche*, Lyon, 1558, p. 83; see also *Description*, where Symeoni returns to a discussion of the significance of medals and their ability to conjure up an idea of a Rome which had otherwise disappeared from view, pp. 78 ff.

38 Symeoni, *Description*, p. 38.

39 Symeoni *Les Illustres Observations*, pp. 81–2; Fulvius, *Antiquitatis urbis*, ff. 167 ff.; and Mauro, *Delle antichità di Roma*, p. 32. The ultimate source is Suetonius.

40 Symeoni, *Illustratione*, pp. 145, 148; Onufrius Panvinius, *De ludis circensibus. De triumphis* (ed. used, Venice, 1600) was authoritative.

41 Symeoni, *Illustratione*, sig. A3r.

42 Ibid., p. 154; Symeoni also had kind words for Roville, ibid., p. 49.

43 Symeoni, *César renouvellé*, pp. 11, 15, 60 and 73; and *Les Illustres Observations*, p. 84.

44 This quotation comes from the 'Apologia generale', Symeoni's manuscript autobiography, and is cited in Renucci, *Un Aventurier des lettres*, p. 87. In addition, Symeoni was in touch with many erudite contemporaries, for example André Alciat to whom a letter survives on the meaning of certain enigmas, *Epitome*, ff. 27v–28.

45 Symeoni's references to the Pantheon (Du Choul, *Discours*, p. 7), which he refers to as the temple of Agrippa, are typical of his approach, which was designed to throw into relief the magnificence of Rome.

46 Symeoni is here translating from the original composition, which was in Latin. He appended the poem to a letter addressed to Carnavalet from Vanves 'la mi-caresme de l'an 1553' (mid-Lent in the year 1553), *Epitome*, ff. 58v–59. The letter to Guidi is in the same volume, f. 24v.

47 For a discussion of this text, see Chapter 8.

48 This is the Italian version of *La Description de la Limague*; the passage is on p. 83.

49 The two medals are analysed by Symeoni on pp. 84–5 in *Les Illustres Observations*.

50 Ibid., p. 95. The comparison with the château d'Anet occurs on p. 102.

51 The details of the comparison can be found in the letter Symeoni wrote to the duc de Guise (le 1er jour de février, 1553), *Epitome*, ff. 53–4.

52 Symeoni, *Illustratione*, p. 152.

53 Symeoni, *Description*, pp. 8–9; the pain and nostalgia that he felt at the sight of such ruins is recorded in a manuscript which survives in Turin, 'Le Origine et le antichità di Lione', which he dedicated to the duc de Savoie.

54 The title was coined by Gabriel Chappuys who translated the work as *Dialogo pio et speculativo* and he chose one of the themes in this miscellany for it. His text, divided into seven chapters, was published by Renucci as his *thèse complémentaire* to *Un Aventurier* in 1944. A copy of Chappuys' translation was later owned by a pupil of Cujas, interested in antiquities, Chaduc (1560–1638).

55 The villas of Cicero and the Younger Pliny were famous in the Renaissance and much imitated by French and Italian princes. The clearest description of such a place can be found in Pirro Ligorio's reconstruction of Hadrian's villa at Tivoli of which several copies survive; the text I have consulted is in the British Library, Add. Ms 22001.

56 For the cultural context in which Symeoni's work at Vanves fits, see Liliane Châtelet-Lange, 'Le "Museo di Vanves" (1560). Collections et musées de sculpture en France au XVIe siècle', *Zeitschrift für Kunstgeschichte*, vol. 38, 1975, pp. 266–85; and our discussion in Chapter 5, p. 181 ff.

57 Antoine III du Prat had been consistently praised by Symeoni in his works but the extolling had never led to a permanent appointment in his household although the *prévôt de Paris* was evidently a connoisseur and owned a large library. The ties with Guillaume du Prat with whom Symeoni had returned to France from Italy in 1546 were much closer and the writer spent many happy hours in the winter months at Beauregard. For details on these matters, see Renucci, *thèse complémentaire, Un Aventurier*, pp. vi–ix. It is surprising that Du Prat failed to respond to Symeoni's

efforts since he was a learned man with more than 1,300 books in his library, including many manuscripts; see M. Connat and J. Megret, 'Inventaire de la bibliothèque des Du Prat', *Bibliothèque d'Humanisme et Renaissance*, vol. 3, 1943, pp. 72–128.

58 Symeoni's extended epitaph is on pp. 127–31 of the *Description*.

59 See R. Descimon, 'Les Ducs de Nevers au temps de Blaise de Vigenère ou la puissance de faire des hommes puissants', *Blaise de Vigenère, poète et mythographe au temps de Henri III*, Paris, 1994, pp. 13–37, Cahiers V.L. Saulnier, no. 11; Vigenère even designed motifs for the decoration of the duchesse's apartments, see Henri Zerner, *L'Art de la Renaissance en France*, Paris, 1996, p. 255. For an account of Vigenère's life which is still valid, see Denise Métral, *Blaise de Vigenère, archéologue et critique d'art*, Paris, 1939.

60 Published in Paris, Abel l'Angelier, 1586. The *Traicté* was the third of three projects on the *Secrétaire*, two others having been stolen from Vigenère in Turin.

61 Ibid., f. 292v.

62 Vigenère, *Les Décades de Tite Live*, col. 769. References will be given to this work as follows: L. plus the column number.

63 Ibid., Du Choul is mentioned L. 1549–50; and Porcacchi and Giraldi L. 886–7. In her book, Métral has traced many sources used by Vigenère, but she adds, p. 112, 'Il est difficile de mesurer l'étendue de ses emprunts' (It is difficult to assess the full scope of his borrowings).

64 Other reconstructions of Ligorio which Vigenère used may be found L. 879–80; 880–1.

65 According to Jean François Maillard, Ligorio invented the devices for the entry of Henri III into Mantua (1574) of which Vigenère published a detailed account in 1576; see Maillard's article, 'De la Maquette autographe à l'imprimé. La somptueuse et magnifique entrée du roi Henri III à Mantoue par Blaise de Vigenère', pp. 71–90, in *Le Livre dans l'Europe de la Renaissance* (Colloque de Tours, no. 28), Paris, 1988.

66 For another reference to the Farnese collection, see L. 1526–8.

67 Although the emphasis throughout is on service to his *concitoyens*, he is aware of the learned audience: 'des gens doctes, auxquels tout mon principal but s'étoit de plaire' (of learned people whom my principal task was to please) L. 887.

68 *Les Commentaires de César*, Paris, 1576, f. 152v. Future references to this work will be to C. followed by the folio number.

69 In an extensive passage at the beginning of *Les Commentaires* (C. ff. 100–100v), Vigenère discusses the style of Caesar and its reputation, then he goes on to differentiate the style of Marot and Ronsard; in doing so, he shows how keen his powers of differentiation were.

70 Antoine du Verdier, *Prosopographie ou description des personnes illustres tant chrestiennes que profanes*, Lyon, 1589, p. 2573.

71 See Métral's discussion of Vigenère's too ready acceptance of false inscriptions, *Blaise de Vigenère*, pp. 118–26.

72 C. sig. ü iij, 'pour le regard du langage, s'il ne vous satisfait de tous points, vos cognoissez le stile de l'autheur. Parquoy vous aurez regard, s'il vous plaist à la contrainte où ie me suis asservy, qui m'empescha en cest endroit d'estre moymesme, n'y à moy' (as far as language is concerned, even if it does not satisfy you on all points, you will recognize the style of the author. You will please appreciate the constraints under which I work which prevent me both from being

myself in this respect and responsible to myself alone).

73 For other examples of Vigenère's descriptive power, see the article of François Secret, 'Blaise de Vigenère à l'hôtel de Bellevue', *Bibliothèque d'Humanisme et Renaissance*, vol. 21, 1969, pp. 115–27.

74 On Vigenère's lively reaction to the sights of Rome, see G. Répaci-Courtois' article, 'Blaise de Vigenère et l'expérience des arts visuels', pp. 101–10 in *Blaise de Vigenère, poète et mythologue, au temps de Henri III*, Paris, 1994, Cahiers V.L. Saulnier, no ii. Denise Métral's pioneering work, *Blaise de Vigenère*, remains fundamental to any assessment of Vigenère's contribution to the history of art.

75 L. 700; on his return from Rome, Vigenère dictated to Jean Cousin the content of the decorative devices for the chamber of Marguerite de Bourbon, see F. Lesure, 'Blaise de Vigenère et Jean Cousin (1550)', *Bibliothèque d'Humanisme et Renaissance*, vol. 9, 1947, pp. 109–13; the date given by Lesure to this transaction will need to be revised.

76 The same idea is developed in the 1637 edition of *Les Images*, published by Sebastien Cramoisy: 'Ains de nous monstrer et faire voir comme dans un miroir tout le train de la vie humaine' (thus, to show us clearly, as in a mirror, the whole sequence of human life), p. 19; unless otherwise stated, all future references to *Les Images des deux Philostrate* will be to the 1578 edition, and will be given thus: P. followed by the folio number.

77 The examples are taken from *Les Images*, ff. 41, 282v and 478 respectively. Thevet had also provided a description of the Farnese Hercules in his *Cosmographie*, II, f. 731v.

78 Vigenère only translated Volume I; the rest was done by Antoine de la Faye, a Protestant minister who died in 1618.

79 The woodcut for the first chapter, for example, reappears opposite f. xciii and elsewhere.

80 I. de Amelin, *Les Concions et harengues de Tite Live*, Paris, 1557.

81 Vigenère, *Trois dialogues*, f. ++, v; cited in Métral, *Blaise de Vigenère*, p. 45.

82 L. 1039, 'Que s'ils ne se rapportent du tout à l'original, il faut partie importer celà à l'incommodité du bois, dont la taille n'est iamais si certaine et naïfve que du métal' (If they do not match the original, you must attribute that to the awkwardness of the wood whose cut is never as certain nor as sharp as in metal). There are several complaints by Vigenère about the inadequacy of woodcuts, see the figure of Aeneas fleeing from Troy, L. 1256.

83 For the method of conjecture, see my article, 'Conjecture, reshaping, and the creative process', pp. 213–40 in *(Ré)interprétations: études sur le seizième siècle*, Michigan Romance Studies, XV, Ann Arbor, 1995, ed. John O'Brien.

84 See L. 467, 515, 805 for examples.

85 Other references to the use of conjecture in the *Commentaires* can be found ff. 100, 100v, 103v. In some instances, Vigenère used the term with the meaning of *drawing*, that is a drawn hypothesis.

86 *Les Images* (1597 edn), sig. ã ij v, 'Car il s'est veu en ce siecle des conceptions aussi relevées, et des labeurs aussi mignardement élabourez, qu'aucuns autres de ces anciens temps.' (Because our century has witnessed inventions as bold and workmanship as delicately handled as any examples from olden times.)

87 *La Suite de Philostrate* (1602 edn) ff. 103–5v; and L. 814.

88 L. 814 and *La Somptueuse et Magnifique Entrée*, pp. 5, 8–9, 29.

89 Vigenère, *La Suitte*, ff. 95v–110.

90 L. 727, 'un petit satyre de marbre tout rompu et rapiecé mais l'un des

plus excellens chefs d'oeuvre qui se puisse voir, comme je l'ay ouy autrefois de la bouche propre de Michel Lange' (a tiny marble satyr all broken and mended and yet one of the finest *chefs d'oeuvre* that can be found, as I heard from Michelangelo himelf).

91 Although he was referred to in the seventeenth century; Jacques Deyron (for instance) regarded him as authoritative and constantly quoted him to justify his own claims, *Des Antiquités de la ville de Nismes*, Nîmes, 1663, pp. 11, 27, 100, 138.

92 Métral's overall assessment of Vigenère's contribution was favourable: 'Blaise de Vigenère contribue puissamment à faire connaître l'antiquité à la jeunesse studieuse' (Blaise de Vigenère contributes powerfully to giving the studious young generation a knowledge of antiquity), *Blaise de Vigenère*, p. 75; and later, ibid., p. 110, 'Ses annotations ne sont pas de simples commentaires, elle sont des recherches' (his annotations are not simple commentaries but researches).

93 Arnaldo Momigliano, *Essays in Ancient and Modern Historiography*, Oxford, 1977, ch. 13, 'The first political commentary on Tacitus', pp. 205–30.

94 Lipsius left Belgium in August 1568 and departed from Rome in April 1570; for details of his journey, see J. Ruysschaert, 'Le Séjour de Juste Lipse à Rome (1568–70) d'après ses *Antiquae lectiones* et sa correspondance', *Bulletin de l'Institut Historique Belge de Rome*, vol. 24, 1947–48, pp. 139–92.

95 All these names are cited by Albertus Miraeus in his biography (p. lj) printed at the beginning of Lipsius' *Opera omnia*, 4 vols, Antwerp, 1637. All references to Lipsius' work are to this edition unless otherwise stated.

96 The principal authors studied in the Vatican Library were Seneca, Tacitus, Plautus and Propertius; they are all cited by Miraeus, op.cit.

97 Miraeus gives few details (ibid., p. lj) 'sed otium et omne liberum tempus dabat inspectioni lapidum, locorum veterum, et si quid in Urbe aut viciniam visendum esset aut noscendum' (he gave over his leisure and free time to the scrutiny of stones, ancient places and what could be seen and should be known in the vicinity of the City).

98 Lipsius, *Opera omnia*, III, p. 586, 'itaque ut veram peregrinationem laudo, susceptam maturo iudicio . . .' (also praised true peregrination as encouraging mature judgement).

99 The letter is well known and can be found in Lipsius, *Opera omnia*, II, pp. 20–2.

100 Normand Doiron in *L'Art de voyager. Le déplacement à l'époque classique*, Paris, 1995, gives Lipsius' text and a French translation, pp. 211–17; he also comments extensively, drawing out the points on *innutrition* (intellectual nourishment).

101 Jean Jehasse, *La Renaissance de la critique: l'essor de l'humaniste érudit de 1560 à 1614*, Saint-Etienne, 1976, has provided a thorough analysis of Lipsius' works; the passage cited is on p. 275.

102 *De admiranda*, Book 1, ch. 2, Lipsius, *Opera omnia*, III, p. 376.

103 'Ipsa urbs, orbis compendium et epitome' (this city, the epitome and compendium of the whole world), *De admiranda*, Book 3, ch. 3, ibid., p. 424.

104 *De admiranda*, Book 4, final chapter, ibid., p. 473, where he cites Aristides' text extensively; see also p. 423.

105 Jehasse (*La Renaissance de la critique*, p. 358) has translated the 'Advice to the Reader' as follows: 'Combien est admirable la bienvieillence de Dieu pour cette ville! Quand elle

lui a arraché la force des légions, elle lui a donné celle des lois; quand elle n'a plus voulu qu'elle commandât par les armes, elle l'a gratifiée du culte: aussi l'a-t-elle faite encore l'honneur, la protection, la colonne du monde.' (How wonderful is the goodness of God towards this city! When He took away the force of the Legions, He gave her the power of law; when she could no longer dominate by arms, He gratified her with religious cult; thus has she continued to be the honour, protection and column of the world.)

106 La Popelinière, *L'Histoire des histoires*, p. 249 'Jule Cesar . . . Lypse pourtant trouve à redire en son style' (Julius Caesar: yet, Lipsius has found fault with his style); p. 265 'Tite Live . . . Lypse toutesfois apres les autres, le recognoist paresseux, froid et manque en plusieurs endroits: mesme ennuieux de redites et choses superflues' (yet Lipsius, like others, saw his as lazy, cold and deficient in many places: even boring with his repetitious and excessive statements).

107 For a discussion of Tacitus' work as a theatrical representation of the life in Lipsius' own day, see Gerhard Oestreich, *Neostoicism and the Early Modern State*, Cambridge, 1982, pp. 61 ff.

108 Passage commented on by Jehasse, *La Renaissance de la critique*, p. 267, who follows with a detailed discussion of the moral and intellectual implications of Lipsius' work for his contemporaries. Pierre Corneille was to see the relevance of these messages, and 'similitudo et imago . . . temporum nostrum' (comparison with and image of our time) formed the point of departure for Terence Allott's treatment of 'Tacitus and some late plays of Corneille', *Journal of European Studies*, 1980, pp. 32–47.

109 On the practical dimensions of

Lipsius' writings, see Mark Morford, *Stoics and Neo-Stoics*, Princeton, 1991, p. 15.

110 See Jehasse, *La Renaissance de la critique*, pp. 253 ff., for a discussion of Lipsius' works as a dictionary of antiquities.

111 *De admiranda* in Lipsius, *Opera omnia*, III, p. 423; see also Jehasse's discussion, *La Renaissance de la critique*, pp. 574 ff.

112 C. Navitel's article, 'Juste Lipse antiquaire', in C. Mouchel (ed.), *Juste Lipse (1547–1606) en son temps. Actes du colloque de Strasbourg, 1994*, Paris, 1996, pp. 275–93.

113 This scientific method is confirmed in *Electa II* (1585). The method is discussed by J. Ruysschaert, *Juste Lipse et les Annales de Tacite*, Turnhout, 1949; and by Morford, *Stoics*, p. 147, who underlined the vastness of Lipsius' knowledge and his accuracy in matters of language and grammar; his attention to the fluidity and dynamics of epistolary conversation was studied by E.C. Dunn, 'Lipsius and the art of letter writing', *Studies in the Renaissance*, vol. 3, 1956, pp. 145–56. Lipsius' use of secondhand scholarship was exposed by C.O. Brink in a fundamental article, 'Justus Lipsius of the text of Tacitus', *Journal of Roman Studies*, vol. 41, 1951, pp. 32–51.

114 Lipsius, *Opera omnia*, I, pp. 13–30.

115 Navitel, 'Juste Lipse, antiquaire', *passim*, has an interesting discussion of Lipsius' inability to deal precisely with the devastated sights of Rome, and Lipsius' avoidance of description in his own words.

116 Anthony Grafton translated and commented upon this passage in similar vein, in the chapter on 'The Renaissance', *The Legacy of Rome*, ed. Richard Jenkins, New York, 1992, pp. 97–123.

117 The references are as follows: Lipsius, *Opera omnia*, III; Serlio pp. 434, 585 and 591; Biondo p. 444; Sigonio pp. 440 and 589;

Mercurialis p. 440; Panvinius p. 444; Leandro Alberti p. 445; Fulvius p. 563; and Vitruvius p. 565.

118 Montaigne's borrowings are chiefly in *Des Coches* (III, 6); chs 10 and 17 particularly attracted his attention.

119 See the paragraph which Montaigne added to the *Apologie* in 1588 (II, 12, p. 578 of the Presses Universitaires de France edition, of the *Essais*, Paris, 1965). For a recent appraisal of the influence of Montaigne and Lipsius upon each other, see the article of M. Magnien, 'Montaigne et Juste Lipse', in *Juste Lipse*, ed. Mouchel, pp. 423–52.

120 *Les Oeuvres de C. Cornelius Tacitus, chevalier romain*, Paris, 1582, sig. ã ij.

121 Ibid., p. 603, 'i'ay suivy la pluspart des corrections latines de Iustus Lipsius comme du plus curieux et net de tous ceux qui ont touché à nostre Tacitus' (I have followed the majority of the Latin corrections of Justus Lipsius as the most learned and clear of all those who have dealt with our Tacitus).

122 Momigliano, *Essays in Ancient and Modern Historiography*, p. 207.

123 Jehasse, *La Renaissance de la critique*, p. 561.

124 Cited at length and translated from the original text by Pierre Laurens in his article, 'Le Dialogue des orateurs de Juste Lipse', in *Juste Lipse*, ed. Mouchel, pp. 103–15.

Chapter 5 Visions Transported

1 Greene, *The Light in Troy*.

2 The respect for classical architectural values, evident in the work of Peruzzi, has been examined by J.J. Gloton, 'Transformation et réemploi des monuments du passé dans la Rome du XVIe siècle', *Mélanges d'Archéologie et d'Histoire*, vol. 74, 1962, pp. 705–58.

3 Archibald Alison, *Essays on the Nature and Principles of Taste*, Edinburgh, 1790, p. 25. Later, in the same essay (p. 65), he argued that the feelings of beauty and sublimity could be aroused by a trivial thing; 'a trifling circumstance' (as he put it) was capable of inflaming the imagination.

4 For a discussion of the pervasive interest in ruins, see Roland Mortier's history, *La Poétique des ruines en France*; and for modern attention to fragments and ruins, Lawrence D. Kritzman (ed.), *Fragments: Incompletion and Discontinuity*, New York, 1981.

5 Poggio himself lamented in most eloquent terms the ruined state of the city which conjured up past glories, see Mortier, *La Poétique*, pp. 32 ff.

6 Silius Italicus, *Punica*, Loeb Library, London, 1927, 2 vols, ch. x, ll. 576–90; ch. xii, ll. 518–20, 580–1.

7 Nicolas Bralion, *Curiosités de l'une et l'autre Rome*, Paris, 1659, p. 7.

8 Vasari, *Lives of the Painters*, IV, p. 1, life of Antonio da San Gallo (*c.* 1480–1546).

9 Marliani, *L'antiquità di Roma*, Rome, 1548, sig. ii.

10 Vigenère, *Traicté des chiffres*, pp. 336–336v.

11 See Hermann Egger, *Die Römische Verduten*, 2 vols, Vienna and Leipzig, 1931, II, plate 26.

12 To cite but one example, at Villers-Cotterêts, a staircase with its coffered vault is decorated with scenes from Colonna's book, see Robert J. Knecht, *Francis I*, Cambridge, 1982, p. 257; for the influence of art on Colonna, see C. Hülsen, 'Le illustrazioni della *Hypnerotomachia Poliphili* e le antichità', *Bibliofilia*, vol. 12, 1910–11, pp. 161–76, and for the influence of Colonna's work on art, Anthony Blunt, 'The *Hypnerotomachia Poliphili* in seventeenth-century France', *Journal of the Warburg and Courtauld Institutes*, vol. 1, 1937, pp. 117–37. Colonna's poor grasp of classical forms is discussed

by Rowland, *The Culture of the High Renaissance,* pp. 60–7.

13 F. Colonna, *Discours du songe de Poliphile*, Paris, 1546, p. 7. Other laments on linguistic deficiences may be found on pages 14, 46v and 73. All references are to the facsimile edition, published by Les Libraires associés, 1963.

14 For similar close links between text and image in the work of Ligorio, see Gaston, *Pirro Ligorio*, p. 14.

15 See Paul S. Wingert, 'The funerary urn of Francis I', *Art Bulletin*, vol. 21, no. 4, 1939, pp. 383–400.

16 P. Pietrasanta, 'Di Fontanbleo a Francesco Re di Francia', Bibliothèque Nationale, Ms it. 1043. Du Choul, 'Antiquitez romaines', ff. 37–8.

17 Symeoni, *Les Illustres Observations*, p. 95; and Van Buchel, *Journal*, pp. 159–66.

18 See Jean Martin's preface to the French translation of Vitruvius, *Architecture* [1553], and his comments f. 120; Van Buchel, *Journal*, p. 130; Colonna, *Discours*, ff. 7, 14; De L'Orme *Le Premier tome* f. 136v; and Germain Pilon, pp. 360–1 in *Germain Pilon et les sculpteurs français de la Renaissance. La Documentation française*, Paris-Louvre, 1993. Martin's own translation of Vitruvius was heavily criticized by Jean Gardet in his *Epitome ou Extrait abregé des dix livres d'architecture de Marc Vitruve*, Toulouse, 1559.

19 Prévost's drawings are preserved in the Bibliothèque Nationale, Estampes, Eb 7a, and were done between 1535 and 1538; see Henri Zerner's article, 'Du Mot à l'image', *Traités d'architecture*, ed. Jean Guillaume, Tours, 1985, pp. 288–94.

20 On Pierre Jacques whose album is in the Bibliothèque Nationale, Estampes, Fb 18a Rés. in 4, see A. Geffroy, *L'Album de Pierre Jacques de Reims*, Rome, 1890; and Salomon Reinach, *L'Album de Pierre Jacques,* *sculpteur de Reims, dessins à Rome 1572 à 1577*, Paris, 1902.

21 Inventory of 'Ponce Jacqueau, sculpteur et architecte du roi', in Grodecki, *Archives nationales*, II, p. 101, no. 618. In the library were also Labacco's description of Italy, three of Serlio's books and two copies of Jean Cousin's *Livre de perspective*; additionally '20 pieces de pourtraictures apres l'Enthiquité de Rome faictes à la main et au pinceau' (20 images of the antiquities of Rome drawn by hand and by the pen), and 'Ung Teatre du Colizet de Rome avec 2 pourtraictz de villes' (a Colosseum Theatre in Rome with 2 images of towns).

22 See Heulhard, *Rabelais, ses voyages* . . . , p. 80 where he cites Rabelais' confirmation of his friendship with Philibert.

23 References to measurements occur additionally in *Premier tome*, ff. 145v, 147v, 152v and 169.

24 De L'Orme, *Nouvelles inventions*, f. 34, and he added: 'Et diray hardiment que ie croy qu'il y a cent ans que François n'en a plus apporté et recouvert que moy: pour la commodité que i'ay euë de visiter telles antiquitez.' (And I will say boldly that I believe that no Frenchman in the last hundred years has rediscovered and brought to light more than I have, through the convenience I have had of visiting such antiquities.)

25 Philibert wrote (ibid., f. 162) 'C'est une eglise bastie de plusieurs sortes de colonnes accompagnees de Chapiteaux Ioniques fort differens les uns des autres et ramassez de plusieurs edifices et ruines des antiquitez pour edifier ladicte eglise.' (It is a church built with several sorts of columns, plus Ionic capitals very different one from the other and picked up from several buildings and ancient ruins for the erection of the said church.)

26 Philibert adds: 'vous sçavez que toutes nouvelles escritures et inventions ne sont iamais sans difficulté et labeur' (you appreciate that all new kinds of writing and inventions are never without work and difficulty) (ibid., f. 87v); in offering an example from Hadrian's villa 'comme vous pouvez enrichir vos moulures' (from which you can enrich your mouldings) Philibert apologizes for the ineptitude of the engraver.

27 For discussion of Philibert's view of the status of the artist see A. Cecarelli Pellegrino, *Le 'bon Architecte' de Philibert de L'Orme. Hypotextes et anticipations*, Paris, 1996, and Philippe Potié, *Philibert de L'Orme: figures de la pensée constructive*, Marseille, 1996.

28 Philibert refers to Vitruvius as 'architecte le non pareil' (incomparable architect) and as 'grand et incomparable auteur' (great and matchless author) (ff. 16v, 62).

29 Philibert's sensitivity to his status was played upon by courtiers; for the most recent account of his contretemps with Ronsard who played a joke upon him, see Ceccarelli Pellegrino, *Le 'bon Architecte'*, pp. 31–4, and Potié, *Philibert de L'Orme*, pp. 45–6.

30 Vigenère, *Commentaires de César*, 1589, f. 142, thought that the invention was inspired by the Rialto bridge in Venice; see also *Les Images*, f. 143, and Métral, *Blaise de Vigenère*, p. 167.

31 See Philibert's claim, 'Nous avons une infinité de beaux traicts en France, desquels on ne tient aucun compte, pour ne les entendre' (We have an infinity of fine features in France which are not taken notice of because they are not understood), *Premier tome* f. 124v.

32 See Grodecki, *Archives nationales*, for numerous references to Philibert de L'Orme and his work for royal patrons.

33 See Blunt, 'The *Hypnerotomachia Poliphili*', p. 45.

34 See the discussion of David Thomson in Jacques Androuet du Cerceau, *Les Plus Excellents Bastiments de France*, Paris, 1988, pp. 270–2.

35 The reference to 'à l'antique' occurs in the dedication (dated 1564) 'que j'ay mesurée à l'antique dedans Rome' (which I measured in Rome, according to the antique). The royal *privilège* was signed in 1563 and the 1568 edition says it is the second impression of the work. On the classicism of Bullant's published work, see Yves Pauwels, 'Les Antiques romains dans les traités de Philibert de L'Orme et Jean Bullant', *Mélanges de l'Ecole Française de Rome*, vol. 116, no. 2, 1994, pp. 531–47.

36 He adds in the dedication: 'plus duisant et convenable pour artisans qui besognent au compas et à l'esquierre' (more suitable and appropriate for those craftsmen who work with compass and set-square). The British Library copy of the *Reigle générale* was owned by a mason from Villepreux, named Guerin.

37 It is worth citing the whole poem since it serves to summarize the efforts of several generations of French architects who sought to transport knowledge of Roman forms into France:

> Gentilz ouvriers, qui d'un soing curieux
> Allez cherchant ès plus vielles reliques
> Les vrais pourtraictz des bastimentz antiques
> Elaborez d'un art industrieux:
> Sans autre part les espritz soucieux
> Vous travailler, pour en voir les practiques:
> Venez icy, et aux proffitz publiques

Imitez-en les plus laborieux.
    Si qu'or-avant on voye en-
        my la France
Maintz beaux Pallais
    d'orgueilleuse apparence
Ne ceder point aux
    Babyloniens:
    Comme or'*Bullant* en diverse
      maniere
Vous en prescript la forme
    singuliere
Sur le patron des ouvriers
    anciens.

[Friendly workmen who, with attentive care, go searching among the ancient remains for those true images of old building elaborated with such delightful skill: Without your mind being bothered with seeing the practical side, come here and, for general benefit, imitate the most intricate. So that shortly one might see in France many fine palaces of noble appearance, yielding nothing to the Babylonians: As now *Bullant*, in diverse manner, prescribes for you the unique form based on the model of craftsmen of old.]

On Bullant's deliberate references to classical motifs in his architectural practice, see Yves Pauwels, 'Jean Bullant et le langage des ordres: les audaces d'un timide', *Gazette des Beaux Arts*, vol. 129, 1997, pp. 85–100.

38 The same giant pilasters were used at Chantilly and at the hôtel d'Angoulême, see Thomson, *Renaissance Paris*, p. 152.

39 Dated '22 janvier 1571', the document refers to the creation of three bronze figures (Peace, Felicity and Justice) designed to adorn the sepulchre which was to contain Montmorency's heart; the document is published in Grodecki, *Archives nationales*, II, p. 134, nos 678–82. It must be stressed that the title 'architecteur' was frequently adopted by artists at this time, see Bernard Palissy's *quittance* (1564) signed 'architecteur et ynventeur des grottes figulines de monseigneur le connestable' (architect and inventor of decorated grottoes to my lord the *connétable*), published in Edouard Rahir's edition of *Architecture et ordonnance de la grotte rustique de Mgr le duc de Montmorency* [La Rochelle, 1563], Paris, 1919.

40 Catherine de' Medici, *Lettres*, IX, p. 29, 10 août 1586.

41 Details concerning Boissard's life and his sojourns in Italy are given in Auguste Castan's article, 'Jean-Jacques Boissard, poète latin, dessinateur et antiquaire', *Mémoires de la Société d'Emulation du Doubs*, décembre 1874, pp. 65–91.

42 The seventeen drawings by Boissard for an entry into Metz were destroyed in 1944; see Christian Callmer, 'Un Manuscrit de J.J. Boissard', *Opuscula Romana*, IV, Lund, 1962, pp. 47–59, p. 49. For an analysis of the entry see Paulette Choné, *Emblèmes et pensée symbolique en Lorraine (1525–1633)*, Paris, 1991, pp. 710–19.

43 See J.-J. Boissard, *Antiquitatum Romanorum*, Frankfurt, 1597–1602, Part I, vol. I, pp. 48–9. Boissard tells an amusing story of how, having contrived to stay in the Carpi gardens after the gates were locked, he worked all night on copying the images on the reliefs and marbles; see Castan, 'Jean-Jacques Boissard', pp. 67–9.

44 The manuscript dedicated to Charles de Lorraine is in Stockholm, press mark S.68; another and larger manuscript of inscriptions can be found in the Bibliothèque Nationale, Ms lat. 12509 from the Coaslin Library. Many of Boissard's notes and drawings were burned in 1587 when the Lorrains invaded Montbéliard where, on his return from Rome, he had left many

belongings in the care of his sister; see *Antiquitatum*, III, dedication to Ghoer, and Castan's comments, 'Jean-Jacques Boissard', pp. 73–4.

45 Theodore died in 1598 and the work was completed by his son Robert and by Jacques Granthomme; see Choné, *Emblèmes*, p. 707.

46 Raymond Chevalier, 'Le Voyage archéologique au XVIe siècle', Céard and Margolin (eds) in *Voyager à la Renaissance*, pp. 357–80; pp. 368–9 for specific reference to Boissard.

47 F. 175 of *Inscriptionum antiquarum*, Bibliothèque Nationale, Rés. J 468bis.

48 FF. 12–14, 26, 169 and 174 in the published version; f. 335 in the Paris Latin version, Bibliothèque Nationale, Ms lat. 12509; and f. 113 in the Stockholm manuscript.

49 For details, see note 44 above.

50 Boissard, *Antiquitatum*, part 5, sig. ★3v where Boissard identifies the particular expertise of each name mentioned. It should be noted that the 1627–28 editions of Boissard's work give the parts and content in a different order.

51 Bibliothèque Nationale, Ms lat. 12509, f. 336v.

52 Ibid., f. 12.

53 Callmer, 'Un Manuscrit', p. 50.

54 Choné, *Emblèmes*, pp. 708–9.

55 On Chevalier see note 46 above; Bruce Mansfield's condemnation occurs on p. 97 of his *Phoenix of his Age: Interpretations of Erasmus, c. 1550–1750*, Toronto, 1979.

56 A very good idea of the extent of use of prints in design at this time can be gained from Anthony Wells-Cole, *Art and Decoration in Elizabethan and Jacobean England*, New Haven, 1997.

57 The growth in the collecting of prints has been traced by David Landau and Peter Parshall, *The Renaissance Print*, New Haven, 1994; see also Henri Zerner, 'A

propos de faux Marcantoine. Notes sur les amateurs d'estampes à la Renaissance', *Bibliothèque d'Humanisme et Renaissance*, vol. 123, 1961, pp. 477–81; and Michael Bury, 'The taste for prints in Italy to *c.* 1600', *Print Quarterly*, vol. 2, 1985, pp. 12–26.

58 Lafréry arrived in Rome in 1540 and for the first three or four years worked with Salamanca. The history of Lafréry's establishment was recounted by François Roland, 'Antoine La Fréry, 1512–1577', *Mémoires de la Société d'Emulation du Doubs*, 1910, pp. 320–78.

59 The engravings are numbered 38 and 51 respectively in the British Library copy of the *Speculum Romanae magnificentiae* (C.77 i 11) with dates from 1519 to 1575.

60 Dinsmoor, 'Sebastiano Serlio's literary remains', p. 64.

61 See D. Lowry's analysis of this copy, 'Notes on the *Speculum Romanae Magnificentiae* and related publications', *Art Bulletin*, vol. 34, 1952, pp. 46–50.

62 Salamanca's album is preserved in the British Library manuscripts (Cotton, Augustus III), ff. 53–120. Additional single sheets are pasted into the Earl of Crawford's copy; see Lawrence R. McGuiness, *Catalogue of the Earl of Crawford's 'Speculum' now in the Avery Architectural Library*, New York, 1976.

63 Bibliothèque Nationale, Ms Dupuy, 490, ff. 143–144, cited in the catalogue, *I Francesi a Roma. Residenti e viaggiatori nella città eterna del Rinascimento agli inizi del Romanticismo*, Palazzo Braschi, May–June 1961, p. 64, no. 106.

64 As Landau and Parshall point out, the images are 'interpretations rather than representation of early sculpture', *The Renaissance Print*, p. 305. On the British Library copy nearly all the major ancient buildings are shown as reconstituted, see

plates 4, 6, 9, 11, 21, 22, 23, 24, 25, 31, 35, 36, and so on.

65 For this process consult my article, 'Conjecture, reshaping and the creative process', pp. 215–40.

66 These anonymous drawings and engravings can be found in the Bibliothèque Nationale, Estampes Ed 8a; typical examples of a landscape in ruins set within elegant cartouches are nos R144368 and R144437.

67 Plate 59 in catalogue, *L'Ecole de Fontainebleau*, Paris, 1972.

68 Ibid., plate 61. There are other drawings from the same catalogue with similar features by Léon Davent (plate 397); yet other examples of entire drawings devoted to depicting ruins can be seen in anonymous engravings: Bibliothèque Nationale, Estampes Ed 8 nos 144437 and 144438 are characteristic of this taste. Cousin's *Liber Fortunae. Centum emblemata et symbola centum*, Paris, 1568, contains many designs where ruins dominate the background (see plates 11, 13, 15, 17, 23, 89).

69 There is one example of such a picture by Hermanus Posthumus in the prince of Lichtenstein's collection, see Nicole Dacos, 'L'Anonyme A. de Berlin: Hermanus Posthumus', in H. Wrede and R. Harprash (eds) *Antiken Studium und antiken Zeichnungen in der Renaissance*, Mainz, 1989, pp. 61–80.

70 The illuminations, mostly painted between 1547 and 1553, are shown in the catalogue, Thierry Crépin-Leblond, *Livre d'heures royaux*, Paris, 1993. The *Heures de Henri II* are preserved in the Bibliothèque Nationale, Ms lat. 1429 as are the *Heures de Dinteville*, Bibliothèque Nationale, Ms lat. 10558. Du Cerceau's designs for the interior decoration of palaces show this inspiration; an example for a chimneypiece is in Bibliothèque Nationale Estampes, E 041622.

Léonard Thiry's engravings showing ruined landscapes are gathered together in Bibliothèque Nationale Estampes, Ed 8a, fol. Rés.

71 See Métral, *Blaise de Vigenère*, p. 187.

72 See Pierre Desiré Roussel, *Description du château d'Anet*, Paris, 1875.

73 See Jean Guillaume, *La Galerie du grand écuyer*, Paris, 1996, pp. 39, 51, 65 and 79, where he argues that no prints of Rome were available at this date.

74 Serlio, *Tutte l'opere*, 1619, ff. 67v–68; particularly striking is the round temple on f. 78v of Montmorency's Book of Hours. Serlio's publications were probably responsible for the late sixteenth-century phenomenon of ruined landscape pictures painted in Venice, see Cecil Gould, 'Sebastiano Serlio and Venetian painting', *Journal of the Warburg and Courtauld Institutes*, vol. 25, 1962, pp. 56–64.

75 The *Heures d'Anne de Montmorency* are preserved at Chantilly, Musée Condé, Ms 1493, Du Cerceau's *Vues des monuments antiques* can be found in the Bibliothèque Nationale, Estampes, Ed 2h. Another example of adaptations of the Tempietto can be seen in Du Cerceau's engravings, Bibliothèque Nationale, Estampes, Ed 8 no. E 039819. The importance of circular structures evoking a higher order is discussed in William A. McClung, *The Architecture of Paradise: Survivals of Eden and Jerusalem*, Berkeley and Los Angeles, 1983, and in Rudolf Arnheim, *The Dynamics of Architectural Form*, Berkeley, 1977, pp. 81–7.

76 The sequence of paintings celebrating the Massacre of St Bartholomew is discussed in Loren Partridge and Randolph Starn's 'Triumphalism and the Sala Regia in the Vatican', *'All the World's a Stage'. Art and Pageantry in the Renaissance and Baroque*, ed. Barbara Wisch and Susan Scott-Munshower,

University Park, Pennsylvania, 1990, pp. 80–1.

77 Cited by Bruno Tollon, 'Nicolas Bachelier', *Germain Pilon et les sculpteurs français*, Paris-Louvre, 1963, pp. 338–62.

78 The self-portrait is in the Fitzwilliam Museum, Cambridge; the Hercules appeared in a series engraved by Philip Galle, see Brown, 'Marten van Heemskerck', pp. 49–60.

79 The picture was listed in an inventory taken in 1556, see Jean Ehrmann, *Antoine Caron. Peintre des fêtes et des massacres*, Paris, 1986, p. 21. On the political dimension represented by the picture, see G. Lebel, 'Nouvelles précisions sur Antoine Caron', *L'Amour de l'Art*, vol. 19, 1938, pp. 172–80.

80 Ehrmann, *Antoine Caron*, pp. 30–1; many of the engravings were done by Nicolas Béatrizet, see Bibliothèque Nationale, Estampes R 149096–149198. Caron must also have known the engravings of Du Cerceau, for in *Arcs de triomphes* (Bibliothèque Nationale, Estampes, Ed 2l pet.fol. no. E 041251) he had depicted the interior of the Colosseum intact and with spectators viewing a show. Clearly, Caron borrowed from multiple sources, from coins and medals as well as from engravings; for this aspect, see Geneviève Monnier and William McAllister Johnson, 'Caron Antiquaire. A propos de quelques dessins du Louvre', *Revue de l'Art*, no. 14, 1971, pp. 22–30.

81 Illustrations of these pictures may be found in Ehrmann, *Antoine Caron*, pp. 114–15, 118–19, 124, 125–6.

82 W.H. Ward, *French Châteaux and Gardens in the Sixteenth Century. Reproduction of Contemporary Drawings by J. A. Du Cerceau*, London, 1909, p. 1. For a comprehensive overview of Du Cerceau's work, see Heinrich Adolf Geymüller, *Les Du Cerceau: leur vie et leur oeuvre*, Paris, 1887. Whether or not Du Cerceau visited Rome is still a matter of dispute; it is to be hoped that we shall soon have David Thomson's authoritative work on Du Cerceau to settle matters of this kind.

83 He refers to this request in the dedication to Catherine of *Leçons de perspective positive*, Paris, 1576.

84 In his dedication to Henri II, Du Cerceau announced that his aim was to provide examples of architecture: 'Qui sera pour enrichir et embellir de plus en plus cestuy vostre si florissant Royaume: lequel de iour en iour on voit augmenter de tant beaux et sompteux edifices, que doresnavant vos sujects n'auront occasion de voyager en estrange païs, pour en veoir de mieux composez. Et d'avantage vostre Maiesté prenant plaisir et delectation, mesme à l'entendement de si excellens ouvriers de vostre nation, il ne sera plus besoin avoir recours aux estrangiers.' (Which will enrich and embellish more and more this your flourishing kingdom in which, from one day to the next, one sees the number of fine and sumptuous buildings increase, such that – in the future – your subjects will not have to travel to foreign parts to see the best designed. And, moreover, your Majesty enjoying and delighting in the capacity of the workmen of your own nation, will no longer have to have recourse to foreigners.) Bibliothèque Nationale, Estampes, Ed 2m, pet. fol.

85 As David Thomson has observed, *Renaissance Paris*, p. 90, the caryatid portico (adapted from Vitruvius to create an antique monument within the royal palace) was the first attempt to build on a monumental scale, and permanently.

86 See Geymüller, *Les Du Cerceau*, p. 285; a comparison between Hieronymus Cock's work and the

engravings of Du Cerceau show the latter to be faithful copies.

87 Bibliothèque Nationale, Estampes, no. E 039643.

88 Du Cerceau, *Les Plus Excellents Bastiments de France*, 1988 edn, p. 120. It has to be recognized that many of Du Cerceau's depictions are what was intended to be built; not all the French palaces were finished as he projects them.

89 Many works had a pronounced technical orientation such as the *Livre d'architecture*, 1559 (translated into French in 1609); Vigenère records his appreciation of the work of father and son in *Les Images*, p. 855.

90 I am grateful to the Librarian of Eton College for having allowed me access to the College's copy of this rare book.

91 Pen drawings by Du Cerceau of many objects which he made available in print are preserved in the library of the Ecole des Beaux Arts; they are listed in the catalogue *Le Dessin en France au XVIe siècle*, Paris, 1995, p. 168 and pp. 303–6.

92 Du Cerceau, *Oeuvres* (published 1884–91) in two volumes with *héliogravures* by Edouard Baldus, II, *Cheminées*, f. 16; *Meubles*, ff. 15 and 20. These engravings are in the Bibliothèque Nationale Estampes, Ed 8 and Ed 2g, nos E 040505–6; E 041617 ff.; E 040216; E 040222.

93 For examples, see pp. 18, 22 and 29 of Du Cerceau, *Oeuvres*, ed. Edouard Baldus, and Bibliothèque Nationale, Estampes, no. E 040548.

94 See Bibliothèque Nationale, Estampes, no. E 040587. Such examples could easily be multiplied.

95 These are described by Geymüller, *Les Du Cerceau*, in his category H, p. 117. A manuscript in the Vatican Library, said to have belonged to Francesco Barberini, has fifty pen and wash drawings 'faictz a plaisir a la mode des antiques' (freely done, according to the ways of the

ancients), see I. Toesca, 'Drawings by Jacques Androuet du Cerceau in the Vatican Library', *Burlington Magazine*, vol. 98, January–December, 1956, pp. 153–7.

96 For an account of this process in the Rome of Nicholas V which is relevant to later reconstructions, see Burroughs, *From Signs to Design*.

97 The translation of Petrarch's poem used here is that by Thomas Bergin and Alice Wilson, New Haven, 1977. *Africa* first appeared in the *Opera omnia* edition of 1501, published in Venice.

98 The translation of the letters used here is that of Aldos Bernardo, *Rerum familiarum*, New York, 1975. The letters were first printed in Venice in 1492, under the title *Epistoli familiares*.

99 This knowledge has been studied by Jacks, *The Antiquarian*, pp. 35–40.

100 As Mazzocco has put it, 'He is not interested in the ruin *per se*, but in its power to evoke the great events of classical history', p. 356 in 'Petrarch, Poggio and Biondo: humanism's foremost interpreters of Roman ruins', *Francis Petrarch, Six Centuries Later: a Symposium*, ed. A. Scaglione, Chicago, 1975, pp. 354–63, and his article, 'The antiquarianism of F. Petrarca', *Journal of Medieval and Renaissance Studies*, vol. 7, 1977, pp. 203–24.

101 For an elaboration on the different rhythms in Petrarch's vision of ancient Rome, see my paper, 'Involuntary memory: responses to Rome in the Renaissance', given at Potsdam, Einstein Forum, 9 March 1998.

102 Both Jacks, *The Antiquarian*, and Catherine Edwards, *Writing Rome: Textual Approaches to the City*, Cambridge, 1996, pp. 27–8, have used Freud in analysing literary responses to the idea of the city; Edwards refers briefly to Petrarch's Rome, pp. 9–10.

103 Cited by Burns, 'Pirro Ligorio's

reconstruction', pp. 19–92; put another way, and writing about a younger architect, 'the ruins of Roman buildings in the Eternal City enabled Bramante to revolutionize architecture', Stinger, *The Renaissance in Rome*, p. 281.

104 Biondo, *Roma triumphans*, edn used, Brixia, 1482. The order of Biondo's literary production has now been fixed, see A. Mazzocco's analysis of *Roma triumphans*, 'Some philological aspects of Biondo Flavio's *Roma triumphans*', *Humanistica Lovaiensis*, vol. 28, 1979, pp. 1–26. Biondo's influence has been studied by Stinger, *The Renaissance in Rome*, pp. 235–91, 382–92. The *Roma triumphans* was translated by Lucio Fauno in 1544 and printed in Venice by Michele Tramezzino.

105 See Weiss' discussion, *The Renaissance Discovery of Classical Antiquity*, pp. 66–8.

106 On the range of Biondo's sources, consult Mazzocco, 'Some philological aspects', pp. 18–25; see also Dorothy M. Robatham, 'Flavio Biondo's *Roma instaurata*', *Medievalia et Humanistica*, vol. 1, 1970, pp. 203–16.

107 Biondo, *Roma instaurata*, I, lxxvi; translated in Jacks, *The Antiquarian*, p. 117.

108 Biondo, *Roma instaurata*, edn used, Venice, 1503, f. xxxviiii; there was a Paris edition of *Roma triumphans*, published in 1537.

109 The address to the pope is also available in *Latin Writings of the Italian Humanists*, ed. F.A. Gragg, New York, 1927, pp. 140–5.

110 From Jean Martin's translation of Alberti, *L'architecture*, Paris, 1553, f. 4.

111 *The first Boke of Architecture made by Sebastioni Serly*, printed for Robert Peake, London, 1611.

112 Ibid., f. 38v, 'Among the ruines of Rome are many things found out, the which a man cannot make nor imagine what they have beene . . .';

on envisaging the whole structure, see his remarks on St Peter's, f. 15v.

113 Ibid., f. 10. With regard to a temple at Tivoli which was so ruinous that it had lost half its walls and its doors, Serlio explains: 'but I have drawne it out thus, to make the more show, because I judge it had been so; neither can you see any windows in the walls, no sides, nor yet beyond, although I have placed them here in the ground, where I thought best'.

114 See Mandowsky and Mitchell, *Pirro Ligorio's Roman Antiquities*, pp. 44 and 50, for a discussion of Ligorio's interest in revivifying the past.

115 In reconstructions, there was a general tendency to inflate, see Gaston, *Pirro Ligorio*, pp. 14–16.

116 Some preliminary investigation into the use of conjecture for creative purposes is attempted in my article, 'Conjecture, reshaping and the creative process'.

117 Translated and cited by Burns, 'Pirro Ligorio's reconstruction', pp. 31–2.

118 Ligorio, Naples Ms XIII 137; photocopy in the Warburg Institute, vol. XI; translated and cited by Mandowsky and Mitchell, *Pirro Ligorio's Roman Antiquities*, p. 42.

119 It is worth quoting the whole passage, as Vasari pinpoints the criteria by which contemporaries judged Falconetto's quality: 'He thus designed and copied all these antiquities [in Rome and on his return to Spoleto] completing them as though he found them entire, restoring them to perfection in his drawings that is to say, being able to furnish the parts wanting, with the utmost truth and in all their integrity, by means of the information supplied to him by such portions and members as were found still remaining in their places; all which he did with such care and exactitude in the measurements and with such perfect justice of propor-

tion, that he avoided all liability to errors, nor did he commit such, in any part whatever', *Lives of the Painters*, III, p. 437.

120 An idea of the regularity of publication of Palladio's text can be gained from Simona di Marco, *Viaggi in Europa, secoli XVI–XIX: catalogo del fondo 'fiammetta Olschki'*, Florence, 1990; and Giovanni Sicari, *Bibliografia delle guide di Roma in lingua italiana dal 1480 al 1850*, Rome, 1991; and Schudt, *Le guide*, who cites sixty-three editions.

121 Peiresc, for instance, recommends their use to Aubéry, *Correspondance*, VII, pp. 228 and 231.

122 For an assessment of Palladio's scholarship, see R. Wittkower, *Architectural Principles in the Age of Humanism*, Milton Keynes, 1971, pp. 62–88, and H. Spielmann, *Andrea Palladio und die Antike*, Munich and Berlin, 1966.

123 Alain Schnapp cites John Aubery's remark that just as Pythagoras had been able to calculate Heracles' height from the length of his foot, 'ainsi parmi ces ruines y-a-t-il suffisamment de traces pour avoir une idée de la grandeur des monuments de nos ancêtres' (thus, among the ruins, there are sufficient traces to gain a fair idea of the greatness of the monuments of our ancestors), *La Conquête*, p. 193.

124 All English texts are taken from the 1721 translation, *The Architecture of A. Palladio*, 4 volumes, published in London.

125 Ibid., IV, vii, pp. 56–7; ix, pp. 60–1; xii, pp. 63–4; x, pp. 61–2.

126 Cotgrave, *A Dictionarie of Frenche and English Tongues*, London, Adam Islip, 1611, gives 'to judge, imagine & divine' among the various meanings of *conjecture*.

127 Rudolf Wittkower, *Disegni de le ruine di Roma e come anticamente erano*, 2 vols, Milan, 1963, and Henri Zerner, 'Observations on the *Disegni de le ruine*', *Art Bulletin*, vol.

48, 1965, pp. 507–12; both agree that the manuscript dates from 1574, although Zerner challenges Du Pérac's authorship.

128 See De Nolhac, *La Bibliothèque*, p. 65.

129 Mandowsky and Mitchell, *Pirro Ligorio's Roman Antiquities*, p. 355.

130 See Jean-Louis Farrary, *Onofrio Panvinio et les antiquités romaines*, Ecole française de Rome, 1996.

131 The text must have been long in preparation for by the time the *I Vestigi* engravings were published the baths of Diocletian were no longer the ruins which Du Pérac showed them to be, but transformed into a church.

132 Du Pérac's drawings were greatly valued and collected right into the seventeenth century; see Schnapper, *Curieux du Grand Siècle*, II, pp. 258–9, for ownership by La Noue in 1625 and 1631.

133 Bibliothèque Nationale, Ms fr. 382, f. 1.

134 Louvre, Cabinet des Dessins, nos 26372–476.

135 Examples of Du Pérac's indications of the place where the marble original might be found are: ibid., 26489, vases on a monument and its inscription, 'nella via Appia dove sono le ruine di Calatia' (on the Appian way where there are the ruins of Calatia); or ibid., 26445, three drawings 'trovata nel monte Celio incontra a S. Stefano rotundo verso Tramontana nella vigna di Sr. L.Luca de Massimi' (found on mount Celio opposite St Stephens, towards Tramontano in the vineyard of Signor L. Luca de Massimi).

136 The winged Mercury: ibid., no. 26419; the four versions of Diana, no. 26430.

137 See McGuiness, *Catalogue*, pp. 173–97.

138 Du Pérac, *I disegni*, manuscript published by T. Ashby, 1916 f. 71.

139 Bibliothèque Nationale, Ms fr. 382, f. 32v.

140 The significance of the juxtaposition of fragments and whole miniatures is discussed by John Elsner, 'The house and museum of Sir John Soane', J. Elsner and R. Cardinal, *The Cultures of Collecting*, London 1994, pp. 155–76. The interplay of ruins and construction can be seen in Joseph Gandy's watercolours of the Bank of England and other monuments built by Sir John Soane: see *John Soane*, ed. Richardson and Stevens.

141 Thevet, *La Cosmographie universelle*, I, f. 373v.

142 P. Petrasanta, 'Di Fontanbleo a Francesco Re di Francia', Bibliothèque Nationale Ms it. 1043, f. 10; Du Choul, 'Antiquitez romaines', f. 37; and Du Cerceau, *Les Plus Excellents Bastiments*, f. 3v.

143 Van Buchel, *Journal*, pp. 160–5. For the works done at Fontainebleau under Henri II, see Maurice Roy, *Artistes et monuments de la Renaissance en France*, 2 vols, Paris, 1929, I, pp. 244–60.

144 The description of Pius II's visit in 1461 can be found in Florence A. Gragg, *Memoirs of a Renaissance Pope*, London, 1960, p. 193; for other visits, see MacDonald and Pinto, *Hadrian's Villa and its Legacy*, pp. 207, 212.

145 'Descrittione delle superba & magnificentissima Villa Tiburtina Hadriana', British Library, Add. Ms 22001 is a copy (*c.* 1600) of the Paris manuscript, Bibliothèque Nationale, Ms it. 625, entitled 'Trattato dell'antichità di Tivoli e della villà Adriana, fatto di Pirro Ligorio patririo Napolitano Romano, e dedicato all'Illust. et Pegmo Hippolito secondo cardinal di Ferrara'. It was published in part by Graevius in 1723, *Thesaurus antiquitatem et historiarum Italiae*, and again in 1751 with plans by Francesco Contini, *Ichnographia*, Rome.

146 Ligorio excavated the villa further in 1560 and 1566. A detailed inventory made on the death of the cardinal of Ferrara in 1572 shows that thirty-eight statues from Hadrian's villa adorned the palace at Tivoli; see Macdonald and Pinto, *Hadrian's Villa and its Legacy*, p. 289.

147 For a full analysis of these different elements, see ibid., pp. 48–111.

148 See David R. Coffin, *The Villa in the Life of Renaissance Rome*, Princeton, 1979.

149 De L'Orme probably visited the site with his patron, Cardinal Marcello Cervini, amateur archaeologist who excavated the villa: see Macdonald and Pinto, *Hadrian's Villa and its Legacy*, p. 215.

150 Audebert, *Voyage d'Italie*, II, pp. 69–88, for the description of his visit to Tivoli.

151 Montaigne, *Journal*, pp. 129–30. T. Ashby has studied the statues, 'The Villa d'Este at Tivoli and the collection of classical sculptures which it contained', *Archaeologia*, vol. 61, 1908, pp. 219–56.

152 Audebert, *Voyage d'Italie*, II, p. 73. Corroborative evidence comes from a manuscript (written in 1571) and published by David Coffin in his study, *The Villa d'Este*, pp. 25–6, 142–8. R.W. Lightbown published extracts from Audebert's account, 'Nicolas Audebert and the Villa d'Este', *Journal of the Warburg and Courtauld Institutes*, vol. 27, 1964, pp. 164–90, and shows Audebert's reliance on Du Pérac's engraving.

153 Monsieur de Monconys, *Journal des Voyages*, pp. 454–5; Coffin, *The Villa d'Este*, p. 323; Pierre du Val (*Le Voyage et la description d'Italie*, Paris, 1656) had also given an admiring account of the fountain of Rome, pp. 269–70.

154 David Coffin discusses these summer debates in *The Villa d'Este*, pp. 335–6.

155 There were many other notable retreats built between 1540 and

1570; similar palaces with large collections and/or grottoes were La Bâtie, built for Claude d'Urfé (1501–68), see Daniel Vallat (ed.), *Claude d'Urfé et La Bâtie. L'Univers d'un gentilhomme de la Renaissance*, Montbrison, 1990; Saint Maur des Fossés, constructed for Cardinal du Bellay: see De L'Orme, *Nouvelles inventions*, f. 52v; and Ecouen, built by Jean Bullant for the *connétable* de Montmorency, and a large grotto (which was never installed) designed by Bernard Palissy and described by him as a 'monstruosité' in *Architecture et ordonnance de la grotte*.

156 Symeoni, *Les Illustres Observations*, sig. A2v.

157 Ibid., p. 95.

158 Thevet, *La Cosmographie universelle*, I., f. 579v: 'Meudon, recommandable pour les antiquitez que j'ay veües dedans, et pour sa crotesque, garnie de tant de statues et effigies antiques de marbre, que de bronze' (Meudon, notable for the antiquities which I have seen inside, and for its Grotesque furnished with so many statues and ancient marble and bronze effigies).

159 G. Colletet, *Antiquitez de la ville de Paris*, Paris, 1577, f. 200v; J. Rabel, *Les Antiquitez et singularitez de Paris*, Paris, 1588, f. 177v; and E. Cholet, *Remarques singulieres de la ville, cité, et université de Paris*, Paris, 1614, p. 111; Estienne de la Boétie also composed 'Ad Musas, de antro Medono', and dedicated the poem to Charles de Lorraine; it was edited by Montaigne in 1571, and given in a modern edition by P. Bonnefon, *Les Oeuvres complètes d'Estienne de la Boëtie*, Bordeaux and Paris, 1892, pp. 244 ff.

160 Lestocquoy, *Correspondance des Nonces en France, Lenzi et Gualtiero*, no. 91.

161 Philibert de L'Orme also stated that he was building a grotto at Monceaux in 1556, *Premier tome*, f. 250. On the prevalence of this form

in France in the sixteenth century and the influence of Serlio, see Golson, 'Serlio, Primaticcio and the architectural grotto', pp. 95–108.

162 These details are given in Roy, *Artistes et monuments*, I, pp. 482–4; and in P. Biver, *Histoire du château de Meudon*, Paris, 1923, p. 32.

163 See Anne-Marie Lecoq, '"Queti et Musis Henrici II. Gall. R." Sur la Grotte de Meudon', who cites Vigenère's testimony, p. 101, *Le Loisir lettré*, ed. Fumaroli, Paris, 1996, pp. 93–115.

164 Van Buchel, *Journal*, pp. 92–3.

165 Symeoni, *Les Illustres Observations*, sigs A2v–A3.

166 Belleforest, *La Cosmographie*, f. 278; Belleforest's text is an augmented edition of Munster's *Cosmography*.

167 Pierre de Ronsard, *Oeuvres complètes*, ed. Gustave Cohen, 2 vols, Paris, 1965, I, p. 955.

168 Michel Bouterone, *Le petit Olympe d'Issy*, Paris, 1609, cited in Roy, *Artistes et monuments*, I, pp. 483–4.

169 Details are provided by De L'Orme, *Premier tome*, ff. 250–1:

> Hunc tibi, Francisci, assertas ob
>   Palladis arteis,
> Secessum, vitas si forte palatia,
>   gratae
> Diana et Charitis, et sacravere
>   Camoena.

> [Here François, in this quiet place protected by the arts of Pallas, live Diana, the Graces, and the Muses who dedicate the palace to you.]

170 Cited by Corrozet, *Les Antiquitez* f. 200v, who wished to emphasize its significance: 'il est important de reciter sur le devant dudict lieu, dedans la cornice, est escrit en lettres d'or.' (It is important to note that in the front of the place, on the cornice, is an inscription written in gold letters.)

171 Ronsard, *Oeuvres complètes*, I, pp. 955–7. It should be noted that his evocation of the Grotto is exact in

its detail; Pallas and Bacchus guarded its entrance. The poetic and philosophical atmosphere of the place was emphasized in early histories of Meudon; Antonio le Roy, in his title *Floretum philosophicum seu iudus Meudonianus* (Paris, 1654) joins Meudon and Philosophy, and in a poem which sees the place as a symbol of contented minds – *Extremum grati animi symbolum in Meudonium* – he expatiates on the palace filled with marble, pictures and portraits (of Aristotle and of Plato).

172 Liliane Châtelet-Lange has studied Symeoni's manuscript closely, 'Le "Museo de Vanves"'. She suggests that Symeoni was influenced by Giovio through his friend Doni; a French influence must also be considered as Symeoni knew the major places where antiquities were displayed in France.

173 Bibliothèque Nationale, Ms fr. 306.

174 Series of tapestries were woven in the early seventeenth century based on the drawings commissioned by Houël; see S. Béguin, 'La Suite d'Arthémise', *L'Oeil*, vol. 38, 1959, pp. 32–9, and Ehrmann, *Antoine Caron*, pp. 51–6; Fouquet owned eleven pieces of tapestry made from Caron's designs, Schnapper, *Curieux du grand siècle*, II, p. 225.

175 Not all the drawings which survive are by Caron; some are by Henri Lerambert, others possibly by Niccolò dell'Abate. See the discussions of Béguin and Ehrmann.

176 He makes this explicit when he goes on to suggest that the drawings he has commissioned to accompany the manuscript should be turned into tapestries 'pour l'ornement de vos maisons des Tuileries' (for the decoration of your Tuileries palace) (Houël, 'Histoire de la reine Arthémise', f. 9).

177 On this parallelism, see the depiction of Catherine as Arthemise during the Paris entry of Charles

IX, *Entry of Charles IX* (1571), ed. F.A. Yates, Amsterdam, 1974, p. 15 and f. 14v; the articles of Sheila ffolliott should also be consulted: 'Biography from below: Nicolas Houël's *Histoire d'Arthemise*', *Proceedings of the Annual Meeting of the Western Society for French History*, vol. 13, 1986, pp. 90–8; and 'Catherine de' Medici as Artemisia: figuring the powerful widow', *Rewriting the Renaissance*, ed. M. Ferguson, R. Quilligan and N. Vickers, Chicago, 1985, pp. 227–41, 370–6.

178 Ehrmann, *Antoine Caron*, pp. 52–83, gives an analysis of those drawings that survive; although these are now well known, no one has considered the text overall.

179 Rome is the factor which brings text and drawings together and which argues against William McAllister Johnson's suggestion that text and design are autonomous, 'Manuscrits, maquettes et albums inédits: Antoine Caron et la suite d'Arthemise', *Cahiers V.L. Saulnier*, no. 6, Paris, 1989, pp. 121–9.

180 See Ehrmann, *Antoine Caron*, pp. 58–63, and Plates 30–41.

181 There are distinct similarities with the tomb Catherine had built for Henri II. In a recent paper, 'Henri II et les arts', Ian Wardropper drew attention to the base designed for the king's heart and its Roman motifs, Colloque du Louvre, septembre 1997. Van Buchel has left a detailed description of Henri II's tomb, *Journal*, pp. 133–4.

182 Chapter 11 of Book 4 is devoted to an evocation of Queen Arthemise's house in the country. Pliny provided two descriptions of his villas: his Tuscan villa in *Natural History*, Book 4, chapter 34, pp. 30–1; and his house at Laurentian, *Letters*, vol. I, Book 2, ch. 17, to Gallus.

183 La Croix du Maine, *Bibliothèque*, p. 347, where he wrote of the *Histoire d'Arthemise*: 'Cette histoire n'est encores en lumiere: elle se voit au

cabinet dud. sieur Nicolas Hoüel laquelle il a composee par le commandement de la Roine Mere du Roy, et a fait une despense infinie, et presque incroïable, pour rendre cette histoire parfaite et accomplie de tous poincts: Ie ne sçay pas quelle recompense il a receu pour ses travaux, mais ie sçay bien qu'il y a employé la plus part de son industrie, et de ses moyens.' (This History is not yet published; it can be seen in the study of Nicolas Hoüel who composed it by order of the Queen Mother and who has spent infinite, almost unbelievable, sums to make it perfect and finished from every point of view. I do not know what recompense he has had for all his work, but I do know that he has expended on it most of his time and means.)

184 Cited in full by La Ferrière, *Le XVIe Siècle*, pp. 300–1.

Chapter 6   Fragments and Wholes

1 All three volumes were published by Fédéric Morel in Paris in 1558.

2 On the reverberations, see Margaret W. Ferguson, 'The afflatus of ruin: meditations of Rome by Du Bellay, Spenser, and Stevens', *Roman Images*, ed. Annabel Patterson, Baltimore, 1984, pp. 23–50, and Malcolm Smith's introduction to his edition of the *Antiquitez de Rome*, Binghamton, New York, 1994.

3 In this context, Dorothy Coleman's work on Du Bellay's allusiveness is fundamental, *The Chaste Muse: A Study of Joachim du Bellay's Poetry* (Medieval and Renaissance Authors, 3), Leiden, 1980.

4 Greene, *The Light in Troy*, ch. 11, pp. 221–41; Gilbert Gadoffre saw *l'idole de Rome* as a spiritual entity whose influence continued to circulate throughout Europe as if

Rome were still intact, *Du Bellay et le sacre*, Paris, 1978, p. 101.

5 MacPhail, *The Voyage to Rome*, pp. 38–94 on Du Bellay.

6 Tucker's argument in *The Poet's Odyssey* is very complex and founded on rich associative material from publications which Du Bellay would have known. It has to be questioned whether their undoubted relevance (in the general associative sense) proves the negative reading of *Les Antiquitez* which Tucker favours: see especially pp. 137, 177 and 181 ff.; see also his contribution in Georges Cesdron (ed.), *Du Bellay. Actes du Colloque International d'Angers du 26 au 29 mai, 1989*, 2 vols, Angers, 1990, 'Du Bellay, Janus Vitalis et Lucain: la trame des mots dans *Les Antiquitez* ou plus un *Songe* et dans quelques vers analogues des *Poemata*', I, pp. 149–60. For a similar viewpoint, John McClelland, 'Les *Antiquitez de Rome*: discours rhétorique, discours historique, discours personnel', ibid., I, pp. 191–200.

7 Cited in Gadoffre, *Du Bellay et le sacre*, p. 86. On Du Bellay in Rome, Dickinson, *Du Bellay in Rome*, is still an important source. For some more recent indications see Richard Cooper, 'Poetry in ruins: the literary context of Du Bellay's cycles on Rome', *Renaissance Studies*, vol. 3, no. 2, 1989, pp. 156–66.

8 Margaret Ferguson has written most persuasively on the living quality of so-called dead texts, and on the powerful presence of ancient writers in Du Bellay's poems, 'The Exile's *Defence*', *Publications of the Modern Language Association*, vol. 93, 1978, pp. 275–89.

9 Although for the purposes of my argument these two poems are discussed first, there is no evidence to show that they were composed before some of the *Regrets* or indeed *Les Antiquitez*.

10 Du Bellay paid tribute to Louis de Bailleul's profound knowledge and to his friendship in an epigram where the poet exhorts his friend to read the *Romae descriptio* to the end and to enjoy again the fruits of their walks: Epigram 27, published with a French translation in Joachim du Bellay, *Oeuvres poétiques*, VII, *Oeuvres Latines. Poemata*, Paris, 1984, pp. 96–9.

11 Ad Janus Avansonium, apud summum pont. oratorem regium, Tiberis, Du Bellay, *Poemata*, VII, pp. 44–53. On the importance of Roman poets' influence on this poem, and of Virgil in particular, see James S. Hirstein, 'La Rome de Virgile et celle du 16e siècle dans *Ad Janum Avansonium apud summum pont. oratorem regium, Tyberis* de Joachim Du Bellay', *Acta Conventus Neo-Latini Sanctandreani*, Proceedings of the 5th International Congress of Neo-Latin Studies, St Andrews, 1982, Binghamton, New York, 1986, pp. 351–8.

12 For similar imperial pretensions, see my discussion in *Ideal Forms*, pp. 9–50.

13 Letter dated 14 October 1559, and edited by Pierre de Nolhac, *Lettres de Joachim Du Bellay*, Paris, 1883, p. 35.

14 Notably, Robert Griffin, *The Coronation of the Poet. Joachim du Bellay's Debt to the Trivium*, Berkeley, 1969, p. 124; Malcolm Quainton, 'Morte peinture and vivante peinture in *Les Antiquitez de Rome* and *Les Regrets*', *Renaissance Studies*, vol. 3, no. 2, 1989, pp. 167–77, and 'Les Regrets: une poétique de Parade', *Du Bellay*, ed. Cesdron, I, 249–59; and D. Russell, 'Du Bellay's emblematic vision of Rome', *Yale French Studies*, vol. 47, 1972, pp. 98–109.

15 The significance attached to poetry by Du Bellay can be gauged by the status of the poets he destines for his palace; all the great names are there: Homer and Virgil, Petrarch and Ronsard, *Les Regrets*, sonnet CL (ll. 9–14). Each poet will have his own particular design to match his individual style:

> Chacun aura sa forme et son architecture,
> Chacun ses ornemens, sa grace et sa peinture. (ll. 12–13)

> [Each one will have his own form and architecture, each one his ornaments, his grace and paintings.]

16 Jacques de Vintemille translated Herodian's text from Poliziano's Italian version *L'histoire d'Herodian*, (available in many editions, Paris, 1529, 1539, 1544 and 1551), and published in Lyon, G. Roville, 1554.

17 Letter dated 1 March 1528 and cited by Julia Haig Gaisser, *Catullus and his Renaissance Readers*, Oxford, 1993, pp. 113–14.

18 Cited in John O'Brien, *Anacreon Redivivus: a Study of Anacreonic Translation in Mid-Sixteenth-Century France*, Ann Arbor, 1995, p. 58. Lipsius' reconstitutions of authentic texts are also covered with indications of *coniectura*.

19 This impression may arise from the thoroughness and impressiveness of Anthony Grafton's investigations of Scaliger's work, see *Joseph Scaliger, Volume I: Textual Criticism and Exegesis*, Oxford, 1983; *Volume II: Historical Chronology*, Oxford, 1993.

20 Auguste de Thou mentions the close friendship of Scaliger and Panvinius to whom he refers as 'si cher à Scaliger, qui l'avoit connu à Rome, et qui l'aimoit par rapport à sa patrie, et à la grande connoissance qu'il avoit des antiquités Romaines, sacrées ou profanes' (so beloved by Scaliger who knew him in Rome and who revered him because of his country and his deep knowledge of the antiquities of Rome, both sacred and profane),

De Thou, *Mémoires*, I, p. 33. We noted earlier (Chapter 4, p. 115) Vigenère's strong support for Scaliger's 'conjectures'.

21 Reported by J. Jehasse, *La Renaissance de la critique*, p. 194.

22 The approach adopted by Scaliger is the same as that used by Dosio in his drawings of Rome, see above, Chapter 2, note 46.

23 Cited in Grafton, *Scaliger*, I, pp. 158–9.

24 Anthony Grafton, *Renaissance Readers and Ancient Texts*, Cambridge, Mass., 1991, p. 103.

25 For a preliminary analysis of *Les Antiquitez* in the context of ruins, see my article 'Conjecture, reshaping and the creative process', pp. 226–30.

26 V.L. Saulnier concurs with this reading of the implications of the title, see 'Commentaires sur les *Antiquitez de Rome* de Joachim du Bellay', *Bibliothèque d'Humanisme et Renaissance*, vol. 12, 1950, pp. 114–43, especially pp. 138–41.

27 The extent to which the connections drawn by Du Bellay between the poet and the king in *Les Antiquitez* are based on political concerns is set out by C. Skenazi, 'Le Poète et le roi dans les *Antiquitez de Rome* et *le Songe* de Du Bellay', *Bibliothèque d'Humanisme et Renaissance*, vol. 60, 1998, pp. 41–55.

28 Du Bellay reiterated and expanded the plans articulated here in his second sonnet, which ends:

> Quand à moy, pour tous je
>   veulx chanter
> Les sept costaux Romains, sept
>   miracles du monde.

> [As for me, I want to sing (above all) the seven hills of Rome, the seven wonders of the world.]

29 See Tucker's report of Henri Estienne's notations on his copy collected together in Appendix C of *The Poet's Odyssey*, p. 237, and the discussion in his Chapter 4, pp. 175 ff. That poets in the sixteenth century saw inspiration as communing with souls long dead can also be seen in Robert Garnier's liminary poem to Thevet's *Les Vrais Pourtraits*, sig. c i,

> Tu descens indomtable au
>   profond des Enfers,
> Pour les antiques Dieux
>   ressuciter au monde,
> Qui logeoyent enfermés dans
>   une nuit profonde,
> Comme Esprits inconneus,
>   d'oubliance couvers.

> [Invincible, you descend to the depths of Hell/ to bring back to the world the ancient gods/ who sojourn wrapped in the dark cloak of night/ Like unknown spirits covered in forgetfulness.]

30 The translations from *Les Antiquitez* are taken from Edmund Spenser's *Ruines of Rome*, appended to Malcolm Smith's edition of Du Bellay's *Antiquitez de Rome*.

31 There is now a mass of articles on the influence of Vitalis' poems on Rome on other sixteenth-century poets, and on influences he himself absorbed; most are given in Tucker's 'Bibliography' (pp. 263–85) and he has himself contributed significantly to these researches, pp. 105–73. Malcolm Quainton has provided a reassessment of Du Bellay's originality in this complex area of intertextuality, 'Du Bellay and Janus Vitalis', *French Studies Bulletin*, no. 38, Spring 1991, pp. 12–15. All this discussion emphasizes the need, in the domain of locating inspiration, to pay as much attention to written sources as to visual ones.

32 For a discussion of this kind of transmutation into symbols, see Griffin, *Coronation of the Poet*, p. 125.

33 On the complex meanings of monument/tomb, see E. MacPhail, 'The Roman tomb or the image of the tomb in Du Bellay's *Antiquitez*', *Bibliothèque d'Humanisme et Renaissance*, vol. 48, no. 2, 1986, pp. 359–72.

34 There is the same kind of word play in Du Bellay's adaptation (sonnet 7) of Castiglione's poem 'Superbi colli'.

35 Jerry C. Nash, 'Cette *beauté non pareille*: Du Bellay et l'écriture de l'impossible', Cesdron (ed.), *Du Bellay*, I, pp. 15–28, has demonstrated how Du Bellay's use of *adynaton* assured the transformation of 'non pouvoir en pouvoir'; through this use, the inability to signify becomes affirmation of meaning; the same point is made several times in Michel Deguy's celebration, *Tombeau de Du Bellay*, Paris, 1973.

36 There has been extensive debate as to the meaning and resonances of *idole*: Gadoffre, *Du Bellay et le sacre*, p. 101, sees it as a kind of *fantôme* signalling the presence of the ancient city 'comme si Rome était encore debout' (as if Rome was still standing); Tucker, *The Poet's Odyssey*, pp. 206–14, has examined a range of texts associated with Plotinus in order to present a diminished significance for *idole* which represents, in his version, an inferior vestige, the pure 'idole' having been absorbed into 'le grand tout'. In my view, Tucker underestimates the reverberative power of the concept.

37 The power of renewal which came from gazing at the ruins is well expressed by Giovanni Botero in his praise of Rome: 'we imagine [what] that city was when she flourished and triumphed, if now, while she lieth thus defaced and is none other than a sepulture of herself she allureth us to see her, and feedeth us insatiably with the ruins of herself', cited from the 1606 translation of *Delle cause della grandezza della citta* [Venice, 1589], and printed in D. and P. Waley, *Giovanni Botero. The Reason of State*, London, 1956, p. 230.

38 Greene, *The Light in Troy*, pp. 235–8, has written cogently on the act of reaching out being already a process of reviving and restoring. Jodelle, too, in a *chanson* written for the seigneur de Brunel, saw that Time (although destroyer of all beautiful things)

> Nous laisse voir
> Dedans quelque ruine
> La beauté grande, et l'art d'un
>   édifice,
> Qui par les traits de quelque
>   frontispice
> Tout entier se devine

[gives us a glimpse in some ruin/ of the great beauty and artifice of a building/ which from some traces on a frontispiece/ allows us to guess at the whole structure],

E. Jodelle, *Oeuvres poétiques*, ed. E. Balmas, 2 vols, Paris, 1965, I, p. 354.

39 This self-reflective dimension of Du Bellay's poetry has been well analysed in Tucker, *The Poet's Odyssey*, *passim*; and by François Rigolot with respect to *Les Regrets*, 'Du Bellay et la poésie du refus', *Bibliothèque d'Humanisme et Renaissance*, vol. 36, no. 3, 1974, pp. 489–502, where he demonstrates that the poet's satirical appraisal of Rome leads to what he terms 'un esprit poétique en miettes' (a poetic spirit in pieces).

40 To cite two examples: Gadoffre, *Du Bellay et le sacre*, used *Le Songe* as an important part of his argument to establish Du Bellay's religious preoccupations in his poetry; Heather Ingman tried to solve the puzzle by having recourse to alchemical processes, 'Du Bellay and

the language of alchemy in the *Songe*', *Modern Language Review*, vol. 82, part 4, October 1987, pp. 844–53.

41 Critics have noticed the difference in the description of Rome in the two series; see, especially, Richard A. Katz, 'The collapse of the city: the *Vision* of the *Antiquitez de Rome*', *L'Esprit Créateur*, Fall 1979, pp. 12–20; and Cooper, 'Poetry in ruins', pp. 156–66.

42 Charles Bené has persuasively argued the presence of the *Apocalypse* in these poems where the same precious materials and the same symbolic meanings can be found: 'Bible et inspiration religieuse chez Du Bellay', Cesdron (ed.), *Du Bellay*, I, pp. 177–87. It should be noted, however, that the tradition of describing elaborate and transparent buildings in literature is a long one; see David Cowling, *Building the Text. Architecture as Metaphor in Late Medieval and Early Modern France*, Oxford, 1998, which begins with such a description from an anonymous *Conqueste du chasteau d'amours*.

43 Van der Noot's publications are reproduced by Malcolm Smith in his edition of *Les Antiquitez de Rome* along with the woodcuts, pp. 119–35; see also Simone Dorangeon, 'Les Complaints de Spenser et l'héritage de Du Bellay', in *Du Bellay. Oeuvres critiques*, no. 20, vol. I, *Du Bellay devant la critique de 1550 à nos jours*, Tübingen, 1995, pp. 175–82; and S.M. Poliner, 'Du Bellay's *Songe*: strategies of deceit, poetics of vision', *Bibliothèque d' Humanisme et Renaissance*, vol. 43, 1981, pp. 509–25, where she discusses the similarity between the images in Du Bellay's sequence and those in emblem books.

44 Du Bellay, *Poemata*, I, p. 447 (Courbet edition of *Poésies françaises et latines*, 2 vols, Paris, 1918):

> Carmina principibus gaudent, plausuque theatri,
> Quique placet paucis, displicet ipse sibi;

translated and discussed in Yvonne Bellenger, *Du Bellay: les Regrets qu'il fit dans Rome*, Rome, 1975, p. 444.

45 In addition to her analyses in *The Chaste Muse*, *passim*, on this point, Dorothy Coleman's article, 'Allusiveness in the *Antiquitez de Rome*', *L'Esprit Créateur*, Fall 1979, pp. 3–11, should be consulted, as well as Alex. L. Gordon's work, 'Styles of absence and presence: *Les Antiquitez* and *Regrets*', *Crossroads and Perspectives: French Literature of the Renaissance*, ed. Catherine M. Grisé and C.D.E. Tolton, Geneva, 1986, pp. 21–30.

46 The Latin text is given by Malcolm Smith, p. 10, note 3 of his *Joachim du Bellay's Veiled Victim*, Geneva, 1974.

47 This translation by Colletet of Sainte Marthe's original Latin text is given in Bellenger, *Du Bellay*, p. 267.

48 Spenser's translations are discussed by Malcolm Smith, *Antiquitez de Rome*, pp. 10–14, and in his commentaries on each translated poem, and in Dorangeon's article, 'Les Complaints', see note 43 above.

49 Smith, *Antiquitez de Rome*, p. 13, where he adds that Spenser's translations of Du Bellay's sonnets found echoes in Shakespeare's sonnets.

50 The specific changes introduced by Jan van der Noot are discussed by Smith, ibid., pp. 12–13. Other uses by Protestant writers of Du Bellay's text will be explored below, in Chapter 7.

51 A. Ceccarelli Pellegrino, 'Du Bellay e il Poliphilo, lettura pluri-isopica del *Songe*', *Studi di letteratura francese*, vol. 19, 1992, pp. 65–95, draws parallels between these images and the illustrations in Colonna's book.

52 *Roma* is depicted on p. 131 of Smith's edition.

53 Claude de Pontoux, *Les Oeuvres*, Lyon, 1579, p. 148.

54 Ibid., pp. 304–5.

55 Geneviève Demerson has studied the detail of La Jessée's dependence on *Les Regrets* in her critical edition of *Les Jeunesses* (composed between 1571 and 1578, and published in Antwerp in 1583), Société des textes français modernes, Paris, 1991; Jean Vignes provides a nuanced view of the parallels between the two works, both linguistic and thematic, in his article, 'Le Pastiche des *Regrets*'.

56 Hennequin's poems were published by Denis du Pré in 1579; the most obvious borrowings from Du Bellay occur on sig. A iijr, ff. 4v, 8r and 10r.

57 The same tones of hopeless lament can be found in the poems of Clovis Hesteau de Nuysement, *Les Oeuvres poétiques*, I and II, 2 vols, ed. Roland Guillot, Geneva, 1994, and in particular in 'Les Gemissemens de la France', dedicated to Henri III and published in 1578, ibid., pp. 124–5, ll. 69–86.

58 Goulart's poems were published alongside those of other Protestant writers in *Poemes chrestiens et autres divers auteurs recueillis et nouvellement mis en lumière par Philippe le Pas*, n.p., 1574.

59 Ibid., sonnet 15 (p. 182), 'Tout ce que Rome tient de sa gloire première' (all that Rome has of her pristine glory), is a close interpretation of *Les Antiquitez*, 3, while the following poem (no. 16, p. 182) underlines the recording power of the engraver's tool, 'Du burin qui combat le temps injurieux' (of the steel which challenges injurious Time), and draws general moral lessons from the ruins portrayed.

60 Françoise Joukovsky drew attention to the influence of Du Bellay on Nicolas Ellain in *La Gloire à la*

Renaissance, Geneva, 1969, p. 310; in a more recent article, she has somewhat modified her original view, arguing that critics have overplayed the impact on Ellain's poems of *Les Antiquitez* and *Les Regrets*, ' "Bellai sumos inter celebrande poetas", Les *Elegies* et les *Sonnets* de Nicolas Ellain', in *Du Bellay. Oeuvres critiques*, no. 20, vol. 1, 1995, pp. 165–73.

61 Cited by Malcolm Smith, *Antiquitez de Rome*, p. 519; or indeed, the words 'finir en rien' (end in nothing) and 'tombeau' (tomb) which reverberate in Ronsard's liminary verses to Hamelin's translation of Livy (1559).

62 Françoise Joukovsky discussed a poem by Gadon in *La Gloire*, p. 311, noting the influence of Du Bellay and the poet's predilection for violent themes. As far as I know, other critics have ignored his work.

63 Gadon announced this fact himself in his poems: *La Marguerite. Les Paysages, plus sonnets faicts à Rome*, Paris, 1573:

> N'y ayant autre aquest, ce m'est
>   grace bien grande
> D'estre sorty de Rome, en
>   l'aage de vingt ans,
> Sans y laisser la barbe . . .
>   (f. 22v)

[having gained nothing else, it is very gratifying to me to have got out of Rome at twenty without leaving my beard there.]

64 The contamination of France by Rome is explored in the opening poem of Gadon's sonnets written while he was in Rome and which begin on f. 20v of *La Marguerite*.

65 Gadon links the freedom of the city (granted to those who settled in Rome) to murder:

> Que les deux fondateurs, iadis
>   vindrent aux mains,

L'un pour avoir failly, occis sur
  ceste douve?
Feu-ce icy qu'on donna la loy
  d'impunité,
A chacun qui viendroit habiter
  la cité?

[the two founders came here once to do battle, one left dead upon this ditch for having failed. Was it here that the law of impunity was given to each one who came to live in this city?]

66 The poet not only claims this transfer of power but also argues that it will be augmented 'sous un Roy qui l'acroist et restore' (under a king who increases and restores it) (f. 21, l. 8).

67 See note 31 for preliminary comment on Vitalis' epigrams; in 1982 Raymond Skyrme announced an unnoticed fifteenth-century prototype of Vitalis' poem (and, incidentally of Janus Pannonius' second Epigram which he wrote on Rome), '"Buscas en Roma a Roma": Quevedo, Vitalis, and Janus Panvinius', *Bibliothèque d' Humanisme et Renaissance*, vol. 44, pp. 363–7; in 1985 and 1986, Tucker discussed the importance of Vitalis for Du Bellay, 'Sur les *Elogia* de Janus Vitalis et les Antiquitez de Rome de Joachim du Bellay', *Bibliothèque d'Humanisme et Renaissance*, vol. 47, no. 1, pp. 103–12; 48, no. 3, pp. 751–6; in 1989, John R.C. Martyn argued that a Portuguese poet might have been a source for both Du Bellay and Vitalis, 'André de Resende, original author of *Roma prisca*', *Bibliothèque d'Humanisme et Renaissance*, vol. 51, no. 2, pp. 407–11; and finally in 1992, Tucker argued for the continuing legacy of Vitalis (despite Martyn's claims), '*Roma rediviva*: André de Resende, Joachim du Bellay, and the continuing Legacy of Janus Vitalis' Roman Diptych', *Bibliothèque d'*

Humanisme et Renaissance, vol. 54, no. 3, pp. 731–6.

68 Translated from Des Masures' *Carmina* (Paris, 1557) and cited (p. 150) by Olivier Millet, 'En la façon que m'a décrit Masures, l'oeuvre de Louis des Masures, un point de vue latéral sur celle de Joachim du Bellay', in *Du Bellay. Oeuvres critiques*, vol. 1, no. 20, 1995, pp. 149–63.

69 E. Pasquier, *Les Recherches de la France*, 2 vols, Paris, 1723, II, ix, col. 237; it should be noted that Montaigne owned a volume of *Epigrammata* which contained Vitalis' poems, see Tucker, 'Sur les *Elogia* de Janus Vitalis', pp. 108–9.

70 It is noticeable that Vitalis' poem is so well known that Doublet does not have to specify which Latin epigram he is translating, Jean Doublet, *Elégies*, Paris, 1559, ff. 53v–54.

71 De L'Orme, *Premier tome*, f. 152.

72 Cited in Richard G. Maber, *The Poetry of Pierre le Moyne (1602–1671)*, New York, 1982, p. 241.

73 Bergeron, 'Le Voyage d'Italie', f. 37.

74 Jean-Jacques Bouchard's text has been published by E. Kanceff, *Journal de voyage*, 2 vols, Turin, 1977; the passage cited is from II, p. 424; Montaigne's reference to the lack of bells in Rome occurs in his *Journal*, p. 98.

75 On this aspect of Du Bellay's aim to seek 'something objective beyond his own crushing sense of the ephemeral', see K. Lloyd Jones, 'Du Bellay's journey from *Roma Vetus* to *La Rome Neufve*', *Rome in the Renaissance*, ed. Ramsey, pp. 301–19.

76 The drumbeat and the rich and subtle resonances of the name 'Rome' have been discussed by Coleman, *The Chaste Muse*, pp. 102–3, and by Griffin, *Coronation of the Poet*, p. 90.

77 For the extent to which this process

of incorporation featured in Latin poetry (especially in the Roman poets), see David O. Ross Jr., *Backgrounds to Augustan Poetry: Gallus Elegy and Rome*, Cambridge, 1975.

78 An earlier version of this section of the chapter was given at the Glasgow colloquium on Montaigne, 'L'Art du décousu dans les Essais', and is now in press. Translations from the *Essais* are given from Michael Screech's text, *The Complete Essays* published by Penguin, London, 1987. Quotations are taken from the Presses Universitaires de France, Paris, 1965 edition where the different states of composition are marked A, B and C respectively.

79 Preconditioned visions of Rome, gained from reading, have been a major theme in this book; on Montaigne's preparation specifically, see my study of 'Involuntary memory', and Françoise Charpentier, 'La Rome de Montaigne, modèle et intercesseur', *Montaigne et l'Italie. Atti del congresso internazionale di studi di Milano–Lecco, 26–30 ottobre, 1988*, ed. E. Balmas, *Biblioteca del Viaggio in Italia*, no. 38, Geneva, 1991, pp. 351–62.

80 Montaigne, *Journal*, ed. Rigolot, p. 90. Montaigne had obliged his companions to rise in the early hours, 'Nous en partismes lendemain trois heures avant le jour, tant il [Montaigne] avoit envy de voir le pavé de Rome' (We left three hours before daybreak, so keen was Montaigne to see the streets of Rome).

81 See Zachary S. Schiffman's essay, 'Montaigne's perception of ancient Rome: biography as a form of history', *Rome in the Renaissance*, ed. Ramsey, pp. 333–44. For a recent assessment of Montaigne's journey in the context of other voyages in the Renaissance, see F. Rigolot (ed.) *Montaigne Studies. An Interdisciplinary Forum*, vol. V, nos 1–2, Chicago, 1993.

82 Daniela Boccassini has compared Montaigne's text with drawings made of the ruins of Rome by Heemskerck, Serlio and Scamozzi. Her interest is to show how artists and writers shared the same feelings of regret at the loss of the past: 'Ruines montaigniennes', *Montaigne Studies*, ed. Rigolot, pp. 154–91.

83 Montaigne, *Journal*, p. 101.

84 Ibid., p. 99.

85 The uplifting effect of the ruins and what they represented was set out for Philippe de Launoy by Lipsius in his letter dated 3 April 1578, given and translated by Anthoine Brun (1619) in Normand Doiron, *L'Art de voyager*, pp. 211–17. Here is a flavour of his advice: 'l'on te monstrera la demeure de Pline, ou celle de Virgile et de Properce . . . de combien de joye interieure sera meslee ceste veüe, lorsque les ombres de ces grands personnages se representent non seulement à l'esprit, mais presque aux yeux . . . et que nous touchons les lieux qu'ils ont tant de fois touché[s].' (They will show you Pliny's house, or that of Virgil or Propertius . . . how much inner joy will be mixed with such sights, when the shades of these great men are present not only to the mind but also almost to the eyes . . . and that we can touch the places they once touched.) See also our discussion in Chapter 4, pp. 122–3.

86 Montaigne, *Journal*, p. 92.

87 See my earlier discussion, 'Contradictory impulses', pp. 392–409.

88 Montaigne's awareness of the successive periods of construction in Rome and the resultant multi-layered character of the city is close to the use Freud was to make of such superimposed processes. See the discussion in Chapter 5, pp. 162–3. To my knowledge, Irène S. Mayer was the first who perceived

a connection between the mind/ city analogy offered by Freud and Montaigne's own superimposition of images: 'Montaigne's cure: stones and Roman ruins', *Modern Language Notes*, vol. 97, no. 4, May 1982, pp. 958–74; it has also been touched on by Tom Conley in 'A sucking of cities: Montaigne in Paris and Rome', *Montaigne Studies. An Interdisciplinary Forum*, vol. 9, 1997, pp. 167–86, where – having fused Freud and Montaigne – he argues that Montaigne is both Paris and Rome.

89 In Augustus' Rome, classical quotation and archaizing elements could be found everywhere, see Zanker, *The Power of Images*, pp. 258 ff.

90 See Mary McKinley, *Words in a Corner*, Lexington, 1981, pp. 15 ff., where she recognizes that borrowings from authors like Ovid, Horace or Virgil raised the larger issues of the relationship of the parts to the whole, and her book *Les Terrains vagues des 'Essais': itinéraires et intertextes*, Paris, 1996, *passim*.

91 Often the borrowings were maxims which usefully summed up a particular stage in the argument and gave authority to it. Their interpretative power has been examined by François Rigolot, 'Montaigne's maxims: from the discourse of the other to the expression of self', *L'Esprit Créateur*, vol. 22, no. 3, Fall 1982, pp. 8–18; on Montaigne's borrowings more generally, see Christine Brousseau-Beuermann, *La Copie de Montaigne*, Paris, 1989. In his often ironic references to the assembling of fragments, Montaigne may also have been thinking about the taste for *Centos*, and of Ausonius' dismissive comment: 'Centon: c'est un pur travail de mémoire: rassembler des lambeaux épars et former un tout de ces découpures, cela peut mériter un sourire plutôt qu'un éloge.' (*Centon* is a pure work

of memory: assembling scattered fragments and making a whole out of the cuttings; that merits a smile more than an encomium.) Ausonius nonetheless penned a magnificent piece, fabricated in this way, for the emperor Valentian (AD 350). For this strange tradition, see Octave Delepierre, *Centoniana ou Encyclopédie du Centon*, The Philobiblon Society, X, 1966–67.

92 The equilibrium thus achieved through commonplaces is explored in Lipsius' writing by Ann Moss, 'Vision fragmentée et unitaire: les *Politiques* et les recueils de lieux communs', p. 375 in Mouchel (ed.) *Juste Lipse*. On contemporary assigning of the *Essais* to the genre *miscellanea*, see her article, 'Du lieu commun à la maxime: de la Renaissance au monde classique', *Romanica Wratislaviensia*, vol. 36, 1991, pp. 43–52.

93 See Michel Jeanneret's article 'Myths of antiquity', *Modern Language Notes*, vol. 110, no. 5, December 1995, pp. 1043–53, where he shows that in order to make the ancient heritage more accessible texts were dismembered and cut up into mobile units that could be recycled. The importance of the context of Montaigne's borrowings was first discussed by Mary McKinley, 'Text and context in Montaigne's *Essais*: the example of Ovid's *Metamorphoses*', *L'Esprit Créateur*, vol. 20, no. 1, Spring 1980, pp. 46–65.

94 Ann Moss, *Printed Commonplace-Books and the Structuring of Renaissance Thought*, Oxford, 1996, analyses the longevity of Aristotle's views and their adaptation to writing and organizing thought in the Renaissance. The metaphor was also used by Seneca, who may have been Montaigne's direct source and where the importance of digestion is emphasized: *Epistles to Lucilius*, no. 84, Loeb Library, London,

1928–35, p. 279, 'We also, I say, ought to copy those bees, and sift whatever we have gathered from a varied course of reading, for such things are better preserved if they are kept separate; then, by applying the supervising care with which our nature has endowed us – in other words, our natural gifts – we should so blend those several flavours into one delicious compound, that even though it betrays its origin, yet it nevertheless is a clearly different thing from that whence it came . . . We must digest it; otherwise it will merely pass into the memory and not into our very being.'

95 See his advocacy of being a naturalist, borrowing and transforming those 'thefts', 'les desguisant et difformant à nouveau service' (masking it and distorting it to serve a new purpose), with a turn of the wrist, in *De la physionomie* (III, 12, 1056).

96 B. Beugnot (ed.), *Jean-Louis Guez de Balzac. Les Entretiens* [1657], 2 vols, Paris, 1972, II, pp. 289–90, Entretien xviii, 'a Monsieur Gaudrilland, conseiller du Roy en ses Conseils, et President d'Angouslesme'.

97 On the alertness of the reader, see McKinley, *Words in a Corner, passim*, and *Les Terrains vagues, passim*; and Gisèle Mathieu-Castellani's article, 'Intertextualité et allusion: le régime allusif chez Ronsard', *Littérature*, vol. 55, 1984, where she shows how a residual fragment taken from another text has the reverberative power to recall the whole work from which it came. On the other hand, Estienne argued that a line of poetry might have a very specific meaning in the original text and acquire a different meaning when it has been isolated and placed in a new context: see Ann Moss' discussion, *Printed Commonplace-Books*, p. 198.

98 La Popelinière, *L'Histoire des histoires*, p. 219.

99 For Montaigne's recourse to the examples of painters whose powers of representation he clearly admired, see *De l'experience* (III, 13, 1076), 'Je laisse aux artistes, et ne sçay s'ils en viennent à bout en chose si meslée, si menue et fortuite, de renger en bandes cette infinie diversité de visages, et arrester nostre inconstance et la mettre par ordre.' (I leave it to the artists, and I do not know if even they will manage to bring it off in a matter so confused, intricate and fortuitous, to arrange this infinite variety of features into groups, pin down our inconsistencies and impose some order.)

100 Montaigne in a later edition supplied the quotation from Seneca's *Epistles to Lucilius*, Loeb Library, 1928–35, no. 118, which he has adapted: 'Miramur ex intervallo fallentia'.

101 Jean-Yves Pouilloux, *Montaigne et l'éveil de la pensée*, Paris, 1995, p. 73.

102 For the persuasive power of discontinuous modes of writing in the *Essais*, see John D. Lyons' discussion in Chapter 3 of his book, *Exemplum. The Rhetoric of Example in Early Modern France and Italy*, Princeton, 1989, pp. 118–53; and on the pleasure derived from recognition of old texts within the new, Moss, *Printed Commonplace-Books*, p. 256.

103 See Montaigne's complaint about words being such a source of persecution in *Du dementir* (II, 18, 667).

104 *Dire à demy* (only saying half the meaning) is well explored by Gisèle Mathieu-Castellani in her essay, 'L'Intertexte rhétorique: Tacite, Quintilien et la poétique des *Essais*', J.J. Supple (ed.), *Montaigne et la rhétorique. Actes du colloque de St Andrews, 28–31 mars, 1992*, Paris, 1995, pp. 17–27.

105 Floyd Gray, *Montaigne bilingue*, Paris, 1991, has emphasized how Montaigne's apparent denigration of his work is, in fact, a metaphoric way of drawing attention to its fragmented nature, see especially pp. 49 ff., and Chapter 6 'Otium/ negotium', pp. 121 ff.

106 The natural tendency of the mind to lift itself out of present realities was noted by Montaigne in one of his earliest essays, 'Nous ne sommes jamais chez nous, nous sommes tousjours au delà' (we are never 'at home': we are always outside ourselves) (*Nos affections s'emportent au dela de nous*, I, 3, 15).

107 The most devastating criticism of man's excessive ambitions founded on ignorance and incompetence is made in the final sentence of *De la vanité* (III, 9, 1000–1): 'Il n'en est une seule si vuide et necessiteuse que toy, qui embrasse l'univers; tu es le scrutateur sans connoissance, le magistrat sans jurisdiction et apres tout le badin de la farce.' (No one is as empty and needy as you, who embrace the universe: you are the seeker with no knowledge, the judge with no jurisdiction and, when all is done, the jester of the farce.)

108 For this developing conception of the self in the Renaissance, see Daniel Russell's article: 'Conception of self, conception of space and generic convention: an example from the *Heptameron*', *Sociocriticism*, nos 4–5, 1986–87, pp. 159–83.

109 Pouilloux has some admirable pages on these habits, *Montaigne*, pp. 173 ff.: 'Il nous faut, à nostre tour, du courage et la force pour résister à la tentation de réduire le livre que nous lisons à une unité et une complétude rassurantes' (in our turn we must have the courage and tenacity to resist the temptation to reduce the book that we are reading to a reasoning unity and fullness); see also Stephen Rendall's article, 'In disjointed parts/par articles décousus', in Kritzman (ed.) *Fragments*, pp. 72–82, and André Tournon, 'La Segmentation du texte: usages et singularités', *Editer les 'Essais' de Montaigne*, ed. Claude Blum et André Tournon, Paris, 1997, pp. 173–95.

110 On reading the *Essais*, see Terence Cave, 'Problems of reading in the *Essais*', in I. McFarlane and I. Maclean (eds), *Montaigne. Essays in Memory of Richard Sayce*, Oxford, 1982, pp. 133–66, and my book, *Montaigne's Deceits*, London, 1974, where I show that the oblique strategies developed by Montaigne required, for their understanding, the partnership of the reader. The extent of this partnership is explored by Françoise Joukovsky, 'Qui parle dans le livre III des *Essais*?', *Revue d'Histoire Littéraire de la France*, 1988, pp. 813–27.

111 I have discussed Montaigne's deliberate distancing of his writing from contemporary habits in *Montaigne's Deceits*; see also Floyd Gray's observations on the pleasure of reading what he terms 'une écriture tournoyante', *Montaigne bilingue*, p. 144, and Daniel Martin's *L'Architecture des Essais de Montaigne. Mémoire artificielle et mythologique*, Paris, 1992, p. 170, where he argues that the reader of Montaigne's text deciphers the writing as though it were a painting, 'en regardant partout et en même temps' (looking everywhere and at the same time).

112 For another interpretation of 'le corps monstrueux', see Gisèle Mathieu-Castellani, *Montaigne, l'écriture de l'essai*, Paris, 1988, ch. 5, 'L'essai, corps monstrueux', pp. 221–40.

113 See McGowan, 'Contradictory impulses', for a discussion of Montaigne's admiration for these forms of spectacle.

114 Lipsius, *De amphitheatro liber*, Antwerp, 1584, incorporated in the *Opera omnia*.

115 Montaigne seems not to have known at the time that the paintings were by Mantegna. On the disposition of the pictures when they were housed in the palace of San Sebastiano and their use for political purposes, see C. Malcolm Brown, 'The Palazzo di San Sebastiano (1506–12) and the art patronage of Francesco II Gonzaga, fourth marquis of Mantua', *Gazette des Beaux Arts*, vol. 129, 1997, pp. 131–80.

116 Quintilian, *Institutes of Oratory, (Institutio Oratoria)*, 2 vols, Bohn's Libraries, London, 1909, vol. 2, Book 11, ch. 17, p. 336.

117 Cicero, *De finibus*, Book 5, ch. 2, pp. 395–6. For further development of the interplay of remembrance and observation, see my paper 'Involuntary memory'.

118 Cicero, *De legibus*, Book 2, ch. 2, pp. 373–4. Atticus speaks: 'For we are in some strange way affected by the very places that carry imprints [*vestigia*] of those whom we love or admire. My beloved Athens delights me not so much by the stunning monuments or the exquisite works of antiquity found there, but rather by recalling to my mind great men – where each one lived, where he used to sit and carry on disputations, why I even enjoy looking on their graves.'

119 Citizenship of Rome was not easy to obtain; as Frenchmen, only Muret and Longueil achieved this honour. See the remarks of La Croix du Maine, *Bibliothèque*, p. 305.

Chapter 7 Negative Responses and Reverse Appropriation

1 Francesco Guicciardini, *Considerations on the Discourses of Machiavelli*, (composed 1530), ed. Cecil Grayson, in *Selected Writings*, Oxford, 1965, Book 2, p. 197; see also in the same *Selected Writings*, Guicciardini, *Ricordi*, no. 110: 'what a mistake always to be citing the ancient Romans'.

2 Erasmus, *Ciceronianus*, first published Bâle, 1528; in the *Collected Works of Erasmus*, XXVIII, ed. A.H.T. Levi, Toronto, 1986, translated by Betty I. Knott, pp. 431–2.

3 René de Lucinge's full development of his ideas on past/present comparisons is given in *La Manière de lire l'histoire*, Paris, 1614; ed. Michael J. Heath, Geneva, 1993, pp. 98–101; Lucinge began to formulate these ideas in *De la Naissance, durée et chute des estats*, Paris, 1588; ed. Michael J. Heath, Geneva, 1984, p. 116, where he resisted detailed analysis of lessons that might be learned from the past (Greeks and Romans), 'mais je les lairray, comme trop reculees de nous, pour m'attacher à celles qui nous sont familieres et voisines' (but I'll leave them aside as being too remote for us, so that I might dwell on those which are closer and more familiar).

4 Most recently, Jean Balsamo has studied this complex phenomenon of the love/hate relationships between France and Italy in the Renaissance. Although his research has concentrated on the last three decades of the century, his work makes clear that influence and rejection are also finely balanced at other periods: *Les Rencontres des Muses: italianisme et anti-italianisme dans les lettres françaises de la fin du XVIe siècle*, Paris and Geneva, 1992. For an overview of anti-Italian feeling at the French court in the sixteenth century, see Lionello Sozzi's comprehensive article, 'La Polémique anti-italienne en France au XVIe siècle', *Atti della Accademia delle Scienze di Torino*, vol. 106, 1972, pp. 99–190.

5 Already in 1565, with *Le Traicté de la conformité du langage françois avec*

le grec, Henri Estienne had sought to extol the expressive power of French; his *Deux Dialogues du nouveau langage françois italianizé et autrement desguizé*, Paris, 1578, targeted the nefarious influence of Italian, especially on courtiers, on their speech and behaviour. For an up-to-date exposition of Estienne's work and its consequences, see Pauline M. Smith's edition of the *Deux dialogues*, Geneva, 1980; in this context, her book *The Anti-Courtier Trend in Sixteenth-Century French Literature*, Geneva, 1966, should also be consulted. Gentillet's attack on Machiavelli, *Discours contre Machiavel*, was published in 1576.

6 De l'Hospital, *Poésies complètes*, pp. 3–14, 134–6.

7 See André Thevet, *La Grande et Excellente Cité de Paris*, Paris, 1881, p. 5: 'Paris fust en essence, voire et avant que Priam fust né. Par ce moyen vous voyez l'antiquité de ceste ville devancer Rome, et la pluspart des autres de par deça.' (Paris was in embryo even before Priam was born. By this means, you observe that the antiquity of the city predates Rome, and the greater part of other cities too.) The search for French origins and traditions was well launched by the middle of the century; typical examples of scholars' research are Claude Fauchet, *Recueil des antiquitez gauloises et françoises*, Paris, J. du Puys, 1579, and Pierre de la Ramée, *Liber de moribus veterum Gallorum*, Paris, 1559, translated into French the same year by Michel de Castelnau as *Livre des moeurs des anciens gaulois*, and reissued in 1581 as *Traitté des meurs et façons des anciens gaulois*, Paris, Denys du Val.

8 Estienne Pasquier's prejudice against Rome (although he was deeply knowledgeable about the city and its history) was undoubtedly formed as a counterbalance to his preoccupations with the ori-

gins and value of all things French. Letter to Sebillet, in *Les Recherches*, 2 vols, Paris, 1723, II, no. xi, cols 19–22; to Paul de Foix, *Lettres familières*, ed. D. Thickett, 3 vols, Geneva, 1974, III, p. 91; dedicatory note to the cardinal of Lorraine, *Les Recherches*, II, cols 27–8.

9 *La Chasse de la beste romaine* is a depressing work of unrelieved vituperation; it was published in La Rochelle in 1611. St Bernard's famous invective was well known; it is cited in La Popelinière, for instance: *L'Histoire de France*, 2 vols, Paris, 1581, f. 194v, and was used in attacks on Rome, in Italy and in France: see Frederick J. McGuiness, 'The rhetoric of praise and the new Rome of the Counter Reformation', Ramsey, *Rome in the Renaissance,* pp. 355–70. Another variation occurs in Louis des Masures' *Babylone ou la ruine de la grande cité*, Geneva, 1563, where Rome is 'la pute' (the whore), sig. Biii.

10 There has been much debate about whether or not Jodelle visited Rome in his youth and disliked the experience. No facts have so far emerged; see the *mise au point* in Jodelle, *Oeuvres poétiques,* I, p. 264.

11 The wolf theme is used in a second epigram written against Rome: 'Non ego Romulae miror quod pastor in urbe'. The satirical ingenuities of Buchanan have been discussed by Philip Ford in his article, 'Du Bellay et le sonnet satirique', in Yvonne Bellenger (ed.), *Le Sonnet à la Renaissance des origines au XVIIe siècle*, Paris, 1988, pp. 205–14.

12 Pierre de Lestoile records in his *Mémoires-Journaux* how Monsieur de Rohan was given a passport to reside in Rome eleven days, and how the son of Du Plessis Mornay 'eust envie comme beaucoup d'autres de la Religion de voir Rome et le pape' (desired, like

many other Protestants, to see Rome and the pope); although he went disguised, his real identity was detected and he had to flee the city precipitately: *Mémoires-Journaux*, VII, pp. 200 and 202.

13 Gregory Martin visited Rome from the end of 1576 to July 1578 when he taught at the English Hospice; his account of his stay, *Roma sancta*, was not published until 1968, Rome; passages cited pp. 10 and 54; for further information on his views, see Lino Pertile, 'Montaigne, Gregory Martin and Rome', *Bibliothèque d'Humanisme et Renaissance*, vol. 50, no. 3, 1988, pp. 637–59. For Filleul's satire (dated 1560), see F. Joukovsky, *La Gloire*, p. 310.

14 For attention to ruined remains in France, see Richard Cooper's article, 'Poetry in ruins'.

15 Bernard Palissy wrote of Xaintes, 'où j'ay beaucoup profité, et après plusieurs secrets de mon art de geometre et architecture, à cause de certains edifices et ruines antiques qui sont en ladicte ville construictes du temps de Cesar . . .' (where I have greatly benefited, and in several secrets of the art of geometry and architecture, by reason of certain buildings and ancient ruins which were erected in the said town at the time of Caesar), *Architecture et ordonnance de la grotte*, not paginated; Michel de l'Hospital, *Oeuvres complètes*, ed. P.J.S. Duféy, 5 vols, Paris, 1824–26, V, pp. 273 and 275; De Thou, *Mémoires*, I, p. 86; and André Thevet, *La Grande et Excellente Cité de Paris*, pp. 25–6.

16 In the sixteenth century, Champier, Rubis, Paradin and Du Choul established the foundations of our knowledge of Lyon's origins; their work was reviewed critically in the seventeenth century by Claude François Menestrier, *Histoire de la ville de Lyon*, Lyon, 1669, and by Jacob Spon, *Recherche des antiquités et curiosités de la ville de Lyon*, Lyon, 1675, who maintained that the antique remains gave a good notion of the excellence of ancient architecture, that they were incorporated into new building operations and were thus the basis of new creative activity, pp. 40, 44, 79 and 163.

17 Braun and Hogenberg, *Civitates orbis terrarum*, *Liber primus* and *Liber secundus*.

18 De Thou, *Mémoires* I, p. 89; regarding visitors from abroad, see the comment of André Thevet, 'Or il n'est point annee que ce lieu de Nymes ne soit visité pour ses raretez, tant des Italiens que des Flamens ou Allemans' (not a year goes by without this place, Nîmes, being visited for its rareties, by Italians, Flemings or Germans), *Cosmographie*, p. 536. The same authors also praised Roman remains at Arles and at Orange, and the oratorian Joseph Guis published *Description des Arenes ou de l'amphitheatre d'Arles*, Arles, 1665.

19 Jean Poldo d'Albenas, *Discours historial de l'antique cité de Nîmes*, Lyon, 1560; passage cited, sig. ★5. By the seventeenth century, sentiments of pride and praise had become more inflated; Jacques Deyron's *Des Antiquités* is largely based on earlier work – that of Poldo d'Albenas, Vigenère and Lipsius; he gives measurements of all the ancient buildings, and refers to attempts made by his countrymen to 'faire un parallele accomply de l'ancien Nismes avec la vieille Rome' (to draw a perfect comparison between Nîmes and ancient Rome), p. 138.

20 Poldo d'Albenas, *Discours*, ch. 16, pp. 73–80, for the depiction and discussion of the *Maison quarrée*; the following chapter focuses on the *Temple de la Fortune*, treated in the same manner, while Chapter 18 studies 'De la Fontaine, tour Romaine et pont du Gard'.

21 Elie Vinet, *L'Antiquité de Bourdeaux*

et de Bourg, Bordeaux, 1574, opposite B1 and B2. An augmented edition came out in 1574, published by Simon Millanges. Elie Vinet, who taught at the collège de Guyenne for nearly fifty years, had many volumes relating to Rome in his library which he had liberally annotated (see Louis Desgraves, *Elie Vinet, humaniste de Bordeaux, (1509–1587)*, Geneva, 1977). Vinet's erudition and his determination not to let his imagination take hold were much respected by his contemporaries; Belleforest's tribute gives the flavour: 'il y a un excellent personnage de nostre temps, auquel je doy respect et reverence pour avoir ouy soubs luy estant escolier à Bourdeaux, a sçavoir maistre Hélie Vinet, rare en doctrine, et des plus curieux rechercheurs des antiquitez gauloises qu'autre qui vive en ce Royaume' (There is a splendid person of our time to whom I owe respect and reverence for having been his scholar at Bordeaux, that is – Maître Elie Vinet, wise and knowledgeable, and one of the most ardent searchers after French antiquities living), *La Cosmographie*, p. 117. The Palais Tutelle was destroyed in 1677.

22 Pierre de Brach, 'Hymne de Bordeaux' (dedicated to Ronsard), in *Poèmes*, Bordeaux, 1576, ff. 70–89v. In a sonnet addressed to the mayor of Bordeaux, De Brach similarly compares the founding of Rome and its growth with that of Bordeaux, ibid., f. 152v.

23 Louis Le Roy, *Consideration sur l'histoire françoise et l'universelle de ce temps dont les merveilles sont succinctement recitées*, Paris, 1570, p. 5.

24 This perhaps explains why Book 1 'Les Misères' of Agrippa d'Aubigné's epic *Les Tragiques* is so difficult to absorb; its accumulation of fearful scenes of carnage has a deadening effect, even though the author seeks to arouse horror and sympathy.

25 Reported by Brantôme, *Oeuvres complètes*, 8 vols, vol. 3, pp. 369–70, and by Lestoile, *Mémoires-Journaux*, I, pp. 49–50: 'La place rendue non seulement fust desmantelée, mais aussi tous les forts rasés et la tour de Melusine ruinée.' (Not only was the place dismantled, but all the forts were razed to the ground, and the tower of Melusine destroyed.)

26 The influence of Du Bellay on these sonnets of Odet de Turnèbe (*Les Sonnets sur les ruines de Luzignan*, 1579, nos 3, 5 and 6) has been discussed by Marie-Madeleine Fontaine, 'Les *Antiquitez* chez les Dames des Roches', *Du Bellay. Oeuvres et critiques*, no. 20, vol. I Tübingen, 1995, pp. 197–208. The works of Madeleine and Catherine Des Roches have recently been edited, *Oeuvres*, ed. Anne Larsen, Geneva, 1993.

27 Jean de la Jessée does not refer specifically to Du Bellay, but in his poems (*Les Jeunesses: les premieres oeuvres*, Antwerp, C. Plantin, 1583), he makes explicit the comparison with Rome on several occasions, such as when addressing La France, he writes: 'Quand je pense aus malheurs de ta civille rage,/ France, ie te compare à l'Empire Romain' (when I think of the evils of civil strife/ France, I compare you to the Roman Empire), p. 167.

28 Hennequin, *Regrets sur les misères*. For other poets influenced by Du Bellay and who imitated his ternary structures, anaphora and antitheses, see the article of Marguerite Soulié, 'L'Imitation des sonnets de Du Bellay chez deux poètes protestants du XVIe siècle [Bernard de Montméja, Simon Goulart] voulant témoigner leur foi', *Du Bellay. Oeuvres et critiques*, no. 20 vol. I, Tübingen, 1995, pp. 183–95.

29 Jacques Bailbé has drawn attention to the frequency – from 1560

onwards – with which French writers saw parallels between their situation and that of Rome, 'Les Guerres civiles de Rome dans la littérature française du XVIe siècle', *Congrès de Rome*, Association Budé, 2 vols, Paris, 1975, II, pp. 520–45.

30 Louis Le Roy, *Exhortation aux François pour vivre en concorde et ioüir du bien de la paix*, Paris, 1570, p. 19. There was a glimmer of hope in 1570 that peace might last, therefore parallels such as these drawn by Le Roy appeared practical; the hostilities broke out again, however, with the Massacre of St Bartholomew.

31 On Caesar's emptying of the Roman treasury, see Vigenère, *Commentaires de César*, pp. 126v and 129v.

32 Louis Le Roy, *Les Politiques d'Aristote*, Paris, 1568; F. Morel had issued separately Book 5 *Des Changements* two years earlier; the quotation is taken from Le Roy's commentary on 'le monde à l'envers' (the world upside down), p. 546; much of Le Roy's commentary is inspired by Sallust, *Works: The Conspiracy of Catiline*, where, in Chapter 16, Cato drew attention to this kind of slippery morality (p. 107 of the Loeb edition).

33 De l'Hospital, *Oeuvres complètes*, II, p. 188, 'Le But de la guerre et de la paix – pour exhorter Charles IX à donner la paix à ses subjects, 1570'.

34 Pierre de La Place, *Traitté de la vocation et manière de vivre à laquelle chacun est appellé*, Paris, 1561, f. 44; De l'Hospital, *Oeuvres complètes*, I, pp. 387–8, and V, p. 227; De l'Hospital, *Poemata*, pp. 174 and 211. These points had been elaborated by Lucan in the *Pharsalia*, Book 1, ll. 158–70.

35 Pasquier, *Lettres familières*, II, à Monsieur Bigot [1560–61], II, p. 2.

36 De l'Hospital, *Oeuvres complètes*, V, pp. 30–1.

37 Pasquier, *Les Recherches*, II, cols 97–8. Le Roy, in his preface to Book 5 of Aristotle's *Politics*, also hoped to persuade the French to learn from others and to restrict military operations to those against foreigners and not on French soil, *Les Politiques d'Aristote*, p. 543.

38 Brantôme, *Oeuvres complètes*, IV, p. 310.

39 In addition to pamphleteers, to D'Aubigné and Brantôme, Garnier (see below), Montaigne (*Des livres*, II, 10, 410–11), 'J'ayme aussi Lucain, et le practique volontiers . . .' (I also like Lucan, and read him frequently) and Du Bellay were very familiar with Lucan's work; on Du Bellay's debt to the *Pharsalia* and its commentators, see Tucker, *The Poet's Odyssey*, pp. 58–63, and Appendix H; and F.M. Chambers, 'Lucan and the *Antiquitez de Rome*', *Publications of the Modern Language Association*, vol. 60, 1945, pp. 937–48. Brantôme's translations are collected together under the title *Opuscules divers* in his *Oeuvres complètes*, V, pp. 353–68. The popularity of Lucan is also attested by the fact that episodes from his epic were depicted on the walls of French castles, at Ancy le Franc (for instance), see Joukovsky, *La Gloire*, p. 89.

40 Jean de Serres, *Memoires de la troisiesme guerre civile en France, sous Charles IX*, n.p., 1570, address to the reader, sig. ★ii; De Serres has avoided Lucan's urge to rub his readers' noses in the gory details of civil war.

41 The co-presence of the ideal and the ruin of Rome in the *Pharsalia* is discussed by Matthew Leigh, *Lucan. Spectacle and Engagement*, Oxford, 1997, pp. 82–99.

42 Pierre de Ronsard, 'Continuation du Discours', 1562, II, p. 557; for the detail of the influence of Lucan on *Les Tragiques*, see Jacques Bailbé, 'Lucan et d'Aubigné', *Bibliothèque d'Humanisme et Renaissance*, vol. 22, 1960, pp. 320–37.

43 Le Roy, *Les Politiques d'Aristote* on Book 5, p. 550.

44 Jacques Grévin, *Sonnets inédits de Grévin sur Rome*, ed. Edouard Tricotel, Paris, 1862, no. 7. On their discovery, see L. Pinvert's edition of *Théâtre complet et poésies choisies de Jacques Grévin*, Paris, 1922, pp. xliii–xlv. F. Belivaqua Caldari studied these poems in 'I sonnetti di Jacques Grévin su Roma', *Studi romani*, vol. 22, 1974, pp. 36–59.

45 Jacques Grévin, *César* (*c.* 1560), ed. Ellen S. Guisberg, Société des Textes Français, Paris, 1971, shows that Grévin translated about 50 per cent of Muret's text (composed *c.* 1544).

46 Grévin, *Théâtre complet*, pp. 338 and 341; the latter text reads:

Troye, le grand tombeau de la
    Grèce féconde,
Et Romme, la terreur du
    demeurant du monde,
D'eux-mesmes ont esté en la
    fin le tombeau.

[Troy, the great tomb of populous Greece/ And Rome, terror of the rest of the world/ Were both – through their own actions – finally entombed.]

47 Criticism of the papacy is also sharp in sonnet 18 where Time:

Afin de se venger te faict voir
    les Romains,
Reduits honteusement sous le
    pouvoir d'un moine.
    (ll. 13–14)

[in order to avenge herself, shows you the Romans/ Shamefully reduced [and] under the power of a monk.]

48 Apollo is given the same treatment in sonnet 21: instead of the god who inspires poetic fury,

Quelque part que tu sois, tu
    portes les malheurs,
Les froides pauvretéz, ruines et
    disetes. (ll. 3–4)

[wherever you be, you will carry misfortune/ Cold poverty, ruin and penury.]

49 On the dating of the composition of Garnier's plays, see Maurice Gras, *Robert Garnier, son art et sa méthode*, Geneva, 1965. I have touched on many of the themes discussed here in my essay, 'Rome in some plays of Robert Garnier', *Myth and its Making in the French Theatre. Studies Presented to W.D. Howarth*, ed. E. Freeman, H. Mason, M. O'Regan and S.W. Taylor, Cambridge, 1988, pp. 12–29.

50 Estienne's claims for the usefulness of history are made in his dedication to Sir Philip Sidney of his edition of Zozime; they are cited in Jehasse, *La Renaissance de la critique*, p. 234.

51 Robert Estienne published *Porcie* in 1568, and added to it various preliminary verses, including two sonnets of his own; the second elaborated on the warning 'France, appren par ces vers [those of Garnier] . . . / Que les malheurs d'autruy te puissent profiter' (France, learn from these verses/ that the ills of others can benefit you). The political context of Garnier's play has been set by Gillian Jondorf, *Robert Garnier and the Themes of Political Tragedy*, Cambridge, 1969. Garnier also explored the ravages of civil war in his *Hymne de la Monarchie* (1567), *Oeuvres complètes*, ed. L. Pinvert, 2 vols, Paris, 1922, pp. 407–22; issued separately in 1567 by G. Buon.

52 The phrase was coined by Dorothy Coleman in her book *The Chaste Muse*, pp. 108–9.

53 There are many variations on the theme of self-destruction; the most forceful occur in *Cornélie* where the heroine accuses Rome directly as having been responsible for Caesar's destructive nature: 'C'est toy, Rome, qui l'as nourri trop

indulgente' (It's your fault, Rome who indulged him in his upbringing) (l. 809), and that accusation of weakness is turned by Cassius into a full-blooded attack on the city's culpable intentions:

Misérable Cité, tu armes contre
 toy
La fureur d'un tyran pour le
 faire ton roy;
Tu armes tes enfans, injurieuse
 Romme,
Encontre tes enfans pour le
 plaisir d'un homme.
 (ll. 1055–8)

[Miserable City, you arm against yourself/ The Fury of a tyrant by making him king/ Injurious Rome, you arm your children/ Against your children for the pleasure of a mere man.]

54 The same ironic comparisons are made by Cicéron in *Cornélie* in the opening scene of Act II.

55 Marie-Madeleine Mouflard, *Robert Garnier*, 2 vols, Paris, 1961, has studied the influences of Lucan and Seneca on Garnier's work, I, pp. 130–70; of the former, she writes that Garnier 'le possédait à fond' (knew his work, in depth), p. 140.

56 For a more detailed discussion of the Triumph, see Chapter 8, p. 312–42.

Chapter 8   *Two Distilled Models of Rome*

1 On the significance of surviving testimony and its influence, see Gruen, *The Image of Rome*.

2 A revealing account of historians' attitudes to the Caesar concept, concentrated in particular on Augustus, is provided by Emilio Gabbo, 'The historians and Augustus', in *Caesar Augustus*, ed. Fergus Millar and Erich Segal, Oxford, 1984, pp. 61–88.

3 See Zwi Yavetz, 'The *Res Gestae* and Augustus', *Caesar Augustus*, ed. Fergus Millar and Erich Segal, Oxford, 1984, pp. 1–36, and her *Julius Caesar and his Public Image*, London, 1983, where she gives a thorough analysis of the measures (political, administrative and social) adopted by Caesar to ensure his success; see also Gruen, *The Image of Rome*, pp. 92–112.

4 An account of Roman preoccupations with fame and self-projection is given in Braudy, *The Frenzy of Renown*, where the key classical texts discussed are from Livy, Caesar, Horace and Virgil.

5 Petrarch was of particular interest since he radically changed his views on Caesar (from critical to approving) after he had studied the *Commentaries*. Hans Baron has charted this changing attitude in 'The evolution of Petrarch's thought: reflections on the state of Petrarch studies', *Bibliothèque d'Humanisme et Renaissance*, vol. 24, 1962, pp. 7–41.

6 The title specifies the use of medals (reconstituted) *excuitiquis numismatibus restituae*; the volume, first published in Bruges in 1563, was based on coins found in many French collections which are listed in the text. It went into many editions.

7 Nicolas Rapin, *Oeuvres*, Paris, 1610, p. 213. Cicero's prototype for praise of an emperor is drawn in the oration for Marcellus, translated by N.H. Watts, Loeb Library, London, 1914, pp. 415–51.

8 Du Chesne's translation is analysed by Robert Bossuat, 'Traductions françaises des Commentaires de César à la fin du XVe siècle', *Bibliothèque d'Humanisme et Renaissance*, vol. 3, 1943, pp. 252–411; for a discussion of different interpretations of *le fantôme de Rome*, consult Ph. Henza, 'Comment peindre le passage du Rubicon', *Présence de*

César. Hommage au doyen M. Rambaud, ed. Raymond Chevalier, Paris, 1985, pp. 56–65.

9 The tapestry designs were inspired by French translations of the *Commentaries*, see Guy Delmarcel, 'Présence de César dans la tapisserie des Pays-Bas méridionaux', *Présence de César*, ed. Chevalier, pp. 257–61.

10 Referred to by many; see, for example, Antoine de Laval, *Desseins et professions nobles et publiques*, Paris, 1605, who cites Augustus as a precedent which French kings might well follow, p. 6: 'Auguste fit embellir son Palais des statues de tous ceux qui avoient bien mérité de la Republique, qui avoient apporté quelque avancement à l'Empire du peuple Romain avec des inscriptions contenant ce que chacun d'eux fait de remarquable' (Augustus embellished his palace with statues of all those worthy of the Republic, who had brought some progress to the Empire of the Roman people, with inscriptions containing everything remarkable that each one of them had done). For a discussion of this tradition, see my article: 'Le Phénomène de la Galerie des portraits des illustres', *L'Âge d'or du Mécénat' (1598–1661)*, Colloque international CNRS (mars 1983), Editions du CNRS, Paris, 1985, pp. 411–22.

11 See Michel Hano's article, 'L'Image de César dans les peintures du XVe au XIXe siècles', *Présence de César*, ed. Chevalier, pp. 305–28. The iconographic tradition of illustrious men in France owed much to the development of parallel series in Italy, see Luciano Cheles, 'The "Uomini Famosi" in the "Studiolo" of Urbino: an iconographic study', *Gazette des Beaux Arts*, vol. 102, 1983, pp. 1–7; and Theodor E. Mommsen, 'Petrarch and the decoration of the Sala Virorum Illustrium in Padua', *Art Bulletin*, vol. 34, no. 2, 1952, pp. 95–116.

12 Orsini's series of portraits and biographies was assembled over a long period, see Eugene Duyer's study, 'André Thevet and Fulvius Orsino: the beginnings of the modern tradition of classical portrait iconography in France', *Art Bulletin*, vol. 75, 1993, pp. 467–80.

13 Further details can be found in Rosanna Pavoni, 'Paolo Giovio et son Musée de Portraits à propos d'une exposition', *Gazette des Beaux Arts*, vol. 105, 1985, pp. 109–16.

14 Thevet, *Les Vrais Pourtraits*, sig. ã iv r: 'et à dire la verité les pourtraits et images ont une energie et vertu interieure à nous faire chérir la vertu et detester le mal' (and to tell the truth, portraits and images have an energy and inner quality which make us cherish virtue and detest evil).

15 The *Historia augusta* was first printed in 1475; most readers used either the Aldine edition (Venice, 1516) or that published by Erasmus two years later. Plutarch's *Lives* were translated in their entirety by Jacques Amyot and first published under the title *Les Vies des hommes illustres*, Paris, 1559; at least ten printings in French followed before the end of the sixteenth century.

16 On princely collections of the twelve Caesars, see Schnapper, *Curieux*, II, p. 44: 'Qui n'a pas sa série des Douze Césars'; a Venetian jeweller, Antonio Fontana, in 1583, for example, had a set of stucco made to resemble bronze, Peter Thornton, *The Italian Renaissance Interior, 1400–1600*, London, 1991, p. 269.

17 *Un Traicté des douze Cesars*, printed immediately after *Les Nouvelles et Antiques Merveilles*, Paris, 1554; Fontaine's account owed much (as he admitted) to the work of Guillaume Budé from which he cites frequently, *De Asse et partibus eius libri quinq.* (first edition, 1514), Lyon, S. Gryphivs, 1550.

18 Joannes Baptista Egnatius, *Caesarum vitae post Suetonium conscriptae*, 2 vols, Lyon, 1551.

19 Aeneas Vico, *Omnium Caesarum verissimae imagines*, Venice, 1552; Jacques de Strada, for instance, referring to Sadolet, Grolier, Huttichius and Munster, also published his ambitious *Epitome thesauri antiquitatem hoc est* at Lyon in 1553 (the biography of Caesar occupies the first twelve pages), while G.B. Cavalieri published his engravings and Antonio Ciccarelli's text *Le vite degli imperadori Romani* in Rome as late as 1590. See also Pedro Mexia, *Le vite di tutti gl'imperadori, di Giulio Cesare insino a Massimiliano*, Venice, 1558.

20 Aeneas Vico, *Ex Libri xxiii commentariorum in vetera imperatorum romanorum numismata*, Venice, 1560.

21 These are the precise terms used by Le Pois in his *Discours*, p. 37: 'perpétuer la memoire de leurs noms' (to perpetuate the memory of their names), and p. 40, in the elucidation of the meaning of *icones*: 'Les effigies des hommes ne se dressoyent point, sinon à ceux, qui par quelque cause signalée méritoyent immortalité.' (Effigies were not made for men unless they had merited immortality through some just cause.)

22 *Les Faicts des romains* was originally conceived as a history of the twelve Caesars, yet nearly all the manuscripts (at least fifty-nine of them, according to Jeannette M.A. Beer) end with the death of Caesar, Beer, *A Medieval Caesar*, Geneva, 1976, p. xv.

23 See P. Mayer, 'Les Premières Compilations françaises d'histoire ancienne', *Romania*, vol. 14, 1885, pp. 3–81.

24 Jeannette Beer's book, *A Medieval Caesar*, rehearses all the aspects of this appropriation. The habit of classicizing Christian and chivalric forms and vice versa is studied by

Sydney Anglo, 'Humanism and the court arts', *The Impact of Humanism on Western Europe*, ed. Anthony Goodman and Angus Mackay, London, 1990, pp. 66–98.

25 Jean-Claude Margolin lists the many printed editions in his article, 'Glareau, commentateur du *De Bello Gallico*', *Présence de César*, ed. Chevalier, pp. 183–212; and, with respect to manuscripts, Virginia Brown notes 'approximately 240 humanistic codices', 'Portraits of Julius Caesar in Latin manuscripts of the Commentaries', *Viator*, vol. 12, 1981, pp. 319–55.

26 Caesar, *Les Commentaires de Jules César*, Paris, 1539, f. ii.

27 Pierre de la Ramée, *Liber de Caesaris militia*, Paris, 1559, translated into French by Pierre Poisson, 1584. De la Ramée's method, by which he identified the ideas, analysed and rearranged them, is examined by Claude-Gilbert Dubois, 'César et Ramus', *Présence de César*, ed. Chevalier, pp. 109–18.

28 Caesar, *I Commentari di C. Giulio Cesare, con le figure in rame de gli alloggiamenti, de' fatti d'arme, delle circonvallationi delle città, et di molte altre cose notabili descritte in essi*, Venice, 1575. Palladio also prepared drawings for the *Histories* of Polybius. On both these works, see the article by J.R. Hale, 'Andrea Palladio, Polybius and Julius Caesar', *Journal of the Warburg and Courtauld Institutes*, vol. 40, 1977, pp. 240–55; reprinted in *Renaissance War Studies*, London, 1983, pp. 471–86, where he shows that Palladio endorsed Baldelli's view that Caesar 'is, as it were, the mirror for our lives as far as military affairs are concerned, in which we can see images of how we should conduct ourselves both publicly and privately', p. 476.

29 Atticus goes on to stress how Caesar chiefly acquired his language and his studied nonchalance, 'and brought it to its present per-

fection by a studious application to the most intricate and refined branches of literature, and by a careful and constant attention to the purity of his style', Cicero, *Brutus, or the Remarks on Eminent Orators*, Bohn edition, London, 1871, p. 477.

30 *De provinciis consularibus*, Loeb Library, *The Speeches of Cicero*, translated by R. Gardner, London, 1958, p. 607; *Philippics II*, John Rutherford's translation, London, 1799, pp. 219–98, citations from p. 297.

31 Pliny (the elder) had contributed many lineaments to Caesar's portrait, 'sa vivacité et promptitude, qui estoit plus soudaine que le feu' (his vivacity and his speed which was quicker than fire), 'Louenges de Jules César', *L'Histoire du monde*, put into French by Antoine du Pinet, 2 vols, Lyon, 1566, I, p. 267.

32 Lisa Jardine and Anthony Grafton, 'How Gabriel Harvey read his Livy', *Past and Present*, vol. 129, 1990, pp. 30–78.

33 Brantôme, *Oeuvres complètes*, V, p. 356.

34 Jardine and Grafton, 'Gabriel Harvey', pp. 36–42; Sidney read his Machiavelli with Thomas Preston, Master of Trinity Hall, Cambridge.

35 See Margolin, 'Glareau', pp. 183–212.

36 Brantôme is the source for these details, *Oeuvres complètes*, I, p. 433, and II, p. 243; Symeoni, *César renouvellé*, f. 53v, 'les Commentaires de Cesar . . . tant necessaires que sans les tenir tous par coeur, i'oseray dire . . . qu'il est quasi impossible de bien sçavoir et faire la guerre' (the Commentaries of Caesar . . . so necessary that without having them by heart (if I may say) . . . it is virtually impossible to know how to wage war well).

37 Monluc, *Commentaires*, p. 341 (1555): 'Il me sembloit, lorsque je me faisois lire Tite Live, que je voyois en vie ces braves Scipions' (It

seemed when I heard Titus Livius read to me that I saw these Scipios as though in life). He cites Livy frequently, see pp. 268, 269, 327, 331 and 341.

38 Ibid., p. 22: 'Le plus grand capitaine qui ait jamais esté, qui est Cesar, m'en a monstré le chemin' (The greatest captain who has ever been, who was Caesar, showed me the way); p. 779 for the confirmation of Monluc's actions by reference to Caesar.

39 Louys Papon, 'Discours à Lesdiguières, 1597', British Library, Ms Harleian, 5256, f. 16; Postel seems also to have used the verb in his *Histoire memorable* (f. 69r), cited in R.E. Asher, *National Myths in Renaissance France*, Edinburgh, 1993, p. 54.

40 As early as 1530, the point is made by Guillaume Michel de Tours in his dedicatory preface to Charles, duc du Vendomois, of his translation of Suetonius, *Des Faicts et gestes des douze Cesars* (Paris, 1530): sig ã ii, '[Les *Commentaries* sont un] moyen d'animer les couraiges des princes car enflant quelques bonnes vertuz on les veult imiter et faire comme fit nostre dessus dit Cesar' (The *Commentaries* are a means of arousing the courage of princes, because by listing a few virtues, one wants to emulate them and do as our aforesaid Caesar).

41 For a discussion of the importance of ancient Roman forms for Renaissance popes in practice see Stinger, *The Renaissance in Rome*; for the references to Julius II and Erasmus' wry comments on his imperial pretensions, see pp. 236 and 383. Caesar Borgia's motto was 'aut Caesar aut nihil', discussed in François d'Amboise, *Recueil de devises*, Paris, 1620, pp. 22–3.

42 For the extent of Maximilian I's ambitions, see the study by Paul Gwynne, '"In alter Caesaris": Maximilian I, Vladislav II, Johannes

Michael Nagonius and the *renovatio Imperii*', *Renaissance Studies*, vol. 10, no. 1, 1996, pp. 56–71; on Charles V, see Stefano Ambrosio Schiappalaria, *La vita di C. Julio Cesare*, Antwerp, 1578; and for Holy Roman Emperor Rudolf II, Walter S. Melion, 'Memorabilia aliquot Romanae stremutatis exempla: the thematics of artisanal virtue in Hendrick Goltzius' *Roman Heroes*', *Modern Language Notes [Myths of Antiquity]*, vol. 110, no. 5, 1995, pp. 1090–134.

43 This bias has been examined by Bossuat, 'Traductions' pp. 275–88.

44 See Robert W. Scheller, 'Imperial themes in art and literature of the early French Renaissance: the period of Charles VIII', *Simiolus: Netherlands Quarterly for the History of Art*, vol. 12, 1981–82, pp. 5–69, and Bonner Mitchell, *The Majesty of State*, Florence, 1986, where he considers the imperial imagery used for both Charles VIII and Louis XII, pp. 61–80, 97–104 respectively.

45 The portrait, drawn after a design by Primaticcio, is reproduced by Scaillerez, *François Ier*, pp. 54–5, fig. 34.

46 There are three surviving manuscripts: Demoulins, 'Commentaires de la guerre gallique', British Library, Harleian Ms 6205; Bibliothèque Nationale, Ms fr. 13429; and Chantilly, Musée Condé, Ms 1139. Until Anne-Marie Lecoq's analysis of them in her *François Ier imaginaire*, they were virtually ignored by historians.

47 Caron's drawings are in the Louvre, Cabinet des Dessins, RF 29752 8–19.

48 Ferrand de Bez, *Le Grand Triumphe magnificque des parisiens*, Paris, n.d., sig. A ij:

Jules Caesar, grand empereur
   romain . . .
Il est bien vray, que les aultres
   Caesars

En grand honneur furent en
   toutes pars.
Mais Jules est par dessus tous
   loué . . .
Car tu es plus que Caesar,
Car tu espans la paix dessus la
   terre . . .
Ta grand Vertu Jules Cesar
   surmonte.

[Julius Caesar, great Roman emperor . . ./ It is true that other Caesars/ In all parts were held in great esteem/ But Julius is praised above all others . . ./ because you are greater than Caesar/ Because you spread peace above the land/ Your great Virtue surpasses Caesar.]

49 Cited pp. 76–7 by Pierre Champion, 'Henri III et les écrivains de son temps', *Bibliothèque d'Humanisme et Renaissance*, vol. 1, 1941, pp. 43–172.

50 There is a manuscript version (Bibliothèque Nationale, Ms fr. 20034) which has the French text followed by a Latin translation, ff. 15 onwards.

51 For the frequency of reference to Caesar and to Rome, Jean Bodin, *Six Livres de la Republique*, Paris, 1579, I, p. 37; III, pp. 10 and 37; IV, pp. 16, 28, 32 and 46; V, p. 101; and VI, p. 155. Jean Céard has discussed Bodin's interest in Rome and in Caesar in 'Rome dans la *Methode de l'Histoire* de Jean Bodin', *Congrès de Rome, Actes de l'Association Budé*, Paris, 1975, pp. 758–70. On Le Roy's comparative method, see Philippe Desan, 'La Logique de la différence dans les traités d'histoire', *Logique et littérature à la Renaissance*, ed. Marie-Luce Demonet-Launay and André Tournon, Paris, 1994, pp. 101–10. Caesar is cited as remarkable everywhere in Lipsius; the references to his genius occur in *De Militia*, V, 8 and *Magnitudo*, IV, 4, and in *Of*

Constancie, ch. XV, trs. J. Stradling, London, R. Johnes, 1595, p. 168. For an overview of Lipsius' admiration for Caesar, see R.H. Schryvers, 'La Présence de César dans Juste Lipse', *Présence de César*, ed. Chevalier, pp. 239–45.

52 The conception of Lucan's poem as opposition to Caesar's work is examined in detail by Jamie Masters, *Poetry and Civil War in Lucan's 'Bellum Civile'*, Cambridge, 1992.

53 Niccolò Machiavelli, *Discourses*, translated by Leslie J. Walker, 2 vols, London, 1950, Book 1, ch. 10, pp. 237–8. The popularity of Machiavelli's work in France can be gauged from the number of editions of the *Discorsi* published in French; the first was in 1571, others followed in 1573, 1577, 1578, 1579, 1586 and 1597. It was just the kind of judgement cited in the text that was picked up by French writers during the wars of Religion, see *Le Tocsin contre les massacreurs en France*, Rheims, 1577, pp. 208–9. For Machiavelli's repeated references to Caesar, see Roger Baillet, 'César chez Machiavel', *Présence de César*, ed. Chevalier, pp. 67–76. Machiavelli's view of Caesar was tempered in the *Arte della guerra* where his good generalship and deeds are recorded.

54 Champier's views are set out by Richard Cooper in chs 12 and 13 of *Literae in tempore belli*, pp. 269–302.

55 La Boëtie, *Oeuvres complètes*, pp. 38–9.

56 Cicero, *Letters to Atticus*, Loeb Library, translated by E.O. Winstedt, 2 vols, London, 1913, II, pp. 5–7.

57 The quotations are taken from Dio Cassius' *Roman History*, Loeb Library, London, 1961, translated by Ernest Cary, Book 3, pp. 39, 71; 4, p. 57. Plutarch similarly stressed the duplicity of both men: 'Il y avoit longtemps que

César s'estoit proposé de ruiner Pompée, et que Pompée de son costé s'estoit proposé de ruiner César', *Les Vies*, pp. 260–1. (Caesar intended to ruin Pompey from a long way back, and Pompey – for his part – aimed to ruin Caesar.)

58 C. Velleius Paterculus, *Compendium of Roman History*, Loeb Library, London, 1924, Book 2, ch. 49, p. 486.

59 The quarrel between Bracciolini and Guarini has been studied by Hans Baron, *The Crisis of the Early Italian Renaissance*, Princeton, 1986, against the background of earlier receptions of Caesar (Dante – favourable; Petrarch – much more ambiguous), pp. 50–66.

60 For a discussion of this kind of artefact, see my *Ideal Forms*, pp. 102–14. An example of a drawing on this subject may be found in Jacob Bean, *Fifteenth and Sixteenth-Century French Drawings in the Metropolitan Museum of Art*, New York, 1986, no. 343. A further indication of the interest in the struggle between Caesar and Pompey is seen in the libraries of the time: Claude d'Urfé (for example) owned a vellum manuscript 'enrichy de figures' (enriched with images) entitled 'Histoire de Jules César et de Pompée' *Claude d'Urfé et La Bâtie*, ed. D. Vallat, Montbrison, 1990, pp. 188–9.

61 The verbal resonances of Lucan and their relevance to Du Bellay's complex interpretation of Rome are discussed in detail by Tucker, *The Poet's Odyssey*, pp. 150–6.

62 Budé does not see Pompey and Caesar as rivals, and does not mention their contestation, perhaps because the structure of his work favours a chronological set of great men/exemplars for the instruction of a monarch. The references to Pompey occur on pp. 123–30, on Caesar pp. 110–11, *L'Institution du prince* [Paris, 1547], published in *Le*

Prince dans la France des XVIe et XVIIe siècles, Paris, 1965.

63 Symeoni, *César renouvellé*, pp. 52–3.

64 De l'Hospital, *Poemata*, 'Ode au Cardinal de Lorraine', IV, p. 166.

65 According to Balmas, the poem was composed about 1561–62; it is printed on pp. 293–345 in vol. II of her edition of Jodelle, *Oeuvres poétiques*.

66 Cited ibid. II, p. 480 note.

67 Gentillet, *Discours contre Machiavel* [Geneva], 1576; Geneva, 1968, pp. 62 and 471.

68 Raymond Chevalier assembled all the relevant passages from the *Essais* in 'Montaigne lecteur et juge de César', *Présence de César*, ed. Chevalier, pp. 91–107; the wider perspective of Rome is stressed by Zachary S. Schiffman, 'Montaigne's perception of ancient Rome', pp. 345–53.

69 Montaigne's copy of Caesar's *Commentaries* with manuscript notes is preserved at Chantilly (*C. Julius Caesaris commentarii*, Antwerp, C. Plantin, 1570); his copy of Dio Cassius is in the Library at Eton College. The actual dates of Montaigne's reading of Caesar are inscribed on his copy: he began on 25 February and finished on 21 July 1578.

70 All quotations and references from Montaigne's *Essais* are to the Presses Universitaires de France edition, 1965, and the translations are from Michael Screech's text of *The Complete Essays*.

71 Passage cited at the head of the essay largely devoted to Caesar, Montaigne, *L'Histoire de Spurina*, I, 33, p. 728.

72 Montaigne's comparison of Alexander and Caesar was taken, unaltered, by Simon Goulart in his extension of Plutarch's *Lives* (second edn, 1587), see Jacques Pineaux, 'Un Continuateur des *Vies parallèles*: Simon Goulart de Senlis (S.G.S.)', *Fortunes de Jacques Amyot, Actes du colloque international*, Melun,

April 1985, ed. J.M.A. Beer and D. Lloyd-Jones, Paris, 1986, pp. 331–42.

73 *Un Traict de quelques ambassadeurs*, I, 17, 72. Clearly, Caesar's indulgence in writing in detail about his engineering capacities irritated Montaigne for he returned to the topic again in *Observations sur les moyens de faire la guerre de Julius Caesar* (II, 34, 738).

74 The same mutual understanding between Pompey and Caesar is sketched out in *Comme nous pleurons et rions d'une mesme chose*, I, 38, 233. John D. Lyons, *Exemplum*, p. 127, sees this evocation of Caesar and Pompey as a fabrication.

75 The complex function of Montaigne's use of quotations has been studied by Mary McKinley, *Words in a Corner*.

76 Muret's play, *Caesar*, dedicated to Jean Brinon, was published in 1553 in Paris; Jacques Grévin's *César* was performed at the collège de Beauvais on 16 February 1561.

77 Suetonius, *Des faicts*, ch. 37, p. 51; Appian, *Des Guerres des Rommains*, I, ch. 66, pp. 507–9 (the Triumph of Scipio); Dio Cassius, *Des Faictz et gestes insignes des Romains*, translated by Claude Deroziers, Paris, 1542, ff. lxxxi–lxxxiii; Plutarch *Les Vies*, I, pp. 604–7. Monroe E. Deutsch has studied *The Apparatus of Caesar's Triumphs* (n.p., n.d) and has explained the reasons why particular woods were used in specific triumphs, revealing their political relevance as well as the rarity of the materials used.

78 'Les Commentaires de Cesar', Bibliothèque Nationale, Ms fr. 38; see discussion on p. 292 of this chapter.

79 See Chapter 7, pp. 280–2.

80 There has been much work on the sources available to Mantegna for his composition of the *Triumphs of Caesar*. See in particular: Andrew Martindale, *The Triumphs of Caesar*, London, 1979; Ronald W. Light-

bown, *Mantegna*, London, 1986; and Jane Martineau (ed.), *Andrea Mantegna*, London and New York, 1992.

81 These woodcuts are discussed in detail by Jean Michel Massing, 'The *Triumph of Caesar* by Benedetto Bardone and Jacobus Argentoratensis: the iconography and influence', *Print Quarterly*, vol. 7, 1990, pp. 2–21. A set of Jacopo de Strasbourg's engravings is in Paris, Bibliothèque Nationale, Estampes, Ea. 11 rés.

82 See Martindale, *Triumphs*, p. 100.

83 Ibid. Simon Vostre, *Heures à l'usage de Lyon* [1502], pp. i–xv, republished Paris, 1520, and *Heures à l'usage de Rome*, Paris, 1508, ff. i–xiv. The complete suite from *The Triumphs of Caesar* was not engraved from the paintings until the end of the century (1598–99) when they were done by Andreani.

84 See Brown, 'The Palazzo di San Sebastiano', *passim*; Blaise de Vigenère, *La Somptueuse et Magnifique Entrée*; Montaigne, *Journal*, p. 59.

85 On Gaillon and for the transported engravings, see Martindale, *Triumphs*, p. 99 and Appendices I and II; the Caen entry is mentioned by Joukovsky, *La Gloire*, p. 423.

86 Mario Equicola, *Commentari mantuani*, n.p., 1521, ff. Vvii–Vviii v. It is from Equicola that we learn that a room was specially constructed for the *Triumphs*.

87 For this detail, see Hano, 'L'Image de César', p. 319.

88 The generalized distribution of images from *The Triumphs of Caesar* has been studied by Jean Michel Massing, 'The *Triumph of Caesar*', and his 'Arnould Poissonier of Tournai and his "huit pièces du triumphe de César" for Margaret of Austria', *Artes Textiles*, vol. 11, Ghent, 1986, pp. 69–74. Gabriel Symeoni, *Dialogue des devises d'armes et d'amours du sieur Paulo Iovio, dis-cours de M. Louys Dominique sur le mesme subject, et devises heroiques et morales de G. Symeoni*, Lyon, 1561, dedicated to Catherine de' Medici, pp. 120–1, 228.

89 The literature on the Triumph is vast; for the most recent information, see Robert Baldwin, 'A bibliography of the literature on triumph', *'All the World's a Stage': Art and Pageantry in the Renaissance*, 2 vols, University Park, Pennsylvania, 1990, ed. Barbara Wisch and Susan Scott-Munshower, I, pp. 359–85; W. Weisbach, *Trionfi*, Berlin, 1919, remains fundamental. For the origins of the early evolution of the Triumph, see S. Versnel's book, *Triumphus*, Leiden, 1970. On the pictorial remains of the Triumph, see Peter J. Holliday, 'Roman triumphal painting: its function, development, and reception', *Art Bulletin*, vol. 79, 1997, pp. 130–47.

90 For Rome and empire experienced as one organism, see Mazzolani, *The Idea of the City*, p. 121. The links between Rome's destiny and the Triumph are exposed by Charles L. Stinger, 'Roma triumphans: triumphs in the thought and ceremonies of Renaissance Rome', *Medievalia et Humanistica*, vol. 10, 1981, pp. 189–201.

91 Renaissance specialist studies on independent elements of triumphal forms were listed in Chapter 1; for modern works, see (as an example) G.C. Picard, *Les Trophées romaines. Contribution à l'histoire de la religion et de l'art triomphal de Rome*, Paris, 1957, considered by MacCormick, *Art and Ceremony*, as the most complete study of a single type of triumphal monument.

92 For the potential latent in familiar images, see the discussion of Nelson Goodman, *Languages of Art: an Approach to a Theory of Symbols*, Indianapolis, 1968, p. 268, and David Freedberg, *The Power of Images*, Chicago, 1989, p. 234.

93 Ilja M. Veldman, *Maarten van Heemskerck and Dutch Humanism in the Sixteenth Century*, Amsterdam, 1977, has given a detailed analysis of the Dutch allegorical triumphs, largely the work of Heemskerck and D.V. Coornhert; see especially ch. 4, 'Dirck Volkertsz, Coornhert and Heemskerck's allegories'. There were also engraved examples in France: see the oval designs of *Lussuria* and other vices by Léon Davent, British Museum, Print Room, 1864–5–14–254.

94 For Limosin's work, see Sophie Baratte, *Léonard Limosin au musée du Louvre*, Paris, 1993, pp. 64 and 84, and Andrew Carnduff Ritchie, 'Léonard Limosin's *Triumph of the Faith*, with portraits of the House of Guise', *Art Bulletin*, vol. 21, no. 3, 1939, pp. 238–50, where he discusses a painted enamel in the Frick collection.

95 The appropriateness of triumphal forms to sixteenth-century court organization and especially to the prince is discussed in my *Ideal Forms*, *passim*; Guillaume Budé, among others, saw the French court with the king enthroned as a theatrical spectacle, *L'Institution du prince*.

96 Robert Payne, *The Roman Triumph*, London, 1962, also rehearses unresolved issues such as the *Porta triumphalis*, the oath of allegiance, and whether or not the Triumphator was to be seen as the embodiment of Jupiter. These issues are still the subject of scholarly dispute, see Versnel, *Triumphus*, pp. 56–93, 132–254.

97 See Versnel's discussion, ibid., pp. 356–83.

98 An attempt at defining 'triumphalism' has been made by Partridge and Starn, 'Triumphalism'.

99 For a discussion of the dynastic considerations which lay at the origin of this arch, see R. Brilliant, 'The arch of Septimus Severus in the Roman Forum', *Memoirs of the American Academy in Rome*, vol. 29, 1967, pp. 271 ff.

100 On the spread of arches across the empire and their functions, see Mazzolani, *The Idea of the City*, p. 196, and Michael McCormick, *Eternal Victory. Triumphal Rulership in Late Antiquity, Byzantium and the Early Medieval West*, Baltimore, 1990, pp. 25–50.

101 D.R. Dudley, *Urbs Roma. A Source Book of Classical Texts on the City and its Monuments*, Aberdeen, 1967.

102 Giovanni Rucellai was so impressed by the arches in Rome that, on his visit there in 1450, he began to compile a list of them, see Weiss, *The Renaissance Discovery of Classical Antiquity*, p. 73.

103 Serlio, Book 3, 1544, f. 50v; *Tutte l'opere*, 1619, f. 99v.

104 For the pope's determined imperialism, see Stinger, 'Roma triumphans', pp. 189–91, and ch. 5, 'The *Renovatio Imperii* and the *Renovatio Romae*', *The Renaissance in Rome*, pp. 235–91, 385–92.

105 Chrysoloras' letter was written about 1411 and is translated in Phyllis Pray Bober and Ruth Rubinstein, *Renaissance Artists and Antique Sculpture*, Oxford, 1986, pp. 210–11.

106 On the eye's memory and its ability to remake, see Goodman, *Languages of Art*, pp. 7–8; Paulette Choné has discussed the passion for covering the surface of arches with symbols, *Emblèmes*, pp. 357–63. For an example of the liberal use of such images (often borrowed from Horapollo), see Gervase Hood's analysis of 'James I's entry into London (1604)', *Across the Narrow Seas. Studies in the History and Bibliography of Britain and the Low Countries*, ed. Susan Roach, London, 1991, pp. 67–81.

107 Zanobio Ceffino published a French account of Charles V's entry, *La Triumphante Entrée de l'empereur*

Charles le 5e faicte en la cité de Rome, Rome, 1536, where he makes clear the interaction of ancient and modern triumphal arches; the role of the *conservatores* is studied by Bonner Mitchell, 'The SPQR in two Roman festivals of early and mid-quattrocentro', *The Sixteenth Century Journal*, vol. 9, no. 4, 1978, pp. 95–9.

108 The rivalry between Florence and Rome is set out by Janet Cox-Rearick, *Dynasty and Destiny in Medici Art*, Princeton, 1984.

109 Colonna, *Discours*, ff. 13, 99, 101, 113, 121v–2.

110 French drawings by Androuet du Cerceau, Etienne Delaune, Etienne du Pérac and Antoine Caron can be found in quantity in the Bibliothèque Nationale, Estampes; examples are given in *L'Ecole de Fontainebleau* (catalogue, 1972), nos 35, 45, 61, 74 and 80.

111 Perugino and Pinturicchio also incorporated triumphal arches into the decorations they painted for the Vatican: see Maurizio Fagiolo dell'Arco (ed), *The Vatican and its Treasures*, London, 1983, pp. 96, 101 and 104–5.

112 G. Carandente, *I trionfi*, n.p., 1963, published several *chars de triomphe* from *cassone*; triumphal forms on tapestries have been studied by Henri Zerner, *L'Art de la Renaissance*, pp. 225–7; H.C. Marillier, *The Tapestries at Hampton Court Palace*, London, 1931; and Sophie Schneelbalg-Perelman, 'Richesse du garde-meuble parisien de François Ier: inventaires inédits de 1542 et 1551', *Gazette des Beaux Arts*, vol. 78, 1971, pp. 253–304.

113 For the influence of Alberti on both Italian artists, see R. Wittkower, 'Alberti's approach to antiquity in architecture', *Journal of the Warburg and Courtauld Institutes*, 1941, pp. 1–18; 'Principles of Palladio's architecture', ibid., 1944, pp. 102–22; and Jean Gabol, *Leon Battista Alberti. Universal Man in the Early Renaissance*, Chicago, 1969.

114 A reproduction of such a keyhole can be found in the standard guide, Le *Château d'Ecouen*, ed. Alain Erlande-Brandenburg, Paris, 1988, p. 66, where a dresser designed as a series of triumphal arches can also be seen, p. 96.

115 Triumphal arches in books and manuscripts illustrate well the European dimension: see H.F. Bouchéry, 'Des Arcs triomphaux aux frontispices des livres', *Les Fêtes de la Renaissance*, ed. Jean Jacquot, 3 vols, Paris, 1956, 1960, 1975, I, pp. 431 ff.; Margery Corbett and Ronald Lightbown, *The Comely Frontispiece: the Emblematic Title Page in England, 1550–1660*, London, 1979; and T. Krea (ed.) *Renaissance Painting in Manuscripts. Treasures from the British Library*, New York, 1983. Innumerable French manuscripts have frontispieces *à l'antique*; see, as examples, Bibliothèque Nationale, Ms fr. 1683, 1738, 4800, 4962, 13429 and Ms fr. 9152 by François Merlin who inserts each of his prayers within a triumphal arch. Other examples are given in Anthony Grafton (ed.), *The Vatican Library and Renaissance Culture*, New Haven, 1993.

116 For example, see Bertolotti, *Artisti francesi*, pp. 160–1, where he discusses a triumph in ivory, and p. 170 where he shows the triumph of Cosimo II in onyx; Veldman, *Van Heemskerck*, discusses the jewel case decorated with triumphs which belonged to Paola Gonzaga; see Bober and Rubinstein, *Renaissance Artists*, p. 200, for the sardonyx cameo depicting the Triumph of Tiberius; and the *Grand Camée de France* which is now in the medals department of the Bibliothèque Nationale (Bab. 264, Plate XII). Charles IX's present was engraved in Simon Bouquet's account of *L'Entrée de Charles IX* (Paris, 1571),

ed. F.A. Yates, Amsterdam, 1974, opposite f. 53v.

117 See my *Ideal Forms*, and Alastair Fowler, *Triumphal Forms*, Cambridge, 1970.

118 Dionysius of Halicarnassus praised the simplicity of Romulus' three triumphs (*The Roman Antiquities*, trs. Edward Spelman, 4 vols, London, 1758. I, pp. 284–5, 318 and 321); his comments on contemporary events are highly critical: 'But, in our time, these triumphs are become very expensive and ostentatious and attended with theatrical pomp, that seems calculated to show their riches rather than their virtue', p. 285.

119 Appian appeared in Latin translation in 1452 and was reissued many times, translated into French by Claude de Seyssel in 1544; Plutarch was published in Latin in 1482, and in Italian in 1491. Some *Lives* were put into French for François I, and Jacques Amyot's translation came out in 1559.

120 Claude Deroziers translated Dio Cassius' *Des Faicts et gestes insignes des Romains* which he published in Paris in 1542. Suetonius' text was first published in Rome in 1470; thereafter there were very many editions as well as adaptations, many of which remained in manuscript.

121 Biondo relied on ancient sources to paint his glorious picture of ancient Rome in *Roma triumphans* where he provided transcriptions and paraphrases of them; Valturius devoted the final book of *De re militari* (edn used, Paris, C. Wechel, 1532) to a study of the Triumph, detailing its ornaments (ff. 355–7) which aroused astonishment because of their number and richness, the merits of the Triumphator (ff. 367–70), the significance which Romans attached to the general's good fortune (*felicitas*) (ff. 372–5), and the games which followed (ff. 376–83). Alexandri ab Alexandro

concentrated a miscellany of information into the six books of the *Genialium dierum* (edn used, Paris, Vascosan, 1549) where he examines the political and military context of the Triumph, its characteristics and its decline.

122 Onufrius Panvinius' *De ludis circensibus. De triumphis romanorum veterum*, Venice, 1550, was enhanced with many illustrations; Francesco Modius, *Pandectae triumphales*, Frankfurt, 1586, provided information about the nature of the Triumph and followed this with details on each emperor's Triumph; Julius Caesar Boulenger's title indicates the comprehensive character of his enterprise, *Liber de spoliis bellicis, trophaeis, arcubus triumphalibus et pompa triumphi*, Paris, 1601; Vigenère's extensive comments on triumphs are from col. 991 to col. 1012, *Les Décades*; and Giacomo Lauro reconstructed his *Triumphus* (sig. A 6) from the study of ancient monuments, *Antiquae urbis splendor*, Rome, 1612. For a general discussion of the decline in the power of imagery in public spectacle, see Sydney Anglo, *Images of Tudor Kingship*, London, 1992.

123 The number of manuscripts is given by Konrad Eisenbichler (among others), p. xii of the essays he edited jointly with Amilcare A. Iannucci, *Petrarch's Triumphs. Allegory and Spectacle*, Ottawa, 1990. For particularly beautiful French manuscripts, see Myra D. Orth, 'The *Triumphs* of Petrarch illuminated by Godefroy le Batave', *Gazette des Beaux Arts*, vol. 104, 1984, pp. 197–206, and E. Golenistcheff-Koutouzoff, 'La Première tradition des *Triomphes* de Pétrarque en France', *Mélanges offerts à Henri Hauvette*, Paris, 1934, pp. 107–12.

124 Their homogeneity was established by Prince d'Essling and E. Müntz, *Pétrarque: ses études d'art, son influence*

sur les artistes, ses portraits et ceux de Laure, les illustrations et ses écrits, Paris, 1902; and has been further studied by Carandente, *I trionfi*, pp. 24–52, and in the many illustrations in his book.

125 On François Robertet, see C.A. Mayer and D. Bentley Cranch, 'François Robertet: French sixteenth-century civil servant, poet and artist', *Renaissance Studies*, vol. 2, no. 3, 1997, pp. 208–22.

126 Louis XII's manuscript is in the Bibliothèque Nationale, Ms fr. 594 (dated 1503); that of Anne de Montmorency, Ms fr. 20020; and Claude d'Urfé's copy is noted in the inventory to his library, see *Claude d'Urfé et La Bâtie, l'univers d'un gentilhomme de la Renaissance*, ed. Daniel Vallat, Montbrison, 1990, pp. 188–9. Printed editions were dedicated to Bauffremont (prose translation, Paris, 1514); Scève (Italian text, Lyon, 1550); and Marguerite de Valois (paraphrases of Petrarch done by Guillaume Bélliard, Paris, 1578).

127 The sculpted frieze at the hôtel de Bourgthéroulde is mentioned by several writers, but the most comprehensive study is *Rouen: l'hôtel de Bourgtheroulde: demeure des Le Roux*, text by Isabelle Lettéron and Delphine Gillot, Rouen, 1996.

128 The commentaries on the Triumphs were sometimes so extensive that they occupied 90 per cent of the page; see, for example, Petrarch, *Triomphi di Meser Francesco Petrarcha, con la loro optima spositione*, Venice, 1519.

129 Zygmunt G. Baranski, 'A Provisional Definition of Petrarch's *Triumphi*', *Petrarch's Triumphs*, ed. Iannucci and Eisenbickler, pp. 63–83 where he also noted (p. 67) 'the triumph brought with it an astonishingly broad range of artistic, ideological and even biographical connotation'.

130 Many examples could be cited: a typical composition was that of André Valladier, invented for the entry into Avignon of Henri le Grand, *Labyrinthe royal de l'Hercule gaulois triumphant*, Avignon, 1601.

131 The layered meanings of the arch of Constantine are analysed in full by P. Pierce, 'The arch of Constantine', *Art History*, vol. 12, 1989, pp. 387–418.

132 Payne traces this evolution, *Roman Triumph*, pp. 13, 36–44, 85–146.

133 McCormick has analysed the development of the Triumph outside Rome, as well as noting the concentration on the emperor's vision of his state, *Eternal Victory*, pp. 84–90.

134 L.M. Bryant, *The King and the City in the Parisian Royal Entry Ceremony: Politics, Ritual, and Art in the Renaissance*, Geneva, 1986, has shown how traditions and changing attitudes to royal power and to the authority of the *Parlement* wrought changes in the capital city.

135 Much good work on French triumphs can be found in the three volumes of *Les Fêtes de la Renaissance*, edited by Jacquot; for the period prior to the one discussed, see Bernard Guenée and Françoise Lehoux, *Les Entrées royales françaises de 1328 à 1515*, Paris, 1968.

136 Philibert de L'Orme discusses the arch on several occasions, *Premier tome*, ff. 197, 232–3, 245v–6.

137 References to Vitruvius abound in French accounts of Triumphs as though he were the ultimate arbiter of true classical style, although his authority was sometimes questioned. The 1549 entry into Paris may be taken as an example; the *Registres* specified 'selon la reigle qu'en baille messire Leon Baptiste Albert, qui faict monstrer l'ouvrage de trop meilleure grace que celle de Vitruve' (according to the rules given by maître Leo Battista Alberti who showed the work to be of greater elegance than that of

Vitruvius), cited by I.D. McFarlane in his facsimile edition [Henri II], *L'Entrée . . . à Paris*, Binghamton, 1982, p. 38. In Spain, the same habit applied; for the entry into Toledo (1560), the author of the account declared that Vitruvius' rules had been faithfully followed for the construction of the arches, otherwise (he commented) it would have been difficult to build them.

138 Caution also has to be exercised with respect to engravings (and especially woodcuts) which, because of the medium, frequently simplified and, thereby, falsified the record.

139 Richard Cooper has shown how Maurice Scève altered his text on several occasions, and he has drawn attention to the severe discrepancies in the texts which describe the entry of Henri II into Lyon in 1548 and the associated festivities; see his introduction and facsimile edition, [Henri II], *L'Entrée . . . à Lyon*, Arizona, 1997.

140 Lecoq, *François Ier*, pp. 357–8. On imperial pretensions in sixteenth-century France, see Frances A. Yates, *Astraea*, London, 1977; and also my *Ideal Forms*, ch. 4, pp. 121–58.

141 Henri IV received an identical gift in 1595.

142 See Bryant, *The King and the City*, p. 189, who discusses this change.

143 [Charles IX] *L'Entrée . . . à Paris*, 1571, facsimile edition of Simon Bouquet's account with introduction by Frances A. Yates, Amsterdam, 1974, f. 52v, 'Dans ce chariot estoit assize Cibelle mère des Dieux, representant la Roine mere du Roy, accompaignee des Dieux Neptune, et Pluton, et deesse Iunon, representans Messeigneurs freres et Madame seur du Roy.' (In this triumphal car sat Cybele, mother of the gods, representing the Queen Mother, accompanied by the gods Neptune and Pluto,

and the goddess Juno representing my lords and my lady, brothers and sister to the king.)

144 The engraved records of the 1549 entry into Paris are in the Bibliothèque Nationale, Estampes AA1 rés; the citation from Paradin can be found in his *Histoire de nostre temps*, Paris and Lyon, 1555, p. 656.

145 Richard Cooper's facsimile edition, [Henri II] *L'Entrée . . . à Lyon*, gives a wealth of scholarly reference; the arch at the Bourgneuf and the sources of its symbolism are discussed, pp. 47–50. Sometimes Scève's text states the origins of the image, such as Androcles and the lion on the first arch, taken from an ancient marble found in Rome (E2 v); Cooper refers the reader to Du Choul's manuscript in Turin for the source, 'Antiquitez romaines', ff. 12 r and v.

146 All these references are found in [Henri II] *L'Entrée . . . à Lyon*, Appendix A. Giorgio Conegrani's dispatch to the duke of Mantua, pp. 301–15; F. Denis Sauvage's appendix to Nicolas Gilles, *Le Second volume des chroniques et annales de France*, Paris, 1549, pp. 325–6.

147 [Henri II] *L'Entrée à Lyon*, H4 v. Serlio was probably the intermediary for the exedra, as Cooper suggests, ibid., p. 61; see Figure 99, p. 336.

148 The trophy is described by Scève, ibid., f. 1–f. 2v, and is engraved on f. 3.

149 Details are in Dudley, *Urbs Roma*, p. 127.

150 Ioannus Stevartus, Scotus, *De adventu Henrici Valesii . . . in metropolini*, Paris, 1549, pp. 10–11.

151 For the entry into Rouen, see my facsimile edition, [Henri II], *L'Entrée . . . à Rouen, 1550*, Amsterdam, 1974. For the several printed sources issued at the time, see ibid., pp. 50–2. There are significant differences in these sources, especially between the manuscript and the

152 The account was possibly written by Claude Chappuys; certainly the invention of the whole scheme can fairly confidently be attributed to him, see my introduction, [Henri II], *L'Entrée*, pp. 44–50.

153 A similar show had been put on at Lyon (1548) which was so successful that Henri II asked them to perform a second time, see [Henri II], *L'Entrée . . . à Lyon*, pp. 39–40.

154 For a discussion of the parallels between Mantegna's *Triumphs* and the Rouen entry, see my introduction, [Henri II] *L'Entrée*, pp. 42–4.

155 Ibid., f. O4v, 'non moins plaisant et delectable que le tiers triumphe de Pompee le grand celebré le jour de sa nativité fut veu des romains superbe en richesses et abondant en despeuilles des estranges nations' (no less pleasing and delightful than the third Triumph of Pompey the Great celebrated on his birthday, seen by the Romans as magnificent in riches and abounding in the spoils of foreign nations).

156 See Victor E. Graham, 'The entry of Henri II into Rouen in 1550', *Petrarch's Triumphs*, ed. Eisenbichler and Iannucci, pp. 403–13.

157 In the triumph of Fame, the printed texts show Roman forms, the manuscript shows contemporary armour, no military trophies, and the car drawn by elephants rather than winged horses, despite what the text says. The manuscript artist may have been more influenced by the tradition of Petrarch's *Triumphs* than the author of the printed account, as elephants frequently appeared with the *Triumph of Fame* (see Petrarch, *Opera*, Venice, B. de Zãni, 1515).

158 For the details regarding Charles IX's entry into Paris, see [Charles IX], *L'Entrée . . . à Paris*.

159 The entry into Moulins was on Tuesday, 26 September 1595, [Henri IV], *L'Entrée du roy en sa ville de Moulins*, Moulins, 1595; the elaborate account was (apparently) written at the request of the king, p. 350.

160 Ibid., p. 26, 'Alexandre et Cesar . . . la gloire et la valeur desquels n'est que l'ombre de celle du Roy' (Alexander and Caesar . . . the glory and value of whom are mere shadows compared to the king). The engraver for the pull-out plate for this entry may have been Jean Perrissin.

161 [Marie de' Medici], *L'Entrée de très-grande princesse Marie de Medici en la ville de Lyon* [4 décembre 1600], Lyon, 1600; the author of this *livret* spells out the hurry and the muddle occasioned by the short notice given; many structures used for the king's entry were refurbished: 'on jugea raisonnable d'y employer celuy [l'appareil] qui l'avoit servi en l'entrée du Roy' (it was thought appropriate to use the apparatus which had been employed for the entry of the king) (f. 10); 'des huict Arcs desseignez il n'y en eut que six sur pied' (f. 11) (of the eight arches planned, only six were built); and the most ambitious design was never made: 'Les nopces de Hercules et de Hebe, une des plus belles pieces de cest appareil demeurat en son crayon, et ne passa le dessein de l'autheur à faute de temps. Ce devoit estre un grand spectacle d'une platte peinture pour couvrir toute l'estendu des maisons de vers le corps de la garde du Change. On y eust representé les champs Elisées, et au milieu un grand pavillon, et soubz iceluy la feste et festin des nopces.' (The wedding of Hercules and Hebe, one of the most beautiful designs for this occasion, was still in its drawn, pencil state, and never got beyond its author's design, for lack of time. It was to have been a grand spectacle in simulated marble pro-

jected to cover the entire surface of the houses near the building of the Garde du Change. There would have been represented the Elysian Fields, and in the middle, a huge pavilion beneath which were the festivities and wedding banquet.) (ff. 67–67v)

In addition the arch at the pont du Rhone was not erected, nor the sixty-four statues of the kings of France.

162 In this way Matthieu fulfils his promise to the reader that he is writing history: that is, an account of what happened; for the arch 'à la Douanne' (at the Customs), was dedicated to the king's victories, and Matthieu, the historian, specifies them: the 'combat d'Arques, 21 septembre, 1589'; Ivry; and 'la [de]route des Espagnols pres Dijon' (the rout of the Spanish near Dijon) ([Henri IV], *L'Entrée . . . à Lyon*, ff. 43–4).

163 For the monuments borrowed from Rome for Leo X's *entrata*, see Anthony M. Cummings, *The Politicized Muse. Music for Medici Festivals*, Princeton, 1992, pp. 67–82.

164 Jean de Luxembourg, *Le Triomphe et les gestes de M. Anne de Montmorency*, ed. L. Delisle, Paris, 1904, presented to François I in 1537, pp. 58–60.

165 Plutarch, *Les Vies*, Amyot, I, p. 606.

166 Appian, *Des Guerres des Rommains*, III, p. 413; see also Plutarch, *Les Vies*, Amyot, II, p. 471.

167 Such criticism could take much cruder forms, particularly in Germany where satirical triumphs of soldiers and peasants were often found at this time; for an example, see Bibliothèque Nationale, Estampes Ea 11 rés.

168 La Popelinière, *L'Histoire de France*, I, ff. 300v–382; writers often had very mixed feelings about triumphal forms. Du Pinet (for example), who admired the Colosseum enormously, was critical of the extravagance that had led to the

construction of such a building and its purposes, *Plantz*, pp. 156–9.

169 For a discussion of Montaigne's love/hate relationship with Rome, and for his views about Roman Triumphs and shows, see my article, 'Contradictory impulses', pp. 402–3.

170 Hotman's text is cited and translated by Bryant, *The King and the City*, pp. 192–3; his thoughts echo those of Michel de l'Hospital expressed in the various *Remonstrances* which he addressed to king and *Parlement*.

171 On Maximilian I's paper triumphs, see Lary Silver, 'Paper pageants: the triumphs of Maximilian I', '*All the World's a Stage*', ed. Wisch and Scott-Munshower, pp. 293–331.

172 For the slavish copying of forms and images in the Renaissance, see Anglo, 'Humanism and the court arts', p. 70.

Coda

1 See Corrozet, *Les Antiquitez*; and Rabel, *Les Antiquitez et singularitez de Paris*.

2 For an analysis of Henri IV's transformation of Paris, see Hilary Ballon, *The Paris of Henri IV. Architecture and Urbanism*, Cambridge, Mass., 1991, especially ch. 6, 'The image of Paris', pp. 212–49.

3 Joukovsky, *La Gloire*, p. 237; poetic inspiration based on the sight of ruins was the subject of a course of lectures given in 1986 which are rich in suggestions, edited by Vincenzo de Caprio, *Poesia e poetica delle rovine di Roma. Monumenti e problemi*, Rome, 1987.

4 Jean-Louis Guez de Balzac, *Oeuvres complètes*, 2 vols, Paris, 1665, I. p. 542.

5 Some of the ideas elaborated here were first discussed in 'Guez de Balzac: the enduring influence of Rome', *Ethics and Politics in*

Seventeenth-Century France, ed. Keith Cameron and Elizabeth Woodrough, Exeter, 1996, pp. 41–55. Balzac was in Rome from 16 September 1619 to 5 April 1622.

6 Jean Jehasse has discussed the continuous rearrangements which Balzac made in his successive editions of his letters, *Guez de Balzac et le génie romain*, Saint-Etienne, n.d., pp. 109, 119–21; for a discussion of Balzac's cultivation of the letter form in order to involve readers in his argument, see Frank Sutcliffe, *Guez de Balzac et son temps*, Paris, 1959, p. 107, and Bernard Beugnot on the deliberate development of an informal style in the letters, *Jean-Louis Guez de Balzac. Les entretiens [1657]*, 2 vols, Paris, 1972, I, pp. xxvii–xxx.

7 Letter dated le 28 décembre 1622 (H. Bibas and K.T. Butler edition of the early letters, 2 vols, Geneva, 1933, henceforth referred to as B & B, I, pp. 122–7). Many shared Balzac's views: La Mesnardière, for example, in his preface to the *Panégyrique de Trajan*, compared the over-zealous quest for the expressions of refined feeling to the search for palaces, circuses and amphitheatres in the ruins of Rome where only names remain and their 'deplorables ruines' (dreadful ruins), cited in Roger Zuber, *Les 'Belles Infidèles' et la formation du goût classique*, Paris, 1968, p. 83.

8 Letter dated le 25 décembre, 1621; B & B, I, pp. 193–6.

9 'Je ne sçay pas à quoy ils pensent de mespriser la force, la vigueur et la lumière de Rome pour n'estre amoureux que de ses maladies et de sa carcasse, que de son sepulchre et de ses cendres' (I don't know what they are thinking of despising the force, vigour and light of Rome as they do in order to engage with her ills and her carcass, her tomb and her ashes), cited by Roger Zuber,

p. 141 in his article, 'Guez de Balzac et les deux antiquités', *XVIIe Siècle*, 1983, pp. 135–48.

10 Letter dated le 25 mars, 1621; B & B, II, pp. 106–8; see also his remarks in the discourse on Romans which he wrote for Madame de Rambouillet, *Oeuvres*, II, p. 424.

11 Letter dated le 3 juin, 1623, B & B, I, pp. 18–21.

12 Letter to Nicolas Bourbon, dated le 25 mars, 1621, ibid., II, pp. 106–8.

13 The claim is made by Méré, *Oeuvres*, 2 vols, Paris, 1692, II, p. 10, lettre IV, cited in Zobeidah Youssef, *Polémique et littérature chez Guez de Balzac*, Paris, 1972, pp. 375–6.

14 See his letter to Richelieu, dated le 12 avril, 1620, B & B, I, pp. 31–3.

15 For an analysis of the consolatory effects of Rome upon Balzac's unstable temperament, see Zuber, 'Guez de Balzac', *passim*.

16 This habit, which Balzac shared with Jean Chapelain, is examined by Youssef, *Polémique*, p. 384.

17 As early as 1623 (letter dated le 4 août, B & B, I, pp. 42–5) Balzac had written to Boisrobert that only his shadow had returned to France; the yearning to have become a citizen of Rome is expressed in a letter to his cousin M. de Brye, dated le 10 mai, 1635: 'Il y a longtemps que j'ay donné mon coeur à l'Italie . . . si j'eusse gouverné ma vie à ma volonté, je serois Citoyen Romain dèz l'an 1620.' (I gave away my heart to Italy a long time ago . . . if I had controlled my life as I would have wished, I would have been a Roman citizen as long ago as 1620.)

18 See above, Chapter 5, pp. 163–5. The civilizing power of Rome also recalls the view of Pierre Bergeron (1601–3) who wrote of the capacity of Rome 'adoucir et polir tant de nations' (to soften and polish so many nations), Bibliothèque Nationale, Ms fr. 5560, f. 4.

19 Guez de Balzac, *Oeuvres*, I, p. 454.

20 Letter to Corneille, dated le 17 janvier, 1643, ibid., p. 675.
21 Jehasse, *Guez de Balzac*, p. 490.
22 For a discussion of the extent to which experience of Rome had helped Balzac to understand more fully his own times, see ibid., throughout, and especially pp. 200 and 390.

23 André du Chesne, *Antiquitez et recherches des villes, chasteaux et places plus remarquables de toute la France*, Paris, 1609, p. 57.
24 Louis d'Orléans, *Les Ouvertures de parlemens*, Paris, 1607, ff. 250–2.

Bibliography

This Bibliography contains only works which have been cited in the text. For primary sources, both place and publisher (where known) are given; for secondary sources, only the place of publication is given.

PRIMARY SOURCES

Manuscripts and engravings

'Atti di vendità delle collezioni del card. du Bellay, Roma 29–30 mai, 1556', Bibliothèque Nationale, Ms Dupuy 264.

Audebert, Nicolas, 'Voyage d'Italie', British Library, Ms Lansdowne, 720.

Béatrizet, Nicolas, Victoria & Albert Museum, Print Room, Dyce Collection, nos 1196, 1197, 1198, 1202 and 1203.

Bergeron, Pierre, 'Le Voyage d'Italie', 1601–3, Bibliothèque Nationale, Ms fr. 5560.

Boissard, Jean-Jacques [Inscriptions], Bibliothèque Nationale, Ms lat. 12509.

Boyvin, Nicolas, 'Miroir hystorial', Bibliothèque Nationale, Ms fr. 15456.

Boyvin, René [Engravings after Thiry], British Museum, Print Room, 1930–T–16–2–12.

——[Designs for ewers], Victoria & Albert Museum, Print Room, M 32.

Caesar, Julius, 'Les Commentaires de Cesar', Bibliothèque Nationale, Ms fr. 38.

Caron, Antoine, 'Histoire françoise de nostre temps', Louvre, Cabinet des dessins, RF 29752 8–19.

——'Histoire de la Reine Arthemise', Bibliothèque Nationale, Estampes, Ad 105 fol. rés.

Charles VIII [Accounts], Bibliothèque Nationale, Ms n.a.fr. 7644 and Ms fr. 11350.

Davent, Léon [Engravings], British Museum, Print Room, 1850–5–27, 2–5, 9–11, 24–25; 1851–2–8–, 94, 117–128, 139–142; 1864–5–14, 252–255.

Delaune, Etienne [Engravings], Bibliothèque Nationale, Estampes, Ed 4a rés in fol.

——[Two Drawings], British Museum, Print Room, 1931–1–4, 1–2; [Engraving of Rome], 1834–8–4–165.

——[Designs for engraved ornament], Victoria & Albert Museum, Print Room, EO 14A [29338–B, 29338–C].

——[Frieze], drawing, Victoria & Albert Museum, Print Room PD 266 [D 39–85].

Demoulins, François, 'Commentaires de la guerre gallique', Bibliothèque Nationale, Ms fr. 13429; British Library, Ms Harleian 6205; Chantilly, Musée Condé, Ms 1139.

Dosio, G.A. [ed.] Christian Hülsen, *Das Skizzenbuch des Giovannantonio Dosio*, Berlin, 1933.

——*Roma antica e i disegni di architettura agli Uffizi*, Rome, 1976.

Du Cerceau, Jacques Androuet [Engravings after the antique] Bibliothèque Nationale, Estampes, Ed 8 & Ed 2 f, g, & h rés.

——*Arcs de Triomphe*, Bibliothèque Nationale, Estampes, Ed. 2 1 pet.fol.; and *Quinque et viginti exempla arcum*, Aureliae, 1549, Victoria & Albert Museum, Print Room, 95 B 94 [E 4633–4658].

——*De Architectura*, 1559, Bibliothèque Nationale, Estampes, Ed 2m pet.fol. rés.

——*Petits et moyens temples* [Orléans, 1550], Bibliothèque Nationale, Estampes, Ed 2d pet.fol.

——*Fleurons, cartouches, cadres, cheminées, meubles*, Bibliothèque Nationale, Estampes, Ed 2e pet.fol.

——*Vues d'optique (Venutissimae optices)*, Orléans, 1551, Bibliothèque Nationale, Estampes, Ed 2d pet.fol.

——*Praecipua aliquot Romanae antiquitatis Ruinarum* [1561], Bibliothèque Nationale, Estampes, Ed 2d pet.fol.

——*Le Livre des édifices antiques romains,* 1584, Bibliothèque Nationale, Estampes, Ed 2j pet.fol.

——[Drawings for *Les Plus Excellents Bastiments de France*], British Museum, Print Room, C 99 a I to VIII.

——*Vues des Monuments antiques*, Bibliothèque Nationale, Estampes, Ed 2h pet.fol.

——*Petites arabesques* [1550], British Museum, Print Room, 2AA* a 13, 1–26; 1850–5–27, 254–263; and Victoria & Albert Museum, Print Room *(grottesche) vocant itali*, Aureliae, 1550, EO 1 [23094, 1–50].

——[Trophies] Victoria & Albert Museum, Print Room, EO 60.

Du Choul, Guillaume, 'Antiquitez romaines', Biblioteca Reale [Turin], Ms Var. 212.

Du Pérac, Etienne, 'Illustrations des fragmens antiques', Bibliothèque Nationale, Ms fr. 382.

——[Drawings], Louvre, Cabinet des Dessins, nos 26372–26476.

——*I Disegni de le ruine di Roma* [1574], ed. T. Ashby, for the Roxburghe Club, London, 1916.

Florisel de Claveson, sieur de Mercurol, 'Voyage', Bibliothèque Nationale, Ms Clairambault 1006.

Foix, Paul de, 'Lettres', Bibliothèque Nationale, Ms Dupuy 712.

Grévin, Jacques [Sonnets sur Rome], Bibliothèque Nationale, Ms fr. 25560.

[Henri II], *L'Entrée du très magnanime tres puissant et victorieux roy de France Henry Deuxisme de ce nom en sa noble cité de Rouen en rithme françoyse*, Rouen, Bibliothèque Municipale, Ms Y 28 (1268).

Hoüel, Nicholas, *Histoire de la reine Arthemise*, Bibliothèque Nationale, Ms fr. 306.

Ligorio, Pirro, *Il primo libro delle antiquità di Roma*, the first of some forty volumes preserved in Rome, Naples, Turin, Oxford and Paris; a facsimile set of the entire corpus in Warburg Institute, Photographic Collection.

——'Trattato dell'antichità di Tivoli', Bibliothèque Nationale, Ms it. 625.

——'Descrittione delle superba & magnificentissima Villa Tiburtina Hadriana', British Library, Add Ms 22001.

Papon, Louys, 'Discours à Lesdiguières, 1597', British Library, Ms Harleian 5256.

Peiresc [Drawings], Bibliothèque Nationale, Ms fr. 9532.

——'Recueil d'Antiquitez', Bibliothèque Nationale, Ms fr. 9530.

——[Collection of drawings], *Antiquitez du cabinet de Peiresc dessinées par le Poussin, Rubens et autres*, Bibliothèque Nationale, Estampes, Aa. 53 and 54 rés.

Petrarch, 'Les Triomphes' [copy owned by Louis XII, and dated 1503], Bibliothèque Nationale, Ms fr. 594.

——'Les Triomphes' [copy owned by Anne de Montmorency], Bibliothèque Nationale, Ms fr. 20020.

Pietrasanta, P., 'Di Fontanbleo a Francesco Re di Francia', Bibliothèque Nationale, Ms it. 1043.

Strada, Jacques de, *Antiquam statuarum tam deorum quam dearum . . . ad vivam depictae atque quam fidelissime repraesentatae*, Vienna, Codex Minatus 21, 2.

Strasbourg, Jacob de [Engravings], Bibliothèque Nationale, Estampes, Ea. 11 rés.

Sully, Maximilien de, duc de, 'Parallèles de César et du roi Henri IV', Bibliothèque Nationale, Ms fr. 20034.

Thevet, André, 'Le grand Insulaire et pelotage' [1583], Bibliothèque Nationale, Ms fr. 15452.

Thiry, Léonard [Engravings], Bibliothèque Nationale, Estampes, Ed. 8a, fol. rés.

Van Heemskerck, Marten, [ed.] Christian Hülsen and Hermann Egger, *Die Römischen Skizzenbücher von Marten van Heemskerck*, Berlin, 2 vols, 1916.

Villeroy, Charles de Neufville de, marquis d'Alincourt, 'Memoire de tout mon voege fait en italie, l'an 1583', Bibliothèque Nationale, Ms fr. 14660.

'Voyage de Provence et d'Italie' (1588–9), Bibliothèque Nationale, Ms fr. 5550.

Woeriot, Pierre, *Antiquarum statuarum urbis Romae, c.* 1560, Bibliothèque Nationale, Estampes, Fb. 7 a Rés.

Printed books

Affagart, Greffin, *Relation de la Terre Sainte, 1533–1534*, ed. J. Chavanon, 1902.

Alberti, C., *Antiquorum statuarum urbis Romae . . . icones*, Rome, 1585.

Alberti, G. B., *L'Architecture de Jean Baptiste Albert*, translated by Jean Martin, Paris, I. Kerver, 1553.

Alberti, Leandro, *Descrittione di tutta Italia*, Bologna, A. Giaccarelli, 1550.

Albertini, Francesco, *Opusculum di mirabilia novae et veteris urbis Romae*, Rome, I. Mazochium, 1510.

Alexandri ab Alexandro, *Genialium dierum*, Paris, Vascosan, 1549 (first edition, 1522).

Alison, Archibald, *Essays on the Nature and Principles of Taste*, Edinburgh, 1790.

Amboise, François de, *Recueil de devises*, Paris, R. Boutonne, 1620.

Amelin, I. de, *Les Concions et harengues de Tite Live*, Paris, M. Vascosan, 1557.

Angelio, Pietro, *Commentarius de obelisco*, Rome, B. Grassij, 1586.

——— *De privatum, publicorumque, aedificorum urbis Romae*, Florence, B. Sermatellium, 1589.

Armagnac, cardinal d', *Lettres du cardinal Georges d'Armagnac*, ed. Tamizey de Larroque, Paris, 1874.

Audebert, Germain, *Roma*, Paris, J. du Puy, 1585.

Audebert, Nicolas, *Voyage d'Italie*, ed. Adalberto Olivero, 2 vols, Rome, 1983.

Baïf, Jean Antoine de, *Oeuvres*, ed. Marty Laveaux, 5 vols, Paris, 1881–90.

Bandole, Antoine de, *Les Parallèles de Cesar et de Henri IV*, Paris, Jean Richer, 1609.

Belleforest, François de, *La Cosmographie universelle*, Paris, Michel Sonnius, 1575.

Belon, Pierre, *Les Observations de plusieurs singularitez et choses memorables*, Paris, G. Corrozet, 1553.

——— *De admirabili operum antiquorum et rerum suspiciendarum praestantia*, Paris, G. Cavallet, 1553.

Bez, Ferrand de, *Le Grand Triumphe magnificque des parisiens*, Paris, N. Buffet, n.d.

Biondo, Flavio, *Roma instaurata* [1446], Venice, B. de Boniniis, 1481; and Venice, B. Venetum de Vitalibus, 1503.

——— *Roma triumphans* [*c.* 1459], Brixia, B. Vercellensem, 1482.

Bodin, Jean, *Six Livres de la Republique*, Paris, I. Du Puys, 1579.

Boissard, Jean-Jacques, *Antiquitatum Romanorum*, Frankfurt, Theodore and Robert de Bry, 1597–1602.

——— *Inscriptionum antiquarum*, Frankfurt, Theodore and Robert de Bry, 1599. Botero, Giovanni, *Delle cause della grandezza della citta* [Venice, 1589], translated by D. and P. Waley, *Giovanni Botero. The Reason of State*, London, 1956.

Bouchard, Jean Jacques, *Journal de voyage*, 1606; ed. E. Kanceff, 2 vols, Turin, 1977.

Boulenger, Jules César, *De circo romano*, Paris, R. Nivelle, 1598.

——*Liber de spoliis bellicis, trophaeis, arcubus triumphalibus et pompa triumphi*, Paris, R. Nivelle, 1601.

Bouterone, Michel, *Le petit Olympe d'Issy*, Paris, 1609.

Bracciolini, Poggio, *De varietate fortunae urbis Romae et de ruina eiusdem descriptio*, Milan, U. Scinzenzeler, 1492.

Brach, Pierre de, *Poèmes*, Bordeaux, S. Millanges, 1576.

Bralion, Nicolas, *Curiosités de l'une et l'autre Rome*, Paris, Edme Couterot, 1659.

Brantôme, Pierre de Bordeilles, seigneur de, *Oeuvres complètes*, 8 vols, Paris, 1822.

Braun, Georgius and Hogenberg, Franz, *Civitates orbis terrarum, Liber primus*, Antwerp, P. Galle, 1572; *Liber secundus*, Antwerp, P. Galle, 1575.

Budé, Guillaume, *L'Institution du prince* [Paris, 1547], published in *Le Prince dans la France des XVIe et XVIIe siècles*, ed. Claude Bontems, Léon-Pierre Raybaud and Jean-Pierre Brancourt, Paris, 1965.

——*De Asse et partibus eius libri quinq.*, Lyon, S. Gryphius, 1550.

Bullant, Jean, *Reigle générale d'architecture des cinq manières de colonnes*, Paris, H. de Marnef and G. Cavellat, 1568.

Caesar, Julius, *Les Commentaires de Jules César*, trs. Estienne de Laigue, Sgr. de Beauvais, Paris, Anthoine Bonnevière, 1539.

——*I Commentari di C. Giulio Cesare, con le figure in rame de gli allogiamenti, de' fatti d'arme, delle circonvallationi delle città, et di molte altre cose notabili descritte in essi*, Venice, Pietro de' Franceschi, 1575.

——*C. Julius Caesaris commentarii*, Antwerp, C. Plantin, 1570 (edition used by Montaigne).

Calvus, Fabius, *Antiquae urbis Romae cum regionibus simulacrum*, Rome, A. Bladum, 1527.

Capgrave, John, *Guide to the Antiquities of Rome* (composed 1450), ed. Francis C. Hingeston, Rolls Series, London, 1858.

Catherine de' Medici, *Lettres de Catherine de Médicis*, ed. La Ferrière, 10 vols, Paris, 1880.

Cavalieri, G. Battista, *Antiquarum statuarum urbis Romae*, Rome, 1561, 1574 and 1594.

——*Urbis Romae aedificorum*, Rome, 1569.

Ceffino, Zanobio, *La Triumphante Entrée de l'empereur Charles le 5e faicte en la cité de Rome*, Rome, 1536.

Charles VIII, *Lettres*, 5 vols, ed. P. Pelicier, Paris, 1898–1905.

[Charles IX] *L'Entrée à Paris, 1571*, facsimile edition of Simon Bouquet's account, with introduction by Frances A. Yates, Amsterdam, Theatrum orbis terrarum, 1974.

Cholet, Estienne, *Remarques singulieres de la ville, cité et université de Paris*, Paris, Jean Le Clerc, 1614.

Ciccarelli, Antonio, *Le vite degli imperadori Romani* [engravings by G. B. Cavalieri], Rome, D. Basa, 1590.

Cicero, *The Philippics*, John Rutherford's translation, London, 1799.

——*Brutus or Remarks on Eminent Orators*, London, Bohn's Libraries, 1871.

——*Letters to Atticus*, Loeb Library, 2 vols, London, 1913.

——*The Speeches of Cicero*, Loeb Library, London, 1958.

——*De Legibus*, Loeb Library, London, 1970.

——*De Finibus*, Loeb Library, London, 1971.

Cock, H., *Praecipua aliquot Romanae antiquitates ruinarum monumenta*, Antwerp, H. Cock., 1550.

Colletet, Guillaume, *Antiquitez de la ville de Paris*, Paris, N. Bonfons, 1577.

Colonna, Francesco, *Discours du songe de Poliphile*, translated by Jean Martin, Paris,

Jacques Kerver, 1546; Les Libraires associés, 1963.

Contarini, Luigi, *L'antiquita, sito, chiese, reliquie et statue di Roma,* Naples, G. Cacchij, 1569.

Corrozet, Gilles, *Les Antiquitez de Paris*, Paris, N. Bonfons, 1550.

Cotgrave, R., *A Dictionarie of Frenche and English Tongues*, London, Adam Islip, 1611.

Cousin, Jean, *Livre de perspective*, Paris, de l'imprimerie de Jean Royer, 1560.

—— *Liber Fortunae. Centum emblemata et symbola centum*, Paris, 1568.

D'Aubigné, Agrippa, *Les Tragiques*, ed. A. Garnier and J. Plattard, 4 vols, Paris, 1932–33.

De la Jessée, Jean, *Les Jeunesses* [Antwerp, 1583], ed. Geneviève Demerson, Paris, Société des textes français modernes, 1991.

De l'Hospital, Michel, *Oeuvres complètes*, ed. P. J. S. Duféy, 5 vols, Paris, 1824–26.

—— *Poésies complètes*, trs. from Latin into French by Louis Baudy de Nalèche, Paris, 1857.

De L'Orme, Philibert, *Nouvelles inventions pour bien bastir et à petis frais*, Paris, F. Morel, 1561.

—— *Le Premier tome de l'architecture*, Paris, F. Morel, 1567–68.

Des Masures, Louis, *Carmina*, Paris, 1557.

—— *Babylone ou la ruine de la grande cité*, Geneva, F. Perrin, 1563.

De Thou, Jacques Auguste, *Mémoires de la vie de Jacques Auguste de Thou*, 16 vols, London, 1734.

Deyron, Jacques, *Des Antiquités de la ville de Nismes*, Nîmes, Jean Plassas, 1663.

[Dio Cassius], *Des Faictz et gestes insignes des Romains*, trs. Claude Deroziers, Paris, A. & C. Les Angeliers, 1542.

Dionysius of Halicarnassus, *The Roman Antiquities*, trs. Edward Spelman, 4 vols, London, 1758.

Discours de la fuite des imposteurs italiens Paris, 1589.

Dosio, Giovanni Antonio, *Urbis Romae aedificorum*, Rome, 1569.

Doublet, Jean, *Elegies*, Paris, Charles l'Angelier, 1559.

Du Bellay, Jean de, *Correspondance du cardinal Jean du Bellay*, ed. R. Scheurer, Société de l'histoire de France, 2 vols, Paris, 1969 and 1975.

Du Bellay, Joachim, *La Deffence et illustration de la langue françoise*, Paris, A. L'Angelier, 1549.

—— *Premier Livre des Antiquitez de Rome Contenant une generale description de sa grandeur, et comme la deploration de sa ruine . . . Plus un Songe ou Vision sur le mesme subiect*, Paris, Fédéric Morel, 1558.

—— *Poematum libri quattuor*, Paris, Fédéric Morel, 1558.

—— *Les Regrets*, Paris, Fédéric Morel, 1558.

—— *Lettres de Joachim du Bellay*, ed. Pierre de Nolhac, Paris, 1883.

—— *Poemata*, in *Poésies françaises et latines de Joachim de Bellay*, 2 vols, ed. E. Courbet, Paris, 1918.

—— *Oeuvres poétiques*, VII, *Oeuvres Latines. Poemata*, ed. G. Demerson, Paris, 1984.

Du Cerceau, Jacques Androuet, *Livre d'architecture*, Paris, B. Prevost, 1559.

—— *Leçons de perspective positive*, Paris, Mamert Patisson, 1576.

—— *Les Plus Excellents Bastiments de France*, Paris, 1576, 1579; presented by David Thomson, Paris, 1988.

—— *Livre des edifices antiques romains*, Paris, 1584.

—— *Oeuvres*, ed. Edouard Baldus, 2 vols, Paris, 1884–91.

Du Chesne, André, *Antiquitez et recherches des villes, chasteaux et places plus remarquables de toute la France*, Paris, Jean Petit-Pas, 1609.

Du Choul, Guillaume, *Discours de la religion des anciens Romains illustré*, Lyon, Guillaume Roville, 1556.

—— *Discours sur la castramentation des Romains, des bains et antiques exercitations*, Lyon, G. Roville, 1557.

Du Pérac, Etienne, *I Vestigi dell'antiquità di Roma*, Rome, Lorenzo della Vaccheria, 1575.

Du Perron, Jacques Davy (cardinal), *Les Oeuvres diverses*, Paris, Antoine Estiene, 1629.

Du Pinet, Antoine, *Plantz*, Lyon, Ian d'Ogerolles, 1564.

[D'Urfé, Claude], *Claude d'Urfé et La Bâtie, l'univers d'un gentilhomme de la Renaissance*, ed. Daniel Vallat, Montbrison, 1990.

Du Val, Pierre, *Le Voyage et la description de l'Italie*, Paris, G. Clouzier, 1656.

Du Verdier, Antoine, *La Bibliothèque*, Lyon, B. Honorat, 1585.

——*Prosopographie ou description des personnes illustres tant chrestiennes que profanes*, Lyon, B. Honorat, 1589.

Egnatius, Joannes Baptista, *Caesarum vitae post Suetonium conscriptae*, 2 vols, Lyon, Seb. Gryphius, 1551.

Erasmus, *Ciceronianus* [Bâle, Froben, 1528], in the *Collected Works of Erasmus*, XXVIII, ed. A. H. T. Levi, Toronto, 1986, trs. Betty I. Knott.

Erizzo, Sebastiano, *Discorso sopra le medaglie antiche*, Venice, nella bottega Valgrisiana, 1559.

Estienne, Henri, *Le Traicté de la conformité du langage françois avec le grec*, n.p., 1565.

——*Deux Dialogues du nouveau langage françois italianizé et autrement desguizé* [Paris, 1578], ed. Pauline M. Smith, Geneva, 1980.

Fauchet, Claude, *Recueil des antiquitez gauloises et françoises*, Paris, J. du Puys, 1579.

Fauno, Lucio, *De antiquitatibus urbis Romae*, Venice, M. Tramezzino, 1549.

——*Compendio di Roma antica*, Venice, M. Tramezzino, 1552.

Favyer, Nicolas, *Figure et exposition des pourtraicts et dictons contenus es medailles de la conspiration des rebelles en France, opprimee et estaincte par le Roy Tres Chrestien Charles IX, le 24 jour d'Aoust, 1572*, Paris, 1572.

Ferrucci, Girolamo, *L'antichità di Roma di Andrea Fulvius antiquario Romano*, Rome, Gir. Francini, 1588.

Fontaine, Charles, *Les Nouvelles et Antiques Merveilles*, Paris, Guillaume le Noir, 1554.

——*Un Traicté des douze Cesars*, Paris, Guillaume le Noir, 1554.

Franzini, G., *Antiquarum statuarum urbis Romae quae in publicis privatisque locii visuntur icones*, Rome, 1583.

——*Palatia procerum Romae urbis*, Rome, G. Franzini, 1596.

——*Templa dea et sanctis eius Romae dicata*, Rome, G. Franzini, 1596.

Fulvius, Andreas, *Illustrium imagines*, Rome, I. Mazzochio, 1517.

——*Antiquitatis urbis*, Rome, M. Sieber, 1527.

Gadon, Adrian de, seigneur de Saussay, *La Marguerite. Les Paysages, plus sonnets faicts à Rome*, Paris, Jean Mettayer, 1573.

Gamucci, Bernardo, *Libro quattro dell'antichita della città di Roma*, Venice, Gio. Varisco e Compagni, 1565.

Gardet, Jean, *Epitome ou Extrait abregé des dix livres d'architecture de Marc Vitruve*, Toulouse, 1559.

Garnier, Robert, *Oeuvres complètes*, 2 vols, ed. L. Pinvert, Paris, 1922.

Gentillet, Innocent, *Discours contre Machiavel* [Geneva], 1576 (re-edition Geneva, 1968).

Gilles, Nicolas, *Le Second Volume des chroniques et annales de France*, Paris, R. Avril pour G. Du Pré and I. de Roigny, 1549.

Goltzius, Heinrich, *Fastos magistratum et triumphorum Romanum*, Bruges, 1561.

——*C. Julius Caesar sive historiae imperatorum caesarumque romanorum*, Bruges, apud H. Goltzium, 1563.

[Goulart, S.], *Poèmes chrestiens et autres divers auteurs recueillis et nouvellement mis en lumière par Philippe le Pas*, n. p., 1574.

Graevius, J.G. (ed.) *Thesaurus antiquitatem et historiarum Italiae*, Leiden, 1723.

Grévin, Jacques, *César* [*c.* 1561], ed. Ellen S. Guisberg, Paris, Société des Textes Français, 1971.

——*Sonnets inédits de Grévin sur Rome*, ed. Edouard Tricotel, Paris, 1862.

——*Théâtre complet et poésies choisies de Jacques Grévin*, ed. L. Pinvert, Paris, 1922.

Guéroult, Guillaume, *Epitome de la corographie d'Europe*, Lyon, Balthazar Arnoullet, 1583.

Guez de Balzac, Jean-Louis, *Les Entretiens* [Paris, 1657], ed. B. Beugnot, 2 vols, Paris, 1972.

——*Oeuvres complètes*, 2 vols, Paris, 1665.

——*Lettres*, 2 vols, ed. H. Bibas and K.T. Butler, Geneva, 1933.

Guicciardini, Francesco, *Considerations on the Discourses of Machiavelli* (composed 1530), ed. Cecil Grayson, *Selected Writings*, Oxford, 1965.

Guis, Joseph, *Description des arenes ou de l'amphitheatre d'Arles*, Arles, François Mesmes, 1665.

Hennequin, Jérôme, *Regrets sur les misères advenues à la France par les guerres civiles*, Paris, Denis du Pré, 1579.

[Henri II], *Actes de Henri II* [1547], Paris, 1979.

——*L'Entrée . . . à Rouen, 1550*, facsimile edition of *C'est la deduction du somptueux ordre* [Rouen, 1551] with introduction by Margaret M. McGowan, Amsterdam, Theatrum orbis terrarum, 1974.

——*L'Entrée . . . à Paris, 1549*, facsimile edition with introduction by I. D. McFarlane, Renaissance and Medieval Texts series, Binghamton, 1982.

——*L'Entrée . . . à Lyon, 1548*, facsimile edition of Maurice Scève, *La Magnificence de . . . l'entrée* [Lyon, 1548] with introduction by Richard Cooper, Renaissance & Medieval Texts series, Arizona, 1997.

[Henri IV], *L'Entrée du roy en sa ville de Moulins*, Moulins, 1595.

——*L'Entrée de très grand . . . Henry IIII . . .*, Lyon, 1595.

——*L'Entrée de très-grande princesse Marie de'Medici en la ville de Lyon*, Lyon, T. Ancelin, 1600.

Hoby, Sir Thomas, *The Travels and Life of*, ed. E. Powell, Camden Society Miscellany, X, London, 1902.

Jodelle, Etienne, *Oeuvres poétiques*, ed. E. Balmas, 2 vols, Paris, 1965.

Labacco, Antonio, *Libro appartenente a l'architettura*, Rome, V. & A. Dorici, 1576.

La Boëtie, Estienne de, *Les Oeuvres complètes d'Estienne de la Boëtie*, ed. P. Bonnefon, Bordeaux and Paris, 1892.

La Boutière (trs.), *Suetone Tranquille, de la vie des douze Césars*, Lyon, Jean de Tournes, 1556.

La Chasse de la beste romaine, La Rochelle, 1611.

La Croix du Maine, François de, *Bibliothèque françoise*, Paris, Abel l'Angelier, 1584.

Lafréry, Antoine, *Speculum Romanae magnificentiae*, Rome, 1573.

La Place, Pierre de, *Traitté de la vocation et manière de vivre à laquelle chacun est appellé*, Paris, F. Morel, 1561.

La Planche, Estienne de, *Les Oeuvres de C. Cornelius Tacitus, chevalier romain*, Paris, Abel l'Angelier, 1582.

La Popelinière, *L'Histoire de France*, 2 vols, Paris, A. H[aultin], 1581.

——*L'Histoire des histoires avec l'idée de l'histoire accomplie*, Paris, M. Orry, 1599.

La Porte, Maurice de, *Les Epithètes*, Paris, veufve la Porte, 1571.

La Ramée, Pierre de, *Liber de moribus veterum Gallorum*, Paris, A. Wechel, 1559 [translated into French by Michel de Castelnau, *Livre des moeurs des anciens gaulois*, Paris, A. Wechel, 1559, reissued as *Traitté des meurs et façons des anciens gaulois*, Paris, Denys du Val, 1581].

——*Liber de Caesaris militia*, Paris, André Wechel, 1559 (translated into French by Pierre Poisson, 1584).

Lauro, Giacomo, *Antiquae urbis splendor*, Rome, 1612.

431

Laval, Antoine de, *Desseins et professions nobles et publiques*, Paris, Abel l'Angelier, 1605.

Le Pois, Antoine, *Discours sur les medalles et graveures antiques, principalement Romaines*, Paris, Mamert Patisson, 1579.

Le Roy, Antonio, *Floretum philosophicum seu Iudus Meudonianus*, Paris, I. Dedin, 1654.

Le Roy, Louis, *Les Politiques d'Aristote*, Paris, F. Morel, 1568.

——*Consideration sur l'histoire françoise et l'universelle de ce temps dont les merveilles sont succinctement recitées*, Paris, F. Morel, 1570.

——*Exhortation aux François pour vivre en concorde et ioüir du bien de la paix*, Paris, F. Morel, 1570.

Lestoile, Pierre de, *Mémoires-Journaux*, ed. G. Brunet et al., 11 vols, Paris, 1875–83.

Ligorio, Pirro, *Libro delle antiquità di Roma*, Venice, M. Tramezzino, 1553.

——*Descrittione della superba et magnificentissima Villa Tiburtina Hadriana*, in *Thesaurus antiquitatem et historiarum Italiae*, ed. J.G. Graevius, Leiden, 1723.

Lipsius, Justus, *Opera omnia*, 4 vols, Antwerp, Balthasar Morel, 1637.

——*Of Constancie*, trs. J. Stradling, London, R. Johnes, 1595.

Louveau, Jean, *Trésor des antiquitez de Jaques de Strada*, Lyon, T. Guerin, 1553.

Lucan, *Pharsalia (The Civil War)*, Loeb Library, London, 1988.

Lucinge, René de, *De la Naissance, duree et chute des estats* [Paris, 1588], ed. Michael J. Heath, Geneva, 1984.

——*La Maniere de lire l'histoire* [Paris, 1614], ed. Michael J. Heath, Geneva, 1993.

Luxembourg, Jean de, *Le Triomphe et les gestes de M. Anne de Montmorency*, ed. L. Delisle, Paris, 1904 (presented to François I in 1537).

Machiavelli, Niccolò, *Discourses*, trs. Leslie J. Walker, 2 vols, London, 1950.

——*Discorsi di Niccolò Machiavelli*, Rome, A. Blado, 1531.

Magny, Olivier de, *Oeuvres*, Paris, 1885; Geneva, Jules Favre, 1969.

Marliani, Bartholomeo, *Liber urbis Romae topographia*, Lyon, Gryphius, 1534.

——*L'antiquità di Roma*, trs. into Italian by Hercole Barbarosa da Terni, Rome, A. Bladum, 1548.

Martin, Gregory, *Roma sancta [1581]*, ed. G.B. Parks, Rome, 1968.

Martin, Jean, *Discours du Songe de Poliphile* [Colonna], Paris, Jacques Kerver, 1546.

——*Architecture de Vitruve*, Paris, H. de Marnef, 1547.

——*L'Architecture de Jean Baptiste Albert*, Paris, I. Kerver, 1553.

Mauro, Lucio, *Delle antichità di Roma*, Venice, G. Ziletti, 1556.

[Medici, Marie de'], *L'Entrée de trèsgrande princesse Marie de Medeci en la ville de Lyon, 1600*, Lyon, T. Ancelin, 1600.

Meilliet, L., *Discours politiques et militaires*, Paris, 1619.

Menestrier, Claude, *Medales illustres des anciens empereurs et imperatrices de Rome*, Paris, Pierre Palliot, 1642.

Menestrier, Claude François, *Histoire de la ville de Lyon*, Lyon, Benoist Coral, 1669.

Méré, chevalier de, *Oeuvres*, 2 vols, Paris, 1692.

Mexia, Pedro, *Le vite di tutti gl'imperadori, di Giulio Cesare insino a Massimiliano*, Venice, G. Giolito, 1558.

Modius, Francesco, *Pandectae triumphales*, Frankfurt, Sigmund Feyerabend, 1586.

Monconys, Monsieur de, *Journal des voyages de monsieur de Monconys*, Lyon, Horace Boissat and George Remeus, 1665.

Monluc, Blaise de, *Commentaires*, ed. Paul Courteault, Paris, Pléiade, 1964.

Montaigne, Michel de, *Essais*, Paris, Presses Universitaires de France, 1965.

——*The Complete Essays*, trs. M. A. Screech, London, Penguin, 1987.

——*Journal de voyage*, ed. François Rigolot, Paris, Presses Universitaires de France, 1992.

Montjosieu, Louis de, *Gallus Romae hospes ubi multa antiquorum monumenta explicantur*, Rome, I. Osmarinum, 1585.

Muret, Marc-Antoine de, *Caesar*, Paris, Veuve Maurice la Porte, 1553.

Nuysement, Clovis Hesteau de, *Les Oeuvres poétiques* I and II [1578], ed. Roland Guillot, 2 vols, Geneva, 1994.

Orléans, Louis d', *Les Ouvertures de par-lemens*, Paris, G. des Rues, 1607.

Palissy, Bernard, *Architecture et ordonnance de la grotte rustique de Mgr le duc de Mont-morency* [La Rochelle, 1563], ed. Edouard Rahir, Paris, 1919.

Palladio, Andrea, *Le antichità di Roma*, Venice, V. Lucrino, 1554.

——*I quattro libri di architettura*, Venice, D. de Franceschi, 1570.

——*The Architecture of A. Palladio*, translation published in London, 1721.

Panvinius, Onufrius, *Respublicae romanae commentarium libri tres*, Venice, Vincenzo Valgrisi, 1558.

——*De ludis circensibus. De triumphis romanorum veterum*, Venice, I. B. Crottum, 1600 (first edition, 1550).

Paradin, Guillaume, *Histoire de nostre temps*, Paris and Lyon, Jean de Tournes and G. Gazeau, 1555.

Paschal, Pierre, *Petrus Paschali oratio de legibus, Romae apud sanctae Eustachium habita*, Paris, M. Vascosan, 1548.

Pasquier, Estienne, *Les Recherches de la France*, 2 vols, Paris, 1723.

——*Lettres familières*, 3 vols, ed. D. Thickett, Geneva, 1974.

Peiresc, Claude-Fabri de, *La Correspon-dance de Claude-Fabri de Peiresc*, ed. Tamizey de Larroque, 9 vols, Paris, 1894.

——*Lettres à Alphonse de Rambervil-liers*, ed. Anne Reinbold, Paris, CNRS, 1983.

——*Lettres à Cassiano dal Pozzo, 1626–1637*, ed. Jean-François Lhote and Danielle Joyal, Adosa, 1989.

Pellicier, Guillaume, *Correspondance politique de Guillaume Pellicier*, ed. A. Tausserat-Radel, Paris, 1899.

Petrarch, *Triomphi di Meser Francesco Petrarcha, con la loro optima spositione*, Venice, B. Stagnino, 1519.

——*Rerum familiarum*, trs. Aldos Bernardo, New York, 1975.

——*Africa*, trs. Thomas Bergin and Alice Wilson, New Haven, 1977.

[Pilon, Germain], *Germain Pilon et les sculpteurs français de la Renaissance. La Doc-umentation française*, Paris-Louvre, 1963.

Pliny, *Letters and Panegyrics*, 2 vols, Loeb Library, trs. Betty Radice, London, 1969.

——*National History*, 10 vols, Loeb Library, 1–5, and 9 trs. H. Rackham, 6–8 W.H.S. Jones, 10 D. E. Eichholz, London, 1940–62.

Pliny (the elder), *L'Histoire du monde*, trs. Antoine du Pinet, 2 vols, Lyon, à la Sala-mandre, 1566.

Plutarch, *Les Vies des hommes illustres*, trs. Jacques Amyot, Paris, M. Vascosan, 1559.

Poldo d'Albenas, Jean, *Discours historial de l'antique cité de Nîmes*, Lyon, Guillaume Roville, 1560.

Polletti, Francesi, *Forum romanorum*, Douai, 1591.

Pontoux, Claude de, *Les Oeuvres*, Lyon, Benoist Rigaud, 1579.

Quintilian, *Institutes of Oratory*, 2 vols, Bohn's Libraries, London, 1909.

Rabel, Jean, *Les Antiquitez et singularitez de Paris*, Paris, N. Bonfons, 1588.

Rapin, Nicolas, *Oeuvres*, Paris, Olivier de Varennes, 1610.

Recueil des histoires romaines extraicts de plusieurs historiographes c'est assavoir Tite Live/Valere/Orose/Justin/Saluste/Cesar/Lucan/Suetone/Eutrope et autres, Paris, 1528.

Rigaud, Jean Antoine, *Bref Recueil de choses rares, notables, antiques, citez, forter-esses principales d'Italie*, Aix, Jean Tolosan, 1601.

Ronsard, Pierre de, *Oeuvres complètes*, ed. Gustave Cohen, 2 vols, Paris, Pléiade, 1965.

Rosinus, J., *Romanorum antiquitatum corpus*, Bâle, 1583.

—— *Romanorum antiquitatum libri decem*, Lyon [Sibille de La Porte], 1585; and *Antiquitatum Romanorum Corpus Absolutissimum*, Amsterdam, Blaviana, 1685.

Roville, Guillaume, *La Première Promptuaire des medalles*, Lyon, G. Roville, 1553.

Sallustius, C.C., *Works of Sallust: The Conspiracy of Catiline*, Loeb Library, London, 1931.

Scamozzi, Vincenzo, *Discorsi sopra l'antichità di Roma*, Venice, F. Ziletti, 1583.

Schiappalaria, Stefano Ambrosio, *La vita di C. Julio Cesare*, Antwerp, A. Bax, 1578.

Seneca, L.A., *Epistles to Lucilius*, Loeb Library, London, 1928–35.

Serlio, Sebastiano, *Il terzo libro*, Venice, 1544.

—— *Tutte l'opere d'architettura*, Venice, D. Scamozzi, 1584.

—— *The First Boke of Architecture made by Sebastioni Serly*, printed for Robert Peake, London, 1611.

—— *Tutte l'opere*, Venice, Giacomo de' Francheschi, 1584; and 1619.

Serres, Jean de, *Memoires de la troisiesme guerre civile en France, sous Charles IX*, n.p., 1570.

Seysell, Claude de (trs.) [Appian], *Des Guerres des Rommains*, Lyon, A. Constantin, 1544.

Sigonio, Carlo, *Historiarum de regno Italiae quinque reliqui libri*, Venice, F. Franciscium, 1591.

Silius Italicus, *Punica*, Loeb Library, London, 2 vols, 1927.

Spon, Jacob, *Recherche des antiquités et curiosités de la ville de Lyon*, Lyon, Antoine Collier, 1675.

Stevartus, Ioannus, Scotus, *De adventu Henrici Valesii . . . in metropolini*, Paris, M. David, 1549.

Strada, Jacques de, *Epitome thesauri antiquitatem hoc est*, Lyon, J. de Tournes, 1553.

Suetonius, *Des Faicts et gestes des douze Cesars*, translated by Michel de Tours, Paris, 1530.

Symeoni, Gabriel, *Epitome de l'origine et succession de la duché de Ferrare . . . avec certaines épistres à divers personnages*, Paris, G. Cavellat, 1553.

—— *Interpretation . . . grecque . . . du monstre d'Italie*, Lyon, Jean de Tournes, 1555.

—— *Les Illustres Observations antiques*, Lyon, Jean de Tournes, 1558.

—— *Illustratione de gli epitaffi e medaglie antiche*, Lyon, Jean de Tournes, 1558.

—— *César renouvellé*, Lyon, B. Prevost, 1558.

—— *Description de la Limague d'Auvergne en forme de dialogue*, Lyon, G. Roville, 1561.

—— *Dialogue des devises d'armes et d'amours du sieur Paulo Iovio, discours de M. Louys Dominique sur le mesme subject, et devises heroiques et morales de G. Symeoni*, Lyon, G. Roville, 1561.

Tarde, Jean, *A la rencontre de Galilée, deux voyages en Italie*, ed. François Moureau and M. Tetel, Geneva, 1984.

Thevet, André, *La Cosmographie du Levant*, Lyon, Jean de Tournes and G. Gazeau, 1554.

—— *La Cosmographie universelle*, 2 vols, Paris, G. Chaudière, 1575.

—— *Les Vrais Pourtraits et vies des hommes illustres*, Paris, la vefve I. Kervert and Guillaume Chaudière, 1584.

—— *La Grande et Excellente Cité de Paris*, Paris, 1881.

Tocsin (Le), contre les massacreurs en France, Rheims, I. Martin, 1577.

Tournon, François de (cardinal), *Correspondance du cardinal François de Tournon*, ed. Michel François, Paris, 1946.

Turnèbe, Odet de, *Les Sonnets sur les ruines de Luzignan*, Paris, F. Morel, 1579.

Valladier, André, *Labyrinthe royal de l'Hercule gaulois triumphant*, Avignon, Jacques Bramereau, 1601.

Valturius, Robertus, *De re militari*, edn used, Paris, Wechel, 1532.

Van Buchel, Arnold, *Journal [1585]*, Paris, 1899.

Van der Noot, Jan, *A Theatre for Worldlings*, London, Henry Bynneman, 1569.

Vasari, Giorgio, *Lives of the Most Eminent Painters, Sculptors & Architects*, translated by J. Foster, 8 vols, London, 1881.

Vasseliev dit Nicolay, Benedit de, *Portrait de la ville, cité et université de Paris avec les faubours di celle dédié au Roy*, Paris, Jean le Clerc, 1609.

Velleius Paterculus, C., *Compendium of Roman History*, Loeb Library, London, 1924.

Veneziano, Agostino, *Recueil de vases*, Paris, 1680.

Veyrel, Samuel, *Indice du cabinet de Samuel Veyrel*, Bordeaux, Pierre de la Court, 1635.

Vico, Aeneas, *Omnium Caesarum verissimae imagines ex antiquis numismata descriptae*, Venice, M. Aldus, 1552.

——*Ex libri xxiii commentariorum in vetera imperatorum romanorum numismata*, Venice, M. Aldus, 1560.

Vigenère, Blaise de, *Les Commentaires de César*, Paris, N. Chesneau, 1576 (a further edition appeared in 1589).

——*La Somptueuse et Magnifique Entrée du roi Henri III à Mantoue*, Paris, N. Chesneau, 1576.

——*Les Images ou tableaux de platte peinture des deux Philostate*, Paris, N. Chesneau, 1578 (later editions, 1597 and 1615, were published by Abel l'Angelier and his widow).

——*Trois Dialogues de l'Amitié*, Paris, N. Chesneau, 1579.

——*Les Décades de Tite Live* [1578], Paris, Jacques du Puy, 1583.

——*Traicté des chiffres ou secretes manières d'escrire*, Paris, Abel l'Angelier, 1586.

——*La Suitte de Philostate*, Paris, Abel l'Angelier, 1602.

Villamont, sieur de, *Voyages*, Arras, G. Baudoin, 1598 and Paris, 1600.

Vinet, Elie, *L'Antiquité de Bourdeaux et de Bourg*, Bordeaux, Simon Millanges, 1574.

Vintemille, J. de, *L'histoire d'Herodian*, Lyon, G. Roville, 1554.

Vitruvius, *Architecture*, translated by Jean Martin, Paris, H. de Marnef, 1547.

Vostre, Simon, *Heures à l'usage de Lyon* [1502], republished Paris, La Sirène, 1520.

——*Heures à l'usage de Rome*, Paris, 1508.

Voyage d'Italie [1606], ed. Michel Bideaux, Geneva, 1981.

Woeriot, Pierre, *Pinax Iconicus. Antiquorum de variorum in sepulturus ritum*, Lyon, Clément Baudoin, 1556.

Zwinger, Theodor, *Methodus apodemica*, Basle, Eusebius Episopius, 1577.

SECONDARY SOURCES

Actes du colloque international à Bordeaux, Montaigne et l'Italie, 1988, published in *Biblioteca del Viaggio in Italia*, no. 38, 1991.

Adhémar, Jean, 'The collection of François Ier', *Gazette des Beaux Arts*, vol. 30, 1946, pp. 4–16.

Allott, Terence, 'Tacitus and some late plays of Corneille', *Journal of European Studies*, 1980, pp. 32–47.

Alsop, J., *The Rare Art Collections*, London, 1982.

Anglo, Sydney, 'Humanism and the court arts', *The Impact of Humanism on Western Europe*, ed. Anthony Goodman and Angus Mackay, London, 1990, pp. 66–98.

——*Images of Tudor Kingship*, London, 1992.

Arnheim, Rudolf, *The Dynamics of Architectural Form*, Berkeley, 1977.

Ashby, Thomas, 'The Villa d'Este at Tivoli and the collection of classical sculptures which it contained', *Archaeologia*, vol. 61, 1908, pp. 219–56.

——'The Bodleian Ms. of Pirro Ligorio', *Journal of Roman Studies*, vol. 9, 1919, pp. 170–201.

Asher, R.E., *National Myths in Renaissance France*, Edinburgh, 1993.

Bailbé, Jacques, 'Lucan et d'Aubigné', *Bibliothèque d'Humanisme et Renaissance*, vol. 22, 1960, pp. 320–37.

——'Les Guerres civiles de Rome dans la littérature française du XVIe siècle', *Congrès de Rome*, Association Budé, 2 vols, Paris, 1975, II, pp. 520–45.

Baillet, Roger, 'César chez Machiavel', *Présence de César*, ed. Chevalier, op.cit., pp. 67–76.

Balas, Edith, 'Michelangelo's *Concetti* (1505) in the château de Blois', *Gazette des Beaux Arts*, vol. 101, 1983, p. 33.

Baldwin, Robert, 'A bibliography of the literature on triumph', '*All the World's a Stage*', ed. Wisch and Scott-Munshower, op.cit., pp. 359–85.

Ballon, Hilary, *The Paris of Henri IV. Architecture and Urbanism*, Cambridge, Mass., 1991.

Balmas, E. (ed.) *Montaigne et l'Italie. Atti del congresso internazionale di studi di Milano–Lecco, 26–30 ottobre, 1988*, Biblioteca del Viaggio in Italia, no. 38, Geneva, 1991.

Balsamo, Jean, *Les Rencontres des Muses: italianisme et anti-italianisme dans les lettres françaises de la fin du XVIe siècle*, Paris and Geneva, 1992.

Baranski, Zygmunt G., 'A provisional definition of Petrarch's *Triumphi*', *Petrarch's Triumphs*, ed. Iannucci and Eisenbickler, op.cit., pp. 63–83.

Baratte, Sophie, *Léonard Limosin au musée du Louvre*, Paris, 1993.

Baron, Hans, 'The evolution of Petrarch's thought: reflections on the state of Petrarch studies', *Bibliothèque d'Humanisme et Renaissance*, vol. 24, 1962, pp. 7–41.

——*The Crisis of the Early Italian Renaissance*, Princeton, 1986.

Bean, Jacob, *Fifteenth- and Sixteenth-Century French Drawings in the Metropolitan Museum of Art*, New York, 1986.

Beatis, A. de, *Voyage du Cardinal d'Aragon, 1517–1518*, Paris, 1913.

Beer, Jeannette M.A., *A Medieval Caesar*, Geneva, 1976.

Béguin, Sylvie, 'La Suite d'Arthémise', *L'Oeil*, vol. 38, 1959, pp. 32–9.

Belivaqua Caldari, F., 'I sonnetti di Jacques Grévin su Roma', *Studi romani*, vol. 22, 1974, pp. 36–59.

Bellenger, Yvonne (ed.) *Le Sonnet à la Renaissance des origines au XVIIe siècle*, Paris, 1988.

——*Du Bellay: Les Regrets qu'il fit dans Rome*, Rome, 1975.

Bené, Charles, 'Bible et inspiration religieuse chez Du Bellay', *Du Bellay*, ed. Cesdron, op.cit., I, pp. 177–87.

Bentley Cranch, D., 'A sixteenth-century patron of the arts, Florimond Robertet, Baron d'Alluye and his "vierge ouvrante"', *Bibliothèque d'Humanisme et Renaissance*, vol. 50, no. 2, 1988, pp. 317–33.

Bertolotti, A., *Artisti francesi in Roma*, Mantua, 1886.

Beugnot, Bernard (ed.) *Jean-Louis Guez de Balzac, Bibliographie générale*, Montreal, 1967; supplément, 1969.

——(ed.) *Jean-Louis Guez de Balzac. Les entretiens [1657]*, 2 vols, Paris, 1972.

Biver, P., *Histoire du château de Meudon*, Paris, 1923.

Blum, C., and Tournon, A., *Editer les 'Essais' de Montaigne*, Paris, 1997.

Blunt, Anthony, 'The *Hypnerotomachia Poliphili* in seventeenth-century France', *Journal of the Warburg and Courtauld Institutes*, vol. 1, 1937, pp. 117–37.

Bober, Phyllis Pray, *Drawings after the Antique by Amico Aspertini. Sketches in the British Museum*, London, 1957.

——'The census of antique works of art known to the Renaissance artists', *Acts of the XX International Congress of the History of Art*, 3 vols, Princeton, 1963, II, pp. 88–9.

——'Francesco Lisc's collection of antiquities. Footnote to a new edition of Aldrovandi', *Essays in the History of Art Presented to Rudolf Wittkower*, London, 1969.

——and Rubinstein, Ruth, *Renaissance Artists and Antique Sculpture*, Oxford, 1986.

Boccassini, Daniela, 'Ruines montaigniennes', *Montaigne Studies. An Interdisciplinary Forum*, V, ed. Rigolot, op.cit., pp. 154–91.

Bonnaffé, E., *Inventaire des meubles de Catherine de Médicis en 1589*, Paris, 1874.

Bossuat, Robert, 'Traductions françaises des Commentaires de César à la fin du XVe siècle', *Bibliothèque d'Humanisme et Renaissance*, vol. 3, 1943, pp. 252–411.

Boucher, Bruce, 'Leone Leoni and Primaticcio's moulds of antique sculpture', *Burlington Magazine*, vol. 123, 1981, pp. 23–6.

Boucher, Jacqueline, *La Cour de Henri III*, Paris, 1986.

Bouchéry, H.F., 'Des Arcs triomphaux aux frontispices des livres', *Fêtes de la Renaissance*, ed. Jacquot, I, op.cit., pp. 431 ff.

Boudon, F. and Blécon, J., *Le Château de Fontainebleau de François Ier à Henri IV*, Paris, 1998.

Bourrilly, V.L., *Guillaume du Bellay, Seigneur de Langey, 1491–1543*, Paris, 1905.

Bowra, C.M., 'Melinno's Hymn to Rome', *Journal of Roman Studies*, vol. 47, 1957, pp. 21–8.

Boyer, Jean, 'L'Influence de Serlio en France: la porte de l'hôtel de Joannis à Aix en Provence', *Gazette des Beaux Arts*, vol. 127, janvier 1996, pp. 11–14.

Braudy, Leo, *The Frenzy of Renown*, Oxford, 1986.

Bresson, Agnès, 'Peiresc et le commerce des antiquités à Rome', *Gazette des Beaux Arts*, vol. 85, 1975, pp. 60–72.

Brilliant, R., 'The arch of Septimus Severus in the Roman Forum', *Memoirs of the American Academy in Rome*, vol. 29, 1967, pp. 271 ff.

Brink, C.O., 'Justus Lipsius of the text of Tacitus', *Journal of Roman Studies*, vol. 41, 1951, pp. 32–51.

Brousseau-Beuermann, Christine, *La Copie de Montaigne*, Paris, 1989.

Brown, C. Malcolm, 'Martin van Heemskerck. The Villa Madonna Jupiter and the Gonzaga correspondence files', *Gazette des Beaux Arts*, vol. 94, 1979, pp. 49–60.

——'Major and minor collections of antiquities in documents of the later sixteenth century', *Art Bulletin*, vol. 46, 1984, pp. 296–507.

——'The Palazzo di San Sebastiano (1506–1512) and the art patronage of Francesco II Gonzaga, fourth marquis of Mantua', *Gazette des Beaux Arts*, vol. 129, 1997, pp. 131–80.

Brown, Virginia, 'Portraits of Julius Caesar in Latin manuscripts of the Commentaries', *Viator*, vol. 12, 1981, pp. 319–55.

Bryant, L.M., *The King and the City in the Parisian Royal Entry Ceremony: Politics, Ritual, and Art in the Renaissance*, Geneva, 1986.

Burns, Howard, 'Pirro Ligorio's reconstruction of ancient Rome', *Pirro Ligorio*, ed. Gaston, op.cit., pp. 19–92.

Burroughs, Charles, *From Signs to Design. Environmental Process and Reform in Early Renaissance Rome*, Cambridge, Mass., 1990.

Bury, Michael, 'The taste for prints in Italy to *c.* 1600', *Print Quarterly*, vol. 2, 1885, pp. 12–26.

Byrne, Janet S., 'Du Cerceau drawings', *Master Drawings*, vol. 15, no. 2, Summer 1977, pp. 147–61.

Cahen-Salvador, Georges, *Un Grand Humaniste, Peiresc*, Paris, 1951.

Callmer, Christian, 'Un Manuscrit de J.J. Boissard', *Opuscula Romana*, IV Lund, 1962, pp. 47–59.

Canedy, Norman W., *The Roman Sketchbook of Girolamo da Carpi*, London, 1976.

Caprio, Vincenzo de, ed., *Poesia e poetica delle rovine di Roma. Momenti e problemi*, Rome, 1987.

Carandente, G., *I trionfi*, n.p., 1963.

Castan, Auguste, 'Jean-Jacques Boissard, poète latin, dessinateur et antiquaire', *Mémoires de la Société d'Emulation du Doubs*, décembre 1874, pp. 65–91.

[Catalogue], *I Francesi a Roma. Residenti e viaggiatori nella città eterna del Rinascimento agli inizi del Romanticismo*, Palazzo Braschi, n.p., May–June 1961.

[Catalogue], *L'Ecole de Fontainebleau*, Paris, 1972.

[Catalogue], *Livres d'heures royaux*, Ecouen, 1993.

[Catalogue], *Le Dessin en France au XVIe siècle*, Ecole des Beaux Arts, Paris, 1995.

Cave, Terence, *The Cornucopian Text*, Oxford, 1979.

——— 'Problems of reading in the *Essais*', *Montaigne*, ed. McFarlane and Maclean, op.cit., pp. 133–66.

Céard, J., 'Rome dans la *Methode de l'Histoire* de Jean Bodin', *Congrès de Rome, Actes de l'Association Budé*, Paris, 1975, pp. 758–70.

——— and Margolin, J.C., *Voyager à la Renaissance*, Paris, 1987.

Ceccarelli Pellegrino, Alba, 'Du Bellay e il Poliphilo, lettura pluri-isotopica del *Songe*', *Studi di letteratura francese*, vol. 19, 1992, pp. 65–95.

——— *Le 'bon Architecte' de Philibert de L'Orme. Hypotextes et anticipations*, Paris, 1996.

Cesdron, Georges (ed.) *Du Bellay. Actes du Colloque International d'Angers du 26 au 29 mai, 1989*, 2 vols, Angers, 1990.

Chambers, F.M., 'Lucan and the *Antiquitez de Rome*', *Publications of the Modern Language Association*, vol. 60, 1945, pp. 937–48.

Champion, Pierre, 'Henri III et les écrivains de son temps', *Bibliothèque d'Humanisme et Renaissance*, vol. 1, 1941, pp. 43–172.

Charpentier, Françoise, 'La Rome de Montaigne, modèle et intercesseur', *Montaigne et l'Italie. Atti del congresso internazionale di studi di Milano–Lecco, 26–30 ottobre, 1988*, ed. E. Balmas, Geneva, 1988, pp. 351–62.

Chastel, André, *Le Sac de Rome, 1527*, Paris, 1984.

Châtelet-Lange, Liliane, 'Le "Museo de Vanves" (1560). Collections et musées de sculptures au XVIe siècle', *Zeitschrift für Kunstgeschichte*, vol. 38, 1975, pp. 266–85.

Chatenet, Monique, *Le Château de Madrid au bois de Boulogne*, Paris, 1987.

Cheles, Luciano, 'The "Uomini Famosi" in the "Studiolo" of Urbino: an iconographic study', *Gazette des Beaux Arts*, vol. 102, 1983, pp. 1–7.

Chevalier, Raymond (ed.) *Présence de César. Hommage au doyen M. Rambaud*, Paris, 1985.

——— 'Le Voyage archéologique au XVIe siècle', *Voyager à la Renaissance*, ed. Céard and Margolin, op.cit., pp. 357–80.

Choay, Françoise, 'Serlio Redivivus', *Bibliothèque d'Humanisme et Renaissance*, vol. 57, no. 1, 1995, pp. 119–25.

Choné, Paulette, *Emblèmes et pensée symbolique en Lorraine (1525–1633)*, Paris, 1991.

Clédat, Louis, 'Le Musée de sculpture du cardinal du Bellay à Rome', *Courrier de l'Art*, vol. 3, 1883, pp. 99–100, 206–7.

Coffin, David R., 'Pirro Ligorio on the nobility of the arts', *Journal of the Warburg and Courtauld Institutes*, vol. 27, 1964, pp. 191–210.

——— *The Villa in the Life of Renaissance Rome*, Princeton, 1979.

——— *The Villa d'Este at Tivoli*, Princeton, 1990.

——— *Gardens and Gardening in Papal Rome*, Princeton, 1991.

Coleman, Dorothy, 'Allusiveness in the *Antiquitez de Rome*', *L'Esprit Créateur*, Fall 1979, pp. 3–11.

——— *The Chaste Muse: A Study of Joachim du Bellay's Poetry* (Medieval and Renaissance Authors, 3), Leiden, 1980.

Conley, Tom, 'A sucking of cities: Montaigne in Paris and Rome', *Montaigne Studies. An Interdisciplinary Forum*, vol. 9, 1997, pp. 167–86.

Connat, M. and Megret, J., 'Inventaire de la bibliothèque des Du Prat', *Bibliothèque d'Humanisme et Renaissance*, vol. 3, 1943, pp. 72–128.

Cooper, Richard, 'Rabelais and the *Topographia Antiquae Romae* of Marliani', *Etudes Rabelaisiennes*, vol. 14, 1977, pp. 71–87.

——— 'Poetry in ruins: the literary context of Du Bellay's cycles on Rome',

Renaissance Studies, vol. 3, no. 2, 1989, pp. 156–66.

——'Collectors of coins and numismatic scholarship in Early Renaissance France', *Medals and Coins*, ed. Crawford et al., op.cit., pp. 5–24.

——*Rabelais et l'Italie*, Geneva, 1991.

——'Gabriel Symeoni visionario', *Studi di Letteratura Francese*, XIX, Florence, 1992, pp. 279–97.

——*Litterae in tempore belli. Etudes sur les relations littéraires italo-françaises pendant les guerres d'Italie*, Geneva, 1997.

Coppens, C., 'Ein Bibliofiel van formaat: Nicolas-Claude Fabri de Peiresc (1580–1637)', *Ex Officina*, no. 2, Louvain, 1990, pp. 89–110.

Corbett, Margery and Lightbown, Ronald, *The Comely Frontispiece: the Emblematic Title Page in England, 1550–1660*, London, 1979.

Costa, Silvia Fabrizio and La Braxa, Frank, 'La Descente de Charles VIII vue par l'humaniste Filippo Beroaldo l'Ancien', *Actes . . . Sorbonne, 1990*, pp. 215–24.

Coste-Messelière, Marie Geneviève de la, 'Pour la République florentine et pour le roi de France: Giovanbattista della Palla, des "orti orecellari" aux cachots de Pise', *Il se rendait à Rome: études offertes à André Chastel*, Paris, 1987, pp. 195–208.

Cottrell, Robert D., *Brantôme. The Writer as Portraitist of his Age*, Geneva, 1970.

Courajod, Louis, *L'Imitation et la contrefaçon des objets d'art antiques au XVIe et au XVIIe siècles*, Paris, 1887.

Cowling, David, *Building the Text. Architecture as Metaphor in Late Medieval and Early Modern France*, Oxford, 1998.

Cox-Rearick, Janet, *Dynasty and Destiny in Medici Art*, Princeton, 1984.

——*The Collection of Francis I: Royal Treasures*, New York, 1996.

Crawford, M.H., Ligota, C.R. and Trapp, J.B. (eds) *Medals and Coins from Budé to Mommsen*, London, 1990.

Crépin-Leblond, Thierry, *Livre d'heures royaux*, Paris, 1993.

Cummings, Anthony M., *The Politicized Muse. Music for Medici Festivals*, Princeton, 1992.

Dacos, Nicole, 'L'Anonyme A. de Berlin: Hermanus Posthumus', *Antiken Studium und antiken Zeichnungen in der Renaissance*, ed. H. Wrede and R. Harprash, Mainz, 1989, pp. 61–80.

Deguy, Michel, *Tombeau de Du Bellay*, Paris, 1973.

Delepierre, Octave, *Centoniana ou Encyclopédie du Centon*, The Philobiblon Society, vol. x, 1966–7.

Delmarcel, Guy, 'Présence de César dans la tapisserie des Pays-Bas méridionaux', *Présence de César*, ed. Chevalier, op.cit., pp. 257–61.

Delumeau, Jean, *Rome au XVIe siècle*, Paris, 1975.

De Nolhac, Pierre, *La Bibliothèque de Fulvio Orsini*, Paris, 1887.

——*Erasme en Italie*, Paris, 1898.

——*Ronsard et l'humanisme*, Paris, 1966.

Desan, Philippe, 'La Logique de la différence dans les traités d'histoire', *Logique et littérature à la Renaissance*, ed. Marie-Luce Demonet-Launay and André Tournon, Paris, 1994, pp. 101–10.

Descimon, R., 'Les Ducs de Nevers au temps de Blaise de Vigenère, ou la puissance de faire des hommes puissants', *Blaise de Vigenère, poète et mythographe au temps de Henri III*, Paris, 1994, Cahiers V.L. Saulnier, no. 11, pp. 13–37.

Desgraves, Louis, *Elie Vinet, humaniste de Bordeaux (1509–1587)*, Geneva, 1977.

Deutsch, Monroe E., *The Apparatus of Caesar's Triumphs*, n.p., n.d.

Deville, J.A., *Compices de Gaillon*, Paris, 1850.

Dickinson, Gladys, *Du Bellay in Rome*, Leiden, 1960.

Di Marco, Simona, *Viaggi in Europa, secoli XVI–XIX: catalogo del fondo 'fiammetta Olschki'*, Florence, 1990.

Dinsmoor, William Bell, 'Sebastiano Serlio's literary remains', *Art Bulletin*, vol. 24, 1942, pp. 55–154.

Doiron, Normand, *L'Art de voyager. Le déplacement à l'époque classique*, Paris, 1995.

Dorangeon, Simone, 'Les Complaints de Spenser et l'héritage de Du Bellay', *Oeuvres critiques*, vol. 1, no. 20, *Du Bellay devant la critique de 1550 à nos jours*, Tübingen, 1995, pp. 175–82.

[Du Bellay], *Du Bellay devant la critique de 1550 à nos jours. Oeuvres critiques*, vol, I, no. 20, Tübingen, 1995.

Dubois, Claude-Gilbert, 'César et Ramus', *Présence de César*, ed. Chevalier, pp. 109–18.

Dudley, D.R., *Urbs Roma. A Source Book of Classical Texts on the City and its Monuments*, Aberdeen, 1967.

Dunn, E.C., 'Lipsius and the art of letter writing', *Studies in the Renaissance*, vol. 3, 1956, pp. 145–56.

Duyer, Eugene, 'André Thevet and Fulvius Orsino: the beginnings of the modern tradition of classical portrait iconography in France', *Art Bulletin*, vol. 75, 1993, pp. 467–80.

Edwards, Catherine, *Writing Rome: Textual Approaches to the City*, Cambridge, 1996.

Egger, Hermann, *Die Römische Verduten*, 2 vols, Vienna and Leipzig, 1911.

Ehrmann, Jean, *Antoine Caron. Peintre des fêtes et des massacres*, Paris, 1986.

Elam, Caroline, 'Art in the service of liberty. Battista della Palla, art agent for François Ier', *I Tatti Studies. Essays in the Renaissance*, vol. 5, 1993, pp. 33–109.

Elsenbichler, Konrad and Iannucci, Amilcare, A. (eds), *Petrarch's Triumphs. Allegory and Spectacle*, Ottawa, 1990.

Elsner, J., *Art and the Roman Viewer*, Cambridge, 1995.

Elsner, J. and Cardinal, R. (eds) *The Cultures of Collecting*, London, 1994.

Erlande-Brandenburg, Alain (ed.) *Le Château d'Ecouen*, Editions de la Réunion des musées nationaux, 1987.

Essling, Prince d' and Müntz, E., *Pétrarque: ses études d'art, son influence sur les artistes, ses portraits et ceux de Laure, les illustrations et ses écrits*, Paris, 1902.

Fagiolo dell Arco, Maurizio (ed.) *The Vatican and its Treasures*, London, 1983.

Farrary, Jean-Louis, *Onofrio Panvinio et les antiquités romaines*, Ecole française de Rome, 1996

Favier, S., 'Les Collections de marbres antiques sous François Ier', *Revue du Louvre et des musées de France*, vol. 24, 1974, pp. 153–6.

Ferguson, Margaret W., 'The Exile's Defence', *Publications of the Modern Language Association*, vol. 93, 1978, pp. 275–89.

——'The afflatus of Ruin: meditations of Rome by Du Bellay, Spenser, and Stevens', *Roman Images*, ed. Annabel Patterson, Baltimore, 1984, pp. 23–50.

ffolliot, Sheila, 'Catherine de'Medici as Artemisia: figuring the powerful widow', *Rewriting the Renaissance*, ed. M. Ferguson, R. Quilligan & N. Vickers, Chicago, 1985, pp. 227–41, 370–6.

——'Biography from below: Nicolas Hoüel's *Histoire d'Arthemise*', *Proceedings of the Annual Meeting of the Western Society for French History*, vol. 13, 1986, pp. 90–8.

Fletcher, Jennifer, 'Marcantonio Michiel: his friends and collection', *Burlington Magazine*, vol. 123, 1981, pp. 453–67.

Fontaine, Marie-Madeleine, 'Les Antiquitez chez les dames des Roches', *Du Bellay. Oeuvres et critiques*, vol. I, no. 20, op.cit., pp. 197–208.

Ford, Philip, 'Du Bellay et le sonnet satirique', *Le Sonnet à la Renaissance*, ed. Bellenger, op.cit., pp. 205–14.

Fowler, Alasdair, *Triumphal Forms*, Cambridge, 1970.

Freedberg, David, *The Power of Images*, Chicago, 1989.

Freeman, E., Mason, H., O'Regan M. and Taylor S.W. (eds), *Myth and its Making in the French Theatre. Studies Presented to W.D. Howarth*, Cambridge, 1988.

Freud, Sigmund, *Civilization and its Discontents*, ed. James Strachey, London, 1982.

Frutaz, Amato Pietro, *Le piante di Roma*, 3 vols, Rome, 1962.

Fumaroli, Marc, *L'âge de l'éloquence*, Geneva, 1980.

——*Nicolas-Claude Fabri de Peiresc, prince de la République des Lettres*, Brussels, 1993.

——(ed.) *Le Loisir lettré*, Paris, 1996.

Gabbo, Emilio, 'The historians and Augustus', *Caesar Augustus*, ed. Fergus Millar and Erich Segal, Oxford, 1984, pp. 61–88.

Gabol, Jean, *Leon Battista Alberti. Universal Man in the Early Renaissance*, Chicago, 1969.

Gadoffre, Gilbert, *Du Bellay et le sacre*, Paris, 1978.

Gaisser, Julia Haig, *Catullus and his Renaissance Readers*, Oxford, 1993.

Gaston, Robert W. (ed.) *Pirro Ligorio, Artist and Antiquary*, Silvana, 1988.

Geffroy, A., *L'Album de Pierre Jacques de Reims*, Rome, 1890.

Geymüller, Heinrich Adolf, *Les Du Cerceau: leur vie et leur oeuvre*, Paris, 1887.

Gloton, J.J., 'Transformation et réemploi des monuments du passé dans la Rome du XVIe siècle', *Mélanges d'archéologie et d'histoire*, vol. 74, 1962, pp. 705–58.

——'L'Influence de Serlio en France', *Traités d'architecture*, ed. J. Guillaume, Paris, 1985, pp. 407–23.

Golenistcheff-Koutouzoff, E., 'La Première tradition des *Triomphes* de Pétrarque en France', *Mélanges offerts à Henri Hauvette*, Paris, 1934.

Golson, L., 'Serlio, Primaticcio and the architectural grotto', *Gazette des Beaux Arts*, vol. 77, 1974, pp. 95–108.

Goodman, Nelson, *Languages of Art: an Approach to a Theory of Symbols*, Indianapolis, 1968.

Gordon, Alex. L., 'Styles of absence and presence: *Les Antiquitez* and *Regrets*', *Crossroads and Perspectives: French Literature of the Renaissance*, ed. Catherine M. Grisé and C.D.E. Tolton, Geneva, 1986, pp. 21–30.

Gould, Cecil, 'Sebastiano Serlio and Venetian painting', *Journal of the Warburg and Courtauld Institutes*, vol. 25, 1962, pp. 56–64.

Gouwens, Kenneth, *Remembering the Renaissance. Humanist Narratives of the Sack of Rome*, Leiden, 1998.

Grafton, Anthony, *Joseph Scaliger, Volume I: Textual Criticism and Exegesis*, Oxford, 1983.

——*Renaissance Readers and Ancient Texts*, Cambridge, Mass., 1991.

——*Joseph Scaliger, Volume II: Historical Chronology*, Oxford, 1993.

——*The Vatican Library and Renaissance Culture*, New Haven, 1993.

Gragg, Florence A. (ed.) *Latin Writings of the Italian Humanists*, New York, 1927.

——*Memoirs of a Renaissance Pope*, London, 1960.

Graham, Victor E., 'Gabriel Symeoni et le rêve impérial des rois de France', *Culture et pouvoir au temps de l'humanisme et de la Renaissance*, Chambéry, 1978, pp. 299–309.

——'The entry of Henri II into Rouen in 1550', *Petrarch's Triumphs*, ed. Iannucci and Eisenbickler, op.cit., pp. 403–13.

Grandmaison, Charles de, 'Bustes antiques envoyées de Rome au connétable de Montmorency, 1554–1556', *Archives de l'art Français*, Documents, IV, Paris, 1855–56, pp. 69–71.

Gras, Maurice, *Robert Garnier, son art et sa méthode*, Geneva, 1965.

Gray, Floyd, *Montaigne bilingue*, Paris, 1991.

Greene, Thomas L., *The Light in Troy*, New Haven, 1982.

Griffin, Robert, *The Coronation of the Poet. Joachim du Bellay's Debt to the Trivium*, Berkeley, 1969.

Grodecki, C., *Archives nationales. Documents du minutier central des notaires de Paris. Histoire de l'art au XVIe siècle*, 2 vols, Paris, 1986.

Gruen, Erich S., *The Image of Rome*, Englewood Cliffs, NJ, 1969.

Grunner von Hoerschnelmann, Suzanne, 'Basilius Amerbach and his coin collection', *Medals and Coins*, ed. Crawford et al., op.cit., pp. 25–52.

Guenée, Bernard and Lehoux, Françoise, *Les Entrées royales françaises de 1328 à 1515*, Paris, 1968.

Guillaume, Jean (ed.) *Traités d'architecture*, Paris, 1985.

—— *La Galerie du grand écuyer*, Paris, 1996.

Gwynne, Paul, '"In alter Caesaris": Maximilian I, Vladislav II, Johannes Michael Nagonius and the *renovatio Imperii*', *Renaissance Studies*, vol. 10, no. 1, 1996, pp. 56–71.

Hale, J.R., 'Andrea Palladio, Polybius and Julius Caesar', *Journal of the Warburg and Courtauld Institutes*, vol. 40, 1977, pp. 240–55; reprinted in *Renaissance War Studies*, London, 1983, pp. 471–86.

Hano, Michel, 'L'Image de César dans les peintures du XVe au XIXe siècles', *Présence de César*, ed. Chevalier, op.cit., pp. 305–28.

Hawthorne, Nathaniel, *The Marble Faun* [first published, 1860], London, 1906.

Henza, Ph., 'Comment peindre le passage du Rubicon', *Présence de César*, ed. Chevalier, op.cit., pp. 56–65.

Heulhard, A., *Rabelais, ses voyages en Italie, son exil à Metz*, Paris, 1891.

Hirstein, James S., 'La Rome de Virgile et celle du 16e siècle dans *Ad Janum Avansonium apud summum pont. oratorem regium, Tyberis* de Joachim du Bellay', *Acta Conventus Neo-Latini Sanctandreani*, Proceedings of the 5th International Congress of Neo-Latin Studies, St Andrews, 1982, Binghamton, New York, 1986, pp. 351–8.

Hobson, A., *Humanists and Bookbinders*, Cambridge, 1989.

Holliday, Peter J., 'Roman triumphal painting: its function, development and reception', *Art Bulletin*, vol. 79, 1997, pp. 130–47.

Hood, Gervase, 'James I's entry into London (1604)', *Across the Narrow Seas. Studies in the History and Bibliography of Britain and the Low Countries*, ed. Susan Roach, London, 1991, pp. 67–81.

Howard, Deborah, *Jacopo Sansovino. Architecture and Patronage in Renaissance Venice*, New Haven, 1975.

Hubaux, J., *Les Grands Mythes de Rome*, Paris, 1945.

Hülsen, Christian, 'Le illustrazioni della *Hypnerotomachia Poliphili* e le antichità', *Bibliofilia*, vol. 12, 1910–11, pp. 161–76.

Hülsen, Christian and Egger, Hermann, *Die Römischen Skizzenbücher von Marten van Heemskerck*, 2 vols, Berlin, 1916.

Impey, O. and McGregor, A. (eds) *The Origins of Museums. The Cabinet of Curiosities in the Sixteenth and Seventeenth Centuries*, Oxford, 1985.

Ingman, Heather, 'Du Bellay and the language of alchemy in the *Songe*', *Modern Language Review*, vol. 82, part 4, October 1987, pp. 844–53.

Jacks, Philip, 'The simulacrum of Fabio Calvo: a view of Roman architecture *all'antica* in 1527', *Art Bulletin*, vol. 72, September 1990, pp. 453–81.

—— *The Antiquarian and the Myth of Antiquity: the Origins of Rome in Renaissance Thought*, Cambridge, 1993.

Jacquiot, J., 'Des Médaillons italiens, diplomates et voyageurs', Céard and Margolin, *Voyager*, op.cit., pp. 115–22.

Jacquot, Jean, *Les Fêtes de la Renaissance*, 3 vols, Paris, 1956, 1960, 1975.

Jardine, Lisa and Grafton, Anthony, 'How Gabriel Harvey read his Livy', *Past and Present*, vol. 129, 1990, pp. 30–78.

Jeanneret, Michel, 'Myths of antiquity', *Modern Language Notes*, vol. 110, no. 5, December 1995, pp. 1043–53.

—— *Perpetuum mobile. Métamorphoses des corps et des oeuvres de Vinci à Montaigne*, Paris, 1998.

Jehasse, Jean, *La Renaissance de la critique: l'essor de l'humaniste érudit de 1560 à 1614*, Saint-Etienne, 1976.

—— *Guez de Balzac et le génie romain*, Saint-Etienne, n.d.

Jenkins, Richard (ed.) *The Legacy of Rome*, New York, 1992.

Jestaz, Bertrand, 'L'Exportation des marbres de Rome, 1535–1571', *Mélanges* d'archéologie et d'histoire, vol. 75, Paris, 1963, pp. 415–66.

Jondorf, Gillian, Robert Garnier and the Themes of Political Tragedy, Cambridge, 1969.

Joukovsky, Françoise, La Gloire à la Renaissance, Geneva, 1969.

——'Qui parle dans le livre III des Essais?', Revue d'Histoire Littéraire de la France, 1988, pp. 813–27.

——'"Bellai sumos inter celebrande poetas", Les Elegies et les Sonnets de Nicolas Ellain', Du Bellay. Oeuvres critiques, vol. 1, no. 20, op.cit., pp. 165–73.

Jullien de la Boullaye, E., Etude sur la vie et les oeuvres de Jean Duvet [1485–c. 1555], Paris, 1976.

Katz, Richard A., 'The collapse of the city: the Vision of the Antiquitez de Rome', L'Esprit Créateur, Fall 1979, pp. 12–20.

Knecht, Robert J., Francis I, Cambridge, 1982.

Krea, T. (ed.) Renaissance Painting in Manuscripts. Treasures from the British Library, New York, 1983.

Kritzman, Lawrence D. (ed.) Fragments: Incompletion and Discontinuity, New York, 1981.

Labrot, Gérard, L'Image de Rome: une arme pour la contre réforme, 1534–1677, Champvallon, 1987.

La Ferrière, comte de, Le XVIe siècle et les Valois: les documents inédits du British Museum et du Record Office, Paris, 1879.

La Fontaine Verwey, H. de, 'Pieter Coecke van Aelst and the publication of Serlio's book on architecture', Quaerendo, vol. 6, 1976, pp. 166–94.

Landau, David and Parshall, Peter, The Renaissance Print, New Haven, 1994.

Laurens, Pierre, 'Le Dialogue des orateurs de Juste Lipse', Juste Lipse, ed. Mouchel, op.cit., pp. 103–15.

Lebel, G., 'Nouvelles précisions sur Antoine Caron', L'Amour de l'Art, vol. 19, 1938, pp. 172–80.

Lecoq, Anne Marie, François Ier imaginaire, Paris, 1987.

——'"Queti et Musis Henrici II. Gall. R." Sur la Grotte de Meudon', Le Loisir lettré, ed. Fumaroli, op.cit., pp. 93–115.

Leigh, Matthew, Lucan. Spectacle and Engagement, Oxford, 1997.

Lestocquoy, J. (ed.) Correspondance des nonces en France, Lenzi et Gualtiero, légation du cardinal Trivultio, Rome, 1977.

Lesure, F., 'Blaise de Vigenère et Jean Cousin (1550)', Bibliothèque d'Humanisme et Renaissance, vol. 9, 1947, pp. 109–13.

Lettéron, Isabelle and Gillot, Delphine, Rouen: l'hôtel de Bourgthéroulde: demeure des Le Roux, Rouen, 1996.

Lightbown, Ronald W., 'Nicolas Audebert and the Villa d'Este', Journal of the Warburg and Courtauld Institutes, vol. 27, 1964, pp. 164–90.

——Mantegna, London, 1986.

Lloyd Jones, K., 'Du Bellay's journey from Roma Vetus to La Rome Neufve', Rome in the Renaissance, ed. Ramsey, op.cit., pp. 301–19.

Lowry, D., 'Notes on the Speculum Romanae Magnificentiae and related publications', Art Bulletin, vol. 34, 1952, pp. 46–50.

Lyons, John D., Exemplum. The Rhetoric of Example in Early Modern France and Italy, Princeton, 1989.

McAllister Johnson, William, 'On some neglected images of the Renaissance diplomatic correspondence', Gazette des Beaux Arts, vol. 79, 1972, pp. 51–4.

——'Manuscrits, maquettes et albums inédits: Antoine Caron et la suite d'Arthemise', Cahiers V. L. Saulnier, no. 6, 1989, pp. 121–9.

McClelland, John, 'Les Antiquitez de Rome: discours rhétorique, discours historique, discours personnel', Du Bellay, ed. Cesdron, op. cit., I, pp. 191–200.

McClung, William A., The Architecture of Paradise: Survivals of Eden and Jerusalem, Berkeley and Los Angeles, 1983.

McCormick, Michael, Eternal Victory. Triumphal Rulership in Late Antiquity, Byzantium and the Early Medieval West, Baltimore, 1990.

MacCormick, Sabine G., *Art and Ceremony in Late Antiquity*, Berkeley, 1981.

McCuaig, William, *Carlo Sigonio. The Changing World of the Late Renaissance*, Princeton, 1989.

Macdonald, William L. and Pinto, John A., *Hadrian's Villa and its Legacy*, New Haven, 1995.

McFarlane, I. and Maclean, I. (eds) *Montaigne. Essays in Memory of Richard Sayce*, Oxford, 1982.

McGowan, Margaret M., *Montaigne's Deceits*, London, 1974.

——'Le Phénomène de la galerie des portraits des illustres', *L'âge d'or du Mécénat (1598–1661)*, Colloque international CNRS (mars 1983), Paris, 1985, pp. 411–22.

——*Ideal Forms in the Age of Ronsard*, Berkeley, 1985.

——'Rome in some plays of Robert Garnier', *Myth and its Making*, ed. E. Freeman et al., op.cit., pp. 12–29.

——'Contradictory impulses in Montaigne's vision of Rome', *Renaissance Studies*, vol. 4, no. 4, 1990, pp. 392–409.

——'Pierre de L'Estoile: amateur collector of medals and coins', *Seventeenth Century French Studies*, 1993, pp. 115–27.

——'Impaired vision: the experience of Rome in Renaissance France', *Renaissance Studies*, vol. 8, no. 3, 1994, pp. 244–55.

——'Conjecture, reshaping, and the creative process', *(Ré)interprétations: études sur le seizième siècle*, Michigan Romance Studies, XV, Ann Arbor, 1995, ed. John O'Brien, pp. 213–40.

——'Guez de Balzac: the enduring influence of Rome', *Ethics and Politics in Seventeenth-Century France*, ed. Keith Cameron and Elizabeth Woodrough, Exeter, 1996, pp. 41–55.

McGuiness, Frederick J., 'The rhetoric of praise and the new Rome of the Counter Reformation', *Rome in the Renaissance*, ed. Ramsey, op.cit., pp. 355–70.

McGuiness, Lawrence R., *Catalogue of the Earl of Crawford's 'Speculum' Now in the Avery Architectural Library*, New York, 1976.

McKinley, Mary, 'Text and context in Montaigne's *Essais*: the example of Ovid's *Metamorphoses*', *L'Esprit Créateur*, vol. 20, no. 1, Spring 1980, pp. 46–65.

——*Words in a Corner*, French Forum, Lexington, 1981.

——*Les Terrains vagues des 'Essais': itinéraires et intertextes*, Paris, 1996.

MacPhail, Eric, 'The Roman tomb or the image of the tomb in Du Bellay's *Antiquitez*', *Bibliothèque d'Humanisme et Renaissance*, vol. 48, no. 2, 1986, pp. 359–72.

——*The Voyage to Rome in French Renaissance Literature*, Stanford, 1990.

Magnien, M., 'Montaigne et Juste Lipse', *Juste Lipse*, ed. Mouchel, op.cit., pp. 423–52.

Maillard, Jean François, 'De la Maquette autographe à l'imprimé. La somptueuse et magnifique entrée du roi Henri III à Mantoue par Blaise de Vigenère', *Le Livre dans l'Europe de la Renaissance*, [Colloque de Tours, no. 28], Paris, 1988, pp. 71–90.

Mandowsky, E. and Mitchell, C., *Pirro Ligorio's Roman Antiquities. The Drawings in Ms. XIII B 7 in the National Library in Naples,* Studies of the Warburg Institute, London, 1963.

Mansfield, Bruce, *Phoenix of his Age: Interpretations of Erasmus, c. 1550–1750*, Toronto, 1979.

Margolin, Jean-Claude, 'Glareau, commentateur du *De Bello Gallico*', *Présence de César*, ed. Chevalier, op.cit., pp. 183–212.

Marillier, H.C., *The Tapestries at Hampton Court Palace*, London, 1931.

Martin, Daniel, *L'Architecture des Essais de Montaigne. Mémoire artificielle et mythologique*, Paris, 1992.

Martindale, Andrew, *The Triumphs of Caesar*, London, 1979.

Martineau, Jane (ed.) *Andrea Mantegna*, London and New York, 1992.

Martyn, John R.C., 'André de Resende, original author of *Roma prisca*', *Bibliothèque d'Humanisme et Renaissance*, vol. 51, no. 2, 1989, pp. 407–11.

Massing, Jean Michel, 'Arnould Poissonier of Tournai and his "huit pièces du triumphe de César" for Margaret of Austria', *Artes Textiles*, vol. 11, 1986, pp. 69–74.

——'The *Triumph of Caesar* by Benedetto Bardone and Jacobus Argentoratensis: the iconography and influence', *Print Quarterly*, vol. 7, 1990, pp. 2–21.

Masters, Jamie, *Poetry and Civil War in Lucan's 'Bellum Civile'*, Cambridge, 1992.

Mathieu-Castellani, Gisèle, 'Intertextualité et allusion: le régime allusif chez Ronsard', *Littérature*, vol. 55, 1984.

——*Montaigne, l'écriture de l'essai*, Paris, 1988.

——'L'Intertexte rhétorique: Tacite, Quintilien et la poétique des *Essais*', *Montaigne et la Rhétorique*, ed. Supple, op.cit., pp. 17–27.

Mayer, C.A. and Bentley Cranch, D., 'François Robertet: French sixteenth-century civil servant, poet and artist', *Renaissance Studies*, vol. 2, no. 3, 1997, pp. 208–22.

Mayer, Irène S., 'Montaigne's cure: stones and Roman ruins', *Modern Language Notes*, vol. 97, no. 4, May 1982, pp. 958–74.

Mayer, P., 'Les Premières Compilations françaises d'histoire ancienne', *Romania*, vol. 14, 1885, pp. 3–81.

Mazzocco, A., 'Petrarch, Poggio and Biondo: humanism's foremost interpreters of Roman ruins', *Francis Petrarch, Six Centuries Later: A Symposium*, ed. A. Scaglione, Chicago, 1975, pp. 354–63.

——'The antiquarianism of F. Petrarca', *Journal of Medieval and Renaissance Studies*, vol. 7, 1977, pp. 203–24.

——'Some philological aspects of Biondo Flavio's *Roma Triumphans*', *Humanistica Lovaiensis*, vol. 28, 1979, pp. 1–26.

Mazzolani, Lidia, *The Idea of the City in Roman Thought*, London, 1970.

Melion, Walter S., 'Memorabilia aliquot Romanae stremutatis exempla: the thematics of artisanal virtue in Hendrick Goltzius's *Roman Heroes*', *Modern Language Notes [Myths of Antiquity]*, vol. 110, no. 5, 1995, pp. 1090–134.

Métral, Denise, *Blaise de Vigenère, archéologue et critique d'art*, Paris, 1939.

Millar, Fergus and Segal, Erich (eds) *Caesar Augustus*, Oxford, 1984.

Millet, Olivier, 'En la Façon que m'a décrit Masures, l'oeuvre de Louis des Masures, un point de vue latéral sur celle de Joachim du Bellay', *Du Bellay. Oeuvres critiques*, no. 20, vol. 1, op.cit., pp. 149–63.

Mirot, L., 'L'Hôtel et les collections du connétable de Montmorency', *Bibliothèque de l'Ecole des Chartes*, vol. 79, 1918, pp. 347–69.

Mitchell, Bonner, 'The SPQR in two Roman festivals of early and mid-quattrocentro', *The Sixteenth Century Journal*, vol. 9, no. 4, 1978, pp. 95–9.

——*The Majesty of State*, Florence, 1986.

Mitchell, Charles, 'Archaeology and romance in Renaissance Italy', *Italian Renaissance Studies*, ed. E.F. Jacob, London, 1960, pp. 455–83.

Momigliano, Arnaldo, *Essays in Ancient and Modern Historiography*, Oxford, 1977.

Mommsen, Theodor E., 'Petrarch and the decoration of the Sala Virorum Illustrium in Padua', *Art Bulletin*, vol. 34, no. 2, 1952, pp. 95–116.

Monnier, Geneviève and McAllister Johnson, William, 'Caron *Antiquaire*. A propos de quelques dessins du Louvre', *Revue de l'Art*, no. 14, 1971, pp. 22–30.

Montaiglon, A. (ed.) Bibliothèque Nationale, Ms fr. 11350, 'Estant des gaiges', *Archives de l'art français*, vol. I, 1851–52, pp. 100–25.

Montembault, Marie and Schloder, John, *L'Album Canini du Louvre et la collection d'antiques de Richelieu*, Paris, 1988.

Morford, Mark, *Stoics and Neo-Stoics*, Princeton, 1991.

Mortier, Roland, *La Poétique des ruines en France*, Geneva, 1974.

Moss, Ann, 'Du lieu commun à la Maxime: de la Renaissance au monde classique', *Romanica Wratislaviensia*, vol. 36, Wroclaw, 1991, pp. 43–52.

——*Printed Commonplace-Books and the structuring of Renaissance Thought*, Oxford, 1996.

——'Vision fragmentée et unitaire: les *Politiques* et les recueils de lieux communs', *Juste Lipse*, ed. Mouchel, op.cit., pp. 375 ff.

Mouchel, C. (ed.) *Juste Lipse (1547–1606) en son temps. Actes du colloque de Strasbourg, 1994*, Paris, 1996.

Mouflard, Marie-Madeleine, *Robert Garnier*, 2 vols, Paris, 1961.

Müntz, E., *Les Antiquités de la ville de Rome aux XIV, XV et XVIe siècles*, Paris, 1886.

Nash, Jerry C., 'Cette *Beauté non pareille*: Du Bellay et d'écriture de l'impossible', *Du Bellay*, ed. Cesdron, op.cit., I, pp. 15–28.

Navitel, C., 'Juste Lipse, antiquaire', *Juste Lipse*, ed. Mouchel, op.cit., pp. 275–93.

Norton, Glyn, *The Ideology and Language of Translation in Renaissance France and their Humanist Antecedents*, Geneva, 1984.

O'Brien, John, *Anacreon Redivivus: a Study of Anacreonic Translation in Mid-Sixteenth-Century France*, Ann Arbor, 1995.

Oestreich, Gerhard, *Neostoicism and the Early Modern State*, Cambridge, 1982.

Oliver, J.H., 'On the Roman Oration of Aelius Aristides', *Transactions of the American Philosophical Society*, vol. 43, part 4, 1953, pp. 871–1003.

Orth, Myra D., 'The *Triumphs* of Petrarch illuminated by Godefroy le Batave', *Gazette des Beaux Arts*, vol. 104, 1984, pp. 197–206.

Paquier, J., *Jerome Aléandre: lettres familières*, Paris, 1909.

Partridge, Loren and Starn, Randolph, 'Triumphalism and the Sala Regia in the Vatican', *'All the World's a Stage'. Art and Pageantry in the Renaissance and Baroque*, ed. Barbara Wisch and Susan Scott-Munshower, University Park, Pennsylvannia, 1990, pp. 23–81.

Patterson, Annabel, *Roman Images*, Baltimore, 1984.

Pauwels, Yves, 'Les Antiques romains dans les traités de Philibert de L'Orme et Jean Bullant', *Mélanges de l'Ecole Française de Rome*, vol. 116, no. 2, 1994, pp. 531–47.

——'Jean Bullant et le langage des ordres: les audaces d'un timide', *Gazette des Beaux Arts*, vol. 129, 1997, pp. 85–100.

Pavoni, Rosanna, 'Paolo Giovio et son Musée de Portraits à propos d'une exposition', *Gazette des Beaux Arts*, vol. 105, 1985, pp. 109–16.

Payne, Robert, *The Roman Triumph*, London, 1962.

Pertile, Lino, 'Montaigne, Gregory Martin and Rome', *Bibliothèque d'Humanisme et Renaissance*, vol. 50, no. 3, 1988, pp. 637–59.

Piaggi, G. de, 'Les Voyages de Brantôme en Italie', *Annales de la Faculté des Lettres et Sciences Humaines d'Aix*, vol. 40, 1966, pp. 79–116.

Picard, G.C., *Les Trophées romaines. Contribution à l'histoire de la religion et de l'art triomphal de Rome*, Paris, 1957.

Picot, Emile, *Les Italiens en France au XVIe siècle*, Bordeaux, 1918.

Pierce, P., 'The arch of Constantine', *Art History*, vol. 12, 1989, pp. 387–418.

Pineaux, Jacques, 'Un Continuateur des *Vies parallèles*: Simon Goulart de Senlis (S.G.S)', *Fortunes de Jacques Amyot. Actes du colloque international*, Melun, avril 1985, ed. J.M.A. Beer and D. Lloyd-Jones, Paris, 1986, pp. 331–42.

Planet, F., 'Jacob Spon et la science des médailles', *Jacob Spon. Un humaniste lyonnais du XVIIe siècle*, ed. R. Etienne and J.C. Mossière, Paris, 1993, pp. 129–36.

Poliner, S.M., 'Du Bellay's *Songe*. Strategies of deceit, poetics of vision', *Bibliothèque d'Humanisme et Renaissance*, vol. 43, 1981, pp. 509–25.

Pomian, K., *Collectors and Curiosities: Paris and Venice, 1500–1800*, Venice, 1990.

Potié, Philippe, *Philibert de L'Orme: figures de la pensée constructive*, Marseille, 1996.

Pouilloux, Jean-Yves, *Montaigne et l'éveil de la pensée*, Paris, 1995.

Pratt, K.J., 'Rome as eternal', *Journal of the History of Ideas*, vol. 25, 1965, pp. 25–36.

Pressouyre, Sylvie, 'Les Fontes de Primatice à Fontainebleau', *Bulletin Monumental*, vol. 127, 1969, pp. 223–39.

Quainton, Malcolm, 'Morte peinture and vivante peinture in *Les Antiquitez de Rome* and *Les Regrets*', *Renaissance Studies*, vol. 3, no. 2, 1989, pp. 167–77.

——'*Les Regrets*: une poétique de Parade', *Du Bellay*, ed. Cesdron, op.cit., I, pp. 249–59.

——'Du Bellay and Janus Vitalis', *French Studies Bulletin*, no. 38, Spring 1991, pp. 12–15.

Ramsey, P.A. (ed.) *Rome in the Renaissance*, Binghamton, 1982.

Rand, Edward K., *The Building of Eternal Rome*, New York, 1972.

Reinach, Salomon, *L'Album de Pierre Jacques, sculpteur de Reims, dessins à Rome, 1572 à 1577*, Paris, 1902.

Rendall, Stephen, 'In disjointed parts/par articles décousus', *Fragments*, ed. Kritzman, op.cit., pp. 72–82.

Renucci, T., *Un Aventurier des lettres au XVIe siècle. Gabriel Symeoni*, Paris, 1943.

Répaci-Courtois, G., 'Vasari, source de Blaise de Vigenère', *Revue de l'Art*, vol. 80, 1988, pp. 48–51.

——'Blaise de Vigenère et l'expérience des arts visuels', *Blaise de Vigenère, poète et mythologue au temps de Henri III*, Paris, 1994, Cahiers V.L. Saulnier, no. 11, pp. 101–10.

Richardson, Margaret and Stevens, Mary Anne (eds) *Sir John Soane. Master of Space and Light*, London, 1999.

Rigolot, François, 'Du Bellay et la poésie du refus', *Bibliothèque d'Humanisme et Renaissance*, vol. 36, no. 3, 1974, pp. 489–502.

——'Montaigne's maxims: from the discourse of the other to the expression of self', *L'Esprit Créateur*, vol. 22, no. 3, Fall 1982, pp. 8–18.

——(ed.) *Montaigne Studies. An Interdisciplinary Forum*, vol. V, nos 1–2, Chicago, 1993.

Ritchie, Andrew Carnduff, 'Léonard Limosin's *Triumph of the Faith*, with portraits of the House of Guise', *Art Bulletin*, vol. 21, no. 3, 1939, pp. 238–50.

Rizza, Cecilia, *Peiresc in Italia*, Turin, 1965.

Robatham, Dorothy M., 'Flavio Biondo's *Roma instaurata*', *Medievalia et Humanistica*, vol. 1, 1970, pp. 203–16.

Robertson, Clare, '*Il gran Cardinale*': *Alessandro Farnese, Patron of the Arts*, New Haven, 1992.

Roland, François, 'Antoine La Fréry, 1512–1577', *Mémoires de la Société d'Emulation du Doubs*, 1910, pp. 320–78.

Romier, Lucien, *Les Origines politiques des guerres de religion*, 2 vols, Paris, 1913–14.

Rosenfeld, Myra Nan, *Sebastiano Serlio. On Domestic Architecture*, New York and Cambridge, Mass., 1978.

Ross Jr, David O., *Backgrounds to Augustan Poetry: Gallus Elegy and Rome*, Cambridge, 1975.

Roussel, Pierre Desiré, *Description du château d'Anet*, Paris, 1875.

Rowland, Ingrid D., *The Culture of the High Renaissance: Ancients and Moderns in Sixteenth-Century Rome*, Cambridge, 1998.

Roy, Maurice, *Artistes et monuments de la Renaissance en France*, 2 vols, Paris, 1929.

Rubin, Patricia Lee, *Giorgio Vasari. Art and History*, London and New Haven, 1995.

Russell, Daniel, 'Du Bellay's emblematic vision of Rome', *Yale French Studies*, vol. 47, 1972, pp. 98–109.

——'Conception of self, conception of space and generic convention: an example from the *Heptameron*', *Sociocriticism*, nos 4–5, 1986–87, pp. 159–83.

Ruysschaert, J., 'Le Séjour de Juste Lipse à Rome (1568–1570) d'après ses *Antiquae lectiones* et sa correspondance', *Bulletin de l'Institut Historique Belge de Rome*, vol. 24, 1947–48, pp. 139–92.

——*Juste Lipse et les Annales de Tacite*, Turnhout, 1949.

Saulnier, V.L., 'Commentaires sur les *Antiquitez de Rome* of Joachim du Bellay', *Bibliothèque d'Humanisme et Renaissance*, vol. 12, 1950, pp. 114–43.

Scaillerez, C., *François Ier et ses artistes*, Paris, 1992.

Scheller, Robert W., 'Imperial themes in art and literature of the early French Renaissance: the period of Charles VIII', *Simiolus: Netherlands Quarterly for the History of Art*, vol. 12, 1981–82, pp. 5–69.

Scher, S.K., *The Currency of Fame*, New York, 1994.

Schiffman, Zachary S., 'Montaigne's perception of ancient Rome: biography as a form of history', *Rome in the Renaissance*, ed. Ramsey, op.cit., pp. 333–44.

Schnapp, Alain, *La Conquête du passé. Aux origines de l'archéologie*, Paris, 1993.

Schnapper, Antoine, *Curieux du grand siècle*, 2 vols, Paris, 1994.

Schneelbalg-Perelman, Sophie, 'Richesse du garde-meuble parisien de François Ier: inventaires inédits de 1542 et 1551', *Gazette des Beaux Arts*, vol. 78, 1971, pp. 253–304.

Schofield, Richard, 'Giovanni da Tolentino goes to Rome: a description of the antiquities in Rome in 1490', *Journal of the Warburg and Courtauld Institutes*, vol. 43, 1980, pp. 246–56.

Schryvers, R.H., 'La Présence de César dans Juste Lipse', *Présence de César*, ed. Chevalier, op.cit., pp. 239–45.

Schudt, Ludwig, *Le guide di Roma*, Vienna, 1930.

Secret, François, 'Blaise de Vigenère à l'hôtel de Bellevue', *Bibliothèque d'Humanisme et Renaissance*, vol. 21, 1969, pp. 115–27.

Sicari, Giovanni, *Bibliografia delle guide di Roma in lingua italiana dal 1480 al 1850*, Rome, 1991.

Silver, Lary, 'Paper pageants: the triumphs of Maximilian I', *'All the World's a Stage'*, ed. Wisch and Scott-Munshower, op.cit., pp. 293–331.

Simonin, Michel, *Vivre de sa plume au XVIe siècle ou la carrière de François de Belleforest*, Geneva, 1992.

Skenazi, C., 'Le Poète et le roi dans les *Antiquitez de Rome* et le *Songe* de Du Bellay', *Bibliothèque d'Humanisme et Renaissance*, vol. 60, 1998, pp. 41–55.

Skyrme, R., '"Buscas en Roma a Roma": Quevedo, Vitalis, and Janus Panvinius', *Bibliothèque d'Humanisme et Renaissance*, vol. 44, 1982, pp. 363–7.

Smith, Malcolm, *Joachim du Bellay's Veiled Victim*, Geneva, 1974.

——(ed.) *Antiquitez de Rome*, Medieval and Renaissance texts and studies, Binghamton, New York, 1994.

Smith, Pauline M., *The Anti-Courtier Trend in Sixteenth-Century French Literature*, Geneva, 1966.

Soulié, Marguerite, 'L'Imitation des sonnets de Du Bellay chez deux poètes protestants du XVIe siècle [Bernard de Montméja, Simon Goulart] voulant témoigner leur foi', *Du Bellay. Oeuvres et critiques*, vol. 1, no. 20 pp. 183–95.

Sozzi, Lionello, 'La Polémique anti-italienne en France au XVIe siècle', *Atti della Accademia delle Scienze di Torino*, vol. 106, 1972, pp. 99–190.

Spielmann, H., *Andrea Palladio und die Antike*, Munich and Berlin, 1966.

Stinger, Charles L., 'Roma triumphans: triumphs in the thought and ceremonies of Renaissance Rome', *Medievalia et Humanistica*, vol. 10, 1981, pp. 189–201.

——*The Renaissance in Rome*, Bloomington, Indiana, 1985.

Supple, J.J. (ed.) *Montaigne et la rhétorique: actes du colloque de St Andrews, 28–31mars, 1992*, Paris, 1995.

Sutcliffe, Frank, *Guez de Balzac et son temps*, Paris, 1959.

Thompson, David, *The Idea of Rome from Antiquity to the Renaissance*, Mexico City, 1971.

Thomson, David, *Renaissance Paris: Architecture and Growth, 1475–1600*, London, 1984.

Thornton, Peter, *The Italian Renaissance Interior, 1400–1600*, London, 1991.

Toesca, I., 'Drawings by Jacques Androuet du Cerceau in the Vatican Library', *Burlington Magazine*, vol. 98, January–December 1956, pp. 153–7.

Tollon, Bruno, 'Nicolas Bachelier', *Germain Pilon et les sculpteurs français*, Paris-Louvre, 1963, pp. 338–62.

Tournon, A., 'La Segmentation du texte: usages et singularités,' *Editer les 'Essais' de Montaigne*, ed. Blum and Tournon, Paris, 1997, pp. 173–95.

Tucker, G.H., 'Sur les *Elogia* de Janus Vitalis et les *Antiquitez de Rome* de Joachim du Bellay', *Bibliothèque d'Humanisme et Renaissance*, vol. 47, 1985, pp. 103–12.

——'Le portrait de Rome chez Pannonius et Vitalis: une mise au point,' *Bibliothèque d'Humanisme et Renaissance*, vol. 48, 1986, pp. 751–6.

Tucker, George H., *Les Antiquitez. The Poet's Odyssey*, Oxford, 1990.

——'*Roma rediviva*: André de Resende, Joachim du Bellay and the continuing Legacy of Janus Vitalis' Roman Diptych', *Bibliothèque d'Humanisme et Renaissance*, vol. 54, no. 3, 1992, pp. 731–6.

——'Du Bellay, Janus Vitalis et Lucain: la trame des mots dans *Les Antiquitez* ou plus un *Songe* et dans quelques vers analogues des *Poemata*', *Du Bellay*, ed. Cesdron, op.cit., I, pp. 149–60.

Vagenheim, Ginette, 'La Falsification chez Pirro Ligorio', *Eutopia*, vol. 3, 1994, pp. 67–114.

Valone, Carolyn, 'G.A. Dosio and his patrons', Northwestern University Dissertation, Northwestern, 1972.

——'Giovanni Antonio Dosio: the Roman years', *Art Bulletin*, vol. 58, 1976, pp. 528–41.

Van der Meulen, M., 'Cardinal Cesi's antique sculpture garden', *Burlington Magazine*, vol. 116, 1974, pp. 14–24.

Veldman, Ilja M., *Maarten van Heemskerck and Dutch Humanism in the Sixteenth Century*, Amsterdam, 1977.

Vermeule, C., 'The Dal-Pozzo album. Drawings of classical antiquities', *Art Bulletin*, vol. 38, 1956, pp. 31–46.

Versnel, S., *Triumphus*, Leiden, 1970.

Vignes, Jean, 'Le pastiche des *Regrets* dans *Les Jeunesses* de Jean de la Gessée', *Du Bellay. Oeuvres critiques*, vol. 1, no. 20, pp. 209–23.

Volpi, C. *Il libro di Pirso Ligorio all' Archivio di Stato di Torino*, Rome, 1994.

Ward, W.H., *French Châteaux and Gardens in the Sixteenth Century. Reproduction of Contemporary Drawings by J.A. Du Cerceau*, London, 1909.

Wardropper, I., 'Le Voyage italien de Primatice en 1550', *Bulletin de la Société de l'Histoire de l'Art Français*, 1981, pp. 27–31.

Weisbach, W., *Trionfi*, Berlin, 1919.

Weiss, R., *The Renaissance Discovery of Classical Antiquity*, Oxford, 1969.

Wells-Cole, Anthony, *Art and Decoration in Elizabethan and Jacobean England*, New Haven, 1997.

Williams, Wes, 'Salad days: revisiting pilgrimage in the sixteenth century', *(Ré)interprétations: études sur le seizième siècle*, ed. John O'Brien, *Michigan Romance Studies*, vol. 15, 1995, pp. 151–76.

——*Pilgrimage and Narrative in the French Renaissance*, Oxford, 1998.

Wingert, Paul S., 'The funerary urn of Francis I', *Art Bulletin*, vol. 21, no. 4, 1939, pp. 383–400.

Wisch, Barbara and Scott-Munshower, Susan, *'All the World's a Stage': Art and Pageantry in the Renaissance*, 2 vols, I: *Triumphal Celebrations and the Rituals of Statecraft*; II: *Theatrical Spectacle and Spectacular Theatre*, Pennsylvania, 1990.

Wittkower, R., 'Alberti's approach to antiquity in architecture', *Journal of the Warburg and Courtauld Institutes*, 1941, pp. 1–18.

——'Principles of Palladio's architecture', *Journal of the Warburg and Courtauld Institutes*, 1944, pp. 102–22.

——*Disegni de le ruine di Roma e come anticamente erano*, 2 vols, Milan, 1963.

——*Architectural Principles in the Age of Humanism*, Milton Keynes, 1971.

Wolfzettel, Friedrich, *Le Discours du voyageur*, Paris, 1996.

Worth, Valerie, *Practising Translation in Renaissance France: the Example of Etienne Dolet*, Oxford, 1988.

Yates, Frances A., *Astraea*, London, 1977.

Yavetz, Zwi, *Julius Caesar and his Public Image*, London, 1983.

——'The *Res Gestae* and Augustus', *Caesar Augustus*, ed. Millar and Segal, op.cit., pp. 1–36.

Youssef, Zobeidah, *Polémique et littérature chez Guez de Balzac*, Paris, 1972.

Zanker, Paul, *The Power of Images in the Age of Augustus*, Ann Arbor, 1993.

Zerner, Henri, 'A Propos de faux Marcantoine. Notes sur les amateurs d'estampes à la Renaissance', *Bibliothèque d'Humanisme et Renaissance*, vol. 23, 1961, pp. 477–81.

——'Observations on the *Disegni de le ruine*', *Art Bulletin*, vol. 48, 1965, pp. 507–12.

——'Du Mot à l'image', *Traités d'architecture*, ed. Jean Guillaume, Tours, 1985, pp. 288–94.

——*L'Art de la Renaissance en France*, Paris, 1996.

Zuber, Roger, *Les 'Belles Infidèles' et la formation du goût classique*, Paris, 1968.

——'Guez de Balzac et les deux antiquités', *XVIIe Siècle*, 1983, pp. 135–48.

Index